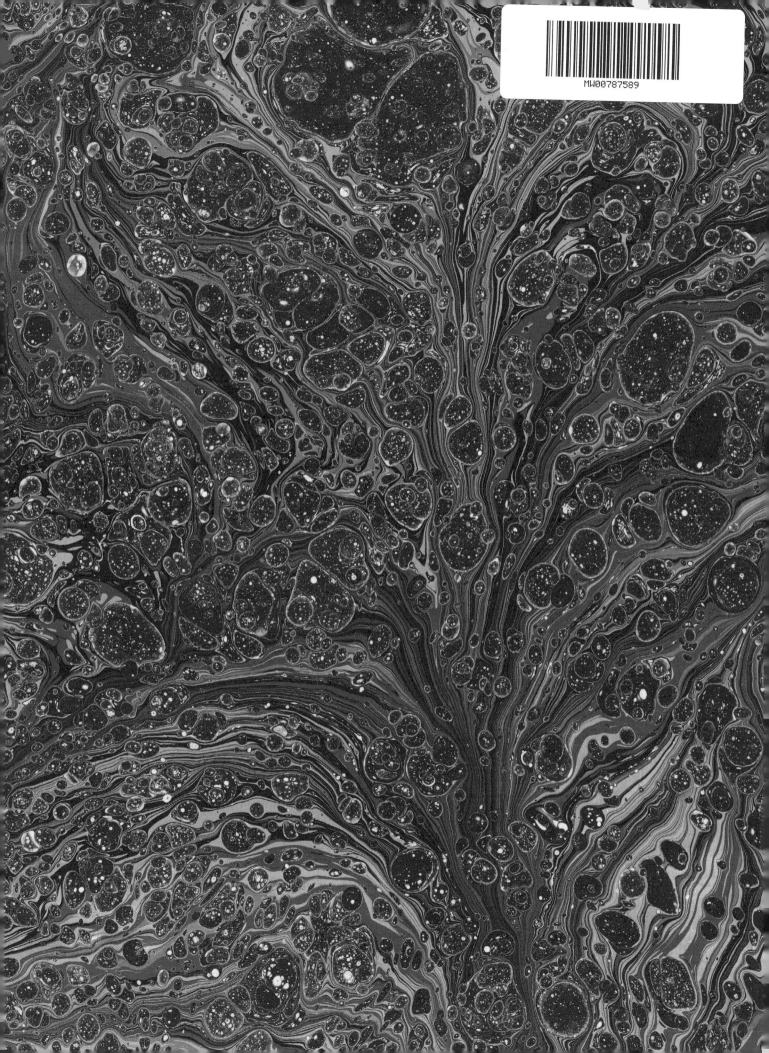

ONE-ELEVEN DOWN

63-9780, an RDT&E F-111A over Texas. *Cover Photo Courtesy of Mike Kaplan*

ONE–ELEVEN DOWN

F-111 Crashes and Combat Losses

Steven Hyre and Lou Benoit

Schiffer Military History
Atglen, PA

Courtesy of Author's Collection

Book Design by Stephanie Daugherty.

Copyright © 2012 by Steven Hyre and Lou Benoit.
Library of Congress Control Number: 2012950185

Printed in China.
ISBN: 978-0-7643-4278-3

We are interested in hearing from authors with book ideas on related topics.

Published by Schiffer Publishing Ltd.
4880 Lower Valley Road
Atglen, PA 19310
Phone: (610) 593-1777
FAX: (610) 593-2002
E-mail: Info@schifferbooks.com.
Visit our web site at: www.schifferbooks.com
Please write for a free catalog.
This book may be purchased from the publisher.
Try your bookstore first.

In Europe, Schiffer books are distributed by:
Bushwood Books
6 Marksbury Avenue
Kew Gardens
Surrey TW9 4JF, England
Phone: 44 (0) 20 8392-8585
FAX: 44 (0) 20 8392-9876
E-mail: Info@bushwoodbooks.co.uk.
Visit our website at: www.bushwoodbooks.co.uk
Try your bookstore first.

CONTENTS

ACKNOWLEDGMENTS

This book could not have been written without the assistance of so many individuals, each providing technical assistance, perspectives, photographs, and shared stories. A great debt is owed to those closely associated with the F-111, and our hope is the finished product will respectfully represent your friends and squadron mates. To the maintainers who toiled endlessly preparing the F-111 for flight, your work, skill, and love for this aircraft are evidence of the best fighter aircraft safety record ever! To the leaders of the F-111 community, the engineers, officers, and senior enlisted, we salute you. To each by name and heartfelt thanks:

Col Arnold Franklin Jr., Col Tom Germscheid, Col Chris McWilliams, Col James Steiber, Air Commodore Kym Osley RAAF, Air Commodore Anker Brodersen RAAF, Air Commodore Gavin Davies RAAF, WGCDR Mike "Boggy Smith RAAF, Lt Col Craig Brown, Lt Col Dick Brown, Lt Col Jack Bauder, Lt Col Walter Manwill, Lt Col Joe Peluso, Lt Col Jerry Kemp, Maj Don Harten, Capt Brad Insley, CMSgt David Sando, CMSgt Greg Weigl, SMSgt Bernard Manfre, MSgt Paul Holmes, MSgt David Phipps, MSgt Tim Gallagher, TSgt Virginia Youngblood, Bill Allen, Joe Betts, Art Hoffman, Ernie Skillern, Don Logan, David de Botton, Doug Loeffler, Mike Jobe, Jim Sorenson, John Smeltz, Anne C. Fuchlow, Sue Ann Wallace, Marcel Benoit, Samantha Benoit, Cassandra Beams, Jeffrey Hyre, Doug Slowiak, Colin Hunter, Kevin Coyne, and General Dynamics Fort Worth, Texas.

Marjorie Brink Coridan: Retired airport consultant, and our personal editor for this book. Thank you for your contributions to civil aviation in America, for your interest in this daunting project, and your professional, constructive critique of this important historical document.

Don Gwynne: For your pursuit of excellence during your career with General Dynamics Fort Worth and for your editorial contributions focused on technical accuracy. Your exemplary dedication to the F-111 Flight Safety Program and this book is appreciated.

To My Wife Dana Benoit for your endless patience, thoroughly constructive reviews, and for naming this book *One-Eleven Down*.

To My Wife Pat Hyre, who is the most patient and wise person I know, a love of 35 years and counting.

Pictures often best tell the story. Without them, the factual text cannot convey any attachment to an aircraft, the individuals involved in a mishap, or reinvigorate fond memories. As such, a great majority of the photographs within these pages were provided by Steven Hyre, Co-Author. These photographs were collected over the years from numerous contributors, including General Dynamics Fort Worth, the United States Air Force, the Royal Australian Air Force, numerous F-111 Fighter Squadron's archives, and fellow F-111 coworkers. The remaining photographs were graciously donated or purchased from aviation photographers and private collections. We have endeavored to accurately acknowledge each of you by name.

DEDICATION

We would like to thank all the employees of General Dynamics Fort Worth (GDFW) for their professionalism and excellence with the engineering and construction of the F-111. The design specifications for this aircraft merged the most advanced aircraft systems technologies then in existence worldwide. The F-111 technologies have led the aviation world into the current generation of unbeatable fighter aircraft. We would like to highlight one GDFW employee who best represents the entire corps of professionals whose combined energies brought the TFX to flight status and then delivered the F-111 to the USAF and RAAF: W.T. "Bill" Allen.

Bill's career spanned over 50 years in aviation. He began by graduating as an Air Corps pilot in 1944. During World War II, he flew B-24s in the 459th Bomb Group in Italy. After the end of the war, he flew acceptance flight tests on a variety of single- and multiple- engine aircraft. In 1950, he graduated from Texas A&M with a degree in Aeronautical Engineering and joined Fort Worth Convair. His career spanned the production of the B-36, B-58, F-111, and F-16 combat aircraft. He remained in the Air Force Reserves flying T-28, T-33, F-80, and F-86 jets. During the F-111 program, Bill had the opportunity to fly the F-111A Terrain Following Radar (TFR) test aircraft and participate in flight operations aboard the USS *Forrestal* aircraft carrier, flying the Navy F-4C Phantom and A-3 Douglas Sky Warrior. Bill's principal General Dynamics assignments included: B-58 Instrumentation Design Group Engineer, F-111 Design Safety Project Engineer, and Manager of F-16 European Co-Production Engineering & Flight Acceptance. Bill retired in 1986 as Senior Project Engineer in Charge of F-16 International Projects.

Bill Allen reveals details about the photograph:

"In September and October 1967, the F-111 Systems Program Office (SPO) authorized flights by Air Force, Navy, and selected company personnel. Phil Oestricher had worked for me at the start of the F-111 program, but was now part of General Dynamics Flight Test. He put me on the list, and we flew together on October 19, 1967, in the TFR test aircraft F-111A 63-9768. This aircraft was unique because it had the Escapac ejection seats. Phil let me take the left seat and I flew the whole flight. We did an aileron roll, TFR penetration, and then 200 foot TFR Hard Ride over the Arkansas test range. We climbed up to altitude and began acceleration to Mach 1.6 where he let me do another aileron roll. The only time he touched the controls was after I pushed both throttles into afterburner and one engine's afterburner didn't light-off. He got it to light-off and we completed the Mach 1.6 run. We returned to Carswell Air Force Base and I did one touch-and-go and then a full-stop landing. I taxied back and asked him to take over and put the bird back in the hanger. I certainly didn't want to screw up after such a thrilling flight. That's the story behind the photograph. One last note, of all the aircraft I have flown in the Army Air Corps and the USAF, the F-111 was by far the easiest. It was an absolute Cadillac!"

Bill Allen (white flight suit) after his flight with Phil Oestricher (far seat) in F-111A 63-9768, the TFR test aircraft. *Courtesy of Bill Allen*

Bill, we dedicate this book to you
and all the lost F-111 crewmembers;
we are eternally grateful!
Bill Allen passed away January 17, 2012,
at the age of 87 –
his professional and technical expertise
will forever be the cornerstone of
One-Eleven Down.

FOREWORD

I was thrilled to hear of the writing of this work, and even more honored to be asked to provide the foreword. Besides having a mishap featured in the F-model section, I was fortunate enough to fly every U.S. model of the Vark except the D, to include the F-111A as a student, the F-111F during Desert Storm and the transition from RAF Lakenheath to Cannon AFB, the F-111G and re-engined AMP F-111E as an FTU IP, and the PACER STRIKE F-111F at the Vark Weapons School. I served at the twilight of the aircraft, but while the time was too short, she had matured into a fabulous weapons system.

Looking back, I grew up in the cockpit of the F-111. I showed up straight out of Undergraduate Pilot Training (UPT) and Lead-In Fighter Training (LIFT) as a snot-nosed, arrogant, know-it-all Lieutenant. But thanks to many instructors and leaders, too many to name, I came to learn humility, and the need to pass on the many lessons this great aircraft, and great community, had taught me. In that cockpit I scared myself (and others!), learned our trade-craft, and experienced loss and the joy of hearing your friends on the radio after a bad night of combat. Ours was a small, tight-knit community, so the losses you read of in this book affected all of us and our families beyond words. This certainly included our support sections, and particularly the maintainers that spent so much time, effort, blood, and skin fixing these amazingly complex machines that we flew and broke. You've never seen a crushed individual until you see a crew chief standing in an empty parking spot, trying to comprehend that his aircraft, and the crew he helped strap into it, are never coming back.

That's why this book is so important; hundreds of us were impacted by each of these losses, and answers are hard to come by. I hope that in reading these accounts, some small measure of understanding is relayed. There are incredible lessons to be learned: not just those specific to the Vark, but for all involved in aviation. And for our lost brothers, it is necessary to remember the efforts that every soul involved placed professionally into making that particular sortie possible; and while the mission may have ended in tragedy, it most certainly did not end in vain.

"To our Fallen, Heroes One and All."
Lt Col Craig F. "Quizmo" Brown, USAFR

Courtesy of Lt Col Craig F. "Quizmo" Brown, USAFR

PREFACE

On a narrow ridge in northeastern Nevada, pine needles filter the fragrant sage-laced wind. Sloping open fields, powdery soil, and half-dollar sized shale support the hardy sage dominated landscape. The exposed rock outcrops are cutting, jagged, inhospitable. This land has seen Indians, prospectors, and ranchers. Occasionally wild horses, elk, domestic sheep, goats, and perhaps cattle have grazed. The remains of a rattlesnake skin are nearby, its owner I will eventually meet in person. Stand, turn, and for a full circle, this is the top of the world. This place is remote, the solitude perfect, the view spectacular, and the memory is forever.

A winter storm lingers in the February sky. Overcast conditions and a setting sun have painted premature darkness. At over 500 mph from the west, an F-111A approaches at low altitude, hugging the terrain on its way toward a simulated attack on the Wendover bombing range, east of where I stand.

The Pequop Mountains rise almost 10,000 feet above sea level, bounding the eastern side of the Ruby Valley. The right seat pilot's intercom confirms the presence of terrain on the attack radar screen. The left seat pilot instinctively glances at the smaller TFR scope to monitor the electronic terrain returns. The pull-up is initiated automatically by the terrain following radar's signal to the autopilot. The two pilots are pushed unnoticed into their seat cushions by the G-force of the pull-up. Accustomed to the sensation of the ride, their attention is focused on the instruments. The pilot's right hand guards the control stick, perhaps squeezing it during the climb. With the left hand, the throttles are eased forward to sustain the climb airspeed. For a moment the silence of the day is interrupted. A flash of lightning, a thunder clap, and then the snow falls slowly, softly, and cold. Night came to this place and then another day.

This book was inspired by my research into the loss of one F-111A in particular, 66-0042. On February 12, 1969, Call Sign Fruity 01 departed Nellis AFB, Nevada, on a training mission and failed to return. Although an extensive air search continued for several weeks, the USAF could not find 042. Almost four months later, a rancher herding goats on the Pequop summit discovered the missing aircraft.

The F-111 aircraft was an engineering marvel for its time. The designers and engineers introduced innovative and ground-breaking technologies that stretched the boundaries of state-of-the-art. The goal and prime directive was the all inclusive fighter. Its size instigated debate about whether it was a fighter or a bomber. Its onboard gun and bomb-bay-mounted air-to-air missiles made it a fighter, but its mission criteria dictated bomber. Ultimately, the Air Force labeled the One-Eleven a fighter to allure the best pilots…but it made history as a bomber! The lyrics of a popular country and western song echo in my ears *"If you could only see me now."*

Even the harshest armchair aviators and critics should be humbled by the history of the F-111, truly one of the penultimate Cold War heroes.

Ironically, the first airplane magazine I ever read as a child was the May 1968 issue of "Flying." I was instantly captured by the artistic drawings, but the theme of the article was a trial featuring the F-111 as the accused. In a multi-count indictment, the author of the article stepped through each complaint. Under trial against the plaintiff naysayers, the jury acquitted the F-111. Reading the article, I couldn't help being fascinated by all the new features this aircraft possessed: swing wings, low bypass turbofan engines, big beefy landing gear, terrain-hugging radar, escape capsule, huge bomb load…and much more. The Air Force, the Navy, the Brits, and the Aussies were getting it. Even the model airplane box top I pinned to the wall showed it decimating the bad guys…the Commies, I suppose. This airplane was just too cool….It could do everything! I decided then and there that I was going to be an Air Force fighter pilot.

Over time the bad press surrounding the F-111 created doubt even in my own mind. I understood the airplane to be something too complex, too ahead of its time, too expensive, and too much trouble mechanically. Yesteryear headlines have always incorrectly prophesied the same story with each different airplane, "….IT WILL NEVER FLY!"

The first 10 years of the F-111A were centered on controversy, confusion, and heartbreak. Through these trials and tribulations, a truly great American fighter aircraft matured. As I researched, I had to unravel information that had been diluted into fiction. However, through detailed research, chasing rabbit trails, and building the puzzle, a clearer understanding of what really happened came to light and the truth was revealed. This book recounts the facts.

Much has been written about the TFX controversies and the F-111's technical problems. Unfortunately, no one author has ever dug deep enough to explain the "Whys?" I searched for answers from every F-111 book, magazine, and historical writing I could find, and not one provided the answers. I did, however, find more questions. The primary purpose of this book is to provide an explanation. Although technical in some cases, the use of photographs and diagrams help in visualizing the exact cause for each F-111 crash and combat loss.

Actually, my real reason for writing this book is the compassion I feel for the families involved. When a military aircraft crashes, the families really never know the why's and how's; to that end, this book was compiled to fill in those blanks.

These historical texts are dedicated to the pilots and their families whose losses were permanent and tragic.

Co-Author Lou Benoit

One of the unique features of the F-111 was the crew escape module; this one is from FB-111A 68-0243. The mishap aircraft departed controlled flight, forcing the crew to eject. The module landed in a forested area near Kirby, Vermont. *Courtesy of Author's Collection*

INTRODUCTION

An aircraft crash scene is utter chaos. Parts are strewn everywhere in widely varied physical sizes, conditions, places, and positions, all which defy the imagination. Finding the cause requires a series of tedious back steps in time. Eventually the clues and a solution come together through scientific analysis, technical explanation, and logical reasoning. To describe the genesis of this book is best illustrated as having found several unmarked boxes, of unconnected pieces, to an unknown puzzle.

The contents revealed within grew exponentially over time while conducting a de facto crash investigation beginning in 2006 regarding the loss of F-111A 66-0042. The main objective during my personal investigation was to provide an answer for the surviving families why 042 did not return from a combined day-night training sortie. A thorough report was written regarding 042's loss, and the family members were grateful for finally knowing why their pilots did not come home. During those years of research, an extensive database for all the F-111 crashes was collected. A new project developed to assimilate these reports into a worthy historical document.

The F-111, like all previous military aircraft, had growing pains. Some of the lessons learned stemmed from destroyed aircraft, bent metal, and unfortunately, fatalities. Each F-111 crash or accident was thoroughly investigated by the USAF; similarly those occurring within the RAAF. The results of these investigations led to changes and improvements of aircraft systems, pilot training practices, flight procedures, and combat tactics. As the aircraft matured during its military career, the F-111's safety record has proven superior to all tactical fighters throughout the world. The general public would be aghast to review the crash and mishap statistics for the F-100, F-104, F-4, and even the F-16 fighters.

Without question, any F-111 accident would fuel and frenzy the naysayers while adding to an unjust controversy. This book is not intended to throw salt on those wounds. Rather, it is dedicated entirely toward recounting the losses; the hows and the whys for each mishap. The basic rules for compiling the text on each major accident were first agreed upon by both authors and all the contributors. Those rules were then chiseled in granite: to be brief, accurate, and factual. There was to be no discussion of forensics or pathological evidence, only a respectful accounting for those involved. In only one mishap is a factual cause of death mentioned. The remaining crashes include the phrase "unsuccessful ejection" or "no attempt to eject," and the conclusion therein should be apparent.

The crash chapters are broken down and separated by each model or version of the F-111: RDT&E / Preproduction, continuing all the way through to the FB-111. For ease of organization, the crashes or mishaps within each chapter are presented in an order of ascending production tail numbers, not by the date of occurrence. The reason we chose this organization was due to the intermingling of crashes between the different F-111 model types over its career. An exception to this plan is found within the chapter covering Combat Losses. These losses are discussed in order of occurrence, as the date of the event was deemed more significant than the tail number sequence. The final chapters are included to highlight some known incidents, to honor the lost aircrews, and to provide a list of the surviving F-111s on display.

The data in the appendix was included to collate all the major accidents, first in order of occurrence, and then a tabulation of the primary causes, location, ejection statistics, and data analysis. Many minor incidents may be missing, but the data presented is by far as accurate as it gets!

Finally, each reader may ask "Where did all the crash information come from?" First and foremost, the "Mishap Scenarios" presented are a direct synopsis from the "releasable" portion of each aircraft's official mishap report. These very brief event descriptions were obtained from the USAF through the Freedom of Information Act (FOIA). The "Findings" portion of the narrative was obtained through pilot interviews, declassified combat reports, technical papers, and abstracts from existing printed materials.

The many pieces of this giant mystery puzzle began to take a form meeting our objectives and providing answers for all the dedicated individuals involved in the F-111's design, manufacture, maintenance, and operation. Lastly, this book is for anyone interested in crash investigation and the history of the F-111. This truly is the last chapter in a remarkable combat aircraft's history, but almost certainly not the last book. However, for now, this book covers all the major crashes and accidents in the F-111's 46 year career, from beginning to end.

Our book's front cover photographs represent the true nature and intent of the F-111; a deep strike, all-weather, interdiction fighter. The 474th TFW F-111As were immediately tested by fire in the highest threat areas of North Vietnam, at night, and single-ship! The cover's top-left photograph recognizes the Cold War contributions of the UK based F-111Es and Fs; truly the first strike option against a Soviet invasion of Europe, followed by stateside Strategic Air Command FB-111As. Just as our inner leaf photograph of 63-9780 serves to remind every reader about the early RDT&E F-111 flight tests, the back cover captures the end; the very last landing of an RAAF F-111C. The Royal Australian Air Force closed the history on this wonderful fighter, being the last to fly and honorably retire the F-111 in grand style on December 10, 2010.

The "Calling Card" portrayed on the bottom center had its origins after the F-111's reintroduction into North Vietnam during Linebacker II. The North Vietnamese called the F-111 "*Whispering Death*". Most F-111 attacks occurred in the middle of the night, and before the noise of the aircraft was registered the bombs were going off. As one NVA officer later said, "*If you saw the F-111, you were already dead*." The F-111's success in combat echoes its mystique; the crews and aircraft were extremely capable of delivering destruction without warning in the highest threat environments!

Lastly, our title had to diverge from all previous books covering the F-111. It had to grasp attention. Just as the bad news of a mishap spreads across an air base - the life changing and gut wrenching news it delivers - the words no one will ever forget once seen or heard: *One-Eleven Down*.

Authors' Disclaimer

The duties of a crash investigation board are to determine the cause of a mishap and make recommendations to prevent a reoccurrence. The board results are based on the weight of the evidence gleaned through expert technical and engineering analysis of the crash site and wreckage. Additional evidence is often derived by witness interviews and surviving pilot debriefs. By strict disclosure laws, the investigation board's entire report will never be made available for public review.

The accident scenarios and findings for each of the F-111 mishaps presented were obtained legally through the Freedom of Information Act (FOIA), unclassified or declassified military documents without copyrights, or existing media sources available to the public. Therefore, the names, dates, places, scenarios, findings, primary causes, and the crash photographs represent the views of the USAF or RAAF, not the authors.

It must be understood by the reader that the entire spectrum of technical analysis leading every F-111 investigation board to a probable cause cannot be printed in a single volume such as *One-Eleven Down*. As a point of reference, the official final report for *each* individual F-111 mishap investigation is similar by volume and weight to this entire book.

1

F-111 SYSTEMS

FLIGHT CONTROLS
CREW MODULE ESCAPE SYSTEMS
ENGINE FIRES AND REVERSE FLOW PHENOMENA
TERRAIN FOLLOWING RADAR

The F-111 flight control system (Figure 1) was technically complex, but superbly designed to handle the entire flight spectrum of the aircraft. To assist the pilot in stability and control, rate gyros and accelerometers within the electronic flight control computers provided continuous automatic damping about the three axes of the airplane: longitudinal, lateral, and directional. The stability automation and dampening significantly reduced the pilot's workload in flight by continuously adjusting to variations in stick and throttle movements, wing sweep, weapon loads, and to external influences, such as turbulence and wind gusts. To maintain stability and control, the flight control computers and autopilot automatically managed trim and control stick feel about all axes to provide a "Cadillac" ride.

Various flight control systems descriptors within the pilot's flight manual, known as the Dash-1, required more than 20 pages detailing the individual functions. Basic details of several specific flight control system components which influenced several mishaps are briefly described, including: the Stall Inhibitor System (SIS), Adverse Yaw Compensation (AYC), and the Central Air Data Computer (CADC).

The primary aircraft control surfaces consisted of a rudder, movable horizontal stabilizers, and spoilers on each wing. Pitch attitude of the aircraft was controlled by symmetrical deflection of the horizontal stabilizer surfaces. Roll attitude was controlled by asymmetrical deflection of the horizontal stabilizer surfaces and assisted by the wing spoilers up to a wing sweep angle of 47 degrees. Yaw control of the aircraft was accomplished by deflection of a rudder surface located on the trailing edge of the vertical stabilizer. Hydraulic servo actuators applied the necessary force to deflect the control surfaces. The pilot's control stick was directly linked to the servo actuators via a control valve. The control surfaces deflected only when hydraulic pressure was available; there was no manual reversion through direct mechanical linkage or leverage.

The Stability Augmentation system employed redundant sensors, electronic circuitry, and electro-hydraulic dampers. Three damper actuators, two horizontal stabilizer actuators (HTSA), and the rudder actuator were supplied by both primary and utility hydraulic systems. Both hydraulic systems were considered stand-alone: independent, yet redundant should one system fail.

A Command Augmentation system utilized pitch and roll dampers to amplify or gain down the pilot's input to provide a near constant relationship between control force and aircraft response throughout the operational envelope.

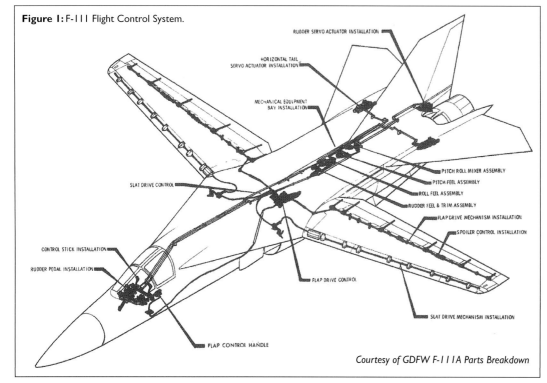

Figure 1: F-111 Flight Control System.

RUDDER SERVO ACTUATOR INSTALLATION

HORIZONTAL TAIL SERVO ACTUATOR INSTALLATION

MECHANICAL EQUIPMENT BAY INSTALLATION

PITCH ROLL MIXER ASSEMBLY

PITCH FEEL ASSEMBLY

ROLL FEEL ASSEMBLY

RUDDER FEEL & TRIM ASSEMBLY

FLAP DRIVE MECHANISM INSTALLATION

SPOILER CONTROL INSTALLATION

SLAT DRIVE CONTROL

CONTROL STICK INSTALLATION

RUDDER PEDAL INSTALLATION

FLAP DRIVE CONTROL

SLAT DRIVE MECHANISM INSTALLATION

FLAP CONTROL HANDLE

Courtesy of GDFW F-111A Parts Breakdown

Pitch Channel: (See Figure 5) Manual control of the aircraft in pitch was achieved by fore-and-aft movement of the control stick. This movement was transmitted along the pitch channel push-pull tubes and bellcranks to the left and right horizontal stabilizer actuator control valves. These valves metered the flow of hydraulic fluid to the actuators, causing the horizontal stabilizers to move symmetrically. Control stick centering and feel forces were provided by the pitch feel springs. The aircraft was equipped with a series pitch trim system to automatically adjust the horizontal stabilizers to the required trim position and minimize transient oscillation errors during autopilot modes and auto TFR operations, as well as to correct for variations in throttle movement and wing sweep.

Roll Channel: (See Figure 5) Lateral movement of the control stick was transmitted to the pitch/roll mixer assembly by a system of push-pull rods and bellcranks. The pitch/roll mixer added the roll commands to the pitch commands and sent summed commands to the left and right horizontal stabilizer control valves and actuators. When the wings were forward of 45 degrees, roll control was aided by the action of two hydraulically actuated spoilers on the top of each wing. There was no mechanical linkage between the control stick and the spoilers. Lateral movement of the control stick caused the stick position transducers to generate electrical command signals which were sent through the feel-and-trim and the wing sweep sensor assembly to the spoiler actuators. At wing-sweep angles greater than 47 degrees the spoilers were locked out. The spoilers not only assisted in roll control during flight; upon landing, automatic extension occurred when the main landing gear struts compressed. The spoilers effectively dumped the wing's lift, increasing the down force on the landing gear which enhanced wheel braking.

Yaw Channel: (See Figure 7) Rudder pedal movement was mechanically transmitted to the rudder control valve. The control valve metered the flow of

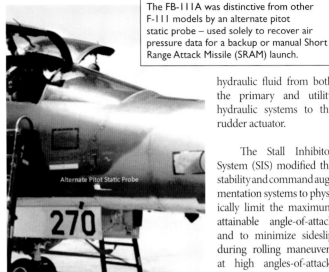

The FB-111A was distinctive from other F-111 models by an alternate pitot static probe – used solely to recover air pressure data for a backup or manual Short Range Attack Missile (SRAM) launch.

FB-111A Alternate Air Data Probe.
Courtesy of Mike Kaplan.

The Beta Probe (β) was also a rotating conical probe that measured the angle of sideslip (AOS). The Beta probe sensed the rotation of the aircraft's centerline from the relative wind, the signal being sent to the SIS computer and then to the AYC. (AOS can be visualized as the directional angle of attack).

Figure 2: Conical AOA or Beta probe.
Courtesy of USAF, ATC Pamphlet 51-3.

The AOA (α) probe is a conical fixture that rotated in relation to the relative wind striking the aircraft in the pitch axis. Air slots in the leading edge captured the airflow and rotated the probe. The transmitter measured the angular displacement of the probe and provided an electrical signal to the SIS and Yaw computers. An identical AOA probe was located in the same position on the opposite side of the forward fuselage.

hydraulic fluid from both the primary and utility hydraulic systems to the rudder actuator.

The Stall Inhibitor System (SIS) modified the stability and command augmentation systems to physically limit the maximum attainable angle-of-attack and to minimize sideslip during rolling maneuvers at high angles-of-attack. The Stall Inhibitor System was added to the flight control system, whereby response to pilot nose-up commands was decreased above 10 degrees angle-of-attack. The SIS was added to the F-111 flight controls system to increase resistance to Roll-Coupled departures and post-stall gyrations. This modification was necessitated after several F-111s were lost due to pilot induced stall AOA departures while maneuvering the aircraft beyond the current stability limits. A SIS modified F-111 could be identified by the addition of an angle-of-attack probe to the right side of the forward fuselage, compared to a non-SIS aircraft with only one AOA probe on the left side of the forward fuselage.

The Adverse Yaw Compensation System (AYC) was added to provide improved turn coordination in the takeoff and landing configurations. This function was provided automatically whenever the slats were extended 70 percent or more. Turn coordination was improved by augmenting the directional stability with a sideslip to rudder feedback. This latter signal produced rudder in the direction of the roll and proportional to the roll rate.

Central Air Data Computer (CADC or CADS) provided aerodynamic intelligence to various control systems. The system consisted of an electromechanical computer which processed raw data from the angle-of-attack probe and transducer (on the left side of the fuselage above the nose wheel well), pitot static probe, and a temperature sensor probe located on the right side of the fuselage above the nose wheel well. The computer utilized raw data: static pressure, pitot pressure, total temperature, and indicated angle-of-attack. The computer transformed the raw data into electrical signal outputs which the various other computers, systems, and cockpit instrumentation utilized. The pitch and roll damper systems accepted inputs form the Combined Air Data Computer (CADC) and the navigation system to provide pitch-and- roll autopilot modes.

Autopilot System: The autopilot operates independently or in conjunction with pilot control application to fly the aircraft during various modes of autopilot flight. The autopilot receives input signals from other systems and computers to provide command signals to the pitch and roll dampers.

Flight Control System Related Air-Data Probes.

FB-111A with Full-Span Double-Slotted Flaps (shown right). *Courtesy of Chris McWilliams*

The photograph below depicts the deployed spoilers on the upper surface of the wing, the extended full-span leading edge slats, and the rotating wing glove fairing on the far right. *Courtesy of Michael A. France.*

Additionally, the autopilot computes and signals the pitch and roll trim actuators to maintain trimmed flight – a portion of the self-adaptive flight control system. The pilot could manually maneuver the aircraft at any time with the autopilot engaged by use of control stick steering. Autopilot commands to the flight controls did not cause control stick displacement. The terrain following radar (TFR) computer supplied the signal commands to the autopilot, which moved the pitch dampers and series trim to maintain the aircraft at a preselected clearance plane above the terrain.

The Wing Flaps were full span, multi-section Fowler-type flaps. Each wing flap was divided into five sections. The four outer sections (main flaps) were mechanically connected and operated as one unit. The inboard section, designated as the auxiliary flap, operated independently from the main flaps. The main flaps were powered by a single hydraulic motor which was connected to a gearbox located in the fuselage section. The hydraulic motor and gearbox assembly drove torque shafts which powered mechanical actuators to raise and lower the flaps. The auxiliary flaps were disabled when either the wing sweep angle switch sensed more than 16 degrees wing sweep, or when the wing sweep handle was at a position greater than 16 degrees. Also, a mechanical interlock locked the flap and slat handle in the UP position when the wing sweep angle was greater than 26 ½ degrees. In operation the slats extended first, then the flaps. Retraction was in the reverse order.

The Variable Sweep wings were moved to and held in position by two hydraulic, motor-driven linear actuators. The actuators were mechanically interconnected to insure positive synchronization. The wings utilized both the Primary and Utility hydraulic systems, either of which could power the sweep mechanism in the event the other hydraulic system failed.

The following diagrams highlight the major components of the F-111 flight control system. The pitch, roll, and yaw systems are referred to as Channels. All information and diagrams were extracted from F-111 model Flight Manuals. Although the different models had slight variations, all the systems operated in a similar manner. Therefore, no model distinction is provided for the individual diagrams.

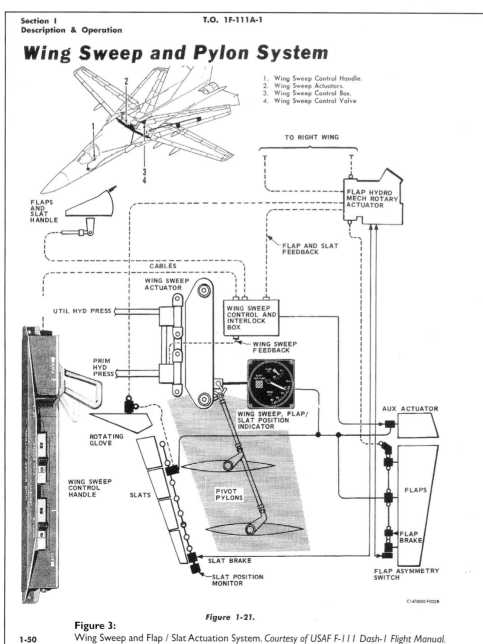

Figure 3:
Wing Sweep and Flap / Slat Actuation System. *Courtesy of USAF F-111 Dash-1 Flight Manual.*

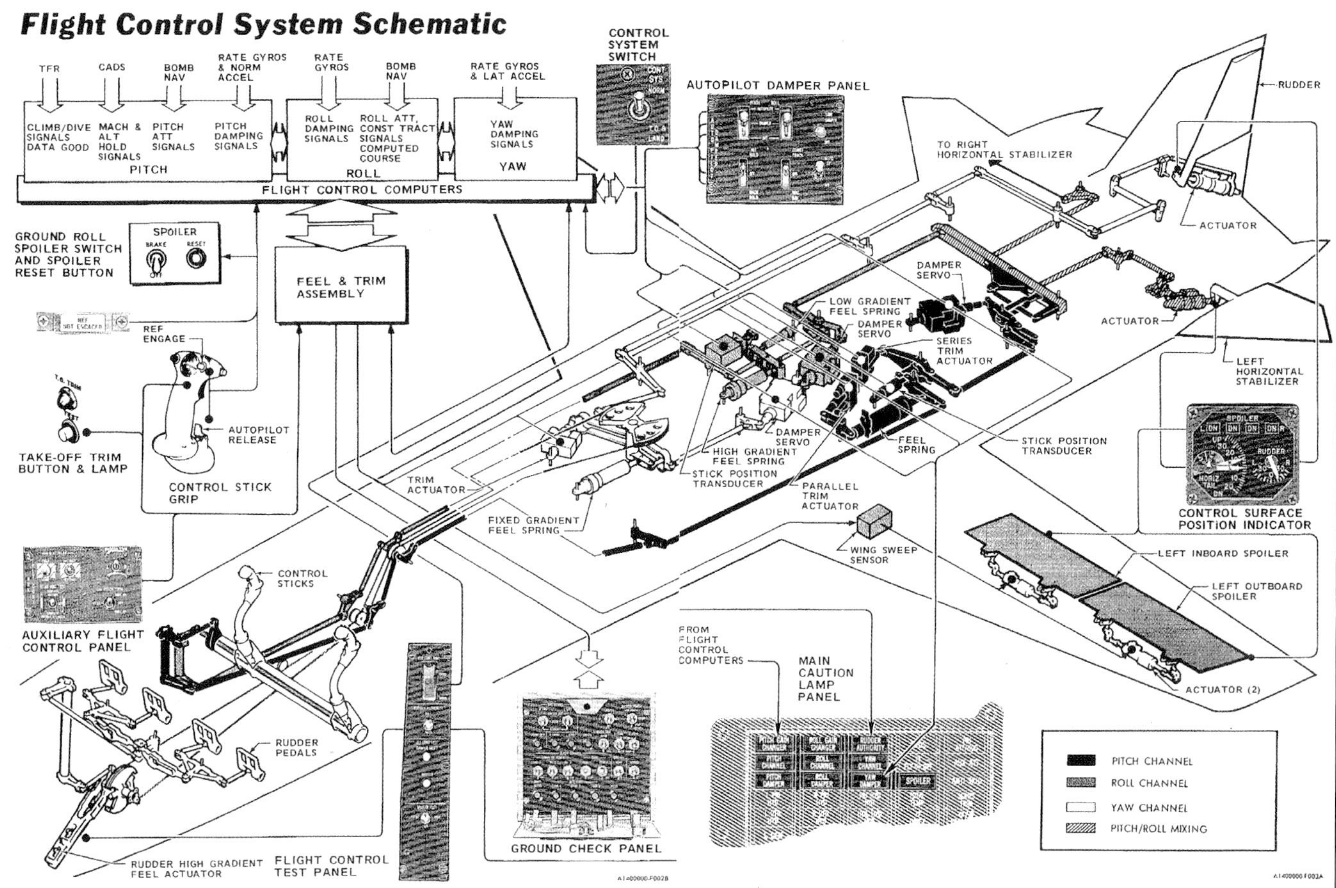

Flight Control System Schematic

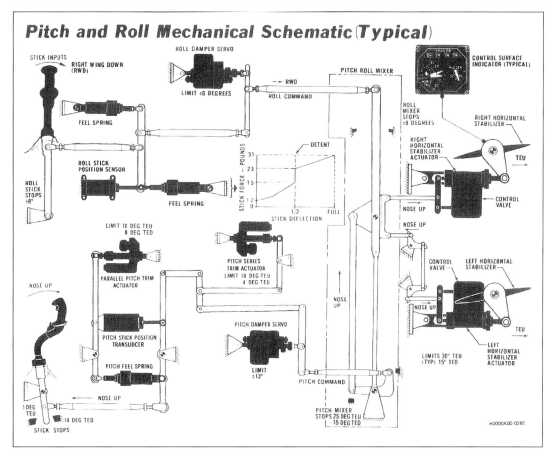

Figure 4: Major Flight Control System Components. *Courtesy of USAF F-111A Dash 1 Flight Manual*

Pitch and Roll Mechanical Schematic (Typical)

Figure 5:
Courtesy of USAF F-111
Dash 1 Flight Manual

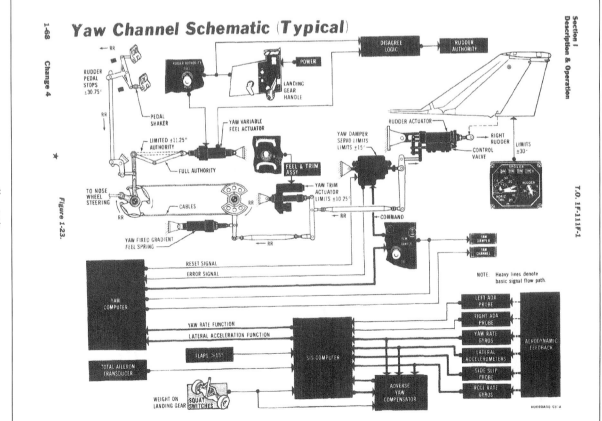

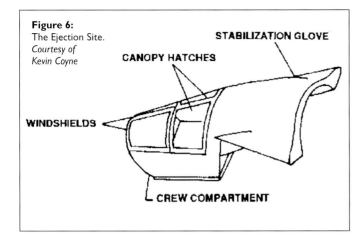

Figure 6:
The Ejection Site.
Courtesy of Kevin Coyne

STABILIZATION GLOVE
CANOPY HATCHES
WINDSHIELDS
CREW COMPARTMENT

F-111 CREW MODULE ESCAPE SYSTEMS

The crew module forms an integral portion of the forward fuselage and encompasses the pressurized cabin and forward portion of the wing glove. Crew entrance to the module is provided through left and right canopy hatches. The system protects the occupants from environmental hazards on either land or water and provides underwater escape capabilities. An emergency oxygen supply system for the crew and a self-contained emergency pressurization system are also available during ejection. However, either system can be manually activated during normal phases of flight as a backup to the associated normal system. Depicted to the right are the major components of the crew module.

The ejection equipment consists of the necessary initiators, severance components, and the rocket motor. Activation of either ejection handle initiator provides an explosive impulse sequenced to lock the pilot's shoulder

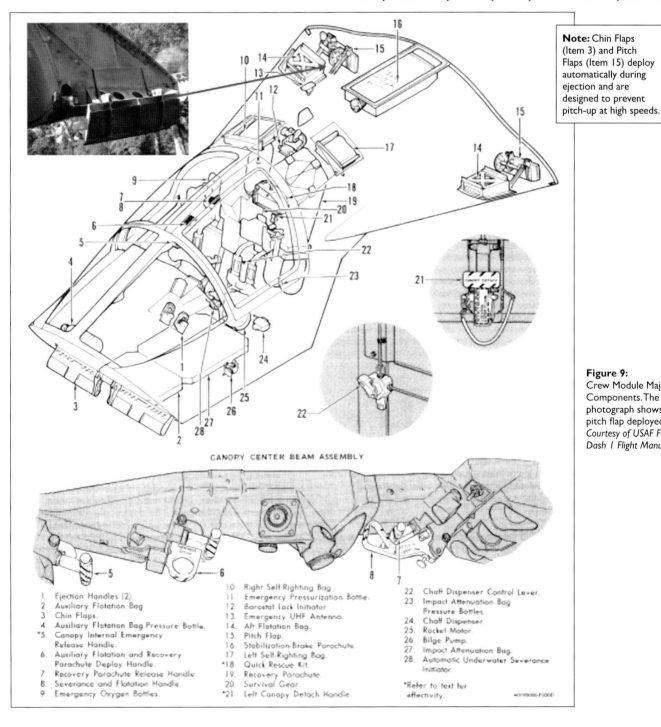

Note: Chin Flaps (Item 3) and Pitch Flaps (Item 15) deploy automatically during ejection and are designed to prevent pitch-up at high speeds.

Figure 9:
Crew Module Major Components. The inset photograph shows the pitch flap deployed.
Courtesy of USAF F-111 Dash 1 Flight Manual.

CANOPY CENTER BEAM ASSEMBLY

1. Ejection Handles (2).
2. Auxiliary Flotation Bag.
3. Chin Flaps.
4. Auxiliary Flotation Bag Pressure Bottle.
*5. Canopy Internal Emergency Release Handle.
6. Auxiliary Flotation and Recovery Parachute Deploy Handle.
7. Recovery Parachute Release Handle.
8. Severance and Flotation Handle.
9. Emergency Oxygen Bottles.

10. Right Self-Righting Bag.
11. Emergency Pressurization Bottle.
12. Barostat Lock Initiator.
13. Emergency UHF Antenna.
14. Aft Flotation Bag.
15. Pitch Flap.
16. Stabilization Brake Parachute.
17. Left Self-Righting Bag.
*18. Quick Rescue Kit.
19. Recovery Parachute.
20. Survival Gear.
*21. Left Canopy Detach Handle.

22. Chaff Dispenser Control Lever.
23. Impact Attenuation Bag Pressure Bottles.
24. Chaff Dispenser.
25. Rocket Motor.
26. Bilge Pump.
27. Impact Attenuation Bag.
28. Automatic Underwater Severance Initiator.

*Refer to text for effectivity.

Crew Module Ejection Sequence

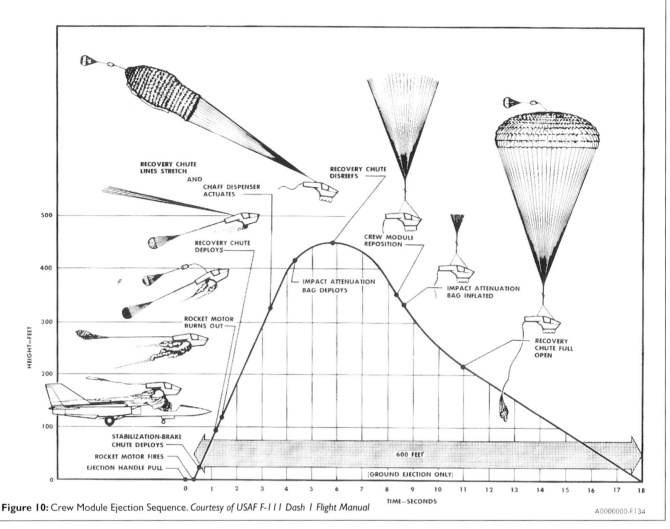

Figure 10: Crew Module Ejection Sequence. *Courtesy of USAF F-111 Dash 1 Flight Manual*

A0000000-F134

harness inertia reels in the retracted position, activate the emergency oxygen and cockpit pressurization system, release the chaff dispenser, activate guillotine cutters, and ignite the rocket motor. Two pressure initiators, which are activated by rocket motor pressure build-up after ignition, are provided to activate the severance components and to deploy the stabilization-brake parachute, the main recovery parachute, and the impact attenuation bag. The severance components consist of the flexible liner shaped charges (FLSC) and explosive guillotine cutters. The FLSC is located around the crew module so that detonation will cut the splice plate joining the crew module to the airplane. FLSC is also used to remove the covers over the parachutes and the flotation, self righting, and impact attenuation bags. The explosive guillotine cutters are provided to sever antenna leads, secondary control cables, and an oxygen line. Quick disconnects located in the crew module floor are used for separation of the normal air conditioning and pressurization system ducts, the flight controls, and the electrical wiring. The rocket motor, located between the crew members and behind the seat bulkhead, provides the thrust to propel the crew module up and away from the aircraft.

The recovery and landing equipment consists of stabilization components and underwater escape components. The stabilization components consist of the stabilization glove, stabilization-brake parachute, pitch flaps, and chin flaps. The stabilization glove section serves to stabilize the flight of the crew module until deployment of the recovery parachute. The chin flaps on the module's lower/forward edge and pitch flaps on the trailing edge of the stabilization glove (see inset photograph, labeled 3 and 15 respectively on Figure 9 next page) assist in maintaining crew module horizontal stability by preventing pitch-up during a high-speed ejection. The stabilization-brake parachute, which is contained in a compartment in the center of the top aft

section of the glove, is used to decelerate the crew module and assist in maintaining stable flight prior to deploying the recovery parachute. The stabilization-brake parachute is a ribbon-type parachute six feet in diameter, and is attached by two bridle cords to the outboard aft sections of the glove section. (Note: The pitch flaps deploy automatically as the module separates from the airframe, requiring no pyrotechnic sequencing.) The main recovery parachute has a ring-sail canopy which is 70 feet in diameter when deployed. The parachute is attached by two bridles to the crew module so that the module will maintain an upright and level attitude during descent. The main recovery parachute is housed in a container between the pilot's seat bulkhead and the aft pressure bulkhead. This container rests on the parachute catapult pan. The catapult forcibly deploys the parachute at a velocity sufficient to ensure proper bag strip-off. A selector monitors the airplane speed to select one of three possible time delays in unlocking a barostat initiator. When below 15,000 feet the barostat initiator, if unlocked, will fire, and in turn fire the catapult to deploy the recovery parachute. The parachute, initially deployed in a reefed configuration, is un-reefed by three cutters which sever the reefing line shortly after line stretch is reached. The landing and flotation components consist of an inflatable landing impact attenuation bag, flotation bags, and self-righting bags. The impact attenuation bag, located in the crew module floor, inflates automatically during descent and serves to cushion the landing impact. Although the crew module is watertight and will float, additional buoyancy is provided by a flotation bag at each aft corner of the glove section and by an auxiliary flotation bag at the front of the crew module. The aft flotation bags are inflated either manually, by use of a T-handle initiator in the cockpit, or automatically, by action of the under-water severance initiator. The auxiliary flotation bag is inflated manually by a T-handle initiator in the cockpit. The pressure source

High Speed Crew Module Ejection Animation. The lower Primary and upper Secondary nozzles have fired. *Courtesy of Author's Video Collection*

The rocket motor (Figure 13) is composed of an upper closure or cap atop a 9" x 58" steel cylinder case and a lower closure or cap. The upper closure directs a portion of the rocket motor thrust through the Secondary (upper) Nozzle, while the Lower Closure directs the majority of the rocket thrust through the fixed Primary (lower) Nozzle. The rocket motor produces 27,000 pounds of total thrust. To avoid excessive "g" forces on the crewmembers, a portion of the rocket motor thrust is diverted to the upper closure through two concentric upper nozzles, the secondary and auxiliary. The small auxiliary nozzle in the center of the upper nozzle fires simultaneously with the lower nozzle. This action provides 500 pounds of thrust to counteract slow-speed crew module pitch up to speeds below 300 knots. At speeds above 300 knots, after a .15-second delay the upper nozzle burst diaphragm is severed by a flexible linear-shaped charge (FLSC) to increase the exhaust-flow area, thus increasing its thrust. Because of the increase in the exhaust-flow area the rocket motor operating pressure is lowered, which results in reduced thrust of 9,000 pounds at the lower nozzle and increases the upper nozzle thrust to 7,000 pounds. This overall decreased thrust extends the operating time and reduces excessive "g" forces.

for inflation of the flotation bags is contained in two storage bottles located in the crew module.

The crew module ejection sequence is initiated when either ejection handle is pulled. The following sequence occurs automatically: Pulling either handle fires an initiator that simultaneously retracts both inertia reels, actuates the emergency oxygen and cabin pressurization systems, activates the chaff dispenser if armed, fires the explosive guillotines, ignites the rocket motor, and unlocks the manual recovery chute deployment handle. Pressure build-up of the rocket motor fires two additional initiators. The first initiator acts as a backup to activate the emergency oxygen and cabin

pressurization system, the chaff dispenser, and guillotines, and also activates the crew module severance system. The Flexible Linear-Shaped Charge (FLSC) detonates and severs the crew module from the airplane. The secondary initiator activates the stabilization-brake parachute and the thrust reducer, and unlocks the barostat initiator. When the barostat initiator is unlocked and senses an altitude below 15,000 feet, it will fire and ignite the Shielded Mild Detonating Cord (SMDC) train to remove the severable cover plate over the main recovery parachute compartment and catapult the main recovery parachute into the airstream. When the severable cover separates from the module, the barostat initiator fires the explosive valves in the impact attenuation bag air bottles, causing the bag to inflate. A third function of the barostat initiator is to erect the emergency UHF antenna and to fire the explosive pin retractor, releasing the repositioning bridle cable, which allows the crew module to assume the correct touchdown attitude. Should the barostat fail, the recovery parachute "Deploy Handle" can be pulled manually.

The stabilization-brake parachute is a 6-foot diameter hemisphere-type parachute that is attached to the crew module at the aft end of the stabilization glove by means of bridle lines. The stabilization-brake parachute is pressure packed around the outer barrel of the main recovery parachute catapult and stored in a compartment on the top aft end of the stabilization glove. After the stabilization/brake parachute deploys the main recovery parachute catapult is fired. This ejects the main parachute aft and upward from the stabilization glove. As the bridle lines pull tight, reefing lines prevent the large main parachute from fully opening until the suspension lines are fully stretched. (The recovery parachute is deployed in a reefed or partially inflated condition to reduce the opening shock of the parachute to the crew module.) When the suspension lines are fully stretched, the reefing line is cut by the reefing line cutter to allow the parachute to fully blossom. When the main recovery parachute is fully open it will appear as shown in the larger illustration in Figure 11.

The crew module initially descends in the nose down attitude seen in the small illustration on the right of Figure 10. A barostatic initiator erects the emergency UHF antenna and fires the explosive pin retractor, releasing the repositioning bridle cable, which allows the crew module to assume a level touchdown attitude, as shown in the larger illustration of Figures 10 and 11.

Displayed above left the module ejection animation is an impression of the crew escape module with both the primary (lower) and secondary (upper) rocket exhausts clearly visible. The representative thrust vectors for both rocket exhausts are depicted in Figure 12 by yellow arrows against the crew module's aft pressure bulkhead. The larger arrow represents the Primary Nozzle exhaust, while the smaller thinner arrow represents the Secondary Nozzle exhaust. Figure 13 depicts a shortened cutaway of the rocket motor.

Note: If the ejection takes place below 300 knots, the stabilization/brake parachute is cut away from the module concurrent with recovery parachute deployment to prevent possible entanglement of the two parachutes.

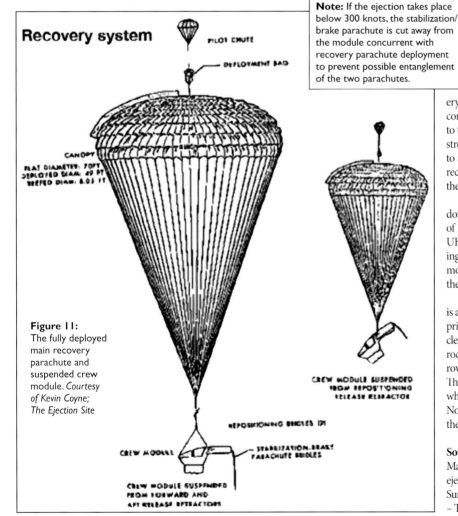

Recovery system

PILOT CHUTE

DEPLOYMENT BAG

CANOPY
FLAT DIAMETER: 70 FT
DEPLOYED DIAM: 49 FT
REEFED DIAM: 8.03 FT

CREW MODULE SUSPENDED FROM REPOSITIONING RELEASE RETRACTOR

Figure 11:
The fully deployed main recovery parachute and suspended crew module. *Courtesy of Kevin Coyne; The Ejection Site*

REPOSITIONING BRIDLES (2)

CREW MODULE

STABILIZATION-BRAKE PARACHUTE BRIDLES

CREW MODULE SUSPENDED FROM FORWARD AND AFT RELEASE RETRACTORS

Sources: T.O. 1F-111A-1, Section-1 of the Pilot's Flight Manual and Courtesy of *The Ejection Site* at http://www.ejectionsite.com, and F-111 Crew Module Escape and Survival Systems by Kevin Coyne. All Art by Kevin Coyne – The Ejection Site

Figure 12: Escape Module Aft Pressure Bulkhead.

Courtesy of GDFW F-111A Parts Breakdown.

Figure 13: Rocket Motor Cutaway (note: shortened for scaling).

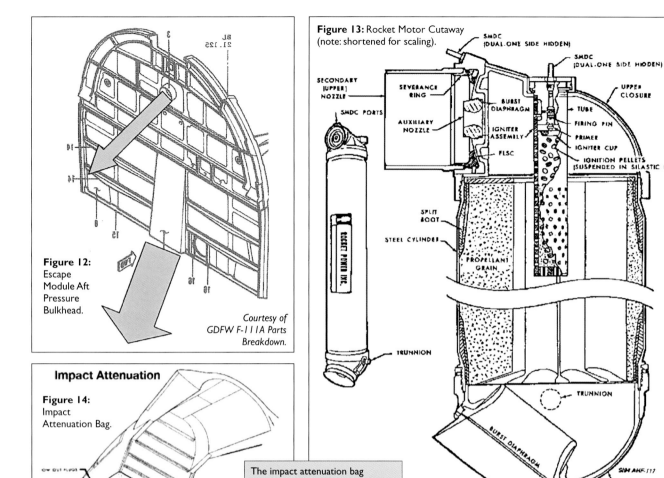

Figure 4-4. Rocket motor.

Courtesy of Kevin Coyne; The Ejection Site

Impact Attenuation

Figure 14: Impact Attenuation Bag.

Courtesy of Kevin Coyne; The Ejection Site.

The impact attenuation bag contains blowout plugs of various sizes. These plugs are retained by shear pins. Upon landing, the pins shear to release the blowout plugs, allowing the bag to deflate. This action reduces the impact shock on the floor of the crew module to tolerable limits.

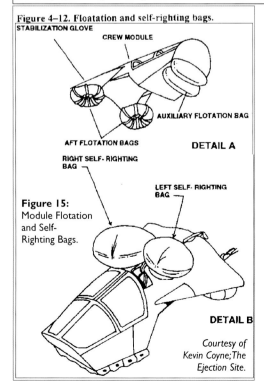

Figure 4-12. Floatation and self-righting bags.

Figure 15: Module Flotation and Self-Righting Bags.

Courtesy of Kevin Coyne; The Ejection Site.

The landing and flotation components consist of an inflatable landing impact attenuation bag, flotation bags, and self-righting bags. The impact attenuation bag, located in the crew module floor, inflates automatically during descent and serves to cushion the landing impact. Although the crew module is watertight and will float, additional buoyancy is provided by a flotation bag at each aft corner of the glove section, and by an auxiliary flotation bag at the front of the crew module. Inflation of the aft flotation bags is accomplished either manually by use of a T-handle initiator in the cockpit, or automatically by action of the under-water severance initiator. Inflation of the auxiliary flotation bag is accomplished manually by a T-handle initiator in the cockpit. The pressure source for inflation of the flotation bags is contained in two storage bottles located in the crew module.

An actual F-111D crew module was restored and enlisted for annual egress and survival training at Cannon AFB, New Mexico. Notice the bean-shaped Life Preserver Unit (LPU) under each of the pilot's arms. The LPUs were a personal flotation device should the module begin to sink. *Courtesy of Chris Woodul*

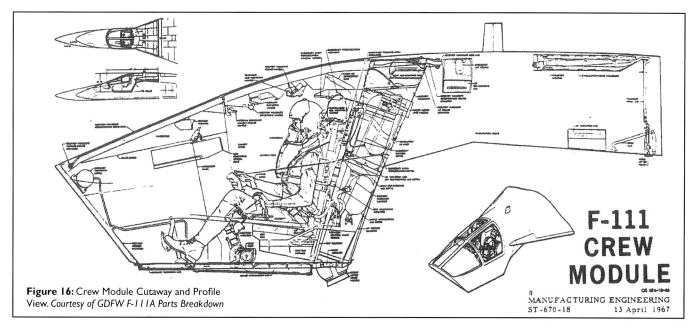

Figure 16: Crew Module Cutaway and Profile View. *Courtesy of GDFW F-111A Parts Breakdown*

F-111
CREW
MODULE

MANUFACTURING ENGINEERING
ST-670-18   13 April 1967

ENGINE FIRES AND
THE REVERSE FLOW PHENOMENA

All F-111 engines were based on the Pratt & Whitney TF-30 Low Bypass Turbofan motor with an afterburner. Although there were several different variants or versions of the engine, the basic form and function of the engine was the same. The earliest version of the TF-30, known as the P-1, was more prone to compressor stalls because of a combination of under-developed engine-inlet integration factors. Unfortunately, the compressor stalls could not be tolerated for flight testing and operational employment of the aircraft. The solution was to develop a less "stall prone" motor known as the P-3 version. Additionally, a number of significant engine intake engineering changes were required to help solve the compressor stalls, the most noteworthy being the shift from the original Triple Plow I intake to the Triple Plow II. Within the early Triple Plow I intakes, the boundary layer intake splitter was given an outward bulge, while the interior of the intake was fitted with vortex generators to disturb the airflow to meet the engine face in a more uniform flow pattern. The motor itself required changes to the mechanized fuel control, variable stator vanes, bleed air control valves, and the exhaust nozzle and intake spike scheduling to better handle the airflow problems associated with the F-111's

entire spectrum of flight: from zero airspeed at brake release to Mach 2.5 at 50,000 feet – a daunting operating envelope for any engine – but even more so for this first-ever afterburning turbofan.

Inherent to any jet engine are the high RPM centrifugal forces on the compressor and turbine blades, high internal operating pressures and temperatures, and the threat from foreign object ingestion. Engine technology in the TF-30 still lagged the high demands placed on the motor. Engine failures occurred, and although most were minor, some were catastrophic disintegrations. In those cases fragmented blades usually penetrated the exterior engine case, punctured fuel and hydraulic lines, and went into the centerbody fuel tank, which the engines straddled. The blade shrapnel triggered an engine bay fire that was sustained by the punctured fuel, oil, and hydraulic lines, or by holes punctured in the fuel tank itself. In almost all cases the fire within the engine bay rapidly burned through hydraulic lines, depleting the pressure and resulting in loss of aircraft control. An additional problem was later discovered by the path followed by the inflight fire. The flames were sucked into the aft centerbody through the ventilation louvers, burning through the rudder controls and causing a hard-over rudder and loss of aircraft control. This external fire moved into the aft centerbody of the fuselage, torching through exposed hydraulic lines and the rudder push-pull tube – a problem described and defined as the Reverse Flow Phenomena.

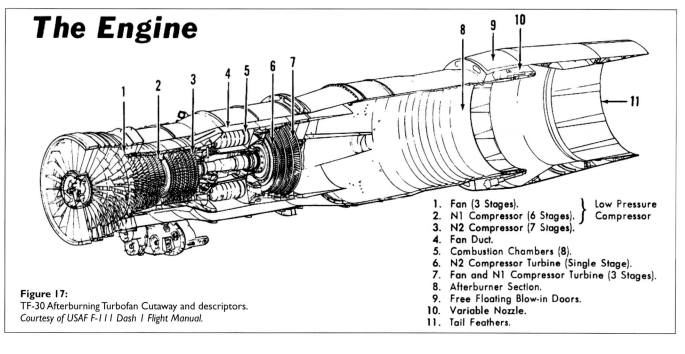

The Engine

1. Fan (3 Stages).
2. N1 Compressor (6 Stages). } Low Pressure Compressor
3. N2 Compressor (7 Stages).
4. Fan Duct.
5. Combustion Chambers (8).
6. N2 Compressor Turbine (Single Stage).
7. Fan and N1 Compressor Turbine (3 Stages).
8. Afterburner Section.
9. Free Floating Blow-in Doors.
10. Variable Nozzle.
11. Tail Feathers.

Figure 17:
TF-30 Afterburning Turbofan Cutaway and descriptors.
Courtesy of USAF F-111 Dash 1 Flight Manual.

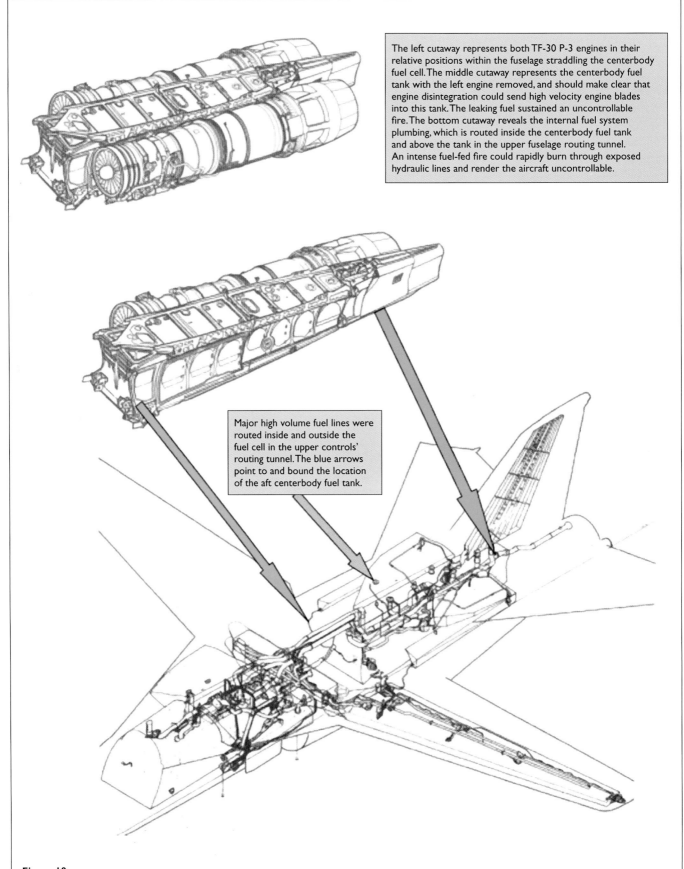

The left cutaway represents both TF-30 P-3 engines in their relative positions within the fuselage straddling the centerbody fuel cell. The middle cutaway represents the centerbody fuel tank with the left engine removed, and should make clear that engine disintegration could send high velocity engine blades into this tank. The leaking fuel sustained an uncontrollable fire. The bottom cutaway reveals the internal fuel system plumbing, which is routed inside the centerbody fuel tank and above the tank in the upper fuselage routing tunnel. An intense fuel-fed fire could rapidly burn through exposed hydraulic lines and render the aircraft uncontrollable.

Major high volume fuel lines were routed inside and outside the fuel cell in the upper controls' routing tunnel. The blue arrows point to and bound the location of the aft centerbody fuel tank.

Figure 18:
Diagram shows relationship of engines, centerbody fuel tank, and major fuel lines.

Actual Mishap Photograph of External Fire Damage on F-111A 67-0053. The aft fuselage centerbody louver duct was intended to provide ventilation for the upper controls routing tunnel and the vaft centerbody cavity, however...

well as the rudder control push-pull tube to a high velocity flame front (torching) during an engine or fuselage fire. In addition, raw fuel or fuel vapors could also be sucked into the centerbody cavity, causing a flame front once ignited.

Combustible fumes and/ or fire would enter the louvers (on either side of the aft centerbody section) and a "Reverse Flow" flame front (Red Arrow) was drawn forward through the upper body Flight

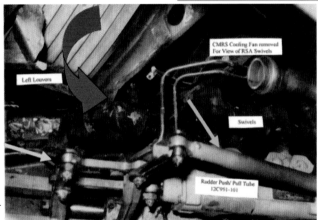

The visible low pressure region above the fuselage of an RAAF F-111C. *Courtesy of Author's Collection via Colin Hunter.*

The Reverse Flow Phenomena

The photo above shows GDFW Engineer Bill Allen (green shirt) investigating 053's aft fuselage centerbody. The inset text box and arrow focus on the ventilation louvers. Though the aft fuselage centerbody louver was intended for air to be drawn out by engine exhaust gas efflux, the extremely low pressure or negative pressure regions due to lift in the over-wing region actually sucked air through the louver and into the Rudder Servo Actuator Bay, then forward through the upper fuselage controls routing tunnel. The reverse flow phenomena exposed the Primary and Utility hydraulic lines, as

Interior View of Rudder Servo Actuator (red arrows indicate forward flow direction of flame front). *Courtesy of Bill Allen*

Blue vertical arrows on the inset aircraft diagram show suction due to lift.

The curved red arrows on the aft fuselage cutaway demonstrate the beginning of the Reverse Flow Phenomena.

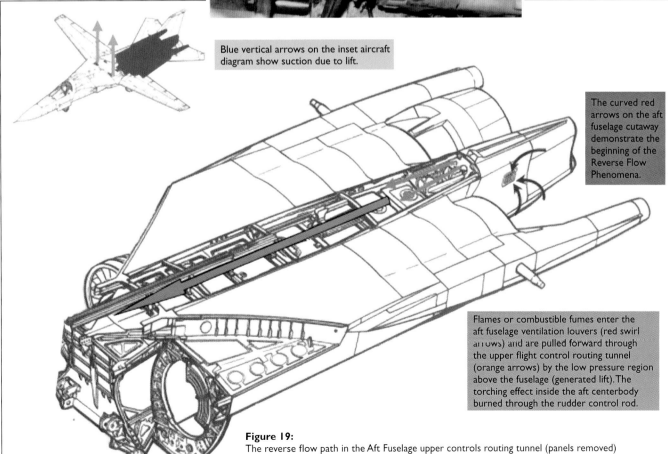

Flames or combustible fumes enter the aft fuselage ventilation louvers (red swirl arrows) and are pulled forward through the upper flight control routing tunnel (orange arrows) by the low pressure region above the fuselage (generated lift). The torching effect inside the aft centerbody burned through the rudder control rod.

Figure 19:
The reverse flow path in the Aft Fuselage upper controls routing tunnel (panels removed)
Courtesy of GDFW F-111A Parts Breakdown

Control Routing Tunnel. The "Blow Torch" effect would burn through the rudder push/pull tube (Blue Arrow) and the rudder control linkage (Green Arrow) would fall backwards, resulting in a rudder hard-over to the right. (Reference center photograph on previous page.)

The negative pressure region developed above the upper fuselage is graphically illustrated by a RAAF F-111C pulling "Gs" on the previous page during a low altitude fly-by. The sun angle and high humidity assist by visually exposing the intensity of the "vacuum" pulling air forward through the aft centerbody louvers and into the upper flight control routing tunnel.

Several Related
Reverse Flow Phenomena Incidents

1. 11 Sept 1968 F-111B BuNo 151971 (A2-02)
Point Mugu NAS Pacific Range aircraft making 20,000 foot MSL run monitored by tracking radar. Radar track indicated progressive right ground track with reducing airspeed. The aircraft went into a steep descent as airspeed slowed to approximately 150-180 knots. The aircraft impacted the water in a near vertical descent. Ejection attempts were out-of-the-envelope. Cause: Undetermined. (Suspected cause was failed hard-over right rudder.)

2. 18 Jun 1972 F-111A 67-0082 (A1-127)
Eglin AFB, Florida. Two minutes after takeoff, while departing Eglin, the aircraft was engulfed in flames. The crew apparently lost control and were forced to eject. The ejection was unsuccessful when the main chute remained in a full reefed condition and the crew module impacted the water. The reefing line cutter failed to actuate and did not cut the reefing line. Investigation indicated the F-1 fuel tank cap was loose and vented fuel. The aft flow of fuel ignited, engulfing the fuselage. Fire damage on the rudder indicated the rudder was in the full right hard over position.

3. 11 Jan 1973, F-111E 68-0024 (E-34)
RAF Upper Heyford: Shortly after takeoff, the left engine FIRE warning light illuminated. The engine was shutdown and fire agent discharged. The FIRE warning light went out. Shortly thereafter a severe right yaw was experienced. The pilot maintained control by maintaining a left bank. The wingman rejoined and reported slats down and a full right rudder. The mishap crew extended the gear and the aircraft suddenly rolled right uncontrollably. The crew ejected safely. The cause was determined to be failure of the left engine afterburner Zone-1 secondary fuel manifold. Reverse flow into the aft centerbody caused failure of the rudder control input link and a hard-over right rudder.

4. 4 May 1973, F-111A 67-0053 (A1-98)
Nellis AFB: A student pilot was executing a missed approach and advanced the power on both engines to Military power, and then into afterburner. The left engine FIRE warning light illuminated. Nellis Tower and the Runway Supervisor both reported to the crew that they were on fire. The instructor pilot took over, shut the left engine down, and depressed the FIRE push button. The fire was extinguished and the instructor pilot made a safe single engine landing. The cause of the engine fire was the left engine afterburner hydraulic fuel pump ruptured and the fuel spray was ignited by the afterburner. Fortunately, survival of this aircraft for post flight investigation revealed the fire damage trail that provided an explanation for the cause of a number of other F-111 major accidents – those presented on this page, in particular.

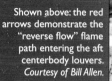
Shown above: the red arrows demonstrate the "reverse flow" flame path entering the aft centerbody louvers. *Courtesy of Bill Allen.*

The aft centerbody louvers (Figure 19 and photo above) were intended to utilize the vacuum generated by the high velocity jet exhaust, to draw cooling air aft through the upper body flight control routing tunnel and into the aft centerbody cavity, and then to exit out of the louvers. Unfortunately the opposite flow pattern occurred, resulting in the loss of several F-111s.

The photograph to the right, accompanied by the previous page's photographs and cutaways, should help visualize the reverse flow phenomena. As the aircraft maneuvers under positive G, an intense low pressure region is generated above the fuselage. The developed vacuum pulls air through the louvers, into the aft centerbody cavity, and into the upper fuselage flight control routing tunnel. The intense swirl effect in the aft centerbody cavity caused a torching effect that burned through the Rudder Push/Pull Tube–causing an uncommanded full rudder deflection known as a Hard-Over Rudder. Thereafter, the pilot had insufficient asymmetric horizontal tail and spoiler deflection to maintain directional and lateral control.

Upper controls routing tunnel with panels opened. A view looking aft towards the vertical tail. The red arrows indicate the forward flow followed by a high velocity flame front. *Courtesy of Bill Allen.*

5. 8 May 1973, F-111A 67-0083 (A1-128)
Takhli Royal Thai Air Force Base: The aircraft experienced a left engine fire on takeoff. The pilot reduced power and the oil low light came on, as the oil pressure indicated 20 psi. The engine was shut down and the FIRE push button was activated. The FIRE light went out after the fire agent discharged. The pilot landed with 24 MK-82 bombs loaded. Landing gross weight was 70,000 pounds. Left wheel brakes caught on fire after the aircraft was turned off the runway. The fire was extinguished by Fire Department personnel. There was evidence of intense fire damage in the aft centerbody, including rupture of the fuel dump line.

6. 15 May 1973, F-111E 68-0008 (E-18)
RAF Upper Heyford: The mishap aircraft was on a low-level at 450 knots when it ingested a large bird into the right engine. The ingestion was followed by an explosion and FIRE light. A short time later the "Wheel Well Hot" light came on. The crew climbed to 2500 feet and ejected safely after aircraft control became erratic and then uncontrollable. The bird impact to the right inlet spike caused the rupture of the F-2 fuel

tank wall, resulting in fuel loss. The flight crew stated that the aircraft was definitely on fire.

7. 6 June 1975, F-111A 66-0034 (A1-52)

Nellis AFB, Peach Springs, AZ: Twenty minutes after takeoff on a TFR low-level, the crew heard and felt a thump. The crew aborted TFR flight and made a shallow climb. The right engine FIRE light illuminated with smoke in the cockpit. The FIRE push button was pressed and agent discharge activated. The crew declared an emergency. Approximately eight minutes after the FIRE light came on, the aircraft became uncontrollable. The crew ejected successfully but sustained back injuries on ground impact. The cause was determined to be failure of the 14th and 15th stage high pressure compressor disk, which ruptured fuel lines. The fuel mixture ignited on contact with the hot engine exhaust nozzle. Fire in the aft centerbody adjacent to the rudder post failed both primary and utility hydraulic lines. The crew ejected safely after loss of flight controls.

8. 22 Dec 1975, FB-111A 68-0290 (B1-62)

Plattsburgh AFB, NY: While on a low-level RBS run at Loring RBS range, the mishap crew experienced catastrophic failure of the left engine. The throttle was reduced to idle and a climb initiated. No indication of fire was apparent to the aircrew. Fire was observed by ground personnel. The pilot experienced a slight left yaw followed by right yaw and a rolling moment which became uncontrollable. The crew ejected safely at 2000 feet AGL. A fan blade penetrated the engine case and ruptured the center fuel tank wall. A nacelle fire exited and burned through the aft centerbody side wall, failing the rudder input control link.

F-111 TERRAIN FOLLOWING RADAR (TFR)

A little over 40 years ago, an automated hands-off terrain following radar (TFR) system was hailed as a "modern marvel." Today such technology is passé, hardly a novelty in the era of stealth aircraft and the newest generation of fighter aircraft. In the 1960s, however, the F-111's leap in technology answered the USAF's urgent quest for an all-weather interdiction fighter/bomber. To fully understand the TFR and the mishap events, it is appropriate to discuss its mechanical function and history. Without the TFR derived capability, the USAF variant of the F-111 would hardly have made headlines. The TFR was therefore one of the pivotal systems of the F-111's all-weather capability.

The F-111A was not the only aircraft to incorporate TFR, nor was it the first. The Grumman A-6 Intruder, McDonnell Douglas RF-4C, and the Republic F-105D and F models deployed to Vietnam with contour mapping and terrain avoidance radars prior to the F-111A.

The F-111's unique capability is differentiated from these aircraft by a fully automated command guidance system capable of maintaining a specific Terrain Clearance Altitude (TCA). The F-111 was also the first combat aircraft to employ digital electronics which enabled integrating the autopilot, TFR, and Bomb-Nav systems.

The primary function of the TFR is to detect terrain features ahead of the aircraft, and convert the terrain slope into digital

commands for the autopilot to fly the aircraft "hands off." The TFR in the F-111 is complemented by the Low Altitude Radar Altimeter (LARA), later known as the CARA, which provides instantaneous vertical height to the TFR Computer for maintaining a pre-selected altitude. With the TFR, the F-111 could better penetrate enemy air defenses by exploiting very low altitudes in all weather, especially at night. The "all weather" capability of the TFR will be called into question; however, the night terrain following capability made the F-111 one of the most tactically effective aircraft in the Southeast Asian night environment.

NOTE: *The TFR pitch commands may also be used directly by the pilot for manual terrain following. Climb or dive indications are displayed on the Heads-Up and Attitude Director Indicator to guide the pilot along the desired terrain contour.*

In Figure 17 below, the two green lines protruding from the nose of the F-111 roughly depict the TFR vertically oriented scan pattern. The small tan arrow extending vertically below the F-111 depicts the low altitude radar altimeter (LARA). The dashed arc line in the diagram below represents the TFR Computer's derived flight path or "contour" to maintain the TCA.

The following pages are presented as a familiarization tour of the basic TFR components, their cockpit locations, and basic switchology descriptions. For the interested reader, it is essential to become familiar with the switches and displays described to fully understand their impact in several of the mishap sequences. To that end, briefly scan the diagrams and pictures for ease of understanding, or refer back to this chapter later for amplified information.

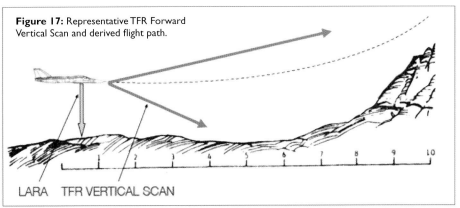

Figure 17: Representative TFR Forward Vertical Scan and derived flight path.

LARA   TFR VERTICAL SCAN

An F-111D with radome and avionics compartment access doors open. *Courtesy USAF.*

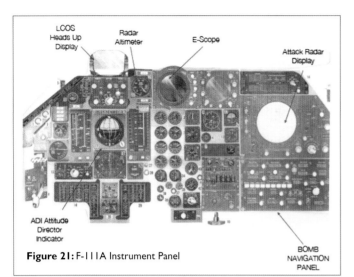

Figure 21: F-111A Instrument Panel

In the photograph on the previous page, the radome is opened to the right side of the aircraft, and the avionic access doors are opened upward in a clam shell manner. The aircraft is configured with two small side-by-side TFR antennas (channels) and the larger Attack Radar Set (ARS) antenna above. Only one of the TF channels is operated in the TFR mode; the opposite antenna is in a TFR Standby or operated in other ground mapping modes. The Attack Radar Set (ARS) was operated by the WSO. The antennas are mounted on a gyro-stabilized Roll Pedestal that kept the antennas level to the horizon up to 60 degree bank turns.

The individual modules within the avionics bay were known as Line Replaceable Units (LRUs). If an avionics system malfunctioned the LRU could be replaced with a functioning unit, quickly returning the aircraft to service.

Terrain Following Radar (TFR)
The terrain following radar (TFR) transmits a radio frequency pulse through a vertically scanning antenna to achieve accurate signal processing for terrain avoidance commands. The TFR consists of left and right antenna receivers (channels), synchronizer transmitters, power supplies, and computers in a dual channel configuration. Each channel may be operated independently of the other in any one of three modes: Terrain Following (TF), Situation Display (SIT), or Ground Mapping (GM).

TFR Displays (Figure 22)
In the TF mode, the range scale on the bottom of the E-scope is *non-linear*; ranges up to two miles are displayed over three-fourths of the scope, and the remaining one-fourth of the scope displays returns up

to 10 miles. In this manner, the close returns are displayed with clearer definition than those at greater range. The elevations of the terrain returns along the ground track being flown are displayed vertically on the scope. The pilot interprets the display by observing the furthest terrain moving from the right side of the scope to the left, the nearest terrain. Figure 22 (TFR E-Scope) shows a solid curved line displayed on the scope, which provides a terrain clearance reference. The slope of the cursor will vary with the speed of the airplane, terrain clearance setting, the type of ride selected, and the current pitch and angle of attack. The fuzzy line below the terrain clearance reference is the TFR's detected terrain returns. As higher terrain approaches the terrain clearance line, the TFR Computer will command a climb to maintain the gap between the solid line and the fuzzy terrain returns. As terrain falls away on the back side of a ridge or mountain the gap increases; the TFR will command a push-over to descend, closing the gap.

In the Situational Awareness (SIT) and Ground Mapping (GM) modes, the terrain viewing scales can be displayed in a 5-, 10-, or 15-nautical mile scale. There is no terrain following or avoidance guidance commands provided to the TFR Computer by the channel being operated in SIT or GM modes. The dual channel configuration of the TFR antennas (reference previous F-111D photograph) allows one antenna to be operating in TF mode while the other is operating in SIT, GM, or TF standby. The SIT and GM modes provide the pilot a forward hemisphere-horizontal sweep view of the terrain ahead. The SIT mode provides the pilot with a horizon-and-up view, while GM provides a horizon-and-down navigation view.

Terrain Following Mode: The AUTO TF mode allows the airplane to be guided automatically at a preselected terrain clearance altitude. Climb and dive signals generated by the TFR Computer are displayed on the Attitude Director Indicator (ADI), lead computing optical sight (LCOS - Heads Up Display), and to the flight controls via the Autopilot. The desired terrain clearance altitude can also be maintained "manually"; however, the pilot flying must control the aircraft pitch and dive by following pitch steering commands on the Attitude Director Indicator and LCOS.

During terrain following flight, the system has a built-in minimum terrain clearance threshold. Should the aircraft descend below "68 percent" of the selected terrain clearance altitude, the TFR Computer will initiate a "fly-up." Fly-up commands are displayed on the pilot's ADI and LCOS in the AUTO and Manual TF modes. In AUTO TF, the *autopilot* will pull the aircraft's nose up. In Manual TF, the *pilot flying* must initiate the climb. The fly-up command is described in the flight manual as a "2g" (incremental) pull-up. A fly-up is also commanded if the aircraft exceeds the TFR bank limit of 45 degrees or the pitch limit of +/- 25 degrees.

The operating TFR antenna oscillates only in the vertical plane (Figure 23, + 8º above / -32 º below the horizon) in the terrain following mode. Antenna tilt *cannot* be adjusted in the TF mode.

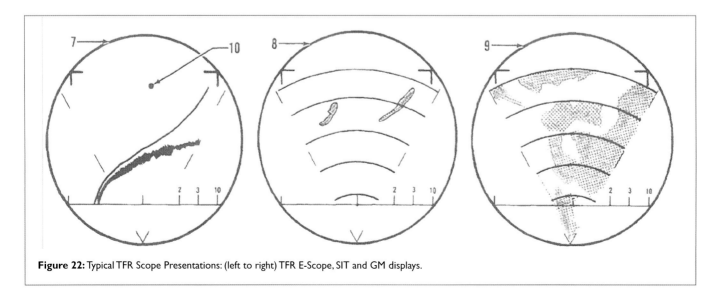

Figure 22: Typical TFR Scope Presentations: (left to right) TFR E-Scope, SIT and GM displays.

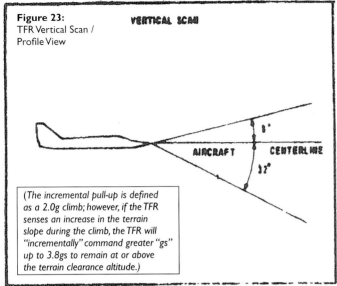

TF MODE

VERTICAL SCAN

Figure 23:
TFR Vertical Scan /
Profile View

AIRCRAFT   CENTERLINE

(The incremental pull-up is defined as a 2.0g climb; however, if the TFR senses an increase in the terrain slope during the climb, the TFR will "incrementally" command greater "gs" up to 3.8gs to remain at or above the terrain clearance altitude.)

Figure 24:
TFR Scan as viewed from above

The TFR's vertical scan pattern is less than one degree wide. Although the TFR beam is 8.20 degrees wide, it is composed of two separate beams that overlap by .65 degrees. The precise center or overlap (Fig 24) of the two beams is where the TFR's scan pattern derives terrain returns. The TFR scan does not provide obstacle clearance to the left or right of the scan pattern. This capability allows the F-111 to fly through narrow canyons or valley passes but limits the turn rate and radius during TF flight.

Known TFR Anomalies

After a review of the F-111A's history, in which several early F-111s were lost, particularly in Southeast Asia, there was a trend of six TFR anomalies which could have contributed to the loss of these aircraft. These six anomalies include: (A) E-Scope Blanking; (B) Weather Induced Climbs / Fly-ups; (C) LARA Override; (D) LARA range limits and break-lock; (E) TFR bank and turn rate/radius limitations; and (F) Bypass Switch Failure. Each of these anomalies will be discussed in the following pages.

(A) E-Scope Blanking

The earliest versions of the APQ-110 TFR did not incorporate a method to suppress rain echoes in the terrain following system. Rain echoes (caused by droplets of water) could exceed the TFR's amplitude detection threshold. Depending on the density of the rain shower, the TFR's transmitted signal could be absorbed by the rain storm or interpreted as a terrain return. In the case of rain storm absorption, the TFR is unable to detect terrain hidden by light rain storms or low density precipitation diffusing or absorbing the radar signal. In the case of false ground echoes, the TFR system interprets heavy or dense rainfall as terrain and initiates a climb maneuver.

The most common TFR anomaly was the phenomenon known as E-Scope Blanking, which has two aspects. The first: light to moderate rain showers absorbed the TFR's energy, thereby masking the presence of terrain (Fig 26). The second: weakly reflecting terrain features are below the TFR's detection amplitude and deflect or absorb radar returns, and the TFR displays gaps or blanks in the terrain return (Fig 27 Example 1 and 3). In both situations too little radar energy is returned to the TFR, and a "blank" terrain profile is displayed, a very dangerous condition.

Though the Dash-1 noted the problem with E-Scope blanking, the severity of the problem was not always apparent or experienced by the flight crews trained in the desert southwest. Unfortunately, it was not until after Constant Guard V, where true Category III TFR testing revealed the full measure of the problem (See Chapter 6, *Constant Sweep Narrative*).

Ultimately, the APQ-110 TFR Computer could not discriminate between smooth terrain features that deflected or diffused the TFR's transmitted signal and weather conditions that absorbed the transmitted signal. In both cases the TFR Computer was unable to generate a

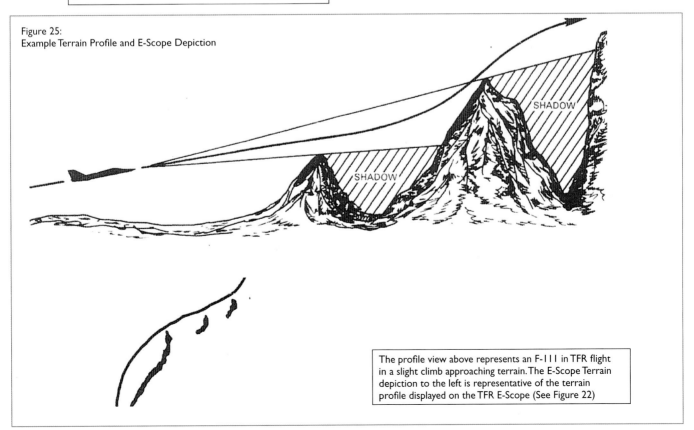

Figure 25:
Example Terrain Profile and E-Scope Depiction

SHADOW

SHADOW

The profile view above represents an F-111 in TFR flight in a slight climb approaching terrain. The E-Scope Terrain depiction to the left is representative of the terrain profile displayed on the TFR E-Scope (See Figure 22)

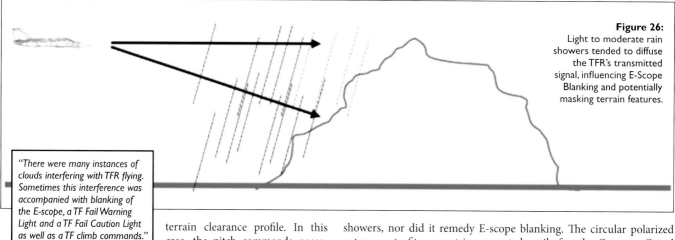

Figure 26:
Light to moderate rain showers tended to diffuse the TFR's transmitted signal, influencing E-Scope Blanking and potentially masking terrain features.

> *"There were many instances of clouds interfering with TFR flying. Sometimes this interference was accompanied with blanking of the E-scope, a TF Fail Warning Light and a TF Fail Caution Light as well as a TF climb commands."*
> *(429TFS Historical Summary 2 7 Sep – 22 Oct 72)*

terrain clearance profile. In this case, the pitch commands necessary to accomplish safe terrain following flight were inhibited.

(B) Weather Induced Climbs / Fly-Ups

The *second* TFR anomaly was influenced by dense precipitation. Heavy rain showers had such high return signal strength that the TFR interpreted the rain shower as terrain, generating a command line that exceeded the 25 degree pitch limit of the TFR. If the TFR exceeded the pitch limits of +/-25 degrees, a fly-up signal would ensue. The pilot then had to override the fly-up and stop the aircraft from attempting to overfly the rain shower or thunderstorm (Figure 25). The flight manual familiar to all USAF pilots is the Dash-1. Even the earliest versions of the flight manual warned pilots of the hazard:

Test flights were flown prior to the Combat Lancer deployment with a "circular polarized" antenna that attempted to solve some of the TFR's problems in the presence of rain showers. However, it was found that the circular polarized antenna only resulted in a small improvement in *light rain showers*; it was not a sufficient fix for moderate to heavy rain showers, nor did it remedy E-scope blanking. The circular polarized antenna retrofit was not incorporated until after the Constant Guard V deployment in 1973, where F-111 crews also experienced E-scope blanking.

(C) LARA Override (Figure 29)

The third known anomaly with the TFR occurred while flying over flat featureless (low reflective) terrain. The absence of terrain returns could cause the TFR to enter LARA Override. During flight along a low-level route, if insufficient forward video is present between 3,500 and 4,500 feet, the LARA takes over to maintain the terrain clearance in an altimeter override mode, more commonly known as LARA Override.

In the LARA Override mode, the terrain clearance altitude is maintained solely by the radar altimeter, not by the TFR-generated command line. The TFR Computer uses the desired set clearance altitude (command line) and the TFR antenna's "down-look angle" at the bottom of the scan (minimum detection range 3,500 to 4,500 feet) to triangulate "height above terrain." If no terrain is detected (angular range data), the TFR cannot determine height and reverts to LARA-derived altitude only. If the LARA detects an incursion below

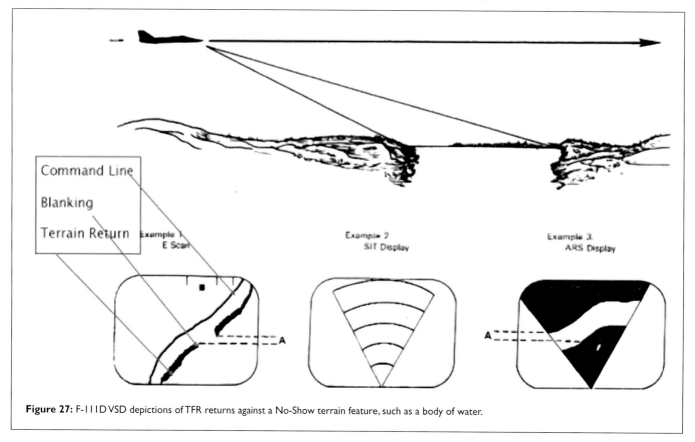

Command Line
Blanking
Terrain Return

Example 1
E Scan

Example 2
SIT Display

Example 3
ARS Display

Figure 27: F-111D VSD depictions of TFR returns against a No-Show terrain feature, such as a body of water.

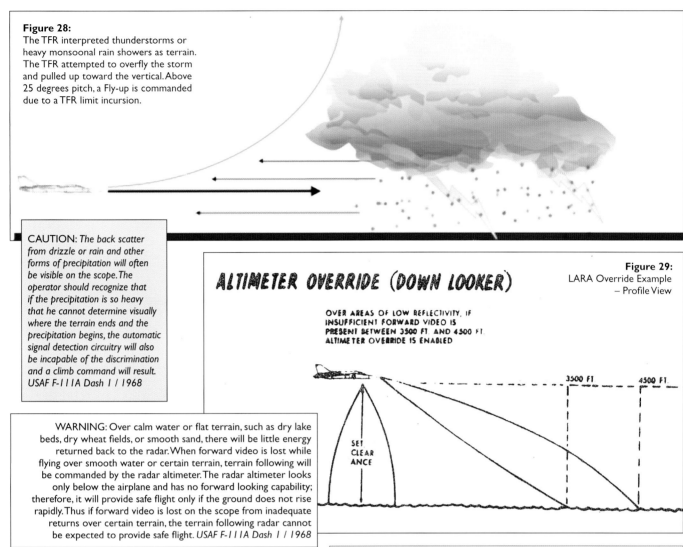

Figure 28:
The TFR interpreted thunderstorms or heavy monsoonal rain showers as terrain. The TFR attempted to overfly the storm and pulled up toward the vertical. Above 25 degrees pitch, a Fly-up is commanded due to a TFR limit incursion.

CAUTION: *The back scatter from drizzle or rain and other forms of precipitation will often be visible on the scope. The operator should recognize that if the precipitation is so heavy that he cannot determine visually where the terrain ends and the precipitation begins, the automatic signal detection circuitry will also be incapable of the discrimination and a climb command will result. USAF F-111A Dash 1 / 1968*

WARNING: Over calm water or flat terrain, such as dry lake beds, dry wheat fields, or smooth sand, there will be little energy returned back to the radar. When forward video is lost while flying over smooth water or certain terrain, terrain following will be commanded by the radar altimeter. The radar altimeter looks only below the airplane and has no forward looking capability; therefore, it will provide safe flight only if the ground does not rise rapidly. Thus if forward video is lost on the scope from inadequate returns over certain terrain, the terrain following radar cannot be expected to provide safe flight. *USAF F-111A Dash 1 / 1968*

Figure 29:
LARA Override Example – Profile View

ALTIMETER OVERRIDE (DOWN LOOKER)

OVER AREAS OF LOW REFLECTIVITY, IF INSUFFICIENT FORWARD VIDEO IS PRESENT BETWEEN 3500 FT. AND 4500 FT. ALTIMETER OVERRIDE IS ENABLED

SET CLEARANCE

3500 FT.   4500 FT.

the 68% minimum altitude threshold, a climb command or fly-up will occur. With the exception of the D and F model F-111s, there was no indication to the F-111A crew that the TFR system was in a LARA Override mode. The F-111A Dash-1 noted this phenomenon with a warning (Yellow Text Box above).

LARA Override was particularly dangerous while flying over water, as the TFR could not accurately determine height due to the absence of solid terrain returns. The LARA signal was either diffused or absorbed by the water, or the LARA signal penetrated the flat surface of smooth water, returning inaccurate height readings leading to insidious descents. If the radar and barometric altimeter were not monitored and compared to the expected altitude, the aircraft could easily enter an insidious descent and crash into water or terrain with a low reflectivity.

(D) LARA Range Limits and Break-Lock (Figure 30 and 31)
The fourth known TFR anomaly was caused by the operational limitations of the LARA, resulting in LARA Break-Lock. The LARA ranging and data input to the TFR Computer was designed with a system limitation that caused a fly-up if the aircraft exceeded +/- 25 degrees of pitch, 45 degrees of bank, or exceeded an absolute altitude (AGL) or a slant range of 5000 feet. Even as early as the first deployment to Vietnam (Combat Lancer), the LARA's limited range was identified as a combat operations deficiency. During the second deployment to Vietnam (Constant Guard V), aircrews noted that the LARA's capabilities were often exceeded while negotiating the steep Karst terrain, or while performing anti-aircraft defensive threat reactions. As depicted in Figure

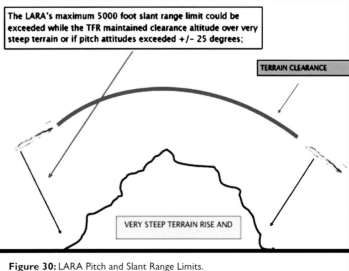

The LARA's maximum 5000 foot slant range limit could be exceeded while the TFR maintained clearance altitude over very steep terrain or if pitch attitudes exceeded +/- 25 degrees;

TERRAIN CLEARANCE

VERY STEEP TERRAIN RISE AND

Figure 30: LARA Pitch and Slant Range Limits.

30, the TFR's terrain contour could result in LARA break-locks during climbs and descents over steeply rising terrain, particularly when the LARA's maximum 5000 foot slant range was exceeded while climbing to overfly or while descending on the downward side of terrain. In these break-lock cases, though, the TFR system responded correctly and commanded a fly-up. The LARA break-locks were more of a nuisance than a significant problem in these situations.

In the extremely rugged terrain of North East Laos and Northwest Vietnam, the 474TFW crews experienced numerous fly ups in their

Photograph of Rugged Karst Terrain typical to Southeast Asia. *Courtesy of Internet Geography*

aircraft due to cresting the top of mountains where the terrain falls away so sharply on the back side that the radar altimeter rings out at 5000 feet before the TFR can bring the crew down the hill. The system works as designed in this circumstance and the crew would get a fail light on both TFR channels and at the same time get an automatic fly up. Source: 474th FW History – Volume I

During surface-to-air missile (SAM) threat reactions at low altitudes, F-111 flight crews initially believed that aggressive maneuvering to defeat SAM threats was a higher priority than remaining within the AUTO TFR and LARA's restricted envelope (See also *Constant Sweep Report*, Chapter 6). These aggressive maneuvers naturally caused fly-ups that could easily exceed the 45-degree bank limitation. Aircrews later came to realize that unprotected TFR flight at low altitude was a greater hazard than the SAM threat. The crews adopted the practice of remaining at low altitude under TFR control or terminating TFR flight and climbing to the MEA during threat reactions. (*The climb to the MEA required the crew to override the TFR with the autopilot release lever, execute hard turns, and then reengage the TFR and descend back to low altitude.*)

(E) TFR Turn Rate/Radius Limitation (Figure 32)
The fifth TFR limitation was exceeding the *maximum rate of turn*. During Automatic TFR flight, the maximum bank angle was limited to 10-degrees in order to limit the rate-of-turn within the TFR's forward scan and minimum obstacle detection range. The F-111's TFR antenna was not designed with a look-into-turn or expanded azimuth search capability. This limiting feature was initially beyond state of the art technologies, and as a result, the TFR was given a turn rate limitation.

Safe terrain following flight is reliant on obstacle detection in the direction of flight, whether directly ahead, or approaching from the side if in a banking turn. The terrain/obstacle detection range must be

sufficiently ahead of the aircraft to allow for terrain detecting, avoidance, and computing the contouring profile. Depending on the aircraft's present airspeed, turn rates are established by the aircraft's bank angle. The steeper the bank, a greater turn rate is developed by the aircraft. Unfortunately, the same criterion affects the TFR's detection range. In straight and level flight, the TFR is attempting to detect terrain between its maximum range of 10 NM and its obstacle avoidance range of 1 to 3 NM ahead of the aircraft. The narrow beam width of the TFR's forward scan cannot detect terrain or obstacles if the rate of turn exceeds the minimum obstacle detection range, generally not less than one (1) mile. For turning flight, an obstacle will usually enter the TFR coverage sector through the side, where the range may be significantly lower than that required for normal terrain following. As a result, the terrain clearance protection of the TFR is defined by the maximum bank angle capability of the TFR. Depicted in Figure 32 are examples of the bank angle capabilities of the TFR system. Green is safe, Blue requires visual lookout, and Red means No TF protection available – completely the pilot's responsibility.

(F) Bypass Switch Failure (Figure 34)
The sixth anomaly associated with the TFR was attributed to a failure of the Bypass Switch and or circuitry. The problem was hazardous, whereby the aircraft continued the descent nose low and crashed, or entered an undetected descent under automated TFR control and crashed. In most instances the crew detected the problem and recovered before terrain collision. To initiate TFR flight, the flight crew would conduct a normal Blind Letdown profile (Figure 33). The initial descent required the aircraft be established at an altitude above 5000 feet AGL (Above Ground Level). Once the pilot engaged the TFR the TFR Computer commanded a pitch-over, which the crew would monitor hands-off. As the aircraft descended the pilot monitored a number of parameters, including TFR commands and responses, to ensure the proper and safe operation of the system. If any of the checks and TFR responses were incorrect, the pilot had to assess whether safe TFR operations were possible and reattempt the blind letdown or abort TFR flight entirely. The TFR system also incorporated its own fault detection circuitry, which under normal conditions commanded a fly-up, commanded a fly-up maneuver for a limit incursion, or inhibited TFR operation entirely. If during low altitude TFR flight a fault was automatically detected or the crew noticed a problem, a fly-up command or fly-up maneuver was flown to abort away from the low-level and reach a safe altitude. If the reason causing the fly-up was determined and corrected, the crew could resume TFR operations

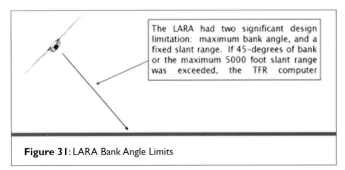

The LARA had two significant design limitation: maximum bank angle, and a fixed slant range. If 45-degrees of bank or the maximum 5000 foot slant range was exceeded, the TFR computer

Figure 31: LARA Bank Angle Limits

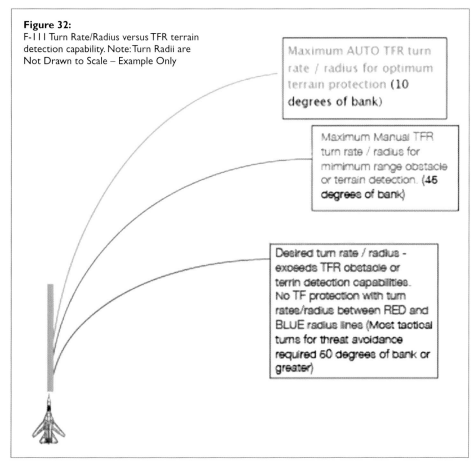

Figure 32:
F-111 Turn Rate/Radius versus TFR terrain detection capability. Note: Turn Radii are Not Drawn to Scale – Example Only

Maximum AUTO TFR turn rate / radius for optimum terrain protection (10 degrees of bank)

Maximum Manual TFR turn rate / radius for mimimum range obstacle or terrain detection. (45 degrees of bank)

Desired turn rate / radius - exceeds TFR obstacle or terrin detection capabilities. No TF protection with turn rates/radius between RED and BLUE radius lines (Most tactical turns for threat avoidance required 60 degrees of bank or greater)

from below 5000 feet AGL using the Blind-Letdown maneuver shown in Figure 35. Thorough technical discussion of the problems attributed to the Bypass Switch (Figure 34) follows and is discussed by former GDFW Technical Representative Don Gwynne. The Bypass switch issue discussed may have occurred during combat operations in Southeast Asia. The details include the system operation prior to retrofit of the Low Altitude Monitor (LAM) system but before Desert Storm. The integration of the Low Altitude Radar Altimeter (LARA) system with the Terrain Following Radar (TFR) system required that GD/FW link the two systems using a Bypass Switch, mounted on the left console Miscellaneous Switch Panel. To understand the functions of the Bypass Switch, consider the following: the LARA provided radar altitude (height above ground directly below the aircraft) from zero to 5,000 feet above ground level (AGL). When the aircraft was more than 5,000 feet AGL, the LARA was not "In Track" and output was zero. Among the TFR Computer's many input requirements, it needed a LARA signal labeled "Hr", i.e., radar altitude. It also required a 28 volt dc (Vdc) discrete signal from the LARA denoting "On and In Track".

If the value of Hr coming to the TFR Computer was not greater than 68% of the selected Set Clearance Plane (SCP, set on the TFR Control Panel: 200', 300', 500', 750', or 1000'), then the TFR Computer would declare TF Fail and a fly-up command would be issued (For FB-111A, the value was 83% instead of 68%).

If the 28 volt dc "On and In Track" discrete was not received, the TFR Computer would declare TF Fail and a fly-up command would be issued.

Consider the problem of wanting the TFR to provide guidance for a "Blind Let Down", i.e., TF descent from an altitude greater than 5,000' AGL. Since the LARA is not In Track above 5,000', and since the Hr value when not In-Track is zero, the TFR Computer would have to declare TF Fail, and instead of flying down to the selected SCP, a TF Fail fly-up would be the result.

Enter the Bypass Switch. Multiple sets of switch contacts inside the Bypass Switch provided a solution to the Blind Let Down problem, as follows:

The Bypass Switch was spring loaded to the NORM (normal) position, where the LARA/TFR interface functioned as described above. If placed to the BYPASS position, however, things changed. The switch would only hold in the BYPASS position if the solenoid coil within the switch was powered by an "On and Not Track" signal from the LARA. Above 5,000' AGL, the Bypass Switch would be solenoid-held in the BYPASS position. Below 5,000' AGL, however, the "On and Not Track" signal would be lost when the LARA began tracking the ground and the Bypass Switch was no longer solenoid-held in BYPASS, dropping back to the NORM position automatically.

With the Bypass Switch in BYPASS the TFR Computer was satisfied, because a 28 volt dc signal from the Bypass Switch replaced the LARA's "On and In Track" signal and a fixed reference voltage replaced the Hr radar altitude signal. The reference voltage equated to an Hr value of 1850 feet AGL, which was high enough to satisfy the 68% or 83% test circuits.

With a simulated 1850 feet Hr value being received, and with a simulated "On and In Track" discrete being received, the TFR Computer would dutifully generate an approximately 10 degree dive command, and the Blind Let Down commenced as desired. As the aircraft descended below 5,000' AGL, the LARA would "ring in" and begin tracking the ground. At this time, the Bypass Switch should drop back to the NORM position, and since the actual Hr value of approximately 5,000' AGL would now be received by the TFR Computer, the computed dive angle increased slightly to approximately 12 degrees. Crews were expected to monitor for the additional 2 degree push over passing down through 5,000' AGL as an indication things were working normally.

Potential Failure Scenarios Involving the Bypass Switch circuitry:

1. Physical sticking of the Bypass Switch in BYPASS position. If the Bypass Switch fails to automatically drop back to the NORM position as the LARA rings in below 5,000' AGL, consider the situation: the 68% (or FB, 83%) check will always pass, due to the simulated 1,850' AGL Hr value being received at the TFR Computer input circuits from the Bypass Switch contacts. So the monitor within the TFR Computer checking that the aircraft doesn't descend significantly below the SCP has been defeated. The monitor within the TFR Computer checking that the LARA is "On and In Track" is also defeated. In this condition, the aircraft will still fly good TF, so long as forward video is being received from the TFR Antenna-Receiver. But if forward returns are lost (e.g., over smooth water, snow, sand, etc.) the TFR Computer will begin flying the aircraft lower, in an effort to get the Hr signal value to equal the SCP command. But the Hr value is stuck at 1,850 feet AGL, so the TF will command a continual descent into the non-reflective terrain, and no 68%/83% fail-safe fly-up will save the situation, because it is also seeing a constant Hr value of 1,850' AGL. Unless the crew detects the situation before ground impact, CFIT would be the logical result.

2. Soldered connections on the bottom of the Bypass Switch, underneath the Miscellaneous Switch Panel, were initially not protected against moisture or corrosion. This was not much of a problem at GDFW, Edwards, or Nellis, but became significant in Southeast Asia (SEA). Fungus development between the solder terminals on the bottom of the Bypass Switch was capable of providing "sneak paths", by which the TFR Computer input circuits might see incorrect values for Hr, even with the Bypass Switch in NORM, leading to the same

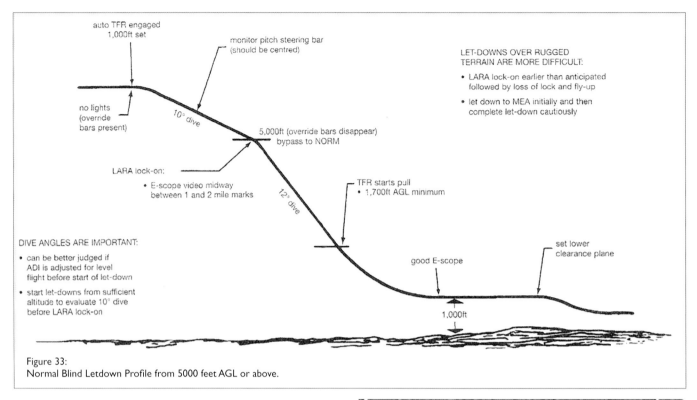

Figure 33:
Normal Blind Letdown Profile from 5000 feet AGL or above.

fly down results as described above. This potential was eventually recognized and corrected by cleaning and then coating the solder terminals with a varnish compound. Even later, a different P/N switch having protected terminals within a connector was eventually retrofitted.

The LARA had two significant design limitations: maximum bank angle and a fixed slant range. If 45-degrees of bank or the maximum 5000 foot slant range was exceeded, the TFR Computer commanded a fly-up.

3. Early versions of the Bypass Switch were manufactured with an internal RTV sealant which released traces of acetic acid as it cured, which could result in internal corrosion of the switch contacts, again creating the potential for incorrect values of Hr going to the TFR Computer. A different Part Number (P/N) Bypass Switch was designed and retrofitted. Additionally, a new Line Replaceable Unit (LRU) dubbed the Low Altitude Monitor (LAM) was developed and retrofitted, which protected against these potential failure modes involving the Bypass Switch.

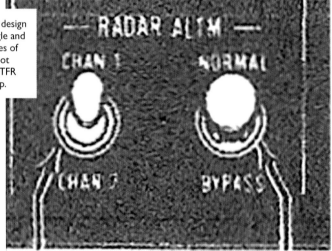

Figure 34: Radar Altimeter Channel Selection and Normal / Bypass Switch.

The LARA Multiplexing Unit (LARA MUX) replaced the original manual selection of the Radar Altimeters (one of two) to an automated switching system and comparator. The LARA MUX unit allowed both radar altimeters to operate simultaneously and performed a comparison of the two signals, ensuring the altitude data did not differ by more than a fixed percentage. The original Radar Altimeter switch design (left switch on Figure 34) allowed the selection of only one Radar Altimeter at a time. A problem with this design could occur on occasion; the Radar Altimeter would freeze on one ranging altitude, sending the same altitude data to the TFR Computer. The TFR Computer accepted the input but could continue to descend, looking for the normal 5000 foot "Lock-on" during a Blind Letdown (Figure 33), or the aircraft could descend below the 68 percent fail-safe fly-up without any warning to the pilot. If the pilot was not paying attention the aircraft could crash. The solution incorporated a new LARA channel select switch with an AUTO position which allowed the LARA MUX to operate both Radar Altimeter Receiver / Transmitters (R/T) simultaneously. The pilot still had the option to use either LARA individually.

The Low Altitude Monitor (LAM) incorporated the LARA Multiplexing Unit and detected: (1) faults in the TFR's computed set clearance plane circuitry; and (2) a failure of the Bypass Switch to not automatically switch from Bypass (above 5000 feet AGL) to Normal when the Radar Altimeter had actually "Locked-On" to 5000 feet slant range.

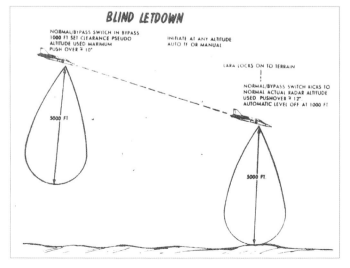

Figure 35: Blind Letdown profile initiated below 1000 feet AGL.

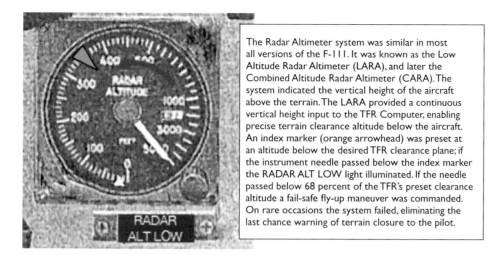

The Radar Altimeter system was similar in most all versions of the F-111. It was known as the Low Altitude Radar Altimeter (LARA), and later the Combined Altitude Radar Altimeter (CARA). The system indicated the vertical height of the aircraft above the terrain. The LARA provided a continuous vertical height input to the TFR Computer, enabling precise terrain clearance altitude below the aircraft. An index marker (orange arrowhead) was preset at an altitude below the desired TFR clearance plane; if the instrument needle passed below the index marker the RADAR ALT LOW light illuminated. If the needle passed below 68 percent of the TFR's preset clearance altitude a fail-safe fly-up maneuver was commanded. On rare occasions the system failed, eliminating the last chance warning of terrain closure to the pilot.

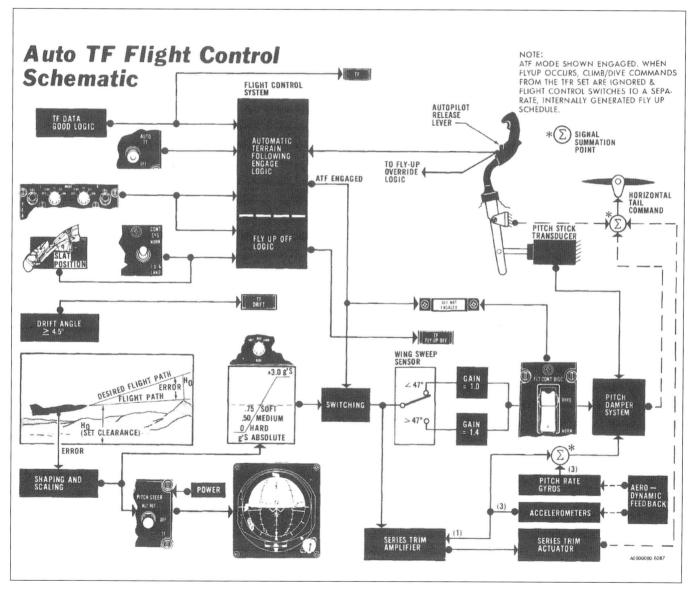

Figure 37: F-111A Automatic TFR Computer and Flight Control Schematic.

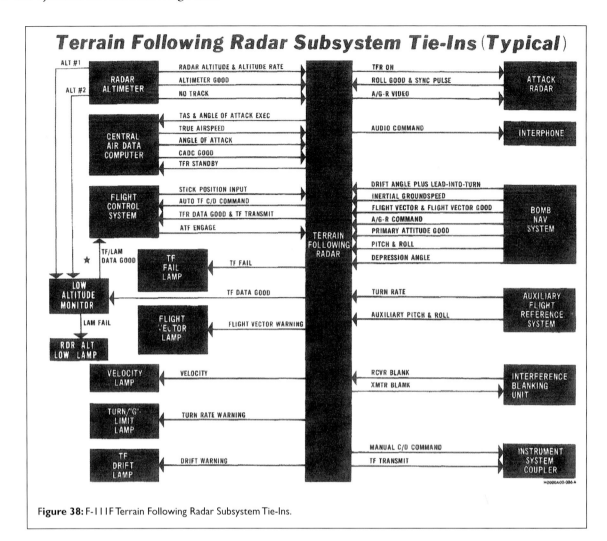

Figure 38: F-111F Terrain Following Radar Subsystem Tie-Ins.

2

RESEARCH, DEVELOPMENT, TEST & EVALUATION (RDT&E) PRE-PRODUCTION, AND F-111B MISHAPS

An aircraft salvage and recovery crane lifting 63-9774 after crash landing. *Courtesy of Don Gwynne.*

63-9769 F-111A #4 GD/FW Production Run # A1-04
USAF Delivery Date June 29, 1965

Crash Scenario
On May 18, 1968, aircraft 63-9769 crashed while conducting an air show routine for the Holloman AFB, New Mexico, Armed Forces Day celebration. During a Low Speed, High Angle of Attack (AOA) flyby in a landing configuration (landing gear down), the aircraft's forward airspeed fell below the total "clean wing" lift capability. The aircraft entered a sink rate that could not be reduced with available engine thrust, and the aircraft abruptly settled onto the runway near the Base Operations building and main taxiway. The subsequent hard landing collapsed the Nose Landing Gear (NLG) and the aircraft received major structural damage.

Findings
Although the aircraft was configured for slow flight, flaps, slats, and landing gear down, the airspeed decreased unabated. The aircraft's subsequent high angle of attack during the low speed pass resulted in the aircraft entering the Region of Reversed Command, whereby the thrust available (even in full afterburner) could not overcome the Lift-Over-Drag (L/D) max ratio. The aircraft could only be recovered by sacrificing altitude (reducing AOA and subsequent lift and drag) to gain airspeed. At such a low altitude this action was not possible, and the pilot could neither maintain altitude nor accelerate to regain flying airspeed. The aircraft entered an unrecoverable rate of descent and crashed slightly nose low with sufficient force to cause major structural damage. The pilot was uninjured and walked away.

Courtesy Author's Collection

Crew
Pilot: Mr. Frederick J Voorhies
WSO: None (Right Seat Ballast)
Call Sign: Swing 6
Time of Crash: 1304 MDT
Mishap Board President: Col Jack Beckelman
Assigned Unit: On Bailment from the USAF to GD/FW
Aircraft Statistics: 229 Flights 420.2 Flight Hours
Crash Result: Aircraft Destroyed; airframe trucked to AMARC and parts later were donors to the GDFW F-111 restoration program – "Vark Hospital."

63-9774 F-111A # 9 GD/FW Production Run # A1-09
USAF Delivery Date February 16, 1966

Crash Scenario
On January 19, 1967, aircraft 63-9774 was on final approach to Edwards AFB, California, when it crashed approximately 1.25 NM short of Runway 04. The mishap aircrew approached with a 50 degree wing sweep. The landing configuration should have called for a 16- or 26-degree sweep with slats and flaps extended for adequate lift. The aircraft settled onto the dry lake bed and caught fire. After the crash landing the left seat pilot, Lt Col Don McCance, was dazed and had difficulty extricating himself from the cockpit. The right seat pilot, Major Herbert Brightwell, got out and ran to the other side of the aircraft to help. While standing in a pool of aviation fuel a fire ignited, and Major Brightwell received fatal burns. Lt Col McCance received significant burns but survived.

Findings
The pilot did not position the aircraft's variable geometry wings to the forward position and did not configure the wings (slats and flaps down) for landing in accordance with checklist procedures.

Additionally, the translating intake cowls were in the "closed" or cruise flight position, not in the "open" Takeoff and Landing position. The aircraft was unable to maintain flight without the high lift devices deployed while at a slow approach speed and aft wing sweep. The aircraft continued an unrecoverable descent and crashed short of the runway. This was the first USAF F-111 mishap, and it was significant at the time, because the variable geometry wing position selector handle moved opposite the wing motion in the first eleven (11) RDT&E aircraft. The investigation team believes the pilot made a human factor error by moving the wing position selector handle in the direction he wanted the wings to move (forward); however, the existing wing sweep mechanization moved the wings aft. Although the flap handle had been moved to the down position, the flaps remained up due to an override mechanism which prevented flap deployment at the aft wing sweep. On this aircraft and the first eleven F-111s there was no automatic activation mechanism on the translating cowls, no wing sweep position warning, and no stall warning device. The absence of configuration indicators or improper configuration warning lights or horns compounded the pilot's lack of understanding of the improper configuration.

Courtesy Author's Collection

Courtesy Bill Allen

63-9780 F-111A # 15 GD/FW Production Run # A1-15
USAF Delivery Date August 21, 1966

Crash Scenario

On October 19, 1967, aircraft 63-9780 was on loan to General Dynamics Fort Worth (GDFW) for a Category I Test Flight when it crashed 14 NM west of Bowie, Texas. The aircraft was on its 113th flight, and was equipped with an experimental 30 inch gap speed brake which was designed to achieve greater stability and fewer buffets than the standard production design. At 39,300 feet and 1.77 Mach the pilot extended the speed brake to 80 degrees. Within 10-12 seconds the crew heard a

loud clunk, followed by primary hydraulic system failure. The test pilot retracted the speed brake, which was followed a few seconds later by another two loud thumps. At the time both engines were in afterburner, but the left engine instruments indicated a compressor stall and the left engine spike was noted to be "off schedule." The left engine throttle was retarded to idle, while the right engine was retarded to the Military power setting. Two (2) minutes and 2 seconds after the thumps were first heard utility hydraulic pressure was also lost. With total loss of all hydraulics aircraft control was impossible and the aircrew ejected.

Note: This was the first fully successful use of the F-111 capsule ejection system.

Findings

A train of hydraulic system pressure losses were caused by structural failure of the test speed brake support bracket. The left engine compressor stalls were indirectly related to the speed brake failures. Compressor stalls were very common in the early pre-production F-111As delivered without the more advanced Triple Plow II intakes and the less stall prone TF30-P-3 engines common to airframes A1-19 and on. In flight regimes at high Mach, G-loading, and AOA, or in high thrust demand flight profiles, the consequent disturbed air flow entering the intake system was incompatible with the current engine design flaws. These early RDT&E and *Preproduction* aircraft were extremely susceptible and intolerant of airflow distortions entering the intake. The disturbed air flow continued down the duct to the engine face, leading to violent compressor stalls within the TF-30 P-1 engine. These RDT&E and *Preproduction* airframes were devoid of an automatic Compressor Bleed Valve Control, which in later models manually opened above Mach 1.6 to bleed air from the engine compressor to prevent compressor stalls.

The speed brake failure may have induced yawing which then induced an airflow distortion, precipitating the compressor stalls. Even though the compressor stalls could have been cleared in flight by the pilot, the catastrophic internal destruction created within the wheel well as the test speed brake slammed closed contributed to hydraulic failures that resulted in the loss of control. With loss of hydraulics pilot initiated flight control movement is impossible and the aircraft had to be abandoned.

Note: The first eleven (11) aircraft required field modifications to reverse this human factor design flaw. Production Aircraft Number 12 and on were configured during production with the wing's sweep following the direction the hand-grip was moved.

Crew

Pilot: Lt Col Donovan L McCance Survived
WSO: Maj Herbert F Brightwell Received Fatal Injury
Call Sign: 774
Time of Crash: 1304 MDT
Assigned Unit: 6510th TW / 6512th Test Squadron AFFTC Edwards AFB, California
Aircraft Statistics: 108 Flights 193.25 Flight Hours
Crash Result: Aircraft Destroyed / One Fatal Injury after landing

Crew

Pilot: Mr. David J Thigpen
WSO: Mr. Max E Gordon
Call Sign: Swing 7
Time of Crash: 1810 CDT
Assigned Unit: On Bailment from the USAF to GD/FW
Mishap Board President: Col James P Hagerstrom
Aircraft Statistics: 113 Flights 278.35 Flight Hours
Crash Result: Aircraft Destroyed, Capsule is on display at the USAF Museum Wright-Patterson AFB, Ohio

The following narrative of the mishap ejection sequence was written by civilian test pilot David Thigpen:

Courtesy Author's Collection

Throughout the aircraft's maneuvering on its own I had my left hand on the throttles and my right hand on the control stick. Prior to ejection I did lower the seat, lower the helmet visor, assumed an erect position in the seat with my feet flat on the floor, and locked the shoulder harness. I think at ejection my hands were on the controls as described. Max had his left hand on the ejection handle. The aircraft made one last pitch up, with the nose 20 to 30 degrees above the horizon and the wings in a relatively level position. At 27,600 feet, 280 KIAS, with both throttles at idle, 72 degrees wing sweep, and after approximately 55 minutes of flight, I asked Max to pull the handle. He did it.

There was a short delay (estimated 1/3 second) after pulling the handle before anything happened. The linear shaped charge fired, followed immediately by the main rocket motor. I could not distinguish the sound of the two firings; however, the overall noise gave me the impression of a large cannon firing. Almost immediately the cockpit air was contaminated to a moderate degree with gases and fumes which I suspect resulted from the charges firing. The forces during ejection were firm but not excessive. I would estimate the normal acceleration to be between 12 and 14 "gs". From my previous experience of ejecting from an F-8 using a Martin-Baker ejection seat, I would estimate these forces to be comparable, if not a little less. It was not a sharp impulse, but rather a smooth acceleration away from the airplane. During this sequence I was not tossed around against my restraining harness but depressed firmly against the seat. My head and hands did not flail around or hit anything, and my feet remained planted on the floor. Also, there were no loose objects tossed around the cockpit. Shortly after separation, I had the sensation that the module had pitched up to an attitude of 50 to 70 degrees nose up. To the best of my knowledge the module did not roll or tumble, or have excessive yaw perturbations at this time or at any time during our descent. During the initial phase after ejection we did not have visual contact with the aircraft or with the ground. My impression was that the module described a parabolic trajectory until established in a nose down dive. There was no sensation of "0 g" flight during this phase or the subsequent descent. My oxygen mask remained in position during the ejection. With the stabilization chute deployed, the module stabilized in a 50 to 70 degree nose down attitude. There were no rolling or pitching forces felt during this free fall, although some yawing of the module may have been present. There was a mild longitudinal tugging produced by the stabilization chute. Occasionally the stabilization chute could be seen from the module. The restraint harness

remained locked until main parachute deployment. I mentioned that for ejection I sat erect and pressed back in the seat with the shoulder harness locked. I do not recall the automatic harness retraction devices forcing me back in the seat, but I'm certain that they did. During the descent, the control stick remained in an essentially neutral position and did not flail around in the cockpit.

Shortly after we were stabilized in our free fall I became concerned about the welfare of Max. I had not observed any response from him since ejection. On severance from the aircraft we lost power to all instruments and systems, including the intercom. The only instruments we noted still functioning were the clock, cabin altimeter, and test altimeter. With the shoulder harness restraining me back in the seat, the pilot's panel camera obstructed my observing Max. There was some wind noise, and with my oxygen mask on I was unable to communicate with him. So I removed my mask for communicating and was subsequently able to determine that he was okay. The foul gases were still persisting in the cockpit. The odor was of an acid nature, only slightly pyrotechnic, and the color was musty brown. It was disagreeable in smell and mildly irritating to the eyes. The intensity was comparable to a cigarette smoke filled room, although visibility was not significantly impaired. I replaced my mask but removed it on several other occasions in order to communicate.

Emergency oxygen was provided automatically on ejection, and I believe the emergency pressurization was automatically activated. I recall no sensation of rapid decompression or pressure changes. I manually activated both emergency oxygen and emergency pressurization as a precautionary step.

During our descent prior to the main parachute opening I could see the abandoned F-111 through the left transparency. I saw the airplane on three or four occasions for durations of 4 to 6 seconds each time, and then it would disappear behind my left shoulder. This resulted in the sensation that I was in a slow right turn. If the module was swinging at all it was of a small magnitude and I was not aware of it. The airplane was descending approximately at the same rate as we were, and it appeared to remain essentially level with us. I could see the silhouette of the module that was missing from the airplane. I don't recall seeing the underneath side of the airplane or being able to determine if the external pods were intact, nor was I able to see any fluids, etc. I was able to determine that there was no smoke or flame emanating from the aircraft. I estimate that the airplane was some 200 to 400 yards to the south of our position (the module was orientated basically on a westerly heading).

Author's Note: An interesting anecdote was revealed during an interview with Bill Allen, GDFW Systems Safety Engineer: the Army Liaison aircraft noted by David Thigpen was travelling cross-country and just happened to be passing by the area when the Army pilot spotted the module descending under the main parachute. The Army pilot reported rather emphatically to air traffic control, "*THERE'S A SPACE CAPSULE DESCENDING NEAR MY POSITION!*" At the time, it was not well known the F-111 was equipped with an escape pod, but every pilot was tuned-in with the well publicized Apollo Moon Program.

Additionally Bill Allen, to whom this book has been dedicated, revealed during an interview that this mishap occurred on the same day as his F-111 flight with Phil Oestricher (also as told in this book's Dedication to Bill Allen). Bill was so excited about his F-111 flight, he took his girlfriend out to the GDFW engineer's favorite restaurant, ecstatically relating his experience to his future wife. Unfortunately, a short time after sitting down to eat, the restaurant manager informed Bill that he must return immediately to his work place. Only after arriving back at work was Bill informed about this crash and designated the lead investigator for General Dynamics. Bill said, "One of the most exciting days in my life was interrupted by the crash of Number 15."

FIRST DEMO OF CREW ESCAPE MODULE - F-111A #15
19 OCT. 1967

First use of the F-111 Capsule Ejection System. *Courtesy GDFW.*

The attitude of the airplane was primarily nose down (20 to 50 degrees) and appeared to be falling in a spiral pattern. Occasionally the nose would pitch up to the horizon and then fall back through, all while it was turning. The maneuvers the airplane was describing reminded me of a movie I had seen some six weeks ago of the wind tunnel spin model tests.

The main parachute deployment occurred as we were descending through approximately 14,000 feet. There was a sharp pop noise just as the main chute was being pulled out. I watched the repositioning bridle being snapped up from the module center beam, and in short order the module was repositioned to a relatively level attitude and the rapid rate of descent broken to a more comfortable rate. My shoulder harness remained locked during the phase, however, I unlocked it shortly after the chute deployed. The physical sensation of this repositioning and deceleration to me was comparable to sliding down a long slide and bottoming out at the bottom of the slide where it ends. Again, there were no loose objects flying around the cockpit.

The attitude of the module in this configuration was essentially level, possibly slightly nose up 5 to 10 degrees. There may have been some mild swings, possibly not; in any case, I was not at all concerned with module oscillations during this descent. Looking up, I could see the large parachute, main riser, and connecting suspension lines, and all appeared to be intact, with the exception of a small tear (approximately one foot square) in the main canopy. During this descent I observed both the cabin altimeter and the test altimeter to be functioning. I first noticed them at approximately 12,000 feet, and they appeared to be tracking together within a couple of hundred feet. Max timed the rate of descent from 10,000 feet to 4,200 feet for a lapsed time of 4 minutes 56 seconds. I lost visual contact with the airplane when the main chute deployed; however, later I did spot a place on the ground from which a considerable amount of grey smoke was coming and assumed that to be the place the aircraft impacted.

From our vantage point we commanded an excellent view of the terrain beneath us. I had the sensation that we were suspended in the gondola of a large balloon. We still had a significant amount of disagreeable gases in the module, so I unlocked and opened the left canopy hatch and locked it approximately 1 ½ feet open. Seeing this caused no adverse characteristics Max opened the right hatch. There was almost a complete absence of sound except for light wind noises. The draft we created purged the cockpit of all foul gases. I looked out over the side and was better able to evaluate the pasture we were descending into. I estimate that we had the hatches open for the descent between 6,000 feet and 4,000 feet. The vertical wind velocity outside was like a mild breeze of about 10 knots. We did not have a significant drift (after landing I would estimate the surface winds to be about 6-8 knots out of the southwest). At about 4,000 feet we closed and locked both hatches. At this point we recovered the condensed checklist and reviewed the emergency procedures after ejection.

In preparation for ground impact the oxygen mask was replaced, visor lowered, and shoulder harness locked. I was in the process of repositioning myself firmly back in the seat when we contacted the ground. I had about 1/5 of my weight supported by my arms pushing up and aft at that moment. I was pleasantly surprised that the ground impact forces were substantially less than I was anticipating. It felt in the order of 10 to 12 gs, or somewhat less than the ejection forces. The module did not bounce, but I did feel the ground impact attenuation bag deflate. The module had 4 or 5 knots of drift to the north (we were orientated on a westerly heading on ground impact), and this was just enough to cause us to roll to the right after the vertical deceleration. The module came to rest after rolling about 135 degrees from the vertical, suspending me somewhat inverted in the harness. Immediately I pulled the severance and flotation handle and Max pulled the parachute release handle.

After all motion stopped I proceeded to abandon the module. Now that we were both safely on the ground there was no sense of urgency, and we did not hasten to get out. I was able to open the right canopy hatch without any difficulty and lay it back across the ground, exposing about a three foot opening. After releasing my left lower torso restraint, I had some problem in reaching the right release. I could have done it if the situation required it; however, rather than strain a muscle or something, I asked Max to unsnap me, and he did. Then, supporting myself upside down, I unsnapped the chest strap and oxygen hose and crawled from the module. Just as I was clearing the module, I heard a sharp "pop" as the self righting bag was inflating. We had landed in an open field covered with brush and weeds approximately 50 feet from a dirt road. The parachute had collapsed over and was suspended by a power line pole on our side of the road. The site of the aircraft crash was not visible from our position, but was approximately 2 ½ to 3 miles southwest of us. Max walked to a nearby (500 yards) ranch house and telephoned the company. An Army aircraft made several low passes over us and we responded to let him know we were O.K. Neither one of us suffered any serious ill effects as a result of this accident.

Signed D.J. Thigpen, Engineering Test Pilot

63-9783
F-111A # 18 GD/FW Production Run # A1-18
USAF Delivery Date August 18, 1966

Mishap Scenario
On August 13, 1968, the mishap aircraft F-111A 63-9783 was scheduled for a test flight to jettison an empty 600-gallon fuel tank and pylon from external stores position # 7. The test was scheduled for a 0700 L drop at the Edwards AFB Precision Bombing Range, PB-2. The jettison conditions for the test were .75 Mach (446 KCAS), 2000' AGL, and 26 degrees wing sweep. The test was flown as scheduled. Tank separation appeared normal, and the tank did drop 10 to 15 feet below the aircraft. However, after the drop the tank initially moved inwards towards the fuselage and then started to roll right. When the tank reached approximately 15 feet below the aircraft, the nose of the fuel tank began to rise and the tank pitched up rapidly to about a 60 degree angle. As the nose of the tank pitched up, the tank also climbed until it impacted the mishap aircraft. The fuel tank nose penetrated the aft fuselage fuel tank, causing considerable damage. A successful landing was accomplished on Edwards AFB, California, Dry Lake Bed Runway 23.

Courtesy of the USAF

Findings
The external fuel tank design connected the fuel tank and its aerodynamic support fairing to the wing swivel by means of a cap pylon. The external fuel tank was suspended to the cap pylon by two jettison hooks. When jettisoned, the jettison hooks released the fuel tank in a stabilized manner, and the nose of the tank pitched down as designed. Unfortunately, the tank's light weight (ratio of volume to mass), stabilization tail fin configuration, the fuel tank's center of

gravity, and the fuel tanks aerodynamic support pylon all contributed to a flight dynamic, resulting in a pitch-up shortly after the separation trajectory. As seen in the photographs below, the fuel tank struck the aircraft in the aft fuselage fuel cell. The pilot shut down the right engine after noticing the engine oil pressure had dropped to zero. The collision caused substantial damage to the aft fuselage. The fuel tank and pylon were later modified to a single forward ejector that influenced a pitch-down when the tank was jettisoned. Thereafter, the production external fuel tanks tumbled nose down and away from the aircraft.

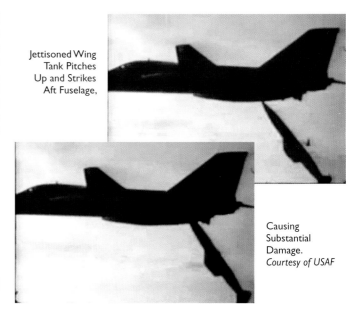

Jettisoned Wing Tank Pitches Up and Strikes Aft Fuselage,

Causing Substantial Damage.
Courtesy of USAF

Crew
Pilot: Mr. Frederick J Voorhies
WSO: Mr. Grover C Tate, Jr.
Call Sign: 9783
Time of Incident: 0706 PDT
Mishap Board President: Capt Floyd B Stroup
Assigned Unit: 6510th TW / 6512 TS Edwards AFB, California
Aircraft Statistics: Unknown
Mishap Result: Major structural damage. Aircraft repaired and returned to service.

65-5701 F-111A # 19 GD/FW Production Run # A1-19
USAF Delivery Date: April 28, 1967

Crash Scenario
On January 2, 1968, while assigned to Edwards AFB, California Test Center, aircraft 65-5701 experienced a fire in the weapons bay while conducting Category II Live Fire testing of the M61-A1 Gatling Gun. While over the Edwards Gunnery Range adjacent to Rogers Dry Lake, the crew began to smell fumes after the first hot pass and could hear the gun cycling. Four more hot passes were made, and then while attempting the 6th hot pass the aircrew heard live rounds cooking off, and the chase aircraft reported smoke trailing the aircraft and the crew experienced flight control gyrations below 1000 MSL. The mishap pilot was able to maintain control of the aircraft for a time and began a 5-10 degree climb. The chase aircraft reported the first signs of a fire, and as the aircraft passed 5000 MSL, control was lost and the crew successfully ejected 13 NM SE of Edwards AFB, California.

Findings
The live 20mm rounds cooked off in the weapons bay, causing shrapnel and fire damage. The exposed hydraulic lines that powered the gun system were ultimately ruptured and resulted in loss of hydraulic pressure to the flight controls. Loss of control ensued and the crew was forced to eject. The F-111 had no backup means to power the flight controls, nor was there a capability for the pilot to fly the aircraft manually. Once

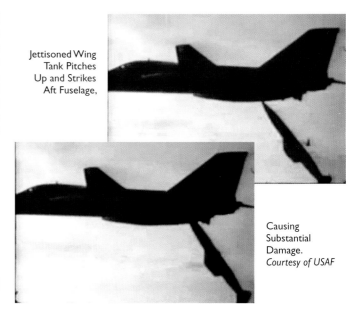

Courtesy of GDFW.

hydraulic pressure to the servo actuators was lost the aircraft departed controlled flight.

Crew
Pilot: Maj Joseph B Jordan
WSO: Col Henry W Brown
Call Sign: 5701
Time of Crash: 1421 PST
Mishap Board President: Col Joseph R Myers
Assigned Unit: 6510th TW / 6512th TS AFFTC Edwards AFB, California
Aircraft Statistics: 84 Flights 207.7 Flight Hours
Crash Result: Aircraft Destroyed / Successful Ejection

65-5703
F-111A # 21 GD/FW Production Run # A1-21
USAF Delivery August 24, 1967

Crash Scenario
On September 11, 1972, at Edwards AFB, California, aircraft 65-5703 crashed while performing USAF CAT II / Phase II scheduled syllabus testing for the Stall / Post Stall / Spin Prevention program. While over the Edwards Spin Area, the mishap crew had completed one spin recovery and then climbed back to altitude for the second spin test. The mishap crew entered

into the test profile at 37,200 feet MSL, which required a left 2.0 g turn with an abrupt pull-up to 10.0 AOA at 270 KIAS. The aircraft departed controlled flight with 28.6 degrees angle of attack (AOA), 12.2 degree aircraft nose right (ANR). and 246 knots indicated airspeed (KIAS). The pilot applied recovery control (full forward stick) immediately after

the nose sliced violently to the right. The aircraft stabilized in a spin to the right, passing 31,750 feet MSL, at which time the pilot applied recovery controls, rudder against the spin, and ailerons controls with the spin. The pilot sensed the spin breaking passing 25,800 feet, where the pilot neutralized the controls but maintained full forward stick. At 22,000 feet neutral rudder was applied, at which time the AOA was -46.7 degrees, 22 degrees nose right, and airspeed 200 KIAS. The pilot felt that adequate control was not regained because of residual oscillations. The spin recovery chute was deployed, inflated, and then abruptly separated from the aircraft,

A rare photograph showing 5703's escape module shortly after landing. *Courtesy of Bill Allen.*

which had 5.3 degrees AOA, 16 degrees left roll, and 240 KIAS. Passing 12,000 feet, the aircraft commander (AC) ejected the module in the High Speed mode. Separation and deployment of the escape system was successfully accomplished. The aircraft continued in a near vertical dive with a slight roll to the left until impact. The aircraft crashed 12 NM North of Edwards AFB in Kern County, California.

Findings:
The pilot was conducting a stall/post stall/spin prevention test utilizing pilot handbook recovery procedures. On the second spin test, the aircraft departed rapidly, then entered a right oscillatory spin. Recovery controls were applied and the spin appeared to be broken. Before recovery could be completed the aircraft again entered an out-of-control condition. After passing through 20,850 feet the recovery chute was deployed, inflated, and immediately separated from the aircraft. Conditions at maximum chute load were AOA 5.5 degrees, Beta 16 degrees aircraft nose left, airspeed 240 KIAS, and dynamic pressure 163 psf. With the aircraft still in a vertical dive passing 12,000 feet, the crew module was ejected. The pilot manual states that if spin recovery is not completed by 15,000 feet – EJECT! Post crash analysis of telemetry video revealed that the aircraft had actually recovered from the spin and remained in a vertical dive with a slight left roll until impact. According to the test pilot, aircraft control was not adequately regained because of residual oscillations. The post crash investigation also revealed the F-111's Category II stall/post-stall/spin prevention program was started before the USAF fully understood the spin recovery parachute system limitations. At the time of the mishap, these limitations were incompatible with the out-of-control envelope of the aircraft.

Note 1: Spin chutes are packed in a ballistic canister, typically mounted under or on the most-aft (tail) portion of the aircraft. Deploying a spin chute breaks the aerodynamic stall, which restores the aircraft to controlled flight. Activating/deploying the chute creates enough drag to yank the tail up, forcing the nose down and breaking the stall.

Note 2: Release or jettison of the spin recovery parachute after the spin recovery is normally accomplished by the pilot: typically a manual and/or hydraulic-release mechanism backed up by an explosive-bolts system.

Note 3: Fighter aircraft drag chutes were connected to a release hook, which in turn was attached to the airframe via a backup shear pin. This design allowed a "fail-safe" means for the chute to break away from the aircraft minimum flying airspeed, generally between 225-250 knots. Whether the topic F-111 spin chute or follow-on spin recovery systems for the F-111 had a shear pin, backup could not be determined by the author.

Crew
Pilot: Maj Charles P Winters
Observer: Sgt Patrick S Sharpe
Call Sign: Snowman 11
Time of Crash: 1159 PDT
Mishap Board President: Maj Gen Homer K Hansen
Assigned Unit: 6510th TW / 6512th TS AFFTC Edwards AFB, California
Aircraft Statistics: 124 Flights 232.2 Flight Hours
Crash Result: Aircraft Destroyed / Successful Ejection Initiated

151971
F-111B #2 Grumman Production Run # A2-02
U.S. Navy Delivery Date October 24, 1965

Crash Scenario
On September 11, 1968, F-111B (Tail # 151971, the 2nd F-111B) crashed. The aircraft had departed the Hughes Aircraft Company, Culver City Airport, California, and was lost at sea during a captive Phoenix Missile tracking flight off Point Mugu, over the Pacific Missile Range. After 57 minutes of flight, while at 20,000 feet in level flight, the pilot reported "*We are having problems.*" During the next 40 seconds the pilot experienced loss of control of the aircraft and transmitted the following: "*I seem to have a hard right rudder that I can't handle. We are going into a spin. We are going to ditch.*" The aircraft collided with the ocean surface at a very high rate of descent eleven seconds later. The impact splash, followed by fire and smoke, was observed by the chase F-4. Light weight honeycomb skin, flap segments, and sections of upper fuselage panels were recovered, but provided very little indication of the cause of the accident. Salvage of the main wreckage was not considered feasible due to the excessive depth of approximately 700 fathoms (4200 feet), soft mud bottom, and rough open seas. This particular F-111B was equipped with ejection seats, and at least one of the test pilots onboard may have attempted ejection. An orbiting F-4 chase aircraft observed a partially inflated parachute on the water surface 1/2 mile from the crash scene. It is also possible the parachute was forcibly ejected from the ESCAPAC seat during the impact sequence. Crash Coordinates: 90 nautical miles bearing 260 degrees from Point Mugu, California / N34 03 / W120 52. Mysteriously, a piece of the left hand flap washed up onto a beach in Oahu, Hawaii, 18 months later.

Findings
Analysis of the aircraft track, gyration motions, and altitude data were taken from a radar plot, captive missile telemetry, and height finding radar. The aircraft appeared to have experienced a malfunction in the rudder channel which produced a large nose right yaw and accompanying large right rolling moments. Both engines stalled, causing a loss of electrical power to the radar beacon after the aircraft entered various gyrations. The aircraft described several small radius turns during the descent following the rolls at altitude, which resulted in an erratic ground track. These small radius turns were made by the aircraft in a stalled flight condition, but not in a fully developed spin.

During the investigation, all conceivable system failures that could have caused the airplane to react as described by the test pilot were appraised. These included full up spoilers on one wing, maximum differential deflection of the horizontal stabilizers, single engine failure, and full rudder deflection. The preponderance of data indicated the most likely cause was from a rudder hard-over event.

A test was conducted using the GDFW flight control simulator and assisted in revealing a potential source of the problem. The rudder servo actuator could position the rudder full right, depending on the disconnect point or failure mode in the rudder control rods. The flight path and control difficulties experienced in the simulation closely approximated those of the mishap aircraft up to the point where control was lost.

The mishap sequence revealed that the pilot maintained wings level flight for 40 seconds after the malfunction commenced, indicating adequate controllability, initially. During this time the airspeed decreased rapidly from 375 knots to 248 knots, indicating either the pilot moved the throttles to idle, loss of thrust due to yaw induced compressor stalls, or from increased drag from applied counteractive controls. When the aircraft's speed was approximately 248 knots, the airplane commenced a series of three rolls to the right. The pilot reported going into a spin, but this is unlikely due to the existing high airspeed and only a small loss in altitude. Seventeen seconds later the airspeed had decreased to 186 knots, and the airplane made a rapid turn of about 150 degrees to the right. The airplane then flew approximately 10 more seconds on a constant heading between a series of gyrations, indicating the pilot

Courtesy of Grumman Aerospace.

had regained some degree of control. Twenty-three seconds later the aircraft again made a rapid nose low turn. The pilot quickly recovered, calmly stating "*Ok, we are going to ditch.*" The aircraft impacted the water 11 seconds later.

Figure I:
Rudder Servo Actuator Cutaway. *Courtesy of U.S. Navy Mishap Report.*

The cause of the accident was attributed to an uncontrollable rudder due to material failure or disconnection of the rudder control rod at the rudder servoactuator's control linkage. The rudder servoactuator is mounted at such an angle to the centerline of the airplane that any discontinuity in the rudder control linkage in level 1 "g" flight will result in aft movement of the control valve actuator by force of gravity, causing the rudder to move to the right. Maintenance history note: the rudder servo actuator was removed on 4 June 1968 for modification. This modification included installation of a tab washer as a redundant locking device for the servo valve input rod end jam nut. The rudder servo actuator was reinstalled on 6 June 1968. The aircraft continued to fly sorties for the Hughes Aircraft Company test division, however, the investigation noted the rudder servo actuator linkages were not periodically inspected (nor required) for integrity during that time.

Reference Only: for a detailed explanation of how a rudder hard-over incident could also occur, see Engine Fires and the Reverse Flow Phenomena in Chapter 1. A rudder control rod burn through was the common link in six USAF F-111 aircraft losses, and later surmised to be a probable cause for this USN F-111B mishap. Fuel fumes and intense heat could collect in the aft centerbody cavity and ignite during afterburner usage, or from an uncontained exhaust nozzle fire, and cause rudder control linkage failure and/or Primary and Utility hydraulic line failure.

Why the two crew members did not eject earlier remains undetermined. The last radio transmission "OK, we are going to ditch" was at an altitude of 3000 to 5000 feet above the water. There was no rushing air noise in the transmission indicating that one of the crew members had already ejected. Shortly thereafter the aircraft entered a steep descent, either due to loss of control or lack of control when the pilot released the controls to eject. At this point, the aircraft attitude placed the ejection sequence out of the envelope. The aircraft impacted the water 11 seconds after the last radio transmission.

Crew
Pilot: Mr. Bart Warren, Hughes Aircraft Company Test Pilot
WSO: Mr. Tony Byland, Hughes Aircraft Missile Control Officer
Call Sign: Bartender 201
Time of Crash: 16:52L / 21:52Z
Assigned Unit: Hughes Aircraft Company, Culver City, California
  Aircraft Statistics: 121 Flights 172.5 Flight Hours
Crash Result: Aircraft Destroyed / Ejection may have been attempted; however, determined to be out of the envelope.

Courtesy of Bill Allen.

151972
F-111B #3 Grumman Production Run # A2-03
U.S. Navy Delivery Date December 20, 1965

Crash Scenario

On October 6, 1969, F-111B (Tail # 151972, the third F-111B) departed Hughes Aircraft Company's Culver City Airport, California, to conduct captive carry flight parameter tests for the Phoenix Missile on the overwater Pacific Ocean test range. During a hard turn and airspeed acceleration, the aircraft became almost uncontrollable in the pitch axis. The test pilot was able to maintain a controlled pitch attitude by remaining in a constant turn and holding full forward stick pressure. Without the test pilot remaining in a bank, the aircraft would have either entered a loop and/or stalled in a steep climb, resolving into loss of controlled flight. The test pilot controlled the aircraft in the pitch axis using variations in pitch trim and engine thrust. After nearly a half hour of turning, the test pilot decided to dump fuel and attempt an emergency landing at Point Mugu NAS. The "emergency" runway at Point Mugu had arresting cables capable of recovering the heavy F-111B.

As the aircraft touched down, the arresting hook snagged the approach end arrestment cable just as the aircraft bounced back into the air (the pilot was barely able to control the arrival sink rate which contributed to the bounce). With the aircraft rapidly decelerating from the restraining force of the cable engagement, the nose began an uncontrollable slow pitch over and a hard landing ensued. The impact collapsed the nose landing gear strut, which damaged the hydraulic system, inducing loss of steering control. The aircraft departed the runway surface and a fire broke out in the nose landing gear bay. Although the fire was quickly extinguished, the Missile Control Officer received third degree burns to his exposed body parts after he opened

his canopy in an attempt to egress. The aircraft was heavily damaged but deemed repairable. Eventually the aircraft was repaired and made a single ferry flight from Culver City, California, to NAS Lakehurst, New Jersey, where it finished its career rather ignominiously, using the airframe and its engine thrust to test jet barrier deflectors.

Findings

A wing pivot panel (approximately 2 feet by 3 feet) covering the left wing sweep mechanism separated in flight. The panel edge penetrated the upper fuselage skin, precisely jamming the pitch control mechanism for the horizontal stabilizers. During the landing approach to Point Mugu, the aircraft's minimum controllable rate of descent contributed to a bounce. The aircraft became airborne after the arresting hook snagged the cable. The airborne trajectory and restraining arrestment cable imparted an uncontrollable nose down rotation. The aircraft crashed with sufficient force to cause major structural damage to the nose landing gear and wheel well area. A nose wheel well fire then ensued.

Crew

Pilot: Mr. George J. Marrett, Hughes Aircraft Company Test Pilot
MCO: Mr. Bill Bush, Hughes Aircraft Company Missile Control Officer
Call Sign: Bloodhound 103
Assigned Unit: Hughes Aircraft Company, Culver City, California
Aircraft Statistics: 366 Flights 541.4 Flight Hours
Crash Result: Aircraft Retired from Phoenix Missile Test program. Scrapped at Naval Air Test Facility Lakehurst, New Jersey, in December 1971

151973
F-111B #4 Grumman Production Run # A2-04
U.S. Navy Delivery Date July 25, 1966

Crash Scenario

The F-111 test program suffered its second crash on April 21, 1967 at the Grumman Flight Test Center, Peconic River Facility, Long Island, New York. This aircraft was BuNo #151973, the fourth F-111B and a Navy RDT&E variant. The purpose of the scheduled test flight was for an inflight refueling test and a familiarization flight for Mr. Wangeman in this version of the F-111B. At about 1357L, the aircraft took position for take-off and applied power. During the run-up to takeoff power, the engines' compressor stalled a couple of times, but this was not an uncommon experience in the RDT&E aircraft. The afterburners were selected and a normal lift-off and gear and flap retraction were accomplished. An F-4B chase aircraft followed. Approximately eight seconds after commencement of gear retraction and at 225 feet AGL, the mishap aircraft experienced dual compressor stalls and both afterburners blew out. The aircraft maintained a nose high attitude and entered a high rate of descent to the point of impact, 7500 feet along and

F-111B Number 4 with captive-carry Phoenix missiles mounted on the wing swivel pylons. *Courtesy of Grumman Aerospace Archives*

130 feet left of Runway 14. After sliding 160 feet, the aircraft burst into flames while rotating 120 degrees nose left. The aircraft finally came to a stop in an upright position, 600 feet from the initial impact point. After 70 seconds with the aircraft engulfed in flames, the escape module was rocket propelled to a point 360 feet, at a 10 o'clock position from the aircraft nose, bounced twice, and ended in an inverted position.

On a normal takeoff, the inlet cowl fairings would be opened when an extra volume of air was needed by the engines at high thrust demand. As the aircraft accelerated, the intake cowls would be closed as the forward velocity of the aircraft provided sufficient ram air pressure to satisfy the engines. In this accident, the intake cowls closed prematurely during gear retraction, causing the engines to compressor stall and flameout. This test aircraft was equipped with an escape capsule. At some point after the engines stalled and the aircraft began a descent, Mr. Donnell, in the right seat, initiated a capsule ejection. Unfortunately, there was a failure or series of failures in the ejection initiator sequence that prevented the capsule from ejecting and the test pilots were killed.

Findings

The probable cause was blamed on double engine compressor stalls and afterburner blow-out on takeoff induced by the engine inlet cowls closing upon gear retraction. The pi-

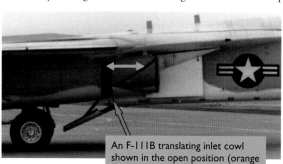

lot flying the aircraft had incorrectly positioned the inlet cowl switch to the "Closed" position during preflight checks. In this position, the cowls are open on the ground and inflight as long as the landing gear handle remains down. Once the landing gear handle is moved up, the cowls close in approximately seven to nine seconds.

An F-111B translating inlet cowl shown in the open position (orange arrow). The forward/aft motion (green arrow) of the translating cowl was pilot controlled by a switch. With gear down, or with weight on the main wheels, the cowls opened automatically, or would remain open regardless of the cockpit switch position. *Courtesy of Author's Collection.*

The purpose of the translating inlet cowls is to provide an additional volume of air into the inlets. The inlet cowls were moved forward (open) and aft (closed) by electrical motor driven actuators, opening a gap in the nacelle fairing. This gap enabled an increased volume flow rate into the intake, meeting

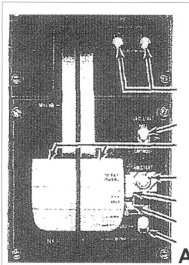

Figure 2: F-111B, Pilot's Throttle Quadrant. *Courtesy of NATOPS F-111B Flight Manual.*

airflow demands for the engines during slow speed-high thrust situations, such as takeoff. (*The permanent fix saw the replacement of the translating cowls with free floating blow-in doors that required no pilot actuation or electrical / mechanical systems interplay.*)

To operate the cowls, there was a single switch that operated both cowls simultaneously. The Number 5 F-111B, in which Mr. Wangeman had flown as an observer, contained a three-position switch labeled OPEN, AUTO, and CLOSE. The Number 1 F-111B, in which Mr. Wangeman had flown several flights as pilot, contained a set of three position momentary switches spring loaded to the center position, The forward position was EXTEND, the center was OFF, and the aft position was RETRACT. In order to cycle the cowls in the Number 1 aircraft, the pilot was required to hold the switches for the full

The translating cowl switch (**Figure 2 labeled A**) was located at the base of the throttle assembly and only on the left seat pilot's console. The right seat pilot in the F-111B had no control stick or throttle quadrant on the center console. The switch positions on the mishap aircraft were: Store (fwd), Open (center), and Close (aft).

The translating inlet cowls were moved by the pilot's switch actuation. Electrical motor driven actuators moved the cowls to the open or closed positions. Position of the inlet cowls was indicated by two green lights that went out when the cowls were closed.

The mishap investigation determined the cowls were open at the start of the takeoff sequence, but closed 9 seconds after the gear handle was placed up, precipitating compressor stalls and afterburner blow-out.

A

Store: is a ground handling position permitting maintenance crews to close the cowls regardless of the landing gear handle position.

Open: The cowls remained open regardless of gear handle position.

Close: in the mishap aircraft, this position contained circuitry which automatically opened the cowls whenever the landing gear handle was put to the down position. However, the cowl "Close" position also automatically closed the cowls *when the landing gear lever was placed up.*

9-second cycle time; the cowls remaining in the position as commanded, although the switch spring-loaded to OFF.

In the mishap aircraft, the position switch remained in the position selected and did not self-return to the OPEN position. The functional discontinuity in the switches between the three versions Mr. Wangeman had flown set up the pilot error. Mr. Wangeman most likely understood that the aft position of the cowl switch (CLOSED) kept the cowls open on the ground, but did not assimilate that, upon gear retraction, the cowls would now "automatically" close.

The investigation concluded that the primary cause of the accident was failure of the pilot to properly position translating cowl control switches prior to takeoff. Additional causes included: (1) failure of aircraft designers to provide an adequate warning system to alert the pilot as to which specific aircraft system was causing or about to cause a catastrophic loss of power; (2) failure of the flight test management to provide adequate training of and rigid checklist procedures to be followed by test pilots; and (3) failure of the test aircraft designers for not considering the human factors element in the cowl switch function. Between the different versions of the F-111A and B there was a built in "booby trap" in the cowl control system.

Crew

Pilot: Mr. Charles E. Wangeman, Grumman Test Pilot
MCO: Mr. Ralph H. Donnell, Grumman Test Pilot
Call Sign: Grumman 67
Time of Crash: 1359L
Assigned Unit: Grumman Flight Test Center, Peconic River Facility, Long Island, New York
Aircraft Statistics: 53 Flights, 89.1 Flight Hours
Crash Result: Aircraft Destroyed / Unsuccessful Ejection attempt due to system malfunction

Note 1: This was the third incident to result in an official recommendation to redesign the cowl position warning system. The first instance was from an inflight incident reported by the Air Force Flight Test Center (AFFTC) at Edwards AFB, California, in May 1966. The second was the fatal crash of F-111A 63-9774, in which the inlet cowls were also closed during an approach to land. The crash investigation board for that mishap recommended the substitution of blow-in doors for the translating cowls.

Note 2: Later RDT&E versions replaced the OFF position with an AUTO position that moved the cowls to open automatically when the gear was down or when the speed was less than .44 Mach. Additionally, the AUTO position would close the cowls only when the gear was up and a speed of .5 Mach was exceeded.

Note 3: After the engines compressor stalled, the aircraft settled with a high sink rate toward the ground in a nose up/tail first impact. The sink rate was estimated to be 40 feet per second. The force of the impact fatally injured the pilots, and an explosive fire broke out thereafter, enveloping the wreckage. The intensity of engulfing fire cooked off the capsule rocket motor, ejecting the module away from the wreckage.

Note 4: Although test pilot Mr. Donnell initiated an ejection sequence while airborne and prior to impact, the capsule failed to separate from the aircraft due to a design deficiency of the ejection initiator unit. 70 seconds after the crash, the escape capsule self-ejected away from the fuselage. The investigation report also stated the crew module had been severely damaged by the combined effects of structural failure at impact and the intense heat of the fire prior to self-ejecting.

3

F-111A 1966 MODELS AND EF-111A MISHAPS

A two-ship of EF-111As launch on a Desert Storm combat mission. *Courtesy of Author's Collection.*

66-0025
F-111A # 43 GD/FW Production Run # A1-43
USAF Delivery Date: February 13, 1968

Mishap Scenario
On June 20, 1975, the mishap aircraft departed single-ship on a scheduled 2.5 hour qualification/instrument check ride sortie. The mission was planned for a Nellis stereotype route consisting of a Nellis One SID departure to Bryce Canyon TACAN on the 205 degree radial at 70 NM, which serves as the anchor point for the Foxtrot One MOA. Pre-flight, engine start, taxi, and take-off at 1000 local were accomplished without any unusual occurrences. Basic maneuvering, including transition (chandelles) and instrument pattern work, was initiated 40 NM east of Las Vegas. Chaps 01 accomplished several practice instrument approaches at both Nellis AFB and McCarran International Airport in Las Vegas, Nevada. Chaps 01 returned to Nellis AFB for the final instrument approach, which was to include a simulated missed approach and go around to the Nellis overhead pattern. Chaps 01 was at 1 NM when GCA advised him to execute previously issued missed approach instructions. The mishap pilot acknowledged with a "Roger" and began his go-around. Simultaneously, calls were received over UHF radio indicating that the aircraft was on fire. Ejection was initiated immediately. After capsule separation, the aircraft began a dive and slight roll to the left and impacted on the left edge of the runway, just past mid-field. It exploded on impact, covering the runway with fire and debris. The capsule landed to the right of the runway, abeam the GCA facilities. The crew escaped with minor injuries.

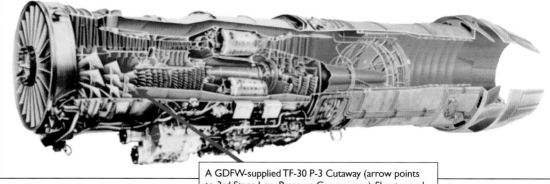

66-0025 on the assembly line at GDFW. *Courtesy of Author's Collection.*

A GDFW-supplied TF-30 P-3 Cutaway (arrow points to 3rd Stage Low Pressure Compressor). Shorter and thinner blades to the right of the Low Pressure Section are those of the High Pressure Compressor Section. Beyond the combustion burner cans are the turbine blades, followed by the afterburner section and exhaust nozzle. *Courtesy of GDFW TF-30 Training Phamplet.*

Findings
Investigation revealed the Number-2 engine's third stage fan disc retaining tangs failed in fatigue as a result of excessive vibration. The third stage compressor disc's vibration originated from wear between the second to third stage air seals and the associated second stage disc. The third stage fan blades then dislodged and grenaded internally due to the high engine RPM, penetrating the compressor fan case. Fragmentation ruptured the engine fuel lines and the aft centerbody fuel tanks, causing massive fuel leaks. The leaking fuel ignited from contact with superheated engine areas, resulting in a severe inflight fire. The fire's intensity caused loss of hydraulics and loss of aircraft control.

Crew
Pilot: Col William F Palmer
WSO: Lt Col Robert L Tidwell
Call Sign: Chaps 01
Time of Incident: 1156 PDT
Assigned Unit: 442nd TFTS / 474th TFW Nellis AFB, Nevada
Aircraft Statistics: 479 Flights and 1,195.3 Flight Hours
Mishap Result: Aircraft Destroyed / Successful Ejection

A nighttime engine trim pad run-up test to full afterburner! *Courtesy of Ivan H. Dethman Collection.*

66-0026
F-111A # 44 GD/FW Production Run # A1-44
USAF Delivery Date: February 14, 1968

Mishap Scenario
On March 13, 1984, the mishap aircraft F-111A 66-0026 was scheduled for a Fighter Weapons Instructor Course (FWIC) Surface Attack (SA-4) sortie. Syllabus events included defensive tactics to defeat an air threat and low altitude ingress, pop-up, and roll-in to an off-axis diving weapons deliveries. Mishap aircraft took off as lead of a two ship with number two on his wing. While maneuvering 16 minutes after take-off, the mishap aircraft experienced an accelerated stall, failed

Courtesy of Don Logan Collection

66-0029
F-111A # 47 GD/FW Production Run # A1-47
USAF Delivery Date: March 31, 1968

Mishap Scenario
On September 1, 1971, the mishap aircraft F-111A 66-0029 was scheduled to fly Carlsbad 213 low-level-route, culminating in practice bomb runs on the Melrose Bomb Range. The mishap aircraft was lead in a two-ship flight and departed Cannon AFB, New Mexico, at the scheduled time. TFR checks were performed and an automatic TFR commanded blind-letdown was initiated to 1000 AGL at 480 KTAS. The wings were swept aft to 48-degrees as the aircraft entered the Carlsbad 213 low-level route. The mishap pilot elected to fly directly over the Salt Flat TACAN station to accomplish an exact Inertial Navigation System (INS) update. After passing over the station, the pilot started a 10-degree left bank turn to intercept a 139-degree heading and track to entry point Alpha on the Carlsbad 213 route. Approximately 20 NM northwest of point Alpha, the mishap pilot glanced down into the cockpit to check mileage to the target, and to ascertain his position on the route map. When he looked up, he saw an object (a turkey vulture) come through the right windscreen. The entire right windscreen and right canopy glass failed and fell off the aircraft. The pilot was unable to maintain control of the aircraft as a result of wind blast effects agitating fragmented glass particles, contributing to temporary blindness and disorientation. The situational shock at low altitude induced the pilot to initiate a successful ejection sequence.

> **Author's Note:** Regarding the photograph right, the black and blue cylindrical objects on the avionics panel (windscreen absent after the bird strike) are thermoses placed there by members of the GDFW crash investigation team. They are not a part of the F-111 escape module, although many a pilot would have graciously welcomed a shot of high-dollar Glen Fiddich Scotch after such a violent experience and ejection!

Findings
The aircrew was flying at approximately 500 feet AGL on automatic TFR when the bird struck the right wind screen. Wind screen failures were significant in the F-111 community. A number of failures led to redesign of a more bird-tolerant windscreen which had lasting effects for all future fighters. Bird strikes / wind screen failures accounted for the downing of at least 8 F-111s. The F-111's high speed capability and its low-level ingress mission subjected the F-111 and its crews to the bird hazard.

Crew
Pilot: Maj Donald M Severance
WSO: Capt Edward Silverbush
Call Sign: Canard 01
Time of Incident: 1423 MDT
Assigned Unit: 522nd TFS / 27th TFW Cannon AFB, New Mexico
Aircraft Statistics: 239 Flights 610.4 Flight Hours
Mishap Result: Aircraft Destroyed / Successful Ejection

Courtesy of Bill Allen Collection.

Courtesy of 474th TFW Archives

to recover, and impacted the ground. The mishap aircrew attempted an unsuccessful ejection. Aircraft impacted 53 NM from Mountain Home AFB, Idaho, on the 207 radial. (N 42 24 25 W 116 41 10)

Findings
The mishap occurred only 16 minutes after takeoff. With the present fuel load at the time of the mishap, the aircraft was still considered heavy-weight. During the low altitude maneuvering, high-G turns require combinations of pitch, roll, and yaw flight control inputs. An accelerated stall could occur with little or no warning if the pilot's applied aft stick inputs were abrupt, thereby overshooting the AOA limits, which exceeded the capabilities of the Stability Augmentation System (SAS). The situation is aggravated by an aft wing sweep. At low altitude, with hard maneuvering, some G-induced disorientation is present and can interfere with the pilot's decision and assessment whether to attempt recovery or eject. Natural instinct is to attempt recovery first, and the ejection attempt was too late and out of the envelope.

Crew
Pilot: Capt David Kirk Peth
WSO: Capt Steven F Locke
Call Sign: Zip Gun 01
Time of Incident: 0944 MST
Assigned Unit: 389th TFTS / 366th TFW Mountain Home AFB, Idaho
Aircraft Statistics: 1085 Flights 2563.9 Flight Hours
Mishap Result: Aircraft Destroyed / Fatal Crash / Unsuccessful Ejection

66-0032
F-111A # 50 GD/FW Production Run # A1-50
USAF Delivery Date: March 29, 1968

Crash Scenario

On May 8, 1968, 60 NM northeast of Nellis AFB, in Lincoln County, Nevada, over Range III-4, Aircraft F-111A 66-0032 crashed during a Weapons System Training Flight (WST-1). The mishap crew had just initiated a standard TFR letdown. During the TFR-controlled descent, the aircraft was crossing a ridge line which bounded a valley area. After passing 5000 feet MSL, the aircraft pitched up violently, followed by a hard right roll. The TFR system was "paddled off" with no effect. Neither crew member could regain control of the aircraft and said the stick(s) appeared to be frozen. During the pitch and roll maneuvers, the nose of the aircraft started to yaw to the left and right. At some time in this violent uncontrolled maneuver, structural failure of the Right Boom Glove region of the escape module occurred. The aircraft commander (AC) ejected the module utilizing the right seat ejection handle when the aircraft was nose down 30-40 degrees with 120 degrees of right roll at 2800 AGL. Ejection sequence and escape module deployment functioned correctly despite the severe damage to the module glove region.

Courtesy of Bill Allen Collection.

Findings

The material weld failure of the input spool rod end to the control valve of the HTSA contributed to loss of aircraft control. The findings for this mishap were of major significance to the entire F-111 program. The results and technical analysis by GDFW and the mishap investigation team led the USAF toward readdressing the probable cause for the Takhli Combat Lancer accident involving F-111A 66-0017 on May 30, 1968. During the investigation, the pilots involved with this accident and the Combat Lancer crash were brought together at Nellis AFB and at GDFW to discuss the control problems they experienced prior to ejecting. Their technical discussions regarding the aircraft motions and loss of flight control were similar. Using an F-111 flight training simulator and a

Notice the absence of the escape module's stabilization boom in the photograph below. The stabilization boom failed structurally during the ejection sequence. Courtesy of Bill Allen Collection.

Separation of the HTSA control input link from the dual booster valve caused the abrupt leading edge down control input. See also Combat Loss 66-0017, Hotrod 76, Chapter 6. Courtesy of Bill Allen and GDFW mishap report.

flight control test stand, GDFW engineers replicated the violent pitch and roll maneuvers by disconnecting the HTSA rod end from the actuator. The failed HTSA input rod end allowed the right horizontal tail to drive full trailing edge up (TEU), resulting in the uncontrollable flight condition. The rod end had failed due to a minor manufacturing defect in the joint weld of the control valve linkage. Additionally, the findings for this mishap established the true cause for the Combat Lancer accident involving 66-0017 in 1968: incorrectly attributing a foreign object (tube of fuel tank sealant) jamming the flight control's pitch-roll-mixer assembly.

Crew
Pilot: Maj Charles E. Van Driel
PWSO: Maj Kenneth E. Schuppe
Call Sign: Hulu 16
Time of Incident: 1220 PDST
Assigned Unit: 4527th CCTS /
    474th TFW Nellis AFB, Nevada
Aircraft Statistics: 13 Flights
    28.05 Flight Hours
Incident Result: Aircraft Destroyed /
    Successful Ejection

66-0034
F-111A # 52 GD/FW Production Run # A1-52
USAF Delivery Date: April 15, 1968

Crash Scenario

On June 6, 1975, near Mohave County, 7 NM south-southeast of Peach Springs, Arizona, aircraft F-111A 66-0034 crashed during off-station training flight from Nellis AFB to McClellan AFB, California. The flight plan was to depart Nellis AFB via the Prescott 327 low-level route and onto the Holbrook, AZ, Radar Bomb Scoring (RBS) site. At 1332 L with wings level and 483 KTAS and TFR engaged, both crew members heard a muffled thump. The mishap aircraft commander terminated TFR flight and began a shallow climb, sweeping the wings forward to 26 degrees. The Primary and Utility hydraulics caution lights illuminated, along with the Right Generator and Engine Over-Speed warning lights. In the process of accomplishing Emergency Action checklist procedures, the

Courtesy of Bill Malerba via Don Logan Collection

crew found the right engine throttle frozen and were unable to shutdown the engine. All three flight control damper lights illuminated with the further loss of the primary hydraulic system. The aircraft began a slow

66-0040
F-111A # 58 GD/FW Production Run # A1-58
USAF Delivery Date: August 1, 1968

Crash Scenario
On September 23, 1968, aircraft F-111A 66-0040 crashed on final approach for landing, 1300 feet short of runway 03L at Nellis AFB, Nevada. The flight crew stated that while configuring for landing approximately one-half mile short of the approach end of the runway, the aircraft began a smooth continuous climb and would not respond to stick or power corrections. As the aircraft approached an abnormally high nose up attitude of 45 degrees of pitch (and stall AOA), the aircraft entered a left turn. Finding the aircraft uncontrollable, the WSO initiated the ejection sequence. The escape module sequence and separation worked correctly. The capsule landed 1100 feet south of the aircraft fuselage impact area, 250 feet short of Runway 03L over-run, and rolled onto its side.

Findings
The investigation determined that the aft fuselage fuel tank fuel indicator was inoperative prior to takeoff. This malfunction resulted in an undetected and extreme aft center of gravity (c.g.) fuel imbalance. Unknown to the pilot, the failed fuel quantity indicator disabled the automatic transfer of fuel from the aft to the forward fuel tank. The only indication the pilot would have of the aft c.g. was to observe the Control Surface Position Indicator needles (see inset below) for the horizontal tail, indicating full trailing edge down. During the landing approach to Nellis, the flight crew was unable to maintain control of the aircraft with the extreme aft c.g. At this point the nose started up, and further nose down command from the system merely drove the stick to the aft position. The crew was forced to eject. Due to the F-111's self-adaptive trim feature and flight control stability augmentation system, all signs of the developing aft-heavy condition were masked. When the pilot configured to land the auto trim system automatically removed all trim compensation (gains), and the nose of the aircraft began a slow uncontrollable pitch up. Due to the limited forward stick travel and commensurate reduced movement of the horizontal stabilizer, full forward stick force could not correct the pitch-up. Loss of control ensued.

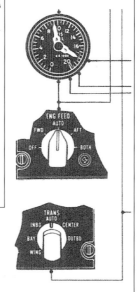

Figure 1: Diagram of the Control Surface Position Indicator. *Courtesy of USAF F-111A-1 Pilot's Manual*

Figure 2: Fuselage Fuel Quantity Indicator. *Courtesy of USAF F-111A-1 Pilot's Manual.*

Courtesy of Author's Collection.

Author's Note: the pilot did not recognize the Flight Control Position Indicator (Figure 1) was at the full Trailing-Edge-Down (TED) position, or that the fuselage fuel quantity indicator (Figure 2) was displaying an incorrect fuel balance.

The pilot had completed a self-test of the fuel quantity indicator on the ground prior to takeoff, which failed; however, the pilot elected to fly the aircraft anyway. At the time of this mishap the Pilot's Flight Manual, T.O. 1F-111A-1, did not tell the pilot that the actual position of the needles within the Fuselage Fuel Quantity Indicator (Figure 2) moved micro-switches, enabling the automatic fuel balancing system's operation. If the actual position of the Forward and Aft indicator needles were incorrect due to a fuel quantity sensing or an internal indicator problem, the automatic fuel transfer system was incapable of correcting an imbalance. In the case of this mishap the fuel quantity indicator had a fault, and a severe aft fuel imbalance was undetected by the pilot.

Author's Note: both mishap pilots were flight instructors at Nellis AFB due to the U.S. Navy and Australian Air Force purchasing the F-111. The U.S. Navy successfully terminated the F-111B program two months prior to this mishap, on July 10, 1968. Deliveries of all 24 Australian F-111s were withheld until development problems and static fatigue testing was completed. The RAAF F-111Cs were stored at GDFW until released in March 1973.

Crew
Pilot: Lt John M Nash U.S. Navy
PWSO: Flt Lt Neil M Pollack
    Royal Australian Air Force
Call Sign: PASHTO 01
Accident Board President: Col F.B. Clark
Time of Incident: 1448 PDT
Assigned Unit: 4527th CCTS / 474th TFW
    Nellis AFB, Nevada
Aircraft Statistics: 16 Flights
    35.6 Flight Hours
Incident Result: Aircraft Destroyed /
    Successful Ejection

---

roll to the left. Control stick input did not counter the movement. The mishap aircraft commander initiated the ejection sequence. The escape module ejection sequence worked correctly and the aircrew successfully ejected from the aircraft.

Findings
The right engine High Pressure Compressor rotor drum failed catastrophically, causing several compressor blades to penetrate the engine case. Either the compressor blade shrapnel ruptured the main engine fuel manifold or cut an engine fuel supply system line. The high-pressure, high-volume fuel flow sustained an uncontrollable inflight fire. The uncontained fire caused loss of hydraulics which resulted in loss of aircraft control. The crew was forced to eject after the aircraft became uncontrollable approximately eight minutes after the first indications of fire.

Investigation revealed a fuel line was ruptured by the disk segments from the 14th and 15th stage compressors. A combustible

mixture of fuel and air was carried aft by secondary airflow in the engine bay and ignited upon contact with the right engine exhaust nozzle. The resulting fire damaged hydraulic lines adjacent to the rudder post and failed the primary and utility hydraulic systems, causing loss of aircraft control.

Crew
Pilot: 1Lt Martin L Perina
PWSO: Maj Merle D Kenney
Call Sign: Ned 70
Accident Board President: Col Joseph E Clarkson
Time of Incident: 1328 MST
Assigned Unit: 430th TFS / 474th TFW Nellis AFB, Nevada
Aircraft Statistics: 619 Flights 1585.8 Flight Hours
Incident Result: Aircraft Destroyed / Successful Ejection

Courtesy of Ray Lock via Don Logan Collection

66-0042 F-111A # 60 GD/FW Production Run # A1-60
USAF Delivery Date: April 30, 1968

Crash Scenario

On February 12, 1969, F-111A 66-0042 was on a combined day/night TFR low-level and practice bombing sortie. This was an F-111A transition sortie for the mishap pilot. During the day portion of the mission, the mishap aircraft had completed a right 90 degree heading change in Manual TFR toward the Wendover Range, Utah, for a dry RBS simulated attack. Shortly after completing the turn, the aircraft began a stabilized climb to overfly terrain directly ahead. The aircraft hit the rising terrain 700 feet from the summit in a shallow nose-up climb. Weather in the vicinity of the rising terrain most likely obscured the summit. A setting sun and a thick overcast were also present. During the next 24 hours, a heavy snowfall buried the wreckage. The wreckage was found four months later by a rancher herding goats to a high pasture.

Findings

The mishap crew had planned and executed a hard 90 degree turn to the east prior to commencing a simulated bomb run on the Wendover Range. During this hard turn, the mishap pilot may have exceeded the LARA bank angle limit of 45 degrees. This action induced a TFR commanded Fly-Up maneuver which the pilot had to override and reset prior to resuming TFR flight. While in the process of resetting the TFR, the aircraft was approaching rising terrain. The mishap crew began a stabilized climb and entered a low cloud ceiling which obscured the mountain's upslope and summit. With the TFR overridden, terrain

A portion of the escape capsule, *Courtesy of Mike Jobe.*

avoidance protection is nonexistent except for illumination of the Radar Altitude Low warning light, activated by a preset index marker on the Radar Altimeter instrument face. Illumination of the warning light with the TFR overridden does not command a terrain avoidance fly-up; therefore, recognition and recovery from this event is the sole responsibility of the pilot flying. Unfortunately, the shallow climb angle established during the route abort set up a terrain collision dynamic which was not ascertained or recognized by the crew. The result was controlled flight into terrain (CFIT).

Crew

Pilot: Capt Robert E Jobe
WSO: Capt William D Fuchlow
Call Sign: Fruity 01
Accident Board President: Col William J Hentges
Time of Incident: 1640 MDT
Assigned Unit: 4527th CCTS / 474th TFW Nellis AFB, Nevada
Aircraft Statistics: 60 Flights 238.1 Flight Hours
Mishap Result: Aircraft Destroyed / Fatal Crash / No Ejection Attempted

The results from the official USAF Mishap Report were unknown and no longer exist. Co-author Lou Benoit spent four years (2006-2010) hiking to and researching this mishap as a personal hobby. He received much assistance from Mike Jobe, son of the mishap pilot; co-author Steven Hyre; and a former GDFW crash investigator, Bill Allen. As a friend of the families whose loved ones perished, the author found an answer to the crash and wrote a detailed mishap report to help the families understand why 66-0042 crashed. During those years of research, a tremendous library of F-111 related information was catalogued. Sharing that information is now deeply embedded within this book.

Impact site for 66-0042. The USAF pilot walking uphill in the left portion of the photo is looking in the direction of travel; the aft sweep of the right wing created a gouge, visible on the right side of the photograph. The aircraft crashed in a shallow nose-up skipping impact, and thereafter the aircraft disintegrated. *Courtesy of Bill Allen Collection.*

The vertical stabilizer from 66-0042 with a bronze memorial plaque attached. *Courtesy of Mike Jobe.*

A remnant section of the wing box, *Courtesy of Mike Jobe.*

Flight view from a position approximately one-half mile to the impact location marked by a yellow dot. The TFR should have responded to the abrupt face just short of the impact location, triggering a climb. Unfortunately, the pilot flying may have overridden the TFR, leading to the Controlled Flight into Terrain (CFIT) mishap. *Courtesy of Google Earth.*

Image © 2009 DigitalGlobe
Image State of Utah

© 2009 Tele Atlas

40° 55.594' N   114° 35.873' W   elev 8261 ft   Eye alt   8297 ft

66-0043
F-111A # 61 GD/FW Production Run # A1-61
USAF Delivery Date: July 24, 1968

Crash Scenario
On March 4, 1969, aircraft F-111A 66-0043 crashed while performing chase duties for another F-111 that was on a Functional Check Flight (FCF). After 35 minutes of routine flight the mishap aircraft was slowed to 220 Knots True Air Speed (KTAS) in a one "g" wings level climb attitude. Angle of Attack (AOA) indicator was at 14 degrees, aircraft altitude was 19,000 feet MSL. A light buffet was experienced when the alpha was 18 degrees, oscillating to 19 or 20 degrees. There was no rudder pedal shaker experienced. Forward stick was applied, and the aircraft began to yaw right and then yawed violently. The aircraft rolled right and then left, and as the gear warning horn sounded at 10,000 feet MSL, which was about 5000 feet AGL, the aircrew ejected the module near Texas Dry Lake, North of Nellis AFB, Nevada.

Findings
The pilot and Instructor Pilot (IP) misinterpreted a post stall gyration as a spin and placed the aircraft in a flight condition at an altitude too low for recovery. Contributing factors in almost all stall/spin divergence scenarios are timely detection/recognition and recovery procedures.

The primary cause in this mishap was the wrong configuration for the slow flight speed regime. The maximum AOA per the flight manual is 15 degrees clean and 18 degrees configured. The pilot manual also states that "for all wing sweeps, for most flight conditions, there will be a tendency to diverge or oscillate in roll and yaw. To recover, full forward stick application is required to reduce the AOA below 15 degrees without applying any roll or rudder controls. When asymmetric rudder and / or lateral control are applied at stall, spin entries should be expected for all configurations. Crossed controls at or before accelerated stalls should likewise produce abrupt entries into erect or inverted spins." (*F-111A-1 Pilot Manual, 1968-1969*)

Crew
Pilot: Maj William Baechle
IP: Maj Edward P Schmitt
Call Sign: POW WOW 08
Accident Board President: Unknown
Time of Incident: Unknown
Assigned Unit: 430th TFS / 474th TFW Nellis AFB, Nevada
Aircraft Statistics: 161 Flights 749.1 Flight Hours
Incident Result: Aircraft Destroyed / Successful Ejection

Courtesy of Author's Collection.

66-0045
F-111A # 63 GD/FW Production Run # A1-63
USAF Delivery Date: July 29, 1968

Crash Scenario
On May 12, 1982, F-111A 66-0045 was lead in a two ship continuation training sortie to IR 307 low-level route after aerial refueling in AR 610. The crew planned to then proceed to Saylor Creek Bombing Range for practice weapons deliveries. Launch was on time, and all events were flown as scheduled up through range entry. Upon range entry, the flight executed a pre-briefed lead change and two level passes were made. The flight requested a target change, and was advised to depart the target area while range personnel moved equipment. The flight moved to a VFR holding pattern 6 NM east of the target area at 7000 MSL and 480 KIAS. Approximately 5 ½ minutes later, the mishap crew declared a Mayday for a right engine fire. One minute later they noticed a Wheel Well Hot Light and lowered the landing gear utilizing the Alternate Gear extension checklist, because only one hydraulic pump on the left engine was operating. The mishap crew radioed at 1258L that they were losing hydraulic pressure, and at 1259L said hydraulic pressure had returned. At 1300L the crew made a successful ejection. Aircraft impact location was 27 NM on the 124 degree radial from Mountain Home, Idaho, TACAN.

Findings
A violent explosion was felt, followed by hydraulic problems. Shortly thereafter, control was lost and the crew successfully ejected. Investigation revealed the right engine number-1 fan hub failed due to low cycle fatigue. Rotating parts from the hub penetrated the fan

Courtesy of Doug E. Slowiak / Vortex Photo-Graphics Collection.

case, damaging nearby fuel and hydraulic fluid lines. These flammable fluids entered the engine through the rupture and exploded in the high pressure compressor section, sending a pressure wave through the 16th stage bleed air duct and stalling the left engine. The left engine recovered. The pressure wave over-pressurized and ruptured the bleed air ducting just forward of the aft wheel well bulkhead. The failure also triggered an uncontained fire, disabling the Primary and Utility Hydraulic systems, which resulted in loss of aircraft control.

Crew
Pilot: Maj Francis B Morris
WSO: Capt George Earles III
Call Sign: Sulk 85
Accident Board President: Col William J Hentges
Time of Incident: 1301 MDT
Assigned Unit: 389th TFTS / 366th TFW Mountain Home AFB, Idaho
Aircraft Statistics: 1232 Flights 3007.8 Flight Hours
Mishap Result: Aircraft Destroyed / Successful Ejection

66-0052
F-111A # 70 GD/FW Production Run # A1-70
USAF Delivery Date: August 18, 1968

Crash Scenario
On July 31, 1979, F-111A 66-0052 crashed while on a student upgrade training sortie. The mishap aircraft was Number-2 in a formation of two. The mishap occurred on the student's sixth syllabus required transition sortie. The flight departed Mountain Home AFB, Idaho, at 1056 local time, and proceeded directly to the Paradise Military Operating area for syllabus wing work. At some point during the wing work, the mishap aircraft flew through the jet wash of the lead aircraft while the instructor pilot was demonstrating the "close trail" formation position (a position directly behind and slightly below the lead aircraft) and experienced dual engine compressor stalls. The mishap aircraft then entered into a flat spin and crashed at approximately 1121 local time. Impact with the ground was upright, nose high, with a slight left bank. The aircraft wreckage was located 72 NM southwest of Mountain Home AFB, near Malheur, Oregon. The aircraft had a high sink rate and negligible forward velocity at the time of impact indicative of a spin. For an unknown reason ejection was not attempted.

Findings
The lead aircraft was flying a series of Lazy-8 type in-trail maneuvers which Number-2 was attempting to follow and remain in position. The mishap aircraft fell out of position due to differences in the aircraft's gross weights. During the maneuver, the lead instructor pilot realized the formation would exit the bottom of the assigned area (15,000 feet MSL) if the maneuver continued. Without warning the lead instructor initiated an aggressive 12 degree AOA recovery to level flight. The abrupt change in the lead aircraft's flight path resulted in the mishap student perceiving a need for evasive action in order to maintain safe aircraft clearance. While attempting to avoid the lead aircraft, the mishap student inadvertently allowed his aircraft to pass through the lead aircraft's jet wash, which resulted in an airflow distortion progressing through the intakes and into

Courtesy of Don Logan Collection.

the compressor section of both engines. The turbulent airflow induced dual engine compressor stalls, followed by simultaneous engine flame-outs. Both electrical generators of the mishap aircraft dropped off line as a result of decreasing rpm. Loss of hydraulics pressure to the flight controls and the pilot's immediate corrective flight control inputs may have aggravated and contributed to the resultant loss of control. Either the crew had become incapacitated by the centrifugal g-forces of the uncontrolled departure and spin, or they were completely overwhelmed by the multiple system failures and out-of-control situation. In either case, collision with the terrain occurred without an ejection attempt for an undetermined reason.

Crew
Pilot: 2Lt Larry E McFarland
WSO: Capt Myles D Hammon
Call Sign: Sulk 82
Accident Board President: Col Richard A Jones
Time of Incident: 1121 MDT
Assigned Unit: 389th TFTS / 366th TFW Mtn Home AFB, Idaho
Aircraft Statistics: 726 Flights 1883.5 Flight Hours
Mishap Result: Aircraft Destroyed / Fatal Crash / No Ejection

---

66-0054
F-111A # 72 GD/FW Production Run # A1-72
USAF Delivery Date: August 15, 1968

Crash Scenario
On April 13, 1983, the mishap aircraft was scheduled for a transition (TR) training sortie. Syllabus requirements included aerobatics (chandelles, lazy 8's, barrel rolls), stall recoveries, unusual attitude recoveries, nose-

high recoveries (also known as vertical recoveries), and no flap / no slat approaches. The crew consisted of a student Aircraft Commander (AC) in the left seat and an Instructor Pilot (IP) in the right seat. The mishap aircraft took-off at 1346 MST and proceeded to the Paradise Military Operating Area (MOA). At 1427 MST, the mishap aircrew initiated a successful ejection. The aircraft impacted the ground 73 miles from the Mountain Home AFB, TACAN (MUO CH 87), on the 194-degree radial near Whiterock, Nevada. The crew was picked up by an Air Force

66-0054 shown in flight while on loan to the 27th TFW. *Courtesy of Author's Collection.*

66-0054 is seen during heavy Depot Maintenance at the Sacramento Air Logistics Center, McClellan AFB, California. *Courtesy of Author's Collection.*

Rescue and Recovery Service helicopter dispatched from Mountain Home AFB Idaho.

Findings

During flight, the Stall Inhibitor System (SIS) circuit breakers popped and the crew continued on with the sortie. During the recovery attempt from the nose high unusual attitude (at approximately 17,000 feet MSL), the aircraft was rolled to near inverted. The nose was pulled back down, and the aircraft was then rolled toward the horizon and wings level with increasing back stick pressure. The airspeed was approximately 300 knots. As the nose came up the aircraft yawed right, the instructor took control, the aircraft yawed left, and then remained out of control. The crew then ejected at 10,000 feet MSL. Investigation concluded the stall warning horn did not work because the landing gear/stall warning circuit breaker was found shorted internally. The IP demonstrated both a nose high recovery and an unusual attitude recovery with a 26 degree wing sweep before telling the student pilot to close his eyes for an unusual attitude recovery. The student pilot initiated a nose high recovery, but he did not sweep the wings forward from 40-degrees in accordance with the F-111A transition phase manual. The IP did not intervene during the recovery.

The F-111 was originally manufactured with only one Angle of Attack (AOA) probe mounted on the left side of the fuselage. To increase the stability-and-control characteristics of the flight control system, the SIS computer and a second AOA probe were added on the right side of the aircraft. The SIS modification enhanced the stability-and-command augmentation systems by physically limiting the maximum attainable AOA, and to minimize sideslip during rolling maneuvers at high AOA. An AOA limiter in the SIS computer acted through the pitch damper and series trim systems to provide positive speed stability at AOAs above 10 degrees.

To prevent the pilot from exceeding the AOA limits, the system increases the amount of aft stick force and travel required to achieve AOAs *above* 10 degrees. If full aft stick is held the maximum attainable AOA will be approximately 20 degrees, but the AOA limiting function causes a nose-down command to the horizontal stabilizers, which causes the aircraft to descend in relation to the power setting. The system was not infallible, and large abrupt cross controlling or rapid reversals at or near the maximum AOA could force the aircraft into a departure from controlled flight.

Additionally, without the SIS (circuit breakers popped in this mishap), AOA limiting is removed and large or abrupt stick inputs at high AOA resulted in an overshoot of the AOA limits. Note: The F-111's departure from controlled flight characteristics and spin recovery procedures were extremely tenuous. At AOAs greater than 15 degrees, roll angle and yaw divergence oscillations required prompt and proper recovery control inputs.

Crew

Pilot: 2Lt John M Dahl
PWSO: Maj John T Shealy
Call Sign: Horse 91
Accident Board President: Col Richard A Bedarf
Time of Incident: 1427 MST
Assigned Unit: 389th TFTS /366th TFW Mountain Home AFB, Idaho
Aircraft Statistics: 1,266 Flights and 3,104.3 Flight Hours
Incident Result: Aircraft Destroyed / Successful Ejection

66-0058
F-111A # 76 GD/FW Production Run # A1-76
USAF Delivery Date: September 6, 1968

Crash Scenario
On October 7, 1975, F-111A 66-0058 crashed during a two-ship night Terrain Following Radar (TFR) practice nuclear strike sortie. The mission was scheduled for practice Radar Lay Down (RLD) bomb deliveries on Nellis AFB Range 65 (R-4806). The scheduled local departure would take the mishap sortie to Range 65 via Low Level High Speed (LAHS) Route 334. The mishap aircraft began the Automatic TFR descent while the wingman entered a 360-degree turn to provide five minutes (40 miles) separation. The mishap aircrew checked in with Fatness 5, the Nellis Range 65 control officer, at approximately 1954L, 18 miles from bomb release. Fatness 5, the range controller, cleared the mishap aircraft onto the range and instructed the crew to report a 60-second final. At about this time, the mishap aircrew experienced a massive engine failure and fire. The mishap aircraft continued toward the target. The range control officer expected to see the mishap aircraft's rotating beacon; instead, a large fireball was observed by range tower personnel. The aircrew did not attempt to eject and were killed.

Findings
The aircraft experienced a catastrophic failure of the Number-2 engine during a night TFR flight at approximately 400 feet AGL. The pilot disengaged the Automatic TFR mode when indications of a serious inflight emergency became apparent. While preoccupied with completing corrective actions to cope with the emergency, the crew allowed the aircraft to descend below safe terrain clearance altitude. Neither crew member attempted to eject and were fatally injured. Investigation revealed a blade in the Number-2 engine fan section failed and penetrated an adjacent fuel tank, resulting in a massive fuel leak and subsequent fire.

Courtesy of Don Logan Collection.

The mishap crew apparently paddled off the TFR and became distracted by events in the cockpit. The mishap aircraft impacted 30 feet below the top of a hill rising 320 feet above the valley floor, one-quarter mile left of the desired target run-in line, and 5.7 miles short of the planned nuclear practice target. This mishap demonstrates the failure of the crew to maintain aircraft control during an inflight emergency, and to immediately abort the route by climbing. Unfortunately, both crew members focused their attention on the engine failure rather than terrain clearance. Without terrain clearance protection provided by the TFR, or by operating at the Minimum Enroute Altitude (MEA), this mishap was a classic Controlled Flight Into Terrain (CFIT).

Crew
Pilot: Capt Ralph D Bowles
WSO: Maj Merle D Kenney
Call Sign: Tasty 15
Accident Board President: Col Samuel Huser
Time of Incident: 1956 PDT
Assigned Unit: 428th TFS / 474th TFW Nellis AFB, Nevada
Aircraft Statistics: Unknown
Mishap Result: Aircraft Destroyed / Fatal Crash / No Ejection Initiated

View of approximate flight path looking south toward the Range 65 Target. *Photograph Courtesy of Google Earth.*

66-0044
EF-111A GRUMMAN CONVERSION NUMBER A-14
USAF Delivery Date: July 28, 1983

66-0044 Shown on takeoff with the 42nd ECS at RAF Upper Heyford. *Photograph Courtesy of Mike Kaplan.*

Crash Scenario
On June 17, 1996, the mishap aircraft was on a single-ship night Terrain Following Radar (TFR), low-level electronic combat training sortie. Approximately one hour into the flight, while on the low-level route IR 107 at 1000' AGL, the mishap crew noticed an unusual orange glow reflecting off the ground underneath the aircraft. Although they had no abnormal instrument indications, the mishap crew felt uncomfortable with this situation and elected to exit the low-level route. The mishap aircraft was in a 5-10 degree climb when the mishap pilot noticed a flashing fire light for the right (# 2) engine. The mishap pilot performed emergency procedures for an engine fire inflight; however, the fire light remained illuminated. While passing 9400' MSL (5000' AGL), the mishap Electronic Warfare Officer (EWO) squawked emergency and the mishap pilot initiated a level off. While initiating the level off, the mishap pilot noticed that an abnormal amount of forward stick force was required to push-over and hold the aircraft's attitude. The aircraft then began an uncommanded roll to the right. The mishap pilot informed the EWO that the aircraft was becoming uncontrollable and to prepare for ejection. The mishap pilot made a MAYDAY call on the local approach frequency and then switched the radio to GUARD frequency and retransmitted the same MAYDAY call. The EWO initiated ejection at approximately 90-110 degrees of bank and 278 KIAS at 10,500' MSL. The ejection sequence was normal and the crew received only minor injuries. The aircraft impacted in steep terrain on the side of a mesa approximately 1.5 miles from the crew capsule landing site. Another EF-111A (BASH 01) operating in the area initiated a SAR (Search and Rescue) orbit, and directed two New Mexico State Police officers and a local rancher to the downed aircrew by relaying radio calls through the

Cannon AFB SOF, and to the police dispatch. The aircraft crashed on the T-4 Ranch at an elevation of 4734', 14 NM northwest of Tucumcari, New Mexico. Coordinates were (N 35 14.5 / W 103 57.8)

Findings
The mishap aircraft experienced a right (# 2) engine fuel duct segment failure. The raw fuel and fumes within the hot engine bay ignited into an uncontrollable fire. The internal nacelle fire burned through hydraulic system lines within the engine bay, depleting system pressure and resulting in a subsequent loss of aircraft control.

Crew
Pilot: Capt James D Wingo
WSO: Capt Don R Watson Jr.
Call Sign: Jamup 2
Time of Incident: 2152 L
Accident Board President: Col Craig R Dedrick
Assigned Unit: 429th ECS / 27th TFW Cannon AFB, New Mexico
Aircraft Statistics: Unknown
Mishap Result: Aircraft Destroyed / Successful Ejection

66-0056   EF-111A GRUMMAN CONVERSION NUMBER A-23
USAF Delivery Date: April 3, 1984

Crash Scenario
On April 2, 1992, EF-111A 66-0056 crashed shortly after take-off. The mishap aircraft departed Runway 09 at RAF Upper Heyford, United Kingdom, on a single-ship mission at 1505 L. After takeoff, the mishap aircraft developed a fire in the aft fuselage area. The mishap aircrew safely ejected. The aircraft impacted the ground and was destroyed in a car-park at Barton Hartshorn (Finmere), United Kingdom, which is 7 NM from RAF Upper Heyford.

Courtesy of Scott Wilson.

Courtesy of Author's Collection.

Findings
A "Y" shaped fuel system distribution duct on the backbone of the aircraft failed. The uncontained fuel was ignited by the hot engine exhaust and rapidly engulfed the aft section of the aircraft. Shortly thereafter, the crew noticed the pitch damper and hook down caution lights illuminate, and the aircraft began an uncommanded right roll. As a result of the massive fire, the crew ejected from the out-of-control aircraft, which then entered a flat spin and crashed.

Crew
Pilot: Capt Jeffrey N Coombe
WSO: Capt David E Genevish
Call Sign: Unknown
Time of Incident: 1507 BST
Assigned Unit: 42nd ECS / 20th TFW RAF Upper Heyford, United Kingdom
Accident Board President: Col Dean W Radueg
Aircraft Statistics: Unknown
Mishap Result: Aircraft Destroyed / Successful Ejection

4

F-111A 1967 MODEL MISHAPS

F-111A 67-0089. *Photograph Courtesy of Doug E. Slowiak / Vortex Photo-Graphics.*

Courtesy of Tom Brewer via Don Logan Collection.

67-0036
F-111A # 81 GD/FW Production Run # A1-81
USAF Delivery Date: August 28, 1968

Crash Scenario
On April 24, 1972, F-111A 67-0036 crashed during a local training sortie over "Canyon Alpha," a local Nellis AFB, Nevada, maneuvering area. This was mission AC-1 (the student pilot's first flight in the F-111), which called for familiarization in aircraft control and transition maneuvers. At a point in the sortie, the student was requested to perform a rudder roll using rudder and pitch controls only. The first attempt was unsuccessful, so the crew placed the flight control system switch to the Takeoff and Land position, i.e. to have full rudder authority. On the second attempt, as the roll was started, the crew members noticed the Angle of Attack (AOA) had increased to 12-degrees, and the Instructor Pilot (IP) felt and observed a departure from normal flight and immediately took control to recover the aircraft. The IP noticed the AOA had increased beyond 25-degrees and that the aircraft was rapidly losing altitude. Passing below 9000 feet MSL at 4400 AGL, the student pilot

The Flight Control System Switch, labeled 2, is shown in the NORM position. The T.O. & LAND position is intended to be used for configuring the flight control system for landing in cases where the landing gear handle can't physically be moved to the DOWN position. Inflight, the T.O. & LAND position allows the rudder authority to go from the maximum flight position of 11¼ degrees to 30 degrees, or full authority; however, that was not its intended use. A separate Rudder Authority Switch (Figure 2 below) should have been used by the IP for this purpose.

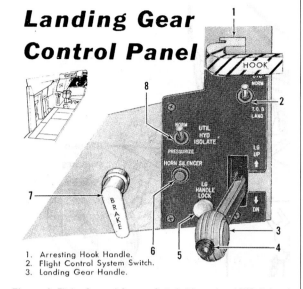

Figure 1: Flight Control System Switch; Normal and T/O & Land (labeled 2). *Courtesy of F-111A Dash-1 Pilot's Manual*

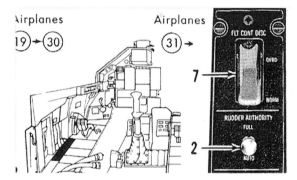

Figure 2: Rudder Authority Switch Labeled 2 with cockpit location highlighted in black.

initiated ejection after confirming that the instructor was in the proper ejection posture. The ejection sequence and module separation in the low-speed mode were successful. The aircraft crashed onto a canyon wall, while the capsule landed 3100 feet north on a rocky, jagged 40- to 50-degree slope. When the module landed it hesitated, and then slid 55 feet down the slope and came to rest on the capsule's right hand side. The crew released the main chute and the capsule slid an additional 64 feet, coming to rest inverted. The crew then exited the module via the left capsule hatch.

Findings
The instructor pilot intentionally placed the Flight Control System Switch on the Landing Gear Control Panel (Figure 1/Item 2) in the Take-off and Landing (T.O. & LAND) position, an inappropriate position for the configuration of the aircraft. Pilot rudder inputs thereafter exceeded the directional control capabilities of the aircraft.

The subsequent departure from controlled flight and the pilot's inability to recover were irreversible.

Crew
Pilot: Capt Richard W Dabney Jr
WSO: Capt Donald R Joyner
Call Sign: Trig 01
Accident Board President: Col Thomas E Lacy
Time of Incident: 0925 MST
Assigned Unit: 442nd TFTS / 474th TFW Nellis AFB, Nevada
Aircraft Statistics: 221 Flights 586.3 Flight Hours
Mishap Result: Aircraft Destroyed / Successful Ejection

Accident Crash Site. Courtesy of Author's Collection.

67-0040
F-111A # 85 GD/FW Production Run # A1-85
USAF Delivery Date: October 28, 1968

Crash Scenario
On July 11, 1973, F-111A 67-0040 crashed during a local training sortie over the Nellis AFB, Nevada, F-2 training area. This was mission AC-1 (the first flight in the F-111) for the mishap right seat pilot, which called for familiarization in aircraft control and transition maneuvers. The aircraft entered the training area with the mishap aircraft commander or Instructor pilot in the left seat in control. Various flight maneuvers from the syllabus were accomplished. Later in the flight the student pilot in the right seat assumed control, making a turn back to the center of the F-2 training area. About five seconds after straight and level flight was achieved, with airspeed of 480 KTAS and an altitude 1500 feet AGL, the right windscreen and hatch glass suddenly imploded. The pilots became disoriented and were unable to regain control of the aircraft due to windblast effects and atomized glass particles temporarily blinding them. The aircrew then initiated a successful ejection sequence. The module landed two miles west of the aircraft impact site in Zion National Park, five miles north of Springdale, Utah.

Findings
This was the second of eight F-111s which suffered a windshield loss or disintegration due to a bird strike penetrating the windscreen and/or structural failure of the windscreen. An instantaneous windblast at 480 KTAS caused obvious shock to the flight crew's bodies, and the pressure on the head and eyeballs caused instantaneous disorientation. Ejection was the immediate response due to the pilots' inability to assess what had happened to the aircraft. Crews revealed in testimony that they immediately concluded the aircraft had either been in a mid-air collision or had disintegrated due to structural failure during the last maneuver. Author's Note: Only the F-111Fs received a shatter-proof polycarbonate windscreen. All previous F-111s retained the glass windscreen.

Crew
Pilot: Maj Robert N Hopkins
WSO: Maj Kirby F Ludwick
Call Sign: Chaps 01
Accident Board President: Col William L Strand
Time of Incident: 1409 PDT
Assigned Unit: 442nd TFTS / 474th TFW Nellis AFB, Nevada
Aircraft Statistics: 402 Flights 1029.2 Flight Hours
Mishap Result: Aircraft Destroyed / Successful Ejection

The capsule came to rest on the steep slope of the rugged terrain in Zion National Park, Utah. The crew survived without significant injury. *Photograph courtesy of Bill Allen Collection.*

Courtesy of Bill Allen Collection.

67-0043
F-111A # 88 GD/FW Production Run # A1-88
USAF Delivery Date: October 29, 1968

Crash Scenario
On May 22, 1969, F-111A 67-0043 departed Nellis AFB, Nevada, via the Carp-1 Standard Instrument Departure procedure and proceeded to the Wilson Creek high altitude corridor toward the OB-29 military entry point. After a TFR letdown, the mishap aircraft was to proceed to the Holbrook, Arizona, Radar Bombing Scoring (RBS) range. After the simulated bomb run, the mishap aircraft would egress the range (level off was at 1000AGL and 480 KTAS), set wing sweep to 45 degrees, and engage the TFR. Approximately 11 minutes into

Courtesy of Bill Allen Collection.

Courtesy of Author's Collection.

the letdown a bird impacted the left windscreen, which became fractured and crazed. At this point the canopy began to fail in approximately a double-fist sized area. Shortly thereafter, the glass failed inward and debris caused disorientation as a result of broken glass particles and glare shield debris entering the cockpit. The aircraft commander, after attempting unsuccessfully to communicate with the WSO, decided to eject. The pilot had to feel blindly with his hand to locate the ejection handle. The ejection sequence was successful.

Findings

This mishap was the second of several windshield failures in the F-111. In the first incident, the aircraft was able to recover to Nellis AFB. This mishap was the first bird strike and subsequent windshield failure that resulted in the loss of the aircraft. Just prior to ejection, the pilot noticed two separate inward bulges develop at the top edge of the windshield. The pilot ducked forward just as the windshield failed. Both pilots reported that debris swirled about the cockpit, most attributed to small pieces of the velveteen glare shield. The pilots reported the wind noise inside the cockpit to be "horrible." Without being able to communicate with each other via the intercom, and unable to ascertain the attitude or altitude, Capt May initiated a successful ejection sequence.

Ultimately, the investigation teams led the USAF and General Dynamics to establish realistic design and test requirements for aircraft windshield and canopy bird resistance. The F-111's mission for Terrain Following Radar and low-level high speed missions exposed the F-111 to birds' natural environment for extended periods of time.

Crew

Pilot: Capt Kent M May
WSO: Maj John C Morrow
Call Sign: Soon 31
Time of Incident: 0955 PDT
Assigned Unit: 429th TFS / 474th TFW Nellis AFB, Nevada
Aircraft Statistics: 60 Flights 238.1 Flight Hours
Mishap Result: Aircraft Destroyed / Successful Ejection

See Also: For similar type accidents:

F-111A	67-0043	(A88)	22 May 1969	
F-111A	67-0069	(A114)	13 Apr 1971	
F-111A	66-0029	(A47)	1 Sept 1971	
F-111F	71-0892	(F68)	6 June 1973	Landed Safely
F-111A	67-0040	(A85)	11 July 1973	
F-111E	68-0081	(E91)	5 Mar 1975	
F-111E	68-0060	(E70)	5 Nov 1975	
F-111C	A8-133	(D1-09)	29 Sep 1977	
F-111E	68-0019	(E29)	9 Aug 1984	

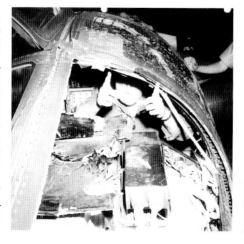

This photograph shows the left forward windscreen and instrument panel glare shield missing. Visual examination at the scene was unable to detect bird remains. Not until the remnants of the windshield and the canopy bow were examined by General Dynamics through microscopic analysis, were bird remains detected. *Courtesy of Bill Allen Collection.*

Courtesy of Tom Brewer via Don Logan Collection.

67-0049
F-111A # 94 GD/FW Production Run # A1-94
USAF Delivery Date: November 26, 1968

Crash Scenario

On December 22, 1969, F-111A 67-0049 was Number-2 in a three-ship local air to ground conventional weapons training sortie on Nellis AFB Gunnery Range 5 near Indian Springs, Nevada. The flight established contact with the range controller and entered the bombing range at 6500 MSL. Two attacks were made, dropping bombs on the dive bomb circle, and another two attacks on the skip bomb panel. The flight switched to the rocket attack panel, and on the fourth rocket attack the mishap aircraft crashed. Subsequent investigation revealed that fatigue failure via carbon deposit on the left wing pivot fitting caused the wing to break off during the rocket attack. The left wing failed catastrophically 18 inches outboard of the pivot point, and this induced an abrupt left rolling moment. The right wing was struck by the severed left wing, causing secondary failures of both these structures. The vertical stabilizer was also struck by pieces of the left over-wing fairing or wing pieces. The mishap aircraft went into a violent roll. The crew initiated an ejection sequence nose down and inverted, but the aircraft was too low for proper chute deployment.

Findings

This accident received the most extensive technical investigation during the F-111 program. However, the determination of the cause of the accident was identified within the first few minutes after arrival at the crash site. The investigators noticed a dark half-moon shaped fracture face on the left wing pivot fitting which caused the wing pivot to fail during the high-G pullout from the rocket pass. The largest concern centered on the D6ac steel wing pivot fitting, and the forging process of all D6ac high strength steel forged components in the F-111 construction. The immediate problems in determining how to detect such cyclic fatigue cracks within a completed and enclosed aircraft structure were so immense that the cost and complexity therefore nearly terminated the F-111 program. However, the broad investigation by General Dynamics, the F-111 Systems Program Office (SPO), the USAF Scientific Advisory Board, and the many subcontractors involved in manufacturing of the wing pivot forging were instrumental in the outgrowth of the Cold Proof Loads Test Program. This was a process that literally froze the completed aircraft while hydraulic lifts applied loads to the wings, much like those experienced by the airframe in flight. The test applied full structural design limit loads on each F-111 in the fleet, demonstrating that the complete aircraft met load limit conditions.

Crew

Pilot: Lt Col Thomas J Mack
WSO: Maj James L Anthony
Call Sign: Advice 02
Accident Board President: Brigadier General John H Buckner
Time of Incident: 0731 PST
Assigned Unit: 428th TFS / 474th TFW Nellis AFB, Nevada
Aircraft Statistics: 46 Flights 107.4 Flight Hours
Mishap Result: Aircraft Destroyed / Fatal Crash / Ejection out of Envelope

After considerable research by experts, including the Air Force Scientific Advisory Board, the SPO implemented a Cold Proof Load Test (CPLT), in which every F-111 was subjected to a +7.33g and -2.4g load in specially-designed structural ground test facilities in which the entire F-111 structure was cold-soaked to -40 degrees Fahrenheit before the load was applied. The Cold Proof Load Test facilities were unique to the F-111. This type of test had never been used on any other aircraft. The theory was that any undetected flaw in the structure, including the wing pivot, would cause a failure in these conditions.

If the structure passes the cold proof load test, it is cleared for the next several hundred flight hours. The Air Force tested all aircraft that had been built before December 1969 (about 200) and continued to cold-test each new F-111 (grand total of 562). Twenty-three Australian F-111Cs were produced from August 1969 to November 1969 before the wing-pivot failure and crash in December 1969. Delivery was delayed until spring 1974, until all the aircraft could be proof-tested. Virtually all the active F-111s were proof-tested at least three times, since cold proof load testing was repeated at intervals as low as 1500 flight hours. Utilizing this proof load testing, numerous failures (11 major) were detected and fixed, thereby avoiding the loss of aircraft had the failures occurred in flight. The cost of the testing was estimated at about 100 million dollars.

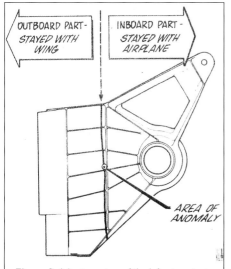

Figure 3: A bottom view of the left wing pivot forging. The Area of Anomaly is also designated in the larger photograph at the top of the page as: ORIGIN. *Courtesy of Bill Allen Mishap Report.*

Close-up of the undetected forging flaw in the left wing pivot forging. *Courtesy of Bill Allen Mishap Report.*

Bottom right two photos represent Cold Proof Load Tests (CPLT) at British Aerospace Filton Plant, Bristol, England. An F-111 airframe undergoing the applied load test, warping the wings to the aircraft load limit, thereby validating the aircraft could survive the full structural design load limit. The wings were flexed over 48 inches during this test. *Courtesy of Author's Collection.*

Courtesy of Author's Collection.

USAF Mishap Photograph Courtesy of GDFW via Bill Allen Collection.

67-0053
F-111A # 98 GD/FW Production Run # A1-98
USAF Delivery Date: November 20, 1968

Accident Scenario
On May 4, 1973, the mishap aircraft F-111A 67-0053 was scheduled as lead aircraft on a two-ship flight being flown by the 442nd TFTS. The mission was a student training syllabus sortie (AC-5), requiring low-level TFR, dry range passes, formation training, and multiple VFR overhead and simulated emergency patterns. The route of flight was low-level route Blythe 336 to Range I-5, followed by recovery back at Nellis AFB, Nevada. All training on Range I-5 was accomplished, and formation training was done on the return to Nellis AFB. The mishap aircraft entered the normal VFR traffic pattern via the Nellis Flex reentry route for runway 21R. Two touch-and-go landings were accomplished. On the third landing, about halfway down the runway, zone-two afterburner was selected. As the afterburner lit, the left engine FIRE light illuminated. Afterburner operation was immediately terminated on both engines, and the left engine was retarded to idle and then to shutoff. The instructor took control of the aircraft as the student depressed the fire agent discharge for the left engine extinguishing system. The fire light remained on for another 30 seconds. The crew made a wide turn and landed single engine. Fire damage to the left speed-bump and afterburner nozzle was found after shut down.

Findings
The left engine fire was created by fuel released from a crack in the engine afterburner hydraulic pump case. The high pressure fuel spray exited the engine bay and was apparently ignited by the afterburner as no evidence of any other ignition source or area within the engine nacelle was found. Examination of the external surface of the aft fuselage centerbody revealed positive evidence of flame flow directly aft and up into the left hand aft centerbody louver. The fire propagated internally going forward around the base of the vertical fin resulting in intense heat damage to the rudder push-pull tubes. Reference Chapter 1, Engine Fires and Reverse Flow Phenomena.

Courtesy of Marty Isham Collection

This accident was a very significant mishap, because the resulting investigation led to a clearer understanding into a total of eight separate F-111 mishaps, all having similar characteristics. Six of the eight aircraft lost experienced loss of control, apparently due to a hard over-right rudder. Two of the eight aircraft had significant fire damage in the aft centerbody but were able to land safely. The common link in the six aircraft lost was evidence that a fire entered the aft centerbody, causing rudder control link failure and/or Primary and Utility hydraulic line failure. The safe recovery of this particular aircraft (0053) was extremely important because it provided General Dynamics and the USAF an opportunity to see firsthand how the fire path moved into the aft centerbody area. The investigation also revealed intensity of the fire in the area of the rudder actuator, both sides of the vertical stabilizer, and in the upper fuselage controls routing tunnel. An F-111D was instrumented to measure the velocity of the airflow through the Rudder Servo Actuator bay. The reverse airflow velocity was recorded at 135 mph, which resulted in the USAF sealing off the aft centerbody louvers!

Crew
Pilot: Capt Robert S Pahl
WSO: Capt Thomas M Heyde
Call Sign: Chaps 03
Time of Incident: 1853 PDT
Accident Board President: Lt Col Everett D Harner
Assigned Unit: 442nd TFTS / 474th TFW Nellis AFB, Nevada
Aircraft Statistics: Unknown Flights Unknown Flight Hours
Mishap Result: Aircraft received significant fire damage but was repaired and returned to service

---

67-0055
F-111A # 100 GD/FW Production Run # A1-100
USAF Delivery Date: August 24, 1968

Crash Scenario
On November 12, 1974, the mishap aircraft F-111A 67-0055, Sigma 71, was scheduled to fly a night high altitude instrument / navigation leg to rejoin with a KC-135 tanker for air refueling in AR-316. The mishap aircraft departed single-ship, but was to rejoin with his wingman, Sigma 72, into a two-ship formation and proceed to the air refueling track. The plan after refueling was for the mishap aircraft to split-up the two-ship and continue with individual training. The mishap aircraft would then return to Nellis AFB to practice instrument approaches and landings. The mishap aircraft entered the refueling track at 18,000 feet MSL. The mishap crew saw a red rotating beacon and believed this to be the tanker, call sign TOFT 51. The mishap aircraft approached and collided with a civilian Turbo Commander 690A that was not seen on radar by Salt Lake Center due to an Identify Friend or Foe (IFF) mode filter. The civilian pilot was killed. The mishap F-111 crew initiated a successful crew module ejection. Although the crew module was damaged by the collision, the sequence and module separation was unhampered.

Findings
Due to a drift in the F-111's INS position, the mishap crew entered the Air Refueling Track several miles northeast of the desired entry point and outside the track's protected airspace. Comparative position communications between the tanker and those of the F-111 crew matched reasonably well. However, the F-111 crew had obtained a radar lock and a visual sighting of the civilian aircraft's beacon, which contributed to the misidentification of the Turbo Commander as the tanker. The mishap crew failed to validate by Air-to-Air TACAN

Courtesy of Author's Collection

ranging, communications with Salt Lake Center Air Traffic Control, and the tanker TOFT 51 their exact position. The crew assumed the civilian aircraft was the tanker and attempted a rejoin using visual clues. The ground track of the mishap aircraft is recreated in Figure 4 to follow.

Crew
Pilot: Capt Peter R Granger
WSO: Capt Paul D Sperry
Call Sign: Sigma 71
Accident Board President: Col Robert M Keith Jr.
Time of Incident: 1804 MST
Assigned Unit: 442nd TFTS / 474th TFW Nellis AFB, Nevada
Aircraft Statistics: 441 Flights 1113.5 Flight Hours
Mishap Result: Aircraft Destroyed / Successful Ejection

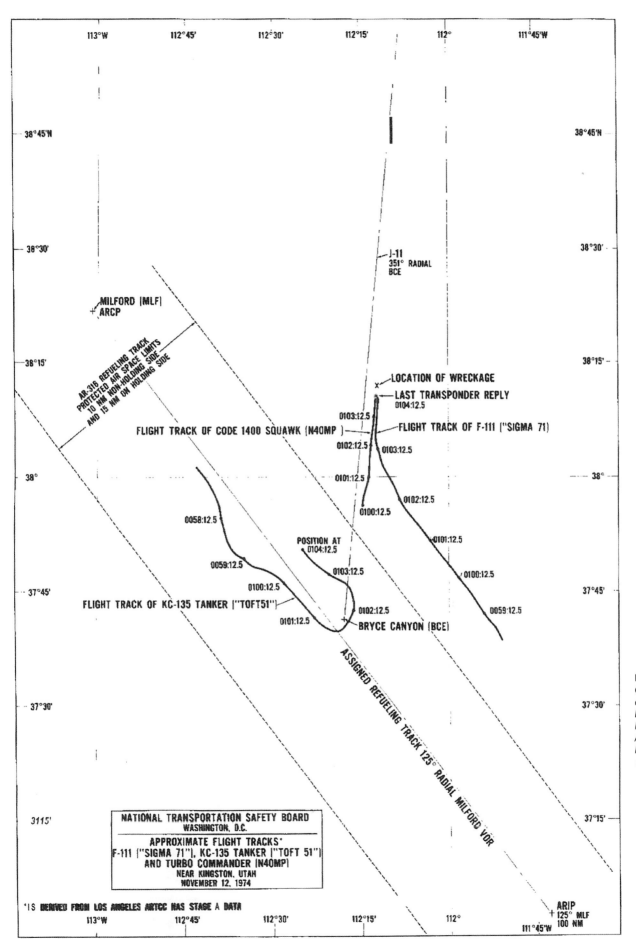

Figure 4:
Courtesy of NTSB Report NTSB-AAR-75-12, November 12, 1974

67-0059
F-111A # 104 GD/FW Production Run # A1-104
USAF Delivery Date: November 26, 1968

Crash Scenario

On January 4, 1979, the mishap aircraft was #2 in a two-ship, day strike student upgrade training syllabus sortie. The crew consisted of a student Aircraft Commander in the left seat and an Instructor Pilot in the right seat. The planned mission was to depart Mountain Home AFB, Idaho, and fly a low-level route, and proceed to the Saylor Creek bombing range. Takeoff was at 1003L, and as the mishap aircraft climbed, approximately 13-14 minutes after level-off at FL 210, the mishap crew declared an In-Flight Emergency (IFE) for a left engine fire. Bold Face emergency procedures for the engine fire and shutdown were accomplished. The mishap aircraft was radar vectored back toward Mountain Home AFB via Salt Lake Center. The instructor pilot began a descent from Instrument Meteorological Conditions (IMC) to Visual Meteorological Conditions (VMC). Shortly after passing 15000 MSL, the aircraft began an uncommanded roll to the right. The instructor pilot initiated the ejection sequence. The mishap aircraft crashed 43 NM west on the 268 radial from Mountain Home AFB TACAN in Owyhee County, 11 miles west of Murphy, Idaho. The ejection sequence and module separation were successful.

Findings

The engine failure and inflight fire were due to a High Pressure Compressor (HPC) disk exploding through the engine case and causing an uncontained fire. The fire burned through the Rudder Control push/pull tube due to the reverse flow phenomena, causing loss of control. Investigation revealed the left engine scavenge passages in the 9th stage stator vanes were blocked by coking. As a result, the number-2 and 3-

Courtesy of Don Logan Collection

bearing compartment became flooded with oil. The oil was forced past the center tube air seals and then into the N-2 compressor rotor drum. The oil in the drum area auto-ignited, subjecting the Number 14- and 15-compressor disks to excessive heat. The disks failed, and a portion of the Number 14 disk penetrated the engine case and the aft fuel tank, resulting in a massive fuel leak and intense fuselage fire. The roll and yaw push-pull tubes failed from excessive heat, resulting in loss of aircraft control.

Crew

Pilot: Capt Gary E Ryker
WSO: Capt William J Locke
Call Sign: Unknown
Accident Board President: Col William D McWilliams III
Time of Incident: 1019 MST
Assigned Unit: 391st TFS / 366th TFW Mountain Home AFB, Idaho
Aircraft Statistics: 940 Flights 2356.8 Flight Hours
Mishap Result: Aircraft Destroyed / Successful Ejection

67-0060
F-111A # 105 GD/FW Production Run # A1-105
USAF Delivery Date: November 26, 1968

Crash Scenario

On April 7, 1976, the mishap aircraft F-111A 67-0060 departed Nellis AFB flying toward the low altitude, high speed training route #317 south of the Wilson Creek TACAN. TFR checks were made, and a TFR letdown from 15000 MSL was accomplished. As the throttles were advanced in anticipation of a level-off at 1000 AGL, the crew heard a loud thump. The aircraft commander (AC) initiated a climb and observed the left engine fire warning light. Bold Face emergency procedures were accomplished by shutting down the #1 engine with the engine fire bottle extinguishing system. The engine FIRE warning light remained illuminated, indicating the fire

Courtesy of Author's Collection

was not extinguished. The mishap aircraft commander observed flames from the left wing root area. The Weapon System Officer (WSO) initiated the ejection sequence at 12,800 feet MSL, and the ejection sequence and capsule separation were successfully made. The aircraft crashed 25 NM southeast of Ely, Nevada (N 38 53 01 / W 114 36 01).

Findings

During an Auto TFR low-level flight, the crew experienced a distinct thump as the throttles were advanced during level off. The pilot initiated a climb and observed illumination of the left engine fire warning light. The engine was shutdown, however, the fire light remained illuminated and the pilot observed flames on the left side of the aircraft, aft of the wing root. Investigation revealed the engine breather pressure had exceeded the pressure in the high pressure compressor drum for an undetermined reason. The high pressure forced oil past the air seals at the front of the compressor center tube into the compressor drum. As a

result, the air/oil mixture was ignited by hot metal surfaces in the vicinity of the 14th and 15th stage disks, and the high intensity fire softened the inner webs and bores of the 14th and 15th stage disks. When the throttles were advanced, the weakened disks failed and disk segments penetrated the engine cases and the saddle fuel tanks, resulting in an uncontrollable engine bay fire.

Crew

Pilot: Capt Benjamin L Alexander
WSO: 1Lt Robert J Short
Call Sign: Doxy 53
Accident Board President: Col John W Gordon
Time of Incident: 0820 PST
Assigned Unit: 429th TFS / 474th TFW Nellis AFB, Nevada
Aircraft Statistics: 750 Flights 1910.6 Flight Hours
Mishap Result: Aircraft Destroyed / Successful Ejection

67-0071
F-111A # 116 GD/FW Production Run # A1-116
USAF Delivery Date: February 27, 1969

Mishap Scenario
On February 17, 1973, F-111A 67-0071 was assigned to Detachment 1, 430th TFS, and was deployed to Takhli RTAFB, Thailand, in support of Operation "Constant Guard V." The mishap aircraft was involved in a collision that occurred during a Beacon Bombing Pathfinder Mission while leading a flight of F-4s over central Laos. A formation change was required after Igloo 50 (67-0098) experienced INS failure while attempting to release ordnance flying on Igloo 47's (67-0071) wing. During the change of lead the two aircraft collided. Igloo 50 jettisoned his ordnance near Udorn RTAFB and returned to Takhli RTAFB with major damage to both wings and leading edge slats. Igloo 47 requested vectors from "Brigham" to a KC-135 tanker that provided fuel while evaluating his situation. After a controllability check, the crew of "Igloo 47" made a successful barrier engagement on Runway 30 at Udorn RTAFB, Thailand.

Findings
During a night ingress, the crew experienced some difficulty with the attack radar system. To preclude an air abort, the pilot requested assistance from another F-111 flight crew that had completed the target run and were egressing the area. This pilot joined on his wing to monitor the bomb drop and to be sure that their system was working properly. Approximately two minutes prior to release, the attacking pilot was unable to acquire

Courtesy of USAF.

the target on radar and directed the other pilot to assume the lead of the formation. During the formation change the two aircraft collided. The right wing of the attacking aircraft and the left wing of the assisting aircraft were damaged. (See Also Mishap for F-111A 67-0098)

Crew
Pilot: Maj Richard S Skeels
WSO: Capt Robert P McConnell Jr
Call Sign: Igloo 47
Accident Board President: Col John F Rhemann
Time of Incident: 0854 GOLF
Assigned Unit: Det 1 430th TFS / 347th TFW Takhli RTAFB, Thailand
Aircraft Statistics: 336 Flights 853.7 Flight Hours
Mishap Result: Aircraft received major damage but was repaired and returned to service

67-0072
F-111A # 117 GD/FW Production Run # A1-117
USAF Delivery Date: March 14, 1969

Mishap Scenario
On February 21, 1973, F-111A 67-0072 was assigned to Det 1, 430th TFS, deployed to Takhli RTAFB Thailand in support of Operation "Constant Guard V." The mishap aircraft was scheduled for a night medium altitude combat bombing mission. At 0126L, the aircrew taxied to the EOR (End-of Runway) for bomb arming and pre-takeoff visual inspections. The flight crew requested take-off clearance from the Takhli tower and were instructed to taxi onto Runway 18 and hold. At 0127L, the crew was issued departure instructions and advised to use the right side of the runway because of rubber removal compound on the left side of the runway at the departure end. Engine run-up checks were accomplished and the afterburner take-off roll started at 0129L. The take-off run appeared to be normal until sparks were observed trailing the aircraft. After approximately 2600 feet of travel, the aircraft veered right and departed 4000 feet down on the right side of the runway and caught fire. The aircraft came to rest 4800 feet from the departure end and 100 feet west (right) of Runway 18, with the nose pointed 062 degrees. The flight crew successfully ground egressed the aircraft.

Findings
During a night takeoff roll at the estimated rotation speed of 135 knots, the right main landing gear dropped, allowing the right wheel to fold as during retraction. This caused the right end of the right landing gear

assembly lateral beam to fall to the runway. The induced drag caused the aircraft to veer to the right. The pilot could not control the veer using full left rudder and full left brake. The aircraft departed the right side of the runway, where both nose gear tires came off with subsequent immediate collapse of the nose strut due to overstress. The aircraft began a slow, clockwise horizontal rotation as it slid along the ground. It struck and demolished the 5000 foot remaining marker. A fuel line or fuel tank was ruptured. The fuel was ignited and fire engulfed the aircraft. The two crew members safely egressed the cockpit and ran like Olympic sprinters! The ensuing fire cooked off and detonated the 24 externally mounted MK-82 weapons, totally destroying the aircraft. Investigation revealed a main landing gear joint / pivot pin failed during the take-off roll. The main landing gear collapsed, causing the aircraft to veer off the runway and slide to a stop. Additionally, an inspection of the landing gear was not properly performed on the landing gear stabilizer rod attachment pin, which resulted in the pin not being changed prior to the failure.

Crew
Pilot: Capt Charles E Sudberry
WSO: 1Lt Eric R Puschmann
Call Sign: Igloo 55
Time of Incident: 0130 GOLF
Accident Board President: Col Cecil D Crabb
Assigned Unit: Det 1 428th TFS / 474th TFW Takhli RTAFB, Thailand
Aircraft Statistics: 476 Flights 1180.9 Flight Hours
Mishap Result: Aircraft Destroyed

Courtesy of USAF.

67-0073
F-111A # 118 GD/FW Production Run # A1-118
USAF Delivery Date: March 7, 1969

Courtesy of Gerald McMasters via Don Logan Collection.

Crash Scenario

On January 19, 1982, the mishap aircraft F-111A 67-0073 was scheduled as lead of a three-ship, low-level, surface attack tactics student training syllabus sortie. The crew members of the mishap aircraft were an instructor pilot (IP) in the left seat and a student weapons systems officer (WSO) in the right seat. The assigned wingman's aircraft was delayed for a maintenance issue, so the mishap aircraft elected to take-off as a single-ship. The mishap aircraft took off at 1501 L and declared an emergency (IFE) one minute and 22 seconds later, with Mountain Home AFB departure control indicating the presence of a left engine fire. The mishap aircraft leveled off at 5500 feet MSL and initiated a left turn. Mountain Home approach recommended a left turn for vectors to an ILS Runway 30 final approach course. Two (2) minutes and five (5) seconds into flight, the mishap aircrew experienced a hard over rudder. The aircraft entered a steep bank to the right and went nearly inverted. The aircrew initiated a successful ejection at approximately 2900 feet MSL. The mishap aircraft impacted the ground 18 NM west of Mountain Home AFB in Ada County, Idaho, on the 288 degree radial. (N 43 12 01 W 116 12 01)

Findings

Shortly after takeoff, the aircraft caught fire due to an F-2 fuel tank leak. The fire could not be extinguished, and the crew ejected at 1500 feet AGL after experiencing control problems. Investigation revealed improper repairs were made to the upper skin of the F-2 fuel bay tank at an undetermined time. Over time moisture entered one of the improperly repaired areas, corroded the honeycomb core, and weakened the inner fuel cell skin. During the mishap aircraft's takeoff, the fuel tanks pressurized and the pressure ruptured the weakened fuel cell skin, allowing fuel to escape and catch fire. The fire propagated forward to the leaking fuel cell and burned into the aft centerbody and left engine nacelle. The fire eventually burned through the rudder push-pull tube, resulting in loss of aircraft control and forcing the crew to eject.

Crew

Pilot: Lt Col Roland J McDonald Jr
WSO: 1Lt Alan D Walker Jr
Call Sign: NOMEX 71
Time of Incident: 1505 MST
Accident Board President: Col Lester G Frazier
Assigned Unit: 391st TFS / 366th TFW Mountain Home AFB, Idaho
Aircraft Statistics: 1181 Flights 2918.8 Flight Hours
Mishap Result: Aircraft Destroyed / Successful Ejection

67-0079
F-111A # 124 GD/FW Production Run # A1-124
USAF Delivery Date: March 26, 1969

Mishap Scenario

On January 21, 1981, the mishap aircraft was the lead aircraft of two F-111As scheduled for a Surface Attack Tactics (SAT) sortie on the Nellis Range Complex in Nevada. Take-off from Mountain Home AFB was scheduled for 1100 L, with a bombing range time of 1150-1230L. The flight lead had pre-coordinated for practice instrument approaches at Tonopah test airfield, within the Nellis Range Complex, following completion of the SAT bombing mission, with a land time at Mountain Home AFB, Idaho, of 1330L. Take-off was on time at 1115L; climb out, level off, and descent into the Nellis Range were uneventful. After the first practice approach at the Tonopah Test Airfield, the mishap aircraft experienced multiple emergencies, consisting of: stuck flaps, wheel well hot warning light, primary hydraulic hot warning light, left and right primary hydraulic failure, and a right engine fire warning light. All emergency checklist procedures were accomplished, and a no flap, single engine landing was made at the Tonopah Test Airfield. The mishap aircrew egressed after landing, and base fire department personnel extinguished the main wheel well fire.

Photograph shows the extensive fire damage to the aft wheel well, fuselage bulkhead, and engine bay.

All photos courtesy of Author's Collection

Findings

The aircraft experienced failure of a secondary "hot bleed" air duct, introducing extremely hot and high pressure bleed air into the engine bay and a consequent back-flow into the main landing gear wheel well. The bleed air eventually melted exposed electrical wires, initiating arcing which ignited a fire. The multiple system failures were a result of the fire burning all exposed combustible fluids and components. The fire damage to the wheel well and aft fuselage was severe, requiring the USAF to partially dismantle the aircraft and ship it to GDFW (Vark Hospital) for restoration.

Arrow points to the broken secondary "hot bleed" air duct.

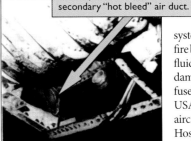

Crew

Pilot: Maj Daniel P Kallenbach
WSO: 1Lt Harry E Pauley
Call Sign: Davit 21
Time of Incident: 1143 PST
Assigned Unit: 390th TFS / 366th TFW Mountain Home AFB, Idaho
Aircraft Statistics: Unknown
Mishap Result: Aircraft received major structural damage, aircraft rebuilt and returned to service.

67-0079 at GDFW undergoing a 13 month rebuild. The aircraft was returned to flight status and later retired from the USAF on September 18, 1990.

67-0080
F-111A # 125 GD/FW Production Run # A1-125
USAF Delivery Date: April 7, 1969

Courtesy of USAF

Crash Scenario

On March 11, 1976, the mishap aircraft F-111A 67-0080 departed Nellis AFB, Nevada, as Number-2 in a scheduled day four-ship, low-level, heavyweight ordnance delivery and Radar Warning Receiver (RWR) and Electronic Counter Measures (ECM) tactics training mission. Takeoff, departure, and cruise to the low-level entry point were normal. The formation entered the Blythe #336 low-level route at 0751L. TFR flight and inert ordnance deliveries were normal. At 0836L, the flight checked in with the Electronics Warfare Range controller and was cleared to work the ECM site. The flight practiced ECM tactics on the range until 0859L. Shortly after 0900L, an emergency beeper was heard on Guard Frequency (243.0 MHz) and a large column of smoke was observed by range officials. The mishap aircrew had initiated the capsule ejection system; ejection sequence and module separation were successful, the capsule landing 600' from the impact area.

Findings

After exiting the low-level passes against the ECM threat emitter, the mishap pilot fell well behind his briefed position of 1000 feet in trail. He began a climb to reduce the closure and to prevent overtaking the lead aircraft, while simultaneously maneuvering to regain his proper position. During this maneuver, the mishap pilot lost sight of lead and banked the aircraft a number of times to regain visual contact. After the third bank, the aircraft stalled and departed controlled flight. Due to insufficient altitude for recovery, the pilot initiated ejection. The pilot

was operating with a wing sweep of 51 degrees, which contributed to the post-stall gyrations and departure.

The F-111A could enter into a flight regime, with marginal control characteristics leading to a departure from controlled flight with little or no aerodynamic clues being provided to the pilot. The artificial stall warning system may have been inoperative with a wing sweep aft of 50 degrees. The WSO did not advise the pilot when critical airspeed and AOA were approached. In maneuvering to regain visual with his flight leader, the pilot flew the aircraft into a flight control regime from which recovery was impossible. The possibility that an uncommanded electrical input to the flight control system may have contributed to the accident was also noted.

Crew:

Pilot: Capt Paul F Reitschel
WSO: 1Lt Gary L Fullington
Call Sign: Tasty 12
Accident Board President: Col Thomas J Hickey
Time of Incident: 0900 PST
Assigned Unit: 430th TFS / 474th TFW Nellis AFB, Nevada
Aircraft Statistics: 767 Flights 1933.6 Flight Hours
Mishap Result: Aircraft Destroyed / Successful Ejection

67-0082
F-111A # 127   GD/FW Production Run # A1-127
USAF Delivery Date: April 17, 1969

Courtesy of Tom Brewer via Don Logan Collection.

Crash Scenario

On June 18, 1972, the mishap aircraft F-111A 67-0082 was on a scheduled training flight. Takeoff from Eglin AFB, Florida, was normal. RAPCON (Radar Approach Control) gave the pilot instructions to turn to 350 degrees approximately four miles from the airfield. This call was acknowledged. Three more transmissions were made by RAPCON, but none were acknowledged by the mishap flight crew. Two (2) minutes and thirty-seven (37) seconds after takeoff the pilot stated "Let's Go." Witnesses observed the aircraft making unusual maneuvers and the aircraft descending downward in a ball of fire. The module separated at an altitude of 5484 feet AGL. The capsule's main parachute failed to open completely and "streamed." The module crashed into the water, killing the crew. The aircraft crashed 90-degrees nose down into the Gulf of Mexico in about four feet of water. Crash site was 12 NM on the 095 degree radial from Eglin AFB, Florida.

Courtesy of Author's Video Collection

Findings

During a planned stop at Eglin AFB, Florida, the refueling crew could not fill the aircraft using the normal single point refueling receptacle. The transient refueling crew elected to use the over-wing gravity filler ports to accomplish the refuel. Unfortunately, the filler cap for the F-1 fuel tank had not been reinstalled, or was incorrectly installed after the refueling operation was complete. During the preflight walk-around, the flight crew had not noticed, nor verified the proper installation of the over-wing caps. On takeoff, voluminous fuel siphoned from the open over-wing fuel port, atomizing as it flowed aft over the backbone of the aircraft. The raw fuel spray was subsequently ignited by the afterburners, sustaining an uncontrollable external fire. Loss of flight control ensued. The crew initiated an ejection,

followed by module separation. Unfortunately, the main parachute failed to fully deploy prior to the escape module crashing into the ocean. During the wreckage recovery and subsequent investigation, fire damage on the rudder was consistent with a full right hard-over position, a consequence of the reverse flow phenomena. The original mishap report for 67-0082 had noted the reefing line cutters failed to cut the reefing lines, preventing the main chute from inflating. However…

Following the July 14, 1980 crash of a Cannon AFB F-111D (68-0139), GDFW and SMALC reexamined the evidence surrounding the unsuccessful ejection involving this F-111A, 67-0082. Although it was not understood at the time of the 1972 crash, there was strong reason to believe that the escape module's main parachute had failed to fully deploy due to entanglement with the stabilizing and brake parachute bridle. Investigators noticed a similarity between the two mishaps when comparing the mishap photographs of 67-0082 and 68-0139. The same abrasion marks seen at the confluence of the bridle were most likely transferred as a result of entanglement with the main parachute. The entanglement occurred due to the trailing angle of the stabilization and brake parachute and trajectory of the main chute when catapulted out of the escape module. *(Continued to following page)*

The escape module often achieved an extreme nose-up pitch attitude during ejections at low airspeeds (a function of the rocket motor thrust vector and low speed crew module aerodynamics); the aft and perpendicular vector of the two chutes contributed to the entanglement: see inset photograph.

A subsequent modification was a fleet-wide retrofit to pyrotechnically sever the stabilization and brake chute bridle simultaneously with main chute catapult/deployment. This retrofit eliminated the potential for further entanglement.

Crew
Pilot: Col Keith E Brown
WSO: Lt Col James D Black
Call Sign: Flick 79
Accident Board President: Col Lynwood E Clark
Time of Incident: 1046 CDT
Assigned Unit: 430th TFS / 474th TFW Nellis AFB, Nevada
Aircraft Statistics: 237 Flights 609.4 Flight Hours
Mishap Result: Aircraft Destroyed / Fatal Crash /Unsuccessful Ejection

67-0083
F-111A # 128 GD/FW Production Run # A1-128
USAF Delivery Date: April 17, 1969

Crash Scenario
On November 30, 1977, the mishap aircraft F-111A 67-0083 was the flight lead for six F-111s on a day Red Flag ground attack mission to the Nellis AFB range complex. The mishap aircraft departed from Mountain Home AFB, Idaho, and entered into the low-level route uneventfully. The mishap aircraft arrived in the target area and made a brief radio call at a point 5 ½ miles short of the target. No further transmissions were heard. The mishap aircraft was observed several times during a planned toss weapons maneuver and during the egress recovery. The aircraft skip hit during a loft recovery and impacted the ground at 1330 L approximately 2 NM southwest of the target in Nye County, 36 NM East of Goldfield, Nevada. No ejection was attempted.

Findings
During the recovery maneuver from a loft/toss weapons delivery, the mishap pilot allowed the aircraft pitch attitude to reach an excessively nose low position from which there was insufficient altitude to complete a pull-out. The aircraft collided with a terrain rise in a nose-up, wings level attitude, at a high rate of speed, and disintegrated. The cause was Controlled Flight Into Terrain (CFIT).

Courtesy of Author's Collection

Crew
Pilot: Capt Arthur L Stowe
WSO: Maj Loreley O Wagner
Call Sign Cub 21
Time of Incident: 1330 MST
Assigned Unit: 389th TFTS / 366th TFW Mountain Home AFB, Idaho
Aircraft Statistics: 816 Flights 2095.1 Flight Hours
Mishap Result: Aircraft Destroyed / Fatal Crash / No Ejection Attempt

67-0089
F-111A # 134 GD/FW Production Run # A1-134
USAF Delivery Date: May 10, 1969

Mishap Scenario
On August 14, 1975, the mishap aircraft F-111A 67-0089 was scheduled for a day, low-level ground attack Instructor Pilot (IP) upgrade training sortie utilizing high speed low-level Route 334. The mishap aircraft was Number-2 of a two-ship formation flying out of Nellis AFB, NV. After departing Nellis AFB, Nevada, the mishap crew was to proceed to Nellis Range 62 and Range 65 for practice bomb drops. Aircraft start-up and taxi to Runway 21R was uneventful. In the formation takeoff position on the runway, the mishap crew advanced the throttles into the afterburner position in preparation for takeoff. The right engine exploded, causing a large fire that engulfed the aft fuselage. The fire was observed by the mishap crew via the hatch rear view mirrors, as well as the lead aircraft. The lead aircraft aborted his takeoff and proceeded to taxi down the runway to remain clear of the fire. The mishap crew performed emergency shutdown procedures and then safely exited the aircraft.

Findings
Investigation revealed the Number 2 engine's third stage fan disk retaining tangs failed in fatigue. The cause was traced to excessive vibration of the third stage compressor disk and the associated wear between the second to third stage air seals and the second stage disk. Third stage fan blades became dislodged and penetrated the compressor fan case, cutting engine fuel lines and puncturing the aircraft fuel tanks,

Courtesy of Don Logan Collection.

causing massive fuel leaks. The leaking fuel ignited from contact with superheated engine areas, resulting in a severe fire.

Crew
Pilot: Capt Wayne C Spelius
WSO: Capt Donald R Westbrook
Call Sign: Trick 02
Accident Board President: Col Kenneth G Frank
Time of Incident: 1518 PDT
Assigned Unit: 442nd TFTS & 430th TFS / 474th TFW Nellis AFB, Nevada
Aircraft Statistics: Unknown
Mishap Result: Aircraft sustained serious damage, but was later repaired at GDFW and returned to service

67-0093
F-111A # 138 GD/FW Production Run # A1-138
USAF Delivery Date: July 30, 1969

Courtesy of Brian C. Rogers

Ground Accident Scenario
On November 9, 1982, a ground related accident occurred to aircraft F-111A 67-0093. The aircraft was scheduled for a live load weapons delivery training sortie. The aircraft was loaded with 24 MK-82 bombs and was parked at the Mountain Home AFB, Idaho, remote hot weapons pad with several other 366th wing aircraft, all being prepared for that day's mission. The accident aircraft had a Gaseous Oxygen (GOX) leak in the Center Suit Mask Panel (CSMP), located in the aft portion of the cabin between the pilot and WSO seats. This discrepancy was repaired some time during the night by Environmental Technicians. The repaired item was the GOX servicing core, a common bench stock or over-the-counter item that resembles a core one might find in a car tire. The crew chief, at or around 0855 L, attempted to service the GOX system. During this procedure, a fire erupted in the cockpit at the CSMP. The fire expanded, and after attempts to extinguish the fire, participants evacuated the area. The fire burned through the capsule floor and aft into the F-1 fuel tank, the nose gear collapsed, and fuel gravity fed into the fire. The aircraft became engulfed in fire, and as the fire spread out to the wings, low order detonation of the weapons occurred. The aircraft was totally destroyed, and violent explosions sent debris a great distance. The cockpit oxygen regulator was later found 4600' away on the base golf course.

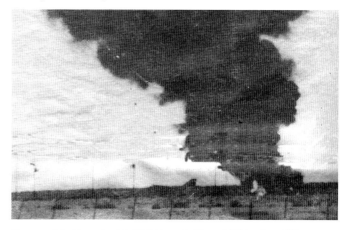

Courtesy of the November 10, 1982 Mountain Home AFB Wing Spread Newspaper

Findings
The GOX (Gaseous Oxygen) core (similar to an inner tube air valve) was installed incorrectly. At some point in time the proper GOX core had been replaced, utilizing a nearly similar, but incorrect, tire core as a suitable substitute. Unfortunately, the substitute tire core was not intended for high-pressure systems. The correct core is gold in color and has an "H" stamped on the end, signifying it as a high-pressure core. The GOX servicing procedures called for a two man operation, purging the supply hose from the GOX cart, bleeding the pressure off the hose, and then connecting it to the aircraft. After these procedural steps were followed, the GOX is added slowly by raising the pressure to a minimum of 1800 psi. All servicing procedures were incorrectly

performed inadvertently setting up the classic "fire triangle": (1) Gaseous Oxygen, (2) high-pressure air provided heat, and (3) dust particle expansion in the cockpit, which provided the fuel, directly contributing to the explosion.

No Call Sign: Ground Incident
Time of Incident: 0900 MST
Assigned Unit: 391st TFS / 266th TFW Mountain Home AFB, Idaho
Aircraft Statistics: 1191 Flights / 2815.8 Flight Hours
Accident Results: Aircraft Destroyed / Crew Chief received minor burns

---

67-0094
F111A # 139 GD/FW Production Run #A1-139
USAF Delivery Date: May 12, 1969

Courtesy of Don Logan Collection.

Mishap Scenario
On June 16, 1973, F-111A 67-0094, assigned to Det 1, 430th TFS, was deployed to Takhli RTAFB Thailand in support of Operation "Constant Guard V." The mishap aircraft was involved in a midair collision approximately 41 NM northwest of Phnom Penh, Khmer Republic (Cambodia), on the Phnom Penh TACAN 323 degree radial. The mishap aircraft was "Popper 11," flying 67-0094 in a "route" formation position (approximately one wingspan distance) from the lead aircraft "Zest 12" flying 67-0108. The two-ship flight was turning right to a heading of 300 degrees magnetic toward an initial point (IP), a preparatory alignment to a "Pathfinding" bomb run. The mishap aircraft was at 14,400 feet MSL when a collision occurred with a third aircraft in the area, 67-0111 "Whaler 21." Although the mishap aircraft 67-0094 lost 4.5 feet of the right wing tip, the aircraft remained controllable. Post-collision, the crew jettisoned its ordnance and proceeded to a refuel track to top off the fuel tanks and then safely recovered at Takhli RTAFB. Whaler 21, in aircraft 67-0111, became uncontrollable and ejected successfully.

Findings
The crew of 67-0111 (mishap aircraft) was on a day VMC level bombing mission near Phnom Penh, Cambodia, when the crew of F-111A 67-0094 collided with them in mid-air. The crew of 67-0094 had been unable to strike their primary target because of an instrument malfunction and coordinated to rejoin to the right wing of the mishap aircraft (67-0111).

The intention of both crews after the rejoin was to use standard path-finding procedures to complete 094's bombing mission. The pilot of 67-0094 was in a 30-degree right bank turn back towards the initial point (IP), where the rejoin and formation change was to occur. During the turn, the right wing of 67-0094 collided nearly head-on with the fuselage of the mishap aircraft 67-0111. At the time of the collision, 67-0111 was straight and level approaching the release point for their bombing run. The pilot of 67-0094, with approximately five feet of the right wing tip missing, returned to base. The crew of mishap aircraft 67-0111 ejected successfully and were recovered.

The tactical air control system operational in the accident airspace was insufficient to adequately separate, direct, control and/or monitor F-111 bombing missions, considering the high density of air traffic at the time of the accident. The numerous communication requirements on diverse radio channels contributed to a cockpit workload which limited VFR surveillance. The physiological capability of either aircrew to visually acquire the oncoming aircraft and to take evasive action was minimized as a result of the near head-on aspect and rapid closure rate. *(Continued on the top of the following page.)*

Crew

Aircraft:	F-111A /67-0108	F-111A/67-0094	F-111A/67-0111
Pilot:	Capt Larry D Crocker	LtCol Clarence J Beaudoin	Maj Charles R Stolz
WSO:	Capt Robert J Dingman	Capt Thomas D Evans	1Lt William R Roberts
Call Sign:	Zest 12	Popper 11	Whaler 21

Accident Board President: Col Michael S Muskat

Time of Incident: 0907 L

Assigned Unit: Det 1 430th TFS / 474th TFW Takhli RTAFB, Thailand

Aircraft Statistics: Unknown			
Status:	No Damage	Damaged	Destroyed

Mishap Result: The damaged wing of 67-0094 was replaced and the aircraft returned to service.

Right wing damage to 67-0094.
Close-up of Right Wing Damage. *Courtesy of Bill Lassiter.*

67-0097
F-111A # 142 GD/FW Production Run # A1-142
USAF Delivery Date: May 27, 1969

First Mishap Scenario

On 12 November 1969, the mishap aircraft F-111A 67-0097 was flying on a low-level Navigation / Bombing mission. The pilot had released his bombs and was departing the local bombing range 100 NM northwest of Nellis AFB, Nevada, when the right engine oil hot caution light came on. At the time of the incident, the engine was at 90% RPM. The pilot followed checklist procedures and advanced the throttle for two (2) minutes, then retarded it to idle. The light did not go out after 10 seconds per the checklist. The crew then completed emergency procedures and placed the right throttle to the cut-off position. The right engine did not shut down, but the oil hot light went out. The crew returned to Nellis AFB, and after landing attempted to again shut the right engine down. The crew chief was able to manually close the fuel shut-off valve in the main wheel well, flaming-out the engine.

Findings

The fire was caused by a nacelle ejector bleed air duct failure. The high temperature / high velocity engine bleed air ignited combustible materials in the vicinity, dislodging a piece of the heat shielding material. Further investigation revealed a piece of burned heat shield had lodged in the main fuel control, preventing throttle movement to the cut-off position and inhibiting a normal engine shut-down. The airframe sustained significant structural damage.

Crew
Pilot: Capt Richard M Matteis
WSO: Capt Harry J Richard
Call Sign: Unknown
Time of Incident: 1030 PST
Assigned Unit: 429th TFS / 474th TFW Nellis AFB, Nevada
Aircraft Statistics: Unknown
Mishap Result: Aircraft sustained fire damage, but was repaired and returned to service

Second Mishap Scenario

On March 26, 1980, the mishap aircraft F-111A 67-0097 was scheduled for a single-ship training mission to include practice ordnance delivery, low-level navigation, and Advanced Handling Characteristics (AHC). The mishap aircraft departed Mountain Home AFB, Idaho, at 1053 L and proceeded to the Saylor Creek Bombing Range area. Radar contact was lost with the mishap aircraft 1112:22L at a point 6.3 NM from the accident site. The aircraft crashed at approximately 1114L 31 NM southeast of Mountain Home AFB, ID. At the time of ground impact, the aircraft was in an upright attitude with little forward velocity and a high sink rate. The left engine was in afterburner, and the right engine was in a stalled condition. Just prior to the crash, an unsuccessful ejection attempt was initiated with the right seat ejection handle. The crew was killed when the capsule hit the ground.

Findings

The mishap pilot was performing a low altitude rolling maneuver, and as the pilot completed the roll in a 15- to 20-degree dive, at or below 3500 feet AGL. The right engine then rolled back for an undetermined reason, resulting in a compressor stall as afterburner was selected. The pilot may have induced the compressor stall by generating excessive yaw during the rolling maneuver. The pilot initiated a single engine dive recovery, but he aerodynamically stalled the aircraft at an altitude that precluded recovery. The WSO initiated an ejection, but the sink rate exceeded the safe escape envelope.

During the low altitude recovery maneuver, the mishap pilot retarded both engines to idle in an attempt to clear an engine compressor stall in the right engine. With heads down and accomplishing checklist procedures, the pilot failed to maintain control of the aircraft and entered an unrecognized deceleration. During the emergency, the slow speed of the aircraft transitioned to a sink rate towards terrain, which the mishap crew recognized too late for recovery. With just the left engine operating in afterburner, there was insufficient thrust to recover the developed sink rate and accelerate to a safe flying airspeed. The aircraft collided with the terrain and was destroyed (CFIT). The ejection attempt was out of the safe sequence and recovery envelope.

Crew
Pilot: Maj Joseph G Raker
WSO: Capt Larry A Honza
Call Sign: Able 21
Accident Board President: Col Richard A Jones
Time of Incident: 1114 MST
Assigned Unit: 390th TFS / 366th TFW Mountain Home AFB, Idaho
Aircraft Statistics: 1097 Flights 2178.8 Flight Hours
Mishap Result: Aircraft Destroyed / Fatal Crash / Unsuccessful Ejection

Courtesy of Brian C. Rodgers

67-0098
F-111A # 143 GD/FW Production Run # A1-143
USAF Delivery Date: June 11, 1969

Mishap Scenario #1

On February 17, 1973, F-111A 67-0098, assigned to Det 1, 430th TFS, was deployed to Takhli RTAFB Thailand in support of Operation "Constant Guard V." The mishap aircraft was involved in a mid-air collision that occurred during a Beacon Bombing Pathfinder mission while leading F-4s over central Laos. A formation position change was required after the INS (Inertial Navigation System) failed on the mishap aircraft F-111A Call Sign Igloo 50 (67-0098). After the lead change, and while established in a formation position on the wing of Igloo 47 (67-0071), the two aircraft collided. The collision occurred while both aircraft were attempting to drop weapons. The crew of Igloo 50 jettisoned their ordnance near Udorn and returned to Takhli with major damage to both wings and leading edge slats. Both wings were replaced at Udorn, RTAFB.

Findings

During a night ingress, the crew experienced some difficulty with the bomb-navigation system. To preclude an air abort, the mishap pilot requested assistance from another F-111 flight crew that had completed the target run and were egressing the area. This pilot joined on his wing to monitor the bomb drop, and to be sure that their system was working properly. Approximately two minutes prior to release the attacking pilot was unable to acquire the target on radar, and directed the other pilot to assume the lead of the formation. During the formation change the two aircraft collided. The right wing of the attacking aircraft and the left wing of the assisting aircraft were damaged.

Crew

Pilot: Capt Glen G Perry Jr.
WSO: Capt Kenneth M Alley
Call Sign: Igloo 50
Time of Incident: Unknown Golf
Accident Board President: Col John F Rhemann
Assigned Unit: Det 1429th TFS / 474th TFW Takhli RTAFB Thailand
Aircraft Statistics: Unknown
Mishap Result: Aircraft received major structural damage, repaired and returned to service.

Mishap Scenario # 2 – Aircraft 67-0098

On October 8, 1982, the mishap aircraft F-111A 67-0098 was scheduled as number two in a three-ship training mission to include low-level navigation, tactical formation, a practice weapons delivery at Eagle Range on the Utah Test and Training Range (UTTR), and then return to Mountain Home AFB, Idaho, for individual practice approaches. The number three (#3) aircraft was to remain with the formation through range departure, then proceed single-ship on a pre-planned cross country sortie. The mishap aircraft began its takeoff roll at 1111L, with 20 second spacing behind the lead aircraft. Shortly after takeoff, the mishap aircraft experienced uncommanded flight control inputs. The pilot was able to recover and positioned the aircraft downwind for landing. A short time later the mishap aircraft pitched up and departed controlled flight. The mishap flight crew initiated ejection from the aircraft 6.3 NM southeast of Mountain Home AFB, Idaho. Both crew members sustained major back injuries during capsule touchdown when the inflatable impact attenuation bags failed to deploy.

Findings

During takeoff, the aircraft entered an uncommanded 135-degree right roll. The pilot recovered the aircraft to wings level by turning off all flight control damper switches and continued a climb away from the runway. The CADC and SIS caution lights illuminated and the cockpit filled with smoke. The left instrument panel appeared to be completely inoperative

67-0098 in a Takhli RTAFB Revetment. *Courtesy of USAF via Roger Peterson.*

(ADI and Instrument tapes frozen). The flight crew began to dump fuel and leveled at 4000 feet AGL / 250 knots in a left orbit over the airfield when the aircraft again pitched up. Control could not be recovered and the crew ejected. Investigation revealed a depot maintenance field team had incorrectly installed TCTO 1168, resulting in nine AC power leads being loosely attached to the AC power panel. The mishap sortie was the first flight after being returned to the unit. Sporadic electrical inputs from the loose leads caused an uncommanded flight control input and ultimately an uncommanded, uncontrollable pitch up and departure from controlled flight.

The Alternating Current power contactor leads were left under-torqued during a previous depot maintenance visit. The contactor leads eventually worked loose over time, causing power fluctuation which affected the flight control computers. Investigation of the escape capsule's impact attenuation bag revealed that the supply line spud fitting had become unbonded from the bag at some time prior to the mishap. During the ejection sequence, the impact attenuation bag failed to inflate, which resulted in an extremely hard landing, injuring the WSO and severely injuring the pilot.

Crew

Pilot: Col Ernest L Coleman
WSO: 1Lt Scott L Springer
Call Sign: Nomex 65
Accident Board President: Col John W Gordon
Time of Incident: 1118 MDT
Assigned Unit: 391st TFS / 366th TFW Mountain Home AFB, Idaho
Aircraft Statistics: 1002 Flights 2315.2 Flight Hours
Mishap Result: Aircraft Destroyed / Successful Ejection

Courtesy of Robert Pickett via Don Logan Collection.

67-0101
F-111A # 146 GD/FW Production Run # A1-146
USAF Delivery Date: June 16, 1969

Mishap Scenario

On August 2, 1982, the mishap aircrew was on a cross-country sortie and had departed from Offutt AFB, Nebraska, on the last leg of an off-station training mission. The mishap crew entered IR 307 low-level route at Point A over southwest Montana, and had almost completed the planned portion of the low-level route when both aircrew members noted a large bird just prior to impact. The bird, later identified as a golden eagle, hit the lower right canopy hatch, the right module glove leading edge, and the right engine inlet spike, and then was ingested into the right (#2) engine. While climbing, the crew simultaneously initiated Bold Face emergency action procedures for a right engine FIRE light and right engine bleed duct fail light. The warning lights went out, but were followed shortly thereafter by primary hydraulic system failure. The mishap crew was diverting to Pocatello Municipal airport, Idaho, when Salt Lake Center advised them that Fanning Field in Idaho Falls was closer. The mishap crew confirmed its suitability for landing an F-111A and changed their destination to Fanning Field. After sighting the field, the mishap aircrew lowered the slats and flaps utilizing back-up emergency systems, and landed utilizing the single engine with hydraulic systems failure checklists. The aircraft was stopped near the departure end of the active runway and shutdown. Emergency response personnel with assistance from other airport sources manually pushed the 73,000 pound aircraft clear of the active runway.

Findings

The mishap aircraft ingested a bird into the right (#2) engine intake over southwest Montana. This caused the right engine to fail catastrophically. The second stage fan failed and ejected numerous fan blades through the case. Fan blades penetrated the aft fuel tanks and cut hydraulic/oil lines. The 12th and 16th stage bleed air lines were also cut, releasing a flow of hot air into the engine bay. A fire developed in the right saddle fuel tank, right engine nacelle, right engine afterburner control, and constant speed drive oil cooler area. The aircrew accomplished all emergency procedures and successfully diverted to Idaho Falls / Fanning Field Airport with guidance from Salt Lake Center air traffic control. After landing and shutdown on the runway, a commercial airliner also reported inbound to Fanning Field with an emergency. The airport manager quickly enlisted 40 civilian workers to hand-push the F-111

67-0101 shown while assigned to the 389th TFS while TDY to Nellis AFB. *Courtesy of Author's Collection via Albert Green.*

aircraft off the runway. 67-0101 was substantially damaged as a result of the bird strike and subsequent inflight fire, requiring extensive repairs.

Crew

Pilot: Maj William D Patton
PWSO: 1Lt Christopher A Singalewitch
Call Sign: Alton 02
Time of Incident: 1202 MDT
Accident Board President: Col Jack R Gray
Assigned Unit: 390th TFS / 366th TFW Mountain Home AFB, Idaho
Aircraft Statistics: Unknown
Mishap Result: Aircraft sustained major structural damage / repaired at GDFW Vark Hospital

67-0101 after GDFW Restoration. *Courtesy of Author's Collection.*

Courtesy of Author's Collection.

67-0102
F-111A # 147 GD/FW Production Run # A1-147
USAF Delivery Date: June 20, 1969

Crash Scenario

On January12, 1988, the mishap aircraft F-111A 67-0102 was scheduled as Number-2 in a two-ship sortie. This sortie was a repeat upgrade ride for the student pilot to complete a non-effective portion of the training syllabus from the previous sortie. Planned events included air work in the Mountain Home AFB, Idaho, Paradise Military Operating Area (MOA), and then rejoining to tactical formation for low-level maneuvering and practice bombing events on the Saylor Creek Bombing Range. After the bombing mission, the aircraft were to return to Mountain Home AFB for individual practice approaches. The mishap aircraft took off single-ship two minutes after the lead aircraft. Shortly after take-off, departure control advised the mishap aircrew that their right hatch appeared to be open. Approximately one minute after take-off, a nose high, high AOA attitude was reached with the landing gear down and the flaps at 19 degrees. The mishap aircraft began a left, nose low roll. At approximately 175 feet AGL, 24 degrees nose low and 132 degrees left bank, the right ejection handle was pulled. The aircraft was below the minimum terrain clearance for ejection required for these parameters. Both crew members were fatally injured.

Courtesy of Tom Brewer via Don Logan Collection.

Findings

During takeoff, the right cockpit canopy hatch opened. Because of wind blast, the crew became disoriented and failed to maintain aircraft control. For an unknown reason, the crew allowed the aircraft to enter a nose high stall and subsequent departure from controlled flight. The only logical reason for the unexplained climbing maneuver after takeoff is that the pilot may have thought that pulling gs and slowing simultaneously might allow the right-seat pilot to pull the hatch closed. Approximately one minute later, from a nose high AOA with the landing gear down and the flaps at 19 degrees, the mishap aircraft departed controlled flight. Ejection was initiated outside of the envelope in an inverted position.

Crew

Pilot: Capt Robert A Meyer Jr.
WSO: Capt Frederick A Gerheart
Call Sign: Honest 02
Accident Board President: Col William M Latulipe
Time of Incident: 1423 MST
Assigned Unit: 389th TFTS / 366th TFW Mountain Home AFB, Idaho
Aircraft Statistics: 1618 Flights 3719.7 Flight Hours
Mishap Result: Aircraft Destroyed / Fatal Crash / Unsuccessful Ejection

F-111C #A8-127 GD/FW Production Run # D1-03
USAF Delivery Date: August 30, 1969
RAAF Delivery Date: June 1, 1973

Crash Scenario

On September 13, 1993, the mishap aircraft F-111C A8-127 was scheduled to lead a 3-ship night sortie, each aircraft departing in 10 minute intervals. The plan was an Auto TFR strike mission against a land strike target near Guyra, New South Wales. Each aircraft was to execute an auto-toss weapon delivery profile against a simulated target. The mission profile was planned to regain proficiency in night operations, as the squadron's aircrews had not conducted night operations for some time due to other squadron commitments. The mishap occurred 23 minutes into flight on the first simulated target attack. Weather in the target area, reported by the second aircraft in 10 minute trail, was layered broken clouds, with the first layer at 400 feet AGL, and the second layer was entered shortly after the pull-up for the TOSS bomb delivery. The mishap aircraft ingressed toward the target on Auto TFR, and the pilot initiated the pull-up in military power for the weapon delivery profile. The plan was for a 3-g pull-up to 15 degrees nose high, but it appeared the pilot had difficulty achieving the required g loading for the climb; recorded TF audio indicated aircraft dive commands. At 20-25 degrees nose up, the Auto TF system commanded a failsafe fly-up with accompanying TF fail audio, probably due to breaching the 25 degree pitch limit of the TFR system. The pilot then rolled the aircraft to the right in a climbing turn to complete the auto-toss maneuver. Approaching the apex of the climb, the aircraft was overbanked and the Pave Tack system went into memory point track, thereby precluding tracking of the target by the navigator. The roll was then reversed to reduce the bank angle, with the aircraft reaching a nose down pitch attitude greater than 25 degrees. As the pilot rolled out on the egress heading, the aircraft impacted the ground wings level, 25 degrees nose low, at 483 knots.

Findings

The most probable cause for the accident was the pilot failed to disengage the Auto TF system during the pull-up for the auto-toss

Courtesy of Author's Collection.

weapons delivery, and through task saturation and loss of situational awareness, placed the aircraft in a descent angle that was too steep at such a low altitude. Compounding in the mishap sequence were lack of proficiency for the type of attack being flown with night conditions and weather factors contributing to spatial disorientation and task saturation. The combined effects significantly reduced the pilot's situational awareness during a very critical phase of flight — the recovery profile. The mishap sequence of events resulted in Controlled Flight Into Terrain (CFIT). Additionally, the pilot paddled-off the TFR system to terminate the Fly-Up condition, which overrode any further TF directed terrain protection. After a TFR commanded fly-up, the TFR system requires procedural steps to reset in order to reestablish any TF mode for flight. The mishap pilot should have immediately aborted the recovery to a recognizable, wings level attitude, or continued a climb to regain aircraft control and situational awareness.

Crew

Pilot: Flt Lt (Pilot) Jeremy. McNess
WSO: Flt Lt (Navigator) Mark. Cairns-Cowen
Call Sign: Buckshot 18
Time of Incident: Unknown
Mishap Board President: Unknown
Assigned Unit: #1 Sq / 82 Wing, RAAF Amberley, Australia
Aircraft Statistics: Unknown
Mishap Result: Aircraft Destroyed / Fatal / No Ejection Attempted

F-111C # A8-128 GD/FW Production Run # D1-04
USAF Delivery Date: August 30, 1969
RAAF Delivery Date: June 1, 1973

Crash Scenario

On April 2, 1987, the mishap aircraft F-111C A8-128 departed East Sale, Victoria, and was scheduled to lead a 2-ship night sortie that began before sunset as an F-111 formation public relations photo shoot (filmed by a chase aircraft), and then separate for an 8 NM radar trail night sortie back to Amberley. The sortie was the final handling test (FHT) for the student navigator prior to completing the F-111C Conversion Course. It was the first F-111 FHT conducted by the pilot since his F-111C Qualified Flying Instructor (QFI) conversion. Prior to the briefing, the two QFIs for the mission decided to simulate "dying" at the Evans Head air weapons range to assess the student navigator's reaction to the situation. The aircraft took off as planned, completed the photo shoot, separated to 8 NM trail, and completed the first planned auto weapon delivery profile attack against a simulated land strike target. The weather was predominately good, but the evening was dark due to limited moonlight. The mishap aircraft ingressed the target at 200 feet AGL on Auto TFR with speeds between 480 and 540 knots. Following simulated weapons release, for an unknown reason, the aircraft continued on attack heading for about 4 seconds longer than normal before turning to egress heading. The aircraft did not achieve a wings level attitude above maneuver safety height (4,000 feet MSL), and in the latter stages of the turn, the aircraft over-banked and commenced a 10 degree descent. At some stage, one of the crew set 400 feet on the SCP on the TFR control panel and 325 feet with the indexer on the radar altimeter. Between 2.5 and 3 seconds before ground impact, the aircraft commenced an Auto-TF Fly-up. The aircraft then impacted the ground.

Courtesy of 82 Wing Photographic RAAF

Findings

The most probable cause of the accident was the crew lost situational awareness with respect to altitude during a critical phase of flight. It was determined that the mishap crew was not wearing g-suits, and may have suffered from minor g-induced spatial disorientation in the night conditions. The crew had entered an Auto TF flight mode, and the TFR was controlling the aircraft at the time of the mishap. The investigation revealed that the acceptable nose down attitude during the post attack escape maneuver was 5 degrees, but some crews used 10 degrees nose down. The mishap board also determined that there were variations of pilot scan priorities during TF letdowns. Some pilots concentrate almost entirely on the Attitude Director Indicator (ADI) to the exclusion of the TFR E-Scope or altimeters. Based on the nose down attitude of the mishap aircraft, there would have been significant ground echo penetration of the Zero Clearance Line on the E-scope during the incident aircraft's post attack egress descent. When the radar altimeter needle passed below the preset index marker, a Fly-up command was directed. Apparently, a climb in response to the fly-up command was initiated but interrupted by ground impact. The descent to such a low altitude in night conditions gave the crew no margin for error during the recovery profile, resulting in Controlled Flight Into Terrain (CFIT).

Crew
Pilot: Flt Lt (Pilot) Mark "Speed" Fallon
WSO: FLGOFF (Navigator)
    William X. Pike
Call Sign: Falcon Sabre 1
Time of Incident: Unknown
Mishap Board President: Unknown
Assigned Unit: #6 Squadron /
    82 Wing RAAF Amberley, Australia
Aircraft Statistics: Unknown
Mishap Result: Aircraft Destroyed / Fatal /
    No Ejection Attempted

Accident Area near Tenterfield, New South Wales, Australia. *Courtesy of RAAF.*

F-111C # A8-133 GD/FW Production Run # D1-09
USAF Delivery Date: September 22, 1969
RAAF Delivery Date: July 12, 1973

Crash Scenario
On September 29, 1977, the mishap aircraft F-111C A8-133 was scheduled to conduct a day single-ship sortie that was the first bombing sortie flight for the student pilot in the Operational Conversion Course. The mission included maritime operations, automatic TFR flight, and simulated practice bombing at Evans Head air weapons range. During the downwind leg at 2,000 feet MSL for the second bombing pass, the aircraft experienced at least three pelican bird strikes on the cockpit windscreen. The student pilot and instructor pilot became disoriented from the fragmentation of the windscreen, bird remains, and high velocity air flow injected into the cockpit. The instructor pilot initiated ejection with the aircraft at 520 knots, 720 feet MSL, nose and right wing down.

Courtesy of Author's Collection.

Findings
Penetration of the windscreen by large birds most likely incapacitated the student pilot. The instructor pilot was extremely disoriented from windblast and debris, but was able to initiate the ejection sequence. The ejection sequence was outside the capabilities of the escape module, and the sequence was interrupted by ground impact.

Crew
Pilot: Flt Lt Student Pilot A. P. "Phil" Noordink
WSO: SQLDR Instructor Pilot John Holt
Call Sign: Falcon 32
Time of Incident: Unknown
Mishap Board President: Unknown
Assigned Unit: 6th Squadron, RAAF Amberley, Australia
Aircraft Statistics: Unknown
Mishap Result: Aircraft Destroyed / Unsuccessful Ejection

See Also: For similar type accidents:

F-111A	67-0043	(A88)	22 May 1969
F-111A	67-0069	(A114)	13 Apr 1971
F-111A	66-0029	(A47)	1 Sept 1971
F-111F	71-0892	(F68)	6 June 1973 Landed Safely
F-111A	67-0040	(A85)	11 July 1973
F-111E	68-0081	(E91)	5 Mar 1975
F-111E	68-0060	(E70)	5 Nov 1975
F-111C	A8-133	(D1-09)	29 Sep 1977
F-111E	68-0019	(E29)	9 Aug 1984

F-111C # A8-136 GD/FW Production Run # D1-12
USAF Delivery Date: September 22, 1969 RAAF Delivery Date: July 12, 1973

Crash Scenario

On April 28, 1977, the mishap aircraft F-111C A8-136 was scheduled to conduct a day single-ship sortie that was to include maritime operations, automatic TFR flight, simulated land strike target attacks, and practice bombing at Evans Head air weapons range. During the approach for the second land strike target attack, with military power selected, the right engine oil hot caution lamp illuminated. The pilot immediately retarded the right throttle to idle. In accordance to emergency checklist procedures, the pilot then advanced the right throttle into minimum afterburner to better cool the engine oil. The oil hot caution lamp extinguished. The pilot made the decision to divert to RAAF Amberley. While in the climbing turn to divert, the pilot deselected afterburner and the oil hot caution lamp illuminated a second time. The pilot again selected afterburner and the oil hot light went out. This process was repeated several times with no resolution of the problem. The crew then heard and felt a loud explosion approximately 14 minutes after the first engine oil hot indication. The pilot attempted to shut down the right engine but could not move either throttle. The pilot then noticed that the landing gear warning light and right engine fire warning light were illuminated. The right engine fire warning push button was depressed, which extinguished the light. The pilot then tried to force the right throttle closed, but both throttles were jammed. The right engine fire warning light illuminated a second time, at which time the pilot actuated the agent discharge switch, but the fire light remained on. The aircraft then entered an un-commanded right roll and then a hard right yaw. The pilot was unable to regain control and initiated ejection.

Findings

The catastrophic failure of a hot engine bleed air duct developed into an uncontrollable and uncontained fire. The severity of the fire resulted in an aft fuselage fuel tank explosion, loss of all hydraulics, and loss

Courtesy of RAAF

of aircraft control: see detailed description of inflight engine fire and reverse flow phenomena, Chapter 1.

Crew

Pilot: Capt William H Baker USAF
WSO: Flt Lt David Clarkson
Call Sign: Falcon 33
Time of Incident: Unknown
Mishap Board President: Unknown
Assigned Unit: # 6 Squadron 82 Wing RAAF Amberley, Australia
Aircraft Statistics: Unknown
Mishap Result: Aircraft Destroyed / Successful Ejection

F-111C A8-137
GD/FW Production Run # D1-13
USAF Delivery Date: September 22, 1969
RAAF Delivery Date: October 1, 1973

Crash Scenario

On August 24, 1979, the mishap aircraft F-111C 67-0137 was scheduled as Number-3 of a 4-ship day sortie that was to include maritime strike operations operating from RNZAF Ohakea airbase, New Zealand, taking part in an Australian/New Zealand Exercise. During an afterburner takeoff roll, the aircraft experienced a double engine surge and afterburner blowout due to ingestion of surface water thrown up by the nose wheel. During the takeoff roll, the aircraft's performance was normal through the 120 knot acceleration time check. At 130 knots, the aircraft had traveled 2,100 feet down the 7,000 foot long runway when the crew heard a loud bang. The mishap crew experienced a noticeable loss of thrust, and the navigator noticed the engine nozzle position indicators closing, an indication that the afterburners had most likely blown out. Neither crew member noticed whether the engine instruments were still operating at military thrust, or whether they were "rolling back," indicating a flameout. The mishap pilot attempted to relight the afterburners by cycling both throttles to military and then back into AB. At approximately 3,800 to 4,000 feet remaining the pilot aborted the takeoff, 25 knots beyond refusal speed, because he judged there would be insufficient runway remaining to accelerate to takeoff speed. The mishap pilot initiated an abort above refusal speed on a wet runway that was not equipped with an arrestment cable system for the F-111C. The mishap Navigator recognized the aircraft would be unable to stop within the remaining runway length and initiated an ejection. The aircraft departed the prepared surface and was destroyed by a post-crash fire.

An excellent photograph capturing water "kick-up" by the nose wheel during takeoff on a wet runway. *Courtesy of RAAF via Al Curr.*

Findings

The entire east-west aligned runway slopes to the south, and was designed for water to drain toward the southern side. During the takeoff roll, the mishap pilot remained aligned with the south side of the runway, rather than correcting to the centerline in accordance with standard procedure. Unfortunately, it was the south side of the runway that had a heavier concentration of pooled water, which was agitated by the nose wheel tires. It was determined that the F-111C was not equipped with "chined" tires, which may have reduced the amount of water kicked-up and then ingested by the engines. Neither crew member recognized whether the engines were running at military power, or whether the aircraft was continuing to accelerate. The unfortunate result was a high speed, heavy weight abort with hydroplaning conditions. The combination exceeded the stopping capability of the aircraft's braking system.

Crew
Pilot: FLGOFF M. Kelly
WSO: Flt Lt (N) A. Curr
Call Sign: Buckshot Colt 3
Time of Incident:
Mishap Board President:
Assigned Unit: 1st Squadron, RAAF Amberley, Australia
Aircraft Statistics: Unknown
Mishap Result: Aircraft Destroyed / Successful Ejection

Courtesy of RAAF via Al Curr.

F-111C A8-139 GD/FW Production Run # D1-15
USAF Delivery Date: September 25, 1969 RAAF Delivery Date: October 1, 1973

Crash Scenario
On January 28, 1986, the mishap aircraft F-111C A8-139 was scheduled as the lead aircraft of a 4-ship night sortie that was to practice maritime strike operations against Royal Australian Navy ships. The mission involved simulated AGM-84 Harpoon anti-ship missile attacks by three of the four aircraft. The fourth aircraft was to provide strike direction and targeting information against the target ships. Each aircraft was operating independently, as the takeoff times were staggered by 30 minute intervals. Weather in the area was mostly overcast, with cloud bases at 2500 feet and tops at 5500 feet. Night conditions were very dark, with no moon or background lighting. During the mishap aircraft's second simulated attack, the aircraft crashed into the ocean approximately 52 NM east of Moruya, New South Wales. The briefed tactics for the maritime strike included a climb from low-level up to 8000 feet Above Sea Level to acquire the target ship, simulate a Harpoon weapon launch, and then fly the weapon's flight profile toward the target ship to provide the Navy maximum training value. For the post-weapon's launch descent, the pilot wanted to try a new "non-standard" tactic of simulating the rapid free fall descent of the Harpoon missile to 300 feet above sea level, and then accelerating at low altitude to achieve the missile's known performance characteristics. The briefed descent profile was to be in idle power with the speed brake extended, however, the use of the speed brake was rescinded by the flight authorizing officer. Target over-flight was to be at 300 feet above sea level on the first attack. The second and last attack for each aircraft would be conducted simultaneously, with the next or follow-on aircraft attacking the target ships for the first time. The follow-on aircraft was to fly the attack at 300 feet above sea level, with the aircraft attacking the second time flying at 800 feet above sea level. The mishap aircraft made a "Bruiser" radio transmission, indicating that they had simulated the launch of a Harpoon missile on their second attack. A short time later the fourth aircraft, providing strike direction, observed three fireballs on the ocean surface. The fourth aircraft initiated a radio check for all formation members, and number one did not check in.

Findings
For an undetermined reason, the mishap aircraft impacted the water near the bottom of the post missile launch descent profile or shortly after leveling off. Post-accident flight profile reconstruction indicated that a very high rate of descent (approximately 20,000 feet per minute) with a nose down attitude of 20 degrees would be required to achieve the missile's known speed of descent with an idle F-111 engine power setting. Apparently, the TFR was not in use to simulate the Harpoon missile's profile, and may have prevented collision with the water. However, the rate of descent and nose-down pitch angle from launch altitude gave the crew no margin for error during the recovery profile, resulting in Controlled Flight Into Terrain (CFIT).

Crew
Pilot: Flt Lt (Pilot) S. Erskine
WSO: Capt (Navigator) D. Angell, USAF Exchange Officer
Call Sign: Buckshot Colt 1
Time of Incident: Unknown
Mishap Board President: Unknown
Assigned Unit: 1st Squadron, RAAF Amberley, Australia
Aircraft Statistics: Unknown
Mishap Result: Aircraft Destroyed / Fatal / No Ejection Attempted

RAAF F-111C's in deep storage for nearly five years at GDFW. *Courtesy of GDFW.*

F-111C A8-141 GD/FW Production Run # D1-17
USAF Delivery Date: September 30, 1969
RAAF Delivery Date: October 1, 1973

Crash Scenario

On October 25, 1978, the mishap aircraft F-111C A8-141 was scheduled as Number-2 of a 4-ship day sortie that was to include maritime strike operations operating from RNZAF Ohakea airbase, New Zealand, taking part in an Australian/New Zealand Exercise called LONGEX '78. During recovery from an auto-toss weapon delivery profile, the wheel well hot caution light illuminated. The pilot deselected afterburner, pulled both throttles to idle, and completed the emergency procedures of extending the speed brake to ventilate the wheel well. The pilot also selected the air source selector knob to the off position, which closes the 16th stage engine bleed air check and shutoff valves. The landing gear was then extended to minimized fire and/or heat damage to the landing gear unit and wheels. While diverting to land the wheel well hot light went out, however, the forward equipment hot caution light and then the low equipment pressure caution light illuminated. While accomplishing the procedures for these caution lights, the wheel well hot light illuminated again. The mishap crew decided to dump fuel to reduce gross weight for landing. During the fuel dump, a chase aircraft reported an apparent reversal of flow of the dump plume, and an intense fire started immediately in the wheel well. Fuel dumping was terminated, however, the fire continued in the wheel well. The right engine instruments began to fluctuate, including the illumination of the left and right fuel pressure caution lights and right engine oil hot caution light. A loud thump was heard emanating from the rear of the aircraft. The pilot then initiated a successful over-water ejection and the aircraft crashed into the ocean.

A8-141 Crew Module afloat at sea during recovery. *Courtesy of RAAF.*

Findings

Because the aircraft was lost at sea, resolution of the actual cause could not be positively determined. However, most of the evidence pointed to a failure of the 16th stage high pressure bleed air duct in the wheel well area. Though fuel dumping was the prudent option to perform, the forward flow of fuel vapors may have contributed to the uncontained and uncontrollable fire. The fire effects resulted in an aft fuselage fuel tank explosion. With the aircraft on fire, the pilot made the correct decision to eject.

Author's Note: Although fuel dumping was based on acceptable principles to reduce landing weight, the extended speed brake induces an airflow reversal (aft to forward) under the fuselage, pulling raw fuel and vapors toward the wheel well. Additionally, with the Air Source Selector Knob in OFF or EMER, or with the landing gear extended, the fuel tanks are not pressurized, resulting in a low velocity dump rate, more readily exposing the dumped fuel to the air flow reversal pattern.

Crew
Pilot: Wing Commander D. Rogers
WSO: Flt Lt (N) P. Growder
Call Sign: Falcon Sabre 1
Time of Incident: Unknown
Mishap Board President: Unknown
Assigned Unit: 6th Squadron, RAAF Amberley, Australia
Aircraft Statistics: Unknown
Mishap Result: Aircraft Destroyed / Successful Ejection

Courtesy of 82 Wing Photographic RAAF

F-111G A8-291 GD/FW Production Run # B1-63
USAF Delivery Date: June 30, 1971
RAAF Delivery Date: October 22, 1993

Crash Scenario

On April 18, 1999, the mishap aircraft F-111G A8-291 was scheduled to lead a 2-ship night maritime strike sortie, each aircraft practicing simulated AGM-84 Harpoon anti-ship missile attacks against naval task force ships positioned to the southeast of Aur Island, in the South China Sea. Weather at the time of the mishap included medium and high-level cloud layers with little moonlight. The planning for the attack was performed by the mishap navigator and the navigator in the other aircraft assigned to the mission. A late change in routing had been received by the tasking authority, effectively allowing free movement of the aircraft in the exercise area. Neither navigator updated the original attack maps to include changes to the attack heading and study of the target area island obstacles. Neither pilot in the mission engaged in detailed mission planning due to other Wing duties. The briefed tactic was to ingress at low-level and split the formation up to fly either side of Tioman Island (inside the 10 NM restricted area) to use terrain shielding and minimize detection by the naval task force. The formation was then planning to turn back onto the attack heading and climb to acquire and designate the target ships. After simulating launch of the Harpoon, the aircraft were to fly the missile's flight path at low-level for a simultaneous target over flight. During the briefing a discussion was made concerning the larger Tioman Island, but no mention was made of the two smaller islands, which include Aur Island, that the mishap aircraft impacted during the ingress. The mishap aircraft utilized TFR during the low-level over-water segment to the split-up point, but during the targeting phase the pilot disengaged the TFR system. The wingman decided to fly all low-level segments in TFR as a consequence of the pilot's lack of currency and the crew's concern for obstacles in the South China Sea operating area.

Findings

The most probable cause for the accident was the pilot's failure to engage the Auto TF system while operating in a night, overwater environment, with island obstacles in the operating area. Lack of mission planning by the mishap pilot influenced a lack of awareness of the terrain obstacles, while a lack of proficiency contributed to misprioritization of tasks and loss of situational awareness. Also, contributory was the F-111G was not Harpoon capable and required the navigator to effect a time consuming work-around procedure to set up the aircraft systems to relay simulated weapon release indications. The navigator was therefore unable to monitor terrain obstacles on the attack radar set while preoccupied with setting up the Bomb-Nav system for the simulated Harpoon launch. At five seconds before impact, the radar altimeter's low altitude audible warning sounded and the radar altitude bars were visible in the attack radar – a display unique to the F-111G. The pilot may have visually sighted the island obstacle and initiated a climb; however, the aircraft impacted trees on a ridge on the island, destroying the aircraft. Controlled Flight Into Terrain (CFIT)

Crew
Pilot: Flt Lt Anthony "SHORTY" Short
WSO: SQLDR Stephen "NIGE" Hobbs
Call Sign: PISCES 01
Time of Incident:
Mishap Board President:
Assigned Unit: 6th Squadron, RAAF Amberley, Australia
Aircraft Statistics: Unknown
Mishap Result: Aircraft Destroyed / Fatal / No Ejection Attempted

6

COMBAT LOSSES

COMBAT LANCER
VIETNAM WAR – 1968

The U.S. Air Force program to prepare both the F-111A and combat crews for the first deployment to Vietnam was titled *Harvest Reaper*. The initial batch of combat ready Production F-111As were referred to as *Harvest Reaper* modified.

The HARVEST REAPER modifications were added to the first 13 Production aircraft as they moved through the Forth Worth assembly line, and included: APS-109/ALR-21 wide band radar threat detection receiver/cockpit display, QRC-160-S Wide Band Noise Jammer, ALE-28 Chaff and Flare Dispenser, ALQ-41 I Band Track Breaker, ALR-23 Aft-Looking Infrared Receiver, installation of the M-61A-1 cannon in the weapons bay, installation of a single AIM-9 trapeze and launch rail, and a lizard green underbelly paint scheme. A unique Combat Lancer tail flash was also applied. The Harvest Reaper airframes were A1-30 through A1-43. A1-30 was considered an RDT&E asset and remained at Edwards AFB for flight test duties. Production F-111As A1-31 and on were delivered directly to Nellis AFB, Nevada. The initial cadre of pilots in the F-111A had all logged 100 flight hours prior to the Combat Lancer deployment. Each pilot and pilot WSO were exceptionally qualified for the deployment.

For a brief period, the USAF acknowledged that the news media may have compromised the F-111's combat training and deployment preparations by openly using the Harvest Reaper name in association with F-111 testing. The conclusion was apparent regarding the inevitable deployment to Vietnam. For a matter of two months, the USAF attempted to disassociate the F-111 flight training program with a combat deployment and changed the code name to **Combat Trident**. When the USAF staff agencies discovered the new code name was causing more confusion within the Air Force communications channels than to the media, cooler heads prevailed and the original Harvest Reaper title was reinstated (Source: CSAF Message 011316Z Sep '67). Many authors have mistakenly associated the Harvest Reaper and Combat Lancer programs as a Limited Operational Test & Evaluation (OT&E) of the F-111. The expediency to place the F-111 into combat, with only six aircraft, for such a short duration, contributed to this error. There was no official tasking on the Harvest Reaper crews to operate within any specific guidelines to "test or evaluate" the F-111 as a weapons system satisfactory to USAF standards; the objective of an OT&E. The duration of the Combat Lancer deployment was cut short due to losses, not the end of an OT&E program.

When the F-111s finally departed for Vietnam, the deployment and employment phase was code named **Combat Lancer**. Only six F-111 aircraft were sent to Vietnam, of which two were lost in the first two days of flight operations. After the second loss, two attrition replacements and crew were sent to Takhli. One of these replacement aircraft was lost, bringing the Combat Lancer losses to three.

After the third loss of a Combat Lancer aircraft combat operations were stopped, however, the F-111 crews flew seventy-one (71) of ninety-seven (97) scheduled training missions in Thailand and Laos. Of the twenty-six (26) missions not flown, eight (8) were cancelled by higher headquarters, four (4) were cancelled by squadron operations, five (5) were maintenance non-aircraft availability, six (6) were due to ground aborts, and three (3) air aborts (*Source: General Dynamics Fort Worth Division Memo, 23 July 1968*).

67-0072 with 24 MK-82s in a Takhli RTAFB Revetment, waiting for a night mission. *Courtesy of USAF.*

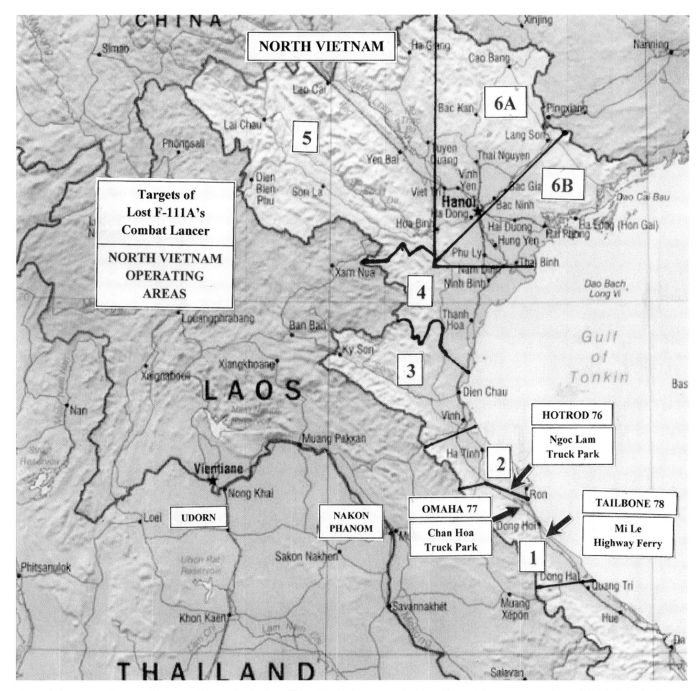

Figure 1: Approximate location of the assigned targets for the three (3) lost Combat Lancer aircraft. Note: The crash locations are not depicted. *Map by Author Lou Benoit.*

Combat Lancer operational statistics: a total of eighty-eight (88) combat missions were scheduled, with fifty-five (55) flown into North Vietnam arriving in the target area. Of the 55 missions, 50 were low altitude deliveries, and 5 were from medium altitude (15,000 feet). A total of (741) MK-117 Low Drag / 117R High Drag, (4) MK-118, and (8) MK-84 weapons were dropped. Of thirty-three (33) cancellations, fifteen (15) were cancelled by higher headquarters, five (5) were ground aborts, eight (8) were air aborts, and two (2) missions were air recalled by higher headquarters. Only three (3) aircraft were lost during combat missions, and one of these was an accident.

Radar film scores were obtained on forty-one (41) of the missions. Camera failures and/or failure to press photo switch at release, or failure to properly set the intervalometer (*the bomb rack release sequence time*) accounted for the fourteen (14) missions that were not scored. Based on radar film scores, the Circular Error Probable (CEP) was 100 feet. CEP, by definition, is the farthest impact distance from the desired aim point for one half of the strikes. For that era in aircraft technology, at night, while at low altitude, this is exceptional, and demonstrated the effectiveness of the F-111.

Missions averaged 2.5 flight hours, with approximately 10,000 lbs. fuel remaining on return to Takhli RTAFB. Enemy actions detected during the fifty-five missions consisted of fourteen (14) ground fire (estimated to be 37mm or less anti-aircraft type) and twelve (12) SAM radar detections. Ground fire was usually behind the aircraft. Several barrage type volleys were observed prior to run-in, but no radar aircraft tracking anti-aircraft fire was observed.

The five (5) medium altitude (15,000 foot) missions were executed after the loss of the three aircraft and prior to termination of combat operations. On all 5 missions, the F-111s dropped MK-117s or MK-84s by synchronous navigation radar; a method using the aircraft's attack radar tracking control to position the radar cursor on the target. Additionally, these five medium altitude missions used "Iron Hand" support aircraft consisting of B-66 ECM and / or F-105 Wild Weasel Shrike equipped escorts.

The following pages document the known facts associated with each of the three Combat Lancer aircraft lost.

66-0022 F-111A # 40 GD/FW Production Run # A1-40
USAF Delivery Date: January 26, 1968

Combat Loss Scenario
F-111A 66-0022, Omaha 77
The first loss occurred on March 28, 1968. Omaha 77 was flown by Major Henry MacCann as aircraft commander and Captain Dennis Graham as pilot weapon system officer. The aircraft departed Takhli RTAFB on a Rolling Thunder combat mission against the Chan Hoa Truck Park in RP 1 (N 17 32 11, E 106 29 12) at 0403 hours local time. The aircraft checked in and was positively identified by Brigham (CRC at Udorn RTAFB). Omaha was then handed off to Invert (CRC at Nakhon Phanom RTAFB) at 0445L while flying at 1,000 feet AGL, 50 nautical miles west of Invert. Invert had radio contact and positive identification with Omaha through decoding of the IFF/SIF. Invert received five (5) radio transmissions from Omaha 77 between 0445L and 0448L. The aircraft passed four (4) miles north of Invert. Invert lost contact but re-identified the aircraft, which was flying heading 085 degrees at 1,000 feet AGL. It appeared Omaha 77 entered into a figure eight holding pattern 60 to 65 miles east of Invert's position. Invert transmitted seven traffic advisories to Omaha 77 between 0450L and 0513L when Omaha 77 passed over Invert. Omaha 77 did not acknowledge any transmissions. It appeared that Omaha 77 was tracked westward toward Invert. When on a TACAN bearing of 135 degrees and seven miles from Invert, Omaha 77 was again positively identified. The aircraft then turned to a heading of 210 degrees and proceeded southwest. All radar returns from Omaha 77 were lost at 0530L, 190 degrees, and fifteen to twenty miles from Invert. Search and Rescue efforts produced negative results and the aircrew members were listed as Missing in Action. (*Excerpt from: Safety Section VIII, Combat Lancer Interim Report, 15 March – 15 June 1968*)

Note: late in 1989 the wreckage was discovered in the Phu Phan mountain range of Northern Thailand, and the crew's remains were recovered and returned.

The most likely cause for this combat loss was due to Controlled Flight Into Terrain (CFIT) while operating on TFR attempting to penetrate weather at night enroute to the target. The aircraft did not arrive in the target area.

Crew
Pilot: Maj Henry E MacCann
PWSO: Capt Dennis L Graham
Call Sign: Omaha 77
Time of Incident: 0635 Golf
Assigned Unit: Det1 428th TFS /
       474th TFW Nellis AFB, NV
Aircraft Statistics: 40 Flights
       103.8 Flight Hours
Incident Result: Aircraft Destroyed /
       1st F-111 Lost In Combat/
       No Ejection Attempted

67-0072 with 24 MK-82s in a Takhli RTAFB Revetment, waiting for a night mission. *Courtesy of USAF.*

Authors Note: The photograph shows F-111A 66-0022 (A1-40), the 40th production F-111A, under construction at GDFW. All Harvest Reaper modifications were installed while on the Fort Worth production line. The Harvest Reaper modifications included the full threat warning and counter-measures suite; equipment all previous Pre-production F-111As did not have.

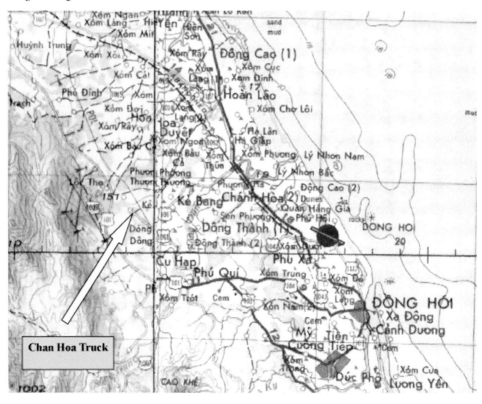

Figure 2: Intended Target for Omaha 77. *Map by Lou Benoit.*

66-0022 on the GDFW Production Line. *Courtesy of GDFW.*

A Harvest Reaper modified, Combat Lancer F-111A in a Takhli RTAFB revetment. *Courtesy of USAF.*

66-0017 F-111A # 35 GD/FW Production Run# A1-35USAF Delivery Date: November 28, 1967

Combat Loss Scenario
F-111A 66-0017, Hotrod 76
On 30 March 1968, F-111A 66-0017 was assigned to Det 1 428th TFS and deployed to Takhli RTAFB, Thailand, while in support of Operation Combat Lancer. This was the second F-111A lost, call sign Hotrod 76. The aircraft was flown by Major Alexander A. Marquardt as aircraft commander and Captain Joe W. Hodges as pilot weapon system operator. Hotrod 76 departed Takhli RTAFB on a Rolling Thunder combat mission against the Ngoc Lam Truck Park (N17 49 00 and E 106 07 09) at 1910L hours. The mission progressed past Korat RTAFB and Ubon RTAFB under GCI control. Hotrod 76 then began the turn to the next checkpoint after passing Ubon RTAFB, where the aircraft commander engaged the Terrain Following Radar (TFR) and began an Automatic TFR letdown. At this time, the aircraft experienced an uncommanded pitch-up while descending through 6,000' MSL. Auto TFR had been selected, and the wings were swept to 38 degrees. At 480 knots true air speed (KTAS) and 80% engine throttle, the flight crew attempted to reverse the abrupt pitch and roll by disengaging the TFR with the stick paddle switch. These attempts did not clear the discrepancy, and the pitch-up continued to 30 degrees nose high, with the aircraft rolling off on one wing. The aircraft commander applied full military power and full forward stick pressure. Aileron input aggravated roll control, and the aircraft rocked 60 to 135 degrees of bank in both directions. Applying full afterburner brought the aircraft to a momentary level flight attitude, and then aircraft control was again lost. The mishap aircrew ejected at

5,630 feet MSL, 232 KTAS, with 18 degrees of dive and 45 degrees left wing low. The successful ejection of the capsule was accomplished 65 NM from Nakhon Phanom, Thailand, on the 185 degree radial, near Mukdahon, Thailand. The aircrew members sustained no injuries and were recovered 2.5 hours after ejection. (*Excerpt from: Safety Section VIII, Combat Lancer Interim Report, 15 March – 15 June 1968*)

Crew
Pilot: Maj Alexander A Marquardt
PWSO: Capt Joseph Hodges
Call Sign: Hotrod 76
Time of Incident: 2010 L
Mishap Board President: Col Edward W Szaniawski
Assigned Unit: Det1 428th TFS / 474th TFW Nellis AFB, NV
Aircraft Statistics: 48 Flights 139.5 Flight Hours
Incident Result: Successful Ejection / Aircraft Destroyed / The wreckage was recovered and buried on Takhli RTAFB after the investigation was completed.

(*The following narrative is an interview excerpt from William T Allen, GDFW F-111 Design Safety Engineer and lead accident investigator 1966-1975*)

Hotrod 76 was the second aircraft lost, and is the only Combat Lancer crash designated as a major aircraft accident. An aircraft accident board was convened at Nakhon Phanom RTAFB, and subsequently moved to Takhli RTAFB to investigate the loss. This board determined the primary cause of the accident to be a maintenance factor, in that a foreign object, a tube of solidified fuel tank sealant located at the accident scene, had lodged in the flight controls' pitch-roll mixer assembly located in the upper fuselage routing tunnel, causing loss of control.

Note: The accident board president asked a GDFW flight control expert, "In what part of the flight controls could a tube of sealant lodge and cause the uncontrolled flight?" The GDFW expert had not been allowed to visit the crash scene, but surmised that an object in the pitch-roll mixer could cause the jammed controls. It was on this statement that the investigation team concluded the primary cause.

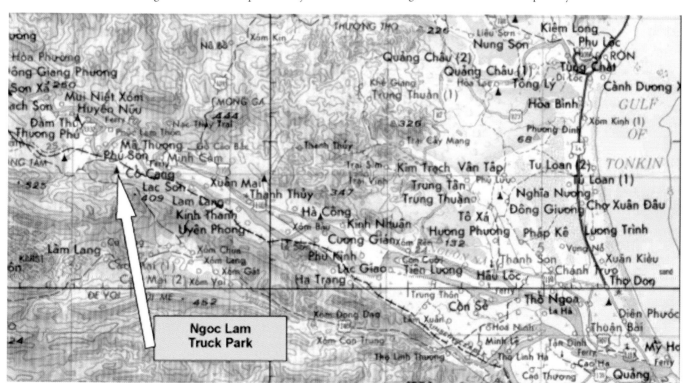

Ngoc Lam Truck Park

Figure 3: Intended Target for Hotrod 76. *Map by Lou Benoit.*

Subsequent to this Combat Lancer accident, another F-111A was lost at Nellis AFB, Nevada, under similar circumstances. The cause of the Nevada accident was attributed to material failure of the Horizontal Tail Servo Actuator (HTSA) rod end of the valve input spool assembly.

GDFW determined the uncontrolled pitch and roll motions of the aircraft were not caused by an object impeding movement of the flight controls, but rather material failure of a major flight control component. The GDFW engineers deemed it "unlikely" that a single tube of fuel tank sealant could have been floating around in the control routing tunnel for any period of time. The most likely location to find an errant sealant tube would have been inside one of the fuselage fuel tanks, where the tank sealant was applied during manufacturing. GDFW engineers were denied an opportunity to analyze the sealant tube at their Fort Worth laboratories to verify the presence of JP-4 fuel infused into the sealant. If the sealant tube was left in the fuel tank over any extended period of time, trace indications of JP-4 would remain in varying depths inside the sealant. If the sealant tube had jammed the control mixer, metallurgical and lubricant identifiers would have remained.

Unfortunately, in order to reinforce their position that the sealant tube was the probable cause of the accident, the accident board directed Major Marquardt to return to General Dynamics Fort Worth, where the sealant tube theory could be demonstrated. A sealant tube, like the one found at the crash scene, was placed in the pitch roll mixer mechanism of a Flight Control Engineering Test Stand. Major Marquardt then manipulated the flight controls of the simulator while flying the TFR descent profile. Major Marquardt stated that the control stick felt similar to what he experienced in the accident. The investigation team then concluded it was, in fact, the sealant tube.

General Dynamics' engineers agreed in principle when an object is placed in the pitch/roll mixer, the pilot will get control stick feedback. However, they were dismayed that the theoretical assumption of the sealant tube theory overruled a thorough scientific analysis. In the end, though, the exercise was proven irrelevant, when six weeks later F-111A 66-0032 (A50) crashed on May 8, 1968. The cause was material failure of the input rod-end at the point where the rod connects to the servo control valve of the Horizontal Tail Servo Actuator (HTSA). The rod-end became disconnected due to a manufacturing defect, causing the horizontal stabilizer to deflect full trailing edge up, leading to an uncontrollable flight condition for the pilots.

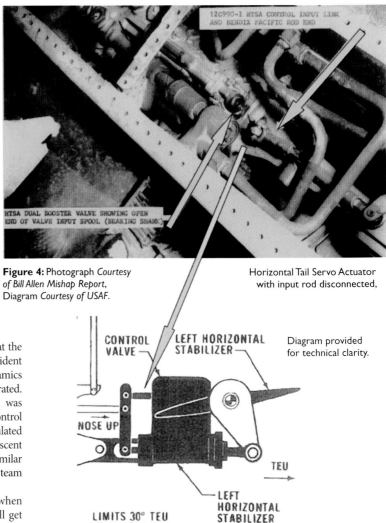

Figure 4: Photograph *Courtesy of Bill Allen Mishap Report*, Diagram *Courtesy of USAF*.

Horizontal Tail Servo Actuator with input rod disconnected,

Diagram provided for technical clarity.

Author's Note: a minority report submitted by a GDFW Investigator at Takhli suggested the flight controls were jammed after the inflight loss of an over-wing fairing access panel. The large panel was found several miles along the route of flight prior to the crash site. The minority report suggested the over-wing panel separated and penetrated the upper controls' routing tunnel panels, damaging the pitch-roll mixer assembly. GDFW countered that the panel most likely separated and fell off during the series of violent uncontrolled oscillations the aircraft followed in response to the material failure of the HTSA control valve spool.

66-0024
F-111A # 42 GD/FW Production Run # A1-42 USAF Delivery Date: January 29, 1968

Combat Loss Scenario
F-111A 66-0024, Tailbone 78

The third loss, Tailbone 78, was flown by U.S. Navy Lieutenant Commander David L. Cooley as Aircraft Commander, and Lieutenant Colonel Edwin D. Palmgren as pilot weapon system operator. Lt Col Palmgren was also the Combat Lancer Operations Officer. Tailbone departed Takhli RTAFB at 1858L on 21 April 1968. The aircraft was on a Rolling Thunder combat mission against the Mi Le Highway Ferry (N17 19 27 and E 106 37 45). Dressy Lady, the call sign for the U.S. GCI site, monitored the initial portion of the flight. The fragged weapons load-out was (12) twelve MK-117R retarded bombs and 1 AIM 9B missile in the weapons bay. By agreement with the Thai government, the portion of flight over Thai airspace would have been conducted at an MEA of 10,000 feet. Upon crossing the Mekong River and entering

Combat Lancer / Harvest Reaper modified F-111As on the Nellis AFB ramp. *Courtesy of Author's Collection via Ivan H. Dethman.*

Laotian airspace, the crew would have descended to 500 feet AGL and maintained that altitude using TFR.

Radar hand off was made to Lion (GCI site) with the aircraft on schedule and experiencing no apparent difficulties. Lion had a good skin paint (radar contact), positive friendly IFF, and radio contact until hand off was made to Alleycat (Airborne Command and Control Center) at 1959L. Alleycat maintained radio contact with Tailbone for approximately five minutes before handing them off to Waterboy (GCI site at Don Ha, South Vietnam) at 2004L. The coordinates of Tailbone 78 at this time were N 16 16 and E 106 07. Alleycat queried Waterboy at 2025L concerning Tailbone's progress, twenty-one minutes after handoff. Tailbone made no radio contact with Waterboy. The absence of radio contact could have been due to terrain masking between Waterboy and the flight route of Tailbone 78. The last radar plot on Tailbone 78 was at 1959L by Lion Control in the area of the 050 degree radial and 55 nautical miles from the Ubon TACAN station. Search and rescue efforts produced negative results, and the aircrew members were listed as Missing in Action. (*Excerpt from: Safety Section VIII, Combat Lancer Interim Report, 15 March – 15 June 1968*)

Investigations by the Joint Task Force – Full Accounting (JTF-FA) in 1991 and 1993 found aircraft wreckage 600 meters (1,968 feet) east of the target which has been tentatively identified as "Tailbone 78". Neither remains nor personal effects have been found, and a definitive cause of this loss has never been established. Although SA-2 surface to air missiles (SAM) were observed in Route Pack 1 in 1968, the possibility of a shoot-down was deemed remote. USAF historical records indicate that no F-111s were lost due to SAMs during the second deployment to Vietnam (Constant Guard V) in 1972. The most universally accepted cause was thought to be from a TFR system malfunction. Known to flight crews as E-Scope blanking, heavy rain or flight over smooth reflective surfaces, such as bodies of water, appeared on the E-Scope as the absence of terrain returns. In these instances, the aircraft could lose altitude and crash or fly into rising terrain masked by the rain showers. However, based on the JTF-FA findings, Tailbone 78 arrived in the target area and crashed shortly thereafter.

The most likely cause for the loss of Tailbone 78 was due to fragmentation damage while delivering ordnance on the target. One or more of the high-drag retarding fins on Tailbone 78's bombs may have failed to open during the low altitude bomb drop sequence. (The bomb's nose fuze arming wire is pulled at release, and under normal conditions, the bomb should not arm unless the high drag fins fully open.) Rather than detonating well behind the delivery aircraft, a "slick" bomb explodes on ground impact below and slightly behind the aircraft. At the very low altitudes being flown on TFR, approximately 300 - 500 feet AGL, the aircraft would be within the lethal 1000 foot blast/fragmentation radius. The results are catastrophic; blast and fragmentation damage will take down an aircraft as effectively as a direct hit by a SAM. Bomb delivery ballistics for the MK-117R Retard High Drag bomb permit the delivery aircraft to be 2000 feet or greater away at detonation (depending on delivery height). On the other hand, unretarded bombs released from the aircraft simultaneously with the high drag bombs would overfly the intended target and detonate below the aircraft, bringing the delivery aircraft down within the 1900 feet described in the JTF-SA report.

Crew
Pilot: Lt Cdr David L Cooley USNR Exchange Pilot
WSO: Lt Col Edwin D Palmgren DET 1 OPS Officer
Call Sign: Tailbone 78
Time of Incident: 2015 L
Assigned Unit: Det1 428th TFS / 474th TFW Nellis AFB, NV
Aircraft Statistics: 40 Flights 110.2 Flight Hours
Incident Result: Aircraft Destroyed / Lost In Combat/ No Ejection Attempted

A clamshell-type retarding device fitted to a MK-117R 750-pound high-drag bomb. *Courtesy of Hill AFB Museum.*

Tailbone 78's Fragged Target, the Mi Le Highway Ferry Crossing; now a bridge. *Courtesy of Doug Loeffler.*

Approximate location of the debris field. *Courtesy of Doug Loeffler.*

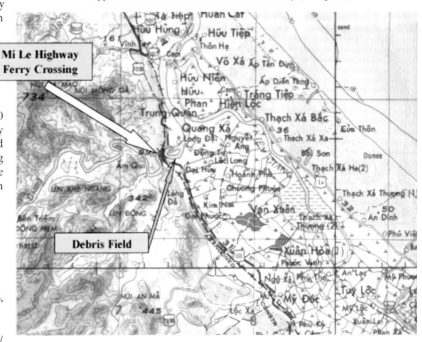

Figure 5: Intended Target for Tailbone 78. *Map by Lou Benoit.*

CONSTANT GUARD V
VIETNAM WAR – 1972

The Nellis AFB, 474th Tactical Fighter Wing (TFW) F-111s returned to Takhli RTAFB and combat operations on September 28, 1972. The concept of operation upon arrival was for six of the newly arrived F-111As to be reconfigured and launch the same evening on strikes in Route Packs 5 and 6. The 474th TFW pilots designated to fly these first combat missions were prepositioned at Takhli a week prior. In preparation for the missions, the pilots were briefed on North Vietnam flying procedures, target area threats, and search and rescue operations. Each of the six crews preplanned their attack routes against ATO fragged targets. These crews were well prepared for the strikes, having current target photographs and hand-drawn radar predictions to assist in target identification.

An F-111A arrives for the second deployment to Vietnam, Constant Guard V, September 28, 1972. *Courtesy of Author's Collection.*

Of the six aircraft readied for a combat mission, one aircraft was a pre-taxi maintenance abort, while (5) F-111s took off. One F-111 crew air-aborted shortly after takeoff as a result of problems, returning to Takhli RTAFB. The four remaining aircraft progressed on their single-ship mission toward their targets. Three of the aircraft completed successful strikes, however, one F-111, Ranger 23, failed to return.

After the loss of Ranger 23, combat operations were put on hold while the 474th TFW conducted a reprisal of operations, which included an evaluation of tactics. All the deployed crews were then required to fly local area orientation low-level TFR training sorties to familiarize them with the Southeast Asia terrain. Though the tactics for employing ordnance in the target area were considered valid and safe, the employment concept for en route procedures was changed. At first, F-111 crews would depart Takhli and fly medium altitude to the Laotian border, then descend to a TFR clearance plane of 1000 feet AGL. A new procedure was adopted where crews descended to a Minimum Enroute Altitude (MEA), providing a minimum of 1000 feet clearance above the highest terrain, five nautical miles on either side of the route leg. The MEA altitudes gave crews the opportunity to proceed without use of the TFR on the initial ingress routing until overflying the mountains bordering Laos and North Vietnam. Thereafter, the crews descended on TFR to 1000 feet AGL terrain clearance and then stepped down to 500 feet AGL prior to entering the anti-aircraft defensive rings.

On October 4, 1972, the 474th TFW returned to combat with a limited sortie rate into Route Pack 1 and Steel Tiger operating areas. By October 13, 1972, the Wing rapidly progressed toward the planned sortie generation rate of 24 aircraft missions per night. (*Project CHECO: The F-111 in Southeast Asia September 1972–January 1973*, 26)

On October 17, 1972, another F-111, Coach 33, disappeared on a mission over Route Package 6. On November 7, 1972, Whaler 57 did not return from a strike against a Route Package 1 target. Finally, on November 20, 1972, a fourth F-111A, Burger 54, was lost. Night F-111 TFR strikes were temporarily suspended.

To fully understand the losses associated with F-111 combat operations, the Chief of Staff of the Air Force, Gen John D. Ryan, initiated three investigations. The first was designated CONSTANT SWEEP, with the objective of determining the cause or causes for the four F-111 losses, which included a review of the previous Combat Lancer losses. The second investigation was titled TAC Project 72A-182U - TFR Operational Test & Evaluation (OT&E), with the urgent mission to fully evaluate the F-111 TFR system and operational procedures being used in the Southeast Asia environment. Lastly, an operational test and evaluation titled F-111 Munitions Delivery Safety and Effectiveness was directed.

During the same time the three investigations into F-111 losses were underway, Linebacker II operations were initiated in December 1972. F-111 night TFR missions were resumed and focused on targets in Route Packs 5 and 6. On the evenings of 18 and 22 December 1972, respectively,

Snug 40 and Jackel 33 were lost (the crew of Jackel 33 successfully ejected). With the loss of Snug 40 and Jackel 33, the total Constant Guard V losses rose to six F-111As spanning three months of combat operations.

Many historical narratives of the F-111's activities in Vietnam have been less than positive, when in fact, the opposite is true. With the F-111, the USAF now had the ability to strike small fixed targets at night in the high threat Route Packs 5 and 6, all without supporting assets. Not until late into Linebacker II were the F-111's true characteristics focused directly on SAM sites and critical logistic nodes. The F-111 attacks also contributed to the suppression of SAM launches prior to approaching B-52 strikes. The precision attack capability of the F-111's attack radar, navigation system, and eventually beacon bombing techniques forcibly denied the Vietcong a period to reconstitute at night. Just over 4,000 combat sorties were flown by 24 F-111s during Constant Guard V, the majority in the last three months of Linebacker II. Due to the controversies surrounding Secretary of Defense Robert McNamara and the F-111 program, the six F-111 losses endured a disproportionate level of media attention during the Vietnam War. In the end the F-111 vindicated itself, having a significant deterrent influence on the Cold War and several U.S. conflicts to follow. Because of its deep strike, all weather penetration capability, the F-111 became a historically significant fighter aircraft; truly the aircraft known to be the *First Strike Option* in a European conflict.

The following historical perspective is a brief compilation of the cause or causes for the six F-111As lost in combat operations during Constant Guard V. The source of the information presented was obtained from the Project CHECO Report: *The F-111 in Southeast Asia September 1972–January 1973*, the *Constant Sweep Report*, Abstract, 22 January 1973, and the *474th TFW History* by Jack R. Hays, 474th TFW Historian, 1 October to 30 December 1972. All documents were declassified and published without copyrights.

This F-111A photograph represents the most common combat configuration of the F-111A in Southeast Asia. The load-out consisted of twenty-four MK-82 Low Drag General Purpose bombs on BRU-3A Multiple Ejector Racks (MERs) mounted on the four swiveling pylons. On the underbelly are the two Electronic Countermeasures (ECM) pods: the ALQ-87 forward and either an ALQ-94 or ALQ-87 aft of the main wheel well. The right side bomb bay was normally loaded with an M-61 Gatling Gun; the aerodynamic fairing for the cannon's rotating barrels can be seen forward of the ALQ-87 ECM pod. Other bomb load configurations were 4 MK-84s or 6 MK-117s. On rare occasions, F-111s employed CBU-58 Cluster Bombs; the exact number of sorties for this weapon is unknown. The real tactical, and even strategic advantage of the F-111 was the aircraft's ability to fly non-stop unrefueled, single-ship, and unescorted from Takhli, Thailand, to Route Packs 5 and 6.

The F-111's best defense was its high speed; however, the terrain following radar (TFR) and the ECM pods greatly enhanced the aircraft's high threat target penetration and egress capability.

A Constant Guard V F-111A in a typical combat configuration. *Courtesy of the USAF.*

COMBAT LOSS INVESTIGATIONS AND REPORTS

After the fourth loss of an F-111A during the Constant Guard V deployment, an investigation team led by Brig. Gen. Charles A. Gabriel, Deputy Operations Director for the USAF Air Staff, was tasked to conduct a "comprehensive inquiry and review of all F-111 losses of undetermined causes." The investigation and report was given the code name Constant Sweep. The Constant Sweep investigation focused only on the specific hazards that may have lead to the F-111 losses. Emphasis was placed on the four F-111s lost during Linebacker; however, two more F-111s were lost during Linebacker II. The investigation concluded the F-111 combat units were accomplishing their assigned missions professionally, although there were F-111-specific operational deficiencies which required solutions.

The first major finding by the Constant Sweep investigation noted that only one F-111A had been lost on a TFR training sortie during the previous 30,000 flight hours of F-111 operations within the United States (see F-111A 66-0042).

The second finding demonstrated that eight F-111s were lost in just 6,000 hours of combat missions in Southeast Asia: two during Combat Lancer in 1968, and six during Linebacker and Linebacker II in 1972. Compared to all previous night operational losses in Vietnam, the loss rate of the F-111 was statistically similar.

The third finding identified that the recent F-111 losses during Constant Guard V operations were similar to those experienced during Combat Lancer, in that: (1) little substantive information was available to precisely establish the causes; (2) the location of the crash was unknown;

and (3) the catastrophic nature of the first six losses (2 during Combat Lancer, 4 in Constant Guard V) precluded a successful ejection.

During the period of the Constant Sweep investigation two more F-111As crashed (Snug 40 and Jackel 33). Snug 40 was lost for an unknown cause, while the last, or sixth F-111, Jackel 33, resulted in a successful ejection. Even though the aircrew was captured and interned as POWs, the cause remained unknown until the crew of Jackel 33 was repatriated at the end of the Vietnam War. Their testimony validated a AAA or small arms fire shoot-down.

The Constant Sweep investigation was unable to certify a specific cause for each of the F-111's combat losses during both Combat Lancer and Constant Guard V. The team, however, determined there was sufficient evidence to indicate a probable cause for each of the six combined losses:

Two of the aircraft apparently crashed in the mountains while attempting to penetrate an area of rain storms that degraded the aircraft's terrain following radar and disoriented the aircrews. Two of the aircraft crashed in the vicinity of the target, having been shot down or crashing during a maneuver to evade enemy defenses, or through self-fragmentation during low altitude weapons deployment. The remaining two aircraft most likely crashed in the Gulf of Tonkin due to a limitation or failure of the Low Altitude Radar Altimeter (LARA) system. (*Project CHECO The F-111 in Southeast Asia September 1972-January 1973*, 55)

Author's Note: The Constant Sweep investigation was nearly complete when Snug 40 was lost and the team did not know Jackel 33 had been shot down.

TFR OT&E (Operational Test & Evaluation)
TAC Project 72A-182U Constant Guard V: OT&E

The F-111 aircraft lost in Southeast Asia were of immediate concern to the USAF, mostly due to the nature of the loss – there was little or no indication of the cause. As such, an Operational Test & Evaluation (OT&E) of the TFR system was ordered to determine whether a series of TFR anomalies or malfunctions could have caused or contributed to the catastrophic loss

of all F-111 aircraft. Major General Richard C. Catledge, Commander of Operations & Test Evaluations at Eglin AFB, Florida, headed the investigation known as TAC Project 72A-182U Constant Guard V: OT&E.

The test aircraft (67-0109) was modified and equipped with a video recorder connected to the TFR system for in-flight recording of the TFR scope and the TF radar derived data. The test aircraft was deployed to Takhli RTAFB and was maintained by the 474 TFW. The

Courtesy of Bill Allen Collection

Photographs taken by an RF-4 Phantom recorded the F-111 TFR Test Flights opposing different Southeast Asia Karst terrain. *Courtesy of Bill Allen Collection.*

Wing also provided an unmodified F-111A on a daily basis to fly the required chase sorties. The test sorties were flown on non-combat profiles, along low level routes within Laos and Thailand, over dense jungle and Karst terrain features similar to those experienced in North Vietnam, and all were conducted during daylight hours. Twelve (12) TFR OT&E sorties were flown to evaluate the TFR performance, of which four (4) were flown with heavy weight ordnance. Two of the test missions were supported by two RF-4C photo reconnaissance aircraft, one recording from a tail chase position and the other recording from a side oblique.

Among the most noteworthy findings of the evaluation were that the TFR in the instrumented test aircraft maintained the selected clearance plane over the jungle canopy, including the tallest live trees in the flight path. The chase aircraft used in the test did not perform as well as the test aircraft; however, no serious differences were noted in that respect. None of the aircraft detected dead or defoliated trees. The test team was unable to duplicate the conditions that had previously caused scope blanking of the attack radar set or the TFR E-Scope. No adverse effects, other than the temporary loss of terrain avoidance capability in the direction of turn, were noted in the operation of the TFR system when the 10 degree bank angle was exceeded. The TFR system on the test aircraft operated properly on all land/water transition flights.

Additionally, the TFR tests avoided all but localized light rain showers and did not plan or attempt TFR operations into heavy rain or thunderstorms.

F-111 Munitions Delivery Safety And Effectiveness
Losses associated with combat employment of the F-111A aircraft raised questions regarding the compatibility of the F-111A with MK-84/MK-82 low drag (LD) and high drag (HD) deliveries. The problem was the unexplained failure of the MK-82 Snake-Eye high drag fins to open during weapons release. Tactical Air Command authorized a five-sortie test at the Tactical Air Warfare Center (TAWC), Eglin AFB, Florida, in order to verify whether combat weapon deliveries had contributed to the catastrophic loss of the F-111.

Weapons release parameters and limitations were established for the test flights; if the potential existed for the delivery aircraft to enter the lethal envelope of any High Explosive (HE) munitions, inert munitions were employed to establish the aircraft's location at bomb impact. The live munitions drops were intended specifically to validate safe separation envelopes depending on delivery altitudes, airspeeds, and current tactics. The test profiles allowed for several dry passes (no ordnance dropped) to determine the pilot's ability to arrive at the specific release conditions prior to the actual test drops.

The project evaluated the release of 12 live MK-82 HD bombs at 500 feet above ground level (AGL) at 480-520 knots true airspeed (KTAS); F-111 level release of 12 live MK-82 LD bombs at 1,500 feet AGL at 480-520 KTAS; F-111 10 degree climb release of four live MK-84 bombs at 800 feet AGL at 480-520 KTAS; and an F-111 level release of four MK-84 bombs at 1,500 feet AGL at 480-520 KTAS (the escape maneuver used was a 30 degree bank/1-G and 60 degree bank/2G turns after release).

Five effective F-111A sorties were flown during the tests; one with four inert MK-84s, and two with four live MK-84 bombs. The remaining two sorties dropped 24 live MK-82 bombs. High speed time correlated tracking cameras were used to track the delivery aircraft from 5 seconds prior to initial drop through all bombs released. Additional high-speed time correlated tracking cameras were used to record bomb impacts.

During October and November 1972, the weapons drop tests demonstrated the Snake-Eye fins failed to open due mostly to an incompatible arming wire swivel link that failed to restrain the arming wires necessary to deploy the high drag fins and fuze arming. The inherent danger at TFR altitudes (300 – 500 feet) is present when the bombs fall "slick" and could potentially detonate with the aircraft inside the lethal fragmentation envelope. (The tail fuze should not arm without the high drag fins deploying, resulting in a dud). Although no F-111s returned with self-fragmentation damage, the remote possibility existed for lethal self fragmentation due to high drag fins failing to fully deploy at release, yet fuze arming occurred.

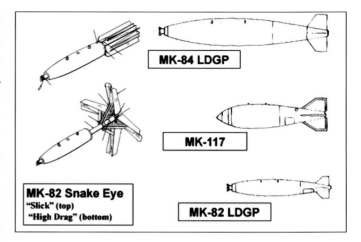

Figure 6. Common weapons employed during Combat Lancer and Constant Guard V. *Courtesy of USAF Technical Order 1F-111A-34-1-1.*

Another F-111A released 12 live MK-82 High Drag bombs at 500 feet AGL and 480 KTAS. Visual observation indicated that all bombs released and impacted on the target range. Nine MK-82 bombs appeared to function normally, however, the remaining three MK-82 high drag fins did not open and the bombs did not detonate. Examination of the aircraft post-flight indicated that on two separate pylon stations, the swivel links were not retained; on three pylon stations the links were broken, and on the remaining pylon stations, the retained arming wires were shorter than the others and some of the swivel links were stretched. Again the source of the problem was a specific series of incompatible swivel links. (A swivel link consists of two low gauge, high tensile strength wire loops [links] connected end-to-end by a loose rivet, allowing the two links to swivel. The links are positioned on the bomb racks to retain or guide the external bomb arming wires.)

The Tactical Air Warfare center evaluators concluded that the MK-84 and the MK-82 High Drag and Low Drag bombs could be delivered safely when the F-111A aircraft was flown within the release parameters prescribed in weapons system and employment Technical Order (1F-111A-34-1-1), or by flying the low-altitude safe escape maneuver after bomb release. (*Tactical Air Warfare Center Report, 1 July 1972 to 30 June 1973, Volume 1*)

Analysis of the Constant Guard V Combat Losses
At the time of the Constant Sweep investigation, only four Constant Guard V F-111's were lost. The initial presumptive findings attributed the losses directly to the night TFR operations seconded only by the intense anti-aircraft defenses. The significant flight hazards associated with low altitude flight at 1000 feet AGL or lower in the rugged Karst type terrain were easily realized. The Karst terrain presented a daunting profile for TFR flight due to the abrupt vertical rise and fall. When confronted by the extreme weather phenomena prevalent in SEA, the operational hazard was exponentially increased.

A typical combat mission from Thailand into North Vietnam was far more treacherous than any training mission experienced in the desert southwest training areas of Nevada and Arizona. Planned ingress routes toward targets in North Vietnam were generally more than 100 NM in length and mostly over mountainous regions. The F-111 combat crews initially employed TFR for a majority of the ingress, believing that the low altitude flight and terrain masking would lead to an undetected penetration of the target area. However, the unrelenting series of climbs and dives associated with the abrupt terrain following profile led to a reprisal of ingress methodology.

The F-111 crews found TFR flight at low altitude for long durations to be fatiguing and somewhat disorienting. Eventually, the 474th TFW proposed and adopted a flight profile at medium altitude to the border above the Karst mountains, and then descended to the MEA prior to entering the target area under TFR control.

Although the medium altitude ingress eliminated most of the terrain hazards, many of the combat crews believed the element of surprise may have been lost when the higher altitudes allowed the North Vietnamese to monitor their ingress by means of long range radar.

Another factor contributing to an increased exposure to anti-aircraft threats was the limited number and concentration of radar significant military or industrial targets. (The F-111 crew used only the attack radar scope to identify the target area, thereafter, placement of the radar cursors on the preplanned target determined the bombing-navigation systems release computations.) The targets suitable for a successful ground mapping radar identification were quantitatively few in number. Therefore tactical planners assumed that North Vietnam would also anticipate where F-111 attacks might occur, and concentrate their air defense systems specifically to engage the F-111's.

Although the night environment eliminated the normal visual aiming of AAA against the F-111, the concentration of targets allowed some AAA batteries to barrage fire towards detected F-111 attacks using radar directed azimuth guidance. Overall, AAA remained a lower threat than anticipated, most enemy gunners responding after the F-111 was clear of the target area.

Author's Note: Later in the Linebacker II campaign, the use of radar beacons, either air-dropped or placed by Special Forces, facilitated F-111 attacks against any target with near-precision accuracy. (The radar beacons were AN/PPN-18 Forward Air Control Transponders – when activated, the transmitted signal is displayed on the F-111's radar screen, allowing precise direct or offset bomb aiming techniques).

Lastly, the monsoonal weather patterns in Southeast Asia were a major hazard confronting F-111 missions into North Vietnam. Combat missions frequently encountered vast regions of intense interlinked thunderstorms as well as unabated heavy rain showers. The level of precipitation encountered was far denser than any F-111 crew had ever experienced in training. The intense precipitation also masked the presence of terrain, preventing detection by the TFR or Ground Mapping radar. These weather conditions had an adverse effect on safe TFR ingress and egress of the target area. Overall, the weather conditions posed a great threat toward survival, perhaps more than any of the anti-aircraft systems.

The terrain, weather, and concentration of suitable targets proved Southeast Asia one of the most difficult combat flying environments in the world. The F-111's night TFR mission amplified the risks crews faced. The Constant Sweep investigation summarized the hazards associated with TFR operation noting: "there was a narrow margin between a successful attack and catastrophic loss."

Operational Factors Influencing Combat Losses
(Low Altitude Operations)

Though possible, a pilot induced loss of control situation was eliminated as a cause for any of the combat losses. The TFR mission, particularly at night, was not an environment for hard dynamic maneuvering, especially near the limits of the flight envelope. Even under the most extreme TFR flight conditions (heavy-weight ordnance load, hard ride mode of the TFR, abrupt climb or dive pull ups) the likelihood of the pilot or the auto-flight system inducing loss of control was considered remote.

Even though the potential for a catastrophic flight control failure such as a hard-over rudder or horizontal tail was possible, the investigation concluded such incidents were rare, noting the crew ejected shortly after loss of control.

The simultaneous loss of thrust in both engines was unlikely, considering engine failure due to heavy rain had not been a problem at any altitudes in the flying history of the F-111. Additionally, dual engine failure would not have caused rapid loss of control in which ejection was impossible. Catastrophic engine failures have resulted in turbine blade penetration of the aft fuel tank, which eventually degraded to an uncontrollable fire and loss of hydraulics. However, even a massive fire would not have resulted in immediate and catastrophic loss of control.

Bird strikes were also discounted as a probable cause of catastrophic loss since the aircrews should have been able to eject even if the windshield had been broken on one side of the cockpit. Though this event would be instantly disorienting, it was believed the aircrew could retain control of the aircraft and initiate a climb out of the TFR environment or to immediately eject. The probability of a bird strike at night, at TFR altitudes between 500-1000 feet AGL, was also deemed a low probability event.

Aircrew Training Deficiencies:

The Constant Sweep investigation revealed the deployed crews had received adequate flight training prior to their arrival in North Vietnam; however this training was limited due to the training environment, i.e. air traffic restrictions, Radar Bomb Scoring range operating limitations, available low level route structures, and the absence of realistic threat emitters of the type and density found in North Vietnam. Therefore, the rather unique combat capabilities of the F-111 could not be fully exploited in training while preparing crews for combat. The low altitude, high speed training routes used by the 474th TFW, could only be flown in visual meteorological conditions, with no less than a 3,000 foot ceiling and five miles visibility. The Constant Sweep Report noted that some crews, who deployed during Constant Guard V, flew their first combat sortie, first heavyweight weapons load, and their first weather TFR flight, all on the same night mission. Although the F-111 training program at Nellis AFB tended to emphasize day/VFR operations, all crews that deployed to Vietnam for Constant Guard V had flown multiple night sorties. One of the night sorties began with a TFR flight initiated over the Pacific Ocean toward the Oregon coastal mountains, TFR low-level across the Sierra Nevada Mountains, and then into the Nellis Range for a live bomb drop. After completion of this stateside training sortie, the most intense flown by aircrews to that date, the 474th deployed to Southeast Asia.

Loss due to Fragmentation Damage:

The Constant Sweep investigation considered the possibility of self-fragmentation resulting in a catastrophic loss. Their eventual conclusions were based on two facts: (1) no combat sorties had returned to Takhli RTAFB with evidence of bomb fragmentation damage, and (2) the fragment damage radius was much greater than the lethal radius. Since the probability for damage was far higher than that contributing to a catastrophic loss, the investigation concluded that a loss due to self-fragmentation was "extremely remote."

The 2000lb MK-84 had a lethal radius of 1,700 feet and a damage radius of 2500 feet, well inside the F-111's TFR flight altitude. The Constant Sweep investigation and the 474th TFW at Takhli noted that the release of ordnance, particularly the MK-84, at a range and altitude less than the damage radius significantly increased the likelihood of self-fragmentation. Preplanned delivery tactics for the MK-84 required a stabilized climb from TFR low level flight to approximately 1,000 feet AGL prior to weapons release. Author's Note: The first two F-111A's lost during Constant Guard V were both loaded with "Slick" MK-84 weapons. The 474th TFW pilots all believed that self-fragmentation was considered the most probable cause for the first two F-111A losses. The 474th TFW also reported several MK-84's were dropped inadvertently during the pre-release arming sequence of the bomb panel. Thereafter, the 474th recognized this danger and limited MK-84 ordnance to medium altitude release until the problem was resolved.

The delivery of low drag weapons in conjunction with a TFR low altitude ingress was always a preferred employment concept. Even though the exposure to self-fragmentation was present, these attacks were considered less hazardous than the vulnerability presented by a medium altitude ingress which increased the exposure of the F-111 aircraft to enemy surface to air defensive systems.

Hung Ordnance and Stores Jettison Limits

A significant and recurring problem was hung ordnance during the release sequence from the troublesome BRU-3A's. This problem resulted in an average of 10 percent of all sorties returning with at least some hung ordnance. Though this problem is not related to the loss of F-111s, hung bombs could conceivably fall off, arm, and detonate during low altitude TFR egress or during the landing phase.

Several aircraft were damaged while jettisoning ordnance during evasive maneuvers. Most often, the BRU-3A bomb racks struck the aircraft during the jettison process causing damage. The Munitions Safety and Delivery Effectiveness OT&E at the Tactical Air Warfare Center noted that most F-111 crews on the Constant Guard V deployment were unfamiliar with the emergency stores jettison limits because these limits had not been established for the current F-111 combat loads.

Additionally, the Constant Guard V crews reported that the unintentional release of the BRU-3A bomb racks during a normal bomb release sequence was a common, recurring, and an unresolved problem. Loss of an F-111 due to collision with its own BRU-3A was considered unlikely.

The photograph above represents a close-up view of the often problematic BRU-3A Multiple Ejector Racks (MERs). The racks are shown mounted on the swivel pylons of a Constant Guard V F-111A in a Takhli RTAFB revetment.

The flight crew had the option to jettison just the bombs, or in an emergency, the racks with the bombs attached. Jettison

BRU-3A Multiple Ejector Rack. *Courtesy of Bill Lassiter.*

limits and procedures were not clearly defined prior to the deployment, and several aircraft were damaged while attempting to deliver ordnance or jettison the stores under excessive G-loads. Additionally, the 474th Wing History noted that nearly 10 percent of all Constant Guard V sorties returned with some hung ordnance.

The MERs could hold six MK-82s / 83s, or 4 "slant" load MK-117's or CBU-58 Cluster Bombs apiece. With the MERs removed, MK-84 2000 pound bombs were mounted directly to the swivel pylon. It should be noted that the MK-117 was only employed during Combat Lancer.

The Constant Sweep investigation and the Tactical Air Warfare Center findings noted:

> Although there are several weapons associated problems which need correction (fin failure, jettison limits, hung ordnance), there is no evidence and little likelihood, that weapons have caused a catastrophic loss. However, further study is required to determine the munitions release problems associated with the BRU-3A's and MK-82 Snake-Eye bombs. Further, it is imperative to investigate a new munition more compatible with the F-111 tactics; the ability to release high drag ordnance reliably at TFR altitudes between 300-500 feet AGL, without danger of self-fragmentation. (*Constant Sweep Abstract 22 January 1973*)

Author's Note: At the time of the Constant Sweep Investigation, none of the F-111 combat crash sites were known, therefore their conclusion regarding "no F-111's were lost due to self-fragmentation" assumed the aircraft crashed en route or during the return trip to Takhli. The author's research and conclusion regarding a self-fragmentation cause for Tailbone 78 during Combat Lancer and Coach 33 during Constant Guard V were based on postwar investigations by the Joint Task Force – Full Accounting (JTF-FA) in 1991 and 1993. Both aircraft arrived at their targets and crashed shortly after attempting to deliver their ordnance.

LARA / TFR Systems Failures

Prior to the Constant Guard V losses, only one TFR related training accident had occurred. This mishap was attributed to pilot error as a result of overriding a TFR fly-up which inhibited terrain avoidance commands. (Author's note: See F-111A mishap for 66-0042). During Constant Guard V, many of the TFR anomalies were known, but not yet fully understood or experienced by all combat crews.

The E-Scope blanking (loss of radar returns) on both the TFR Scope and Attack Radar screen were primarily the result of external attenuation of the radar signal due to weather factors. In the presence of the scope blanking phenomena, normal terrain following climb and dive commands derived by the forward looking TFR antennas were "degraded" to the point that height keeping was derived solely from the low altitude radar altimeter (LARA) inputs. The severity of E-Scope blanking due to rain was not fully recognized prior to the Constant Guard V deployment and may well have contributed to several of the combat losses. Failure of the LARA to maintain height above water or flat featureless terrain, forced the TFR system to enter a LARA Override mode (in the absence

of TFR returns, TFR computer relies entirely on LARA altitude to maintain height above terrain). At the time, it was undetermined whether the LARA signal was absorbed by the low reflective surface of a body of water, or if the LARA ranged off thermoclines below the surface causing a false "high" indication and thence a TFR commanded descent. The 474th TFW recognized that TFR commanded flight over water was hazardous; eventually overwater egresses were prohibited during Linebacker II.

After the Vietnam War, an in-depth investigation by General Dynamics focused on the problems associated with the TFR phenomena. The investigation identified that internal failures of the LARA Bypass Switch may have been a contributing factor. (See Chapter 1, Known TFR Anomalies: (F) Bypass Switch Failure)

In conclusion, during both the Combat Lancer and Constant Guard V deployments, F-111 aircrews were exposed to situations in North Vietnam that were not present in the training environment. The intensity of the night TFR sortie into a high threat combat environment presented a massive task loading on the F-111 crews. Any lapses in judgment or situational awareness could prove fatal.

The loss of Ranger 23, Whaler 57, Burger 54, and Snug 40, were presumed and very likely to have been the result of these TFR system phenomena.

Enemy Air Defenses

The enemy anti-aircraft threat present during low level F-111 strikes into the Route Pack areas, consisted of sporadic small arms fire, undirected anti-aircraft artillery, and radar directed surface to air missile activity.

An early and continuing trend revealed the NVA's AAA reaction to F-111 night attacks, which normally erupted just after weapons release. AAA gunners were understandably unable to determine the correct altitude and azimuth of the attacking F-111s. Most crews reported seeing post-attack barrage fire, in a direction towards the sound of the aircraft rather than into the actual position of the attacker. As F-111 night operations continued during Linebacker II, the AAA gunners eventually aimed down toward the actual 500-feet AGL altitude. Fortunately the detonations were still occurring behind the aircraft.

Despite the low altitudes flown by F-111s, SAM batteries always presented a viable threat, and in fact, were capable of tracking and firing on aircraft as low as 500 feet AGL. By October 22, 1972, F-111s had been illuminated and tracked on more than 70 occasions; in eight encounters a total of 16 SAMs had been fired. Although there were no known losses, one aircraft

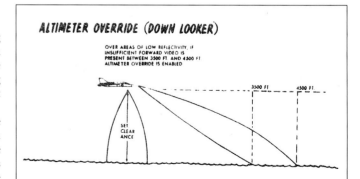

ALTIMETER OVERRIDE (DOWN LOOKER)

OVER AREAS OF LOW REFLECTIVITY, IF INSUFFICIENT FORWARD VIDEO IS PRESENT BETWEEN 3500 FT AND 4500 FT ALTIMETER OVERRIDE IS ENABLED

SET CLEAR ANCE

3500 FT   4500 FT

Figure 7: During over-water flight, the Low Altitude Radar Altimeter (LARA) could fail to provide accurate height measurements to the TFR computer due to the reflective or absorbent natures of bodies of water. Additionally, smooth, flat, terrain or bodies of water reflected very weak returns to the TFR, in which case the TFR went into LARA Override affecting clearance height. *Courtesy of USAF 1F-111D-1 Pilot's Manual.*

had sustained minor damage while others reported near misses. (*Project CHECO The F-111 in Southeast Asia September 1972-January 1973*, 30)

Enemy air defense activities against F-111 low altitude operations could not be discounted as a possible cause for the combat losses. Of 22 reported SAM launches, just one detonated close enough to cause minor fragmentation damage to an F-111. (*Project CHECO The F-111 in Southeast Asia September 1972-January 1973*, 44)

Constant Guard V aircrew reported the Radar Warning Receiver (RWR) detection and electronic counter measures jamming pods (ALQ-94 and ALQ-87) defeated the SAMs, increasing aircraft survivability.

Conclusions

The Constant Sweep Investigation determined it was not possible to establish with certainty the specific cause for any but the last F-111 lost in combat. Although, there was sufficient evidence toward a probable cause for each, it was concluded that no one cause was responsible for all six losses. Two of the aircraft (Ranger 23 and Whaler 57) apparently crashed in the mountains while attempting to penetrate an area of rain storms that degraded the aircraft's radar and disoriented the aircrews.

One of the aircraft (Coach 33) crashed in the vicinity of the target; either being shot down, destroyed by self-fragmentation, or having flown into the ground during maneuvers to evade enemy defenses. The other two aircraft (Burger 54 and Snug 40) most likely crashed in the Gulf of Tonkin due to a limitation or failure of the LARA system. As noted, one aircraft, (Jackel 33) was presumed to have been shot down.

Following the end of hostilities in Vietnam, the Chief of Staff of the Air Force, General John D. Ryan, directed Tactical Air Command, the Tactical Air Warfare Center, and the Air Force Flight Test Center to initiate and conduct Category III Flight Testing – the Operational Test and Evaluation of the F-111. For a number of reasons related to the redesign and incorporation of the Triple Plow II intake, the Recovery Program (Cold Proof Load Testing), and the Vietnam War, traditional Category III Testing of the F-111 prior to entry into operational service had not been conducted.

Reference Figure 5 Regional Map for a synopsis of the lost F-111s during Constant Guard V; the map denotes the assigned targets for these aircraft, not the crash location.

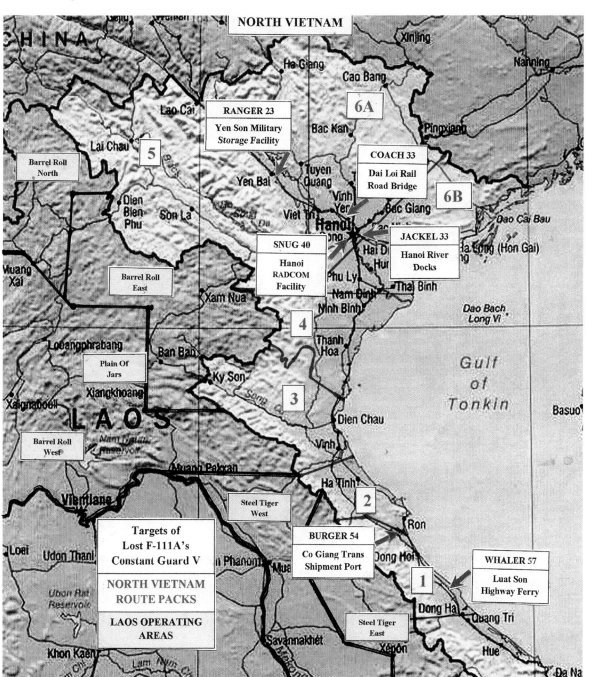

Figure 8:
The map denotes the Air Tasking Order (ATO) assigned targets for the six (6) lost F-111A's during Constant Guard V. The map does not indicate the locations of the combat losses. *Map by Lou Benoit.*

67-0078 F-111A # 123 GD/FW Production Run # A1-123
USAF Delivery Date: April 7, 1969

Combat Loss Scenario
F-111A 67-0078, Ranger 23

F-111 operations against North Vietnam began on the evening of September 28, 1972; just hours after the first deploying aircraft landed a Takhli RTAFB. The Air Tasking Order (ATO), a.k.a. "The Frag," for the evening called for six F-111's to strike six targets in Route Package 5. In accordance with the 474th TFW's F-111 employment concept, these initial night sorties were fragged to penetrate North Vietnam as single-ships at low altitude; with a descent point predetermined by the location of enemy air defense threat sites. The missions were to be flown by aircrews that had deployed in advance from Nellis AFB on 24 September. These initial crews arrived on September 26, 1972.

Ranger 23 was lost near the Laos / North Vietnam border. The last known coordinates were on the 030 Radial at 70 miles from the Udorn RTAFB TACAN or (N 21 35 51 / E104 59 21) in Thailand. The crash site coordinates were (N20 42 44 E 104 06 28) in Northern Laos.

Flight Scenario for Ranger 23:

Ranger 23 was the second aircraft to depart Takhli RTAFB on a strike mission against the Yen Son Military Storage Facility located southeast of Yen Bai in Route Package 5. The flight plan for Ranger 23 included a lengthy portion of TFR flight over extremely rugged Karst areas. This terrain included abrupt variations up to 4,000 feet in passing from mountain peaks to valley floors. There were several 9,000-foot peaks in the vicinity of the flight path, which towered over the typical 5,000 to 6,000 foot peaks in the region. Approximately 4 NM short of the target on the inbound track was a hill rising about 200 feet above the surrounding terrain. The target was adjacent to the Red River and lay in a relatively flat region, but beginning about 2 to 3 NM beyond the target along the extended inbound track, the terrain rose in a series of 300 to 400 foot hills. Enroute weather for Ranger 23 was reported as scattered clouds at 4,000 feet with a second layer of scattered clouds at 12,000 feet; visibility was 7 miles. Other F-111 aircraft encountered numerous heavy thunderstorms in the area. The last radio contact with Ranger 23 was at 2141L, and the last radar contact occurred at 2145L as the aircraft approached the Laotian border. At that time the pilot was deviating from his programmed track to avoid thunderstorms. His last reported altitude was 15,000 feet. U.S. ground based radar coverage at 15,000 feet extended approximately 70 NM beyond the last reflected position. Taking the flight deviation into account, the estimated descent point would have been just north of Barthelemy Pass. On September 29, 1972, after Ranger 23's loss had been officially announced, Radio Hanoi reported a shoot-down of an F-111 in Yen Bai Province. No elaborate narrative or photography was produced to substantiate this claim. However, all F-111 missions on the night of September 28 were fragged against targets in Yen Bai Province. Ranger 23 was last sighted on radar entering a thick line of thunderstorms some 80 miles northeast of Udorn RTAFB. His last radio transmission indicated no problems. It was known that the heavy precipitation from a thunderstorm would 'paint' on the TFR scope and the system would try to overfly the thunderstorm as if it were a mountain. Rather than fly over the storm, F-111 pilots would either circumnavigate the storm or attempt to fly under the storm using TF inputs.

Findings

On September 28, 1972, the F111s returned to Southeast Asia after a prolonged absence following the Combat Lancer deployment. After their arrival at Takhli RTAFB, the USAF planned to quick-turn and launch the F-111s the same night for strikes against North Vietnam. Ranger 23 was flown by pilot Maj. William C. Coltman and Weapons System Officer 1Lt. Robert A. Brett, Jr. Radio contact with the crew was lost in Thailand near the Udorn TACAN. Their target was located on the Red River about 10 miles southwest of the city of Yen Bai. When the aircraft failed to return from their mission, the two were declared missing after their estimated fuel exhaustion time passed. A news release issued by

Courtesy of Tom Brewer via Don Logan Collection.

North Vietnam claimed the downing of an F-111 in the same area near Yen Bai, but made no mention of the fate of the crew. A second North Vietnamese news release, monitored by the BBC in Hong Kong, claimed to have downed an F-111 and captured the crew on September 28, 1972. The USAF acknowledged that Major Coltman and 1Lt Brett were the only F-111 aircrew operating in that area, and a shoot-down was possible. However, the wreckage was later found in Laos on the western slope of a mountain range nullifying the shoot-down claim. The most likely cause for the loss of Jackel 33 was Controlled Flight Into Terrain (CFIT) while under TFR flight control. (*Project CHECO: The F-111 in Southeast Asia September 1972-January 1973*)

Ranger 23 failed to return to Takhli RTAFB on 28 September 1972. Maj William C. Coltman and Lt Robert A. Brett, Jr. were listed as MIA.

Additional Notes:

Major Coltman was the only pilot on the first night of F-111 operations (28 September 1972) with previous combat experience in the F-111A. Major Coltman had flown 6 combat sorties during COMBAT LANCER, the first deployment of the F-111A to Vietnam in 1969.

Crew:

Pilot: Maj. William Clare "Horse" Coltman
WSO: 1Lt Robert Arthur "Lefty" Brett Jr.
Call Sign: Coach 33
Time of Incident: Night Mission Time Unknown
Assigned Unit: Det 1 429th TFS / 347th TFW Takhli RTAFB, Thailand
Aircraft Statistics: 282 Flights and 735.5 Flight Hours
Mishap Result: Killed in Action / Remains returned

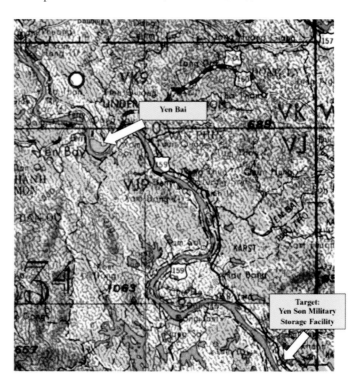

Figure 9: Yen Bai Topographic Map, Target for Ranger 23. *Map by Lou Benoit.*

67-0078, Ranger 23 Search and Rescue (SAR) Debrief:
The following is a transcribed interview with Lt Col. Jack Bauder, USAF (Ret) made in May 1996. "Cactus Jack" later became the Commander of the 523rd TFS flying F-111Ds.

Captain Bauder was flying F-4C's over North Vietnam when called by 7th AF HQ to perform the initial SAR mission for 67-0078—"Ranger 23". "My involvement with the last flight of Ranger 23, an F-111A out of Takhli Royal Thailand Air Base is quite unusual. I was flying F-4's for the 497th Tactical Fighter Squadron "Night Owls" at Udorn RTAFB. We flew single ship, night fast FAC missions—spotting targets for other fighter-bombers in southern North Vietnam. On the night of 28 Sept 1972 I was flying with my roommate, Capt Gordie Tushek. We were working the border between Route PAC 1 and Route PACV2 looking for targets of opportunity. We went to a KC-135 tanker stationed in "Purple Anchor" off the coast of North Vietnam to air refuel. After refueling, we were told by the tanker to contact 7th Air Force Command Center in Saigon for a mission change. We were directed by 7th Air Force to fly to a set of coordinates passed to us and look for a downed aircraft who had been flying as Ranger 23. We proceeded to the area, which I guessed was on the western edge of Route Pack 5 in North Vietnam and set up our search and rescue operation. Our task was to drop flares from our aircraft and look for the downed aircraft and airmen. We also made radio calls on the SAR (search and rescue) frequencies and guard frequency. Because we were taking heavy ground fire, we thought we were close. However, we spent about 30 minutes and found no trace of the crew or their aircraft. We returned to the tanker to refuel again and the SAR mission was cancelled by 7th AF Headquarters. I had

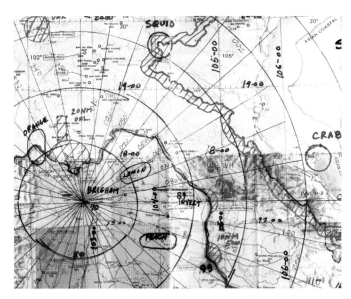

Figure 10: The Udorn TACAN is Brigham, the first circle is at 50 miles… PEACH-LEMON-ORANGE are refueling tracks. The 30-degree radial is above (Lemon refueling track) 70 miles puts the last known coordinates near Laotian border. *Courtesy of Lt.Col. Jack Bauder.*

no idea what kind of aircraft we were looking for that night until I returned to Udorn and looked at the (ATO) Air Tasking Order in our operations center. It was then I learned that the aircraft, call sign Ranger 23, was an F-111A".

67-0066   F-111A # 111 GD/FW Production Run # A1-111
USAF Delivery Date: February 6, 1969

Combat Loss Scenario
F-111A 67-0066, Coach 33
Coach 33 disappeared on October 16, 1972, while on a strike against the Dai Loi Railroad Bridge located about 6.1 NM east southeast of Vinh Yen on the Northwest rail line. The flight was planned for 15,500 feet to the descent point where a 1000 foot MEA was to have been flown until approaching Thud Ridge in Route Pack 6A, then a descent to 500 feet on TFR was planned, followed by bomb release and egress.

The MEA portion of the flight ranged over 6,000 to 9,000 foot peaks inbound and 4,000 foot peaks outbound. The TFR portions were over terrain with variations of 1,000 feet. The final leg into the target paralleled Thud Ridge to the west. The terrain dropped about 600 feet during this run in. Directly on the planned track and about 7.4 NM from the target was a hill rising some 360 feet above its surroundings. Terrain beyond the target was the relatively flat Red River Plain.

Weather enroute and for the target area was reported to include isolated thunderstorms and rain showers. Target area weather was reported to be 1,000 to 1,500 feet broken overcast with 10 NM visibilities under the ceiling. Thunderstorms and lightning were observed by F-111 crews in the area.

Coach 33's flight plan took the aircraft and crew into the heart of the SAM envelope for Route Package 5 and 6A, and came within range of at least five photo-confirmed, occupied SAM sites. An estimated 12 SAM battalions operated in the Route Packages 5 and 6A areas between Yen Bai and Hanoi. There were at least ten 57 mm and two 85 mm guns located along the route to the target area portion of Coach 33's track. Though these high caliber AAA guns presented no threat to the F-111 at low altitude, should a TFR failure have occurred and the aircraft been forced to a higher altitude, the potential for a AAA engagement existed. Numerous light AAA guns (12.7 mm and 14.5 mm) and automatic weapons were also scattered along the track. In addition, photographs taken in July west of Phui Yen (along Coach 33's track) showed two mobile gun systems capable of tracking and firing at an aircraft flying at 500 feet.

Courtesy of Don Logan Collection.

The last known location of Coach 33 was in Laos about 50 NM from the North Vietnamese border, five minutes before its descent scheduled for 2339L. At that point, U.S. radar lost contact. At 0007L, while in the vicinity of Coach 33's fragged target, Coach 27 heard some seemingly normal conversation between Coach 33 and another agency.

North Vietnamese press releases reported an F-111 was shot down by AAA fire in Vinh Phuc Province, northwest of Hanoi and along Coach 33's projected flight path into the target area. On October 18, two photographs purporting to show the wreckage of an F-111 shot down in Vinh Phuc Province were released by Hanoi. On 19 and 20 October Radio Hanoi broadcast details of crew identification papers and claimed Coach 33 to be the 4000th U.S. plane shot down. Subsequently, the U.S. investigating team also received Japanese news film showing the crash site. Analysis of the film confirmed that the wreckage shown was from an F-111. (*Project CHECO: The F-111 in Southeast Asia September 1972-January 1973*)

Coach 33 failed to return to Takhli RTAFB on October 17, 1972. Capt James A. Hockridge and Lt Allen U. Graham were listed as MIA. Last known coordinates (N 21 15 26 / E 105 41 35) were in the vicinity of the target.

Findings
Coach 33 was lost while attacking the Dai Loi railroad bridge near the Phuc Yen Airfield, in Route Pack 6A, North Vietnam. Weapons load was (4) four MK-84, 2,000 pound low drag bombs. Although the area

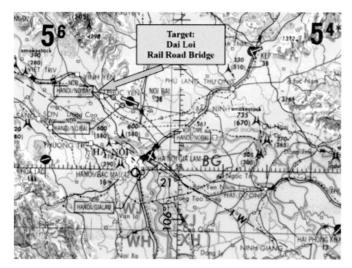

Figure 11: Hanoi and Phuc Yen Area Map.

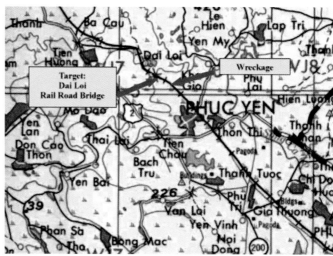

Figure 12: Phuc Yen and the Dai Loi Rail Road Bridge. *Map by Lou Benoit.*

around Phuc Yen and the MIG fighter base were heavily defended with AAA, veterans of the deployment thought the use of Low Drag MK-84's was a causal factor in this loss. While delivering "slick bombs," the pilot must either pull up and "toss" the bombs into the target area, or climb to and remain above the minimum fragmentation envelope during a level straight-through pass. If the pilot failed to climb or the bombs impacted with the aircraft inside the fragmentation envelope, the results were immediately catastrophic, downing the aircraft. Since the aircraft wreckage was located approximately 1600 feet past the target area, the self-fragmentation conclusion is the most likely cause.

Crew:
Pilot: Capt James Allen Hockridge
WSO: 1Lt Allen Upton Graham
Call Sign: Coach 33
Time of Incident: Night Mission Time Unknown
Assigned Unit: Det 1 429th TFS / 347th TFW Takhli RTAFB, Thailand
Aircraft Statistics: 308 Flights and 809.1 Flight Hours
Mishap Result: Killed in Action / In September 1977, the Vietnamese government returned the remains of the two men; Captain Graham's remains were positively identified in October 1977.

67-0063 F-111A # 108 GD/FW Production Run # A1-108
USAF Delivery Date: January 9, 1969

Combat Loss Scenario
F-111A 67-0063, Whaler 57
On November 7, 1972 the combat sortie was fragged for a night, single-ship mission against the Luat Son Highway Ferry and Ford Complex nestled in a populated and forested area where highway 101B crosses over Ben Hai River approximately 24 miles south of the major port city of Dong Hoi, it is 10 miles southeast of the coastline and 9 miles north of the Demilitarized Zone (DMZ), in Quang Binh Province, North Vietnam. The target was in Route Package 1 (RP1) about 6.5 NM southeast of Bat Lake. The mission was planned to takeoff from Takhli, RTAFB, cruise at 15,500 AGL for ingress to a descent point just North of Bartelemy Pass, then fly a 70 nautical mile (NM) long, 1,000 feet AGL minimum enroute altitude (MEA) track to a descent point within approximately 10 NM of the target. At this time the crew was to have used TFR set at 500 feet into the target, returning at 1000 feet TFR from the target to a scheduled climb-out point. They were to return to base at 24,500 feet.

The terrain from the descent point to 10 miles from the target was irregular with mountains and Karst formations along the route. The MEA for this leg was 3,455 feet Mean Sea Level (MSL). Ten miles from the target, where flight planning called for a TFR descent to 500 feet, terrain features were Karst-formations for the first two-thirds of the leg, with the last third being level. About 3 NM enroute to the target was a series of 600-foot hills. Beyond the target the terrain was tidal plain with few significant features. The scheduled return flight plan would have taken the aircraft over similar terrain. Thunderstorms were reported in the target area. Three other F-111s were scheduled into Lower Route Pack I, but aborted due to severe weather conditions. Enroute to the target, the mishap aircraft's flight-path could have encountered isolated AAA units. At approximately 35 NM from the target, Whaler 57's scheduled flight path took it over a heavy AAA concentration estimated to have had one 85 mm, five 57 mm, and twenty-two 23 mm guns. (*Project CHECO: The F-111 in Southeast Asia September 1972-January 1973*)

Courtesy of Dave Menard via Don Logan Collection.

The initial North Vietnamese report of an F-111 shoot down was made the day after the U.S. announced the loss of Whaler 57. This was the first Hanoi report to credit a Western news agency as the source of the report. Whaler 57 failed to return to Takhli RTAFB on November 7, 1972. Major Robert Brown and Robert D. Morrissey were listed as MIA.

Findings
Whaler 57 took off from Takhli at 0219L, November 7, 1972 at 0250L. The aircraft commander checked in with the Airborne Battlefield Command and Control Center (ABCCC), but no position report was given at that time. Two unexplained incidents involving Mode 3 IFF squawks were noted. The first squawk intercepted by U.S. radar was at 0257L and would have placed Whaler 57 approximately 45 NM south of track. The second intercept, at 0408L, one hour and two minutes after the last radio contact, was a Mode 3 Mayday squawk. Investigations of these IFF squawk incidents were not conclusive in tying these transmissions to Whaler 57. Whaler 57 apparently crashed in the mountains while attempting to penetrate an area of heavy rainstorms that degraded the aircraft's radar and disorientated the aircrew. The most probable cause was Controlled Flight Into Terrain (CFIT) influenced by a TFR anomaly known as E-Scope Blanking due to rain showers. Crash site coordinates were (N 17 09 38 / E 106 43 15).

67-0092 F-111A # 137 GD/FW Production Run # A1-137
USAF Delivery Date: May 24, 1969

Combat Loss Scenario
F-111A 67-0092, Burger 54

On November 20, 1972, Burger 54 was fragged to attack the Co Giang Trans Shipment Port on Route 101 approximately 8.5 NM southwest of Quang Khe in Route Pack 1 (RP 1).

The planned flight profile included a descent from 15,500 feet to a tactical MEA prior to reaching the North Vietnamese border. A 1,000 foot AGL TFR ingress was to begin at the initial point (IP) to 10 NM short of the target, followed by a descent to 300 foot AGL for the Auto TFR run in to the target. After the attack, the crew planned a 200 foot AGL egress route toward the Gulf of Tonkin. Once "feet wet" and approximately 20 nautical miles over the ocean, the crew was to return to Takhli at high altitude, going "feet dry" south of the Demilitarized Zone. Burger 54's ingress route crossed terrain with peaks reaching 4,500 feet, located just prior to a Karst region with a concentration of 2,000 foot peaks. Enroute weather was adequate for TFR operations with a cloud deck from 2,000 to 8,000 feet. No significant rain or thunderstorms were forecast or reported along the ingress and strike route. In the target area however, visibility was reported between two and four nautical miles, with both thunderstorms and rain showers. A 1,000 foot cloud deck covered the target region and egress route, above which there was a 20,000 foot overcast.

At 0239L, Burger 54 reached the low-level entry point. From there he descended from 15,500 feet to 3,000 feet at the initial point. The initial point was reached at 0245L, the time of the last radar and radio contact with Burger 54. At this last contact, there were no indications of any problems.

Courtesy of Tom Brewer via Don Logan Collection.

One hour prior to Burger 54's strike, the crew of Burger 52 received RWR indications from three enemy height-finder radars in the same general area as Burger 54's target region. (*Project CHECO: The F-111 in Southeast Asia September 1972-January 1973*)

Burger 54 failed to return to Takhli RTAFB on November 20, 1972. Capt Ronald D. Stafford and Capt Charles J. Cafferrelli were listed as MIA.

Findings

The aircraft was lost during the egress from a target in Route Pack 1. The flight crew planned to egress heading out into the Gulf of Tonkin, north of Da Nang AB, South Vietnam. The crew called "Feet Wet" but the Navy failed to record the call. The failure to relay Burger 54's call inhibited the Search and Rescue effort. After-action analysis of Burger 54's time on target indicated there was no evidence of enemy air defense reaction to the strike, and, North Vietnam did not announce a shoot down following Burger 54s loss.

Several days after Burger 54's loss, pieces of honeycomb wreckage were found along the coastal beaches 14 miles north of Da Nang. Prevailing ocean currents between one-half to one knot propelled the debris between 120 and 240 NM to the beach location north of Da Nang. Although the exact location of impact is unknown, the surmised crash site was reasonably

Crew:
Pilot: Maj Robert Mack Brown
WSO: Capt Robert David Morrissey
Call Sign: Whaler 57
Time of Incident: 0408 Local
Assigned Unit: Det 1 429th TFS / 347th TFW Takhli RTAFB, Thailand
Aircraft Statistics: 333 Flights and 822.1 Flight Hours
Mishap Result: Presumptive Finding Killed in Action / Aircraft Destroyed

Figure 13: Luat Son Target area. *Map by Lou Benoit.*

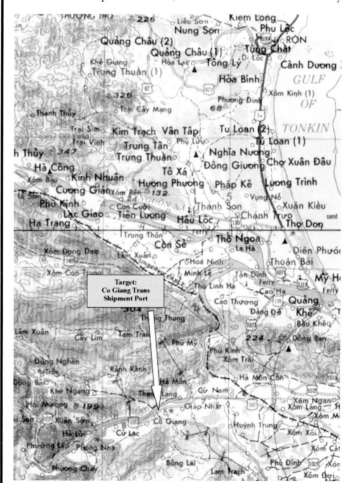

Figure 14: Quang Khe region of Route Pack 1. *Map by Lou Benoit.*

placed within the area of the planned egress. Debris from the mishap aircraft was sent to the Sacramento Air Logistics Center for material-forensic study. The parts were determined to be from an F-111 aircraft. Analysis indicated post-impact fire, 72 degree wing set at impact, and that the crew module probably had not separated at the time of impact.

The most likely cause for the loss was Controlled Flight Into Terrain (CFIT) due to the TFR system entering a mode known as LARA Override during the overwater egress. The crew may have failed to detect and correct a descent which resulted in a collision with the open ocean surface at high speed.

Research Findings:
These findings were documented in a GDFW / SMALC engineering report # 73-511. Evidence backs up the 72-degree wing-sweep and

shallow impact with the water. Veterans that flew with this particular crew recalled that they preferred to egress target areas at 200 feet AGL with the wings swept at 72 degrees, and the engines set at 100% Military power.

Crew:
Pilot: Capt Ronald Dean Stafford
WSO: Capt Charles Joseph Cafferrelli
Call Sign: Burger 54
Time of Incident: Night Mission Time Unknown
Assigned Unit: Det 1 429th TFS / 347th TFW Takhli RTAFB, Thailand
Aircraft Statistics: 344 Flights and 917.2 Flight Hours
Mishap Result: Killed in Action / Aircraft Destroyed

67-0099   F-111A # 144 GD/FW Production Run # A1-144
USAF Delivery Date: June 11, 1969

Combat Loss Scenario
F-111A 67-0099, Snug 40
On December 18, 1972, F-111A 67-0099 assigned to Det 1 430th TFS deployed to Takhli RTAFB, Thailand in support of Operation "Constant Guard V" was scheduled for a "Linebacker II" combat strike on the Hanoi International Radio Communication (RADCOM) Transmitter at 0053L Hanoi time. The last radio call contact was received by an orbiting Moonbeam C-130 Airborne Battle Command and Control (ABCC) aircraft at 0054L hours was after bomb release on the assigned target.

The weather enroute to and at the target area was reported to be 4,000 to 6,000 feet, scattered to broken clouds. No rain or thunderstorms were reported, and visibility was six to ten miles with 91 percent moon illumination.

At 0030L, U.S. radar at Udorn had its last contact with Snug 40. By 0037L, the aircraft was to begin its descent from 19,500 feet. An MEA profile was to continue to the initial point where TFR at 500 feet AGL was to begin. At 0054L, one minute after scheduled time over target, Snug 40 transmitted an off-target call. Another call from Snug 40 was received at 0100L on UHF but there was no radar contact. Further attempts at radio contact were unsuccessful. There was no indication of any problem.

The mishap aircraft had egressed the target area going "feet wet" out over the Gulf of Tonkin and disappeared from all radar contact. No further communications were received. No trace was ever found of the aircraft, and both Ward and McElvain were declared Missing in Action.
Loss Coordinates: N 20 17 00 E 106 36 00

Findings
The loss of Snug 40 and the earlier loss of Burger 54 were similar in that both egressed their assigned target areas over the Gulf of Tonkin under Auto TFR flight control. During post-loss analysis of Snug 40's route, some conflicting information was provided by the Navy as to whether Snug 40 had transmitted a radio call of "feet wet"; an indication that the mishap aircraft reached the water. After this loss however, the USAF restricted the F-111 aircrews from planning or executing "feet wet" exits from their target areas towards the relative safety of the open ocean.

Prior to Snug 40's loss, President Nixon imposed a bombing halt against North Vietnam. During the bombing halt, no night TFR sorties were flown from 20 November to 16 December 1972, a restriction instituted by the USAF after the fourth F-111A loss. During the bombing halt however, all Takhli based F-111's continued to fly daytime combat sorties against the Pathet Lao. After completing their assigned missions, F-111 aircrews were required to operate the TFR system on low-level routes while returning to Takhli.

Aerial bombing resumed into North Vietnam once again in December 1972 (Linebacker II). The USAF simultaneously lifted the night TFR restrictions allowing the Takhli based F-111's to strike military targets in the Hanoi area. Snug 40 was the first night TFR loss of an F-111 after the bombing halt. (*Project CHECO: The F-111 in Southeast Asia September 1972-January 1973*)

Courtesy of Author's Collection.

Snug 40 failed to return to Takhli RTAFB on December 18, 1972. Lt Col Ronald J. Ward and Maj James R. McElvain were listed as MIA.

The cause of this combat loss was most likely Controlled Flight Into Terrain (CFIT) due to the aircraft entering an undetected descent into the water. Speculation leans toward a TFR anomaly known as E-Scope blanking whereby the TFR system reverts to a LARA Override mode to maintain the desired terrain clearance height. In this case, the forward looking TFR has little or no "terrain" returns while operating over open water. In order to maintain a terrain clearance profile, the TFR computer attempts to manage height solely from the radar altimeter. Compounding the problem, the vertically oriented low altitude radar altimeter (LARA) signal had either been absorbed by the water, or the radar altimeter signal penetrated the surface and ranged off thermoclines below the surface, contributing to an undetected and uncorrected descent. The presumption was that the back-up 68 percent fly-up safety feature of the radar altimeter was also not triggered. In this case, when the radio altimeter indicator needle penetrated a preset indexer, set at 68 percent of the selected TFR clearance altitude, the TFR computer should have commanded a fly-up safety maneuver.

Crew:
Pilot: Maj Ronald Jack Ward
WSO: Maj James Richard McElvain
Call Sign: Snug 40
Time of Incident: 0854 GOLF
Assigned Unit: Det 1 430th TFS / 347th TFW Takhli RTAFB, Thailand
Aircraft Statistics: 336 Flights 853.7 Flight Hours
Mishap Result: Aircraft Destroyed / Fatal Combat Loss

LARA Override could occur over flat farm fields, snow fields, and water. The situation was worse over-water because the Radar Altimeters signal was either diffused or absorbed by the water, returning inaccurate height readings. The TFR computer would then initiate a slow descent to the selected ride height. In the dark of night, a crew could easily miss

at 300 feet. The run-in heading was picked up at Duc Noi about

67-0068 F-111A # 113 GD/FW Production Run # A1-113
USAF Delivery Date: February 20, 1969

Combat Loss Scenario
F-111A 67-0068, Jackel 33
On December 22, 1972, F-111A 67-0068 was assigned to Det 1 430th TFS deployed to Takhli RTAFB, Thailand in support of Operation "Constant Guard V." The crew and aircraft were fragged against the Hanoi River Docks in Route Pack 6B, a very high threat target area. Takeoff time was 2100L. The high altitude route to the target area took the crew over *The Plain De Jarres* in Laos into the *Gorillas Head* area of North Vietnam, where a TFR letdown to the low altitude penetration altitude was initiated. The last leg before turning south was on the North Side of "*Thud Ridge.* " Run-in altitude for the target was from the north

Courtesy of Don Logan Collection.

ten miles due north of the Hanoi Dock target, airspeed was 480 knots. A Time-On-Target (TOT) of 2238L was planned. The northwest corner of the *Paul Doumer Bridge* was used for the final attack radar offset aim point (OAP). All 12 Mk-82's were on target. Hanoi confirmed a shoot down and displayed photos of the wreckage on television. The photos provided sufficient evidence that the wreckage was indeed an F-111. (*Project CHECO: The F-111 in Southeast Asia September 1972-January 1973*)

Jackel 33 failed to return to Takhli RTAFB on 22 December 1972. Capt Robert D. Sponybarger and Lt William W. Wilson were listed as MIA and later confirmed to have become POW's.

the insidious descent and impact the water. Over-water transitions were later prohibited in Vietnam.

Don Gwynne, in *GDFW Flight Safety*, notes:

> Another anomaly associated with undetected descents was later attributed to a defect in the LARA Bypass switch. In such cases, internal corrosion caused the LARA Bypass switch to stick in the Bypass position. The whole point of a Bypass Switch is to allow a TFR commanded descent when LARA is ON but not IN-TRACK, i.e., above 5000 feet AGL. (The 28vdc which holds the Bypass Switch solenoid is from the LARA, namely ON and NOT TRACK). As soon as LARA begins tracking the ground descending through 5000 feet AGL, the ON and NOT TRACK 28vdc goes away, and if not physically stuck, the Bypass Switch drops back to the NORM position automatically, and the TFR Computer uses actual LARA radar altitude for 68% checks, etc. instead of the pseudo 1850 foot value provided through the Bypass Switch.

Findings
Upon egress, the aircraft received AAA hits that resulted in a loss of the utility hydraulics, followed by a right engine fire light. At 2238L the crew called "Off Target- with one engine out." Moonbeam, the ABCCC, acknowledged the call. After egressing the target area to the west of Hanoi, total hydraulic failure occurred. The crew was forced to eject at 2240L. The two men evaded the enemy for 4 days, but were eventually captured. The USAF made several attempts to rescue the crew but were repelled by small arms fire. After loss of contact with the crew members the search effort was terminated. Portions of the wreckage and the crew escape module are now found in the Moscow Aviation Museum.

Crew:
Pilot: Capt Robert D Sponeybarger
WSO: 1Lt William W Wilson
Call Sign: Jackel 33
Time of Incident: 2238L
Assigned Unit: Det 1 430th TFS / 347th TFW Takhli RTAFB, Thailand
Aircraft Statistics: 372 Flights 946.8 Flight Hours
Mishap Result: Aircraft Destroyed / Successful Ejection / Crew became POWs

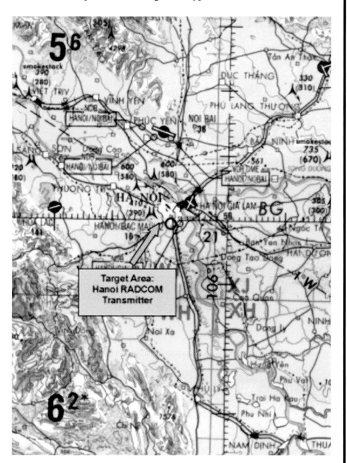

Figure 15: Hanoi Area. *Map by Lou Benoit.*

Jackel 33's Crew Module at the Moscow Aviation Museum. *Courtesy of Moscow Aviation Museum.*

Jackal 33 Bravo (An Overdue Briefing)
By; Charles J. Rouhier

I was a Jolly Green Giant Flight Engineer (FE) participating in the failed rescue of Jackal 33 Alpha, Capt. Robert Sponeybarger, and Bravo, Lt. William W. Wilson December 23 - 26, 1972. In January 1973 I went TDY to Takhli for a conference with the 474th TFW F-111 unit. They asked me to present a briefing on the events of the 26 December 1972 rescue attempt of 33 Bravo at the end of the session. At the completion of the other briefings no one brought up my briefing and I did not volunteer. I believe there were a couple of reasons for this: First, I was a snot nosed kid of 20 at the time and had never spoken before a large crowd before. It scared the hell out of me. Second, it bothered me tremendously that we came so close to rescuing Wilson, but we just were not good enough. There was a lot of guilt over that mission and I did not feel like talking about it. With the departure of the F-111's from the Air Force (AF) inventory it's time for this long overdue briefing. To the Aardvarks who were at Takhli in 1973 I apologize for shirking my duties at that conference.

Jackal 33, crippled by Triple-A over downtown Hanoi on the night of 22 December 1972 exited the target area on a single engine. The crew limped to the first ridge line west and ejected about 17 miles from the edge of Hanoi. I am still not sure of the exact location. If memory serves, 33 Alpha's capture was sometime on the 24th or 25th. On the 24th I was the FE on Jolly 2, Alpha High. Little did we know this mission foretold the events of coming days. The primary hydraulic flight control system failed shortly after crossing the border into North Vietnam (NVN) and a fire started in the left forward electronics bay when the TACAN failed. We aborted and RTB'd to Nakhon Phnom (NKP). The remainder of the force continued, but could not penetrate due to weather. SAR forces were in the area again on the 25th, but weather again prevented a rescue. The night of the 25th the weather cleared sufficiently to allow a rescue attempt on the 26th. We woke about 0300 for briefings and preparations. Included in the rescue package, as I recall, were four HH-53C's, two HC-130's and eight A-7D Corsairs. Other units provided additional support for MIGCAP, SAM suppression, and tankers for the fast movers and AEW. I was the FE on Jolly 1, Alpha Low, on this day. Alpha High was Jolly 2, Bravo Low, Jolly 3 and Bravo High, Jolly 4.

The crew of Jolly 1 was:

Capt. Richard D. Shapiro – Pilot   Capt. Miguel A. Pereira – Copilot "Call sign" Bear
Sgt. Charles J. Rouhier – Flight Engineer   A1C Robert W. Jones – Para Rescue man (PJ), Ramp
TSgt. John R. Carlson – Para Rescue man (PJ), Left window– Combat Cameraman

We departed NKP before first light and proceeded north past Udorn. We crossed into Laos between Vientiane and Pak Sane then proceeded North East around the Plaine-des-Jarres to a holding point just west of the NVN/Laos border. Systems problems kept me busy and I am not sure of our exact route. Just after passing into Laos we test fired the mini-guns. The window gun failed to operate and I spent the next several hours trying to fix the problem. I salvaged parts from the door mounted weapon to repair it. Losing the door weapon is not a problem since the hoist precludes its use. Once we reached our holding point another problem manifested itself. The upper-half of the ramp door kept detaching itself and falling on the PJ standing on the lowered half of the ramp door. Normally, FE's disable the ramp hydraulics during a combat mission and the up-locks keep the upper door in place. This time it did not work and hydraulic power remained on the ramp. This is a risk since the utility hydraulic system supplies this and other non-essential systems. Disabling these systems mitigates the effects of battle damage. Anyway, I continue the story: Sandy's 1 (Lead), 2, 3, and 4 proceeded to the survivor's area to pinpoint his location and suppressed the ground fire. We spent considerable time orbiting waiting for the Sandy's to make the area safe enough for a rescue. The North Vietnamese Army (NVA) had at least two 51 Cal. in

the area and a considerable number of troops. We were confident the NVA knew the location of 33 Bravo and we were heading into a flak trap. We refueled several times waiting for the call from Sandy Lead. If I remember right, about thirty minutes after our last refueling we got a call (we thought from Sandy Lead) to make the rescue. We turned east and crossed the border into North Vietnam at maximum speed and very low altitude. I believe two Sandy's escorted us while the other two stayed with the remaining Jollies in the holding area. We observed numerous bunkers being built into the sides of the mountains as we ingressed. At one point we passed a NVA truck barreling down a mountain road. The driver's surprise to see us lower than him almost caused him to drive off the cliff. To this day, I believe if I had waved at him, he would have. As we reached the Black River the Sandy's laid a smoke corridor across the river to screen us from a 57mm site to the northwest. Several rounds of 57mm passed behind us as we crossed. Sandy 5 announced our arrival in the area to which Sandy Lead responded with something along the lines of "What the hell are you doing here?" We were setup and should have authenticated the call. Murphy was clearly along in spades on this mission. The North Vietnamese sucker us in with the call. Whoever he was, his English was very good. We ended up passing over 33 Bravo's area at about 150 knots since Sandy Lead was not ready to pinpoint his location. We flew around the mountain and this put us briefly over the plains with Hanoi barely visible in the distance.

We came back around the mountain from roughly south. From the time we entered 33 Bravo's area we were taking heavy small arms and 51 cal. At some point during this time the copilot took two small arms' rounds through the right elbow. Nobody was aware of this for some time. One of the Sandy's also reported we were losing a lot of fuel from our left side. As we came back around the mountain Shapiro was trying to slow up the Jolly. The Sandy's were calling for Bravo to pop smoke, telling us to slow down, and trying to suppress the ground fire we were taking. We overshot the survivor again and had to perform a hovering turn to get back into the area. Twice we passed directly over a 51-cal site. The second time over the ramp PJ silenced it. I never saw this weapon, which surprised Bob Jones at the debriefing. Locating 33 Bravo was more important to me than looking for bad guys. The smoke from Bravo's Mk13 had dissipated by the time we got into a hover over his general area. Locating him proved difficult due to the high, blowing elephant grass. I am not sure how long we were in a hover looking for him. It seemed like hours, but was probably only minutes. The whole time we were taking a lot of hits. We could see the NVA moving in on us the entire time. Only the ramp mini-gun was firing. At the debriefing Bob Jones reported NVA under the Jolly firing into the bottom of his gun tub. The window mini-gun was not firing and I was beginning to think Carlson was hit. I eventually heard him firing his CAR-15. I finally spotted 33 Bravo about our 2 o'clock making his way to the Jolly. I directed the pilot over his position and set the penetrator down about three feet from him. He was reaching for the penetrator when our rotor wash knocked him backwards. He was getting up when the pilot pulled power and exited the area. Even though we were taking numerous hits I was not aware of any critical damage to the Jolly. I pulled the penetrator into the Helo, turned and scanned the instruments. Everything appeared to be working, at least from the instruments not shattered by ground fire. There were many holes through the various cockpit windows. I asked Shapiro why we left. He said he had just then heard Bear report being hit. It was the first any of us knew of Bears injuries. Our fuel state at this time was critical and fuel would not transfer from the drops even though everything appeared to be working electrically. The Sandy's were giving us directions to exit the area. I applied a tourniquet to Bear's arm and directed the closest PJ to attend the copilot. I manned Carlson's mini-gun only to discover it had failed again. That's why there was no firing from his side. With Bear out of the seat I jumped in to assist the pilot. All of this occurred prior to re-crossing the Black River. The Sandy's were a tad late laying the smoke and we were on the front edge of the screen as we crossed. No one noticed

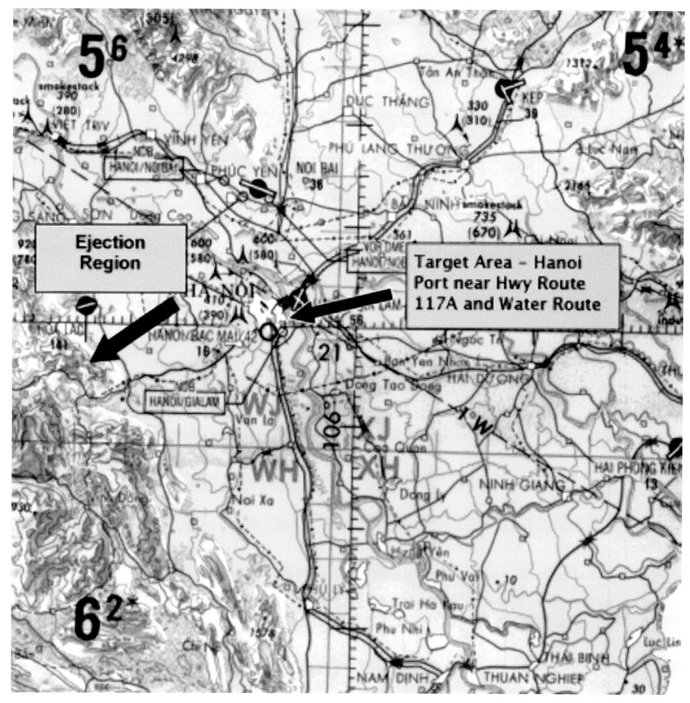

Figure 16: Hanoi Area and Jackel 33's approximate target area and ejection / SAR attempt. *Map by Lou Benoit.*

if the 57 fired at us or not. One of the Kings (forget which) crossed into NVN to give us gas. We rendezvoused with King and Alpha High. The probe would not extend and we had to plug in to King with the probe retracted. This put us very close to the HC-130 with the drogue flying underneath the rotor blades. Turbulence from our abnormal closeness to the HC-130 caused us to disconnect once. The front of the probe had taken one or more hits and the fuel King was sending us right into the slipstream. I do not think any of it made it to the tanks. I told the pilot we did not have any more time for this. The left main showed 0 pounds and the right about 250 pounds. I had no idea if they were accurate or damaged. Alpha High picked a landing site on a mountaintop for us. I believe we had only reached the border at this time. We took more ground fire as we went in for a fast hard landing. I am not sure if the engines flamed out before or as I shut them down. Alpha High landed about fifty yards from us up

the hill. We abandoned the Jolly and got into the High bird. We then left the area and headed home. Due to the late hour the Sandys put 33 Bravo to bed for the night. Jolly 3 and 4 along with several Sandys stayed in the area of our Helo for a while. I believe it was Bravo Low that went back in to see if the Jolly was salvageable. While the PJs were inspecting the Helo they came under ground fire from people moving up the mountain from a village in the valley. They abandon the Jolly and the Sandy's destroyed it. We landed briefly at Udorn to drop Bear off at the hospital. He never came back to the 40th and went directly back to the States. We got back to NKP some thirteen or so hours after we took off, debriefed and went to the hooch. The bombing halted the next day and the Jollies did not attempt another rescue of Jackal 33 Bravo. I believe Jackal 33 Bravo's capture was a couple of days later. I understand assets where directing him to a safer location or possibly into Laos at the time of his capture.

OPERATION "EL DORADO CANYON"
LIBYA RAID — 1986

70-2389 F-111F # 28 GD/FW Production Run # E2-28
USAF Delivery Date: January 12, 1972

Combat Loss Scenario
F-111F 70-2389, Karma 52

Incident Summary-Direct Quote from FOIA
Release prepared by Lt Col Kripner
Defense POW/Missing Personnel Office Analyst Report (USDPMO)
On April 14-15, 1986, Major Ribas-Dominicci, Pilot, and Capt Lorence, WSO, were flying an F-111F (Call Sign KARMA-52) as part of a package of aircraft bombing targets in Tripoli, Libya, during Operation El Dorado Canyon. The F-111 strike came from northwest to southeast in a sequence of widely spaced parallel tracks with specific times over target (TOT). Karma 52's ingress was near the end of the attack package. As Karma 52 began his high-speed ingress toward the target area, some F-111's had completed their attacks and were egressing northwest over the water. During the attack, two aircraft reported a fireball traveling from west to east near Sidi Balal, which impacted near the beach at 1504Z. This was confirmed by a third aircraft, which also reported a fireball near Sidi Balal. A fourth aircraft reported the same fireball and crash as he exited the target area, position estimated to be 10 NM from the beach, near 32-52N/013 00E. Although numerous SAR assets were in the area, no contact was made with Major Ribas-Dominicci's aircraft before or after the crash. Search and Rescue efforts continued late into the night with no wreckage, debris, or capsule parachute spotted. On 16 April, the Air Force determined the aircraft must have disintegrated upon impact with the water. In May 1986 the remains of Major Ribas-Dominicci were found on a beach 40 miles west of Tripoli. Those remains were returned to the U.S. via the Vatican in January 1989. Captain Lorence has been listed as MIA.

Findings
An admittedly controversial task is to define whether Karma 52 was shot down or had crashed during the attack. The conclusion supporting a shallow water impact due to a TFR malfunction or pilot error was surmised simply from the F-111's accident history. During an interview with Remit 31 Alpha, the pilot revealed:

> As I coasted out after attacking my assigned target, still at less than 1,000 feet AGL, I saw what I believed to be an airplane impact the water at a very shallow angle. This impact was at my left, 9-10 o'clock position. I had seen a good bit of low-angle napalm drops in Southeast Asia, and the burning smear of the impact across the water reminded me of napalm. I commented to my right seater, "Somebody just hit the water."

After reading this statement, one could easily assume the aircraft simply crashed into the sea. The interview response does not openly reveal any sign of a shoot-down, such as missiles fired in Karma 52's direction, or witnessing a series of explosions. True also, the F-111 had a history of losses attributed to TFR problems, ungraciously revived by the media each time an F-111 crashed. To dispel the rumors regarding a shallow water impact; at the 540 knots airspeed Karma 52 was flying, a skip hit would not have been a survivable event. Fortunately, evidence indicates an ejection did occur and eye witness accounts support a shoot down.

The first task is to admit the Libyan Air Defense network was both prepared and aggressive in its application of AAA and SAMs. Additionally, rocket launched parachute suspended flares were employed by the Libyan military near the Tripoli shoreline. The flares launches were intended to amplify the visual intensity of the Libyan air defense while causing some distraction and confusion for attackers. This goal was achieved by Libya: Almost all the Libya Raiders reported seeing rocket launched-parachute suspended flares, stating "the flare launches were clearly visible and appeared to remain 'fixed' on their F-111 canopies, much like a guided missile's intercept trajectory."

The next task is to recognize the effectiveness of both the U.S. Navy and USAF Suppression of Enemy Air Defense (SEAD) assets toward actively jamming the SAM search and track threat radar sites. These initial SEAD activities subdued the Libyan defenders into firing the majority of their SAMs in a back-up, unguided manner. Without the SEAD assets, it is almost certain more aircraft could have been shot down.

The F-111 attack was a two-pronged ingress (Figure 18) on either side of Tripoli, with the major force (Remit, Elton, Jewel, and Karma) on a western axis, and a second group (Puffy and Lujac) on an eastern axis. The F-111s departed their tankers and ingressed due south at 1,000 feet toward the Libyan coast. When a series of towers on the coastline were identified, the main force of attackers (Remit, Elton and Karma) turned east (yellow route) and proceeded on a parallel track with the coast line toward Tripoli and the Azziziyah Barracks. (Jewel) spilt southeast (green route), slightly off axis from the main force to attack Sidi Bilal terrorist training camp. The eastern group (Puffy and Lujac) turned west (blue route) at the coast line ingressing overland for an end-around attack on the Tripoli Airport. All the Libya Raiders then egressed north (orange line), feet wet, on a common route back toward the awaiting tankers. The main echelon's overwater attack run was at extremely low altitude (400 feet to as low as 200 feet AGL) – initially below the line-of-sight detection capability from the fixed "inland" SAM locations. During the west to east ingress heading, some of the main force F-111 crews received missile threat warning indications at 400 feet, but descended to 200 feet where the threat indications dissipated, some flew lower still!

70- 2389 shown at RAF Sculthorpe. *Courtesy of Author's Collection via Chuck Pitts.*

The briefed combat Minimum Enroute Altitude (MEA) was 700 feet AGL; an altitude to be flown in the event of TFR and radar altimeter failure. F-111 crews participating in the raid believed Karma 52 did not descend below the 700 foot minimum and may even have ingressed toward Tripoli at 1,000 feet AGL. As Karma 52 approached, his height above the ocean may have allowed an SA-6 missile site to directly engage his aircraft.

Karma 51, flying ahead and to the right of Karma 52's position, assessed in a post flight debrief that his aircraft was locked onto by a SAM (a threat warning display indicating an enemy lock-on and launch audio/symbology). The pilot of Karma 51 did not visually acquire a SAM launch directly at their aircraft requiring a defensive maneuver. Karma 53, aft and to the right of Karma 52, developed a TFR problem and climbed above 400 feet while attempting to reset the TFR. During their ingress, Karma 53's WSO visually acquired a SAM, took control of the aircraft, and executed a break turn into the missile. Once the missile missed them, the WSO returned control to the aircraft commander. The likelihood that Karma 52 was also actively engaged *(locked onto)* by a specific threat system is highly probable.

The pilot of Karma 53 witnessed a bright flash (Karma 52's crash) off to his left during his target run, however he did not report a SAM fly-out across his nose (right to left) toward Karma 52. Karma 53 was also the only F-111 to visually acquire and defend against a SAM launch from his right side. After executing a break turn into the missile, the missile apparently trailed aft and exploded. Because of this SAM engagement, the crew of Karma 53 believes that Karma 52 was shot down by the Libyan defenders.

Ahead of Karma flight but already egressing their Tripoli area targets, Remit flight was in a left turn to north to exit the area. Remit 32 witnessed an airborne explosion off to his left side, followed shortly thereafter by a much larger and more intense explosion on the surface of the water. Remit 32 believes either an SA-6 or SA-8 guided on Karma 52 due to his higher altitude on the ingress. He believed the first explosion was the missile's impact, while the second explosion was the aircraft colliding with the water, detonating the onboard fuel and bombs.

The last task in this narrative is to answer whether an ejection occurred. A capsule ejection might have been witnessed as a short duration rocket blast from over-the-water skyward. However, due to the intensity of the Libyan air defense response and the F-111 crew's task-loading for the attack execution at the time, the ejection event was missed. Most crews only reported seeing Karma 52's explosive impact with the sea. No crews recalled an ejection type event including hearing a Mayday radio call, or hearing the sickening *Weeeep Weeeep* of the Emergency Locator Transmitter (ELT). The ELT may have been turned off, a standard combat procedure.

Because Major Ribas-Dominicci's body was recovered on the Libyan shoreline weeks later, the conclusion leading to a successful ejection and subsequent drowning are very reasonable. An autopsy of Major Ribas-Dominicci conducted by the Armed Forces Medical Examiner reveals the cause of death as drowning (the autopsy finding indicated seawater in Major Ribas-Dominicci's lungs), "There is no evidence of crash trauma except for a fracture of the right heel, such as might be sustained within the crew module during a hard parachute landing." This excerpt should lead the reader to believe an ejection occurred; most likely after the aircraft was hit by a SAM.

Though not discussed in the autopsy, an interview with Remit 31 Alpha revealed there was also a scar on Major Ribas-Dominicci's face. The scar was later linked to and matched the G-suit zipper on the inward side of the right leg. During the ejection sequence, the torso would remain firmly strapped upward in the seat due to the shoulder strap inertia reel locking mechanism. At some point a crushing impact to the floor of the crew capsule drove the right knee upward and the inner leg portion of the G-suit zipper struck Major Ribas-Dominicci's face. Such a hard force would also have been sufficient to break the heel of Major Ribas-Dominicci's foot. What caused a severe impact force on the floor of the crew module? During the attack, there was a 30 to 35 knot surface wind and 10 to 25 foot swells. One pilot reported the sea was foaming! When the crew module descended into the ocean under the main parachute, it would have been drifting near the velocity of the wind. Additionally, the swells may have influenced a hard impact on the forward edge of the crew module causing structural damage, throwing Major Ribas-Dominicci's leg upward. If the module had not been damaged during the shoot-down, or during the ejection due to airframe breakup, the existing sea state could have damaged the module.

The crew module was designed to be water tight and float, essentially a self-contained raft. If the sealed integrity of the capsule had been compromised during the shoot-down, ejection, or landing, sea water would rapidly flood the module's interior. If either crew member opened their canopy in the present sea state, an unstoppable torrent of water would have overcome the buoyancy of the crew module causing it to sink. Thereafter, it is unlikely either crew member could have survived in the sea for any length of time. Eventually, underwater currents slowly assisted in washing the body of Major Ribas-Dominicci ashore. Capt Lorence may have been pulled under with the wreckage; no remains were found.

Crew:
Pilot: Maj Fernando Ribas-Dominicci
WSO: Capt Paul F. Lorence
Call Sign: Karma 52
Time of Incident: 1504 Zulu
Accident Board President: Unknown
Assigned Unit: 494th TFS Aircraft / 495th TFTS Crew / 48th TFW RAF Lakenheath, UK
Aircraft Statistics: 1,286 Flights and 3,294.5 Flight Hours
Mishap Result: Aircraft Destroyed / Lost in Combat / Successful ejection

The combat loss of Karma 52 was due to a successful Libyan air defense missile engagement. The time interval from the low altitude shoot-down, through ejection and water landing, would have been measured in seconds. If the aircraft had crashed without an ejection attempt, it is unlikely that Major Ribas-Dominicci would have been found.

Author's Note: The crew module may have separated from the aircraft, but it does not indicate an entirely successful ejection was achieved. The scar on Major Ribas-Dominicci's face indicates a very hard impact was delivered to the floor of the capsule, most likely when the module impacted the sea surface. Thereafter, egressing a disabled and sinking crew module would have been an extreme survival situation. Both crew members wore Life Preserver Units (LPU), which will keep a survivor afloat once manually inflated. It is unknown whether either crew member successfully evacuated the crew module. Rescue forces in the area would have been challenged to find any crash debris given the current sea state, let alone, two airmen adrift in the crew module or supported by their personal LPUs.

As described in Chapter 1 (The TFR System), the F-111 TFR had a clear history of problems related to maintaining height above water surfaces. At least two F-111As were lost in Vietnam and several additional peace time F-111's crashed at sea due to the TFR anomaly known as E-Scope Blanking and/or LARA Override. It was also assessed that the EF-111 SEAD assets jamming bandwidth of the anticipated SAM missile sites and AAA guidance radars was in the same bandwidth as the F-111's TFR and radar altimeter. It was surmised that the intensity of the jamming caused many of the F-111 crews to experience some TFR / LARA problems during the ingress.

Further Research Findings:
1. Defense POW/Missing Personnel (DPMO) visited Libya and were shown and photographed pieces of an F-111 wing pivot joint or Wing Carry-Through Box
2. DPMO also were shown and photographed two HGU-55/P helmets of the type worn by U.S. aircrew in the 1980s. The helmets have custom molded foam inserts to comfortably fit a pilot's head.

Inbound to the Bab al Aziziya Compound, Tripoli, Libya
The Loss of Karma 52
by Lt Col Dick "Downtown" Brown
14-15 April 1986 0000L Hours

The entire city of Tripoli was now fully visible from about 20 miles away. We were at 200 feet and well above 600 Knots airspeed. The intensity of the AAA fire was surprising. Streams of menacing AAA fire covered the entire sky. I recognized the 57mm cannon fire which came at us in a group of visible tracers. However, the ZSU-23-4's looked like a fire hose and for some reason I remembered that not every round was a visible tracer but one every five or so! That is lots of bullets! There were other types of AAA fire that only added to the intensity. I had already seen several SAM missiles fired starting with a SA-2 some miles from target. The RHAWS scope and audio was lit up and screaming over our headsets yet we focused on the procedures needed to release our four laser guided GBU-10's. Numerous sequential switches needed to be actuated in a well-rehearsed symphony with no mistakes.

My job was to monitor and fly the aircraft, insure we did not hit the ground, and react against the threats with maneuvers, ECM, and chaff and or flares as needed. The WSO was busy finding and refining the steering in order to release the weapons as precisely as possible. The ROE (rule of engagement) were stringent and very specific – make sure you do not miss! Much was at stake since we were attacking a target surrounded by homes, businesses, schools, and hospitals.

Out of the corner of my eye I caught a large flash from something on the shoreline. The flash was preceded by a bright glow that had all the characteristics of a guided SAM and it was in the right vicinity of a known SAM site. I alerted the WSO since the missile was coming from his side. The RHAWS scope confirmed my suspicions and we got ready to react if needed. Suddenly the rocket motor went out and I knew that the missile's rocket motor had served its function and now the missile's maneuvering energy was at its maximum. I had actuated the proper ECM defense measure. As soon as the glow from the missile went out I turned to my WSO and over the interphone counted "1000&1, 1000&2… up to six and shrugged my shoulders knowing that the missile had missed or was not aimed at us. The night sky over Tripoli was lit up with numerous SAM's as if it were a pop bottle rocket convention. Nothing tracking yet - but none-the-less, in the air, always a chance "golden BB" striking any aircraft.

Note: prior to going on the low level portion, I told my Lt. WSO that I would not kill us by not doing my job – just to concentrate on what he had trained for and I would get us back if possible – that is if we survived the intense defenses - I had anticipated would meet us at the target!

I accelerated up to the carriage limit of the weapon in order to have the needed 600 KTAS at release – kinetic energy needed by the 4 GBU-10's to accurately hit the target. I knew that afterburner (AB) was not an option during the TOSS maneuver, and any energy I had at the start of the maneuver in Military power would be all I was going to have. Ahead of me I could see my lead's AB as he approached his TOSS pull up point. I watch as the ZSU-23-4's followed his climb, expecting at any time for them to wipe him out of the air. They missed! My turn was next!

Tripoli was lit up like New York City on a Friday evening and I knew we might be visible to the ground defenses. My impression of the target area was that everyone who owned a gun, sat at a SAM, or AAA site, were shooting up into the air, even if they did not see anything.

We went through the TOSS maneuver which included a 135 degree bank - pull back to the horizon and then a descent

back to TFR altitudes after weapons impact. The AAA was intense and I could see tracers all around my airplane. The city was now so lit up by lights and flares on parachutes that I disengaged the TFR system and started to hand-fly VFR between the taller buildings to avoid the AAA fire. As we rolled out of the TOSS recovery, my WSO shouted, "SAM right 5 o'clock!" I immediately made a 5-g turn, plus dispensed chaff to the left – 45 degrees off of the egress heading. I looked up and saw next to the canopy the rocket motor and fins of what proved to be a SA-8 SAM. It missed - but that was close!

Just then off to my left I saw an enormous explosion above the water, which looked like a napalm bomb igniting as its fuel rolled over the water, followed by a second huge explosion. Then it was dark….at which time I needed to turn back to the northerly egress heading. I knew we had lost friends…. but who was it? Initially I thought it was our number three since night time has a way of misrepresenting distances. I estimated the distance to the shore where the airplane blew up at around 5-6 miles.

The egress was executed as planned and fortunately we found our correct tanker, and got a needed top off of fuel. After all the F-111's had returned, we began a poll, to see who was missing. Initially it was 3 airplanes; but two of them were on the wrong radio frequency. Eventually that got sorted out. However, one was still gone – "who was it?" Probably, a heavy thought on everyone's mind. Two of our friends had paid the ultimate price for freedom that night.

An interesting note: Later, while reviewing the combat tapes, some general commented that our crews sounded so professional, it seemed like they were on an every-day range ride. F-111 crews were that good!

The sky was so clear – resplendent with stars – tranquil - so contrasting to the madness I had just witnessed. Around the tanker orbit on the wings of the KC-10 we flew and heard the radio call that no one wants to hear or will ever forget – "Karma 52, this is Red Crown on guard. If you read come up 243.0." We orbited for around 30 minutes as the lonely radio called out for our friends lost somewhere in the distance. Moments that will live in me and others forever. By now we all knew that "Nando" and Paul were missing, but unsure of their fate. I made a radio transmission to the command tanker and said that I saw them blow up over the water short of the target. The flight home was long and hard – only interrupted by other crews calling out HF frequencies to listen to the now global news of the attack; a view from the BBC's perspective.

Some years later Libya gave back Fernando's body at the request of the Pope. I was now based at Cannon AFB flying the F-111D. My Ops Officer came to me and said we are going to Puerto Rico for a missing man four ship fly by for Fernando's funeral. It was there that I learned from Bianca, Nando's wife, that the body was in indeed Fernando's and the cause of death was drowning. The only injuries that could be discovered were a bruised heel and punctured ear drum. What was surprising is the fact that based on the condition of the Fernando's body they must have ejected - Paul remained in the capsule and it sank. Fernando got free but perished in the gale wind driven seas.

Ever since the raid, I had always suspected that Nando and Paul were shot down by a SAM. Some thought he hit the water, but that could not have happen since his recovered body showed something different. I suspect to this day that he was hit by an SA-6 which would have been right according to what I saw when the airplane blew up. Several of the F-111's had dual Radar Altimeter failures (possibly due to the EF-111A jamming – in my nearly 17 years and 4650 hours in the F-111 I had seen dual Radar Altimeter failure only a few times) which would have made it necessary to hand fly at the 700' MEA – well within the lethal envelope of the SAM-6.

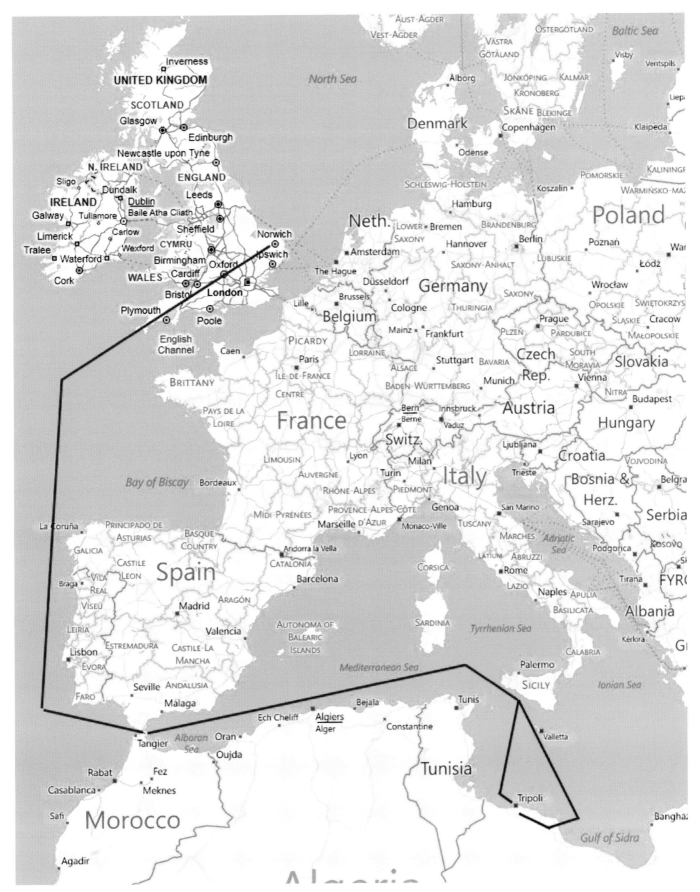

Figure 17: Libya Raid Route of Flight. *Courtesy of Lt Col Dick Brown and Bing.com/Maps.*

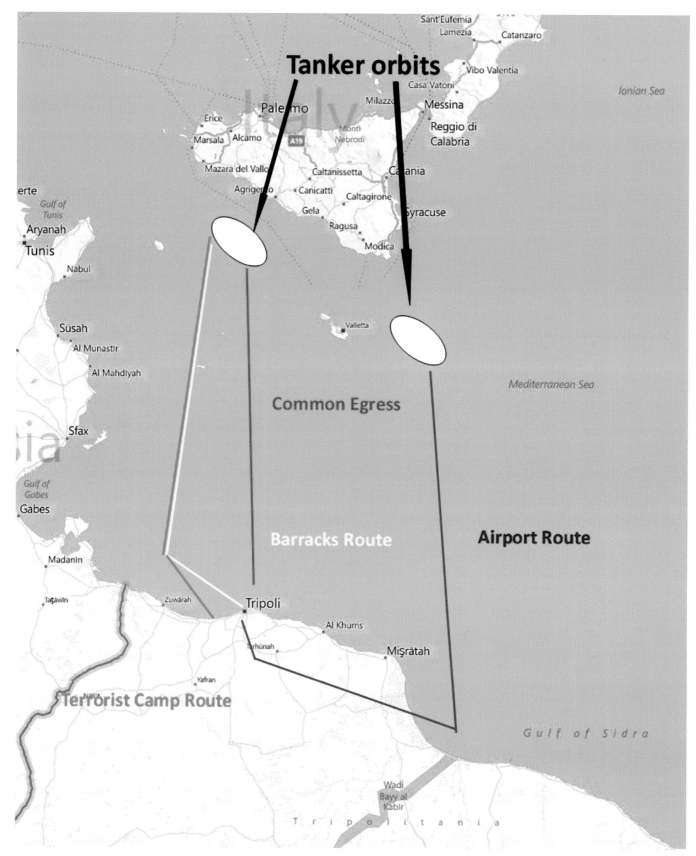

Figure 18: Attack Routes. *Courtesy of Lt Col Dick Brown and Bing.com/Maps*

Bab al Aziziya Compound

Murat Sidi Bilal Terrorist Camp

Tripoli Airfield

Tripoli Airfield. The Three Targets for the Libya Raid. *Courtesy of Lt Col Dick Brown and Google Earth*

What went wrong – some Four Star General decided to attach an additional five aircraft to the four already assigned to our target! We may have had a great plan for the suppression of the integrated air defenses going, but after several aircraft had flown the same attack heading, the defenses quickly figured that out. This was a known fact by the RHAW target tracking audio and visual confirmation by the trailing members of the 9 aircraft after the raid debrief. They had to literally fight their way through not only the AAA, but now the SAMs that were tracking them.

Some asked why we did not change the attack heading for those nine airplanes. It was simply too late in the game and the powers to be had already tasked five additional airplanes which had to be worked into the package - of which an additional tanker refueling requirement was needed. The addition of five more aircraft into the attack plan became a huge undertaking in terms of mission planning; remember, this was to be a 14-15 hour non-stop mission.

One last note – in my opinion the 48th TFW was probably the finest Fighter Wing that was ever formed in my 21 years in the Air Force. The Wing Commander, General Sam Westbrook is one of the finest and most capable leaders I ever had the privilege to serve under. His whole staff was outstanding. Every one of the Squadron Commanders were exceptional leaders and excellent F-111 pilots. My Commander, Remit 31 Alpha, who led the raid, was without a doubt one of the most skilled aviators I ever flew with; his leadership, inspiration, and love of his crews was unmatched. The only guy who could "whoop" him on the bombing range was me (Rooster I hope you see this!). The 48th TFW was indeed unique, a once only experience - in a moment of time – in a moment of history.

Dick "Downtown" Brown
F-111 A, D, E, F Fighter Pilot
6250 hours total and 4650 hours in the F-111

OPERATION "DESERT STORM"

66-0023 EF-111A Grumman Production Number A-17
Grumman Delivery Date: October 7, 1983

Combat Loss Scenario
EF-111A 66-0023, Call Sign Wrench 54

On February 14, 1991, EF-111A 66-0023 was flying a night operational combat sortie during week five of Operation Desert Storm. The aircraft crashed at high speed during the pull-up recovery from a diving descent. The mishap crew had initiated a defensive threat reaction maneuver to a perceived air-threat radar which could not be discriminated; Friend or Foe. The mishap occurred approximately 30 nautical miles northwest of Ar'ar, Saudi Arabia.

Findings

Though not verified officially by the USAF, the mishap EF-111A may have had an IFF (Identify Friend or Foe) discreet mode failure, or an incorrect mode reply when interrogated by a friendly fighter. Presumably, a USAF F-15E operating in Iraqi airspace had locked-onto and continuously tracked the EF-111A as a bogey – an unidentified / unfriendly aircraft. The mishap EF-111 crew responded as trained to the warning receiver's threat display and aural tones (potentially accompanied with a missile launch indication) by executing a defensive threat reaction. The mishap aircrew lost situational awareness with their height above terrain during the maneuver, and crashed. The subject defensive threat reaction maneuver flown by the mishap EF-111 pilot involved pointing the airplane in a steep dive toward the ground, lighting the afterburners, and relying on the TFR system to pull the aircraft out of the dive and level-off above the terrain.

The following written narrative was obtained by a Desert Storm EF-111 pilot:

> Capt Brandt had only been in-theater about a week or two before the accident, and was relatively new to the EF-111. Capt Paul Eichenlaub was an experienced IEWO. This was considered a typical crew setup, old head with a new guy. After a review of all available data, the USAF Accident Board determined the mishap aircraft had been locked-onto by an airborne radar, probably an F-15E. Unfortunately, the RWR in the EF did not discriminate between aircraft types, so all the mishap crew knew was that a new-generation fighter radar was tracking them. The crew entered a defensive maneuver, and descended rapidly, assuming worst case, an Iraqii F-1 or Mig-29 was on their tail. Unfortunately, the mishap crew lost situational awareness of their altitude and flew into the ground. Contributing factors could have included: they may have failed to set up the TFR correctly, or they descended too fast, exceeding the TFR's pull-up capability. It was sad, not only because they died, but somewhat needlessly, because the

66-0023 "Wrench 54" shown at Taif AB, Saudi Arabia during "Desert Storm."
Courtesy of Author's Collection via Denny Pyles.

66-0023 shown at Taif AB, Saudi Arabia (HAS Q-9) during 'Desert Storm."
Courtesy of Author's Collection via Denny Pyles.

Iraqi's had not flown any air combat sorties in the previous two weeks, and we had been briefed on it. (Lt Col. Walter Manwill, USAF, Retired).

Prior to this fatal crash, a Desert Shield deployed EF-111 Squadron Commander flying EF-111 67-0041 barely recovered from the dive while practicing the same threat reaction maneuver. The aircraft presumably clipped a tree top sustaining only superficial damage.

After the crash investigation of 66-0023 was completed, Higher Headquarters USAF ordered the immediate removal of the subject defensive threat reaction maneuver from the Multi-Command Manual (MCM) 3-1 Volume 12, (EF-111 Tactics).

Although the subject EF-111, 66-0023, crashed in Saudi Arabia, the Controlled Flight Into Terrain (CFIT) mishap has been officially attributed to combat operations.

Crew:

Pilot: Capt Douglas M. Brandt
WSO: Capt Paul R. Eichenlaub II
Call Sign: Wrench 54
Time of Incident: 2339 Z
Attached Unit: 48th TFW (P) Taif AB, Saudi Arabia for Operation Desert Storm
Assigned Unit: 42nd ECS / 20th TFW RAF Upper Heyford, UK / 390th ECS Crew
Accident Board President: Col Dean W Radueg
Aircraft Statistics: Unknown
Mishap Result: Aircraft Destroyed / Ejection may have been attempted; however it was well out of the envelope.

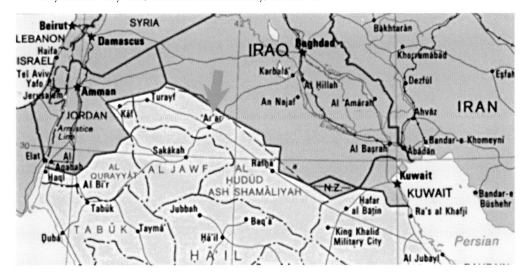

Figure 19:
Area where Wrench 54 went down is near Ar'ar Saudi Arabia, just south of the Iraq border. *Map by Lou Benoit. Courtesy of http://www.freerepublic.com.*

7

F-111D MISHAPS

F-111D 68-0160. *Courtesy of Gerry R Markgraf.*

Courtesy of Author's Collection.

68-0093
F-111D # 9 GD/FW Production Run # A6-09
USAF Delivery Date: January 26, 1972

Crash Scenario
On October 3, 1977, the mishap aircrew was scheduled as Number-2 in a two-ship night continuation training sortie. The pre-flight plan was to fly a low-level navigation route using terrain following radar (TFR) to enter TR-289 low-level route at point LIMA, exiting at Melrose Range, New Mexicao, for three (3) level radar deliveries. The scheduled takeoff at 1800L was delayed for maintenance. As a result, the mishap aircraft departed single ship at 1819L. Due to the delay, the crew changed the route of flight to enter TR-289 at point OSCAR. This placed the mishap aircraft back on time along the pre-planned route. IFR clearance was cancelled at 1840L for route entry. The mishap aircrew contacted Melrose Range at 1920L and read back the range altimeter of 30.25. Crazy 45 and mishap aircraft Crazy 46 worked the range as a flight, as planned. The mishap aircraft's first three range passes yielded scores of no-spot, 90 feet, and no-spot, respectively. A no-spot bomb score

indicates a bomb impact was not observed from the delivery aircraft, even though the range control officer cleared the delivery aircraft for a release. The mishap aircrew made a fourth pass, intending to release the two MK-106 inert high drag practice bombs still remaining in the SUU-20 practice bomb dispenser. The mishap aircraft passed over the target without dropping and the crew transmitted a request for one more pass. That was the last transmission heard. The mishap aircraft crashed at 1930L, six miles south of the nuclear target on the Melrose Range. The crash location was 26 NM from Cannon AFB, on the 234 degree radial, 12 NM west of Floyd, New Mexico.

Findings
The aircraft crashed on the downwind leg after the fifth Radar Lay Down (RLD) pass on the Melrose Bombing Range. The pilot's attention was misdirected to help the WSO solve a bomb release problem. The Terrain Following Radar (TFR) was paddled off, which disconnects the flight control system from the TFR pitch commands and inhibits fly-up protection. The aircraft entered an undetected and uncorrected descent to impact while both crew members were "heads down" and distracted with cockpit tasks. This was a Controlled Flight Into Terrain (CFIT) mishap.

Crew
Pilot: Capt Richard L Cardenas
WSO: 1Lt Steven G Nelson
Call Sign: Crazy 46
Accident Board President: Col Robert I McCann
Time of Incident: 1930 MDT
Assigned Unit: 524th TFTS / 27th TFW Cannon AFB, New Mexico
Aircraft Statistics: 301 Flights and 851.5 Flight Hours
Mishap Result: Fatal Crash / No Ejection Attempt

68-0095
F-111D # 11 GD/FW Production Run # A6-11
USAF Delivery Date: February 29, 1972

Crash Scenario
On February 26, 1976, the mishap aircrew was scheduled for an Instructor Weapons System Operator (IWSO) upgrade sortie. The preflight, engine start, taxi, and before takeoff checks were normal. Takeoff was on time at 1015L from Cannon AFB, New Mexico. The flight progressed normally until approximately 1248L, when the pilot made a transmission that he had a wheel well hot light, followed by a left engine fire light. The crew accomplished bold face emergency procedures but the light remained on. At 1257L the pilot made a radio call that his utility hydraulic pressure was zero. Attempts to lower the landing gear by emergency means were unsuccessful. While preparations were being made for an approach end barrier engagement, a chase aircraft observed smoke and fire in the wheel well area of the mishap aircraft. A successful approach-end barrier engagement on Runway 21 was accomplished at 1319L. Both crew members egressed the aircraft without injury. Pre- and post-crash fire damage was limited to the left main wheel well and cross-over areas between the engines.

Courtesy of C. Ray Reed Collection.

Capt Victor G. Grahn
481st TFTS/17th TFW
Cannon AFB, NM

Lt Col Clarence R. Reed
481st TFTS/17th TFW
Cannon AFB, NM

Courtesy of C. Ray Reed Collection.

Findings
Cyclical chafing between a wire and an exposed hydraulic line resulted in a hydraulic leak, which depleted the Utility Hydraulic system. Electrical arcing present between the errant wire and the leaking hydraulic line ignited and sustained a major fire in the main wheel well. The crew accomplished a wheels-up landing and cable arrestment, which brought the aircraft to a stop. Post crash fire damage was significant; however, the aircraft was rebuilt and remained in active service until retired in June 1992. The WSO wrote a personal recounting of the mishap which has been posted on the following page.

Crew
Pilot: Capt Victor G Grahn
WSO: Lt Col Clarence R Reed
Call Sign: Dryly 62
Accident Board President: Col Jerry W Tietge
Time of Incident: 1319 Local
Assigned Unit: 481st TFTS / 27th TFW Cannon AFB, New Mexico
Aircraft Statistics: 4,388 flight hours
Mishap Result: Major Structural Damage requiring repair at GDFW

A Tail Number I'll Never Forget
by C. Ray Reed

We got to Cimarron as planned and started the first unusual attitude recovery, when the wheel well hot light came on. Vic leveled out the plane and we immediately got a left engine fire light. Whatever happened to the perfect day and the perfect airplane? It's amazing how fast things happen and how fast things can get done. In less than 30 seconds, we went from a safe airplane to a single engine, an engine fire (light still on), a wheel-well hot light and declaring an inflight emergency. Oh, and our voices were at least one octave higher. I didn't have enough fingers for the emergency procedures checklist.

Now a couple decisions had to be made. With single engine, we had to use afterburner to maintain altitude and even though we were above bingo fuel, we wouldn't make it to Cannon AFB if we put the gear down as the wheel well hot light check list called for. Alternates were just as far away as Cannon, so we left the gear up. We were still flying and under control and the cockpit felt like a real safe place. The idea of ejection crossed our minds, but we put that aside for a while.

As we approached Cannon, another F-111 joined up with us. They could see smoke. No surprise. We started to configure for landing and guess what, the gear wouldn't come down. We tried to blow it down, no luck. We blew the flaps and slats down. Next was the tail hook and it came down. They were foaming the runway as we made our first pass to try to shake the gear down, but no luck. Our wingman requested to move over to the left side as he was seeing the rudder kick. He didn't want to be in our way if we suddenly made a roll to the right. Things were getting a little exciting. When he got crossed over, he said he could see flames and that things were falling off the airplane. If we were to eject, now was the time. The next downwind would head us toward Clovis instead of the wide-open spaces. The cockpit was still feeling safe even though we had 17 red and yellow lights on; including the engine fire light and 3 out of 4 hydraulic systems had failed. You don't fly this bird without hydraulics. We decided to go ahead and land. I rechecked my straps and made them as tight as possible and stored everything possible. It's getting close to one choice, but we still had two--eject or land. We came around, but the foam trucks were still on the runway. Vic told them to get out of the way as we made a 360 for our third approach. As we turned northwest, we discussed one more time-- eject or land.

Let's land. We rolled out on final and we were ready to land. Suddenly, the aircraft pitched over. Let me tell you how wide the runway looks. Vic pulled the stick full aft and went full afterburner on he right engine. Can you believe it, the plane leveled out and we

68-0095 shortly before touchdown with the tail hook extended. Clearly visible are the flames exiting the wheel well. The graining snapshot was clipped from the photographer's home movie camera. *F-111 Video Courtesy of Author's Collection via Bob Patusek.*

Fire Damaged Main Landing Gear Wheel Well Looking Aft. *Courtesy of GDFW.*

started dragging the tail hook. It drug over 200 ft. before it engaged the barrier and we settled into the foam. You know what, it was one of the more smooth landings I'd had. Ha! Anyway, we slid about 1200 ft. and the foam ended at about 1000 ft. It got real noisy toward the end of the slide. I opened the canopy, unhooked myself and jumped over the side to the runway. You wouldn't believe how close to the ground the cockpit sits with no wheels. I ran out front for a short distance and looked back to see Vic still sitting on the canopy rail. He was making it, so I started running again. What a flight!

Yes, 095 brought us back and all of us got to fly again, including 095. I think the base temporarily closed down, because there were people everywhere, watching this landing unfold. What a memory maker. The accident board determined that there were maybe 30 seconds of flying time left before the last hydraulic pump would have failed. We wouldn't have been able to make another approach. I'm truly glad we didn't have to eject.

SIGNED: C. Ray Reed
A happily retired Navigator / WSO

68-0098
F-111D # 14 GD/FW Production Run # A6-14
USAF Delivery Date: April 26, 1972

Crash Scenario
On June 8, 1988, the mishap aircraft was Number-1 of a three-ship scheduled for a practice flight lead upgrade sortie. The mishap sortie was scheduled for night aerial refueling in AR-602 track, and a TFR low-level routing with a simulated enroute target on the IR-113 low-level route. The crew was to enter and practice Radar Lay-Down (RLD) and fixed angle deliveries on the Melrose Bombing Range in New Mexico. The mishap flight took off three minutes late and flew to the refueling track. Aerial refueling operations were uneventful. The flight of three flew IR-113 and entered the range from the south. Subsequent passes were flown from north to south in the standard night pattern. The mishap crew went through dry on the second pass, but

Courtesy of Douglas E. Slowiak/Vortex Photo-Graphics.

no reason was given. On the third pass the mishap crew called "final RLD," followed by "make that a fixed angle." Shortly thereafter, the Range Control Officer (RCO) made a "Pull Up, Pull Up, Pull Up" call on the UHF guard frequency. The aircraft crashed 1300 feet right of the run-in line, and 11,000 feet from Melrose target T-20. Crash impact point was 25 NM west of Cannon AFB, New Mexico, at coordinates (N 34 20 00 / W 103 48 50).

Courtesy of Dave Meehan via Don Logan Collection

68-0099
F-111D # 15 GD/FW Production Run # A6-15
USAF Delivery Date: April 14, 1972

Mishap Scenario
On February 10, 1976, the mishap aircraft was scheduled as Number-2 in a two-ship, day, low-level ground attack and air refueling training mission. Preflight, engine start, and taxi checks all appeared normal. No discrepancies were noted by the aircrew or maintenance prior to their late, single ship takeoff at 0815 MST from Cannon AFB, New Mexico. The flight rejoined at 0850 MST and entered Melrose Bombing Range at 0925. Due to the lead aircraft's radar malfunctioning, both aircraft were to delete the radar events and go directly into the dive bombing events from a spacer pass. As the mishap aircraft pulled up to downwind, the right engine FIRE warning lamp illuminated for about a second and then went out. Fire circuitry tested normal. The crew decided to abort the mission and return directly to Cannon AFB. No indications of fire or heat were present until 85 to 100 seconds after the first fire indication, when the right engine FIRE warning lamp came on steady. The right engine was shut off with the throttle, at which time the fire warning lamp went out. The crew continued with the emergency procedural steps and depressed the fire push-button, discharging the fire extinguishing agent. The flight rejoined and returned to base for an uneventful single engine landing.

Findings
Investigation revealed the 16th stage bleed air duct failed at a weld joint in the duct-to-flange mating area. The rupture resulted in vented high pressure, high velocity, and high temperature engine bleed air directly against the heat shield and caused the fire detection system to activate. The heat shield in the immediate vicinity failed due to impact damage from the ruptured duct, allowing hot bleed air to escape through the hole. The slower hot air flow between the heat shield and the engine resulted in the fire detection system deactivating after a few seconds. Hot bleed air continued to flow between the heat shields and the bonded panels, deforming the heat shields inward and buckling the bonded panels, eventually insulating the fire sensing element from the hot bleed air. The aircraft sustained substantial heat damage requiring major repairs.

Crew
Pilot: Capt Jay D Milstead
WSO: Capt James R Hussey
Call Sign: Maggy 68
Accident Board President: Col Bradley C Hosmer
Time of Incident: 0930 MST
Assigned Unit: 523rd TFS / 27th TFW Cannon AFB, New Mexico
Aircraft Statistics: Unknown
Mishap Result: Aircraft suffered major fire damage and was repaired at Cannon AFB, New Mexico by a Depot Field Team

Findings
The mishap flight crew made their first pass from 600 feet AGL and then transitioned to the opposite pattern. On the second pass, the mishap pilot climbed to the MEA and called "Off Dry," meaning no bomb was dropped. On the third and final pass, the aircraft descended below the minimum altitude of 400 feet, skip hit, and then impacted a few hundred yards further down range and disintegrated. The investigation determined the TFR was not engaged and the pilot was hand-flying the aircraft at the time of the accident. A cockpit distraction, absence of terrain clearance protection, and failure to monitor altitude during the bomb run resulted in an undetected slow descent to terrain impact. Additionally, the crew violated command directives for operation on the range at night time. In no circumstances was hand flying below MEA or manual TFR approved at night. The cause of the mishap was controlled flight into terrain (CFIT) due to the pilot not employing the TFR system while operating at low altitude at night. An ejection was not attempted.

Crew
Pilot: Capt Glenn E Troster
WSO: Capt Michael A Barritt
Call Sign: Cubid 12
Accident Board President: Col William S Hinton Jr.
Time of Incident: 2137 MDT
Assigned Unit: 523rd TFS / 27th TFW Cannon AFB, New Mexico
Aircraft Statistics: 1,547 Flights and 3,663.3 Flight Hours
Mishap Result: Aircraft Destroyed / Fatal Crash / No Ejection Attempted

68-0105
F-111D # 21 GD/FW Production Run # A6-21
USAF Delivery Date: May 18, 1972

68-0158
F-111D # 74 GD/FW Production Run # A6-7
USAF Delivery Date: December 18, 1972

Crash Scenario
On March 20, 1973 the mishap aircraft, "Bert 73" 68-0105 and "Bert 74" 68-0158, were scheduled for a two-ship night training sortie. The flight crew of 68-0105 was the designated lead aircraft for the mission. The aircraft were to takeoff at 1900L, conduct aerial refuel in AR602 at 1945L, and then proceed for radar bomb delivery training at the Holbrook, Arizona, RBS site (TOT 2115-2200L). Both aircraft were to fly a night TFR low-level, but due to bad weather, an alternate route was flown to the Holbrook Range at standard IFR altitudes. The mishap aircraft "Bert 73" departed Cannon AFB, New Mexico, at 1910L, with #2 "Bert 74" 30 seconds later. A rejoin was accomplished on the standard instrument departure routing. The flight then proceeded via its flight planned route to the air refueling initial point for the refueling area (AR-602). Air refueling was accomplished without event, and the flight entered the alternate route structure at Tuba City VORTAC. The flight proceeded to the Holbrook RBS Range initial point (IP) at 8000ft MSL. Prior to flight contacting the Holbrook Range controller a lead change was accomplished, with "Bert 74" flying 68-0158, now in the lead. Upon reaching the IP at 2113L, "Bert 74" stated that he intended to make a synchronous delivery on the target. Delivery altitude would be 3000 feet AGL (8000 MSL), with no electronic warfare activity to be exercised. After transmitting post release information, "Bert 74" stated that "Bert 73" 68-0105 would not be making an RBS bomb run due to a failure of his attack radar set. "Bert 74" also informed the range controller that the flight would be orbiting the target area after the RBS attack for a VFR rejoin. Shortly thereafter, "Bert 73" stated that he was one mile in trail of "Bert 74." The Holbrook RBS radar controller noted that "Bert 73" was approximately

Bert 73, 68-0105. *Courtesy of Author's Collection.*

Bert 74, 68-0158. *Courtesy of Author's Collection.*

800 to 1000 yards behind "Bert 74." "Bert 74" made an uneventful bomb run on the target at 2119L release time. He was immediately cleared off the bomb run heading, but maintained this heading (157 degrees magnetic) at 495 KTAS for approximately one minute. After initiating a left turn, a 26 degree wing sweep call was given by "Bert 74." "Bert 73" acknowledged with a "Tally Ho" on "Bert 74," and was advised that Bert 74 would be holding 350 KTS. The rejoin was continued until Bert 73 collided with Bert 74 at approximately 2123L. An explosion was observed at collision, and although both crew modules separated from their respective aircraft, both ejections were unsuccessful.

Crew	68-0105	68-0158
Pilot:	Maj Richard Leon Brehm	Maj William Warren Gude
WSO:	Capt William Ty Halloran	Capt David Carl Blackledge
Call Sign:	Bert 73	Bert 74

Accident Board President: Col Wilford E. Deming, III

Time of Incident: 2123 Local

Assigned Unit: 4427 TFRS / 27th TFW Cannon AFB, New Mexico

Aircraft Statistics:	53 Flights and 142.7 Flight Hours	24 Flights and 68.1 Flight Hours
Mishap Result:	Aircraft Destroyed / Fatal Crash / Unsuccessful Ejection Attempt	Aircraft Destroyed / Fatal Crash/ Unsuccessful Ejection Attempt

Left Wing of Bert "73"–68-105

1). Aerial View of Crash Site. 2). Bert 73's left wing with Bert 74's left engine tail feather embedded; the initial point of impact. 3). Bert 74's Capsule and entangled Main Recovery Parachute. All photos *courtesy of Author's Collection.*

Findings

Although Bert 73 was the designated lead aircraft for the night RBS mission, a failure of his Attack Radar Set (ARS) necessitated a lead change at some point prior to reaching the Initial Point (IP) for the RBS target. Normal night RBS procedures for a flight of two F-111 aircraft with all systems operating calls for the Number Two aircraft to hold IFR at the entry point and establish 12 minute separation, or 96 miles apart, assuming 480 knot speed. Each aircraft then continues individually along the IFR route to the target on a separate clearance. If a rejoin is to be made coming off the target, the first aircraft will hold at the exit point under Air Traffic Control (ATC), awaiting the Number Two aircraft. If no rejoin is made, each aircraft will return to base separately under ATC control.

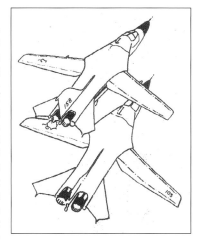

Figure 1: Initial impact with approximately 50 knots overtake.

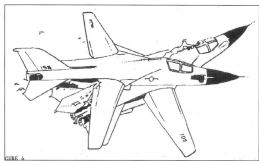

Figure 2: Resultant left yaw and cross-over. *Drawings Courtesy of USAF Mishap Report.*

If a flight intends to depart the IFR Low Level Route as a formation, the normal procedure is to remain in close formation throughout the entire route. Upon entering the RBS range, Bert 73 had not yet achieved the required minimum separation of greater than 1NM to be considered "non-standard" formation, and was not on a separate clearance to operate on the range as a single ship. Bert 73 then attempted a rejoin, contrary to standard operating procedures. While Bert 74 had turned to a heading of 336 degrees, on an approximate downwind leg to the target, Bert 73 continued to rejoin and close on Bert 74 with too much overtake airspeed, insufficient visual reference, and/or inadequate vertical and lateral separation. All factors combined to a moment and a position from which a collision was unavoidable.

Bert 73's left wing collided with Bert 74's left engine nozzle from slightly below. The overtake airspeed and yaw induced motion of the collision which pulled Bert 73 upward while moving forward and yawing left. It appears that both mishap aircraft crews initiated ejection almost simultaneously. Unfortunately, through ejection module sequencing and collision dynamics, both module descent parachutes failed to deploy due to collision damage and entanglement. It could not be fully determined whether Bert 73 actually attempted module ejection, or whether the module separated from the aircraft during the collision. It was determined that Bert 73's recovery parachute had been torn from the module during the impact sequence followed by module separation. Author's Note: both instructor pilots for the two mishap aircraft reported for duty 11.5 hours prior to the mishap. Though this was not discussed in the mishap report narrative, crew fatigue was present, and possibly contributory in the mishap sequence of events.

68-0109
F-111D # 25 GD/FW Production Run # A6-25
USAF Delivery Date: June 8, 1972

Crash Scenario

On February 16, 1979, the mishap aircraft was originally scheduled as Number-2 for a two-ship night low-level training mission, but due to a crew change with the lead aircraft, the scheduled sortie was changed to a single ship mission. The flight plan was to fly low-level and enter IR-111 at alternate entry point "O," then proceed to the Melrose Range, New Mexico. Takeoff was normal, and entry into IR-111 at alternate point "O" was uneventful. After contacting Melrose Range, the mishap aircraft was cleared onto the range and given an altimeter setting of 30.19. In addition, the crew was advised that clearance to drop would not be given until the range control officer had them in visual contact. The Range Officer confirmed visual contact when the mishap aircraft was approximately 8NM north of the target and cleared them hot (permission to release ordnance) for a low toss delivery. The mishap aircrew had a good release on the delivery, and the bomb score was 118 meters at 2 o'clock. During the recovery from the toss delivery, the aircraft departed controlled flight and the crew initiated a successful ejection. The aircraft crashed 2 ½ NM from the target on a bearing of 334 degrees. The crew module landed 1530 feet from the aircraft at 1930L, and came to a rest in a near inverted attitude. The crash coordinates were (N 34 20 50 / W 103 48 50), which are 25NM west of Cannon AFB, New Mexico, on the 253 Degree Radial, 15 miles west of Melrose, New Mexico.

Findings

The mishap crew lost control of the aircraft after a low altitude toss weapons delivery maneuver. The pilot used a low-toss recovery technique which resulted in excessive loss of airspeed and excessive angle of attack, thus leading to a subsequent stall and departure from controlled flight. During the toss recovery, the pilot's finger slipped off the Autopilot override switch. The TFR commanded a fly-up because the aircraft's roll attitude had exceeded the TFR limits. While inverted, the Fly-Up is actually a Pull-Down. The mishap pilot executed a loaded roll reversal to recover, exceeding both AOA and yaw stability limits of the aircraft and contributing to the departure from controlled flight. The Autopilot override switch was later modified to a longer curved handle, eliminating the problem. Understandably, at night, at unusual attitudes, with absence of a horizon and spatial disorientation, all could easily influence a pilot to apply abrupt pitch and roll inputs (loaded roll) in an attempt to recover the aircraft to a recognizable attitude. *(Continued on following page.)*

Crew
Pilot: Capt Michael E Damitz
WSO: Capt Randall C Lambirth
Call Sign: Best 16
Accident Board President: Col Eddy J Doerschlen
Time of Incident: 1930 MST
Assigned Unit: 522nd TFS / 27th TFW Cannon AFB, New Mexico
Aircraft Statistics: 394 Flights and 1,085.5 Flight Hours
Mishap Result: Aircraft Destroyed / Successful Ejection

Courtesy of Author's Collection.

Input by an experienced former F-111 pilot, Capt Brad Insley:

I do remember the 68-0109 crash as Mike Damitz is a good friend. Mike was on a night toss mission because he was running out of night toss currency. He had to fly a night to sortie or he would have to fly with an IP to get recurrent, and the Squadron didn't want to do that. Currency was 180 days at the time but after this accident it was changed to 90 days I believe. The weather was about 200 foot overcast so they were doing the maneuver at night and in the weather. Mike was new to the F-111; he had very small hands which played a part in the mishap. At the time the paddle switch for the TFR was a small short paddle. Pilots with smaller hands had a hard time grasping the paddle switch and their fingers could come off of during the maneuver. The night toss required you to run in on TFR until the pull-up light came on, then paddle off the TFR with your little finger on the short paddle switch and make a 4g wings level pull until bomb release, and then roll 135 degrees (right roll at Melrose) until 135 degrees of turn then roll wings level. After leveling the wings, you would release the paddle switch to return to the TFR low-level for escape. If you slipped off the paddle switch during the maneuver the aircraft would try to fly-up because you have exceeded the TFR limits and in 135 degree bank this would be a downward trajectory. I have small hands and my little finger slipped off the paddle switch all the time. You could override if you knew what was happening. They changed the paddle switch after this to a long curved switch.

The old style paddle switch (Figure 3, labeled 6) was initially very short. The pilot's finger could easily slip off while continuing to maneuver the aircraft and simultaneously attempting to override the TFR. The new "extended" paddle switch depicted in the photograph solved the problem.

Figure 3:
Old Style F-111A Control Stick Grip. Courtesy of 1F-111A Dash-1 Pilot's Manual.

New Style Control Stick Grip. *Photograph Courtesy of Lt Col Dick Brown.*

68-0110
F-111D # 26 GD/FW Production Run # A6-26
USAF Delivery Date: June 9, 1972

Crash Scenario
On January 27, 1982, the mishap aircraft was scheduled for a Functional Check Flight (FCF) following scheduled Depot Maintenance. The mishap aircraft departed McClellan AFB, California, at 0945 PST. After initial climb from an intermediate level-off on departure, the mishap crew heard a loud boom. The aircraft shuddered and the following caution lights illuminated: Right Bleed Duct Fail, Right Primary Hydraulic, Right Utility Hydraulic, and Right Generator. The aircrew performed emergency procedures for engine bleed duct failure (Right Throttle Idle / Air Source Selector Knob to EMER). While performing those steps, the right engine FIRE light illuminated and the emergency procedures (Right Throttle Off / Right Fire Pushbutton Depress / Agent Discharge Switch Up) were accomplished. During a left turn back to base, the wing sweep indicator went from 26 to 72 degrees. The tail hook down light also illuminated. The aircraft began to exhibit increasing right adverse yaw, which was controllable with left stick deflection. Eventually, full left stick and right rudder pedal deflection from either seat had no effect on the aircraft. At this time, the crew realized they had experienced a hard-over rudder and would have to eject. Ejection was successful, and the aircraft crashed and was destroyed. The crash coordinates were 5 NM west-southwest of Woodland, California, in Yolo County (N 38 38 00 / W 121 55 21.7).

Findings
Investigation revealed a pin in the right engine Number 5 combustion chamber was missing, allowing the combustion chamber to shift aft and down relative to the fuel nozzle, disrupting the flame pattern. The abnormal flame pattern created a hot spot that eventually burned through the combustion chamber wall. Escaping hot gases also burned through the chamber inner case and into the Number 4- and 5- bearing scavenge pump area, igniting the lubricating oil. The fire subsequently burned through the diffuser fan duct, engine bay titanium shield and insulation, and the right saddle tank floor, causing the fuel tank to explode. Flames engulfed the aft fuselage and were drawn into the aft centerbody due to the reverse flow phenomena, burning through the rudder push rod and resulting in a hard-over rudder. The fire damage caused loss of hydraulic pressure and loss of flight control.

Crew
Pilot: Capt Jack V Leslie
WSO: Maj Theodore S Sienicki
Call Sign: Unknown
Accident Board President: Col Robert I McCann
Time of Incident: 0953 PST
Assigned Unit: Flight Test / Sacramento Air Logistics Center McClellan AFB, California
Aircraft Statistics: 574 Flights and 1,454.8 Flight Hours
Mishap Result: Aircraft Destroyed /Successful Ejection

Courtesy of Douglas E. Slowiak/ Vortex Photo-Graphics.

68-0113
F-111D # 29 GD/FW Production Run # A6-29
USAF Delivery Date: June 23, 1972

Crash Scenario
On December 21, 1973, the mishap aircraft was scheduled for a training sortie to the Melrose Bombing Range, New Mexico, via the Truth or Consequences VFR Hi-Speed low-level route 289. Low level and TFR were to be utilized with a range time of 1845-1900L. Pre-flight and right engine start was normal, however, the crew experienced slow start-up acceleration on the left engine. Corrective procedures were applied and the engine accelerated normally thereafter. The mishap crew experienced several other minor problems after engine start which required corrective actions prior to departure. Both TFRs would not pass ground checks, as evidenced by ground personnel overhearing aircrew conversation over the interphone. After these delays the mishap aircrew taxied and made a normal takeoff from Cannon AFB, New Mexico, via the Santa Rosa 3 Standard Instrument Departure. Due to the late takeoff, the crew deleted two legs of the planned route and proceeded directly to the bombing range to meet

Courtesy of Author's Collection.

the scheduled range time. The on-range location of the mishap aircraft was established with the Melrose Range Control Officer as the mishap crew departed the initial point (IP) at approximately 1852L (night time conditions). The Range Officer visually sighted the mishap aircraft's lights and issued range clearance onto the range. At 1853, the mishap aircraft crashed 10 NM west of Melrose, New Mexico, and approximately 10 NM north of the Nuclear Target. A fireball was observed at impact. Although the crew module separated from the aircraft, the ejection was unsuccessful.

Findings
Investigation found the Low Altitude Radar Altimeter (LARA) was inoperative during preflight. The mishap investigation team found the TFR was also in standby, and not in a terrain avoidance mode. The TFR would not have worked with a failed LARA; therefore, the crew placed the TFR in STBY and attempted to complete the mission by flying the night range pattern at or above the MEA. The mishap aircraft was traveling in a southwesterly direction when it struck the ground at a shallow angle and skipped. The aircraft grazed the ground, leaving marks gouged into the ground from the aft fuselage strakes several hundred feet short of the initial hard ground impact point. The aircrew attempted an ejection shortly after the hard impact; however, the initial crash forces resulted in

significant damage to the module. The module ejection was in the high speed mode at 406 KTAS indicated. The capsule's main recovery parachute became entangled with the stabilization brake chute and the ejection was unsuccessful. Investigation also determined the crew was unaware that the point of impact was 138 feet higher than the Melrose range target elevation. In addition, the crew failed to obtain the range altimeter setting, an error which placed the mishap aircraft 170 feet lower than their cockpit altimeter indication. The cause of the mishap was controlled flight into terrain (CFIT) due to inoperative / non-use of terrain avoidance equipment and failure of the mishap crew to fly at the correct minimum terrain clearance altitudes.

Crew
Pilot: Capt William K Delaplane III
WSO: 1Lt Robert J Kierce
Call Sign: Age 39
Accident Board President: Col Thomas E Wolters
Time of Incident: 1853L
Assigned Unit: 523rd TFS / 27th TFW Cannon AFB, New Mexico
Aircraft Statistics: 93 Flights with 256.7 Flight Hours
Mishap Result: Aircraft Destroyed / Fatal Crash Unsuccessful Ejection

Portion of Aft fuselage. *Courtesy of GDFW Mishap Files.*

68-0119
F-111D # 35 GD/FW Production Run # A6-35
USAF Delivery Date: August 31, 1972

Courtesy of Author's Collection.

Crash Scenario

On February 6, 1980, the mishap aircraft, F-111D 68-0119, was established on a straight-in final approach to Cannon AFB after completing its assigned mission. The F-111D was descending on the approach with only the speed brake extended. While flying over Ned Houk Park (5.5 NM north of Clovis, New Mexico), the mishap aircraft collided in midair with a civilian Cessna 206 Stationair II (Serial # N7393N) at 1026L. The weather at the time of the collision was clear, with 30 miles visibility. The Cessna had departed Alameda Airport in Albuquerque, New Mexico, and then made a brief enroute refueling stop in Tucumcari, New Mexico, before returning to its home location at the Clovis Municipal Airport. The collision occurred at 5800' MSL, killing both occupants in the Cessna instantly. The Cessna's left wing impacted the right underside of the F-111 between the right wing external bomb rack and the right engine nacelle. The F-111D crew initiated ejection at 1300' AGL in 95 degrees of right bank and 32 degrees nose low at 300 knots. The escape module requires approximately 2000 feet altitude, at these parameters, to function correctly. As a result, the main recovery parachute was considered a streamer when the capsule hit the ground.

Findings

The National Transportation Safety Board (NTSB), report number NTSB-AAR-82-10, determined the probable cause of the accident to be failure of both aircraft to request radar traffic advisories, and the failure of the Radar Approach Control (RAPCON) controllers to observe the Cessna radar target and to issue traffic advisories to the F-111D. The NTSB report faulted the F-111D crew for not "seeing and avoiding" the Cessna. The NTSB report correctly details the WSO was heads down, monitoring the aircraft's radar display for the correct runway alignment, and the F-111 pilot had little or no opportunity to see the approaching Cessna while monitoring his instruments. A student controller and an experienced senior controller working the arrival position in RAPCON had just received a handoff from Albuquerque Center and cleared the mishap F-111 for the approach when the midair collision took place. The Cannon AFB RAPCON controllers did not observe the Cessna as a radar track, nor did a transponder signal from the civilian aircraft (VFR Squawk code 1200) display on the radar screen. The NTSB went through great lengths in a detailed report to use Federal Aviation Regulations (FARs) and Airmen's Information Manual (AIM) procedures to be more critical of the USAF responsibilities for the accident than those of the civilian pilot. Of note, the Cessna was on a VFR flight plan to land at the Clovis Municipal Airport, and the pilot should have become familiar with the arrival flight path of the nearby military base. However, the civilian pilot flew directly through the Cannon AFB arrival corridor without communicating with RAPCON. The Cessna pilot did not make radio contact with the RAPCON controller. As the NTSB report stated, "he was not required to do so." In actuality, the well written and detailed NTSB report missed the big picture: the coveted "See and Avoid" Rules and Procedures can never stop an impromptu meeting between bad luck, the law of averages, and an aberrant failure of the Big-Sky-Theory. Author's Definition of "The Big-Sky-Theory": *In flying – the probability of two aircraft unintentionally occupying the exact same piece of sky simultaneously – is remote; therefore flying an aircraft is inherently safe.*

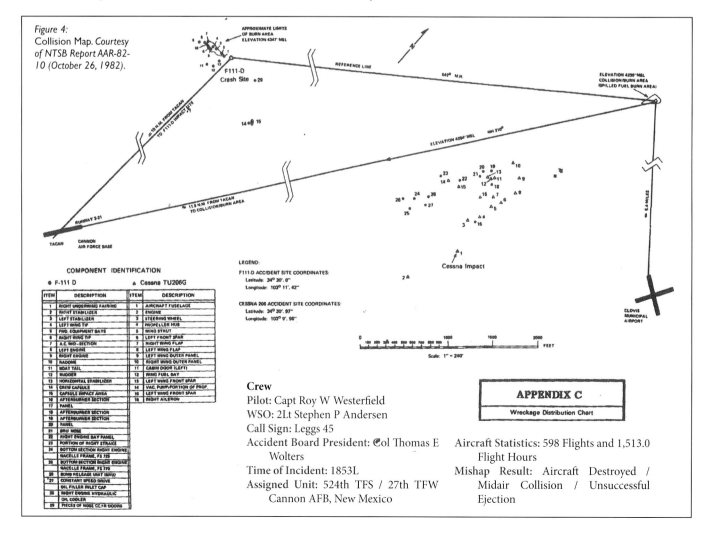

Figure 4: Collision Map. *Courtesy of NTSB Report AAR-82-10 (October 26, 1982).*

Crew
Pilot: Capt Roy W Westerfield
WSO: 2Lt Stephen P Andersen
Call Sign: Leggs 45
Accident Board President: Col Thomas E Wolters
Time of Incident: 1853L
Assigned Unit: 524th TFS / 27th TFW Cannon AFB, New Mexico

Aircraft Statistics: 598 Flights and 1,513.0 Flight Hours
Mishap Result: Aircraft Destroyed / Midair Collision / Unsuccessful Ejection

68-0125
F-111D # 41 GD/FW Production Run # A6-41
USAF Delivery Date: September 18, 1972

Courtesy of Brian C. Rogers.

Crash Scenario
On September 11, 1987, the mishap aircraft departed Cannon AFB, New Mexico, as a single-ship initial qualification check for the Weapons System Officer (WSO). The mission consisted of terrain following and visual low-level, range bombing events and instrument recovery in visual meteorological conditions. The mishap occurred during an actual single engine approach. One of the mishap aircraft's engines had been shut down in accordance with checklist procedures to prevent further damage due to a minor malfunction. While on the visual approach to land the remaining operating engine failed as well. The aircrew ejected, and the aircraft crashed 1.57 NM short of Cannon AFB Runway 22 in an open field at 1408 MDT. The ejection sequence functioned normally and the crew egressed without injury.

Findings
The mishap aircraft was on a straight-in final for Runway 22 with one engine shutdown when the operating engine rolled back to sub-idle. A rapid loss of flying airspeed ensued, accompanied by a developing sink rate.

The F-111 in a landing configuration, flaps and slats down, exhibited a stall characteristic, whereby increasing the Angle-of-Attack (AOA) (aft stick movement to climb or level off) does not increase lift and transition to a climb or, while descending, decrease the rate of descent. Rather, pulling back on the stick drives the aircraft deeper into the stall with a subsequent rapid loss of airspeed.

Due to the low altitude and loss of flight sustaining thrust, the pilot was unable to maintain a stabilized glidepath or arrest an increasing rate of descent. The mishap crew ejected when loss of hydraulic pressure resulted in loss of aircraft control. The mishap aircraft crashed and was destroyed. The capsule bounced after initial contact with the ground and came to rest in an upright position.

Crew
Pilot: Maj John W Sides
WSO: Maj Russell C Stricker
Call Sign: Captor 74
Accident Board President: Col Edward L Chase
Time of Incident: 1408:21 MDT
Assigned Unit: 524th TFS / 27th TFW Cannon AFB, New Mexico
Aircraft Statistics: 1,444 Flights and 3,494.2 Flight Hours
Mishap Result: Aircraft Destroyed / Successful ejection

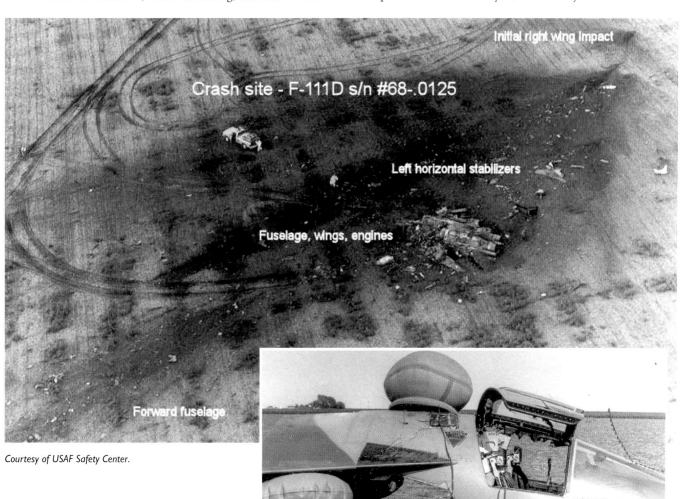

Initial right wing impact

Crash site - F-111D s/n #68-.0125

Left horizontal stabilizers

Fuselage, wings, engines

Forward fuselage

Courtesy of USAF Safety Center.

Courtesy of USAF Safety Center.

68-0127
F-111D # 43 GD/FW Production Run # A6-43
USAF Delivery Date: September 21, 1972

Crash Scenario

On July 7, 1981, the mishap aircrew was flying a night syllabus training mission which included night low-level navigation training on low-level route IR-113, weapons delivery training on Melrose Range, formation practice, and single-ship approaches and landings at Cannon AFB, New Mexico. The mission was uneventful until the mishap aircraft was established on a Precision Approach Radar (PAR) arrival to a touch-and-go on Runway 21 at Cannon AFB. At approximately 5.5 Nautical Miles (NM) from touchdown, the aircrew transmitted to the PAR controller that they had a Wheel Well Hot Caution lamp illuminated and were declaring an emergency. At approximately 2.5 NM from touchdown, the aircrew transmitted that the aircraft was on fire and they would make an approach end barrier engagement. The aircraft made a successful engagement. The aircrew egressed without injury following a rollback of 65 feet due to arrestment cable tensioning. After the tension of the arrestment cable went slack, the cable fell off the aircraft's arrestment hook and the mishap aircraft began rolling without the aircrew and exited the left side of the runway. The aircraft rotated left 225 degrees, heading 345 degrees. Emergency response arrived and extinguished the fire.

Courtesy of Author's Collection.

Findings

The cause was the result of cyclical chafing between a wire bundle and a hydraulic line, eventually creating a small hole and subsequent leak in the hydraulic line. The atomized high pressure hydraulic fluid exiting the hole was ignited by arcing between the chafed electrical wires. The resulting wheel well fire was extensive, causing the left side of the main landing gear to collapse and influencing significant structural bulkhead damage. The aircraft was partially dismantled and transported via C-5A Galaxy to the Vark Hospital at GDFW. At GDFW repairs started March 31, 1982, and were completed July 5, 1984. Repair consisted of utilizing the aft fuselage from F-111F 70-2407 and a new "Water Boiler" bulkhead, as well as incorporating cannibalized parts from other USAF and General Dynamics spares.

Note regarding F-111F 70-2407: this aircraft had been heavily damaged due to a "pre-delivery" engine failure and subsequent catastrophic fuselage fire during an engine test cell run at GDFW (see Chapter 9).

The damaged "Water Boiler" on the bottom left as compared to the new-build replacement. *All Photographs Courtesy of GDFW.*

Crew
Pilot: Capt Ralph R Inman
WSO: Capt George H Stillwell
Call Sign: Maggy 21
Accident Board President: Col Joseph E Stapleton
Time of Incident: 2243 MDT
Assigned Unit: 523rd TFS / 27th TFW
 Cannon AFB, New Mexico
Aircraft Statistics: Unknown
Mishap Result: Aircraft Suffered Major Damage
 / Repaired at GDFW Vark Hospital

68-0130
F-111D # 46 GD/FW Production Run # A6-46
USAF Delivery Date: October 17, 1972

Crash Scenario

On October 21, 1988, the mishap aircraft departed Cannon AFB, New Mexico, at 1143 MDT as lead of a Surface Attack Tactics (SAT) student syllabus mission. During departure, a fire developed in the right (#2) engine. An uncontained and out-of-control fire caused the aircraft to eventually roll left and pitch up due to burn through of the flight control hydraulic systems and lines. The aircrew ejected, and the aircraft crashed into the ground 6 NM southwest of Cannon AFB. The capsule

Courtesy of Douglas E. Slowiak/Vortex Photo-Graphics.

functioned normally and the crew egressed without injury. Crash Coordinates were (N 34 19 00 / W 103 25 00).

68-0131
F-111D # 47 GD/FW Production Run # A6-47
USAF Delivery Date: October 27, 1972

Crash Scenario
On August 23, 1990, the mishap aircraft departed Cannon AFB, New Mexico, as a chase aircraft on a tactical check ride for another 522nd aircraft and crew. The sortie was planned to fly VR-176 low-level route with a transition to VR-1107, and then onto the Melrose Range for a single-ship bombing pass and then return to Cannon AFB. Due to an engine driven generator dropping off-line, maintenance technicians changed the Generator Control Unit (GCU). The mishap aircraft took off late. The mishap crew then flew directly towards Albuquerque to make up for the late departure and entered the VR-176 low-level route on time. After approximately 23 minutes of low-level flight, the crew transmitted "mayday-mayday-mayday" over the radio. The aircraft had become uncontrollable and they elected to eject. The mishap crew received back injuries due to a hard capsule landing. Crash coordinates were (N 33 48 60 / W 107 20 00) approximately 85 NM northwest of Holloman AFB, New Mexico, and 30 NM north of Truth or Consequences, New Mexico.

Findings
The aircraft experienced flight control problems attributed to the Generator Control Unit (GCU) change conducted prior to takeoff. During the low-level portion of the mission, the mishap aircraft experienced an uncommanded roll, accompanied by caution lights, and the control stick moving forward and to the right. The pilot countered the uncommanded maneuver, but the aircraft immediately began another uncommanded right roll that was not controllable. The crew then ejected at 2000 feet AGL. The mishap investigation revealed that a malfunctioning GCU could influence frequency fluctuations that may have caused the flight control computers to malfunction.

F-111 Pilot Dick Brown talks about his flight control malfunction in this aircraft a few weeks prior:

During the setup and preparation for a Defensive BFM sortie with F-15 adversaries, I was using the autopilot pitch and altitude hold. In this mode the stick drives to neutral when engaged and then does not move. All of a sudden the stick started moving aft on its own. I disconnected the autopilot and hand flew – called knock it off and told #2 to keep at a distance. In the meantime, the stick continued driving back on its own and I used afterburner and bank to control speed and pitch. I tried all my flight control tricks and finally I was able to stop the uncommanded aft stick movement. The control stick had reached its TEU (trailing edge up) limits which required me to use almost full forward stick placement against the forward stop to control the pitch axis. I declared an emergency and completed a controllability check, finding I could fly the airplane and command enough pitch using a no slats/no flaps configuration. I was convinced that I could land the airplane at just below nose wheel tire limit speed and engage the approach end barrier. We set up for a straight in approach to land. I instructed the WSO to keep his hand on the top of his ejection handle and if I said "bail-out" he was to pull the handle. When I touched down I had the control stick full forward against the stop, successfully engaging the arrestment cable. When I shut down the engines, the slab was full up. My arm ached for days afterwards because of the force needed to maintain control.

Crew
Pilot: Maj Richard C Davidage
WSO: Capt Valdimar L Smith
Call Sign: Captor 46
Accident Board President: Col Charles H Jackson
Time of Incident: 1055:30 MDT
Assigned Unit: 522nd TFS / 27th TFW Cannon AFB, New Mexico
Aircraft Statistics: 1,681 Flights and 3,806.2 Flight Hours
Mishap Result: Aircraft Destroyed / Successful Ejection

Courtesy of Author's Collection.

Findings
The aircrew heard a loud thump after takeoff and then observed an engine FIRE light. The aircraft simultaneously rolled left, which the pilot countered with right stick and rudder. The flight crew accomplished the emergency action procedures by shutting down the right engine and discharging the fire suppression agent. The FIRE light remained on, and the aircrew experienced an uncommanded pitch-up and hard-over rudder which resulted in loss of flight control prior to ejection. Investigation revealed that a 3rd stage turbine disk failed and penetrated the engine case and centerbody fuel cell. The fuel cell damage resulted in a massive fuel leak that ignited into an uncontrollable fire within the engine bay. The engine bay / nacelle fire caused rudder control rod burn-through due to the reverse flow phenomena.

Crew
Pilot: Capt David A Swanson
WSO: Capt Timothy P Gaffney
Call Sign: Snip 01
Accident Board President: Col Arnold L Franklin Jr.
Time of Incident: 1145 MDT
Assigned Unit: 524th TFS / 27th TFW Cannon AFB, New Mexico
Aircraft Statistics: 1,398 Flights and 3,322.1 Flight Hours
Mishap Result: Aircraft Destroyed / Successful Ejection

68-0132
F-111D # 48 GD/FW Production Run # A6-48
USAF Delivery Date: October 16, 1972

Courtesy of USAF.

Crash Scenario

On March 17, 1988, the mishap aircraft was scheduled as Number-4 in a four-ship tactical low-level sortie to the Melrose Bombing Range near Cannon AFB, New Mexico. The aircraft took-off single-ship at 1542 MST and joined the flight on the Melrose Range. After completing all scheduled range events, the mishap aircraft began a rejoin for range departure. The Range Control Officer (RCO) reported "liquid vapors" trailing from the mishap aircraft. The crew realized that they had a fuel leak via a fuel warning light and made an immediate turn toward Cannon AFB, 25 NM to the east. The pilot shut-down the malfunctioning engine and made a single engine visual straight in approach to Runway 04 at Cannon AFB. The crew attempted to land the plane at too high an airspeed. On initial touchdown, the aircraft bounced and became uncontrollable due to sluggish flight control response. The mishap pilot was able to climb the plane upward in an attempt to gain enough altitude for ejection. The mishap aircrew initiated a successful ejection, and the aircraft crashed onto the runway and was destroyed. The capsule landed approximately 300 feet right of the runway.

Findings

The mishap aircraft was landed single-engine, with the power setting on the remaining engine set at idle, due to the high airspeed on the rushed approach. While in idle power, there was inadequate hydraulic pressure to maintain a safe margin of control over the aircraft. After touchdown, the combined effects of high rate of descent and sluggish flight control response resulted in a pronounced bounce. Before the operating engine could spool up and provide adequate hydraulic pressure for sustained flight the mishap pilot ejected. The pilot determined that he would be unable to control the aircraft before it began an uncontrolled descent. Mishap investigation determined that either the operating engine's hydraulic pump cavitated, or a hydraulic check valve had stuck partially closed, reducing the hydraulic volume flow. Either malfunction could have influenced low system hydraulic pressure, which would result in significantly reduced flight control response.

Note: the pilot flight manual, known as the Dash-1, specifically calls for a minimum of 85% RPM on the good engine to maintain adequate hydraulic pressure. At no time can this be reduced until touchdown.

Crew
Pilot: 1Lt Philip E Walgren
WSO: Maj Juergen Neumann (German AF Exchange)
Call Sign: Unknown (Not Listed on 711)
Accident Board President: Col Robert P Andrews
Time of Incident: 1717 MST
Assigned Unit: 522nd TFS / 27th TFW Cannon AFB, New Mexico
Aircraft Statistics: 1,376 Flights and 3,188.3 Flight Hours
Mishap Result: Aircraft Destroyed / Successful Ejection

68-0136 seen on a TDY deployment to RAF Fairford. *Courtesy of Author's Collection.*

68-0136
F-111D # 52 GD/FW Production Run # A6-52
USAF Delivery Date: November 2, 1972

Crash Scenario

On September 20, 1979, the mishap aircraft was scheduled for a night low altitude toss bombing checkout for the Weapons System Officer (WSO) with an Instructor Pilot (IP) in the left seat. The crew planned for a 1929 MDT takeoff, but due to maintenance problems and a runway change, actual takeoff time was 2039L. In order to make the scheduled range time, the crew elected to enter the low-level route at an alternate entry point 40 NM from the range. While in the base turn for the first low altitude toss delivery, the crew heard a thump and observed an external flash of light. There was no immediate cockpit indication of a problem. Fifteen seconds later a second thump was heard, and another external flash of light was observed by the pilot. The left engine fire warning light illuminated and emergency procedures for an inflight fire were accomplished. The mishap pilot terminated the planned attack maneuver and initiated a climb while turning toward Cannon AFB. After two minutes the fire light went out. The instructor pilot (IP) requested to land on the closest runway (Runway 12) with an approach-end barrier engagement. At seven miles, the Supervisor of Flying

F-111D-52 - BACKGROUND
(S/N 68-136)
F-111D-43 - CREW MODULE (FOREGROUN[...]
(S/N 68-127)

Vark Hospital. *Courtesy of GDFW.*

(SOF) confirmed a small fire on the left side of the mishap aircraft. The aircraft landed at 2101L and made a successful approach-end barrier engagement. After stopping on the runway, the aircraft rolled back 75 feet due to arrestment cable tension. The aft section of the aircraft became engulfed in flames. The mishap aircrew rapidly egressed and the base fire department suppressed the fire in six minutes. The aircraft sustained substantial fire damage during the ground fire.

Findings

The aircraft's left engine (#1) had two second-stage fan blades fail which penetrated the engine compressor case, the left main engine fuel line, and the aft fuel tank. The leaking fuel caught fire and the fire spread throughout the engine bay. The volume of the fuel leaking from

68-0139
F-111D # 55 GD/FW Production Run # A6-55
USAF Delivery Date: **August 11, 1972**

Crash Scenario
On July 14, 1980, the mishap aircraft was scheduled as Number-2 in a three-ship formation. The mission was planned for a 1305L takeoff, low-level training on VR-198 and practice bomb deliveries on the Melrose Range, New Mexico. The instructor pilot (IP) of the mishap aircraft "Vark 22" was observing and grading the pilot of "Vark 21" to flight lead status. The flight took off at 1304 L and proceeded to the entry point for VR-198. Five minutes prior to the planned range entry time of 1345L, the mishap aircraft experienced a right engine (# 2) oil hot light. Vark 21 assumed a chase position on the mishap aircraft while Vark 23 proceeded to the Melrose Range as a single-ship. The mishap aircrew reported they had shut the right engine down and were preparing for a single engine landing. The mishap aircrew configured the mishap aircraft for landing 30 NM out of Cannon AFB TACAN on the 320 radial. The mishap aircraft began a descent from 7,000 MSL to maneuver for a visual straight in approach. At approximately 9 NM north-northeast of Cannon AFB the mishap crew initiated an unsuccessful ejection. Both crew members received fatal injuries and the aircraft was destroyed. Crash Coordinates were N 34 29 50 / W 103 13 00, which is 9 NM north-northeast of Cannon AFB, New Mexico.

Findings
The mishap pilot was unable to maintain a controlled rate of descent with one engine shutdown. It was determined that the remaining engine's afterburner had also failed to light-off, or was selected too late to arrest the sink rate. Without the additional thrust provided by the afterburner, the aircraft entered the "region of reversed command": a flight regime

Vark Hospital. *Courtesy of GDFW.*

the ruptured fuel tank and air flow around the engine reduced the effectiveness of the fire suppression agent. The fire continued to burn, causing substantial airframe damage. The aircraft was dismantled and shipped to the GDFW restoration facility (Vark Hospital) and later returned to service.

Crew
Pilot: Capt Steven J Feaster
WSO: 1Lt Roy A Gilbert
Call Sign: Unknown
Accident Board President: Col Joseph F Hansard
Time of Incident: 2101L
Assigned Unit: 522nd TFS / 27th TFW Cannon AFB, New Mexico
Aircraft Statistics: Unknown
Mishap Result: Aircraft sustained major fire damage to the aft fuselage

Courtesy of USAF.

where there is insufficient thrust to sustain flight without descending in a nose down attitude to gain airspeed. The mishap crew ejected. During the low altitude ejection sequence, the crew module pitched nose-up into the vertical. The brake and stabilization chute was trailing the escape module as designed, but perpendicular to the module's pitch attitude due to the ground velocity vector. When the main recovery parachute was catapulted out of the pod, the main parachute containment bag struck and became lodged in the confluence of the stabilization and brake parachute bridle. Thereafter the main recovery parachute could not inflate, resulting in an unsuccessful ejection attempt. The aircraft settled to the runway in a landing attitude and was destroyed. After this mishap, the USAF modified all F-111 escape modules to release the stabilization parachute simultaneously with the main parachute catapult sequence.

Crew
Pilot: Maj Ulysses S Taylor III
WSO: 1Lt Paul E Yeager
Call Sign: Vark 22
Accident Board President: Col Lester G Frazier
Time of Incident: 1353 MDT
Assigned Unit: 522nd TFS / 27th TFW Cannon AFB, New Mexico
Aircraft Statistics: 495 Flights and 1,304.8 Hours
Mishap Result: Aircraft Destroyed / Fatal crash / Unsuccessful Ejection

Base emergency personnel look at the wreckage of an F-111D from Cannon AFB that crashed Monday afternoon. Both crewmembers of the aircraft died in the accident. (U.S. Air Force Photo by SrA. Kim Caswell)

Courtesy of the Clovis News Journal Files via USAF.

On a better day, 68-0139 sports a new paint job. Courtesy of Ulysses S Taylor IV. No matter how you view a Vark......... it looks fast, even in the chocks!

68-0142
F-111D # 58 GD/FW Production Run # A6-58
USAF Delivery Date: November 30, 1972

Mishap Scenario

On June 25, 1973, the mishap aircraft was scheduled to fly the Las Vegas VR-270 low-level route using Terrain Following Radar (TFR) and then make four night practice bomb runs on the Melrose Bombing Range, followed by recovery back to Cannon AFB, New Mexico. Taxi, last chance inspection, bomb arming, and takeoff were made without incident. The Santa Rosa #3 standard instrument departure was flown on an IFR clearance. The mishap aircraft then proceeded via its flight planned route at 16,000 feet MSL to the entry point for the Las Vegas VR-270 route. Upon arriving at the entry point, the crew had approximately 20 minutes until the scheduled route entry time of 1948L. The mishap crew cancelled the IFR clearance and made two race track orbits in VFR conditions under Albuquerque radar surveillance. The crew then entered and flew the low-level route to the Melrose Range, accomplishing four practice radar bomb deliveries. Prior to departing the range the mishap aircraft climbed to 15,000 feet MSL and proceeded to the Tucumcari VORTAC, and then to the Bellview Initial Approach Fix (IAF) for a TACAN penetration and approach. The crew flew three Ground Controlled Approaches (GCA) without incident. The final approach was a simulated no-gyro (compass heading director simulated out) GCA. The aircraft was configured for the approach on the base leg and all indications were normal. The crew twice detected momentary stick movements during this sequence. A normal touchdown was made. Shortly after touchdown the aircraft began a series of uncommanded pitch oscillations that increased in severity. The third time the nose wheel slammed onto the runway, the nose gear broke off, and the radome impacted the runway. The aircraft scraped the right wingtip, the afterburner nozzles, and then the left wingtip in a violent out of control maneuver. During these gyrations the left main tire blew. The aircraft rebounded into the air and again hit hard on the radome. The right main wheel and tire assembly broke off and the aircraft came to rest on the flattened left main tire and right lateral beam of the landing gear unit. The aircrew shutdown the aircraft and successfully egressed the aircraft without injury. The aircraft sustained substantial damage to the fuselage, landing gear, and radome as a result of the hard landing.

Findings

The Horizontal Tail Servo Actuator (HTSA) main stage spool slide and sleeve assembly (Figures 5 and 6) were found to have galled, causing loss of pilot control authority during the landing attempt. (Galling is caused by excessive friction between two rubbing metal surfaces, resulting in

> True galling of the slide and sleeve within the HTSA servo control valve will result in a hard-over position of the horizontal tail. If the sliding motion of the lands within the sleeve is restricted due to near galling, then a lag motion of the HTSA would result. In this case, the pilot's response to the HTSA position or movement could result in a Pilot Induced Oscillation (PIO) while counteracting the aircraft's response to erratic flight control motions. Correspondingly, the autopilot pitch/roll dampers through the flight control system could introduce uncommanded pitch and roll motions while automatically attempting to maintain the selected or commanded flight parameters.

localized welding of the two surfaces.) Once the slide assembly seized in position the horizontal tail was commanded to a full hard-over condition, which could not be corrected by pilot flight control inputs. Excessive friction between the slide and sleeve may have occurred as a result of (1) unwanted micro-sized particles entering between the extremely tight tolerance (.000165 to .0002 inches) design of the movement area, or (2) due to a very slight misalignment of the servo-valve assembly (Figure 5) applying bending forces on the sleeve (Figure 6). The servo-valve housing was split into two parts at the manufacturing joint. These two parts, the Boost Housing and the Main Body, could be tightened together with a small misalignment and consequent bending force being applied to the sleeve. When the free movement of the slide within

Courtesy of Mike Kaplan Collection.

the sleeve is restricted, a lag or stall motion is transmitted in comparison to the opposite HTSA's movement, causing erratic but in most cases correctable flight control response. However, in several cases the galling seized the slide within the sleeve, resulting in an uncorrectable hard-over horizontal tail.

A hesitation in the slide's movement, or a rapid "un-sticking" of the control valve spool, elicited a lag or an amplified deflection of the horizontal tail control surface respectively. If one surface is lagging in motion or has frozen in place, an asymmetrical or oscillatory condition is set up, compounding the pilot's control problems. To the pilot, the uncommanded or exaggerated pitch, roll, or yawing motions required corrective flight control response. However, when true galling occurred, the cycle resulted in a departure from controlled flight and post-stall gyrations.

Crew
Pilot: Capt Robert D Ramsey
WSO: Capt John C McFarren
Call Sign: Age 15
Accident Board President: Col James N McClelland
Time of Incident: 2226 Local
Assigned Unit: 522nd TFS / 27th TFW Cannon AFB, New Mexico
Aircraft Statistics: Unknown
Mishap Result: Aircraft sustained major damage but was repaired and returned to service.

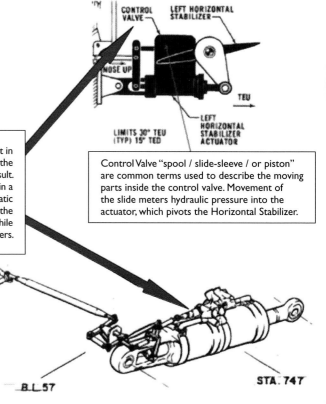

Control Valve "spool / slide-sleeve / or piston" are common terms used to describe the moving parts inside the control valve. Movement of the slide meters hydraulic pressure into the actuator, which pivots the Horizontal Stabilizer.

Figure 5: Horizontal Tail Servo Actuator and Control Valve Spool. *Diagrams Courtesy of F-111A Parts Breakdown and 1F-111A-1 Pilot's Manual.*

A discussion with an F-111 hydraulic system instructor revealed that in normal circumstances, only ounces of stick pressure were required to move the HTSA servo control valve, which commanded minute deflections of the HTSA. An HTSA servo control valve slide that was restricted in movement may now require "pounds" of stick pressure to elicit a control response. This excessive force was usually the result of an approaching galling condition or other problems internal to the control valve spool. The immediate corrective action for the galling problem required USAF maintenance technicians to time the trailing-edge-down (TED) droop of the horizontal tails after the engines were shutdown. If the droop time was too slow, the hydraulic specialist investigated further by checking the control valve spool push-pull resistance. If the resistance was too high, the control valve required replacement. Later, the entire HTSA control valve was redesigned and replaced fleet-wide, eliminating the galling issue. (Source: Bernard Manfre, F-111 Hydraulic System Specialist)

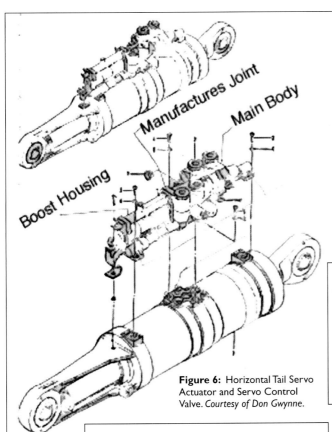

Figure 6: Horizontal Tail Servo Actuator and Servo Control Valve. *Courtesy of Don Gwynne.*

Shown to the left is the Horizontal Tail Servo Actuator, or HTSA. Atop the HTSA is the servo control valve, a two part component made up of the Boost Housing and the Main Body. Deflection of the control stick is transmitted through the pitch/roll mixer to the Boost Housing input rod. A small inner control linkage inside the Boost Housing moves the slide within the sleeve assembly (Figure 7) internal to the Main Body. Figure 6 represents a parts breakdown of the Slide and Sleeve assembly. The slide mechanism is composed of thicker sections known as Lands. Movement of the slide positions the lands in relation to openings in the sleeve, metering hydraulic fluid into or out of the actuator to position the horizontal stabilizer.

The forward-most land was known as the Atmospheric Land. It was on this land that galling occurred. The gap between the atmospheric land and the inner portion of the sleeve had extremely tight tolerances (.000165 to .0002 inches). The introduction of foreign particles or misalignment of the servo-valve may have precipitated the metal to metal friction, and eventual galling. In the worst case, galling caused a localized welding together of the slide and sleeve. Without the free movement of the slide, the affected actuator went to a hard over position, rendering the aircraft uncontrollable and forcing the crew to eject. As a size reference, the inner sleeve is 10.5 inches long and approximately 7/16 inches thick.

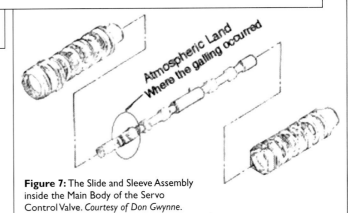

Figure 7: The Slide and Sleeve Assembly inside the Main Body of the Servo Control Valve. *Courtesy of Don Gwynne.*

68-0146
F-111D # 62 GD/FW Production Run # A6-62
USAF Delivery Date: November 30, 1972

Crash Scenario

On September 2, 1977, the mission was the student aircraft commander's initial sortie in the F-111D/F conversion training course. The aircraft departed Cannon AFB, New Mexico, at 0859L on an IFR clearance. The mission progressed normally through the takeoff and departure phase. The crew then entered the Cannon AFB local training area at 0927 MDT. After area entry, the Instructor Pilot (IP) directed the student to practice a series of basic flight familiarization maneuvers which included a demonstration of aircraft roll characteristics at forward and aft wing sweep positions. The first maneuver was an uneventful aileron roll to the right, and was performed at a wing sweep of 40 degrees. The crew then swept the wings to 54 degrees, established an airspeed of 450 KIAS, and entered a second aileron roll to the left. At some point during this maneuver the aircraft became uncontrollable and the aircrew ejected. The aircraft crashed in an open field 10 NM south of Des Moines, New Mexico, 132 NM from Cannon AFB on the 340 degree radial. The crew sustained minor injuries during the ejection sequence; they were picked up by a local rancher and then transported via helicopter to Cannon AFB medical facilities.

Courtesy of Author's Collection via GDFW.

Courtesy of the USAF.

Findings

The aircraft departed controlled flight while executing an aileron roll at 450 knots and 14,500 MSL. The aircraft was configured with a 54 degree wing sweep, and the Flight Control System switch was accidentally left in the Takeoff and Land position and not corrected to the Normal position prior to executing the maneuvers. When the flight control system switch is in Normal and the aircraft is in a clean configuration, the rudder is limited to 11 ¼ degrees deflection left or right of center. In the Takeoff and Land position, the rudder authority

is increased to 30 degrees. Additionally, pitch and roll commands in the T/O and Land position are no longer automatically limited by the flight control computers as flight conditions change. Flight control deflections for a given stick movement were therefore excessive, resulting in the aircraft exceeding AOA and yaw-side-slip limits. In this mishap, the induced AOA and side-slip angles exceeded the flight control computer and the pitch/yaw/roll damper's capability to maintain stability, resulting in a departure and spin. See also: F-111A 67-0036 April 24, 1973, and included figures referencing the T/O & Land switch.

Crew

Pilot: Capt Roy W Westerfield
WSO: Capt Jonas L Blank Jr.
Call Sign: Tempest 12
Accident Board President: Col Donald M May
Time of Incident: 0940 MDT
Assigned Unit: 524th TFS / 27th TFW Cannon AFB, New Mexico
Aircraft Statistics: 259 Flights and 743.1 Flight Hours
Mishap Result: Aircraft Destroyed /Successful Ejection

Courtesy of Gerry R. Markgraf.

68-0160
F-111D # 76 GD/FW Production Run # A6-76
USAF Delivery Date: February 14, 1973

1st Mishap Scenario

On January 22, 1974, the mishap aircraft was scheduled for a routine WSO-4 syllabus training mission, flying the Dalhart VR-207 low-level route using TFR, and then proceeding to the Melrose Bombing Range for practice radar lay-down bomb delivery. Due to a maintenance directed launch delay, the flight took-off and proceeded directly to the range. Range work and recovery were normal. While setting up on a long final approach to Runway 03, at 5800 feet 17 miles out the crew began to configure the aircraft for landing. The leading edge slats extended, but the flaps only extended 2 to 3 degrees and then locked out. The crew declared an emergency and requested vectors for a precision final approach. Initial touchdown occurred approximately 1,100 feet from approach end of Runway 03 and appeared normal. However, moments later the nose came up and the tail bumper made contact with the runway. The aircraft became airborne again for a further 1230 feet still aligned with the runway. A second hard contact with the runway 2,330 feet down occurred, with the left main and nose striking simultaneously, followed immediately by right main contact. During this sequence both main tires blew, followed by the entire right main gear assembly departing the aircraft. The aircraft remained on the runway for another 248 feet before becoming airborne again in a nose high attitude for a further 982 feet. The aircraft returned to the runway, striking the right main axle followed by the left wing. The aircraft continued another 600 feet while shedding the left main gear and the wing hitting the Barrier Arrester Kit (BAK-12) concrete ramping. A fire erupted in the main wheel well area. The crew shut down both engines and then safely egressed the aircraft.

Findings

The aircraft was returning to base for an emergency landing in a slats down no flaps configuration. The pilot selected a wing sweep that resulted in an aft center of gravity condition for the gross weight and landing configuration. The pilot did not use the correct emergency

procedure for the current aircraft configuration, which resulted in an incorrect airspeed and angle of attack at touchdown. The aircraft entered a series of porpoising maneuvers that exceeded the structural capability of the main landing gear, which collapsed both sides of main gear. The aircraft was heavily damaged but eventually repaired at Cannon AFB and returned to flight status.

Crew

Pilot: Capt Robert H Jones II
WSO: Capt George G Giddens
Call Sign: News 75
Accident Board President: Col James R Arthur
Time of Incident: 1700 Local
Assigned Unit: 4427th TFRS / 27th TFW Cannon AFB, New Mexico
Aircraft Statistics: Unknown
Mishap Result: Substantial Damage / Repaired and returned to flight status

2nd Mishap Scenario

On January 22, 1979, the mishap aircraft was scheduled for a night low-level on IR-111 and conventional ground attack sortie. Takeoff, enroute, low-level, and range work were accomplished without incident. Returning to base, the first approach was a non-precision Airport Surveillance Radar (ASR) approach and low approach/go around to Runway 03. During the second approach, the Supervisor of Flying (SOF) directed all aircraft to return to a full stop landing because of deteriorating weather. The mishap aircraft flew a Precision Approach Radar (PAR) approach to a landing. During the landing touchdown, the mishap aircraft experienced a series of pitch oscillations and the pilot executed a maximum power go-round. The crew left the gear extended because of the Pilot Induced Oscillation (PIO) and resultant hard landing. The crew accomplished another precision approach. Touchdown on this landing was normal, but as soon as the nose gear was lowered to the runway, sparks were observed by the mobile controller and SOF. The nose gear collapsed during the landing roll and the aircraft slid down the runway, coming to a stop 4,497 feet down and slightly right of the runway centerline.

Findings

Due to the pilot induced oscillations during the first landing touchdown, the nose landing gear was structurally damaged from the hard nose down impact stress. On the second landing attempt, the nose gear failed structurally and collapsed. After the aircraft was brought to a stop the crew then safely egressed. The collapse caused significant structural damage to the airframe, however, the aircraft was deemed repairable and returned to service. The PIO resulted from an incorrect wing sweep for the weight, fuel load, and configuration, resulting in an aft center of gravity at touchdown.

Courtesy of Douglas E. Slowiak/Vortex Photo-Graphics Collection.

68-0164
F-111D # 80 GD/FW Production Run # A6-80
USAF Delivery Date: January 29, 1973

Crash Scenario
On October 17, 1984, the mishap aircraft was on a formal syllabus training sortie, with the student aircraft commander in the left seat and an instructor pilot in the right seat. Syllabus events called for night terrain following radar on a low-level route to the bombing range and low-level radar weapons deliveries. The sortie was briefed as a two-ship, with the mishap aircraft in the wing position. Due to a maintenance issue

Crew
Pilot: Capt William M Blaesing
WSO: 1Lt Roger F Kropf
Call Sign: Crazy 46
Accident Board President: Col Joseph K Stapelton
Time of Incident: 2214 MST
Assigned Unit: 524th TFTS / 27th TFW Cannon AFB, New Mexico
Aircraft Statistics: Unknown
Mishap Result: Aircraft Suffered Major structural damage and was repaired at Cannon AFB

3rd Mishap / Fatal Crash Scenario
On September 14, 1982, the mishap aircraft "Excit 76" was scheduled as Number-2 in a two-ship formation. The mission was planned for a 2000 MDT takeoff, night low-level training on IR-111, and practice bomb deliveries on the Melrose Bombing Range. The flight took off at 2015 MDT and proceeded as planned to the alternate entry point "J" of IR-111 to make up timing in order to meet the scheduled range time. The lead aircraft, "Excit 75," entered the low-level route first, followed by "Excit 76." During the descent into the low-level route the mishap aircraft crashed. Both crew members were fatally injured and the aircraft was destroyed.

Findings
The aircraft crashed during an Automatic Terrain Following descent into the low-level route. Investigation revealed the TFR system malfunctioned at an unknown time. The malfunction prevented electronic transmission of normal TF climb/dive commands to the flight control system. The specific nature of this malfunction could not be determined. The aircraft failed to level off at the preselected 1000 foot Set Clearance Plane (SCP) and descended through the 68 percent fly-up threshold. A TFR Fly-Up command was generated, but the aircraft pitch series trim response, without positive pitch damper inputs, was insufficient to preclude ground impact. It was also noted that the normal associated warning/caution lights indicating a problem, or warning the pilot of a terrain incursion, did not illuminate. The mishap pilot also failed to respond to secondary indications confirming a system malfunction, or recognize impending ground impact. The pilot also did not intervene manually to control the aircraft prior to ground impact. A survey of F-111 incidents between 1967 and 1976 revealed a number of incidents in which the TFR / LARA failed to level the aircraft during a descent toward terrain as a result of anomalies in the pitch dampers, feel and trim centering unit, TFR Computer malfunctions, and/or LARA malfunctions. In several cases, had it not been for the pilot abruptly overriding the TFR commanded descent, those aircraft would also have crashed.

with the lead aircraft, the mishap aircraft launched single-ship at 1903 MDT. The mishap aircraft entered the IR-113 low-level and impacted the ground at 1945 MDT. The crash occurred on the Holloman AFB, New Mexico, TACAN, 002 degrees radial and 63 NM. An ejection was not attempted. Crash coordinates were (N 33 51 05 / W 105 48 05).

Findings
The mishap aircraft crashed during the TFR portion of the night low-level. An ATC radar track file indicated that the mishap aircraft was seen to have climbed out of the low-level route toward the Minimum Enroute Altitude (MEA), and then descended back onto the route. Speculation and reconstruction of the mishap sequence indicated during the Fly-Up recovery maneuver, the crew became spatially disoriented attempting to recover the aircraft using the simplified attitude indicators on Vertical Situation Display (VSD). The mishap aircraft was initially at the MEA, according to Albuquerque Center air traffic control, and then the radar track file indicated their flight path resembled a 30-degree nose low barrel roll prior to impact. The airplane hit the side of a cliff above 600 KTAS.

Input by F-111 pilot Capt Brad Insley:

The mishap crew was flying in mountainous terrain and apparently had a TFR fly-up. The recovery profile indicated they had reached an extremely nose high attitude and attempted an unusual attitude recovery. The aircraft impacted a mountain before completing the unusual attitude recovery maneuver. The "D" model didn't have a separate TFR scope and used the VSD on the pilot's side to display the TFR information. A simplified Attitude Director Indicator (ADI) overlaid the TFR E-Scope display on the VSD. The simplified ADI consisted of a vertical course displacement, a horizon bar, and a "flying W" for attitude control. Recovery from an unusual attitude on the simplified ADI took some practice. During an unusual attitude recovery, the pilot would normally switch the VSD back from the TFR display to a typical ADI; but this took away the TFR display and required a switch activation. Speculation was the pilot or Instructor Pilot WSO may have attempted an unsuccessful unusual attitude recovery using the simplified ADI (winged W) on the TFR display, shown by a red arrow on the inset F-111D VSD.

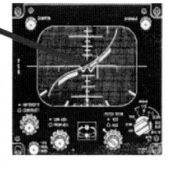

Crew
Pilot: 2Lt Albert H Torn
WSO: Capt Alan J Pryor
Call Sign: Hound 64
Accident Board President: Col Hubert J Carron
Time of Incident: 1945 MDT
Assigned Unit: 524th TFS / 27th TFW Cannon AFB, New Mexico
Aircraft Statistics: 1,272 Flights and 3.175.4 Flight Hours
Mishap Result: Aircraft Destroyed / Fatal Accident / No Ejection Attempt

Crew
Pilot: Maj Howard L Tallman III
WSO: Capt William R Davy
Call Sign: Excit 76
Accident Board President: Col Brian R Williams
Time of Incident: 2040 MDT
Assigned Unit: 524th TFTS / 27th TFW Cannon AFB, New Mexico
Aircraft Statistics: 429 Flights and 1,058.8 Flight Hours
Mishap Result: Aircraft Destroyed / Fatal Crash / No Ejection Attempt

68-0167
F-111D # 83 GD/FW Production Run # A6-83
USAF Delivery Date: January 30, 1973

Crash Scenario

On October 10, 1976, the mishap aircraft was scheduled for a Functional Check Flight (FCF) due to a double engine change. The aircrew took off at 1127L. The FCF progressed normally throughout the subsonic profile. The mishap aircraft entered the supersonic tract at approximately 1158L. A fluctuating right Turbine Inlet Temperature (TIT) gauge, which had been noticed earlier in the mission, stabilized when minimum afterburner was selected. The aircraft commander then selected maximum power and initiated a climb to FL410 while accelerating to 1.85 Mach. After accomplishing the FCF checks at 1.85 Mach, the aircraft commander slowed the aircraft to below 600 KTAS and performed the speedbrake check. During speed brake retraction, the aircraft pitched over violently and began a right roll. The pilot was unable to return the aircraft to level flight, and the crew successfully ejected as the aircraft passed 22,100 feet MSL. The aircraft impacted on U.S. Highway 82 approximately 15 miles west of Hope, New Mexico, and was destroyed. The crew was later picked up by a rescue helicopter and flown to Holloman AFB, New Mexico. The crash site was at 33 miles on the 202 degree radial from the Roswell, New Mexico, TACAN.

Findings

The left Horizontal Tail Servo Actuator (HTSA) control valve had become galled and the control valve stalled and seized, causing an uncommanded pitch-over and rolling maneuver. Under normal flight control, only ounces of control stick pressure will move the slide within the servo control valve sleeve. The maximum breakout force on the control valve spool is 35 pounds of flight control input. A slide that is contacting the sleeve section may result in binding, inducing a lag or erratic deflection of the affected horizontal tail. In a galled state, the HTSA deflects hard-over, resolving into uncorrectable pitch, roll, and yaw oscillations and eventually departure from controlled flight.

Investigation revealed the left HTSA control valve assembly was reassembled incorrectly, resulting in misalignment. The misalignment caused a side load to the control valve slide, inducing metal to metal contact and eventual galling: see also mishap findings for F-111D 68-0142.

Crew
Pilot: Capt Richard J McEwen
WSO: Capt Larry F King
Call Sign: Kino 05
Accident Board President: Col Milford E Davis
Time of Incident: 1213 MDT
Assigned Unit: 523rd TFS / 27th TFW Cannon AFB, New Mexico
Aircraft Statistics: 290 Flights and 817.6 Flight Hours
Mishap Result: Aircraft Destroyed /Successful Mach 1.4 Ejection

Courtesy of C. Ray Reed

68-0173
F-111D # 89 GD/FW Production Run # A6-89
USAF Delivery Date: February 20, 1973

Crash Scenario

On November 18, 1978, the mishap aircraft, "Patsey 05," was scheduled as a single-ship high altitude navigation proficiency sortie from Cannon AFB, New Mexico, to Nellis AFB, Nevada, and return to Cannon AFB, New Mexico. The mishap occurred on the return portion of the cross-country mission. The mishap aircraft took the active runway at Nellis for takeoff, but aborted prior to brake release when intense smoke appeared in the cockpit at high power settings. The aircraft returned to transient alert and shut down. During a two hour airfield closure, the aircrew conferred with Cannon AFB maintenance personnel and arranged a corrective action plan with them. After engine start and troubleshooting smoke ceased the aircraft was cleared for flight. Patsey 05 took off at 1509 PST. At 1521 PST, shortly after level off at FL230, the aircraft had a left engine fire. After initially turning back towards Nellis AFB, Nevada, the aircrew attempted to divert to Mojave County Airport in Kingman, Arizona. At 1531 PST the aircraft became uncontrollable and the aircrew ejected. The aircraft crashed and was destroyed.

Findings

The aircraft was returning from a cross country flight to Nellis AFB, Nevada, when the left engine exploded and the aircraft caught on fire. The explosion and fire were due to failure of a 9th stage high pressure compressor (HPC) air seal due to high cycle fatigue. The failed air seal damaged the 9th stage vanes, over-pressurizing the number 2 and 3 bearing compartments, forcing oil past the bearing seals. The leaking oil passed into the bore area and was ignited in the vicinity of the number 11 compressor disk by heat and sparks from the damaged seal. The 11th stage (HPC) disk failed due to heat softening, and pieces of the disk (shrapnel) penetrated the engine case, aircraft structure, and aft fuel tank. The leaking fuel ignited and entered the aft centerbody due to the reverse flow phenomena, where it resulted in damage to the primary hydraulic system. The fire also caused rudder actuator push-pull rod burn-through, a rudder hard-over, and loss of flight control. The crew successfully ejected.

Crew
Pilot: 1Lt Richard P McKee (522nd TFS)
WSO: Capt Lee A Bauer.(481st TFTS)
Call Sign: Patsey 05
Accident Board President: Col Robert I McCann
Time of Incident: 1632 MST
Assigned Unit: 522nd TFS & 481st TFTS / 27th TFW Cannon AFB, New Mexico
Aircraft Statistics: 658 Flights and 1,656.1 Flight Hours
Mishap Result: Aircraft Destroyed /Successful Ejection

Courtesy of 27th TFW, Cannon AFB, New Mexico, Public Affairs Office.

68-0174
F-111D # 90 GD/FW Production Run # A6-90
USAF Delivery Date: August 31, 1972

Crash Scenario
On May 21, 1976, the mishap aircrew was scheduled to lead a two ship tactical evaluation mission from Cannon AFB, New Mexico. Pre-flight and engine start were normal. Run-up checks were accomplished on the runway, and all indications were normal up to and including selection of minimum afterburner. The mishap crew heard a thump, followed by a rattling noise and moderate airframe vibrations. The wingman then stated "Lead you're on fire - Get out." The aircrew of the mishap aircraft accomplished emergency shutdown procedures and then exited the aircraft without injury.

Findings
A first stage fan blade failed due to a manufacturing defect and penetrated the fan case, rupturing the aft fuel tank. Fuel from the ruptured tank ignited, resulting in major fire damage to the left stabilizer and aft section of the aircraft. The aircraft was shipped to Davis-Monthan AFB, Military Aircraft Storage and Demolition Center (MASDC) after the accident. The aircraft remained in the "Bone Yard" (MASDC) until shipment to GDFW for restoration on August 1, 1979. Repairs were completed June 22, 1984. The aircraft was then returned to service at Cannon AFB, New Mexico.

Courtesy of GDFW

Crew
Pilot: Capt Gregory L Smith
WSO: 1Lt John C Hall
Call Sign: Unknown
Accident Board President: Col Joseph E Clarkson
Time of Incident: 1358 MDT
Assigned Unit: 523rd TFS / 27th TFW Cannon AFB, New Mexico
Aircraft Statistics: Unknown
Mishap Result: Initially the aircraft was classified as "Destroyed," however 68-0174 was restored at the GDFW Vark Hospital and returned to service.

The fuselage is lowered onto the repair platform and alignment jig, "The Fixture."

68-0174 enters GDFW Vark Hospital

Originally **68-0174** was declared destroyed. The cockpit had been completely stripped of useable avionics and components by the USAF parts/supply system for use in operational F-111D's. *All Photographs Courtesy of GDFW.*

8

F-111E MISHAPS

F-111E 68-0003. *Courtesy of Doug E. Slowiak/Vortex Photo-Graphics.*

67-0116
F-111E # 2 GD/FW Production Run # A1-161
USAF Delivery Date: August 30, 1969

Crash Scenario
On October 27, 1976, the mishap aircraft F-111E 67-00116 was scheduled for a supersonic vibration test of internally carried inert weapons. Planned test points were 660 KCAS at 41,000 feet, 20,000 feet, and 6,000 feet AGL. At each point the weapons bay doors were to be opened for 30 seconds to gather telemetry data. The mission briefing, preflight and take-off were normal. The first two test points were flown, but the third one was cancelled. The aircraft returned to base and executed a straight-in approach to Runway 01. During the landing attempt the aircraft began porpoising. The porpoising increased in amplitude and the mishap aircrew initiated ejection; the escape module functioned normally. The aircraft impacted on the runway and came to rest approximately 1500 feet from the departure end of the runway. The escape module impacted on the runway 925 feet short of the aircraft wreckage. The mishap aircrew successfully egressed the capsule. The mishap aircraft sustained major damage to the forward section and was destroyed.

Findings
According to GDFW records, the aircraft was returning to Eglin AFB, Florida, due to a low fuel emergency. The mishap pilot landed too fast and "spiked it on." In layman's terms, this means the aircraft was pushed over to increase the rate of descent and forced hard onto the runway. Generally, a fast forced-on landing results in the nose gear hitting first, which initiates the porpoising between the nose gear and the main gear. The pilot's corrective or countering control stick inputs can aggravate the porpoising motions, and all the while the airspeed is slowing and control effectiveness begins to lag. In a severe porpoise, the aircraft motions and lack of control response may eventually appear uncontrollable.

The best option during a porpoise is to establish and hold a landing attitude and go-around. Unfortunately, the crew did not have this option because of the low fuel state. The pilot had miscalculated the amount of

Courtesy of Tom Brewer via Don Logan Collection.

fuel required to complete the third test run and had to terminate the test due to low fuel. The pilot declared minimum fuel and then emergency fuel while returning to base. During the first approach, communication terminology and interpretation between the tower and the crew were both in error regarding the availability of an arrestment cable versus a net barrier. The mishap pilot initiated an unnecessary go-around due to this breakdown in communication terminology and attempted realignment to another runway. Now critically low on fuel, the pilot inadvertently accelerated to 350 knots during the rushed maneuver to land. Although the excessive airspeed was nearly corrected, the aircraft touched down approximately 50 knots above computed touch-down speed, 3,500 feet down the runway, and entered a porpoise. During the landing, the pilot swept the wings from 26 degrees sweep to 16 degrees (full forward). This action changed the aircraft center of gravity, possibly aggravating the porpoise. The WSO initiated the ejection sequence.

Crew
Pilot: Capt Douglas A Joyce
WSO: Capt Richard M Mullane
Call Sign: Unknown
Accident Board President Col James D Sanders
Time of Incident: 0957 CDT
Assigned Unit: 3214th TS / 3246th TW Eglin AFB, Florida
Aircraft Statistics: 381 Flights 581.8 Flight Hours
Mishap Result: Aircraft Destroyed / Successful Ejection

67-0117
F-111E # 3 GD/FW Production Run # A1-162
USAF Delivery Date: October 13, 1969

Crash Scenario
On April 23, 1971, the mishap aircraft F-111E 67-00117 departed Edwards AFB, California, and had entered the Leach Lake Air-to-Air Gunnery Range. The mishap aircraft was on its 86th mission supporting CAT II Flight Testing, and was on its 22nd gun firing mission. The purpose of this flight was to evaluate operation of the gun port cover and the effects of engine bleed air changes on engine stalls during gun firing. This was a follow-up on a mission performed earlier during the day. The mission was to examine the 300 to 400 knot regime at 20,000 feet within the angle of attack up to the 3 "G" maximum limit. Two firing passes were to be completed; on the second pass the mishap aircraft entered a right turn, which the pilot continued until the aircraft departed controlled flight. Shortly after, the mishap wingman observed a downward nose slice (an abnormal yawing motion) and realized the aircraft was out of control. The mishap crew ejected at 10,200 feet MSL, 6000 feet AGL. The mishap aircraft continued out of control until impact. The crew module impacted 1400 feet southwest of the main aircraft impact point.

Courtesy of GDFW.

Findings
The aircraft was flown into a region of the F-111's flight envelope that increases the susceptibility to departure: heavy positive G-loading and a roll maneuver to execute a turn. The effect is an accelerated stall that, due to the AOA while pulling Gs, the vertical stabilizer can be partially blanked out from high energy airflow over the wing glove and upper fuselage. The rolling motion to turn also introduces an adverse yaw motion. At this point the aircraft begins some minor oscillatory motions (seen with the nose wandering – generally opposite the desired direction of turn) which the pilot may attempt to correct by increasing roll (bank) into the desired direction of turn. The pilot's inputs to correct the oscillation actually aggravate the situation, and the aircraft quickly departs controlled flight due to a roll coupled departure. At low altitude, the aircrew had little option other than to eject. The ejection sequence was initiated within the safe escape envelope. Unfortunately, the ejection attempt was unsuccessful due to pyrotechnic failures in the recovery parachute severable cover panel, which prevented the main recovery parachute from deploying. A fleet-wide inspection of all recovery parachute severable panels immediately followed.

Crew
Pilot: Maj James W Hurt III
WSO: Maj Robert J Furman
Call Sign: Junco 08
Accident Board President: Col Clyde S Cherry
Time of Incident: 1652 Local
Assigned Unit: 6512th TS / 6510th TW Edwards AFB, California
Aircraft Statistics: 97 Flights 152.7 Flight Hours
Mishap Result: Aircraft Destroyed / Fatal Ejection

68-0001
F-111E # 11 GD/FW Production Run # A1-170
USAF Delivery Date: November 26, 1969

Courtesy of Pat Martin via Don Logan Collection.

Crash Scenario
On February 5, 1990, the mishap aircraft F-111E 68-0001 was on a two-ship night surface attack tactics mission. While in a steep transition turn from the base leg to final run-in the aircraft crashed. The mishap aircraft impacted the water on the initial range entry pass near RAF Coningsby, United Kingdom. The aircraft was destroyed and the aircrew were fatally injured. Ejection was not initiated prior to ground impact.

Findings
This mishap occurred during a visually flown turn in a night radar bombing pattern. Loss of situational awareness in the over-water transition area resulted in spatial disorientation influencing an undetected descent into the water. TFR protection was not engaged, nor required if the aircraft remained at or above the Minimum Enroute Altitude (MEA) of 1000 feet AGL. Any night or weather flight requires the pilot to maintain a constant cross-check of the cockpit instruments. Failure to monitor the aircraft's altitude, or to detect a rate of descent below the MEA, placed the aircraft in a perilous trajectory. Unfortunately, the aircraft had entered a steep descending turn and the wingtip caught the water, cartwheeling the aircraft into the ocean. The night conditions, aircraft G-loading in the turn, and possible visual illusions in the over-water transition may all have influenced unrecognized spatial disorientation. This crash was a Controlled Flight Into Terrain (CFIT) mishap.

Crew
Pilot: Capt Clifford W Massengill
WSO: 1lt Thomas G Dorsett
Call Sign: Lay 21
Accident Board President: Col Robert S Pahl
Time of Incident: 1729 GMT
Assigned Unit: 77th TFS / 20th TFW RAF Upper Heyford, United Kingdom
Aircraft Statistics: 1641 Flights 4321.3 Flight Hours
Mishap Result: Aircraft Destroyed / Fatal Crash / No Ejection initiated

68-0003
F-111E # 13 GD/FW Production Run # A1-172
USAF Delivery Date: November 25, 1969

Crash Scenario
On December 19, 1979, the mishap crew was scheduled to fly as Number-2 in a two-ship formation in support of exercise Hammer Blow 18, a United Kingdom tactical low-level flying exercise. The exercise profile was briefed to include a low-level ingress into the Spadeadam Range, using split tactics with an air-to-air TACAN rejoin afterward to proceed low-level to the Otterburn Range, then followed by a return to base. The flight departed at 1005L and decided to go to the Jurby Head Range, located off The Isle of Man, because the eastern ranges were down for weather. The flight held at high level south of the Point of Ayre until approximately 1130L, when range entry was approved. The flight made one pass on the range to increase spacing for single ship deliveries. After the bombing events were completed the two aircraft departed for Burrow Head, with the mishap aircraft rejoining on the lead aircraft while proceeding outbound from the range. The two-ship entered a low-level route. The flight was flying north bound on the low-level routing while stair-stepping down to 500 feet AGL with the mishap aircraft on the right side as briefed. As the flight approached high terrain the wingman was no longer in sight off the flight lead's right wing. The lead aircraft commander looked left as he was beginning a pushover in Auto TFR and spotted the mishap aircraft about 3000 feet away, slightly back and high. The wingman was in a nose up attitude that was higher than the leader, and appeared to be inverted (or nearly inverted), pulling down to the horizon. The lead aircraft commander then lost sight of his wingman due to clouds or terrain. The flight lead again looked left, but did not see the wingman's aircraft and became concerned, because the mishap aircraft was on the wrong side for an upcoming 90 degree tactical right turn. Lead attempted to call his wingman on the radio with negative results. The wreckage was later discovered by a Royal Navy Sea-King helicopter from RAF Prestwick with no survivors.

Findings
The two F-111s were in a line-abreast tactical formation with approximately one mile spacing between them. The mishap wingman changed his position from one side of the formation to the other without informing the flight lead. The lead aircraft, uninformed of the mishap aircraft's new position, flew close to high terrain, inadvertently forcing the mishap pilot to climb over the terrain. As the flight crested the hill, the mishap wingman was seen in an inappropriate nearly inverted attitude, beginning a pull down. The mishap pilot then made a last ditch unsuccessful attempt to avoid ground collision.

The last visual sighting by the flight lead placed the mishap aircraft inverted and pulling down toward the ground.

To properly complete an inverted nose low recovery at low altitude, the pilot must first "unload" the aircraft and roll to an upright attitude. Once upright, the pilot must then execute a wings level pull-up to the horizon. Additionally, if the attempted rolling recovery is a loaded roll (the pilot is pulling aft on the stick and rolling simultaneously), the roll rate is slower, and the maneuver consumes altitude below the aircraft. Unfortunately, the mishap pilot also failed to see the terrain ahead and could not complete the 120 degree rolling slice maneuver in time, flying into the terrain nearly inverted. The cause for this mishap was Controlled Flight Into Terrain (CFIT).

Crew
Pilot: Capt Richard A Heztner
WSO: Capt Raymond C Spaulding
Call Sign: ReRun 16
Accident Board President: Col William T Stanley
Time of Incident: 1143 GMT
Assigned Unit: 79th TFS / 20th TFW RAF Upper Heyford, United Kingdom
Aircraft Statistics: 800 Flights 2076.6 Flight Hours
Mishap Result: Aircraft Destroyed / Fatal Crash / No Ejection initiated

Courtesy of Doug E. Slowiak /Vortex Photo-Graphics.

68-0008
F-111E # 18 GD/FW Production Run # A1-177
USAF Delivery Date: December 18, 1969

Crash Scenario

On May 15, 1973, the aircraft was scheduled for a single-ship training mission, with flight activities to include low-level range deliveries and then an instrument recovery to home base. The mishap aircraft took off from RAF Upper Heyford at 1104 L and proceeded to the training area. About three minutes after entering the low-level route the aircraft ingested a bird into the right engine. Shortly thereafter an engine fire ensued and the crew ejected. The aircraft crashed and was destroyed near Skipness, Mull of Kintyre, close to Macrihanish in western Scotland. Both crew members survived and were recovered without injury.

Findings

The right engine caught fire after a bird strike at 450 knots, followed by an explosion and engine Fire light. A few seconds later a Wheel Well Hot light came on. As control of the aircraft became erratic, the mishap crew climbed to 2500 feet. When the aircraft became uncontrollable the crew ejected safely. The bird impact to the right inlet spike caused rupture of the F-2 fuel tank wall, resulting in fuel loss. The aircrew stated that the aircraft was definitely on fire. The fuel-fed fire entered the aft centerbody, causing rudder control link burn through and failure of the primary and utility hydraulic system pressure: see also Reverse Flow Phenomena, Chapter 1.

68-0008 "On the Boom" during an air refueling mission. *Courtesy of the USAF.*

Crew

Pilot: Capt Andrew J Peloquin
WSO: Maj Ariel Alvarez
Call Sign: Akee 54
Accident Board President: Col John J Knight
Time of Incident: 1204 GMT
Assigned Unit: 79th TFS / 20th TFW RAF Upper Heyford, United Kingdom
Aircraft Statistics: 138 Flights 413.6 Flight Hours
Mishap Result: Aircraft Destroyed / Successful Ejection

Crash investigation team members inspect the crew module. *Courtesy of Bill Allen Collection.*

The capsule in 2007 near Belen, New Mexico, Coordinates are (N 34 45.375 W 107 00.310);At one time, Kirtland AFB in Albuquerque New Mexico, used the derelict module for survival training. *Courtesy of Neal Lawson.*

68-0012
F-111E # 22 GD/FW Production Run # A1-181
USAF Delivery Date: December 13, 1969

Crash Scenario
On October 30, 1979, the mishap crew was scheduled to lead a two-ship day/night, continuation training sortie. The planned mission profile included low-level navigation, night terrain following, weapon deliveries, refueling, night formation approaches, and single ship recoveries at RAF Upper Heyford, United Kingdom. The mishap crew took off after an aircraft swap due to maintenance difficulties at 1712 L. They proceeded to the low-level entry as planned and continued toward the range. Prior to reaching the range, deteriorating weather caused the mishap crew to climb to minimum safe altitude. The crew determined the bombing range was unworkable due to weather and turned south for the refueling track. The mishap crew refueled with a SAC KC-135 and took on 3000 pounds of fuel, then proceeded under radar control to RAF Brize Norton, United Kingdom, for practice approaches. After descending to 4000 feet MSL, they received instructions to go to the holding pattern and hold at maximum endurance fuel flow. The crew then made a radar climb to the hold at FL 230. After one circuit in the holding pattern, the mishap crew reduced the airspeed and entered a left hand turn for the outbound portion of the holding pattern. The aircraft began a slow descent to FL226 during this outbound turn. Approximately two-thirds of the way through the turn, the aircraft began to climb back to FL230 and departed controlled flight at 1932 L. The mishap aircrew ejected and the aircraft impacted the ground in a grove of trees five miles south of Cambridge, United Kingdom. The crew module landed in a field 2.6 miles northeast of the aircraft.

Findings
While established in the holding pattern, the pilot retarded power to slow from 300 KCAS to 250 KCAS with the autopilot engaged. During a left turn on the outbound leg of the holding pattern, the pilot allowed the airspeed to decay further to 210 KCAS. The aircraft began to buffet (stall onset) and lose altitude. The pilot added power and applied aft stick to reduce the altitude loss, which resulted in a rapid increase in angle of attack beyond the maximum allowable AOA. The aircraft departed controlled flight and the crew ejected.

In the holding pattern, the mishap pilot was using the pitch autopilot with the "altitude-hold" sub-mode. Airspeed control is always the responsibility of the pilot, since there are no "autothrottles." As the airspeed slowed (wings were at 26 sweep), the pilot initiated the left turn and the autopilot abruptly disconnected, resulting in a slight pitch up and in an AOA overshoot.

The minimum recommended airspeed for holding in a clean configuration was 280 knots. The minimum flying airspeed with flaps and slats up and with wing sweep 16 degrees to 26 degrees is approximately 250-260 knots. Note: forebody vortices off the elongated nose and the wing glove at high AOA tended to blank the rudder, contributing to a loss of stability. The aircraft would then enter a "post-stall gyration" and normally not enter a spin.

Crew
Pilot: Capt Eugene S Ogilvie
WSO: 1Lt Albert P Manzo
Call Sign: Unknown
Accident Board President: Col Donald F Kaufman
Time of Incident: 1932 BST
Assigned Unit: 79th TFS / 20th TFW RAF Upper Heyford, United Kingdom
Aircraft Statistics: 711 Flights 2017.2 Flight Hours
Mishap Result: Aircraft Destroyed / Successful Ejection

Courtesy of Author's Collection

68-0018
F-111E # 28 GD/FW Production Run # A1-187
USAF Delivery Date: December 13, 1969

Crash Scenario
On January 18, 1972, the mishap aircraft was scheduled for a local landing recurrency mission. The pilot had exceeded the 20th TFW restriction of 21 days between landings for wing aircrew members, and the sortie would also provide USAF required instrument continuation training for both crewmembers. The mishap aircraft departed RAF Upper Heyford at 1126 Zulu. The mission flew as planned via SID 17 to Wallesey TACAN, cruise at FL 270 under positive radar control to Oustan TACAN, Craigowl Hill TACAN, Kinloss TACAN, and enroute penetration for a diverse GCA to RAF Leuchars. The crew made HF contact with the 20th TFW Command Post from overhead Craigowl Hill at 1222Z with systems normal and flight proceeding as planned. The aircraft descended into layered clouds at approximately 12,000 feet MSL, passing through alternating light to moderate rain and clear icing conditions between 10,000 feet MSL and 2,000 feet AGL. Cloud coverage at Leuchars was 1,600 feet AGL, visibility was six miles, no precipitation, and the wind was from 140 degrees at 18 knots. At 1236Z the mishap aircraft was cleared to 2000 feet. The pilot acknowledged the clearance, and stated he was leveling at 2,000 feet. The mishap crew was given a frequency change and checked in with the new controller. The radar controller advised of a temporary loss of radar contact; the controller noted the position of the mishap aircraft 15 miles northwest, and that contact would be reestablished shortly. The mishap

Courtesy of USAF

crew acknowledged. At 1238:40, the radar controller transmitted a turn to heading 170. The mishap aircraft did not acknowledge the heading change and no further contact was made.

Findings
The mishap aircraft crashed and burned 14.5 NM northwest of RAF Leuchars, Scotland, near the village of Coupar Angus. The aircraft had departed controlled flight on the base leg turn of GCA pattern. The mishap crew failed to perform the before landing checklist. The investigation revealed the variable sweep wings were swept to 35 degrees with no slats or flaps deployed. (Normal configuration for landing per checklist procedures: wing sweep 16 or 26 degrees to allow flaps/slats extension.) The deployed flaps and slats increase lift at a lower AOA as the aircraft slows on approach. The pilot must monitor and maintain the sink rate between 700 and 1200 fpm on a standard instrument approach. Note: Recovery from a high sink rate may be impossible at traffic pattern altitudes in a clean configuration (F-111 Dash-1).

68-0019
F-111E # 29 GD/FW Production Run # A1-188
USAF Delivery Date: November 30, 1969

Crash Scenario
On August 9, 1984, the mishap aircrew was scheduled for a Flight Lead Upgrade mission to include air refueling and low-level and range work. The mishap aircraft departed RAF Upper Heyford, United Kingdom, at 0915 L. While on the bombing range a bird struck the aircraft, destroying the radome. Shortly thereafter the aircrew successfully ejected. The aircraft crashed near a lake on the Tain Range, Scotland, 15 NM from RAF Kinloss on the 295 degree radial. Crash Coordinates were (N 57 47 00 / W 00 35 08).

Findings
The mishap aircraft experienced a bird strike on the radome. The debris damaged the engines and the Angle of Attack (AOA) probe for the Stall Warning Inhibitor System (SIS). The loss of the critical flight control systems resulted in an unmanageable situation for the crew. The aircraft departed controlled flight. This was the 7th F-111 lost due to a bird strike.

Crew
Pilot: Capt Ralph J Jodice II
WSO: Maj Paul D Emrich
Call Sign: Roar 21
Accident Board President: Col Robert D Sponeybarger
Time of Incident: 1217 BST
Assigned Unit: 79th TFS / 20th TFW RAF Upper Heyford, United Kingdom
Aircraft Statistics: 1160 Flights 3,076.6 Flight Hours
Mishap Result: Aircraft Destroyed / Successful Ejection

Courtesy of Doug E. Slowiak /Vortex Photo-Graphics.

See Also: For similar type accidents:

F-111A	67-0043	(A88)	22 May 1969
F-111A	67-0069	(A114)	13 Apr 1971
F-111A	66-0029	(A47)	1 Sept 1971
F-111F	71-0892	(F68)	6 June 1973 Landed Safely
F-111A	67-0040	(A85)	11 July 1973
F-111E	68-0081	(E91)	5 Mar 1975
F-111E	68-0060	(E70)	5 Nov 1975
F-111C	A8-133	(D1-09)	29 Sep 1977
F-111E	68-0019	(E29)	9 Aug 1984

Crash Scene Pictures: 14.5 NM northwest of RAF Leuchars, Scotland. All Photographs *Courtesy of USAF via Al Pinto.*

The pilot inadvertently left the wing sweep at 35 degrees while slowing to 210 knots with the speed brake down. The aircraft entered a left bank of approximately 20 degrees in a fairly level attitude, with a slight descent to below 800 feet MSL or 400 to 600 feet AGL. During the last few hundred yards of flight the nose rose to 50 to 60 degrees and the aircraft banked left 30-40 degrees. The nose came left from about 175 degrees to 140 degrees. The aircraft impacted the ground in a nose high left wing low attitude, with the left tail pipe striking the ground first. No ejection was attempted.

Crew
Pilot: Lt Col Floyd B Sweet
WSO: Lt Col Kenneth S Blank
Call Sign: Sewn 11
Accident Board President: Brigadier General Frank L Gailer Jr.
Time of Incident: 1238 GMT
Assigned Unit: 55th TFS / 20th TFW RAF Upper Heyford, United Kingdom
Aircraft Statistics: 141 Flights 362.9 Flight Hours
Mishap Result: Aircraft Destroyed / No Ejection Attempted

68-0024
F-111E # 34 GD/FW Production Run # A1-193
USAF Delivery Date: October 25, 1970

Crash Scenario

On January 11, 1973, the mishap aircraft was scheduled to takeoff from RAF Upper Heyford, United Kingdom, as lead of a two-ship flight. The purpose of the mission was to accomplish local training requirements, consisting of TFR low-level navigation, local range weapons deliveries, instrument approaches, and formation practice. Shortly after take-off, while climbing at 230 KIAS with the landing gear up and the flaps retracting through approximately 15 degrees, the pilot observed a FIRE warning light on the #1 (left) engine. The pilot pulled back on the right engine throttle and disengaged the right afterburner. The WSO reminded the pilot that the left engine FIRE light was illuminated. The pilot then reengaged the right engine afterburner. The left engine was then pulled to idle and then placed to cutoff. The aircrew then completed the emergency procedures by discharging the left engine fire bottle extinguishing agent. The crew then experienced a severe right yaw that required 15 to 20 degrees left bank to maintain directional control. The mishap pilot then made four 360 degree turns to remain close to the airfield while a wingman joined and reported slats down and full right rudder. A controllability check was accomplished, and then the pilot proceeded inbound to land. With the main landing gear down and the nose gear partially down, the aircraft began to roll to the right. The pilot was unable to control the aircraft. As the roll progressed past 90 degrees of bank, the nose dropped below the horizon and the pilot instructed the WSO to eject. The ejection was successful. The aircraft crashed four miles south of Crawley and 24 NM northeast of RAF Upper Heyford, United Kingdom.

Findings

The aircraft experienced a major engine fire shortly after takeoff from Upper Heyford. The fire was due to failure of the left engine zone-1 secondary fuel manifold. Reverse flow of fuel-fed flames into the aft centerbody caused a burn-through of the rudder control rod, resulting in a hard-over right rudder. Control was maintained, however, as the crew flew in large circles. The pilot lost control of the aircraft after a surge-drop in hydraulic pressure when the landing gear was lowered: see also reverse flow phenomena, Chapter 1.

Courtesy of Don Gwynne.

When the gear was lowered the speed brake door opened fully, the main gear dropped from the wheel well, and the nose gear partially extended. The aircraft rolled to the right and could not be controlled. Investigation revealed an intergranular failure which occurred during fabrication brazing operations that caused the left engine Zone-one secondary fuel manifold to fail. This resulted in fuel spillage within the engine nacelle and subsequent fire. A lower B-nut on the pressurization and vent valve sensing line did not remain secured due to improper installation, and fuel from the pressurized aft tank escaped through this line, intensifying the fire. The reverse airflow condition within the fuselage centerbody area allowed the fire to be drawn through the ventilation louvers into the aft centerbody area, causing the rudder control tubing assembly to melt and resulting in a hard-over right rudder.

Crew
Pilot: Maj Robert J Kroos
WSO: Capt Roger A Beck
Call Sign: Sewn 12
Accident Board President: Brigadier General Robert S Cramer
Time of Incident: 0946 Local
Assigned Unit: 55th TFS / 20th TFW RAF Upper Heyford, United Kingdom
Aircraft Statistics: 34 Flights 522.29 Flight Hours
Mishap Result: Aircraft Destroyed / Successful Ejection

68-0040
F-111E # 50 GD/FW Production Run # A1-209
USAF Delivery Date: August 10, 1970

Crash Scenario

On February 16, 1995, the mishap aircraft was scheduled for a training sortie for the mishap Weapons System Officer. The sortie was uneventful up to the base turn for a planned full stop landing on Runway 04 at Cannon AFB, New Mexico. Approximately halfway through the final turn the right engine generator light illuminated. After completing the turn to final approach, the mishap pilot advanced both throttles to maximum afterburner and repositioned the flaps from full down to 25 degree flaps (normal for a single engine approach) while attempting a go-around. The mishap pilot recognized an unrecoverable sink rate developing and initiated the ejection sequence. The ejection was successful, with no significant injuries to the mishap crew. The aircraft crashed 222 feet short of the runway threshold on the main gear, right wing down. The mishap aircraft slid sideways and came to a rest off the right side of the runway threshold, caught fire, and was destroyed.

Findings

This mishap can best be described as the proverbial "between a rock and a hard place." The mishap pilot was practicing an overhead approach with flaps extended when the maneuvering engine rolled back to sub-idle RPM, illuminating the generator light. When the pilot completed the turn to intercept a visual glidepath on the final approach, the lack of normal power response provided an indication

Courtesy of Michael France

of engine status. The pilot then advanced both throttles to maximum afterburner and attempted to reposition the flaps to the appropriate single-engine configuration. The aircraft developed an unrecoverable sink rate before the good engine could spool up to produce flight sustaining thrust. With a loss of thrust in a high drag configuration (flaps, slats, and landing gear down), the pilot must keep the aircraft above minimum flying airspeed by adding power, or he must push the stick excessively forward (reduce AOA and dive to accelerate) – an unnatural response for the situation. On final approach, there is too little altitude to dive and accelerate the aircraft to maintain flying airspeed. With only one engine spooling up, arresting the sink rate without stalling the aircraft is nearly impossible. The pilot is left with two decisions: landing short of the runway with excessive sink rate or eject. In this mishap the pilot chose wisely. The cause of the engine roll-back was due to a malfunctioning fuel control: see also mishaps for F-111A 63-9769 and F-111A 63-9774.

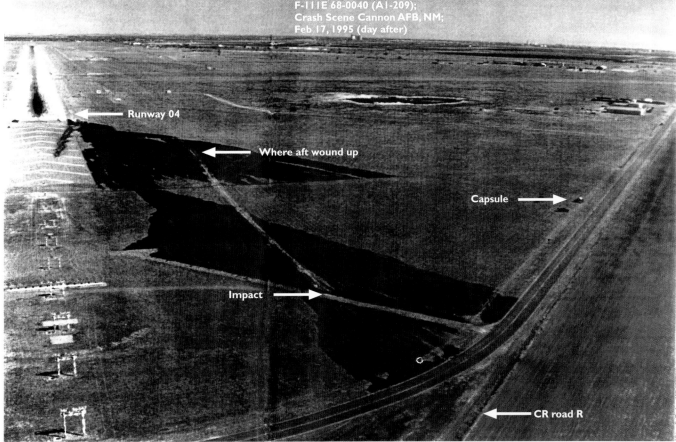

F-111E 68-0040 (A1-209);
Crash Scene Cannon AFB, NM;
Feb 17, 1995 (day after)

Runway 04

Where aft wound up

Capsule

Impact

CR road R

Aerial view of approach to runway. *All Photographs Courtesy of USAF Mishap Report.*

Remains of Aircraft Fuselage and Debris Field.

Top view of aircraft fuselage, notice the forward swept wings, flaps and slats down for landing.

Crew
Pilot: Capt James E Newton II
WSO: 1Lt Randolph L Winge
Call Sign: Hypo 01
Accident Board President:
    Col David R Hall
Time of Incident: 1044 MST
Assigned Unit: 428th TFS / 27th TFW Cannon AFB,
    New Mexico
Aircraft Statistics: Unknown
Mishap Result: Aircraft Destroyed / Successful Ejection

F-111 Pilot and mishap witness Craig "Quizmo" Brown talks about F-111E- 68-0040:

Fig saw the GEN light and started a normal final turn. He then notices the engine rolling back. No bang, no whimper, it just quit when he retarded the throttles at the perch. (*I had the same fuel controller problem while on a night TFR ride at Cannon the previous year while in the right seat; no whimper, it just quit - caused when the fuel controller failed to "full shutoff."*) Half way around the turn, and facing 35 knot head winds, Fig tried to accomplish a single-engine go-around and/or make the runway. The wind made sure the latter didn't happen. Fig had to initiate the ejection. The only reason they got a full chute was the high wind. The same high wind tumbled the capsule until the perimeter fence caught the chute. Fig thought his back might have been hurt so he stayed put while Winge got out and talked to the EOR crew, the first on the scene. The same wind carried the grass fire toward the capsule and Fig finally gave in to the EOR crew's plea to "GET OUT OF THE CAPSULE AND GET IN OUR TRUCK!"

68-0042
F-111E # 52 GD/FW Production Run # A1-211
USAF Delivery Date: October 28, 1970

Crash Scenario
On July 24, 1979, the mishap aircraft was scheduled to fly as Number-2 in a three-ship formation. The purpose of the mission was for the mishap instructor pilot to evaluate the lead pilot for flight lead upgrade training. The sortie profile included a low-level route in the Netherlands and range work in either the Netherlands or United Kingdom, followed by individual Radar Bomb Scoring (RBS) runs and then recovery to home base. The flight departed on time, and the join-up, departure, and low-level were accomplished

Courtesy of Doug E. Slowiak /Vortex Photo-Graphics.

without incident. Two dry pass runs were flown at Vliehors Range in the Netherlands before the flight proceeded back to the United Kingdom because of deteriorating range weather. The flight then proceeded to the Donna Nook Range, holding airspace to await entry into Cowden Range at their scheduled time. Range entry was normal, and after one overhead pass the flight took single-ship spacing on range downwind. At this point, the Number 3 aircraft in the formation departed the range because he did not like the weather, which was below USAFE Command minimums. The lead aircraft and the mishap aircraft made two more dry passes. On the fourth pattern, lead called "Base" (a turn point in the bombing pattern), followed shortly by Number-2. Lead then advised Two that he had a conflict at twelve o'clock. The lead WSO observed Number-2 roll wings level to pass behind them. No further radio transmissions were made by the mishap aircrew. Lead made several orbits before locating the wreckage south of the range. No ejection attempt was made by the mishap crew. The aircraft crashed at sea 1.5 NM north of Withernsea, United Kingdom. Crash Coordinates were (N 55 43 03 / E 000 01 00).

Findings
Maintaining flight parameters in the weather and during over-water transitions without TFR protection is an extremely demanding instrument crosscheck task. The poor visibility eliminated the pilot's ability to make visually derived corrections to the aircraft's attitude, bombing pattern position, and spacing behind the lead aircraft. Additionally, flying in the Number-2 position required all normal cockpit tasks, plus maintaining precise bombing pattern ground track, spacing, and position awareness of the lead aircraft. Any cockpit distraction or attempts to visually acquire number one might have diverted attention from the normal instrument crosscheck. In this mishap, the lead aircraft was on final for a radar bomb pass and recognized that the mishap aircraft had made an early turn to base, and was positioned to pass in front of his aircraft. The lead pilot identified the conflict to the mishap pilot, who then rolled to wings level to reposition and increase separation with the lead aircraft. The mishap pilot then entered a 60 to 70 degree bank turn without correcting a developing descent rate, most likely due to spatial disorientation. The mishap aircraft impacted the water and was destroyed (CFIT).

Crew
Pilot: Capt David W Powell
WSO: Capt Douglas A Pearce
Call Sign: Lay 26
Accident Board President: Col Joseph E Clarkson
Time of Incident: 1215 L
Assigned Unit: 55th TFS / 20th TFW RAF Upper Heyford, United Kingdom
Aircraft Statistics: 714 Flights 1928.6 Flight Hours
Mishap Result: Aircraft Destroyed / Fatal Crash / No Ejection

---

68-0045
F-111E # 55 GD/FW Production Run # A1-214
USAF Delivery Date: August 20, 1970

Crash Scenario
On December 12, 1979, the mishap crew was scheduled to fly a single-ship night mission, to include aerial refueling, Radar Bomb Scoring (RBS), and air-to-ground range work. The mishap aircraft took off and proceeded directly to Spadeadam bomb range for RBS work, completing four passes against four different targets. The first two passes were completed at approximately 1,000 feet above ground level (AGL). The crew accomplished the last two runs at 2,000 feet AGL and 1,640 feet AGL, respectively. The mishap aircraft proceeded directly to Wainfleet Range under Air Traffic radar control. Initial contact was established with Wainfleet Range, and the mishap aircraft

Courtesy of Author's Collection

was cleared to enter the range holding pattern at 4,500 Mean Sea Level (MSL). The crew returned to Air Traffic Radar Control and was cleared to descend to 3000 feet MSL. Descending through 4000 feet, the mishap crew cancelled radar service and reestablished contact with Wainfleet Range. While enroute to the holding pattern, the mishap aircraft was cleared to enter the range, and was informed of another F-111E already in the range pattern. The mishap pilot descended to 1,000 feet AGL while proceeding toward the target area. The aircraft continued past the normal downwind position and called entering downwind at a point approximately three miles east of the active target. This was the last transmission received from the mishap aircraft. The aircraft crashed three miles southeast of the target, approximately 7.5 NM south of Skegness, Lincolnshire, United Kingdom.

Findings
The aircraft crashed shortly after departing the range entry holding pattern to enter the bombing pattern. The aircraft impacted the water in a shallow descent and plowed deep into coastal mud. Wreckage recovery efforts were hindered due to World War II debris blurring search sonar readings. Some debris did wash up on shore. Later recovery attempts produced substantial amounts of the aircraft wreckage. The mishap investigation revealed that the pilot had used nonstandard procedures, including a steep turn, a delayed descent, and a modified ground track to enter the bombing range. As a result, the mishap pilot overflew the downwind leg and entered the range danger area. After realizing the mistake, the mishap pilot disengaged the automatic terrain following radar (TFR) while descending in a left turn to prevent the TFR from triggering an Automatic Fly-up command, and to increase the aircraft's maneuver capability. The pilot then further increased the bank angle to approximately 60 degrees in order to exit the range danger area. The pilot attempted a last-ditch terrain avoidance recovery, but the aircraft impacted the water and was destroyed. Spatial disorientation was a contributing factor.

Crew
Pilot: Capt Randolph P Gaspard
WSO: Maj Frank B Slusher
Call Sign: Lay 40
Accident Board President: Col Thomas A Baker
Time of Incident: 1820 LBST
Assigned Unit: 79th TFS / 20th TFW RAF Upper Heyford, United Kingdom
Aircraft Statistics: 766 Flights 2126.9 Flight Hours
Mishap Result: Aircraft Destroyed / Fatal Crash / No Ejection

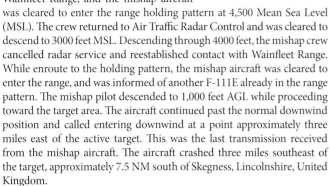

Courtesy of Author's Collection

68-0052
F-111E # 62 GD/FW Production Run # A1-221
USAF Delivery Date: September 30, 1970

Crash Scenario
On September 17, 1992, the mishap crew was scheduled to fly a single-ship day Surface Attack Tactics (SAT) mission. After returning to base, the aircraft crashed 1,720 feet short and west of Runway 09 during a visual flight rules straight-in approach to RAF Upper Heyford, United Kingdom. Ejection was not initiated prior to ground impact. Crash coordinates were (N 51 56 01 / W 001 16 62).

Findings
The pilot was practicing a no flap/slat visual approach in marginal VMC. Maneuvering on short final led to a high sink rate, and despite selection of full afterburner, the aircraft touched down (effectively "landed short") in a field approximately one-quarter mile short of the runway. The WSO initiated ejection after touchdown, but the aircraft collided with a transverse row of approach light poles, causing severe damage to the escape module and rocket motor before the module could separate. Damage to the rocket motor precluded an adequate lofting trajectory, resulting in insufficient time for the main parachute to fully deploy from a reefed status before the module struck the ground.

Crew
Pilot: Capt Jerry C Lindh
WSO: Maj David M McGuire
Call Sign: Lay 43
Accident Board President: Col Walter R Berg
Time of Incident: 1620 BDT
Assigned Unit: 55th TFS / 20th TFW RAF Upper Heyford, United Kingdom
Aircraft Statistics: Unknown
Mishap Result: Aircraft Destroyed / Fatal Crash / Unsuccessful Ejection after initial impact

68-0057
F-111E # 67 GD/FW Production Run # A1-226
USAF Delivery Date: November 21, 1970

Crash Scenario
On April 29, 1980, the mishap crew was scheduled to fly as lead in a two-ship formation in support of an exercise titled DATEX 80. The sortie profile included a low-level route in France, low-level in the United Kingdom (fuel permitting), and return to home station. The flight departed on time. The climb-out, join-up, and level-off were accomplished without incident. During the descent to enter a low-level route, a pre-briefed position change was made in VFR conditions, placing the mishap crew in the wingman position. Shortly thereafter, the flight entered the clouds and maneuvered under radar control. During the weather descent portion of the flight, the mishap aircraft departed the formation. The aircraft impacted the ground and was destroyed 6 NM west of Winborne, Dorset, United Kingdom. There was no attempt to eject. Crash Coordinates were (N 50 47 40 / W 002 08 40).

Findings
The mishap aircraft's spoilers had erroneously extended during a formation descent in Instrument Meteorological Conditions (IMC). The aircrew lost control and ejected out of the envelope. Normally, a roll stick input by the pilot will result in spoiler extension on one wing to aid roll response (the inboard spoilers are locked out at sweeps greater than 45 degrees, and the outboard spoilers are locked out at sweeps greater than 47 degrees). Inflight, the pilot has no capability to extend the spoilers on both wings simultane-

ously. The F-111 Spoiler Monitor System should lock-out all spoilers to the fully retracted position if the left and right spoilers extend simultaneously in flight. This purposeful design measure prevents a gross loss of lift.

If a spoiler inadvertently extends without being commanded and the aircraft starts a roll, the pilot would apply an opposite stick command to maintain wings level. Extension of the spoilers on the opposite wing will cause the spoiler monitor, through a voting process, to cut-off hydraulic pressure to the malfunctioning spoiler and its mate. This action will retract and lock the errant pair of spoilers in the down position and cause the spoiler caution lamp to illuminate. The lock-out will also result in reduced roll power into the locked-out wing. The spoiler monitor could be reset by depressing a Spoiler Reset button. This action caused the spoiler caution lamp to go out and restored hydraulic pressure to the pair of spoilers locked down. Emergency corrective action is to slow the aircraft to a safe speed and attempt to reset the spoilers one time only. Thereafter, the crew could expect a rapid roll transient if the spoiler still failed. A spoiler that was voted out because of an actual failure might not reset. In this case, a failure in the roll computer or the spoiler monitor may have prevented spoiler retraction.

In this mishap, a filter screen in the right spoiler failed, momentarily jamming the right inboard spoiler servo valve, resulting in full-up deflection. As a result of the uncommanded spoiler deflection, the mishap pilot maneuvered out of formation. The mishap pilot delayed recovery from the right bank and allowed the aircraft to enter an unrecoverable, nose-low unusual attitude. Spatial disorientation and/or confusion with the problem contributed to the mishap pilot's error. The mishap crew lost situational awareness with the terrain and crashed. There was no attempt to eject.

Courtesy of Don Logan Collection

Crew
Pilot: Capt Jack A Hines
WSO: 2Lt Richard J Franks
Call Sign: Lay 32
Accident Board President: Col John F
    Manning
Time of Incident: 1128 BST
Assigned Unit: 77th TFS / 20th TFW RAF
    Upper Heyford, United Kingdom
Aircraft Statistics: 801 Flights   2241.2
    Flight Hours
Mishap Result: Aircraft Destroyed /
    Fatal Crash / No Attempt to Eject

All Photographs Courtesy of USAF.

Courtesy of Gerry R. Markgraf Collection.

68-0060
F-111E # 70 GD/FW Production Run # A1-229
USAF Delivery Date: November 30, 1970

Crash Scenario
On November 5, 1975, the mishap crew was scheduled to fly a routine low-level training mission on the Wainfleet Range. While flying this sortie over the bombing range, the mishap aircraft experienced a bird strike approximately five miles southeast of Boston, Lincolnshire, United Kingdom. The bird hit the right windshield, causing catastrophic failure of the right windshield and right canopy glass. Ultimately, both crew members pulled the ejection handles within seconds of each other. Only one ballistic path out of four possible in the two handles burned far enough to initiate the ejection. (This was one of 11 major failures in this particular capsule's ejection sequence.) The WSO suffered no injuries, but the pilot sustained serious back injuries.

Findings
The mishap aircraft was lost during a low-level sortie after a bird impacted the right windscreen, causing catastrophic failure of the

right windshield and the right canopy glass. The cockpit filled with a fog-like debris from the failed windshield, making it impossible for the crew to determine aircraft attitude. The WSO initiated ejection over water and the aircraft was destroyed upon impact. The capsule landed in 3 to 4 feet of water, rolled over, and sank almost immediately due to an onrush of water entering through the broken windshield and the WSO's broken canopy glass. This was the 6th F-111 lost due to a bird strike.

Crew
Pilot: Capt James E Stieber
WSO: Capt Robert L Gregory
Call Sign: Akee 46
Accident Board President: Col Anthony T Sheehan
Time of Incident: 1611 GMT
Assigned Unit: 77th TFS / 20th TFW RAF Upper Heyford, United Kingdom
Aircraft Statistics: 407 Flights1204.3 Flight Hours
Mishap Result: Aircraft Destroyed / Successful Ejection <u>over water</u>
See also for similar type accidents:

F-111A	67-0043	(A88)	22 May 1969
F-111A	67-0069	(A114)	13 Apr 1971
F-111A	66-0029	(A47)	1 Sept 1971
F-111F	71-0892	(F68)	6 June 1973 Landed Safely
F-111A	67-0040	(A85)	11 July 1973
F-111E	68-0081	(E91)	5 Mar 1975
F-111E	68-0060	(E70)	5 Nov 1975
F-111C	A8-133	(D1-09)	29 Sep 1977
F-111E	68-0019	(E29)	9 Aug 1984

F-111E Ejection Narrative by Col Jim Stieber:

I was scheduled as aircraft commander of AKEE 46 on 5 November 1975, Guy Fawkes Day, out of RAF Upper Heyford. Early on, it became clear that only one aircraft would be available and we were rescheduled as a single-ship mission, low-level, to Wainfleet Range. I was crewed with Bob Gregory from our wing weapons shop. Pre-flight briefing was normal and, since we had not flown together before, we spent extra time briefing bird strike procedures. Aircraft confirmation was late due to maintenance issues, so we decided to forego the low-level portion of the mission and proceed directly to Wainfleet Range, in The Wash inlet, on the east coast of England.

Range entry and the first three passes were normal. On the fourth pass, a visual lay down planned for 480 kts, at 200' above the ground, I saw a white flash a few inches in front of the right windscreen. We were at 350' AGL descending and I was a tad hot on airspeed at 499 kts. Impact created the loudest noise I had ever heard, windscreen grazing, and immediate implosion. The sudden wind blast caused the right canopy to depart. So there we were, nose low, no glass on the right side of the cockpit, and a 500 knot breeze coming through the cockpit. That wind created a very dense fog in the cockpit akin to a rapid decompression at altitude. I leaned forward as far as I could with my chin over the stick and tried to acquire a visual reference, any visual reference, with which to orient myself and control the aircraft. I was instinctively, pulling the nose up and, I

All Photographs Courtesy of USAF Mishap Report.

thought, retarding the throttles. (Note: This is an unnatural act. I had in fact, pulled the nose up and pushed the throttles into afterburner.) Simultaneously, the provisions of our bird strike briefing were going through my mind and I was visualizing what I expected Bob to be doing: trying to gain a visual reference, gaining control of the aircraft: and if so, grabbing my wrist to communicate he had some control. After what I thought to be way too long, I reached down, pulled my ejection handle and, for good measure, pulled his. Without any noticeable changes in physiological cues or visibility, I put my hands back on the controls and kept trying to fly blind. The presumption is we had already begun the ejection sequence. At that point, I already was experiencing back and neck pain. Shortly thereafter, things started to quiet down a bit and numerous loud bangs were heard, which were indicative of various panels being blown off, exposing such things as drogue chute, parachute harness, main chute, capsule repositioning, etc. Once in a single point position hanging from the chute, the rest of the three-point harness was exposed and that repositioning of the capsule felt like dropping into a hard chair from a few feet up and created more back pain. Throughout the ejection sequence I was stuck bent over the

stick since my shoulder harness retractor had failed. That was one of 11 major failures in our capsule system that day.

As we descended hanging from the chute, we passed through clouds of smoke/exhaust from the capsule's rocket motor that entered our oxygen masks and caused us to drop the masks on one side. The capsule's emergency oxygen system had failed to actuate as witnessed by a free floating manual activation lever that came out in my hand when I pulled it. We checked the chute for integrity, and each other for injuries which was the first time I mentioned back pain. Bob then noticed we were getting close to the water in the descent, so we donned our oxygen masks, and assumed the impact position. That was a new procedure for capsule impact that had just come out via safety supplement days before this ejection. Water impact was sudden, hard, and felt like falling from the second story of a building sitting in a chair. That impact markedly increased my back pain and knocked the wind out of me. Upon impact the capsule immediately rolled, started filling with water coming in from the right side of the cockpit, and sank. My initial thought as it sank was, "the engineers said it would float!" As we sank, I saw Bob's hand go for his single point harness release, and figured it would be best to wait a moment while he exited through the hole in his canopy before I followed him out. We didn't want to be found stuck in the hole together like Laurel and Hardy stuck in a doorway.

The capsule came to rest in what I thought was an upright attitude, on the bottom of The Wash, in 20-30 feet of water. Thinking that, I proceeded to locate the various chute release and flotation activation handles located on the center beam of the capsule between the canopies. All I kept grabbing was water. Finally, I stuck my right hand out the hole where Bob's canopy should have been and reached over my head and located the outside of my canopy. I traced a path back into the cockpit and found an air vent located between the handles. I proceeded to pull handles with no apparent results. At some point I had a flashback to a TV program of a scuba diver trapped in rocks and thought that would be a terrible way to die. A thought entered my head that breathing water was no worse than air, so I started, without any adverse effects, to breathe in water. I also experienced the pleasant sensations of a near death experience and thought eternity was a pretty good alternative.

About the time I estimated I would pass out, I decided to unstrap, float to the surface (probably unconscious), and Bob and nearby fishermen could revive me. Somehow, I floated out of the capsule, my feet touched bottom, and my head broke the surface, looking up at Bob. I was drowning in water I could stand up in! But I was still drowning. The force of the ejection and my unrecalled pulling on the oxygen hose (the quick disconnect had failed) caused the oxygen mask harness bayonets to separate and jam in their brackets. While holding onto the jagged edges of the bottom of the capsule with one hand, I could pull the mask up just enough to break the seal with my face and take a breath and utter a few ideas to Bob…like, kick the mask off with your boot. In time we freed me from being pulled back under by the oxygen hose and got me up on the bottom of the capsule which, at that point a few minutes after arrival, was even with the surface of the water. You'll notice my initial assumptions at the top of this paragraph regarding the attitude and depth of the capsule were sorely inaccurate. Further, had the handles I was so desperately trying to locate and pull worked, Bob would have been severely injured or worse, since he was sitting on

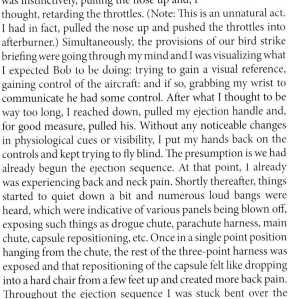

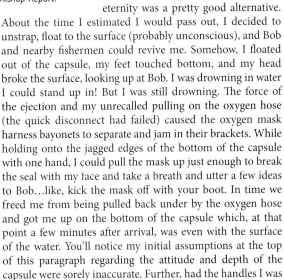

All Photographs Courtesy of USAF Mishap Report.

the exposed bottom of the capsule on the ballistic panels that would have been blown off, and, no doubt, him with them. Everything happens for a reason.

So there we sat, in The Wash, on the bottom of an upside down ejection capsule, at dusk, with the tide coming in fast, and pieces of burning wreckage floating by. I smoked in those days, so it seemed reasonable to pull my cigs out and try to get one lit on burning wreckage. They say nicotine is not addictive?

Within minutes, a one-man commercial fishing boat came along side and, with some difficulty, we got on board. His port did not have a hospital nearby, so he transferred us to a boat operated by two brothers, and they transported us to the harbor at Plymouth where we were met by the police chief who transported us to the Pilgrim Hospital, where we spent the night.

In all, as mentioned, we experienced 11 major failures of the ejection system, many minor ones, and survived. It was a violent ride, at the edge of the ejection envelope, but had we gone out in conventional ejection seats, I fear

the result would have been much worse…testimony to the capsule concept.

My injuries included a broken neck vertebral process, ruptured disc in the neck, 4 compression fractured vertebrae, and disc damage in lower back. Bob had superficial cuts from glass fragments getting under his oxygen mask. We both lost height.

Although I could have lived without this experience, I count myself fortunate to have flown two models of this wonderful, capable aircraft in combat and peacetime. She always delivered and brought me home…one way or the other.

James E. "Steebs" Stieber,
Colonel, USAF (Ret.),
Captain, Southwest Airlines

68-0066
F-111E # 76 GD/FW Production Run # A1-235
USAF Delivery Date: November 25, 1970

Crash Scenario
On July 20, 1990, the mishap aircraft departed Incirlik Air Base (AB), Turkey, as Number-2 of a four-ship flight redeploying after a Weapons Training Deployment (WTD) to RAF Upper Heyford, United Kingdom. Rejoin and climb to FL190 were uneventful. The mishap aircraft developed smoke in the cockpit from the Navigation Computer Unit (NCU). Shortly thereafter the aircraft departed controlled flight. The mishap pilot initiated a successful ejection. The aircraft crashed in a mountainous area and was destroyed 62 NM west of Incirlik AB, Turkey, near Sorgun, Turkey. The WSO did not have any ejection injuries, but the pilot sustained back injuries upon capsule landing. Crash Coordinates were (36 55 00 / E 034 09 00).

Findings
After rejoining to fingertip formation on the flight lead, the mishap WSO noted the inertial navigation system (INS) had frozen, followed quickly by large amounts of smoke emanating from underneath the navigation computer unit (NCU). Attempting to handle this problem, the pilot turned the Yaw and Pitch Dampers off, then turned off the Central Air Data Computer (CADC) in an attempt to clear the smoke. The pilot then allowed the aircraft to enter a left roll and was unable to regain control of the aircraft. The aircraft stalled and departed controlled flight.

Shutting down the NCU or the CADC should not have affected the flight characteristics of the aircraft. However, loss of the pitch damper will result in degrading damping characteristics, as well as the loss of the command augmentation system. Flight in these regimes of the F-111 operating envelope is restricted due to low-stick-force-per "g" response. The combination of low damping and reduced stick force per "g" increased the susceptibility of the pilot to induce oscillations.

Loss of the yaw damper will result in degraded Dutch roll dynamics, a slight, continuous, and uncorrectable nose oscillation.

Courtesy of Michael A. France

Roll inputs should be minimized to preclude excitement of the Dutch roll mode. Attempts to damp the Dutch roll mode through pilot rudder inputs should be minimized to prevent getting in-phase with the oscillations and causing the aircraft to enter a sustained oscillation. During flight with pitch, yaw, or roll damper off, large and/or abrupt stick and/or rudder inputs should be avoided in the damper off axis.

Loss of the pitch, roll, or yaw dampers will not cause loss of pilot actuated flight control authority, however, over-controlling the aircraft or attempting to "chase" the oscillation could aggravate the pilot's ability to remain within the aircraft's Angle of Attack (AOA) stability limits, resulting in a stall or departure from controlled flight.

Crew
Pilot: Capt Robert W Travis
WSO: Capt Richard M Basak
Call Sign: Unknown
Accident Board President: Col Barry L Ream
Time of Incident: 1308 Local
Assigned Unit: 55th TFS / 20th TFW RAF Upper Heyford, United Kingdom
Aircraft Statistics: 2048 Flights, 5346.9 Flight Hours
Mishap Result: Aircraft Destroyed / Successful Ejection

Courtesy of Author's Collection

68-0070
F-111E # 80 GD/FW Production Run # A1-239
USAF Delivery Date: December 30, 1970

Crash Scenario
On October 31, 1977, the mishap crew was scheduled for their second sortie of the day. The mission included night low-level TFR in a United Kingdom low-level area, one pass on a local RBS site, and recovery to home station. The same aircraft and crew flew both sorties as Number-2 in a two-ship formation. The lead aircraft was the same on both sorties as well. Takeoff on the second sortie was flown as a formation departure using 30-second spacing. The join-up and cruise to the descent point were uneventful. Flight split-up for entry into the low-level area was accomplished under radar advisory service. The low-level route progressed normally until approximately 25 NM from the exit point, when the flight lead noticed the Air-To-Air TACAN had broken lock. UHF and HF radio contact with the wingman was attempted without success. Queries with area radar agencies were also futile. The area was closed to further air traffic and lead reversed track and initiated search efforts. The crash site was eventually located and a rescue helicopter was vectored into the area by lead. Rescue personnel onboard the helicopter confirmed no survivors. The mishap aircraft crashed 2 NM northwest of Llangadfan, Wales, United Kingdom, which is 95 miles northwest of RAF Upper Heyford, United Kingdom.

Findings
The mishap aircraft hit the ground at a 12 degree angle following a night TFR low-level mission. The TFR was found not to be engaged, and it was determined that the mishap pilot was hand flying the aircraft when the crash occurred. By supposition there are two contributing factors: fatigue and/or visual illusion. This was the mishap pilot's second mission of the day, with the mishap occurring on the night portion. Mission demands from the first mission, then ground refueling operations, followed by departure and enroute cruise on the second mission may have contributed to fatigue. The second factor, a horizon or light fixation visual illusion, was suspected but cannot be conclusively verified. During the low-level, the mishap aircraft had taken standard night TFR trail spacing between 5 and 10 NM and maintained the position using the radar. Shortly after acknowledgment of lead's call that he was rolling out of the turn following the third steerpoint, the mishap aircraft maneuvered into a 12 degree dive and impacted the ground. Just prior to the crash the mishap aircraft had increased airspeed, establishing a rate of closure on the lead aircraft for an apparent rejoin. It was surmised that the mishap pilot might have interpreted a light on the ground for a light on the lead aircraft, establishing a visual illusion that contributed to the controlled flight into terrain (CFIT) mishap. The mishap pilot had either turned off or paddled off the TFR to complete the rejoin, which eliminated any terrain avoidance capability. The aircraft crashed into rising terrain in a slight descent, resolving into a 12-degree impact angle.

Crew
Pilot: Capt John J Sweeney
WSO: Capt William W Smart
Call Sign: Lay 198
Accident Board President: Col Jerry W Tietge
Time of Incident: 2155 LGMT
Assigned Unit: 79th TFS / 20th TFW RAF Upper Heyford, United Kingdom
Aircraft Statistics: 499 Flights 1394.0 Flight Hours
Mishap Result: Aircraft Destroyed / Fatal Crash / No Ejection Attempt

Aerial View of Crash
site and debris field.
*Courtesy of USAF
Mishap Report.*

*Photographs
Courtesy of USAF
Mishap Report.*

Courtesy of Author's Collection

68-0081
F-111E # 91 GD/FW Production Run # A1-250
USAF Delivery Date: January 31, 1971

Crash Scenario
On March 5, 1975, the mishap aircraft was scheduled for low-level TFR sortie. While descending from 2,000 feet AGL to terrain following radar (TFR) altitude of 1,000 feet AGL, and approximately 9 miles north of Kendal, England, a bird hit the right windscreen. The bird impact caused catastrophic failure of the right windscreen, as well as the hatch canopy glass. The WSO initiated the ejection sequence after he lost his helmet due to the severe windblast. The WSO suffered minor facial lacerations and the Aircraft Commander (AC) suffered a compression fracture of the upper spine during capsule landing. The aircraft crashed and was destroyed 4.5 NM southwest of Shap, Cumberland, United Kingdom.

Findings
The aircraft suffered a bird strike that penetrated the right windscreen, causing pilot disorientation due to high speed wind blast and windshield

glass fragments. Unable to accomplish basic aircraft control or discern the aircraft's attitude, the crew ejected. This was the 5th F-111 lost due to a bird strike.

Crew
Pilot: Maj Richard A Wolfe
WSO: Maj Jay K Miller
Call Sign: Unknown   (Not Listed on 711)
Accident Board President: Col Robert C Karns
Time of Incident: 1112 GMT
Assigned Unit: 55th TFS / 20th TFW RAF Upper Heyford, United Kingdom
Aircraft Statistics: 300 Flights886.7 Flight Hours
Mishap Result: Aircraft Destroyed / Successful Ejection
See also for similar type accidents:

F-111A	67-0043	(A88)	22 May 1969
F-111A	67-0069	(A114)	13 Apr 1971
F-111A	66-0029	(A47)	1 Sept 1971
F-111F	71-0892	(F68)	6 June 1973 Landed Safely
F-111A	67-0040	(A85)	11 July 1973
F-111E	68-0081	(E91)	5 Mar 1975
F-111E	68-0060	(E70)	5 Nov 1975
F-111C	A8-133	(D1-09)	29 Sep 1977
F-111E	68-0019	(E29)	9 Aug 1984

68-0082
F-111E # 92 GD/FW Production Run # A1-251
USAF Delivery Date: January 31, 1971

Crash Scenario
On March 25, 1981, the mishap aircrew planned to depart RAF Fairford, United Kingdom, and climb to FL180, proceed to RAF Upper Heyford, and land when fuel state permitted. Preflight, engine start, and taxi were normal and uneventful. During take-off, events were normal until immediately after liftoff. At that point the stall warning horn was heard and the stall warning light began flashing. The pilot checked the angle of attack (AOA) tape and it was at 20 degrees. Indicated airspeed was approximately 180 knots at this time. The pilot elected to abort the take-off and put the aircraft back on the runway. The aircraft touched down with approximately 3800 feet of runway remaining. The throttles were retarded to idle and brakes were immediately applied. Although the pilot knew there was no barrier available, he extended the tail hook by habit. Both crew members instinctively applied brakes, however, the aircraft could not be stopped in the remaining runway or over-run. It departed the prepared surface right of centerline and came to rest approximately 400 feet past the overrun within the base perimeter. The aircrew egressed the cockpit unharmed.

Courtesy of USAF Mishap Report.

Findings
During the stopover at RAF Fairford, a transient alert maintenance technician hit the AOA Probe with a maintenance stand, which caused the stall warning system to malfunction. Unfortunately, this was only the first link in the chain of events. The mishap pilot failed to detect the damaged probe during the preflight walk around. Next, after rotation to takeoff, the AOA probe subsequently locked in the high AOA position during the takeoff, resulting in an erroneous stall warning immediately after liftoff. The mishap pilot did not cross-check other available instrument information before aborting the takeoff. The aircraft was already airborne and at flying airspeed when the pilot aborted. After setting the aircraft down, there was now insufficient runway to stop

the heavy-weight mishap aircraft on the remaining runway.
Note: the artificial stall warning system is automatically armed by the landing gear squat switch when the aircraft becomes airborne. In this case, the pilot should have continued to fly the aircraft rather than abort. The audible stall warning tone could have been silenced by depressing the landing gear horn silencer button.

Crew
Pilot: 1Lt Timothy E Collins
WSO: Capt Robert N Miglin
Call Sign: Unknown
Accident Board President: Col Jerome E Hughes
Time of Incident: 1328 Local
Assigned Unit: 79th TFS / 20th TFW RAF Upper Heyford, United Kingdom
Aircraft Statistics: Unknown
Mishap Result: Aircraft Sustained Major Damage / Repaired at GDFW Vark Hospital

Heavily damaged nose radome and forward avionics bay. *Courtesy of Author's Collection via Tim Barnett.*

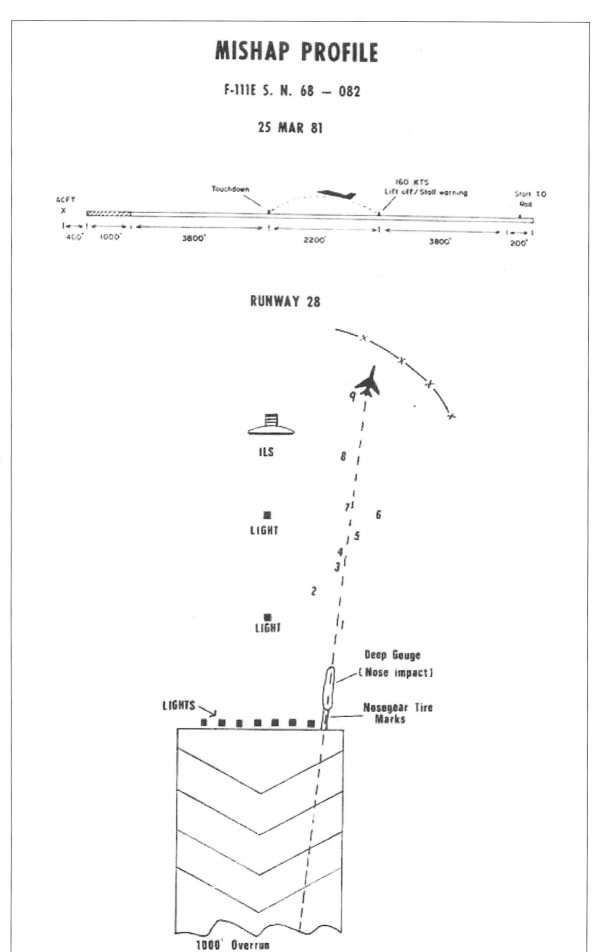

Figure 1:
Profile and Top
View of Mishap
Ground Track.
*Courtesy of USAF
Mishap Report.*

9
F-111F MISHAPS

Pave Tack F-111F over England. *Courtesy of the USAF.*

70-2366
F-111F # 5 GD/FW Production Run # E2-05
USAF Delivery Date: October 1, 1971

Crash Scenario

On December 21, 1983, the mishap aircraft departed RAF Lakenheath, United Kingdom, at 1831Z to fly a routine air refueling mission, followed by Radar Bomb Scoring (RBS) work, practice formation flying, and return to home station for practice instrument approaches. Approximately 46 minutes after take-off and six minutes after departing the tanker, the mishap aircraft requested an altitude block of FL250 to FL270. Shortly thereafter, the mishap aircraft departed controlled flight. The mishap crew successfully ejected, and the aircraft crashed into the North Sea and was destroyed. Crash location was 22 NM north of Flamborough Head, United Kingdom. Crash Coordinates were (N 54 28 00 / W 00 05 00).

Findings

The mishap aircraft was originally part of a two-ship mission, but took off late due to maintenance problems. After takeoff, the mishap aircraft rejoined for night aerial refueling without event. The aircraft departed controlled flight a short time after coming off the tanker. The aircraft had accumulated a history of flight control problems while on a recent Weapons Training Deployment (WTD) to Incirlik AB, Turkey. The crash was the result of loss of control while performing Lazy-8 type maneuvers while the aircraft's gross weight was high. The pitch and roll type maneuvers may have developed into oscillations which exceeded the flight control system's damping capability, complicating aircraft control. The investigation could not determine whether a flight control or flight control computer problem may have preexisted, thus contributing to the actual cause. This aircraft was modified with the SIS computer, which should have prevented the pilot exceeding 20 degrees AOA. However, if

Courtesy of Author's Collection

there was a mechanical malfunction with the flight controls, or the pilot rapidly pulsed the stick, an AOA overshoot was possible. In these possible scenarios, the flight control computers may not have been able to maintain aircraft stability as designed. The aircraft was lost over water and the primary cause was undetermined. However, night spatial disorientation may have influenced the pilot to over-control the aircraft while attempting post-stall recovery procedures.

Crew

Pilot: 1Lt James P Marcouiller
WSO: 1lt Terry A Tatterfield
Call Sign: Seeker 36
Time of Incident: 1920 BST
Accident Board President: Col Dale W Thompson
Assigned Unit: 493rd TFS / 48th TFW RAF Lakenheath, United Kingdom
Aircraft Statistics: 1,180 Flights and 3,109.6 Flight hours
Mishap Result: Aircraft Destroyed / Successful Ejection

73-0714
F-111F # 90 GD/FW Production Run # E2-90
USAF Delivery Date: January 31, 1975

70-2367
F-111F # 6 GD/FW Production Run # E2-06
USAF Delivery Date: October 14, 1971

Crash Scenario

On April 20, 1979, both mishap aircraft (Call Signs Hid 23 [73-0714] and Hid 24 [70-2367]) were scheduled as a two ship low-level training weapons delivery sortie. The aircraft both departed RAF Lakenheath, United Kingdom, at 0911 BST. Pre-flights, engine starts, and taxi and launch were accomplished without incident. Climb and cruise to the low-level entry point for Low Level Area 14 was accomplished. Weather precluded entry into the low flying area, and the formation proceeded to the Tain Range, on the Moray Firth in Scotland, for practice weapons delivery. Range entry and low angle weapons deliveries were conducted. Upon range departure, during rejoin to formation, the two aircraft collided. Both aircrews successfully ejected and were rescued from the water by a local fishing vessel. Both aircraft crashed into the sea and were destroyed. Crash Coordinates were (N 53 51 50 / W 004 00 00) 2 NM south southeast of Donoch, Scotland.

Findings

The mid-air collision between aircraft 73-0714 and 70-2367 occurred during the rejoin after completing range work. Hid 24 failed to monitor closure and ensure flight path deconfliction while on the rejoin line toward Hid 23. The collision resulted in sufficient damage to both aircraft that flight control was lost. The aircrews from both aircraft successfully ejected and made water landings. Hid 23's crew module rolled inverted when the pilot stood up to signal a nearby fishing boat and remained inverted on the water's surface. Hid 24's module initially settled to one side until the crew activated self-righting bags, at which time the module returned to an upright position.

73-0714 shown being delivered to the BAe Bristol, United Kingdom Depot Facility. *Courtesy of Author's Collection via John Godfrey Bae.*

70-2367 as depicted. *Courtesy of the USAF.*

A fishing vessel in the vicinity of the crew modules retrieved both crews. A rescue helicopter from RAF Lossiemouth arrived several minutes later.

Crew:	73-0714	70-2367
Pilot:	Capt Joseph Peluso	Capt Stephen R Ruttman
WSO:	Capt Timothy A Schlitt	Capt Roger L Webb
Call Sign:	Hid 23	Hid 24

Time of Incident: 1055 BST
Accident Board President: Col C.D. Wright
Assigned Unit: 492ⁿᵈ TFS / 48ᵗʰ TFW RAF Lakenheath

Aircraft Statistics:	417 Flights and 1,140.0 Flight Hours	637 Flights and 1,736.0 Flight Hours
Mishap Result:	Aircraft Destroyed / Successful Ejection	Aircraft Destroyed / Successful Ejection

The following narrative was written by Aircraft Commander of 73-0714 (Hid 23), Lt Col Joe Peluso, USAF, Ret:

Our two ship sortie was scheduled as a low-level flight in support of an air defense exercise in Low Flying Area 14 in Scotland. It was to be a relatively tame mission with just a dry (no bombs dropped) level pass on an airfield in Scotland. When we briefed the mission that morning, we were aware the weather would be marginal in the low-level and target area. An alternate mission of practice weapons deliveries in Scotland was briefed to include Low Angle Dive (LAD), Radar Lay Down (RLD) and Visual Lay Down (VLD) passes on Tain and Rosehearty ranges. Tain range is located about 40 miles north of Inverness, Scotland on the Dornoch Firth. Rosehearty range is about 70 miles east of Tain, just west of Fraserburgh, Scotland.

Taxi, takeoff and cruise to the low fly area were uneventful. Shortly after descending into the low fly area, the weather began to deteriorate and we would be unable to continue the mission VFR (visual flight rules). After climbing out of the low fly area we proceeded east to Tain range for our alternate mission. While we did not have any scheduled Tain range time, the range was not occupied and we were allowed to proceed with our practice bombing runs. We were carrying twelve practice bombs that day. Our plan was to drop 6 practice bombs at Tain range then proceed to Rosehearty range to drop the other six.

The weather at Tain range that day was excellent. There were a few scattered clouds with unrestricted visibility and light winds. Our range work went as briefed with two low angle dive (10 degree) passes, two RLD's and two VLD's. I made one extra dry pass to expedite the rejoin. I called "off dry for the rejoin." My wingman acknowledged and called "lead in sight." The plan was to rejoin at 1,000 feet AGL and proceed low-level over water and along the coast to Rosehearty range.

The great thing about flying in the United Kingdom is most of the country is a low fly area with few restrictions. There are however many noise sensitive areas to be avoided especially along the coast. The town of Dornoch just north of Tain was one of those noise sensitive areas. My initial turn off target was to the right in a 30 degree bank turn. As the rejoin progressed I could see I would overfly the Dornoch area and steepened my bank to 45 degrees to stay away from Dornoch. As we continued the turn I asked my WSO (Weapons System Officer) Tim Schlitt how my wingman was doing. He responded with something like "a little fast and ahead of the line, but not bad." Shortly thereafter, as I was looking through the right canopy I saw a blur of an aircraft pass below me. I then looked out my canopy expecting to see my wingman shoot out high and left with the speed brake extended as he tried to slow his forward motion. Instead, I felt my aircraft shudder and start to roll. I scanned the engine instruments thinking maybe I had a double compressor stall because of the vibration. Everything seemed normal except the aircraft continued to roll right despite my control inputs. When my attitude reached about 120 or so

degrees right bank and about 30 degrees nose low I decided I had seen enough and pulled the ejection handles as I told the WSO "we're getting outta here."

As soon as I pulled the ejection handle temporal distortion set in. I distinctly remember seeing bits of the aircraft fly off as the SMDC (shielded mild detonating cord) severed the capsule from the fuselage. This was followed by a bright orange flame starting to envelop the capsule as the rocket motor ignited. The "Gs" created by the rocket motor igniting blacked me out for a few seconds. When I regained consciousness, I looked up to see a beautiful canopy over us. Initially the capsule is in a very nose down attitude. This probably has to do with how the main chute deploys and unfurls. Shortly after the chute is fully deployed, another SMDC line fires to release a riser embedded between the two forward windscreens. This repositions the capsule so it descends in an upright attitude. Although I knew this reposition would occur, it was still very disconcerting to see what appeared as my recovery chute departing the capsule. Everything appeared to function as advertised in the flight manual.

Part of the ejection sequence is to inflate the impact attenuation bag located on the bottom of the escape module. This reduces the impact forces on your body when the capsule hits the ground, or, as in our case, the water. Unfortunately, the only way you have to know if the bag actually inflated is when you hit the ground. Luckily for us, the bag did inflate properly. Despite the bag being inflated, and landing in water, the impact was quite hard. I can only imagine what it would be like on firm ground or if the bag did not inflate. The momentum of the capsule pushed us about ten feet underwater before coming to rest on the surface. There are other inflatable bags around the escape module that help keep it upright and floating.

Poopy suits are normally used by aircrews when flying overwater. Because F-111 crews are supposed to be protected by the capsule we were not required to wear them. There were however poopy suits installed in the capsule that could be donned if necessary. The poopy suits were stored in a cavity on the either side of the capsule. For some reason we were unable to pull the suits out of the cavity. Even if we had, it would have been very difficult to don them. Don't get me wrong, I appreciated not having to fly around in a rubber suit. We were floating somewhat blissfully when I could see a fishing boat in the distance. I opened the canopy hatch on my side so I could get a better look at the boat and hopefully get their attention. Little did I know that they had seen the mid-air explosion and watched as the capsules hit the water. As I stood on the canopy rail to signal the boat my weight caused the capsule to rotate upside down. My WSO scrambled out of the capsule into the very cold water with me. The capsule continued float albeit upside down so we climbed onto the capsule to get out of the water. Unfortunately the forward flotation bag eventually ripped off and departed the capsule at which point the nose of the capsule went underwater, and all that could be seen was the aft flotation bags of the capsule. It took the fishing vessel about ten minutes to get to our position and extract us from the water. It was probably the coldest ten minutes of my life. The water temperature was in the mid-40s. At least I had thermal underwear on under my flight suit which helped retain some heat. My WSO only had on a flight suit and he was extremely cold. The crew of the fishing vessel extricated us from the water, wrapped us in blankets and gave us some hot soup. While the crew attended to us, they motored over to where my wingman's capsule had landed. About that time, a rescue helicopter from RAF Lossiemouth arrived on scene to recover us. The range officer at Tain had also seen the mid-air collision and phoned the rescue squadron. All four crewmembers were transported to RAF Lossiemouth while awaiting transportation back to RAF Lakenheath.

70-2368
F-111F # 7 GD/FW PRODUCTION RUN # E2-07
USAF Delivery Date: October 14, 1971

Crash Scenario
On May 2, 1990, the mishap aircraft departed RAF Lakenheath, United Kingdom, as number two of a two-ship formation which formed part of a ten-ship simulated attack package on RAF Sculthorpe, United Kingdom. The flight from takeoff until just after the planned airfield attack was normal. After recovery from the simulated toss bomb delivery on airfield, the aft fuselage of the mishap aircraft was seen enveloped in a large inflight fire. The lead aircraft advised the mishap crew of the fire. The mishap aircrew initiated a successful ejection, and the mishap aircraft impacted in an open field and was destroyed. Debris from the impact damaged a nearby unoccupied house. Crash Coordinates were (N 52 55 00 / E 000 57 00) 8 NM northeast from RAF Sculthorpe, United Kingdom.

Findings
The aircraft was outbound from the RAF Sculthorpe airfield when the mishap crew heard a loud thump, followed by moderate to severe aircraft vibrations and numerous warning and caution lights. Shortly after shutting down the right engine, the flight lead reported the mishap aircraft was on fire and recommended ejection. Due to a 1st stage fan blade failure, engine fan blades penetrated through the engine case and ruptured the aft centerbody fuel tank. The catastrophic engine failure erupted into an uncontrollable

and uncontained aft fuselage fire. The intensity of the fire rapidly initiated multiple system failures and contributed to loss of control. The aircraft crashed just off Blankey Point, 2 miles from RAF Sculthorpe, United Kingdom.

Crew
Pilot: Capt David E Ratcliff Jr.
WSO: 1Lt Brian W Kirkwood
Call Sign: Rex 62
Time of Incident: 1253 BST
Accident Board President: Col Gregory P Bailey
Assigned Unit: 492nd TFS / 48th TFW RAF Lakenheath, United Kingdom
Aircraft Statistics: 1,692 Flights and 4,269.8 Flight Hours
Mishap Result: Aircraft Destroyed / Successful Ejection

Courtesy of Author's Collection

70-2375
F-111F # 14 GD/FW Production Run # E2-14
USAF Delivery Date: November 8, 1971

Crash Scenario
On July 28, 1987, the mishap aircraft was lead of a two-ship formation of F-111Fs that departed RAF Lakenheath, United Kingdom, at 1018Z, to fly a flight lead upgrade sortie. Prior to departure, the mishap aircraft had a maintenance issue while at the end of runway last chance arming area. The maintenance problem was a left (#1) engine generator falling off line. Checkout and adjustments were accomplished by the launch truck (engine and electrics shop personnel), with proper documentation and release entries annotated in the aircraft forms prior to launch. The maintenance performed was not a factor in the mishap. Weapons deliveries were accomplished on the Wainfleet and Donna Nook ranges prior to descending low-level for a simulated Pave Tack toss bomb attack on a simulated target in Scotland. During the toss recovery procedure the mishap aircraft crashed. Ejection was initiated prior to impact, however, the attempt was out of the envelope. Crash location was Thirlstane Farm, 3 miles east of Lauder, Scotland. Coordinates were (N 55 42 17 / W 02 42 67) 240 NM on the 330 degree radial from RAF Lakenheath.

Findings
During a day toss bomb delivery profile, the pilot entered IMC (Instrument Meteorological Conditions) while executing a rolling recovery from the attack maneuver. The mishap pilot may have succumbed to unrecognized spatial disorientation, as the aircraft exited the low cloud ceiling nose low at over 500 knots. The aircraft was too low to avoid collision with the ground. Cloud bases reported by his wingman, Deuce 32, were 2,700 feet Above Mean Sea Level (AMSL),

Courtesy of Author's Collection via Chuck Pitts.

approximately 1,800ft above ground (AGL) at the time of the accident. It could not be determined whether a failure of the primary flight instruments contributed to this Controlled Flight Into Terrain (CFIT) mishap. The ejection attempt was outside the safe recovery envelope.

Crew
Pilot: Capt Taylor F Stem III
WSO: Capt Phillip D Baldwin
Call Sign: Deuce 31
Time of Incident: 1125 BDT
Accident Board President: Col David J Vogl
Assigned Unit: 493rd TFS / 48th TFW RAF Lakenheath, United Kingdom
Aircraft Statistics: 1,938 Flights and 4,939.6 Flight Hours
Mishap Result: Aircraft Destroyed / Fatal Crash / Unsuccessful Ejection, Out of the Envelope.

70-2377
F-111F # 16 GD/FW Production Run # E2-16
USAF Delivery Date: November 17, 1971

Crash Scenario

On December 7, 1982, the mishap aircraft departed RAF Lakenheath at 1905 GMT on a night training mission. The crew departed and climbed to high altitude enroute to Scotland. The mishap aircrew initiated a TFR Blind Letdown descent at 1952 GMT to begin their planned night low-level flight in the Highlands Restricted Area. The aircraft crashed into a mountain (Sgurr na Stri) on the Isle of Skye at 1,000 feet MSL and was destroyed. No ejection attempt was initiated and both crewmembers were fatally injured. Crash Coordinates were (N 57 11 07 / W 06 08 30).

Findings

The mishap aircraft crashed during a night low-level sortie shortly after performing an Auto TFR descent that initially began over-land and then transitioned to over-water. During the Blind Letdown, the LARA system correctly leveled the aircraft off at 1,000 feet above ground level as designed. Shortly after the level off, the pilot initiated a right turn toward the coast line while level at 1,000 feet above the water. The mishap pilot had just completed the right-hand turn when it hit a cliff. Several factors were present in the chain of events leading to the crash. First, maintenance was incorrectly performed on the TFR antennas, and proper alignment and tuning was not conducted to complete the maintenance action. Therefore, the TFRs were incorrectly calibrated to insure proper operation in avoiding terrain. Without the TFR receiving forward radar signals no terrain was displayed on the pilot's E-Scope, nor transmitted to signal the aircraft to fly-up. The second link in the chain of events was partially blamed on the student WSO. The WSO was scheduled on the mishap sortie with an experienced instructor due to necessary retraining for radar navigation skills. The student WSO's primary duties were to continually update the pilot on route position and verbally communicate approaching terrain features. The pilot's duties are to validate route

Courtesy of Patrick Little via Douglas Slowiak Vortex Photo-Graphics Collection

position and monitor TFR performance versus observed obstacles and terrain approaching on the TFR Scope. The pilot must verify if the TFR commands a climb to overfly the approaching terrain. The WSO had previously demonstrated a tendency to operate the Attack Radar Set (ARS) antenna in a manner that failed to detect navigation update points, and provide terrain awareness information to the pilot. It was assumed by the mishap investigation team that the student WSO again failed to detect approaching terrain and advise the instructor pilot of the hazard in a timely manner. Lastly, the instructor pilot failed to monitor the TFR's performance by conducting the Blind Letdown over-water into a no-show E-Scope return. In any let-down descent, the LARA is the primary piece of equipment until the TFR begins to compute forward video at 35,000 feet slant range. If the letdown is over-water the LARA commands the level-off, which is known to have occurred. After the LARA correctly leveled the descending F-111, the pilot initiated a right turn into approaching terrain and failed to validate E-Scope returns when the aircraft was clearly approaching rising terrain immediately ahead (see depicted route map on the following page). With the absence of forward video on the E-Scope due to the improperly aligned or tuned TFR antennas, the mishap crew failed to detect and overfly approaching terrain. The mishap was the result of Controlled Flight Into Terrain (CFIT).

Note added via pilot interview: the primary terrain avoidance instrument in all F-111s was the Attack Radar. Although it did not do any of the flying, it gave the best indication of approaching terrain and clearance over terrain. Plus, on the cresting of a peak, forward video had to be seen in the ARS before letting the TFR command a descent. The standard call over a peak or ridge was "I have forward video."

Crew

Pilot: Maj Burnley L Rudiger Jr.
WSO: 1Lt Steven J Pitt
Call Sign: Vixen 31
Time of Incident: 1958 GMT
Accident Board President: Col Lawrence W Foley
Assigned Unit: 494th TFS / 48th TFW RAF Lakenheath, United Kingdom
Aircraft Statistics: 941 Flights and 2490.1 Flight Hours
Mishap Result: Aircraft Destroyed / Fatal Crash / No Ejection Initiated

Close-up of the crash site. *Courtesy of USAF Mishap Report.*

Large overview photo of flight path depicted by the red arrow. *Courtesy of USAF Mishap Report.*

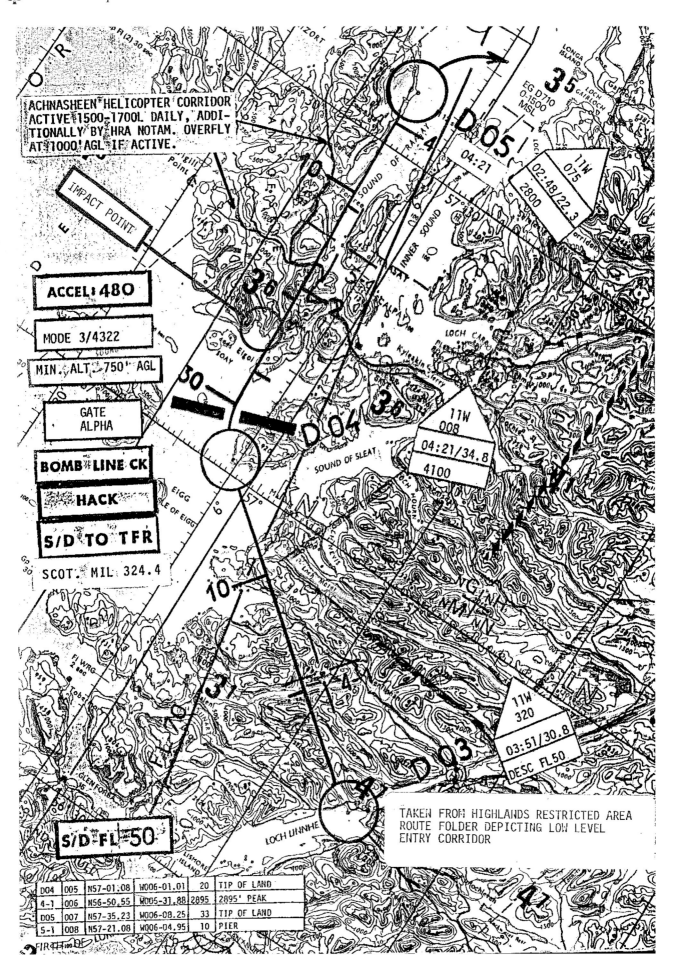

70-2380
F-111F # 19 GD/FW Production Run # E2-19
USAF Delivery Date: November 11, 1971

Shown on the "Hard-Stand" bedded down for the day. *Courtesy of Art Hoffman.*

Crash Scenario

On December 15, 1977, the mishap aircraft was on a Functional Check Flight (FCF) when a utility hydraulic failure occurred. An inflight emergency was declared, and recovery toward RAF Lakenheath was initiated. While enroute, the Utility Hydraulic failure emergency checklist procedures were accomplished. Initial contact was made with the Supervisor of Flying (SOF), and he was informed of the hydraulic failure. At approximately 1225 L, the crew attempted emergency extension of the slats and flaps. The slats extended without any problem, but as the flaps passed the 15-20 degree down position, the mishap aircraft began a pitch up and a left roll. The flaps and slats were retracted and aircraft control was restored. The aircraft commander stated the stick was feeling "funny." It was decided to lower the landing gear, and this was successfully accomplished with the alternate system. A second attempt to lower the slats and flaps resulted in a similar uncommanded pitch up as the slats reached the 20-degree down position. The flaps were returned to the 15 degree down position. Though control was restored, the decision was made to fully retract the flaps and slats and land in a no-slat-no-flap configuration. During a low altitude fly-by over the runway for a visual inspection, the aircraft became increasingly difficult to control, requiring constant forward pressure on the stick to keep the nose down. At 1239 L, the aircraft began a pitch up that could not be overcome by both crewmembers exerting full forward control stick pressure. Afterburner was selected, but pitch attitude and angle of attack continued to increase. At 1240 L the nose sliced to the left and the WSO initiated ejection at approximately 10,000 feet AGL. The ejection

was successful. The aircraft was destroyed on impact. Crash location was 12.5 NM southwest of RAF Lakenheath.

Findings

The mishap aircraft was returning to base with a declared Inflight Emergency (IFE) for Utility Hydraulic failure. Post crash mishap investigation revealed that the right horizontal tail servo actuator (HTSA) mount pin had become loose, causing a split horizontal stabilizer condition and eventually loss of flight control. The F-111's flight control system automatically attempts to trim the aircraft as the airspeed slows or during configuration changes, such as lowering the landing gear, flaps, and slats. With the asymmetric horizontal stabilizers automatically attempting to compensate for the slowing aircraft, uncommanded yaw, pitch, and roll motions occurred due to the erratic movements of the malfunctioning horizontal stabilizer. While the pilot attempted to apply corrective flight control inputs, the corresponding motion of the deflecting horizontal stabilizer was insufficient to correct pitch-ups. The aircraft then slowly climbed to an attitude and airspeed from which the aircraft stalled and control was completely lost. Ejection was the only recourse.

Newmarket Crash Scene. *Courtesy of Jerry Kemp.*

Crew
Pilot: Capt Jerry L Kemp
WSO: Capt Thomas E Bergam
Call Sign: Trest 07
Time of Incident: 1240 LGMT
Accident Board President: Col Donald G Waltman
Assigned Unit: 492nd TFS / 48th TFW RAF Lakenheath, United Kingdom
Aircraft Statistics: 550 Flights and 1,542.5 Flight Hours
Mishap Result: Aircraft Destroyed / Successful Ejection

Pilot's personal story:

It was one of those rare beautiful clear Saturday mornings in East Anglia (Sat. being the reason no other airplanes were airborne) when I was called to do the FCF (functional check flight). Maintenance had been working on 380 all night to finish it up for the flight check. They were hoping to put it on the schedule Monday. We'd both volunteered to do FCFs on weekends (as if we had a choice) and I was told Bergie would meet me at the maintenance hangar. We both loved flying together and an FCF on a beautiful day was icing on the cake. The FCF profile was great fun to fly. The jet was clean and light weight; we did full AB climbs, zoom climbs and zero G accelerations with wings fully swept, a Mach 2 plus run at 50 thousand feet, high G wind-up turns, and basically checked and tested every system and performance parameter on the airplane. Life don't get any better than that over the beautiful English countryside and historic English Channel, in my humble opinion. But I may be a little strange.

The airplane was a hangar queen and besides a double engine change, had had extensive flight control maintenance and other systems work done. It was during the high G wind-up check that the caution and warning panel lit up like a pinball machine. I declared an emergency and requested clearance direct to Lakenheath from Eastern Radar while Bergie got out the Emergency checklist to sort out the problem. We were dealing with flying a sick airplane, the checklist, communicating with each other, Eastern Radar, the SOF (supervisor of flying, a senior officer) and it seems like someone else was on the frequency. I was having sensory overload and was of course task saturated. I told everyone to come up on the SOF frequency so they would stop stepping on each other and to slow down and help get this airplane on the ground, not hinder the effort. The SOF had all the manuals out, the DO (the #2 COL in the wing - Director of Operations) in the tower and was working on a conference call with General Dynamics. This frequency consolidation turned out to be a good decision as the SOF frequency was recorded and helped the accident investigation board a lot. I still have a copy of the tape. The only time I've listened to it since the accident my heart rate increased and my back started to hurt.

Bergie's summary of the final sequence is right on the money. The only thing I'd add is that while they were trying to get another airplane airborne to join in formation with us, the SOF asked me to fly a low approach so he could get a look at the airplane. I told him I'd fly over the field, but wouldn't descend below 5,000 feet because aircraft control was deteriorating, or words to that effect. Base housing was near the runway and I didn't want to chance losing control of the airplane at low altitude near where my family and many others were enjoying a beautiful Saturday morning.

Shortly after the flyover, I was getting intermittent violent feedback through the flight controls and had almost lost it a couple times. I told the SOF we were going to fly out over the Wash (a shallow part of the English Channel) in case we had to give this airplane back to the taxpayers. I didn't use those words, but that was the idea. It was not able to land at that point and I wanted to avoid the populated countryside if possible until we could diagnose the problem. That was my next to last transmission. The airplane then pitched straight up on its own. I selected full AB and tried to get the nose down to preserve flying airspeed. But even with Bergie's help we couldn't overcome stick pressure and regain control. We were passengers at that point. Albeit very reluctant passengers! My last transmission prior to the ejection was: "We're going to have to get out now!" The only problem with that last transmission was that my voice was about five octaves higher and it totally destroyed my Chuck Yeager image. Up until that point I sounded cool and collected.

I remember the nose slice into the inverted spin being very violent, as was the ejection. Then everything slowed down. I saw the aircraft in flames from the cockpit aft, and debris floating away from me in slow motion. I think I was in shock to think we had actually ejected from a multi-million dollar fighter jet. The next thing I remember was the opening shock of the chute and everything coming back to real time. Bergie and I looked at each other and said: "are you ok", simultaneously I think. My back hurt but I was happy to be alive. It seemed about a five minute ride under the chute until the capsule impacted the ground. And when the impact occurred the pain in my back increased about ten fold. I thought it was broken. I still have some pain at times, but considering the alternative, I'm ok with it. I don't think I mentioned it to the flight surgeon because I wanted to get back on flying status ASAP

I hope this wasn't too long and boring, but that's the way I remember the accident. A few more somewhat humorous incidents occurred once we were on the ground with me trying to get out of the capsule, Bergie trying to talk on the Emergency radio and more and more British civilians swarming the site but that is beyond the scope of this I think.

A postscript: About three months later, two good friends and squadron mates, Chuck Kitchell and Jeff Moore, were lost when they ejected from an F-111 after a lightning strike. Their chute didn't deploy due to a rocket nozzle burn through. May God rest their souls. They were good men of great character. The F-111 fleet was grounded to check the rocket nozzles on all escape capsules. Many airplanes had the same potential malfunction including the one we used three months earlier.

"Check-6"
Jerry "Joe Bob" Kemp

WSO's personal story:

Here is some additional information regarding 380. Jerry and I were not scheduled to fly that day, but 380 had just come out of maintenance for double engine change as I recall, and we were directed to do a check flight on it. My pilot and I were a Functional Check Flight crew. When any aircraft had major maintenance performed it was required to be flown and checked out (FCF) before being returned to the squadron. We were informed that there was a check flight and were scheduled to do it.

Preflight was uneventful and we took off. As we were putting the aircraft through some checks, we felt a shudder and several malfunction lights illuminated. After an assessment, we determined that we had a hydraulic failure and then decided to return to base (RTB). As we were in the pattern and configuring the jet for landing, the Vark pitched up and it took both of us to get the nose down. For the next several moments, we were in and out of control. We flew down the runway so the safety officer could take a look at us with the binoculars, but nothing looked out of the ordinary. There were no other jets in the pattern. As we made a climbing turn to the right, the jet pitched up, straight up! The pilot selected afterburner, and for a moment we were riding a rocket. Both of us were pushing forward on the control sticks, but nothing happened. We ran out of airspeed, the aircraft violently stalled, and we entered into an inverted spin. I grabbed the ejection handle, yelled "Sit up Jerry", and pulled. What seemed like a minute later, I heard a loud bang and out we went. The chute deployed and we landed approx. 100 meters from the still smoldering wreckage. A crowd of Brits came over offering us hot tea and apologizing for not having any Brandy! Later we were flown by British helicopter back to RAF Lakenheath. The accident investigation team determined there was a mechanical failure on the right stabilator, which severed hydraulic lines and resulted in intermittent un-commanded pitch inputs. That in a nutshell is what happened.

Regards,
Bergie

Courtesy of Author's Collection

70-2388
F-111F # 27 GD/FW Production Run # E2-27
USAF Delivery Date: December 28, 1971

Crash Scenario

On March 16, 1976, the mishap crew was scheduled for a day conventional ground attack sortie. Pre-flight planning and mission preparation for the mishap sortie began at 0630 MST. Final desk briefing, local flight clearance, and weather forms were completed, and the crew arrived at the aircraft at 0830 MST. Preflight, engine start, taxi, and before takeoff checks were normal. Takeoff was scheduled for 0930 MST. Actual takeoff for the mishap aircraft was 0935 MST, with the wingman delaying his takeoff 17 minutes for quick check inspection and maintenance. Enroute, low-level, range work, and initial recovery of the flight were accomplished as briefed. Turning on a 15 NM final for a PAR approach, the mishap aircraft's right (#2) engine throttle froze at 88% RPM. At 1210 MST, the mishap aircraft accomplished a normal landing on Runway 12 at Mountain Home AFB while the wingman executed a go-around and low approach. After a series of ground roll porpoises, the aircrew successfully ejected approximately 21 seconds down the runway. Capsule touchdown was approximately 700 feet short of the aircraft wreckage, and the aircrew egressed without injury. Post impact fire severely damaged the aircraft.

Findings

The aircraft had a frozen right throttle at 88% RPM power setting. The pilot made a decision, approved by the SOF, to make a visual full stop landing. Four minutes after discovery of the malfunctioning throttle, the pilot landed 600 feet down the runway at a speed well above that recommended for the landing weight and configuration. After flying the nose wheel to the runway, the pilot depressed the right engine fire push-button; however, the engine continued to run for an additional 20 seconds due to available residual fuel. Transitioning visually back to the runway, he noted the nose of the aircraft coming up so he applied forward stick pressure. The nose continued up, and the aircraft became airborne approximately 2 feet. The pilot positioned the stick to hold the aircraft in a landing attitude and tried to fly the aircraft back to the runway. On the third porpoise, approximately 4,000 feet from the approach end of the runway and about 20 feet above the runway, the pilot applied power and aft stick to stabilize the aircraft attitude in an attempt to fly the aircraft back to the runway. This time, rather than the aircraft settling into a normal nose slightly up, main gear first touchdown, the nose rotated downward towards the runway. Due to the decaying airspeed, there was insufficient horizontal stabilizer control authority to correct the downward pitch attitude. Both crew members felt the aircraft would not survive the impact and ejected about 10 feet above the runway and 140 KIAS. The aircraft impacted and burned approximately 5,300 feet from the approach end of the runway. The stuck throttle was determined to be the result of internal binding of the throttle cable control assembly.

Crew

Pilot: Flt Lt Richard E O'Ferrall RAAF
WSO: Capt Joseph D Freeman USAF
Call Sign: Noman 87
Time of Incident: 1210 MST
Accident Board President: Col William F Palmer
Assigned Unit: 390th TFS / 366th TFW Mountain Home AFB, Idaho
Aircraft Statistics: 386 Flights and 1,112.2 Flight Hours
Mishap Result: Aircraft Destroyed / Successful Ejection

Courtesy of Richard E. O'Ferrall

70-2393
F-111F # 32 GD/FW Production Run # E2-32
USAF Delivery Date: January 12, 1972

Crash Scenario

On November 8, 1975, the mishap aircrew was scheduled to fly an Operational Readiness Inspection (ORI) mission for the 366th TFW. Preflight, engine start, and taxi were normal. The mishap aircraft took-off at 0331 MST. The mission was flown as planned through the night weapons delivery portion of the sortie. At the conclusion of the weapons delivery maneuvers, the aircraft began its return to Mountain Home AFB, Idaho. Upon return to the local traffic pattern for a night landing, as the slats were extending, the aircraft yawed violently to the left. The Pilot Weapons System Officer (PWSO), who was controlling the aircraft, attempted to counter the yaw/roll movement with stick and rudder inputs while the pilot attempted to retract the slats. The aircraft then yawed/rolled back to the right, pitching up slightly. When the right rolling motion overshot the desired flight attitude, the PWSO assumed that he and the pilot were both on the controls and fighting each other's inputs. As the aircraft's nose started left again the PWSO noted the pilot was on the controls, so he verbally transferred control to him. As the pilot took control he noted 160 KIAS, selected afterburners, and noted a stall warning. He pushed the stick forward, but no roll or rudder controls were applied. As the left roll continued, the pilot decided to eject and reached for the ejection handle. At this time, the nose sliced down and the roll continued. The mishap aircraft became uncontrollable and the mishap aircrew initiated a successful ejection sequence.

Findings

On two of the four previous sorties prior to the mishap flight, the flight crews had reset intermittent Adverse Yaw Compensation (AYC) malfunctions and did not identify the problem to maintenance technicians. Additionally, the mishap aircraft had a previous history of AYC problems that were not properly analyzed and corrected. Due to tech data confusion between the yaw computer and AYC malfunction

A brand new F-111F (Production number E2-32 on nose gear door) is photographed at GDFW prior to USAF delivery. *Courtesy of Joe Betts Collection.*

analysis, the recurring AYC malfunctions went unrepaired prior to the mishap flight. Shortly after takeoff on the mishap sortie, the crew reset an AYC malfunction in accordance with checklist procedures, but this masked the true nature of the AYC problem. At some time during the accident flight a second AYC malfunction occurred, due to a malfunction in either the Feel and Trim assembly or the Beta probe. During the final approach to land the slow speed, combined with the existing AYC problems, caused the aircraft to yaw and roll to the left, contributing to the crew's loss of control. Disorientation and aircraft oscillations made it difficult for the pilot to locate and grasp the ejection handle. The PWSO initiated the ejection while the aircraft had entered an inverted nose-low attitude at 3,259 feet AGL.

Crew
Pilot: Capt Eddie L Ortego
WSO: 1Lt Richard B Lewis
Call Sign: Unknown
Time of Incident: 0536 MST
Accident Board President: Col Vernon L Frye
Assigned Unit: 391st TFS / 366th TFW Mountain Home AFB, Idaho
Aircraft Statistics: 325 Flights and 906.4 Flight Hours
Mishap Result: Aircraft Destroyed / Successful Ejection

70-2395
F-111F # 34 GD/FW Production Run # E2-34
USAF Delivery Date: January 21, 1972

Crash Scenario

On September 11, 1974, the mishap aircraft crashed during a night Terrain Following Radar (TFR) and Radar Lay-Down (RLD) bomb delivery on the Saylor Creek Bombing Range (R-3202) in Idaho. The mishap aircraft was scheduled to fly the Boise 412 Visual Flight Rule (VFR) high speed low-level route, which terminates at the Saylor Creek Bombing Range. The mishap aircraft took off at 2115 MDT. The night TFR low-level route to the bombing range was flown without any problems. The mishap aircraft completed one successful pass and then reentered the range. During the second pass, the mishap aircraft crashed. Both crew members were fatally injured. The crash location was 44 NM on the 143 degree radial from Mountain Home AFB (TACAN).

Findings

Shortly after the pilot called turning base-to-final for a second bomb delivery pass, the aircraft impacted the ground in a descending right turn. The mishap aircraft crashed short of the intended bomb target on a night practice Radar Lay Down (RLD) bombing run at 2223 MST. Air Traffic Controllers in the base control tower saw a fire ball shortly after they lost contact with the aircrew during the mishap aircraft's second bomb run toward the range target. No ejection attempt was made. The pilot had overridden the TFR while close to the ground in response to a master caution light illuminating during the bombing pass. The master caution light may have illuminated due to an impending engine malfunction, though this fact could not be substantiated. The investigation surmised the pilot paddled off the TFR to prevent an Auto

TFR commanded fly-up during the final phase of the bomb run. Without the TFR providing terrain clearance, the aircraft entered an insidious and undetected descent into a terrain rise. The TFR is "paddled off" by pulling the Autopilot Release Lever on the control stick grip; thereafter the pilot must hand fly the aircraft.

Crew
Pilot: Capt William A Kennedy Jr.
WSO: 2Lt David C McKennon
Call Sign: Chomp 81
Time of Incident: 2223 MDT
Accident Board President: Col Samuel Huser
Assigned Unit: 390th TFS / 366th TFW Mountain Home AFB, Idaho
Aircraft Statistics: 264 Flights and 744 .2 Flight Hours
Mishap Result: Aircraft Destroyed / Fatal Crash / No Attempt to Eject

Courtesy of Author's Collection

Courtesy of Author's Collection

70-2397
F-111F # 36 GD/FW Production Run # E2-36
USAF Delivery Date: January 25, 1972

Crash Scenario

On April 5, 1989, the mishap aircraft was number four in a four-ship Red Flag training sortie over the Nellis AFB, Nevada, range complex. During a ridge crossing, while performing a defensive threat reaction to a simulated AAA site, the aircraft crashed. The defensive maneuver, known as "jinking," requires the pilot to change the aircraft heading and pitch every 2-3 seconds to defeat an AAA gun from tracking the aircraft. During the maneuver, the pilot must simultaneously pull Gs and roll the aircraft to change the aircraft's pitch attitude or heading. A series of these "hard turn" maneuvers can rapidly deplete the aircraft's speed. The pilot must select full "military" power, if not maximum afterburner, to sustain maneuvering speed. If the aircraft is heavily loaded with fuel and/or ordnance, the airspeed will deplete even faster. In this mishap, the mishap pilot allowed the airspeed to deplete to just under 200 knots with the wings swept back to 45-50 degrees. The mishap aircraft entered post stall gyrations seen on the Red Flag ACMI (Air Combat Maneuvering Instrumentation) system as a series of rolls to inverted, first to the right and then to the left. With the wings swept too far aft at the depleted airspeed, the mishap aircrew could not maintain control. The aircraft impacted a ridge crest near Nellis Range Camera S-28. An out of the envelope ejection attempt was made, but the mishap crew was fatally injured.

Findings

During a defensive threat reaction to a simulated AAA site, the mishap pilot began a series of jinking maneuvers to defeat the threat radar track and to spoil a valid AAA gun solution. Unfortunately, the mishap pilot did not appropriately manage the aircraft's airspeed during the series of hard maneuvers, leading to post stall gyrations. The mishap aircraft departed controlled flight at low altitude. There was insufficient altitude and flight control authority to recover the aircraft and to prevent Controlled Flight Into Terrain (CFIT).

Note: members of the 4-ship flight stated that the mishap pilot had rolled upside down for a ridge crossing. While rolling out, the airspeed was too slow for the aft wing sweep (about 54 degrees), which also locks out the roll spoilers. From the resultant nose low attitude there was not enough speed to pull out. His AOA at impact was 30. The WSO initiated an ejection, but the capsule trajectory failed to clear and impacted a ridge.

Crew

Pilot: 1Lt Robert Boland
WSO: Capt James A Gleason
Call Sign: Greebie 54
Time of Incident: 2223 Zulu
Accident Board President: Col Samuel Huser
Assigned Unit: 494th TFS / 48th TFW RAF Lakenheath, United Kingdom
Aircraft Statistics: 1,526 Flights and 3,868.0 Flight Hours
Mishap Result: Aircraft Destroyed / Fatal Crash / Ejection Initiated
    Out of the envelope

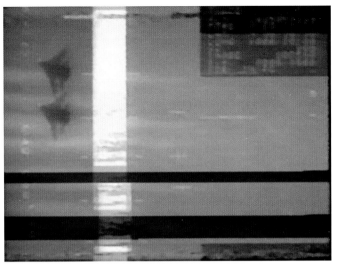

An overlapping split frame image (camera film) of the mishap aircraft just prior to crashing. *Courtesy of Author's Video Collection.*

Initial Impact and ensuing fire. *Photographs Courtesy of Authors Video Collection.*

Courtesy of Author's Video Collection.

70-2407
F-111F # 46 GD/FW Production Run # E2-46
(Never Delivered to the USAF)

Ground Accident Scenario

On February 2, 1972, the accident aircraft was undergoing a routine engine run during pre-delivery preparations for General Dynamics Company and USAF acceptance flight. At approximately 6:30 PM, the accident aircraft experienced an internal failure of the right (# 2) engine during a trim run at Run Station # 5 at the GDFW plant. The failure occurred just as the throttle was retarded from the Maximum Afterburner (AB) to the Minimum AB detent. Turbine blades from the 4th stage penetrated the right and left walls of the aft fuselage A-2 fuel tank. The resulting fire caused extensive damage to the left and right sides of the aircraft, aft of the Main Landing Gear Wheel Well areas.

Findings

The General Dynamics factory investigation determined the internal failure of the TF-30-P100 engine was due to incomplete assembly of the internal turbine case by manufacture (P&W) error. The aircraft was substantially damaged and never repaired to flight status. Undamaged portions of the aircraft were cannibalized and donated to restore other damaged operational F-111s.

Details:

Run Man Unknown
Call Sign: F-46
Time of Incident: 1830 CDT
Accident Board President: Internal to GDFW (Company Safety Officials)
Aircraft Statistics: 0 Flights and 0 Flight Hours
Accident Result: Aircraft never delivered to the USAF / Aircraft parts used in the F-111 "Vark Hospital" Restoration Program

While on the ground during a pre-delivery engine test run-up, the Number 2 engine failed catastrophically. Turbine blades penetrated the aft fuel tank resulting in a fire which caused severe airframe damage before extinguished. *Courtesy of GDFW.*

Accident Scene; Engine Run Station # 5 at GDFW. *Courtesy of GDFW.*

70-2410
F-111F # 49 GD/FW Production Run # E2-49
USAF Delivery Date: March 24, 1972

Crash Scenario

On June 15, 1972, the mishap aircraft was number two in a two-ship flight scheduled for a RHAWS/ECM training mission at Fallon NAS Nevada, Electronic Warfare (EW) Range. The flight was cleared IFR local, with Racer 41 as the flight leader and Racer 42, the mishap aircraft, as the wingman. Aircraft pre-flight, start, taxi, and take-off were normal. Take-off time was 0858 MDT from runway 12 at Mountain Home AFB, Idaho. The crew accomplished an uneventful join-up after take-off, both aircraft making a right turn out of traffic while heading south direct to the Battle Mountain TACAN. Level-off at FL220 was accomplished with the mishap aircraft flying in a loose route position. The flight departed Battle Mountain TACAN on a heading of 213 degrees and started a descent to 15,000 feet. Their IFR clearance was cancelled after departing 18,000 feet and they contacted Fallon NAS tower for permission to contact the ECM

Courtesy of Author's Collection

Range. They received permission, and upon contacting the range were informed that it would not be open for thirty minutes. Lead informed the range that they would hold southeast and started a level turn to the left. Lead instructed the mishap Aircraft Commander to take spacing for some air-to-air work. At some time prior to or during this 25-30 degree bank turn to the left, the mishap aircraft commander

acknowledged the call and began dropping back. Lead rolled out on a heading of 100 degrees and informed the mishap aircraft of his roll-out and heading, but there was no response. Subsequent to being told to take spacing the mishap aircraft started a gentle climb, dropped back approximately one mile behind lead, and then rolled into a left turn. Configuration at this time was as follows: wing sweep 26 degrees, gross

Courtesy of Author's Collection

weight 75,710 pounds, fuel distribution normal with dry wing tanks, wing pylons carried on stations 3 and 6, and a SUU on station 6. The aircraft entered into an uncontrolled roll. On the second roll, the pitch was approximately 70 degrees nose low and the aircraft was rolling in a non-oscillating spin-type maneuver. The mishap aircraft commander checked the instruments and noticed one or two caution lights. His initial response to the uncommanded roll was to release the stick and try to determine what was causing the roll. After two rolls he noticed the stick was chattering, and he positioned the stick to the forward stop centered on the Horizontal Situation Indicator. The pilot turned off the autopilot damper switches with no apparent response. The aircraft made several more revolutions with no recovery indications. The aircrew initiated ejection at 8,400 feet MSL, 4,200 feet AGL with an airspeed of 267 KIAS. The WSO noticed 10 feet of bright flame on the bottom of the aircraft in the nose wheel well area after ejection. Ejection was successful, but the pilot received back injuries. The Crew Module landed, then rolled upside-down. The WSO recovered the UHF emergency radio and contacted lead and Fallon NAS tower. Both crew members were picked up by a Navy rescue helicopter and transported to NAS Fallon.

Findings
The mishap aircraft departed controlled flight at 16,000 feet MSL while purposely increasing the distance between the flight lead. The pilot noticed some caution lights, on which would have been some combination of

roll or yaw channel or damper caution lights. The mishap pilot's initial response to the uncommanded roll was to release the stick and attempt to determine the cause for the uncommanded roll. The stick was chattering, but stopped when the pilot moved the stick full forward and centered on the control panel. The pilot turned off all autopilot damper switches and noticed the aircraft was not responsive to the full forward stick input. The aircraft continued to roll in a non-oscillating spin-type maneuver. The precise cause leading to loss of control was undetermined, but it was likely a flight control component or flight control computer malfunction. The crew initiated a successful ejection. The capsule landed approximately 450 feet north of the main fuselage impact crater and rolled upside down. The mishap pilot suffered back injuries requiring hospitalization. The WSO witnessed a fire in the nose wheel well area during the ejection, which was probably initiated by the capsule rocket motor during the ejection sequence. This was the 1st F-111F operational loss.

Crew
Pilot: Capt Henry R Hutson
WSO: Major John S Sinclair
Call Sign: Racer 42
Time of Incident: 0835 PDT
Accident Board President: Col William R Nelson
Assigned Unit: 4590th TFS / 347th TFW Mountain Home AFB, Idaho
Aircraft Statistics: 24 Flights and 65.6 Flight Hours
Mishap Result: Aircraft Destroyed / Successful Ejection

70-2412
F-111F # 51 GD/FW Production Run # E2-51
USAF Delivery Date: March 23, 1972

Courtesy of Author's Collection via Chuck Pitts.

Crash Scenario

On September 22, 1993, the mishap aircrew was briefed as number two of a three-ship formation for a night, continuation training sortie. The sortie was planned to fly IR-113, then to Melrose Bombing range for multiple passes and return to Cannon AFB for landing. The mishap aircraft took-off late for maintenance problems and flew direct to Tucumcari, then to the alternate entry for IR-113 to rejoin with the flight. The flight entered Melrose Range on time, with the mishap aircraft flying in the number three position. After three uneventful passes on the range, the Range Control Officer (RCO) asked the mishap aircraft commander if he was dispensing chaff. The mishap aircraft commander transmitted back "Terminate," followed by "Knock It Off," after seeing the mishap aircraft on fire. Approximately two minutes later the mishap aircraft commander stated "We are going down and have to get out of this one." The mishap WSO initiated a successful ejection sequence. The

mishap pilot sustained minor back injuries during the ejection process.

Findings

The mishap aircraft's right (# 2) engine disintegrated due to a number 3 bearing failure, causing an internal engine fire. After the Bold Face Emergency Procedures were accomplished, the WSO saw an increasing fire glow outside his canopy window. Both crew members could see the lights at Cannon AFB, and the mishap pilot pointed the aircraft towards the airfield. The continuing fire began affecting the flight controls; the mishap pilot zoomed the aircraft toward 12,000 feet. After achieving a safe ejection altitude, the pilot pushed the nose over and the WSO initiated the ejection sequence. Upon landing, the crew stated they initially had a difficult time, fumbling in the dark, only to discover the "Hit and Run" emergency kit flashlights were inoperative. The mishap WSO had a cell phone, and he called the base to effect their rescue. They spent about an hour waiting for rescue to arrive from Cannon AFB.

Crew
Pilot: Capt Robby A. "KY" Kyrouac
WSO: Capt Gregory "Pud" Wilson
Call Sign: Leggs 12
Time of Incident: 2044:55 MDT
Accident Board President: Col Robert A Stier
Assigned Unit: 522nd TFS / 27th TFW Cannon AFB, NM
Aircraft Statistics: Unknown
Mishap Result: Aircraft Destroyed / Successful Ejection

Crash Scene Photographs Courtesy of Author's Collection via Greg Wilson

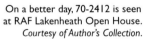

Courtesy of Author's Collection via Greg Wilson.

On a better day, 70-2412 is seen at RAF Lakenheath Open House.
Courtesy of Author's Collection.

The crew module's front bridle cable has failed, placing the pod in a nose down attitude instead of a normal level stance for landing. *Courtesy of Author's Collection.*

The capsule's impact attenuation bags were designed to inflate during the ejection sequence and deflate slowly as the pod touched down, absorbing the impact force. There is no attenuation bag on the forward bulkhead of the ejection module where unfortunately, the impact forces are transmitted directly to the crew members, resulting in injury. *Courtesy of Author's Collection.*

The escape module's rocket motor ignited this spectacular aircraft fire as it separated from the airframe upon ejection. *Courtesy of Author's Collection.*

70-2418 F-111F # 57 GD/FW Production Run # E2-57
USAF Delivery Date: April 24, 1972

Crash Scenario
On February 23, 1987, the mishap aircraft was number two of a two-ship mission which departed Ramstein AFB, Germany at 0826Z. The first leg of the mission was to fly a cross country sortie to RAF Bentwaters, United Kingdom. A planned low-level in the Federal Republic of Germany was over-flown at medium altitude due to poor weather. Weapons deliveries were accomplished at Vliehors Range in the Netherlands, followed by a high altitude return to the United Kingdom. The flight lead coordinated for a formation approach to RAF Bentwaters. On final approach, the mishap aircrew noticed a ten degree horizontal stabilizer split and elected to low approach and return to RAF Lakenheath. On radar downwind, the mishap aircraft experienced an uncommanded left roll. The mishap aircrew ejected and sustained major back injuries when the escape module impacted the ground. The aircraft was destroyed upon impact. Crash Coordinates were (N52 15 35 / E 000 26 20) 8 NM SSW of RAF Lakenheath, near the city of Newmarket.

Findings
The mishap aircraft was returning to RAF Lakenheath when the aircrew experienced a split horizontal stabilizer configuration, which eventually led to loss of control. The asymmetric split in the horizontal tails was caused by a Horizontal Tail Servo Actuator (HTSA) control valve galling. In this scenario, the pilot's normal response to control the aircraft can lead to controllability problems due to the lags or leaps in flight control response. A lag response on one side of the pitch / roll mixer can cause a roll when a pitch is commanded, while a leap or rapid control deflection may occur due to the unsticking of the control valve

or HTSA. The result is a series of uncommanded pitch, yaw, or roll motions when the "sticking" actuator control valve breaks free, moves sluggishly, or remains frozen. The pilot naturally attempts to compensate to control the aircraft, however, the additive lateral or longitudinal stick displacements aggravate control. In this case, the pilot's small flight control movement caused violent pitch and roll motions, rendering the aircraft uncontrollable. The crew ejected. Unfortunately, the forward bridle cable severed due to corrosion and fatigue. The escape module remained in a nose down attitude through touchdown. The capsule's nose down unattenuated collision with the ground during landing caused serious back injuries to both crew members. An amateur photographer captured the burning aircraft, and also the nose down attitude of the capsule as it descended under the main parachute.

Crew
Pilot: Capt Scott E Lewis
WSO: 1Lt Frank E Casella
Call Sign: Trest 01
Time of Incident: 1043 BST
Accident Board President: Col Richard R Riddick
Assigned Unit: 492nd TFS / 48th TFW RAF Lakenheath, United Kingdom
Aircraft Statistics: 1,425 Flights and 6,637.7 Flight Hours
Mishap Result: Aircraft Destroyed / Successful Ejection

The escape capsule's front bridle cable has failed, placing the pod in a nose down attitude, instead of a rather level stance for landing.

The capsule's impact attenuation bags are designed to inflate during the ejection sequence and deflate as the pod touches down. There is no attenuation bag on the forward bulkhead of the ejection module.

72-1441
F-111F # 71 GD/FW Production Run # E2-71
USAF Delivery Date: February 12, 1973

Crash Scenario

On February 4, 1981, the mishap aircraft departed RAF Lakenheath at 1434 GMT on a routine low-level training mission. Pre-flight, taxi, and takeoff were uneventful. Climb and cruise to the low-level entry point over the North Sea were successfully accomplished. After flying low-level, the mishap aircraft proceeded to the Donna Nook Range on the coast of Lincolnshire, United Kingdom, for practice weapons delivery. Upon completing a toss bomb delivery, the crew experienced a problem with the pitch damper, terminated the range work, and began their recovery to RAF Lakenheath. On final approach for landing, the aircrew encountered flight control problems. The aircrew could not regain controlled flight and successfully ejected near East Wrentham, Suffolk, United Kingdom. Both crew members were uninjured. The crew was rescued by a helicopter dispatched from RAF Coltishall. The aircraft crashed into an open field and was destroyed. Crash Coordinates were (N52 29 20 / E 00 49 07), which is 11NM on the 072 radial from RAF Lakenheath.

Findings

The mishap aircraft was on final approach to RAF Lakenheath when a violent and uncommanded nose down pitch motion occurred. The accident investigation determined galling had occurred within the slide/sleeve assembly of the Horizontal Tail Servo Actuator (HTSA). The galling caused the control valve to freeze in a position which drove the right horizontal tail to a full trailing edge down position. The aircraft entered a diving trajectory at a very low altitude. The aircrew ejected due to the suddenness of the pitch down and lack of aircraft response to stick inputs. See also F-111D 68-0142 regarding more detail surrounding HTSA servo actuator control valve galling.

Crew

Pilot: Capt Barry E Horne
WSO: Capt Larry P Apel
Call Sign: Pall 35
Time of Incident: 1602 GMT
Accident Board President: Col Donald G Waltman
Assigned Unit: 494th TFS / 48th TFW RAF Lakenheath, United Kingdom
Aircraft Statistics: 690 Flights and 1,808.5 Flight Hours
Mishap Result: Aircraft Destroyed / Successful Ejection

Courtesy of Pat Martin via Don Logan Collection.

Courtesy of Author's Collection.

72-1444
F-111F # 74 GD/FW Production Run # E2-74
USAF Delivery Date: April 17, 1973

Accident Scenario

On October 29, 1991, the mishap aircraft was lead in a two-ship mission flying a night, low-level, Terrain Following Radar (TFR) surface attack upgrade sortie for the mishap WSO. The mission was being flown in the Highlands Restricted Area (HRA) EGR 610A, North Scotland. The left (# 1) engine experienced a #3 bearing failure, which caused an explosion that sent the entire center section of the motor out the left side of the mishap aircraft. A fire ensued, but was extinguished utilizing "Bold Face" emergency checklist procedures. The engine failure occurred about 25 miles west of Wick, Scotland. The aircrew recovered to RAF Lossiemouth, Scotland. The incident coordinates were (N 58 35 00 / W 004 00 00) 85 NM northwest of RAF Lossiemouth.

Findings

The mishap aircraft experienced a #3 bearing failure in the left (# 1) engine. The catastrophic destruction of the engine caused an explosion and nacelle fire. The nacelle fire was rapidly extinguished, preventing loss of hydraulics and flight control. Although the aft fuselage was substantially damaged, the crew safely landed the aircraft.

Crew

Pilot: Capt Craig E Brown
WSO: 1Lt Jeffrey M Zeller
Call Sign: BOSOX 41
Time of Incident: 1748 BST
Accident Board President: Col Richard M Meeboer
Assigned Unit: 494th TFS / 48th TFW RAF Lakenheath, United Kingdom
Aircraft Statistics: Unknown
Mishap Result: Aircraft suffered major structural damage

Pilot / Aircraft Commander Craig "Quizmo" Brown's recollection:

My WSO, callsign "Fuzzy," and I were BOSOX 41. We were lead of a flight of two on a night TFR surface attack upgrade ride for Fuzzy in the Highlands Restricted Area (HRA). Like most good stories, it was a dark and stormy night--no really! The weather this night was terrible, but the winds were barely within limits but we needed the upgrade sortie for night TFR simulated target attacks for Fuzzy's final ride prior to his Mission Check. We let down near the Isle of Skye and then pressed into the mountains. The winds and turbulence were the worst

72-1447
F-111F # 77 GD/FW Production Run # E2-77
USAF Delivery Date: July 20, 1973

Crash Scenario

On June 23, 1982, the mishap aircraft departed RAF Lakenheath at 1657 BST on a routine low-level training sortie. Pre-flight, taxi, and launch were accomplished without any problems. Climb and cruise to the Highlands Restricted Area for low-level training was uneventful. While low-level, the aircraft experienced flight control problems. The crew was unable to regain controlled flight and successfully ejected from the mishap aircraft. The crew was rescued by a helicopter dispatched from RAF Lossiemouth, Scotland. The mishap aircraft crashed in rugged open terrain 20 NM northwest of Inverness, Scotland and was destroyed. Crash Coordinates were (N57 34 00 / W 04 50 00).

Findings

The mishap aircraft was on a low-level Terrain Following Radar (TFR) flight when the crew experienced a violent pitch and roll when the crew changed the set clearance plane from 500 feet to 750 feet during automatic terrain following flight. The uncommanded control input was caused by a foreign object in the (HTSA) Horizontal Tail Servo Actuator Valve Input Rod. Normally, the flight control system responds to small force inputs from the control stick or from the TFR via the autopilot. The pilot's control inputs are translated through the pitch-roll mixer assembly to a small corresponding movement of the HTSA servo control valve. As the servo control valve moves, a volume of high pressure hydraulic fluid enters the Horizontal Tail actuator, which rotates the Horizontal Stabilizers to influence pitch, roll, or a combination of the two. Due to galling, or in this case the presence of a foreign object within the input rod, more force may be required to cause a deflection of one HTSA than the other, or if it is jammed, the HTSA doesn't move. To the pilot, the stick feedback and control response

Courtesy of K. Kesteloo via Don Logan Collection

could feel sluggish or cause abrupt uncommanded motions to the aircraft. If only one side responds, or responds more rapidly than the other, the aircraft may respond erratically. If the galling actuator or control valve breaks loose a large input is commanded, causing abrupt pitch or roll response – something the pilot is not expecting. The pilot will naturally fight the flight controls, and often these control inputs can influence a number of responses: the control inputs show no response at all, the aircraft moves opposite to expected control applications, or the aircraft moves abruptly with no pilot input whatsoever, all of which appear to aggravate the aircraft's controllability. In this case, the crew could not regain control and decided to eject.

Crew

Pilot: Capt Stanley J Syzbillo
WSO: Capt William S Clendenen
Call Sign: Cuppy 32
Time of Incident: 1820 BST
Accident Board President: Col Stephen H Cowles
Assigned Unit: 492nd TFS / 48th TFW RAF Lakenheath, United Kingdom
Aircraft Statistics: 771 Flights and 2,016.1 Flight Hours
Mishap Result: Aircraft Destroyed / Successful Ejection

I'd ever experienced. During our last target run we felt an extreme jolt and simultaneously the fire lights came on and flames were shooting past the left canopy, which really got our full attention. We knocked it off with a manual fly-up from our 1,000 foot TF altitude and ran the bold face which seemed to put the fire out, but the jet was not performing like she should single engine. We only got to about 8,000 foot MSL and could not hold altitude. We were never going to make it to RAF Leuchars, but Scottish MIL let us know that RAF Lossiemouth was night flying this evening so we headed straight there. We had one shot at the approach and the controller did a perfect job, we broke out of the weather on centerline in a high crosswind. There were a couple of rotating beacons going the other way, turned out to be two RAF rescue helicopters going up into the Highlands to find us. They turned around and followed us in. We planned to take the approach-end barrier but our hook shredded the cable so we rolled to a stop near the far end. We jumped out and ran for the edge of the runway, almost getting killed by a fire truck in the limited visibility! When the fire chief called us back over to the aircraft, this was the first clue we had that we had anything other than a simple engine fire. We saw about a 12' hole in the side of the jet where the failed #3 bearing had exploded and sent the entire center section of the motor out the side of the jet. Had it been the other engine, the evening would have ended differently (which is exactly what happened to KY and Pud at Cannon a couple of years later). The RAF took us to the club, and after the rescue helicopter crews showed

Triple 4 undergoing repair at RAF Lossiemouth. Note: The aircraft was repaired by a Depot Repair Field Team and returned to service. *Courtesy of Craig Brown.*

up it was really a party! When the accident team from Lakenheath showed up the next morning it was still going strong, and they were not impressed with our ability to make friends with our British hosts. So we hung out at Lossies until they were ready to go and they gave us a lift in the aero club Piper they had brought up. I swore never to fly 'cripple 4' again. But, like life in general, never say never. In 1995 I flew my last F-111 flight in Triple-4 while TDY to Nellis with the Weapons School; and she didn't blow up that time!

73-0709 F-111F # 85 GD/FW Production Run # E2-85
USAF Delivery Date: June 6, 1974

Crash Scenario

On April 21, 1977, the mishap aircraft was on an air-to-ground bombing sortie in support of F-111F weapons delivery validation. The aircrew attended a mass mission briefing at 0600 MST and completed their crew briefing immediately following. Both briefings were accomplished in a squadron other than the mishap aircrew's parent squadron. Crew show at the mishap aircraft was 0810 MST, and pre-flight, engine start, and taxi were normal. Takeoff was at 0944 MST. The flight progressed normally, entering the Military Range Complex (China Lake Naval Weapons Center) portion of R-2505 at 0958 PST. On the fifth bombing run and second dive delivery, during the final attack phase, the aircrew ejected from the aircraft. The mishap aircraft impacted 30 NM north of the China Lake Naval Weapons Center. The aircraft was destroyed by impact with the ground. The aircrew ejected successfully and were picked up alongside the escape capsule, 580 feet north of the aircraft impact crater.

Findings

Aircraft control was lost after a Split-S maneuver while executing a Joint Munitions Effectiveness Manual (JMEM) diving attack delivery. The maneuver, described as a "Split-S," was most likely a roll and pull maneuver which placed the aircraft into a dive pointed at the target. The execution of the maneuver requires the pilot to half-roll to inverted, then pull the nose to the approximate desired dive angle, unload the aircraft while inverted to stop the nose in-place, and then complete another half-roll to an upright position. When completed, the aircraft should be pointed at the target on the proper dive angle. The mishap pilot experienced difficulty during the second dive bomb pass after losing sight of the target. While on the third dive bomb run, the pilot performed a split-S maneuver and rolled on final too close to the target and at too low an altitude, stalling the aircraft. The aircraft immediately departed controlled flight. The aircrew ejected

at approximately 2500 feet AGL. Both crew members sustained back injuries when the capsule touched down nose first. Due to an installation error involving crossed Shielded Mild Detonating Cord (SMDC) lines, the forward bridle attachment point was pyrotechnically released. As a result, the capsule remained in an extreme nose down attitude, and impacted without the cushioning effect of the attenuation bag. A fleet-wide inspection of the canopy center beam SMDC installation was subsequently directed by the Sacramento ALC.

Crew

Pilot: Capt Peter G Ganotis
WSO: Capt Harold L Petersen
Call Sign: Noman 67
Time of Incident: 1019 PST
Accident Board President: Col Peter T Kempf
Assigned Unit: 391st TFS / 366th TFW Mountain Home AFB, Idaho
Aircraft Statistics: 272 Flights and 738.5 Flight Hours
Mishap Result: Aircraft Destroyed / Successful Ejection

E2-85 (factory number) shown at GDFW. *Courtesy of Author's Collection.*

73-0715
F-111F # 91 GD/FW Production Run # E2-91
USAF Delivery Date: March 12, 1975

Accident Scenario

On December 12, 1979, the mishap aircraft took off at 1739Z as number two in a two-ship night aerial refueling mission. Weather precluded a tanker rendezvous, so the formation split up to accomplish individual events. At 1900Z, the mishap aircraft returned to RAF Lakenheath in response to a weather recall for increasing strong crosswinds. An enroute descent to a precision approach for a full stop was requested. All portions of the approach were normal until touchdown, when the aircraft started to roll and drift left, at which point the pilot initiated a go-around. The runway supervisory officer observed a small explosion, with sparks coming from the left wheel-well area. In addition, the Runway 24 Barrier Arrestment Kit (BAK)-12 barrier cable was sheared when the left gear spindle struck it at high speed. The mishap aircraft was instructed to refuel with an airborne tanker, Lynn 22, while Runway 06 was foamed and the overrun unidirectional BAK-9 was disconnected. The air refueling tanker, Lynn 22, verified that the left main gear wheel assembly was missing. The mishap aircraft returned to RAF Lakenheath for an approach end BAK-12 cable engagement on Runway 06.

Findings

The aircraft touched down just short of the foam, approximately 1000 feet down the runway and began to drift to the left. The aircraft commander believed he had missed the cable and selected afterburner to initiate a go-around. During rotation, the tail hook engaged the BAK-12 left of centerline, slamming the aircraft back onto the runway and causing severe damage to the airframe. The aircraft came to rest 840 feet from the BAK-12 moorings, and approximately ten feet off the left side of the runway. A small fire ensued in the right glove area, which was extinguished by the fire department. The crew egressed the aircraft

without injury. Investigation revealed a stress crack had developed at a rivet hole in the left, aft section of the left MLG lateral beam. During landing the lateral beam aft lug failed, resulting in separation of the axle, wheel, and brake assembly.

Crew

Pilot: Maj Robert G Little
WSO: Capt Steven J Austin
Call Sign: Trest 56
Time of Incident: 2208 LGMT
Accident Board President: Col Dale W Thompson
Assigned Unit: 492nd TFS / 48th TFW RAF Lakenheath, United Kingdom
Aircraft Statistics: Unknown
Mishap Result: Aircraft Suffered Major Structural Damage / Repaired and returned to service.

Courtesy of Author's Collection.

73-0716
F-111F # 92 GD/FW Production Run # E2-92
USAF Delivery Date: April 15, 1975

Crash Scenario
On November 1, 1982, the mishap aircraft departed Incirlik AB, Turkey at 1245L for a routine Weapons Training Deployment (WTD) mission. Pre-flight, engine start, taxi, and takeoff were uneventful. Departure and cruise to the Konya Range was normal. The crew aborted a hot weapons delivery pass on the Konya Range due to a left engine fire. The fire burned through into the rudder controls, resulting in a hard-over right rudder, and the aircrew could not maintain control. The crew ejected from the mishap aircraft and was rescued by a helicopter dispatched from Konya AB, Turkey. The aircraft impacted on the perimeter 1 NM north of Tomek, Turkey. Crash Coordinates were (N 38 01 30 / E 32 41 00).

Findings
During a Weapons Training Deployment (WTD) sortie, the aircraft had an inflight fire in the (#1) left engine. The uncontained and uncontrollable fire entered the aft centerbody section due to the reverse flow phenomenon, causing rudder control burn through and loss of control. The engine failed due to failure of the Number-3 bearing, resulting in a fire in the bearing cavity. The fire burned through the engine casing, heat shield, and aft fuel tank wall, resulting in a massive uncontrollable fire. The crew was forced to eject. The crew sustained injuries during the ejection due to failure of the forward bridle attachment. The escape capsule impacted in a nose down, unattenuated pitch attitude.

Crew
Pilot: 1Lt Steven J Bowling
WSO: Capt John E Clay
Call Sign: Fort 51
Time of Incident: 1331 Local
Accident Board President: Col John Granskog
Assigned Unit: 492nd TFS / 48th TFW RAF Lakenheath, United Kingdom
Aircraft Statistics: 690 Flights and 1,808.5 Flight Hours
Mishap Result: Aircraft Destroyed / Successful Ejection

Courtesy of the USAF.

Accident Scene on Runway 06 RAF Lakenheath, United Kingdom

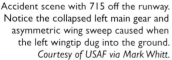
Accident scene with 715 off the runway. Notice the collapsed left main gear and asymmetric wing sweep caused when the left wingtip dug into the ground. *Courtesy of USAF via Mark Whitt.*

73-0717
F-111F # 93 GD/FW Production Run # E2-9
USAF Delivery Date: June 12, 1975

Crash Scenario

On March 29, 1978, the mishap aircraft departed RAF Lakenheath, United Kingdom, at 1506 BST as flight lead of a two-ship formation. Pre-flight, engine start, taxi, and enroute cruise to the Jurby Range (a Royal Air Force air weapons range on the Northwest coast of the Isle of Man) was uneventful. Range practice weapons deliveries and cruise back to RAF Lakenheath local area were also uneventful. On approach to RAF Lakenheath, both aircraft in the formation were struck by lightning. A position change was directed by the mishap aircraft, and the mishap aircraft assumed the right wing position. The formation flew over the airfield and entered the VFR traffic pattern. The mishap aircraft made a radio call saying he was alright and could pitch-out for landing. Shortly thereafter the mishap aircraft departed the formation and the crew ejected. The aircraft crashed and was destroyed. The crew module impacted the ground before the main parachute deployed, fatally injuring the mishap aircrew. Crash Coordinates were (N 52 31 00 / E 00 37 00), which is 1.5 NM east of Methwold, Norfolk, United Kingdom, and 7 NM from Lakenheath on the 027 degree radial.

A "Go-To-War" F-111F with Pave Tack Pod and 4 GBU-10's. *Courtesy of Author's Collection.*

Findings

Both aircraft were struck by lightning while on final approach into Lakenheath. The mishap crews continued without declaring an IFE. A flight lead change was directed, and Hid 34 (the mishap aircraft) assumed the right wing position. The formation flew over the base and entered the VFR traffic pattern. The mishap pilot made a radio call stating the aircraft was okay, and they would pitch out for landing. Shortly after this call, the mishap aircraft pitched down and departed controlled flight. It was determined the lightning strike was conducted through the pitot static system to the central air data computer, and possibly to the essential AC electrical bus, resulting in an erroneous, nose down electrical command to the pitch damper resulting in an uncommanded extreme negative G pushover. The aircraft departed controlled flight, and the aircrew attempted an unsuccessful ejection at 780 feet AGL. Although the ejection was initiated within the ejection envelope, the capsule impacted the ground prior to main chute deployment. The primary cause of the failed ejection sequence was due to the Secondary (Upper) Nozzle separating when the rocket fired. The Secondary (Upper) Nozzle is a pipe which extends from the Upper Closure Cap and directs a portion of the total rocket thrust, depending on the ejection speed mode, beyond the module's aft bulkhead. With the Secondary (Upper) Nozzle missing, the rocket exhaust bloomed inside the aft bulkhead, greatly reducing the overall propulsive force necessary for a low altitude, nose low ejection. If the ejection occurred above 300 knots, the upper nozzle burst diaphragm is severed to increase the exhaust-flow area, thus increasing its thrust. When the upper nozzle diaphragm bursts, this increases the entire exhaust-flow area. The overall effect is a reduction in the rocket motor's operating pressure: a 9,000-pound reduction of thrust at the Primary (lower) Nozzle and an increase at the upper nozzle thrust to 7,000 pounds. Unfortunately, the reduced thrust exiting the Primary (lower) Nozzle on the bottom of the pod and a failure of the upper nozzle resulted in a massive reduction in overall thrust to propel the escape capsule high enough to sustain a successful main parachute deployment. The Mishap Investigation revealed the Secondary (Upper) Nozzle, which is threaded into the Upper Closure Cap housing, had less than one full turn of thread-to-thread contact; too little to contain the high pressure exhaust. When the rocket fired, the secondary nozzle extension was blown off. Without the Secondary Nozzle, the uncontained rocket exhaust bloomed outwards, burning through the capsule's aft pressure bulkhead, contributing to a decreased lifting force. The USAF conducted a fleet-wide inspection and found other escape module rocket motors with the same defect. (For more Escape Capsule details, see Chapter 1.)

Crew

Pilot: Capt Charles H Kitchell
WSO: 1Lt Jeffrey T Moore
Call Sign: Hid 34
Time of Incident: 1640 BST
Accident Board President: Col John F Manning
Assigned Unit: 492nd TFS / 48th TFW RAF Lakenheath, United Kingdom
Aircraft Statistics: 265 Flights and 785.2 Flight Hours
Mishap Result: Aircraft Destroyed / Fatal Crash / Capsule Rocket Motor Nozzle Malfunction

View of the Crew Module's Aft Bulkhead and the Secondary Nozzle Burn-Through. *All photographs courtesy of USAF via Larry Walters Collection.*

View of a normal Module Aft Bulkhead with rocket motor nozzle visible. *Courtesy of Ken Pringle.*

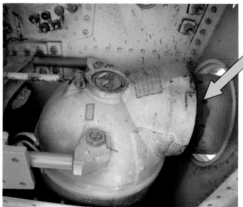

An internal view of the Escape Module's rocket motor upper cap. The arrow points to the "threaded" Secondary Nozzle extension that was blown off when the rocket motor fired due to an installation error. Without the Secondary Nozzle channeling the high velocity rocket exhaust beyond the aft bulkhead, the exhaust bloomed internally and burned through the module's aft bulkhead. The bloomed exhaust thrust was insufficient to propel the Escape Module through a successful ejection sequence.

73-0718
F-111F # 94 GD/FW Production Run # E2-94
USAF Delivery Date: July 23, 1975

Courtesy of David W Ross Collection

Crash Scenario
On October 5, 1977, the mishap aircraft was scheduled for an air defense target sortie in the Federal Republic of Germany (FRG). The crew attended the exercise briefing at 0303Z, four hours and 12 minutes prior to the scheduled 0715Z take-off. The mishap crew arrived at the aircraft at 0600Z. Pre-flight, engine start, and taxi were normal. Take-off was at 0711Z. The first portion of the flight profile was IFR high altitude navigation to Leiphem AB, FRG. At the "TANGO" 183 degree radial / 19 DME, the mishap aircraft started an enroute descent to FL150. At Leiphem they accomplished a further descent, cancelled IFR, and proceeded on the low-level Terrain Following Radar (TFR) navigation route. Contact was made with the Forward Air Controller (FAC) for instructions. After completing the low-level they continued to Initial Point (IP) for the last scheduled event, a simulated weapons release and Electronic Counter Measures training with Ramstein AB Approach (Call Sign Courtroom). The mishap aircraft notified Courtroom that the event would be flown at 3000 MSL, rather than the pre-planned 3600 foot MSL altitude. The pilot later transmitted that the altitude would be 2,500 MSL in order to maintain VMC. At 0856Z, the mishap pilot informed Courtroom that he was aborting the event because he could not maintain VMC, and that he would exit the area and contact Ramstein AB Approach. Courtroom acknowledged and cancelled the event. A short time later the aircraft crashed 1.2 NM southeast of Annweiler, FRG. The aircraft was destroyed on impact and post-impact fire. The aircrew made no attempt to eject and was fatally injured.

Findings
The mishap aircraft air aborted a planned bombing range event due to weather. The mishap occurred while in a 180-degree descending turn at low altitude when the aircraft collided with a small hill. No ejection was attempted. The investigation determined the pilot was attempting a steep-bank turn around a mountain peak with insufficient forward flight visibility. The aircraft entered a steep, nose-low attitude and impacted mountainous terrain at 1,083 feet MSL. Contributing causes are: spatial disorientation, loss of situational awareness with the terrain, below-range minimum enroute altitude (MEA), and the absence of terrain protection during the descending turn. Without the use of the terrain following radar or a preset radar altimeter altitude indexer (to warn of a low altitude situation), there was no backup means of preventing collision with the terrain in marginal VMC. Speculating on the crew's wakeup time through the time of the mishap (seven to eight hours later), fatigue may have been a factor toward influencing spatial disorientation and inattention to the aircraft's attitude and altitude. The mishap was deemed Controlled Flight Into Terrain (CFIT).

Crew
Pilot: Capt Stephen H Reid
WSO: Capt Carl T Poole
Call Sign: F367
Time of Incident: 0958 CET
Accident Board President: Col Ronald G Strack
Assigned Unit: 494th TFS / 48th TFW RAF Lakenheath, United Kingdom
Aircraft Statistics: 285 Flights and 785.2 Flight Hours
Mishap Result: Aircraft Destroyed / Fatal Crash / No Ejection Attempt

---

74-0179 F-111F # 97 GD/FW Production Run # E2-97
USAF Delivery Date: December 4, 1975

Crash Scenario
On September 16, 1982, the crew was flying a low-level route in Scotland when a Wheel Well Hot Light (WWHL) illuminated. The mishap aircraft crashed while on final approach into RAF Leuchars, United Kingdom. The mishap crew had declared an In Flight Emergency (IFE) for a Wheel Well Hot Light. The aircrew then experienced a fire and loss of hydraulics, which caused a left roll and uncontrollable flight. The mishap aircrew successfully initiated the ejection sequence and survived.

The USAF Safety Center via Freedom of Information Act (FOIA) request provided a document (an AF Form 711B) that states: "the crew abandoned the aircraft and that a Wheel-Well Hot Light (WWHL) existed. The mishap aircraft had a loss of utility hydraulic pressure and the aircraft was destroyed."

Findings
Hot compressor air from the engines is bled off and used for various aircraft systems after being cooled, such as air conditioning and pressurizing the cockpit, and cooling the avionics system. The high energy air is carried by ducting from the engine to the air conditioning unit through the main wheel well. The duct was notorious for failing due to vibrations propagating cracks about the welds in the duct. A fire loop is routed along the duct and illuminates the WWHL if a hot air leak is detected. The emergency procedure for a WWHL is to pull the respective throttle to idle (thus reducing the amount of hot air leaking out of the duct) and landing as soon as possible. The aircrew accomplished the emergency checklist and attempted to land at RAF Leuchars. Investigation revealed a 16th stage bleed air duct clamp failed, allowing high temp, high velocity bleed air to enter into the main wheel well. Additionally, due to contamination in the hydraulic/pneumatic system, the utility hydraulic/pneumatic check and shuttle valves were leaking. Loss of utility hydraulic reservoir pneumatic head pressure caused by the 16th stage bleed air duct leak, and leakage in the shuttle valve, resulted in pump cavitation and utility hydraulic pressure loss. When a large demand was placed on the utility hydraulic system during final approach, a left roll began which exceeded the pilot's control authority. Control of the aircraft was lost and the crew ejected.

Crew
Pilot: 2Lt William C. Coutts
WSO: Capt Michael J. Artese
Call Sign: Unknown
Time of Incident: Unknown
Accident Board President: Unknown
Assigned Unit: 495th TFS / 48th TFW RAF Lakenheath, United Kingdom
Aircraft Statistics: 714 Flights and 1,745.7 Flight Hours
Mishap Result: Aircraft Destroyed / Successful Ejection

Courtesy of Author's Collection.

74-0183
F-111F # 101 GD/FW Production Run # E2-101
USAF Delivery Date: June 2, 1976

Crash Scenario
On October 10, 1990, the mishap aircraft was lead of a two-ship night low-level mission to include an enroute level target attack, two night Pave Tack mini-toss range deliveries (dry) in the Askr Range, Saudi Arabia, then recover single-ship back to Taif AB, Saudi Arabia. Pre-flight, engine start, taxi, and take-off were accomplished without any problems. Low level and enroute target attack were flown as briefed, with mishap wingman 9NM in trail. The mishap crew was next practicing night GBU-24 mini-toss deliveries. The first pass was uneventful. However, during the second maneuver the mishap aircraft collided with the ground. The aircraft was destroyed. The aircrew did not attempt to eject and they were fatally injured. The crash coordinates were (N 21 27 00 / E 41 02 00), which is about 27 NM east of Taif AB, Saudi Arabia.

Findings
The mishap aircraft was on a night mission and impacted the ground during a Pave Tack Loft Recovery maneuver. The TFR was paddled off and the mishap pilot was manually flying the aircraft. The pilot most likely succumbed to spatial disorientation during the maneuver and failed to maintain aircraft control by positive instrument maneuvering. If the pilot was attempting to monitor the WSO's Pave Tack targeting via the video display, the distraction may also have contributed to a poor instrument cross check and terrain awareness. The aircraft impacted the ground due to an undetected descent while maneuvering post-attack. The cause was Controlled Flight Into Terrain (CFIT)

Crew
Pilot: Capt Frederick A Reid
WSO: Capt Thomas R Caldwell
Call Sign: Cougar 41
Time of Incident: 0536 Saudi Time
Accident Board President: Col Daniel B Cecil
Assigned Unit: 493rd TFS / 48th TFW RAF Lakenheath, United Kingdom
Aircraft Statistics: 1,432 Flights and 3,430.1 Flight Hours
Mishap Result: Aircraft Destroyed / Fatal Crash / No Ejection Attempt

74-0183 shown during depot maintenance at BAe Bristol, England . *Courtesy of Author's Collection.*

The last F-111 (74-0188) departing GDFW. *Courtesy of Author's Collection.*

74-0188
F-111F # 106 GD/FW Production Run # E2-106
USAF Delivery Date: November 22, 1976

Crash Scenario
On April 26, 1983, the mishap aircraft departed RAF Lakenheath, United Kingdom, at 1153 GMT on a local readiness exercise mission to the Federal Republic of Germany (FRG). Climb out and cruise at FL 250 to Hopsten AB, FRG, was accomplished, followed by a descent to low-level utilizing Hopsten AB radar control. The mishap aircraft cancelled radar control at 1227 GMT and continued the low-level portion of the flight. At 1300 GMT, during low-level egress, the mishap aircraft was seen in a left turn over the east end of Borkum Island, FRG. Seconds later, the aircraft impacted the water and was destroyed. No ejection attempt was made and both crewmembers were fatally injured.

Findings
Automatic terrain following radar was not engaged at the time of the mishap. The investigation revealed the pilot was attempting to hand-fly the airplane at low-level in marginal weather conditions. The pilot, attempting to successfully complete the mission, found a break in the clouds and descended to low altitude (VFR conditions) with Hopsten radar, then cancelled radar service. Once below the clouds with some visual orientation with the water surface, the pilot proceeded inbound toward the German coast, where a fog bank was encountered. During a 45-50 degree bank turn, the aircraft entered an area in which the discernible horizon was obscured by fog and haze. Rather than abort the low altitude flight, or engage the automatic TFR system, the pilot continued hand flying the airplane. Inattention to the apparent altitude and absence of

TFR protection in marginal weather conditions resulted in the pilot flying the aircraft into the water. Controlled Flight Into Terrain (CFIT).

Crew
Pilot: Capt Charles M Vidas
WSO: 2Lt Stephen A Groark
Call Sign: Hair 28
Time of Incident: 1500 CET
Accident Board President: Col Frederick A Zehrer III
Assigned Unit: 492nd TFS / 48th TFW RAF Lakenheath, United Kingdom
Aircraft Statistics: 572 Flights and 1,407.1 Flight Hours
Mishap Result: Aircraft Destroyed / Fatal Crash / No Ejection Attempt

74-0188 being accepted by the USAF. F-111 Pilot Major Don Harten, second from the right, was influential in identifying unresolved problems with the TFR system during Constant Guard V combat operations. *Courtesy of Author's Collection.*

The last production F-111F, 74-0188, leaves GDFW, led by the first F-16. *Courtesy of Author's Collection.*

10
FB-111A MISHAPS

FB-111A 69-6510 Dropping MK-82 High Drag "Ballute" Bombs. *Courtesy of Chris McWilliams.*

67-7194
FB-111A # 8 GD/FW Production Run # B1-08
USAF Delivery Date: November 4, 1969

#1 Mishap Scenario

On November 29, 1971, FB-111A 67-7194, assigned to the 509th Bombardment Wing (Medium), Strategic Air Command (SAC), Pease AFB, New Hampshire, departed on a routine training mission at 1837 EST. Due to deteriorating weather conditions the crew was directed to return to Pease after 3+00 hours of flight. Upon arrival, an instrument penetration to a ground controlled approach was accomplished. Extensive damage occurred when the aircraft departed the edge of Runway 34 during a night landing.

Findings

The aircraft struck runway edge marking signs, causing a fuel leak. The hot brakes ignited a sizable fire that engulfed the main landing gear wheel well and left engine bay. Before the fire was extinguished the aircraft incurred substantial damage. The photo on the following page illustrates the severity of the fire damage.

A GCA penetration was completed and visual contact established at two miles. The aircraft was lined up with the right side runway lights and overcorrected to the left. The pilot corrected back to the right, and was then advised by GCA to go around if he did not have the runway in sight because he was too far left. The pilot disregarded GCA corrections since he had visual contact with the runway. The pilot elected to land, and touched down in a wings level attitude approximately 16 feet left of the runway centerline. The aircraft was pointing to the left of the runway heading and drifting left from a 10 knot crosswind. The aircraft continued along this drifting ground path as a result of hydroplaning. Right rudder correction was applied but was ineffective. The aircraft departed the prepared surface approximately 1400 feet from the touchdown point, where the nose gear failed and the aircraft came to rest on the nose section.

Crew

Pilot: Maj Edwin M Moorman
WSO: Maj James M Brighenti
Call Sign: Unknown Not Listed on 711)
Time of Incident: 2234 EST
Accident Board President: Col Melvin G Bowling
Assigned Unit: 393rd BS / 509th BW, Pease AFB, New Hampshire
Aircraft Statistics: Unknown
Mishap Result: The aircraft was substantially damaged and repaired at GDFW Vark Hospital

They say "lightning never strikes twice." However, the odds say otherwise…

#2 Mishap Scenario

On February 25, 1976, the mishap aircraft (FB-111A 67-7194) was assigned to the 509th Bombardment Wing (Medium) Strategic Air Command (SAC), Pease AFB, New Hampshire. The mission included formation training with wingman enroute to (air refueling track) AR206, where cell refueling was accomplished. The mishap aircraft then entered Low Level route OB-11. After this training was accomplished, the crew rejoined with their wingman and proceeded back to Pease AFB. Mishap aircraft received an enroute descent, followed by radar vectors from Pease RAPCON to PAR final approach. Shortly after passing one mile from touchdown final control advised aircrew twice that they were well below glide path, followed by the transmission "If runway or approach lights not in sight, climb and maintain one thousand three hundred heading three four zero." The mishap pilot replied "I'm visual." This was the last transmission from the mishap aircraft. Due to low visibility and absence of radio contact with the mishap aircraft, RAPCON informed the Supervisor of Flight (SOF) to make a runway check. The SOF started north on runway

The Second Time! *Courtesy of Author's Collection.*

Extensive fire damage to aircraft fuselage. *Courtesy of GDFW Vark Hospital.*

34 and discovered a right main landing gear laying on the right side of the runway, approximately 600 feet from the approach end. After proceeding down the runway, the SOF located the mishap aircraft 4600 feet from the runway threshold just left of the center-line. A fire was present in the main wheel well which was extinguished by base fire personnel. The crew had safely egressed the mishap aircraft when the SOF found them.

Findings

During the return-to-base (RTB) flight, the weather deteriorated below approach minimums. The mishap pilot flew below the PAR approach weather minimums, attempting to gain a visual sighting of the runway and approach lights. The Precision Approach Radar (PAR) controller made two transmissions that the aircraft was well below the glidepath. Neither crewmember was aware of these transmissions, since the mishap aircrew was on the interphone discussing decision height and the sighting of the runway. The mishap aircraft then struck six approach light stanchions beginning at a point 1100 to 600 feet short of the runway over-run, then contacted the overrun 400 feet short of the runway threshold. The main landing gear collapsed 75 feet short of the runway threshold, and the aircraft came to rest 4400 feet down the runway. A wheel well fire was extinguished by the crash crew after both crewmembers egressed the aircraft. The aircraft sustained substantial damage to the main landing gear wheel well, left wing, fuselage, and engine bay doors.

Crew
Pilot: Capt James N Gabriel
WSO: Capt Michael H Labeau
Call Sign: Radon 19
Accident Board President: Col James K Secrest
Time of Incident: 2243 EST
Assigned Unit: 715th BS / 509th BW Pease AFB, New Hampshire
Aircraft Statistics: Unknown
Mishap Result: Aircraft severely damaged / Repaired at GDFW Vark Hospital a second time!

The aft fuselage of FB-111A 67-0160 (an early FB-111A used exclusively for testing at Edwards AFB) was mated to the forward fuselage of 67-7194, along with a spare vertical stabilizer from FB-111A 69-6513. Because GDFW used a conglomeration of parts to rebuild 67-7194, the aircraft was affectionately nicknamed *Frankenvark*. The aircraft was returned to flying status and assigned to the 380th Bombardment Wing (Medium) at Plattsburgh AFB, NY, in September 1980. The aircraft was later converted to an F-111G (primarily by removal of the Boeing AGM-69 Short Range Attack Missile (SRAM) equipment) and assigned to Air Combat Command. The reason for the rebuild and cost involved was justified to maintain the number of strategic bombers allowed by the Strategic Arms Limitation Treaty (SALT). In particular, the FB-111A fleet was limited by the treaty! FB-111 attrition due to accidents reduced the fleet size, necessitating the rebuild before the arrival of the B-1. Many of the FB-111As found a new life after their exit from SAC as F-111Gs. Some of the F-111Gs were subsequently purchased and operated by the Royal Australian Air Force (RAAF).

Courtesy of Chris McWilliams.

Courtesy of Chris McWilliams.

68-0242 at CFB Cold Lake, Alberta, Canada, *Courtesy of Ben Ullings*

68-0242
FB-111A # 14 GD/FW Production Run # B1-14
USAF Delivery Date: September 22, 1970

Crash Scenario
On June 7, 1983, the mishap aircraft was scheduled as number two in a three-ship for a routine Red Flag training mission with a departure from Nellis AFB, NV. Prior to entering IR-126 Low Level Route, the three individual aircrews planned for and increased the trail spacing between each aircraft to approximately five miles. Twenty-seven minutes after low-level entry, the mishap aircraft's left engine Low Pressure Fan hub failed due to metal fatigue. The nature of the failure released the first stage fan blades. The blades penetrated the engine case and ruptured the aft fuel tank. An inflight fire was confirmed by the number three aircraft. The fire quickly became uncontrollable. When the crew noticed deteriorating flight control response a successful ejection was initiated. The aircraft crashed and was destroyed in an isolated desert area of Arizona 42 NM SE of Mesquite, NV. Crash Coordinates were (N 36 19 29 / W 113 36 00).

Findings
The crew heard a loud thump, followed by illumination of the left engine FIRE warning light. The engine fire was caused by an internal catastrophic failure of the low pressure compressor fan hub. The crew could not extinguish the engine fire by performing the checklist procedures. The severely damaged fan blades separated from the fan hub and penetrated through the engine case. The explosive effects caused an uncontrollable engine bay fire. Flight control authority deteriorated rapidly due to burn-through of exposed hydraulic lines. The subsequent loss of hydraulic pressure to the flight control components necessitated an ejection.

Crew
Pilot: Maj Richard B Young
WSO: Capt Raymond A Drogan
Call Sign: Maul 42
Time of Incident: 1613 PDT
Accident Board President: Col Stephen B Croker
Assigned Unit: 393rd BS / 509th BWM Pease AFB, New Hampshire
Aircraft Statistics: 978 Flights and 3,564.6 Flight Hours
Mishap Result: Aircraft Destroyed / Successful Ejection

Courtesy of Tom Brewer via Don Logan Collection.

68-0243
FB-111A # 15 GD/FW Production Run # B1-15
USAF Delivery Date: August 31, 1970

Crash Scenario
On February 2, 1989, the mishap aircraft was involved in a unit directed Emergency War Order (EWO) generation. During that exercise, external fuel tanks were loaded on wing stations 2, 3, 6 and 7. Stations 2 and 7 were subsequently downloaded prior to the mishap flight. The mishap aircraft was scheduled to fly as part of the Bomb Wing's exercise as call sign Heat 22. Scheduled flight items included a Minimum Interval Takeoff (MITO), air refueling in W-102, and low-level activities in IR-800. The mishap aircraft took-off at 1050 EST as number two in a two-ship formation flight. At 1134 EST, the mishap crew requested to return to base. At 1144 EST, the mishap aircraft declared an In Flight Emergency (IFE) with Boston Air Traffic Control Center because of an external stores problem. By 1144 EST, the mishap aircraft started a descent to 10,000 feet MSL. Boston Center radar plots indicate that the last altitude of the mishap aircraft was 13,300 feet MSL. At 1146:15 EST, Boston Center's radar indicated a primary target of the mishap aircraft. After that point Boston Center had no verbal or radar contact with the mishap aircraft. A SAR was initiated, and wreckage from the mishap aircraft was located on a mountainside near Kirby, VT. The crash site was located 70 NM East of Plattsburgh AFB, New York, with coordinates of (N 44 28 00 / W 71 57 00)

Findings
Shortly after takeoff, while leveling off at 19,000 feet MSL, a 600-gallon external fuel tank installed on the #3 wing station pivot pylon swiveled outward. The aft wing sweep position, combined with the surface area of the external tank exposed to the relative wind, caused an uncorrectable yawing force. The aircrew was unable to maintain control and ejected near (Kirby) St. Johnsburg, Vermont. The crew was slightly injured during the ejection sequence.

Crew
Pilot: Capt Randall S Voorhees
WSO: Capt Leonard J Esterly Jr.
Call Sign: Heat 22
Time of Incident: 1147 EST
Accident Board President: Col Gerald K Bishop
Assigned Unit: 529th BS / 380th BWM Plattsburgh AFB, New York
Aircraft Statistics: 1,302 Flights and 4,459.2 Flight Hours
Mishap Result: Aircraft Destroyed / Successful Ejection

Courtesy of GDFW.

68-0253
FB-111A # 25 GD/FW Production Run # B1-25
USAF Delivery Date: August 22, 1970

Crash Scenario
On October 7, 1970 the mishap aircraft was scheduled for a 5.0 hour aircrew training mission to include air refueling, low-level bombing, and practice instrument approaches at Carswell AFB, TX. Prior to takeoff, the low-level mission was cancelled due to weather. The aircraft took off at 1825L and climbed toward the air refueling track. The mishap aircraft received a 12,000-pound off-load of fuel in the Busy Marshall refueling area and then directly returned to Carswell AFB. At 2030L, while enroute, the crew advised the 7th BW Command Post that they had lost the Inertial Navigation System (INS). The mishap aircraft penetrated to Carswell AFB at 2042L on a TACAN-published penetration. The crew made five approaches to Runway 17 (1-GCA PAR / 1-GCA No Gyro /2- ILS). After the last ILS low approach, the aircraft was vectored to 270 degrees at 3,000 feet on a cross-wind leg for the last GCA to a full stop landing. The downwind leg was 350 degrees at 3,000 feet, then a pattern correction turn to 020 degrees, followed by a heading change to 080 degrees for a base leg. The pattern appeared normal to the GCA controller until radar and radio contact were lost on the Carswell TACAN 340 degree radial at 9 NM. The aircraft impacted the ground and was destroyed. The crew escape module separated from the aircraft, however, the ejection was unsuccessful.

Courtesy of Author's Collection.

Findings
During the base to final turn the aircraft stalled and departed controlled flight. The investigation revealed the mishap pilot did not complete the Before Landing checklist and failed to extend the wing slats and flaps. On the downwind leg, the pilot maintained at 230 KIAS and 3,000 feet MSL (2,350 AGL) throughout the turn to base leg. During the right turn to final the aircraft began a descent. The landing gear were down

68-0261
FB-111A # 33 GD/FW Production Run # B1-33
USAF Delivery Date: September 22, 1970

Crash Scenario
On September 18, 1979, the mission was scheduled as a three-ship Red Flag sortie; the first for the mishap crew. The profile consisted of a standardized VFR departure route, visual formation, low-level navigation, and a simulated bomb release on a heavily defended target within the Nellis AFB range complex. After completing the low-level portion of the mission, the mishap crew had planned to rejoin the three-ship and then recover to Nellis AFB. The crew made an on-time takeoff at 1340 PDT. The mission proceeded without apparent difficulty until approximately 1455 PDT. At that time, the mishap aircraft was observed on radar to be exiting the Military Operating Area to the north, away from the other two aircraft they were planning to rejoin with. At approximately 1502 PDT, the lead aircraft reported to the range control group that they had lost radio contact with the mishap aircraft, and informed range control that they were observing a plume of smoke to the north. A surveillance aircraft proceeded to the north, attempting to determine the source of the smoke plume. The smoke and fire were attributed to the crash of the mishap aircraft. No ejection attempt was initiated and the crew was fatally injured. Crash coordinates were (N 37 24 04.41 / W 114 03 25.61), which is 15 ¼ NM north of Pioche, NV, and 120 NM north of Nellis AFB, NV.

Findings
For an unknown reason, the flight crew departed controlled flight after completing their assigned mission on the Nellis Range complex. The investigation assumed the crew failed to visually acquire the other flight members while attempting to rejoin into formation. After the mishap crew realized they had unintentionally passed their element mates, the pilot made an aggressive loaded roll (simultaneous high G pitch rate and roll), attempting to turn the aircraft toward the other flight members that were now heading away from the mishap aircraft's position. During the aggressive maneuver airspeed rapidly depleted, and was too slow for the demanded performance. The aft wing sweep configuration and pilot-applied control response to oscillation influenced departure from controlled flight. The crew remained with the aircraft too long while attempting to recover and collided with the ground. Ejection was not attempted.

Crew
Pilot: Capt Phillip B Donovan.
WSO: Capt William J Full
Call Sign: Not Listed on 711 Report
Time of Incident: 1459 PDT
Accident Board President: Col Allen B Peterson
Assigned Unit: 393rd BS 509th BW Pease AFB, New Hampshire
Aircraft Statistics: 684 Flights and 2,560.0 Flight Hours
Mishap Result: Aircraft Destroyed / Fatal Crash / No Ejection Initiated

Courtesy of Don Logan Collection.

and the throttles were in idle, but the slat and flaps were up. 25 seconds after starting the turn, and a recovery was initiated at 2,200 feet MSL, 1,650 AGL. The airspeed had dropped to 170 to 180 KIAS with 21 degrees AOA. Ten seconds later the AOA was 32 degrees and the aircraft was in a post-stall gyration. Control was lost when the airspeed slowed to a point where wing lift was insufficient to sustain flight. A combination of night-induced spatial disorientation and the oscillations associated with post stall gyrations contributed to the pilot's inability to regain control at such a low altitude. An unsuccessful ejection was initiated out of the envelope.

Crew
Pilot: Lt Col Robert S Montgomery Jr.
WSO: Lt Col Charles G Robinson
Call Sign: Not Listed on 711 Report
Time of Incident: 2142 CDT
Accident Board President: BG Eugene Q Steffes
Assigned Unit: 340th BG Carswell AFB, TX
Aircraft Statistics: 26 Flights and 106.0 Flight Hours
Mishap Result: Aircraft Destroyed /
    Unsuccessful Ejection / Fatal

Courtesy of Author's Collection.

68-0263
FB-111A # 35 GD/FW Production Run # B1-35
USAF Delivery Date: October 30, 1970

Courtesy of Don Logan Collection.

Crash Scenario

On January 30, 1981, the mission was added to the weekly flying schedule as a Functional Check Flight (FCF). It was scheduled as a single-ship sortie to accomplish the required FCF after a double engine change. The mishap crew was to proceed to IR 800 for low-level navigation and simulated bombing practice, then return to home station for landing. Because of pre-flight maintenance delays, the low-level and bombing practice were cancelled prior to take-off. The mishap crew took off at 1356 EST, approximately two hours late. The mission was flown as scheduled, with no significant deviations or known problems, until the return to home station leg. During the enroute descent the aircraft departed controlled flight. Unable to bring the aircraft back under control, the mishap crew successfully ejected without injury. The aircraft crashed 2 NM east of Pease AFB, in the outskirts of Portsmouth, New Hampshire. The crew module landed 1,750 feet east of the crash site near Interstate Highway 95. Crash Coordinates were (N 43 05 00 / W 70 46 00).

Findings

During a descent profile and while in a left turn, the mishap aircrew experienced an uncommanded roll to the left and an associated increase in the AOA. The pilot applied a right stick input which stopped the roll in a 135-degree banked attitude. The pilot then continued to roll the aircraft to the left instead of rolling the nearest way to upright. During the roll, the stall warning tone activated and the pilot noted yaw. The pilot rapidly applied forward stick, inducing inertial coupling. The aircraft departed controlled flight at an altitude too low for recovery.

The mishap aircraft had entered a rapid, unscheduled roll to the left for an undetermined reason. The pilot testified that the aircraft began "snap-rolling motions in one direction." The activity stopped and appeared to recover, but then the rolling continued. The pilot was initially able to correct the rolling motion by applying right rudder,

but the aircraft continued to lose altitude. The uncommanded roll was suspected to be the result of a galled Horizontal Tail Servo Actuator (HTSA) or HTSA servo control valve. The pilot's attempts to stop the rolling motion indicated the flight controls were responding somewhat to manual inputs, albeit grossly. Unfortunately, the automatic characteristics of the stability and command augmentation systems agitated horizontal stabilizer motions. The pilot again responded to stabilize the aircraft but the cycle continued. Due to the galling in the HTSA or HTSA control valve, proper control response was either stalled, sluggish, or exaggerated, all of which contributed to unwanted flight control deflections, rapidly rolling the aircraft. Each roll, and the time spent attempting to recover the aircraft to a stable position, depleted altitude. As the plane approached 4,000 feet AGL, the unpredictability of the aircraft's uncommanded motions and inability to achieve stabilized flight influenced the crew to eject.

Crew

Pilot: Capt Peter Carellas.
WSO: Maj Ronald J Reppe
Call Sign: Salic 16
Time of Incident: 1456 EST
Accident Board President: Col Robert E Reynolds
Assigned Unit: 715th BS 509th BW Pease AFB, New Hampshire
Aircraft Statistics: 682 Flights and 2,472.7 Flight Hours
Mishap Result: Aircraft Destroyed / Successful Ejection

68-0268
FB-111A # 40 GD/FW Production Run # B1-40
USAF Delivery Date: November 17, 1970

Courtesy of Ben Knowles via Don Logan Collection.

Crash Scenario

On October 6, 1980, the mishap aircraft departed Plattsburgh AFB, New York, as Number-2 in a two-ship formation at 2119 EDT. After level-off, the formation lead was changed and the mishap aircraft became the lead aircraft. At the Bangor 199/41 the formation separated to allow the mishap aircraft to enter the low-level route twelve minutes ahead of his wingman. At 2158 EDT, the mishap aircraft entered IR-800 at 17,000 feet. Shortly thereafter the mishap crew requested clearance to make a Tactical Auto TF descent. The request was approved. At the Bangor 103/57 the mishap aircrew reported initiating descent. The mishap aircraft then continued along the planned route until reaching Bangor 134/59. At 2212 EDT, Boston Center lost radar contact with the mishap aircraft. Boston Center and the mishap aircraft's wingman conducted an unsuccessful communications search. At 2230 EDT, Boston Center was advised by the U.S. Coast Guard station at Jonesport, ME, that a citizen had reported seeing and hearing an explosion on the water. A short time later floating wreckage and debris were found, and it was determined it was from the mishap aircraft. Crash Coordinates were 7.4 NM on the 227 degree radial from Coast Guard Station Jonesport, ME (N 44 25 15 / W 67 41 90).

Findings

The aircraft was operating in IMC at an altitude of approximately 1,000 feet AGL as it approached a climb point where a right turn was to begin. For an undetermined reason, the aircraft entered a steep right descending turn and crashed. Ejection was not attempted. The aircraft impacted in 180 foot deep water at night in heavy weather during low-

level route ingress. The actual cause of the crash was never determined. Probable causes could be spatial disorientation, visual illusions, or an uncommanded flight control input. Additionally, if the pilot was distracted with other cockpit tasks while managing the mission, these could influence and contribute to an unrecognized descent. The result was controlled flight into terrain (CFIT).

Crew

Pilot: Maj Thomas M Mullen
WSO: Capt Gary A Davis
Call Sign: Touch 55
Time of Incident: 2212 EDT
Accident Board President: Col James J LeClier
Assigned Unit: 4007 CCTS 380th BW Plattsburgh AFB, New York
Aircraft Statistics: 680 Flights and 2,446.0 Flight Hours
Mishap Result: Aircraft Destroyed / Fatal Crash

68-0266 at RAF Marham, UK *Courtesy of Udo Weisse*

68-0266
FB-111A # 38 GD/FW Production Run # B1-38
USAF Delivery Date: October 29, 1970

Crash Scenario
On February 14, 1977, the mishap aircraft "Orb-16" was the lead aircraft of a two-ship formation from takeoff until low-level entry. This mission was the first time the mishap aircraft had flown after 58 days of ground alert (SAC terminology is First Sortie After Ground Alert, or FSAGA). Scheduled activity included a visual lead formation check, air refueling, low-level navigation, Radar Bomb Scoring (RBS), Electronic Counter Measures (ECM) training, and high and low altitude simulated AGM-69A Short Range Attack Missiles (SRAM) launches, then return to Pease AFB. Prior to launch the air refueling was cancelled. Pre-flight, engine start, and taxi were accomplished without incident. The crew launched at 1827 L and proceeded direct to the entry control point for the Olive Branch 14 (OB-14) or Oil Burner low-level route, accomplishing the formation maneuvering as briefed. The formation was split up, and the mishap aircraft entered OB-14 as a single-ship at 2034L. The aircraft was tracked performing normally until Point J on the planned route. At that point, Atlanta Air Route Traffic Control Center (ARTCC) via Data Analysis Reduction Tool (DART) indicated that Orb-16 had descended to 6,700 feet MSL. The IFR route structure at this point is 7,700 feet MSL. At Point K,

Orb-16 descended to 4,700 feet MSL, where the route structure at this point directs a descent to 6,700 feet MSL. Indianapolis ARTCC voice tapes indicate the mishap aircraft made initial radio contact and reported level at 4,700 feet MSL at Point L, a 6,700 foot MSL level off point on the route. Approximately three minutes later, at 2054L, Orb-16 began impacting large trees atop a mountain peak along the route at approximately 4,500 feet MSL. The aircraft received extensive structural damage on initial tree impact. The aircraft traveled about 1400 feet after initial contact with the trees and then crashed. Debris from the ground impact and subsequent explosion covered an area of more than one mile. Both crew members were fatally injured. No ejection attempt was made. Crash location was 175 NM northwest of Pope AFB, NC, on Beartown Mountain, Russell County, VA.

Findings
The mishap aircraft crashed after a night air refueling during a low altitude instrument route mission. After the refueling was completed, the mishap crew descended one turn point too soon and hit the crest of a mountain. No ejection sequence was initiated. Terrain clearance protection along the low-level route was ensured, provided the crew maintained the minimum altitudes designated for each leg segment. However, the crew failed to verify their position before entering the route, negating the minimum altitude protection on the actual route segment and resulting in controlled flight into terrain (CFIT). The TFR was not used to back up the mishap crew's terrain awareness.

Crew
Pilot: Capt Edward A Riley Jr.
WSO: Capt Jeremiah F Sheehan
Call Sign: Orb-16
Time of Incident: 2054 EST
Accident Board President: Col Richard A Burpee
Assigned Unit: 715th BS 509th BW Pease AFB, New Hampshire
Aircraft Statistics: 436 Flights and 1,650.2 Flight Hours
Mishap Result: Aircraft Destroyed / No Attempt to Eject / Fatal Crash

---

68-0279
FB-111A # 51 GD/FW Production Run # B1-51
USAF Delivery Date: December 31, 1970

Crash Scenario
On July 30, 1980, the mission was scheduled as a single-ship sortie consisting of a standard instrument departure and climb-out to FL 220, inflight refueling, low-level navigation, simulated bombing, fighter aircraft intercept exercises, and multiple approaches upon return to Pease AFB, New Hampshire. An aircraft tail number change was effected by maintenance personnel prior to the mishap crew's arrival. The substitute aircraft was preflight inspected by a buddy flight crew. The mishap aircrew accepted the aircraft, completed all remaining checklist items, and accomplished an on time take-off at 0958 EDT. Enroute to the low-level entry control point was flown as scheduled, with no significant problems noted. During the descent to the low-level corridor, the aircraft entered a maneuver which resulted in an out of control condition. The crew successfully ejected and the aircraft crashed 54 NM north of Bagotville, Quebec, Canada. The escape capsule landed on a log boom in a Canadian lake.

Findings
When the mishap pilot had engaged Auto TFR for the descent to enter the low-level route, the aircraft began an uncommanded roll. As the roll passed 45 degrees of bank, a TFR fail safe fly-up occurred. The pilot over-controlled the aircraft attempting to stabilize the oscillations and entered a roll coupled departure. The pilot did not take adequate steps to reduce the aircraft's increasing pitch attitude, thus reaching a stall AOA. The aircraft stalled and departed controlled flight. The uncontrolled aircraft descended into clouds, and the pilot was unable to regain control. The

Courtesy of GDFW.

WSO initiated a successful ejection. The cause of the uncommanded roll was never determined.

Crew
Pilot: Maj Walter L Mosher
WSO: Capt Jackie T Shallington
Call Sign: Unknown
Time of Incident: 1130 EDT
Accident Board President: Col John A Dramesi
Assigned Unit: 393rd BS / 509th BW, Pease AFB, New Hampshire
Aircraft Statistics: 707 Flights and 2,562.4 Flight Hours
Mishap Result: Aircraft Destroyed / Successful Ejection

68-0280
FB-111A # 52 GD/FW Production Run # B1-52
USAF Delivery Date: January 31, 1971

69-6505
FB-111A # 67 GD/FW Production Run # B1-67
USAF Delivery Date: February 28, 1971

Mid-Air Collision Scenario
On February 3, 1975, both mishap aircraft were scheduled as a two-ship night, low-level, air refueling training sortie. Pre-flight, taxi, and

68-0280 *Courtesy of GDFW.*

takeoff were accomplished without incident after minor maintenance delays (HF Radio on 69-6505 and late refueling from a previous sortie for 68-0280). The flights were uneventful through bomb release over the Ft Drum, New York, Bomb Plot. Boston Center cleared Dowel 46 (69-6505) to FL 220 and told the crew to hold at point D2 (ALB 064/34) to wait for Dowel 45 (68-0280). Dowel 46 had completed one orbit when they heard Dowel 45 get clearance to climb to FL 230 enroute to point D2. Dowel 45 requested initial information from Linda 21, the refueling tanker, but never heard an answer. TACAN air-to-air frequencies were set to effect the FB-111s' rendezvous, but lock-on never occurred. The navigators attempted radar contact, but that was also unsuccessful. Dowel 46 was cleared by Boston Center to turn toward Dowel 45 to effect the join-up, and they compared Bomb Navigation Distance Time Indicator (BNDTI) readouts to estimate their relative position. Boston Center gave Dowel 46 a left turn as Dowel 45 passed abeam, which should have put them in ten mile trail with Dowel 45 in the lead as planned. Dowel 45 slowed to Mach 0.67 (290 KCAS) while Dowel 46 maintained Mach 0.74 (330 KCAS) to aid in the closure. After a vector from Boston Center, the pilot of Dowel 46 saw Dowel 45's anti-collision light and confirmed it by having Dowel 45 turn it off momentarily. At point D2, Dowel 45 turned left to point D3 (ALB 068/51) and told Dowel 46 to cut him off in the turn. Dowel 46 started the cutoff but temporarily lost sight of Dowel 45. During the turn, the pilot of Dowel 45 saw 46's anti-collision light one to two miles at eight o'clock low. Dowel 46 reacquired visual contact during the turn and continued the cutoff by maintaining the light at his 2 o'clock position. As Dowel 45 rolled out toward point D3, the pilot of Dowel 46 believes he crossed behind to Dowel 45's 5 o'clock with about one mile separation. Dowel 45 was concerned that he had not yet confirmed the tanker's altitude,

so he obtained clearance from Boston Center to descend early to the block altitude of FL 180 to 210. Dowel 46 heard this clearance and told Dowel 45 he had him visual, and he was also cleared to descend. Dowel 45 reduced power and began a very slow descent. At this time Dowel 45 planned to descend only to FL 210, but 46 expected the flight to descend to FL 190. The pilot of Dowel 46 began a descent also, and recalled checking his altimeter as he descended through FL 210. During the join-up, the pilot of 46 was devoting almost all of his attention to 45's anti-collision light, the only light he saw. In the descent Dowel 46 checked his Mach and noted that he was 0.70 to 0.71 (about 320 KCAS). Dowel 45 was holding at 270 KCAS, and his slow descent never went below FL 225. Dowel 45 crossed point D3. Dowel 46 estimated his distance to be ½ mile at 5 o'clock, then suddenly realized that he was very close to Dowel 45 and began a rapid right bank to avoid collision. Dowel 46 never saw any part of Dowel 45's aircraft except the anti-collision light. Dowel 46's left wing struck Dowel 45's aircraft in the rear, causing the crew of Dowel 45 to experience a sensation of being pushed. Dowel 45's aircraft immediately entered a rapid uncontrollable roll to the left. The navigator saw a large fireball to his immediate right and reached for the ejection handle, hesitated momentarily, then ejected the capsule. The pilot of Dowel 45 had also decided to eject at this time and was reaching for the ejection handle when ejection occurred. Dowel 45 ejected at 22,480 feet MSL at Mach 0.62 (280 KCAS), approximately 35 degrees nose low inverted on a heading of 052. Dowel 46 was in a 30 to 60 degree right bank when the collision occurred. After the collision the crew of 46 was thrown hard right, indicating that the aircraft entered a hard left roll. They noted fire on the left side of the aircraft and attempted to right the aircraft by applying right rudder and right forward stick movement. After 1 to 5 seconds of control inputs the pilot of Dowel 46 initiated ejection; ejection was at 26,000 feet, Mach 0.43 (110 KCAS), inverted 80 degrees nose high, left wing low on a 315 degree heading. Both ejection sequences were successful and both aircraft crashed near Londonderry, Vermont (1 mile North of Londonderry Vermont/ Albany VORTAC 074/54), 64 miles from Westover, Massachusetts.

Findings
The pre-takeoff flight briefing was rushed because the two crews had to re-plan the bombing profile for changing weather conditions. The formation procedures were not adequately briefed at the pre-takeoff meeting. The crews planned to join-up over the ARIP, which compressed the two-ship rejoin, as well as the pre-refueling tanker rendezvous during a critical phase of flight. After departing the bombing range and proceeding to the Air Refueling Track,

69-6505 *Courtesy of GDFW.*

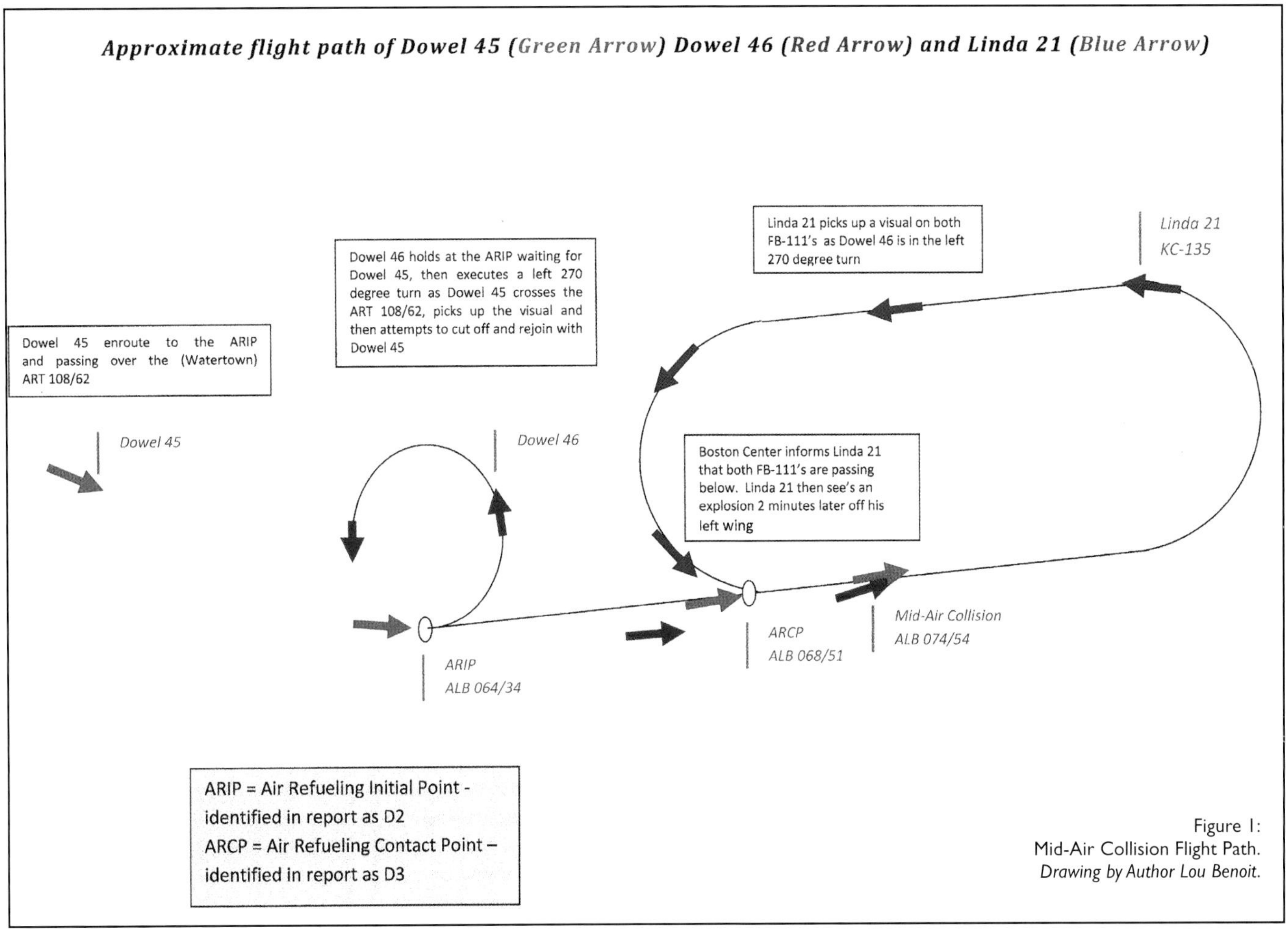

Approximate flight path of Dowel 45 *(Green Arrow)* Dowel 46 *(Red Arrow)* and Linda 21 *(Blue Arrow)*

Linda 21 picks up a visual on both FB-111's as Dowel 46 is in the left 270 degree turn

Linda 21
KC-135

Dowel 46 holds at the ARIP waiting for Dowel 45, then executes a left 270 degree turn as Dowel 45 crosses the ART 108/62, picks up the visual and then attempts to cut off and rejoin with Dowel 45

Dowel 45 enroute to the ARIP and passing over the (Watertown) ART 108/62

Dowel 45

Dowel 46

Boston Center informs Linda 21 that both FB-111's are passing below. Linda 21 then see's an explosion 2 minutes later off his left wing

Mid-Air Collision
ALB 074/54

ARCP
ALB 068/51

ARIP
ALB 064/34

ARIP = Air Refueling Initial Point - identified in report as D2
ARCP = Air Refueling Contact Point – identified in report as D3

Figure 1:
Mid-Air Collision Flight Path.
Drawing by Author Lou Benoit.

Dowel 45 delayed radio contact with his wingman and the tanker to obtain bomb scores. Dowel 45 was slow to account for high tailwinds, which reduced the time available for the two-ship formation join-up. Because Dowel 46 was already holding at Destination 2 (D2 = ARIP), a reversed order of arrival and Dowel 45's high ground speed reduced the amount of time for Dowel 46 to visually or electronically acquire Dowel 45. The crews did not utilize range and closure information by using onboard air-to-air TACAN or radar to assist them in a rejoin. Additionally, off-board aids such as "Close Control" radar vectors from Boston Center, or comparative Bearing/Distance from the Albany VOR were not exploited to assist in the rejoin either. Dowel 45 received clearance to descend from Dowel 46, which led Dowel 45 to believe Dowel 46 was in formation. Dowel 45 descended at a slower rate and was flying 20 knots slower than briefed. There was confusion among all crew members as to the level off altitude. The pilots were transmitting on both UHF radios, rather than allowing the navigators to aid in air refueling communications, causing an unnecessary pilot workload during a critical phase of flight. Dowel 46's navigator was unaware that the pilot was attempting to join in visual formation and provided no practical assistance to the pilot during the joinup. The FB-111A lighting does not provide adequate references to judge distance during a night joinup from the rear. With inadequate visual or electronic closure references, the pilot of Dowel 46 misjudged his closure rate and failed to maintain lateral and vertical separation, leading to the collision with Dowel 45. After the collision, both aircraft went out of control and both crews ejected successfully without injury.

69-6505 Crew Module. *Courtesy of Bill Allen Collection.*

Crew:	68-0280	69-6505
Pilot:	Capt John E Hockenberger	Capt Larry L McMaster
WSO:	1Lt James D Kotton	Capt Donald G Vann
Call Sign:	Dowel 45	Dowel 46

Time of Incident: 2226 EST
Accident Board President: B/Gen Thomas P Conlin
Assigned Unit: 529th BS / 380th BW Plattsburgh AFB, New York

Aircraft Statistics:	287 Flights and 1,077.8 Flight Hours	339 Flights and 1,304.3 Flight Hours
Mishap Result:	Aircraft Destroyed / Successful Ejection	Aircraft Destroyed / Successful Ejection

68-0283
FB-111A # 55 GD/FW Production Run # B1-55
USAF Delivery Date: March 26, 1971

Crash Scenario

On January 8, 1971, the mishap aircraft was lost on a routine USAF Acceptance Functional Check Flight (FCF). The aircraft took off from Carswell AFB, Texas, and crashed close to the north shore of Lake Pontchartrain, approximately 4.5 NM east of Mandeville, Louisiana. The USAF searched for more than one month, sifting through all possible route deviations from the scheduled flight path to no avail. On February 2, 1971 the crash site was discovered by two local Louisiana contractors in heavily wooded marshy swampland. Ejection sequence was initiated but was out of the envelope. Crash Coordinates were (N 30 24 21 / W 89 59 75).

Note: the mishap aircraft was factory new and being flown on a GDFW pre-acceptance flight check. Because the aircraft crashed prior to delivery, an official Air Force Safety investigation report does not exist (USAF Flight Safety Office, Kirtland AFB, New Mexico).

Findings

The accident involving FB-111A 68-0283 was an extremely difficult accident, as it involved an Air Force officer assigned as a GDFW plant representative testing the aircraft TFR system prior to delivery to the USAF. In addition, the crash site was not located for nearly a month after the flight went missing. An extensive search was conducted by the GDFW / AFPR (Air Force Plant Representative) flight operations department and the Air Force Air Rescue Recovery Service without success in locating the missing plane. Two construction workers came across the FB-111 crew module wreckage in a dense pine forest while looking for some construction equipment that had been left in the area. The search effort had been focused along the Carswell Number-3 TFR route that ran from Carswell, across the Oklahoma Ouachita mountains, and terminated just east of Fort Smith, Arkansas. The purpose of the flight was to make a brief recheck of the TFR system for a

TFR discrepancy found prior to final USAF acceptance. For this reason, the initial search area was confined to the Carswell Number-3 TFR route. After the fuel exhaustion time had expired, Air Traffic Control Centers were notified to conduct a review of recorded audio and radar tapes to determine where the missing aircraft, EEL 005, had gone down. The crash occurred on Friday, January 8, 1971, yet it wasn't until Monday morning, January 11th, that an important clue was revealed. A weekday Houston ATC controller had heard about the weekend ATC controllers conducting a tape review to find the missing FB-111. The weekday Houston ATC controller stated that he had talked to and tracked EEL 005 near Grand Isle, in the Gulf of Mexico, and that the crew was low-level out of Carswell and needed to climb through the overcast enroute to Mobile. After hearing this information, the investigation team learned that, before departing on the mishap flight, the flight crew had asked the flightline avionics technicians if the "Purple Route" had been loaded into the navigation computer. This route was Carswell to Matagorda Island, Sabine Pass, Grand Isle, Mobile, Lafayette, Lufkin, and return to Carswell. The wreckage was found near the Slidell Bridge between Pearl River and Lafayette.

The aircraft crashed at high speed and approximately 45 degrees nose low. The crater rapidly filled with water, masking obvious signs of an aircraft crash. An ejection attempt was made by the crew, but it was unsuccessful due to an out-of-the-envelope trajectory. Although about 80 percent of the aircraft wreckage by weight was recovered from the mishap scene, analysis of all the investigation data and recovered parts did not provide the basis for establishing the cause for the accident. The official cause remains "Undetermined."

The nature of the pitch-over and the inability of the pilot to recover may have been due to a catastrophic failure of a Horizontal Tail Servo Actuator or component of the flight control system that "jammed" the flight controls mechanically or hydraulically, preventing recovery.

A review of several FB-111 incidents that resulted in an uncommanded pitch-over provides some clues, but these have been added by the author as conjecture only:

The recovery parachute's white risers are apparent in this aerial photo. *Courtesy of Author's Collection.*

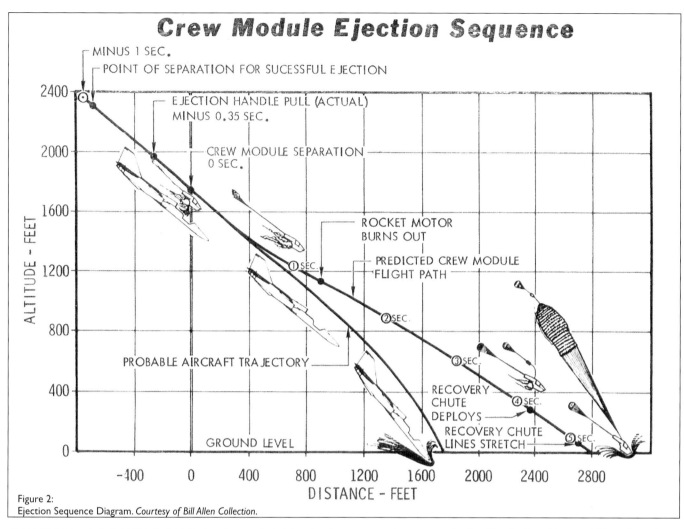

Figure 2:
Ejection Sequence Diagram. *Courtesy of Bill Allen Collection.*

Impact crater as found had quickly filled with water, camouflaging the crash scene. *Photographs Courtesy of Bill Allen Collection.*

1. Material failure of the TFR 83 percent fly-up signal resulted in immediate pitch-over when a lower SCP was selected. At the time of the occurrence, the aircraft descended through 500 feet (the selected SCP) and through the 83 percent LARA indexer (415 feet) without recovering. Additionally, there were no TFR, Channel Fail caution lamps, failure warning lamps, audio, or pitch steering bar indications of a failure, nor was a fly-up commanded. The pilot recovered the aircraft at 300 feet AGL.

2. Reference FB-111 69-6511. While passing 13,000 feet MSL on an instrument penetration, the aircraft rolled left and pitched down. The pilot could not correct the lateral (roll) motion of the aircraft, nor recover from the dive and ejected. A yaw-induced roll could have been the result of a foreign object from some undetermined source lodging in the rudder servo-actuator control valve. The foreign object could have been introduced to the hydraulic system via contaminated fluids during servicing, or by spalling of a hydraulic pump drive shaft bearing. With reference to the F-111 uncommanded maneuvers charts in the appendix, a number of "pitch-down" motions were the result of failed yaw dampers, rudder servo actuators, and rudder hard-overs.

3. An FB-111 was flying on autopilot altitude hold mode at 2800 feet MSL, approximately 2550 feet AGL, when the autopilot commanded a sharp nose down signal. The pilot immediately disengaged the autopilot and was able to recover the aircraft. The aircraft had previously aborted a takeoff for a failed CADC. The CADC was replaced, and on this flight, just prior to the pitch-down, the pilot reported a number of fluctuating instruments, including the airspeed indicator and the angle of attack indicator. Post-flight investigation revealed a bent pin in the CADC connection, and the connector was also not completely seated.

4. Two separate FB-111 incidents which involved an abrupt pitch down while on autopilot were caused by a failed pitch computer.

5. Several FB-111 incidents involved a failed yaw computer which caused an abrupt pitch-over.

Crew
Pilot: Lt Col Bruce D Stocks
WSO: Maj Billy C Gentry
Call Sign: EEL 05
Time of Incident: Late Afternoon
Accident Board President: Unknown probably GDFW Internal
Assigned Unit: GDFW / USAF Crew was from the 4111th BS / 340th BG Carswell AFB, Texas
Aircraft Statistics: 4 Flights and 12.0 Flight Hours
Mishap Result: Aircraft Destroyed / Fatal Ejection

68-0285
FB-111A # 57 GD/FW Production Run # B1-57
USAF Delivery Date: February 27, 1971

Crash Scenario

On October 28, 1977 the mission was scheduled as an initial qualification check with the student pilot in the left seat. The sortie consisted of an instrument departure, visual formation, air refueling, low level navigation and bombing, and a return to Plattsburgh AFB, New York, for traffic pattern activity. Preflight, engine start, and taxi were accomplished without incident. The aircraft took-off at 0808 EDT. The mission proceeded without reported difficulty until approximately 1030 EDT. At that time, and while on the Olive Branch 27 low level route, the crew declared an emergency with the Boston ARTCC, stating they had an engine fire and were proceeding to Loring AFB, Maine. Shortly after this call, the crew stated over the Ashland, ME, Radar Bomb Scoring site (RBS) frequency that they might have to eject. Ejection was initiated at approximately 6,000 feet MSL, and the crew module successfully separated from the aircraft. Shortly thereafter, the aircraft crashed in a nearly vertical attitude into a river and was destroyed. The crew module descended into a densely wooded area, and a portion of a six-inch diameter tree penetrated the floor of the module, bruising the left leg of the instructor pilot, who occupied the right seat. The mishap crew proceeded on foot to a nearby clearing, and at approximately 1230 EDT was rescued by helicopter. Crash location was 6 NM west-southwest of Ashland, Maine, and 34 NM west-southwest of Loring AFB, Maine.

Findings

The mishap sequence started when the left engine afterburner igniter plug failed inflight, opening a hole in the afterburner section. High temperature, high velocity jet exhaust gas formed a perpendicular flame torch which initiated an engine bay and aft fuselage fire. Investigation revealed the left engine combustion chamber's outer case failed due to fatigue originating in the area of the afterburner igniter squirt boss. The resulting explosion ruptured the aft fuselage fuel tank, causing an uncontrollable fire. A portion of the left engine nacelle was blown from the aircraft, creating a ventilation pattern which drew the fire forward to the left engine firewall. The hydraulic shutoff valves on the engine firewall failed to close on activation of the left

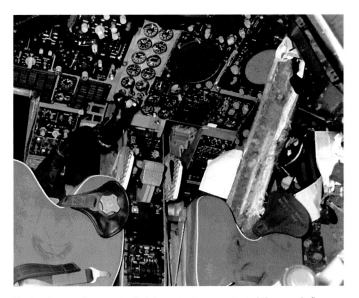

During the parachute controlled descent, a tree penetrated the capsule floor on the WSO's side. *Courtesy of Author's Collection.*

engine fire push button due to heat damage, and subsequently shorted the valve solenoid wiring harness. The fire burned through both the primary and utility hydraulic lines, resulting in loss of aircraft control. Though the ejection sequence was successful, the capsule floor on the WSO's side was penetrated by a spruce tree during landing, injuring the WSO.

Crew

Pilot: Capt John D Miller
WSO: Capt John J Blewitt Jr.
Call Sign: Not Listed on 711 report
Time of Incident: 1034 EDT
Accident Board President: Brig Gen William E Masterson
Assigned Unit: 4007th CCTS / 380th BW, Plattsburgh AFB, New York
Aircraft Statistics: 384 Flights and 1,391.7 Flight Hours
Mishap Result: Aircraft Destroyed / Successful Ejection

68-0290
FB-111A # 62 GD/FW Production Run # B1-62
USAF Delivery Date: February 22, 1971

Crash Scenario

On December 23, 1975, the mishap aircraft was scheduled for a low-level training mission. Pre-flight, engine start, taxi, and take-off were accomplished without incident. At 0920L, the mishap crew took off and flew the Caledonia published instrument departure, leveled off at FL220, and proceeded toward the entry fix for the Oil Burner (OB-27) low altitude route. The aircraft entered the route on time at 1000L, and shortly thereafter started a descent to low altitude. The low altitude portion of the mission was flown normally to a point 60 to 90 seconds

prior to the first scheduled simulated bomb release. At this point, the aircraft commander declared an aborted bomb run because of an apparent engine failure. The mishap pilot climbed and turned northeast towards Loring AFB, Maine. Shortly after this turn to Loring, the pilot experienced a yaw and rolling motion to the right which he was unable to control. During the out of control maneuver, the mishap pilot initiated ejection at 3,660 feet MSL. Ejection occurred at 1103 EST. All portions of the ejection sequence were successful, with no injuries sustained by either crew member. The crew remained in the immediate vicinity of the crew module until they were rescued by helicopter at 1240 EST. The crash site was 5.7 miles west of Ashland, Maine, and 34 NM southwest of Loring AFB, Maine.

Findings

The accident occurred 43 minutes after take-off from Plattsburg AFB during a daytime Radar Bomb Scoring (RBS) attack run. A massive uncontained left engine explosion was caused by fan blades failing for an undetermined reason. The failed blades became dislodged, rupturing the engine case and penetrating the aft centerbody fuel tank. The leaking fuel was ignited and sustained an intense uncontrollable fire in the aft centerbody. The resulting fire burned through the rudder push-pull tube due to the reverse flow phenomena, resulting in a hard over rudder and loss of flight control.

Courtesy of Don Logan Collection;

69-6508
FB-111A # 70 GD/FW Production Run # B1-70
USAF Delivery Date: March 31, 1971

Crash Scenario

On 29 September 1972, the mishap aircraft was scheduled for low-level training on the Oil Burner 23 route and Radar Bombing Score (RBS) training. Engine start, taxi, and take-off at 2356Z were accomplished without incident. Climb out, cruise to the OB-23 entry point, OB-23 activity, and return to the local Plattsburgh area were uneventful, with the exception of minor course deviations for weather to and from OB-23. ARTCC gave clearance for a descent from cruise altitude of FL 210 to 10,000 feet, and then radar hand-off was made to Burlington Approach Control. Burlington approach then cleared the mishap aircraft to 6000 feet, heading of 090 degrees, enroute to the ALTONA intersection (VAL 352/150 for radar pickup for a planned precision GCA low approach to Plattsburgh AFB runway 17. Burlington approach coordinated radar transfer to the Plattsburgh radar pattern controller. During the initial contact, realizing that a dog leg was not possible due to the aircraft's position, the pattern controller issued instructions for a right turn to heading 180 degrees and a descent to 2000 feet. The mishap aircraft crossed the extended radar runway centerline at 12 NM, still apparently on the 090 degree heading. The pattern controller directed a heading change to the right to 210 degrees, then 230 degrees. At this time control was transferred to GCA final controller on the same frequency with the aircraft on the 230 degree heading, descending. The final controller established positive radio contact, directed a left turn to 200 degrees, then attempted to make the final approach intercept by giving a left turn to 170 degrees and then 160 degrees. At this time, the mishap aircraft crossed the final approach course on the 230 degree heading at 7 NM. The aircraft, still descending to 2000 feet, configured for landing/low approach. During or shortly after the GCA turns to 150 and 130 degrees were given, the mishap pilot visually acquired Clinton County Airport runway lights, incorrectly identifying the light pattern as the Plattsburgh AFB runway. The mishap pilot landed at the Clinton County Airport on a 5000 foot runway, ran out of hard surface, and skidded off the overrun into a field.

Crew

Pilot: Capt Robert J Pavelko
WSO: Capt Michael R Sprenger
Call Sign: Not Listed on 711 report
Time of Incident: 1033 EST
Accident Board President: Col Donald E Malrt
Assigned Unit: 529th BS / 380th BW Plattsburgh AFB, New York
Aircraft Statistics: 348 Flights and 1,287.7 Flight Hours
Mishap Result: Aircraft Destroyed / Successful Ejection

inset, courtesy of Bill Allen Collection.

Courtesy of GDFW

Findings

The aircraft was returning from a night sortie in the rain with possible cockpit lighting failure. The pilot mistook the Clinton County Airport for the Plattsburg AFB runway. While attempting to stop the heavy weight aircraft on the runway, the pilot skidded off the runway surface. The unprepared surface slowed the aircraft to a stop; however, the strain of the thick brush collapsed the nose gear. The mishap aircraft was extricated from the runway clear zone and towed by surface roads to Plattsburg AFB for repairs.

Investigation determined the mishap pilot made a slow enroute descent and a lengthy delay in establishing communications with the home field GCI. As a result, the mishap aircraft was in a position, speed, and heading from which the approach controller was unable to provide the pilot normal vectors to final. The pilot was slow to configure the aircraft, and due to excess speed, overshot the normal final approach course. The approach controller attempted to provide vectors back to course. At 8NM from the runway and still descending a stall warning indication was experienced, as evidenced by the AOA tape increasing to +25 degrees, followed by illumination of the stall warning lamp, activation of the rudder pedal shaker, and the audible stall warning tone. The navigator noted illumination of the CADC system caution light. Visible stall departure and buffet were not experienced. Recovery procedures were initiated and aircraft response and control were normal. Stall warnings and indications eventually disappeared. The GCA observed the aircraft to again pass through the precision radar

Courtesy of GDFW

centerline and repeatedly gave heading directions for a left turn. The pilot was distracted by the malfunctions and had apprehensions that his instruments were providing incorrect information, and subsequently declared an emergency. The pilot visually acquired a runway to his left and disregarded GCA corrective instructions. The pilot advised the GCA that he had the field in sight and was going to land. The GCA attempted course and glidepath corrections until the mishap aircraft disappeared off the scope. The mishap pilot landed at a civilian airport with a 5000 foot long runway. The pilot was unable to stop the aircraft on the runway and departed the prepared surface, collapsing the nose gear.

Crew
Pilot: Maj Bennie L Woytovich
WSO: Capt Andrew Z Stepniewski
Call Sign: Prior 47
Time of Incident: 2218 EDT
Accident Board President: Col G.R. Abendhoff
Assigned Unit: 4007 CCTS / 380th BW Plattsburgh AFB, New York
Aircraft Statistics: Unknown
Mishap Result: Aircraft sustained major damage/ Repaired and returned to service

Many versions of the story have been told over the last 30 years, however, Major Ed MacNeil remembers this event very well and tells the story:

On Friday September 29, 1972, an FB-111A from the 380th BW at Plattsburgh AFB landed by mistake on a short runway at the Clinton County Airport in Plattsburgh, New York. The aircraft was crewed by Pilot Maj. Bennie L.Woytovich and Navigator Capt. Andrew Z.Stepniewski. "I'm very familiar with that short flight of 69-6508. This flight became known as the "Polish cross country" as both members of the crew had Polish names. The mission was a CCTS night sortie at KPBG. This was the end of summer and as usual a great deal of construction was in progress. Among other things a significant number of the runway lights were inoperative making the runway appear much shorter than it actually was. The weather on the night of the mishap was terrible - raining like a cow peeing on a flat rock! Shortly after takeoff the CADC malfunctioned which resulted in a lot of warning lights and the accompanying audio. The crew elected to abort the mission and return to KPBG. They requested and received a GCA to runway 17. This approach was controlled

6508 under tow with a safety "braking" tug connected by rope to the arresting hook. *Courtesy of the USAF.*

by a student controller and resulted in the airplane being well right of centerline. At about 2 miles the crew sighted a lighted runway dead ahead and assuming it to be runway 17 at Plattsburgh proceeded to land.

Like most SAC bases, the runway at Plattsburg AFB (KPBG) is far longer than required by an FB-111A. Pilots usually employed aerodynamic braking to slow the aircraft in a nose-up / main landing gear only stance on the runway. When the aircraft has slowed, aerodynamic braking effects are lost, and the nose-gear cannot be held up off the ground by the horizontal tail stabilizers and begins to fall forward or is lowered to the runway by the pilot on the controls. The aircraft is then allowed to roll down the runway before brakes are applied.

Using normal habit patterns after the mishap landing, the (mishap) pilot elected to employ aerodynamic braking only until the aircraft was well slowed down. Unfortunately, he ran off the end of the 5,000-feet runway before slowing very much. The aircraft departed the end of the runway and then down an incline striking several small trees. One drop tank was knocked off and ruptured. When the aircraft came to a stop the pilot directed the Nav to go up the incline and caution rescue personnel to be very careful not to ignite the spilled fuel.

The Nav was an FAA licensed Commercial Pilot but was a bit rattled at this fairly nonstandard arrival. He departed the airplane still wearing his helmet and carrying his bag of secrets. When he reached the top of the incline he noted the airport beacon going green --- white --- green --- white. He knew that this was the designation for a civil airport and since Clinton County was the only airfield near Plattsburgh he then knew exactly where he was. He proceeded across the airfield to the terminal, which was closed, and found a telephone booth. Directly in front to this phone booth was a car containing a young couple. He couldn't see them well as the windows were all steamed up. Reaching in his pocket he discovered that he had two quarters. Dropping a quarter in the coin slot he dialed 0. When the operator answered, he identified himself and asked that she dial the Command Post at Plattsburgh. She informed him that he could dial the number himself. He responded that his hands were still shaking too damn bad and would she just dial it!! The phone in the Command Post (CP) was answered by the NCO Controller who announced that he was unable to talk due to an aircraft emergency and broke the connection. The Nav then deposited his last remaining coin and dialed the CP. At this point the young couple left the area. The same command post controller answered, and before he could break the connection again, the Nav informed him that if he broke the connection again he would personally walk back to Plattsburgh and shoot him! When the situation was explained, a vast contingent departed Plattsburgh AFB for Clinton County".

Soon, security police and base officials arrived and a UH-1N rescue helicopter transported the crew back to Plattsburg AFB while base personnel tried to figure out what to do with the aircraft. State Police and Sheriff's deputies cordoned the area off to civilians and base personnel set up floodlights to begin their inspection. Fuel was removed from the aircraft at the scene as Plattsburg AFB fire trucks stood by. Guards from the base were stationed around the FB-111 until it could be moved. The following Wednesday morning, October.4th, seven Air Force vehicles, five New York State Police cars, a New York State Electric and Gas truck and a New York Telephone truck escorted the crippled FB-111A back to base.

With the wings folded back, the FB-111 was 34 feet wide, making its route home a tricky one. The work crew took Route 3 to Military Turnpike, north on the turnpike to Route 374, east on 374 to Exit 38 of the Northway, south on the Northway to Exit 36 and back to base. The entire operations took four and a half hours. The gas and telephone trucks traveled ahead of the caravan, lifting power and phone lines. Several signs and reflectors had to be cut down to allow clearance, but a base welding team followed the convoy and restored each one. State Police closed off the Northway highway to civilian traffic one intersection at a time while the convoy moved at walking speed until it reached the Northway turnoff. It then picked up speed to 5 miles per hour. Eventually, 6508 was repaired and returned to service.

The Long Journey Home. *Courtesy of the USAF.*

Factory Fresh Roll-out. *Courtesy of GDFW.*

69-6511
FB-111A # 73 GD/FW Production Run # B1-73
USAF Delivery Date: March 16, 1971

Crash Scenario
On June 7, 1976, the mishap aircraft was scheduled as Number-2 in a two-ship low-level training sortie. Preflight checks, engine start, taxi, and takeoff were on time at 0857 EDT. Departure join-up, enroute pre-refueling procedures, and refueling were conducted without incident. Low level entry into Oil Burner-27 (Bangor, Maine) was accomplished, and a normal in-trail bomb run was made. After flying the alternate exit in northern Maine, the mishap aircraft leveled off at 22,000 feet and proceeded back towards Plattsburgh AFB, New York. A line of thunderstorms south and east of Plattsburgh necessitated a deviation to the south. After clearing the weather a turn was made northbound to the Plattsburgh area. The pilot obtained destination weather and requested an enroute descent from Boston ARTCC. While descending from 19,000 feet to 10,000 feet, radio and radar contact was lost. The mishap crew successfully ejected at an altitude of 8120 feet MSL. The crew escape module came to rest on the ground in a wooded area in a steep bank to the right. The crew was picked up by helicopter from Plattsburgh at 1310 EDT. The aircraft impacted the ground in a slight descent 3.3 mile NE of the capsule site in a woody, marshy area. The aircraft cut a 615 foot swath through the trees; the major portion of the wreckage came to rest relatively intact and was engulfed in flames. Capsule coordinates were (N 44 05 40 / W 73 09 10), while the aircraft impact coordinates were (N 44 08 50 / W 73 08 00).

Findings
During the descent profile towards Plattsburg AFB, and at approximately 13,000 feet, the pilot noted his airspeed between 275 to 280 knots, slightly below desired, and then retracted the extended speed brake. Noting a small cloud ahead, the pilot initiated a 20-30 degree bank to the left and entered a yaw induced roll. The pilot countered the uncommanded yaw induced roll with side-to-side (lateral) stick inputs only, and did not apply opposite rudder or forward stick pressure. The pilot noted the aircraft was unresponsive to lateral control inputs and subsequently executed the out of control procedures, which failed to recover the aircraft. Observing that an increasing nose low and turning or spiraling condition was developing, and that the aircraft was passing through 10,000 feet MSL, the aircrew decided to eject. The investigation determined the Horizontal Tail Servo Actuator (HTSA) was damaged during installation on the aircraft 2.5 weeks prior to the mishap, when misinterpretation of the technical orders resulted in the HTSA being incorrectly installed with a side load applied.

Crew
Pilot: Capt Raymond T Wilson
WSO: Capt Richard A Bernardi
Call Sign: Peter 36
Time of Incident: 1200 EDT
Accident Board President: Col Henry W Boardman
Assigned Unit: 529th BS / 380th BW Plattsburgh AFB, New York
Aircraft Statistics: 456 Flights and 1,763.5 Flight Hours
Mishap Result: Aircraft Destroyed / Successful Ejection

11

OTHER KNOWN
F-111 MISHAPS & INCIDENTS

F-111F 70-2415 Main Gear-Up Landing and Cable Engagement at Mountain Home AFB, Idaho. *Courtesy of Don Gwynne.*

F-111A:

63-9771 - on November 14, 1966, the aircraft experienced a ruptured engine compressor disk that resulted in an engine failure and fire during a flight test sortie.

63-9772 - on July 6, 1966, during the first weapons bay bomb drop test, an internally loaded MK-43 bomb hit the weapons bay door and hinge assembly, causing significant structural damage.

66-0011 - on August 21, 1967, the aircraft suffered significant damage in a large hail storm over the Nellis Range while on a training sortie. Crew: Pilot: Capt Joe Hodges, WSO: Capt Phillips, Call Sign: Unknown

66-0012 - on October 30, 1969, while performing chase aircraft duties for a classified project, the aircraft experienced an inflight separation of the Triple Plow II engine inlet splitter plate. The mishap aircraft was assigned to the Air Force Flight Test Center (AFFTC) at Edwards AFB, California. The splitter plate configuration was common to the production F-111As from A1-30 and on. Due to airflow swirl around the aircraft the plate penetrated the F-2 fuel tank, causing significant damage. The aircraft was recovered safely by the mishap aircrew to Edwards AFB without incident. Pilot: Lt Col Michael F McNamara Jr., WSO: 1Lt Howard L Kotlicky, Call Sign: Unknown

Courtesy of Craig Kaston Collection.

NOTE 1: 66-0012 had been modified as a Harvest Reaper Electronic Counter Measures (ECM) test aircraft, and was later used for F-111 flight training service at the Edwards Air Force Base Flight Test Center. Though the damage was repairable, the aircraft could not be repaired into a configuration suitable for squadron level service. Because the aircraft's service with the AFFTC was no longer a viable necessity, it was deemed beyond economical repair. The aircraft was stricken from the inventory and sent to Lowry AFB as a ground trainer. The aircraft is currently on display at the Battle Mountain Air Museum in Nevada.

NOTE 2: 66-0012 was the last of 30 Pre-production and Test F-111As known as Research, Development, Test & Evaluation (RDT&E) aircraft. 66-0012, along with F-111As 5704 and 5708, were used to test the "Harvest Reaper" avionics equipment later installed on the first F-111As deployed to Vietnam for combat operations under the code name Combat Lancer. The first 13 Production F-111As were known as Harvest Reaper modified jets (tail numbers 66-0013 through 66-0025).

66-0013 - on April 22, 1969, near Indian Springs (Weapons Range III-4), 10 NM north of Beatty, Nevada, the mishap aircrew were cruising at 13,000 feet MSL, 378 Knots Indicated Air Speed (KIAS), and 90% throttle selected when the mishap aircrew felt a slight engine surge. Within seconds a larger surge was felt, accompanied by a control stick transient, left generator light, left primary and utility hydraulic lights, and left engine fire light. The mishap wingman "Tartan 02" observed a ten foot sheet of flame and white smoke trailing from the left engine. The mishap aircrew initiated left engine shutdown and fire agent discharge. A single engine approach and landing was successfully accomplished on Runway 03L at Nellis AFB, Nevada. Subsequent investigation reported the left (#1) engine combustion chamber burner can insulator was not installed, causing the fire. **Pilot:** Maj John O Hanford, **WSO:** Maj Grover C Poole, **Call Sign:** Tartan 01

Courtesy of D. Larson via Douglas E. Slowiak/Vortex Photo-Graphics Collection.

66-0018 - on January 23, 1981, the mishap aircraft, while assigned to the 389th TFTS / 366th TFW, experienced a main landing gear (MLG) failure. The aircrew successfully returned to base and accomplished a gear-up BAK-12 barrier engagement with minimal structural damage. The direct cause was an alignment issue with the main gear A-frame support, which allows the gear to disengage from the up-lock assembly. A fleet-wide inspection and fix was issued following this event.

 The aircraft shown during the recovery phase. The photograph on the left shows the aircraft being lifted by a crane, then being placed on jacks stands in the photograph on the right. The landing gear were extended and the jacks removed, and then the aircraft was towed into the hangar for repairs.

Courtesy of Author's Collection.

66-0030 - on March 24, 1978, the mishap aircraft was scheduled to fly an initial Functional Check Flight (FCF) following Programmed Depot Maintenance (PDM) at Sacramento Air Logistics Center (SMALC). The preflight, engine start, and taxi were accomplished without major discrepancies. The mishap aircraft taxied approximately 200 yards, when the aircraft began to settle to the left after the pilot applied moderate brake pressure. The aircraft scraped to a stop, supported by the nose gear and main landing gear door (also the speed brake) and the left engine bay strake panels. The aircrew shut down both engines and egressed the aircraft. **Pilot:** Maj James K Dozier Jr., **WSO:** Capt Brian J Teague. **Call Sign:** Unknown

67-0050 - on January 8, 1975, the mishap aircraft, flying with the 428th TFS out of Nellis AFB, Nevada, experienced a nose landing gear that would not extend. The mishap crew safely landed at Nellis AFB, bringing the aircraft to a stop using a BAK-12 barrier engagement. **Pilot:** Lt Col Carl L Hamby **WSO:** Unknown **Call Sign:** Unknown

Courtesy of Don Logan Collection.

67-0057 - on November 6, 1969, during landing rollout after a successful 3.5-hour training mission, the forward equipment hot light illuminated, but was extinguished by advancing power slightly. The light illuminated again just prior to engine shutdown. Investigation revealed failure of a nacelle ejection bleed air duct. Failure of the duct allowed hot engine compressor bleed air to be discharged into the engine bay, resulting in overheat and mechanical damage to the airframe. Contributing to the mishap, the duct mounting hardware was inadequate and did not provide sufficient adjustment capability to preclude pre-stressing the installation. **Pilot:** Lt Col Donald D Mueller, **WSO:** Capt Brian K O'Riordan, **Call Sign:** Unknown

Courtesy of Author's Collection.

67-0057 (above) photographed sitting on the Nellis AFB flight line. This rear view of the F-111A shows the full droop (nose-down pitch) of the horizontal stabilizers without hydraulic pressure. Additionally, the presence of light in the right engine exhaust nozzle reveals the unique characteristic of the blow-in-door ejector nozzle. The ejector nozzle doors close as the aircraft accelerates toward supersonic speed, capturing additional engine/afterburner thrust from the nozzle. Beyond the blow-in doors are free floating nozzle flaps called "turkey feathers," which expand outward between Mach 0.9 and Mach 2.4 depending on flight conditions, assisting in capturing additional thrust performance.

67-0059 - on November 23, 1972 (Constant Guard V), during combat operations the mishap aircraft's slats and flaps would not extend. The crew accomplished a no slat/flap approach and landing, after which the aircraft's hot brakes ignited a wheel and brake fire.

On April 16, 1973 (Constant Guard V), 67-0059 hit an animal on the runway during takeoff just prior to rotation. The crew executed a go-around and completed a successful barrier engagement, sustaining only minor tail hook fairing damage.

67-0065 Battle Damage (Constant Guard V): the aircraft was damaged on December 29, 1972, after attacking a North Vietnamese Early Warning Radar site at 300 feet AGL with 12 Mk-82s in Route Pack 5 North Vietnam. The aircraft received AAA fire from eight different sites during the target run-in. The aircraft sustained shrapnel damage in the right engine bay door. Crew: Unknown, Call Sign Jumbo 41.

On May 18 or 19, 1980, 67-0065 was flown through the Mount St. Helens ash cloud at 35,000 feet. After landing, the aircraft appeared as though it had been sand-blasted to bare metal with the cockpit glass very cloudy and crazed.

67-0069 Battle Damage (Constant Guard V): on December 27, 1972, during a night attack against the Lan Truoc RADCOM Center at 500 feet, the aircrew observed SAM flashes and felt an impact. The crew initiated a climb and experienced smoke fumes in the cockpit. Shortly thereafter, the Icing Light and an Engine Inlet Hot Light illuminated. Emergency checklist procedures cleared the problems. After recovery, battle damage was found in the left inlet guide vane area, one hole in the left horizontal stabilizer, and in the left saddle tank that caused a fuel leak. Call Sign: Jumbo 42, Crew: Unknown

67-0080 (Constant Guard V): on October 21, 1972, the aircraft incurred damage due to a "tree strike" while landing at Takhli; the landing accident occurred in heavy fog. The crew came in too low during a GCA landing while attempting to land.

67-0083 Battle Damage (Constant Guard V): on December 20, 1972, the aircraft sustained battle damage from small arms fire. The aircraft was repaired and went back into action January 3, 1973. Call Sign: Jackel 23, Crew: unknown.

On May 8, 1973 (Constant Guard V), 67-0083, during takeoff from Takhli RTAFB, experienced a broken fuel line that ignited a fire in the #1 engine bay. The aircrew returned to base with a full fuel load and 24 MK-82 bombs. The aircraft sustained extensive damage to the engine and nacelle area. Crew: Pilot Maj Lester G Frazier, WSO: 1Lt Gary R. Rundle, Call Sign: Jumbo 41.

67-0091 Battle Damage (Constant Guard V): on October 12, 1972, the aircraft sustained damage in an attempt to evade a SAM missile launched over RP 5. The bomb load was jettisoned outside the release envelope, and parts of the bombs or bomb racks penetrated both horizontal stabilizers. Crew: Unknown, Call Sign: Drylot 60.

67-0085 - on March 15, 1988, the mishap aircraft, flying with the 389th TFS, experienced a nose landing gear that would not extend; a safe barrier engagement was successfully accomplished on return to Mountain Home AFB, Idaho. Pilot: Lt Col Brusting, WSO: Capt Keller, Call Sign: Unknown.

Courtesy of Author's Video Collection.

67-0100 (Constant Guard V): on October 21, 1972, the aircraft's right engine disintegrated, causing the aircrew to divert to Udorn RTAFB. Crew: Unknown, Call Sign: Dipper 34.

In February 1991, 67-0100 had a ground mishap due to a fuel purging unit fire that burned the right intermediate fuselage area (Panel 2204). The aircraft was repaired at Mountain Home AFB by placing a patch over the fire damaged area. The aircraft was then shipped to Nellis AFB, Nevada, to become a display in July 1991.

67-0103 Battle Damage (Constant Guard V): on October 23, 1972, the aircraft sustained AAA damage. The aircraft had several bullet holes in the cheek area and engine panels.

67-0106 (Constant Guard V): on May 12, 1973, the aircrew had lightning strike during a combat mission over northern Laos. Crew: Unknown, Call Sign: Jackel 50

67-0109 - this aircraft was modified by GDFW and sent to Takhli RTAFB, and was used for the TFR OT&E testing during Constant Guard V. This aircraft was instrumented and equipped with cockpit cameras to video the TFR test flights. After completion of the tests, the aircraft was returned to the normal configuration and served with TAC until this aircraft was purchased by the RAAF and became A8-109.

67-0112 (Constant Guard V): on 11 October 1972, the aircrew expended 24 MK-82s by jettison while taking evasive action to avoid two SAM launches. The BRUs pickled off, damaging the wings. Aircrew used jinking tactics after the first SAM launch, but no chaff was used. The threat warning receiver missile launch warning lamp went on, then off after the second SAM launch. Aircrew observed a yellow-orange flame and a white halo circle behind them after evading the launches. This aircraft was purchased by the RAAF and became A8-112.

67-0113 - in September 1979, the pilot landed very hard 500 feet short of the runway threshold. The aircraft damage was severe. It sat for three years as a hangar queen and cannibalization bird. The 366th Fighter Wing was ordered to repair the aircraft and return it to flight status in the summer of 1981. This aircraft was purchased by the RAAF and became A8-113.

67-0114 (Constant Guard V): on November 5, 1972, the aircraft had an inflight incident. The aircraft's right strake was broken off after being grazed by a released bomb. This aircraft later was purchased by the RAAF and became A8-114.

August 14, 1978 - an unknown F-111A suffered an uncommanded landing gear retraction during engine shut down at Mountain Home AFB, Idaho. No other details are known.

F-111B:
151972 - in May 1966, while on takeoff from the Hughes Aircraft Company airfield at Culver City, California, an out-of-rig nose gear door closed and cut the nose gear hydraulic lines during gear retraction. With broken hydraulic lines, the pilot had no control over the steering or brakes. On landing, the mishap aircraft began a left turn and ran off the runway. The out-of-control aircraft appeared to be heading for an employee parking lot when the nose gear wheels caught the pavement curb/edge, straightening the heading and averting disaster! The aircraft was repaired and returned to service. Crew: Pilot Charles McDaniels, MCO Barton Warren.

F-111C:
A8-112 - on June 26, 2002, the aircraft experienced an internal fuel tank explosion, requiring 18 months to repair.

A8-114 - on March 3, 1983, the aircraft sustained repairable structural damage to the wing pivot during a display.
On May 26, 1988, during flight, the over-wing fairing separated and struck the vertical stabilizer. The aircraft safely landed.

A8-131 - on March 12, 1986, the aircrew experienced a gun malfunction in the weapons bay. Aircraft landed safely.
On January 18, 1988, the aircraft returned with utility hydraulic failure and made a successful barrier engagement.

A8-143 - on July 18, 2006, the aircraft lost its left main wheel on takeoff. The flight crew did not know one of the main wheels had fallen off and retracted the gear, where it jammed in the up position. Unable to extend the landing gear, the crew landed gear up using a successful barrier engagement at RAAF Amberley. The aircraft was repaired and returned to service. This was the last known major F-111 incident. **Pilot:** PLTOFF Peter Komar, **WSO:** FLTLT Luke Warner, **Call Sign:** Unknown.

Courtesy of 82 Wing Photographic RAAF.

F-111D:
68-0090 - on June 11, 1977, the aircraft experienced a left engine fire while taxiing on the Cannon AFB ramp. The flight crew declared a ground emergency. The aircraft received minor damage.

68-0097 - on March 21, 1978, the aircraft failed to rotate on takeoff. The pilot completed a high speed abort and engaged the departure-end barrier. No other details known.

68-0098 - on May 10, 1975, the left engine rolled back and shut down while on final approach to Cannon AFB Runway 21.

68-0099 - on February 10, 1976, the aircraft had a 3rd stage fan blade failure, causing a main wheel well fire; damage was sustained on the aircraft's emergency generator, emergency generator control unit, and wiring. There was also damage to both hydraulic systems. The aircraft

Mishap aircraft ground track. Refer to 151972 *Courtesy of Tommy Thomason.*

was repaired at Cannon AFB and returned to service. Crew: Capt Jay D Milstead, Capt James R Hussey, Call Sign: Maggy 68.

68-0101 - GDFW Restoration (Vark Hospital). On October 28, 1983, the aircraft had a LOX (Liquid Oxygen) converter explosion and fire that damaged the forward fuselage and escape capsule floor area(s). The aircraft was flown by C-5A Galaxy to the GDFW factory restoration center in January 1984 for repairs. It was returned December 1986 to the 27th TFW after repairs completed.

F-111D-17 (S/N 68-101)
JAN. 1984   (8-37813

F-111D #17 CANNON AFB 15 NOV 83

Courtesy of Author's Collection.

68-0104 - on June 2, 1977, the aircraft experienced a left engine fire over central Kansas. The crew safely recovered to Forbes Field, Salinas, Kansas.

68-0106 - on August 28, 1980, the mishap aircraft experienced a left engine turbine failure during a night sortie. The third stage disk penetrated aft fuel tanks, eventually resulting in an explosion, and the fire crew landed safely at Peterson Field, Colorado. Crew: Pilot Maj Rowland H Worrell III, WSO: Capt John A Osborn, Call Sign: Unknown.
 On July 25, 1975, the crew landed without wheel braking due to total utility hydraulic failure, accomplishing a safe barrier engagement on Runway 14 at Buckley Field (ANG Base), Colorado.

68-0108 - on January 8, 1976, while supersonic, the left horizontal stabilizer disintegrated inflight. The crew maintained control and diverted to Roswell, New Mexico. The aircraft was repaired by 27th TFW personnel and returned to service.

April 1977: 68-0108 had an IFE for jammed landing gear handle while in the Cannon AFB landing pattern.
 June 1977: 68-0108 had right engine flameout while in the Cannon AFB Pattern, IFE, and then BAK 12 Engagement.
 March 1978: 68-0108 had an inflight fire on takeoff from Cannon AFB Runway 21. Landed safely.

68-0110 - on November 27, 1978, portions of the vertical stabilizer fell apart inflight. The crew safely recovered back to Cannon AFB, New Mexico.

68-0111 - on December 1, 1976, the mishap aircraft experienced an uncommanded landing gear retraction during engine start on the Cannon AFB ramp. The landing gear selector valve spool was found to be in the up position.

68-0115 - Date Unknown (1980s). The mishap aircraft had a MK-82 hung-bomb release that severely damaged all left (#1) engine bay panels, as shown in the following two pictures.

Courtesy of Author's Collection.

 On December 8, 1978, 68-0115 had an unknown object destroy the left windscreen inflight; an IFE was declared, RTB.
 On January 21, 1988, 68-0115 experienced a left engine failure and engine bay fire. The crew recovered to Cannon AFB. No other details known.

68-0121 - Date Unknown (1980s). The tail jack slipped from the aircraft jacking point and penetrated through the engine bay and upper aft fuselage, as depicted in the three pictures. (Next page, top).

68-0121 seen with tail jack puncturing the aft fuselage. *Courtesy of Author's Collection.*

68-0129 - on February 5, 1979, the left engine 16th stage bleed air duct ruptured, causing an engine bay fire that necessitated engine shutdown; the crew safely returned to Cannon AFB, New Mexico.

68-0129 - between 16 and 30 December 1985, 68-0129 suffered a nose gear collapse in Dock 4 of the 524th AMU Maintenance complex at Cannon AFB, New Mexico.

Photograph of TSgt Greg F. Weigl briefing Lt Col David Mitchell, 524th TFS Commander on the probable cause. *Courtesy of Author's Collection.*

Courtesy of Author's Collection.

68-0129 - Date unknown (1980s). The aircraft suffered a massive radome failure after a bird strike. Even though cockpit visibility was almost completely obstructed, the flight crew was able to recover the aircraft to Cannon AFB.

F-111D 68-0129 with significant radome damage after a direct hit from a turkey vulture. *Courtesy of USAF.*

68-0133 - on May 31, 1991, the aircraft experienced a bird strike to the intake and a subsequent engine fire. The USAF chose to write off the airframe rather than repair it; it was subsequently scrapped in the local Clovis, New Mexico, area.

*Courtesy of
Author's Collection.*

68-0135 - on May 10, 1977, the aircraft had a primary hydraulic system failure on departure from Cannon AFB; the crew declared an IFE and safely returned to Cannon AFB, New Mexico.

In March 1978, 68-0135 experienced a False Engine Fire Light, causing an AIR ABORT while over the Melrose Bomb Range during a routine training sortie. Safe recovery back to Cannon AFB was accomplished.

68-0136 - on January 15, 1976, the aircrew experienced an uncommanded roll during a low-level descent; the crew declared an IFE and landed safely at Cannon AFB, New Mexico.

68-0138 - on September 20, 1979, the aircraft experienced an aft fuselage fire; no further details are known.

68-0140 - on September 15, 1989, the aircraft suffered a bird strike, structurally damaging the intake. The USAF chose not to repair the aircraft and it was written off. The aircraft then served as the Cannon AFB Weapons Load Training (WLT) Aircraft for "Weapons Load Crew Certification." The aircraft was eventually placed on display at "Veterans Park" in Clovis, New Mexico.

Courtesy of Author's Collection.

68-0142 - on June 25, 1972, the mishap aircraft experienced a galled horizontal tail surface actuator control valve, causing loss of control during landing at Cannon AFB, New Mexico. The crew made a successful BAK-12 barrier engagement without incident. Crew: Capt Robert D Ramsey, WSO: Maj John C McFarren, Call Sign: Age 15

68-0148 - on January 17, 1979, the mishap aircraft had a 9th stage fan blade failure on the right engine during takeoff run-up. The aircrew experienced a major fire engulfing the aft fuselage on the Cannon AFB, New Mexico, runway. The fire was skillfully extinguished by the Cannon AFB Fire Department personnel as depicted in the following pictures below.

Courtesy of Author's Video Collection.

68-0150 - on December 3, 1975, the mishap aircraft had a failure of the Left (#1) engine 10th and 11th stage high pressure compressor rotors, followed by a significant inflight engine and nacelle area fire. The crew safely recovered to Cannon AFB.

 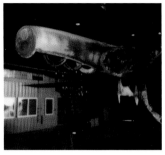

Courtesy of Author's Collection.

On November 7, 1975, **68-0150** had the # 3 flap vane fall off during takeoff roll, resulting in a high-speed abort. The crew safely stopped on the Runway 03 overrun at Cannon AFB.

On January 16, 1978, **68-0150** experienced a rudder failure at Mach 1 airspeed during a routine transition upgrade sortie. Pilot: Capt Tom Rodgers, WSO: 1Lt Junior Hill, Call Sign: Unknown

Courtesy of Tom Rogers via USAF.

68-0152 - on January 9, 1976, the aircraft experienced a primary hydraulic system failure during low-level descent over the LAMAR TACAN 270/30 radial; the crew declared an IFE (In-Flight Emergency) and safely recovered to Cannon AFB.

In March 1978, 68-0152 experienced a 16th stage bleed duct failure. An IFE was declared and the crew safely recovered back to Cannon AFB.

68-0159 - on February 20, 1976, the aircraft had an inflight left engine fire. A left engine fuel control line backed off, causing a fuel leak and inflight engine fire that burned through the engine bay heat shield and afterburner can. It was repaired at Cannon AFB.

68-0168 - on March 26, 1990, the aircraft sustained a significant bird strike on the right forward/center capsule area and radome. The radome disintegrated, which caused debris to be ingested down the intake, destroying the # 1 engine. The # 2 engine was also damaged and was stuck in afterburner. The crew realized that severe damage had been done to the capsule center beam area which eliminated an ejection option. The crew safely returned to Cannon AFB single engine. Crew Pilot Lt Col Hill, WSO: Capt Gregory Wiley, Call Sign: Unknown

NOTE: the aircraft was never repaired. A major depot repair request was received March 29, 1990, but instead the aircraft was stricken and utilized for training Aircraft Battle Damage Repair (ABDR) in the 27th TFW; eventually the airframe was scrapped in the local Clovis, New Mexico, area.

On February 25, 1976, 68-0168's Main Landing Gear Door was lost inflight.

68-0178 - on December 30, 1975, the aircrew had a Lt Engine failure over Tucumcari, New Mexico, TACAN (on the 350/70 radial). An IFE was declared by the crew, and they safely recovered at Cannon AFB.

On June 6, 1978, 68-0178's takeoff was aborted at high-speed for water ingestion after both engines stalled.

68-0180 - on January 6, 1976, the aircraft suffered a 16th stage bleed duct failure in the main gear wheel well. The crew declared an IFE and safely landed back at Cannon AFB.

On January 19, 1978, 68-0180 sustained a left engine diffuser burn through and fire. The crew declared an IFE and safely recovered back to Cannon AFB.

F-111E:

67-0118 - on June 12, 1982, while parked on the ramp at Eglin AFB, a 3000 psi high pressure impact bag inflation bottle in the escape capsule exploded, causing extensive damage to the crew module, lower panels,

capsule floor, F-1 fuel tank, and bulkhead. The aircraft was partially dismantled and loaded onto a C-5 for transport to GDFW. Repair started August 10, 1981, and completed July 1, 1982, at a cost of 1.85 million dollars. The aircraft was returned to the 3246th TFW at Eglin AFB, Florida, after restoration was completed.

Capsule floor damage. *Courtesy of GDFW.*

Mishap Aircraft being unloaded from a C-5A at GDFW. *Courtesy of GDFW.*

68-0038 - on July 20, 1970, during a routine training sortie the aircraft lost part of the left horizontal stabilizer leading edge while at Mach 2. The crew safely recovered back to home station.

68-0039 - prior to USAF delivery from GDFW, the leading edge of the right horizontal stabilizer tore off inflight. This was determined to be the result of improper honeycomb bonding during the manufacturing process at Grumman Calverton, New York.

68-0043 - while at BAe Filton, Bristol, England, the aircraft failed the planned Cold Proof Load Test (CPLT), suffering major cracks in the Wing Carry Through Box (WCTB) and a Horizontal Stabilizer pivot shaft. The aircraft's wings and the WCTB were removed, and the aircraft was placed on a support jig for a major rebuild. A new Wing Box and horizontal stabilizer pivot shaft were installed and the aircraft was returned to service. The CPLT subjected the airframe to loads at 7.33+G and -2.4 Gs at 56-degree wing sweep angle. The loads were applied by

68-0039 Right Horizontal Stabilizer with failed honeycomb leading edge. *Courtesy of Bill Allen Collection.*

hydraulic lifts at the wing pylon hard points and at each wing tip. The applied loads were reacted (held down) through the landing gear, tail hook, and special fittings at the horizontal tail pivot shafts. Testing was done at -40 degrees F to insure that critical flaw defect sizes were reduced, thus the flaw sizes at the service temperature were not at the fracture critical sizes. Testing was done to the full F-111 fleet, as well as new production aircraft. A follow-on series of tests were conducted during Structural Inspection Program (II-SIP) on all in-service aircraft. In the third series of tests, a wing sweep angle of 26 degrees was added in addition to the 56 degree position test.

F-111E **68-0043** being lowered by a crane onto the rebuild jigs. *Courtesy of Author's Collection via John Godfrey-BAe.*

68-0050 (Vark Hospital) - aircraft was substantially damaged in 1985 when a LOX Bottle exploded, damaging the escape capsule, nose wheel well, and avionics bay area. The damage required GDFW factory repairs. Repair started September 1986 and was completed in November 1988.

F-111F:
70-2364 - the mishap aircraft sustained a bird strike to the intake lip and inlet panels. The USAF elected not to repair this aircraft and the airframe was stricken from the inventory. It later became the Portales, New Mexico, "City of Portales" display.

Courtesy of Author's Video Collection.

Courtesy of Orlando Ortega.

70-2370 - on August 6, 1993, during a Red Flag deployment, a routine maintenance engine run was being performed on the Nellis AFB "trim pad" when the mishap aircraft had a fire in the weapons bay. The fire burned the Nuclear Consent and Arming wiring, which can only be rewired from point-to-point without splicing. This task would have taken months of tedious work. The USAF chose not to repair the damage, and the aircraft was subsequently stricken from the inventory and scrapped in place.

The completely stripped down fuselage of **70-2370** being loaded for delivery to an unknown location. **Note:** There is no record that the aircraft hulk was delivered to AMARC at Davis-Monthan AFB; a.k.a. the "Bone Yard".

More 70-2370 -Tear Down (Scrapping) photographs. *Coutesy of MSgt Laurel Leppkk*

Pulling the Right Wing.

The back bone of a "Thunder Vark."

TSgt Tony Snow supervising engine removal.

The stripped out Radome & Avionics bay.

Removing the left wing. All Tear Down and Scrapping pictures are from author's collection. *Photographs Courtesy of Author's Collection via MSgt Laurel Leppke.*

70-2378 - on May 1, 1979, the aircrew experienced an engine fire that burned through into the saddle tank, causing structural damage. The crew safely recovered to RAF Lakenheath, United Kingdom. No other details are known.

70-2384 - on January 17, 1991, during a "Desert Storm" sortie, the mishap aircraft collided with a KC-135 tanker's aerial refueling boom. The bullet fairing on the vertical tail was torn off. The aircraft also sustained damage near the aerial refueling door. The aircraft was repaired at Taif AB, Saudi Arabia, on day 28 of Desert Storm and returned to service. **Pilot:** Capt Dwayne Mathers, **WSO:** Maj Terry Phillips, **Call Sign:** Unknown

On January 29, 1974, an unknown F-111F aircraft experienced an uncommanded nose landing gear retraction during post-flight engine shutdown at Mountain Home AFB; no other details are known.

Courtesy of Author's Video Collection.

70-2387 - on January 28, 1972, the aircraft's main gear would not extend. The crew accomplished a successful barrier engagement at Mountain Home AFB. No other details are known.

70-2401 Battle Damage - on January 17, 1991, the aircraft sustained a bullet groove in the windscreen and a 1" hole in the vertical tail during a Desert Storm combat sortie.

70-2408 - on June 15, 1994, the mishap aircraft hit a 4.5 lb turkey vulture, severely damaging the left engine inlet vortex generators, cowl lip, and nacelle structure. The aircraft damage was substantial and the aircraft was stricken from the USAF inventory. The aircraft sat on the Cannon AFB ramp for a year until it was demilitarized and prepped as a display. It now serves at the Santa Fe, New Mexico, airport (1996).

Courtesy of Steve H. "Gator" Bosang.

70-2413 - on April 10, 1985, the mishap aircrew successfully landed main gear up at RAF Lakenheath. The aircraft was on an FCF sortie. **Pilot:** Maj. Fernando L. Ribas-Dominicci, **WSO:** Unknown, **Call Sign:** Unknown

NOTE: Major Ribas-Dominicci was tragically killed in action during the raid against Muammar Gadhafi during Operation El Dorado Canyon one year later.

71-0888 - fire: 1987-1990 time frame. During a ground maintenance run in Hush House # 1 at RAF Lakenheath, the mishap aircraft had an Environmental Control System (ECS) ground cooling fan disintegrate, causing a fire which damaged main wheel well ECS and electrical systems. The aircraft was repaired at RAF Lakenheath and returned to service.

71-0891 - on June 16, 1995, the 524th TFS aircrew landed low on fuel and without a diversionary airfield in the vicinity of Cannon AFB during a major thunderstorm (seen in the background of the photo). On landing,

71-0891 *Courtesy of Author's Collection.*

the aircraft hydroplaned while braking, sliding sideways and stopping on the BAK-12 barrier.

72-1442 Desert Storm: on January 17, 1991, the aircraft sustained battle damage from AAA fire over an unknown location. Damage: aircraft had a 1½" x ¾" hole in the right side wing glove.

FB-111A:
68-0241 - April 20, 1972, the aircraft's main landing gear failed to extend and performed a barrier engagement at Plattsburgh AFB, New York. Further details unknown.

69-6512 - on August 18, 1971, the main gear would not extend. The mishap crew landed safely with only the nose gear extended at Carswell AFB, Texas. The aircraft was repaired and returned to service. **Pilot:** Lt. Col Bob Russell, **WSO:** Maj. Arben R. Ely, **Call Sign:** Unknown

Courtesy of Author's Collection.

68-0259 - on August 13, 1981, at Nellis AFB, Nevada, a BDU-38 parachute charge went off in the weapons bay, causing an extensive fire. The damaged aircraft was trucked to GDFW, where repairs started September 30, 1981, and were completed February 4, 1983. This was a no crew ground accident.

68-0287 - May 17, 1974, the main landing gear would not extend. The crew landed safely with only the nose gear extended and made a successful barrier arrestment. **Pilot:** Capt Dick Korich, **WSO:** Capt Denny Blodgett.

On February 14, 1974, an unknown FB-111A experienced an uncommanded nose landing gear retraction during an alert exercise engine start (no intent for flight). The landing gear control valve extend/retract spool detent spring had failed. No other details are known.

EF-111A:
66-0021 - on March 6, 1997, the mishap aircraft had a "Takeoff Mishap" while on TDY assignment to Nellis AFB, Nevada. The mishap crew felt a loss of power and aborted their takeoff. The aircraft went airborne about 15 feet off the Nellis AFB runway. The Aircraft Commander (AC) put the EF-111A back down on the runway, and the aircraft then ran through the BAK-12 barrier, tearing it out of the ground. The mishap aircraft departed the runway over-run area, coming to a stop in the sand and gravel. The aircraft sustained a broken main landing gear trunnion, main wheel well structural damage, and Foreign Object Damage (FOD) to the engines during the incident. It was repaired and returned to service.

66-0027 - on August 16, 1995, the mishap aircrew had declared an In-Flight Emergency (IFE) near Dyess AFB, Texas. The electrical power leads on the AC Power Contactor (ACPC) had loosened over time and shorted together. The aircraft lost all electrical power and a small fire was started. The aircrew diverted to Dyess AFB, Texas. The emergency generator also failed on final approach to land, causing loss of aircraft instrument gauges and cockpit lighting during a night landing. The 429th aircrew skillfully landed the disabled aircraft under adverse aircraft conditions. **Crew: Pilot** Capt Hughes, **EWO:** Unknown, **Call Sign:** Unknown.

Repercussions: Fleet-wide inspection of all EF-111A AC Power Contactor (ACPC) components; a Depot facilitated re-do of all EF-111A ACPCs; and a Tech Order change for installation and inspection procedures.

Author's Note: EF-111A 67-0032 had a similar ACPC fire while assigned to the 42nd ECS at RAF Upper Heyford prior to the Gulf War; details are unknown. Source of incident information was SSgt Scott MacManus.

66-0038 - in December 1991, the aircraft suffered Wing Carry-Through Box (WCBT) failure during cold proof test at Sacramento Air Logistics Center (SMALC). The aircraft was trucked to the AMARC storage facility on October 3, 1997.

67-0034 - on November 12, 1991, the left wing failed in upwards bending during a Wing Carry-Through Box (WCBT) cold proof test at the Sacramento Air Logistics Center (SMALC). The aircraft was originally retired, but was eventually repaired and returned to service.

67-0035 - on December 16, 1985, RAF Upper Heyford, United Kingdom, the mishap aircraft experienced an engine fire which caused extensive damage to the aft fuselage area. No other details are known about the incident.

67-0037 Desert Storm - on February 15 or 16, 1991, the aircraft sustained battle damage from several 50 Cal. bullet holes in the left horizontal stabilizer during a combat sortie.

67-0041 Desert Shield - (Between August 1990 and January 16, 1991). The aircraft struck a tree during a low altitude dive recovery; there was no significant damage sustained by the aircraft.

12

PRESERVED F-111S AND CREW ESCAPE MODULES ON DISPLAY

End of the line: RAAF
F-111s are buried (*Australian
Channel 7 News*);
while below, USAF F-111s
await scrapping.

Author's Photo.

F-111A 67-0047, Sheppard AFB, TX. *Sheppard AFB Historian*

F-111A 63-9773, Sheppard AFB, TX. *Mark O. Williams*

F-111A 67-0051 (displayed as 67-0050), Tyler Pounds Regional Airport, TX. *Sheppard AFB Historian*

F-111A 63-9771, Cannon AFB, NM. *Author*

F-111A 67-0056 (location and status unknown). *Sheppard AFB Historian*

F-111A 63-9767. *Museum picture courtesy of Chanute Air Museum, Rantoul, IL*

EF-111A 66-0016, Cannon AFB, NM. *Author*

F-111E 67-0120, Imperial War Museum Duxford, Duxford, England. *Author's Collection via Tim Barnett*

63-9776 (displayed as 66-0022), Mtn Home, ID. *WCDR Mike Shaw RAAF*

EF-111A 66-0039, Davis-Monthan AFB, AZ. *Museum picture courtesy of AMARC*

63-9775, Huntsville, AL. *Museum picture courtesy of United States Space and Rocket Center*

EF-111A 66-0047, Silver Springs, NV. *Steven Clark*

EF-111A 66-0049, Mtn Home AFB, ID. *366th FW Public Affairs*

F-111A 63-9766, Edwards AFB, CA. *Steve H. "Gator" Bosang*

F-111A 66-0012, American Air Power Museum, Long Island, NY. *Joe Arnold*

EF-111A 66-0057, Wright-Patterson AFB, OH. *Museum picture courtesy of the National Museum of the United States Air Force*

F-111A 67-0046, Brownwood, TX. *Sheppard AFB Historian*

F-111A 67-0058, Carl Miller Park, Mountain Home, ID. *Courtesy of the City of Mtn Home, Idaho*

F-111E 68-0030, Davis-Monthan AFB, AZ. *Museum picture courtesy of AMARC*

F-111E 68-0033, Tucson, AZ. *Museum picture courtesy of Pima Air and Space Museum, Tucson, AZ*

F-111A 67-0069, Southern Museum of Flight, Birmingham, Alabama. *Museum picture via Mark Neville*

F-111E 68-0055, Museum of Aviation, Robins AFB, Warner Robins, GE. *Museum picture courtesy of Waymarking.com*

F-111A 67-0057, Dyess Air Force Base Linear Air Park, Abilene, TX. *Sheppard AFB Historian*

F-111A 67-0100, Nellis AFB, NV. *Nellis AFB Public Affairs*

F-111A 67-0067, Wright-Patterson AFB, Dayton, OH. *Museum picture courtesy of National Museum of the United States Air Force*

1). FB-111A 68-0245, March Field Air Museum, March AFB, Riverside, CA. *Steve H. "Gator" Bosang* **2).** FB-111A 68-0244, Davis-Monthan AFB, AZ. *Museum picture courtesy of AMARC*

1). FB-111A 68-0239, K.I. Sawyer AFB, MI. *Museum picture courtesy of K.I. Sawyer Heritage Museum* **2).** F-111E 68-0027, Midland/Odessa, TX. *Courtesy of Commemorative Air Force, Midland/Odessa Airport, Midland, TX*

1). F-111E 68-0055, Museum of Aviation, Robins AFB, Warner Robins, GE. *Museum picture courtesy of Waymarking.com* **2).** F-111E 68-0011, RAF Lakenheath, England. *Dave Riddell*

1). F-111E 68-0009, Davis-Monthan AFB, AZ. *Museum photo courtesy of AMARC* **2).** F-111E 68-0020, Hill AFB, UT. *Museum picture courtesy of Hill Aerospace Museum.*

FB-111A 67-0159, Aerospace Museum of California, North Highlands, CA. *Museum picture courtesy of Aerospace Museum of California*

1). FB-111A 68-0275, Lackland. AFB, TX. *Courtesy of Kelly Field Heritage Museum* **2).** F-111D 68-0140, Clovis, NM. *Author* **3).** F-111A 63-9782 (status unknown), Griffiss AFB, NY. *USAF*

F-111D 68-0092, Yanks Air Museum, Chino, CA. *Museum picture courtesy of Brian C Rogers*

F-111B 152715 Silver Springs, NV. *Courtesy of Steven Clark*

FB-111A 68-0267, Ashland, NE. *Museum picture courtesy of Strategic Air and Space Museum.*

F-111F 70-2390, USAF Museum Wright-Patterson AFB, Dayton, OH. *Courtesy of Author's Collection via Bob Brewster*

FB-111A 68-0248, South Dakota Air and Space Museum, Ellsworth AFB, SD. *Don Logan*

F-111F 70-2364, Portales, NM. *Courtesy of Author's Collection via Orlando*

F-111F 74-0177, Royal Air Force Museum, Cosford, Cambridgeshire, UK. *Courtesy of B. Morrison via Don Logan*

1) FB-111A 68-0287, Lowry AFB, Denver, CO. *Museum picture courtesy of Wings over the Rockies Air and Space Museum, Lowey AFB, CO* 2) Full Scale F-111A Mock-up. *Courtesy of Turners Army Surplus, Hook, TX* 3) FB-111A 69-6509, Whiteman AFB, MO. *USAF / SSgt Jason Barebo*

1) FB-111A 68-0286, Clyde Lewis Airpark, Plattsburgh, NY. *Courtesy of Waymarking.* **2).** FB-111A 68-0284, Eighth Air Force Museum, Barksdale AFB, LA. Mike Kaplan.
3) General Dynamics F-111 Test Article B-4, Hawkins, TX. *Courtesy of Private Owner*

FB-111A 69-6507,
Castle AFB, Atwater, CA.
*Museum picture courtesy
of Castle AFB Museum*

F-111F 70-2409, Santa Fe,
NM. *Steve H. "Gator" Bosang*

Preserved Crew Escape Modules On Display

F-111E 68-0019 (displayed as FB-111A 68-0284), Barksdale AFB, LA. *Mike Kaplan*

F-111A 63-9780 Wright-Patterson AFB, Dayton, OH. *Museum picture courtesy of National Museum of the United States Air Force, Dayton, OH*

1). FB-111A 68-0263 Oklahoma City, OK. *Museum picture courtesy of Kirkpatrick Science and Air Space Museum* 2). F-111F 70-2412 "Pud" & "KY's" Capsule restored, Cavanaugh Flight Museum, Addison, TX (current location unknown). *Courtesy of Chris Woodul* 3). F-111D 68-0125 Cavanaugh Flight Museum, Addison, TX (current location unknown). *Courtesy of Chris Woodul*

1). F-111D 68-0162 Santa Rosa, CA. *Museum picture courtesy of Ron Stout & Pacific Coast Air Museum* 2). F-111E 68-0060 Dumfries, Scotland. *Museum picture courtesy of Dumfries & Galloway Aviation Museum* 3). F-111E 68-008 (Capsule In desert) near Belen, NM. *Courtesy of Neil Lawson*

1). F-111A 67-0068, Moscow, Russia. *Museum picture courtesy of Moscow Aviation Museum* 2). EF-111A 66-0044 (current location unknown). *Courtesy of Ken Pringle* 3). F-111C A8-141 at RAAF Amberley, Ipswich, Brisbane, AU. *David De Botton*

1). EF-111A 66-0056 (photo taken at RAF Upper Heyford two months after ejection). *Don Gwynne* 2). F-111C A8-137, RAAF Museum. *Paul Holmes* 3). Unknown F-111 capsule at SAC Museum, Offutt AFB, NE. *Museum picture courtesy of Strategic Air and Space Museum, Ashland, NE.*

13

F-111 MEMORIAL
"THE ROCK"

Dedication Day, November 16, 1996. *Steve H. "Gator" Bosang*

Author

The F-111 Memorial
Veterans Park; Clovis, New Mexico, Pedestal Display
Dedicated 16 November 1996

"To The Men Who Died Flying the F-111
Defending Our Nation's Freedom"

A Project and Calling note about "The Rock" from Doc- Steven Hyre

"The Rock," as it has become known, was an eight month project undertaken by a small but dedicated group of citizens from Clovis, NM, and Cannon AFB 27th FW USAF personnel. They truly felt this was necessary and long overdue. The F-111 community owes thanks to Mr. Ernest Skillern, Ms. Ernie Kos, Ms. Wendie Glaze, Mayor of Clovis Mr. David Lansford, Clovis Mayor Pro-Tem Mr. Bobby Moreno, Mr. Randy Harris,

F-111D 68-0140 and "The Rock" after dedication, November 16, 1996. *Steve H. "Gator" Bosang*

Lt Col Dale R Hanner, USAF 524th FS CC, and most of all Sra Gary Bayer and Mr. Steve H. Bosang; thanks guys, you helped a vision of the correct thing to do come true. The funds were raised $10.00 at a time via donation and purchase of a short F-111 video called "The Mighty Vark." The F-111 community of aircrew, maintainers, and other professionals that served on the platform jumped with both feet onboard across the planet to support and fund this project. Several local Clovis businesses, through generous donations, helped push the funding over the top. The names on The Rock belong to the ages as our fallen heroes; they stepped up and made the ultimate sacrifice in defense of our nation(s)' (both Australia and the United States) freedom. All those named above as participants in this project were privileged and honored to serve in facilitating this worthy cause to its completion.

Author

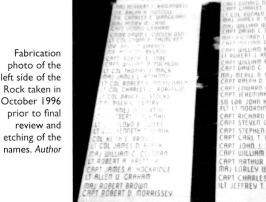

Fabrication photo of the left side of the Rock taken in October 1996 prior to final review and etching of the names. *Author*

Construction Photos of "The Rock"

The Rock being fabricated just prior to etching the original 111 crew names at Glaze Monument Co. in Clovis, NM. Thankfully, prior to the final "proceed order" to complete the work, a diligent search was performed to ensure all the lost F-111 crew members were included. Two additional names (Capt. Randolph P. Gaspard and Maj. Frank B. Slusher) were added, bringing the original etched name total to 113. In 1999, two more names (FLTLT Anthony "Shorty" Short and SQNLDR Stephen "Nige" Hobbs) were added after RAAF F-111G A8-291 crashed and the crew was lost.

Memorial Day 1999

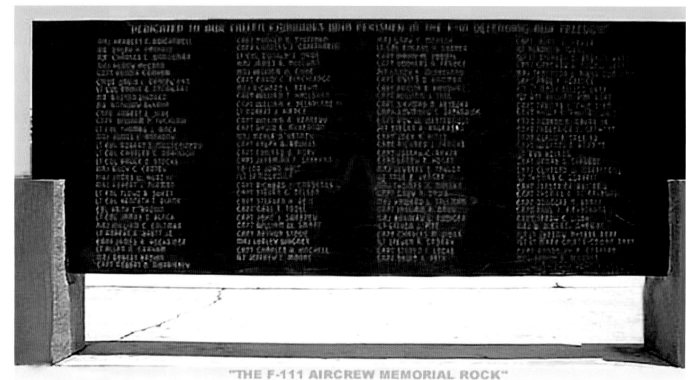

"THE F-111 AIRCREW MEMORIAL ROCK"

Crew Member Names	Aircraft Operator	Model Type	Tail #
Maj Herbert F. Brightwell	USAF	F-111A	63-9774
Mr. Ralph H. "Dixie" Donnell Mr. Charles E. Wangeman	Grumman Aerospace Grumman Aerospace	F-111B	151973
Maj Henry Elmer "Hank" McCann Capt Dennis Lee Graham USAF	USAF	F-111A	66-0022
CMDR David Leo "Spade" Cooley Lt Col Edwin David "Ed" Palmgren	USN USAF	F-111A	66-0024
Mr. Barton Warren Mr. Anthony Byland	Hughes Aircraft Company Hughes Aircraft Company	F-111B	151971
Capt Robert E. Jobe Capt William D. Fuchlow	USAF USAF	F-111A	66-0042
Lt Col Thomas J. Mack Maj James L. Anthony	USAF USAF	F-111A	67-0049
Lt Col Robert S. Montgomery Lt Col Charles G. Robinson	USAF USAF	FB-111A	68-0253
Lt Col Bruce D. Stocks Maj Billy C. Gentry	USAF USAF	FB-111A	68-0283
Maj James W. Hurt III Maj Robert J. Furman	USAF USAF	F-111E	67-0117
Lt Col Floyd B. Sweet Lt Col Kenneth T. Blank	USAF USAF	F-111E	68-0018
Col Keith E. Brown Lt Col James D. Black	USAF USAF	F-111A	67-0082
Maj William Clare "Bill" Coltman 1Lt Robert Arthur "Lefty" Brett JR	USAF USAF	F-111A	67-0078
Capt James Alan Hockridge 1Lt Allen Upton Graham	USAF USAF	F-111A	67-0066
Maj Robert Mack Brown Capt Robert David Morrissey	USAF USAF	F-111A	67-0063
Capt Ronald Dean Stafford Capt Charles Joseph Cafferrelli	USAF USAF	F-111A	67-0092
Lt Col Ronald Jack Ward Maj James Richard McElvain	USAF USAF	F-111A	67-0099
Maj William Warren Gude Capt David Carl Blackledge	USAF USAF	F-111D	68-0158
Maj Richard Leon Brehm Maj William Ty Halloran	USAF USAF	F-111D	68-0105
Capt William K. Delaplane III 1Lt Robert J. Kierce	USAF USAF	F-111D	68-0113
Capt William Arthur Kennedy Capt David C. McKennon	USAF USAF	F-111F	70-2395

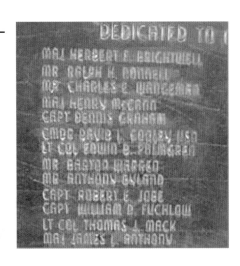
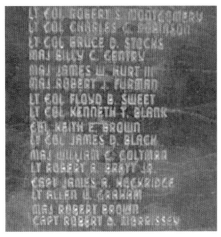
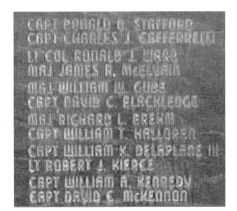

Opposite Page: Memorial Day 1999

Clockwise from top left: 1). "The F-111 Rock." *Author,* 2). "The Bronze Plaque." *Author* 3). (L to R): Lt. Col Bob Brewster, DO, 27th FW USAF; Mayor of Clovis, NM, Mr. David M. Lansford; WGCDR RAAF Mike "Boggy" Smith; Col Tan, RSAF 428th FS CC; and Mr. Steve H Bosang. *Author* 4). "The Rock" and a Listing of all 115 Names for our F-111 Lost Aircrews *Author,* 5). Local Clovis, NM, and 27th FW dignitaries paying their respects to our fallen RAAF F-111 comrades. *Author* 6). RAAF WGCDR Mike "Boggy" Smith giving his eloquent and "heartfelt" dedication speech. Royal Singaporean AF members kindly volunteered "impromptu" for duty in the "Color Guard," enabling all participating countries' colors to be rendered for this solemn ceremony. *Author* 7). "Doc, Boggy, and Gator." *All photos are from the Author Collection.*

Crew Member Names	Aircraft Operator	Model Type	Tail #
Maj Merle D. Kenney Capt Ralph David Bowles	USAF USAF	F-111A	66-0058
Capt Edward R. Riley Capt Jeremiah E. Sheehan	USAF USAF	FB-111A	68-0266
SQNLDR John Holt FLTLT A.P. 'Phil' Noordink	RAAF RAAF	F-111C	A8-133
Capt Richard L. Cardenas Capt Steven C. Nelson	USAF USAF	F-111D	68-0093
Capt Stephen H. Reid Capt Carl T. Poole	USAF USAF	F-111F	73-0718
Capt John J. Sweeney Capt William W. Smart	USAF USAF	F-111E	68-0070
Capt Arthur Stowe Maj Lorley "Skip" Wagner	USAF USAF	F-111A	67-0083
Capt Charles H. Kitchell 1Lt Jeffery T. Moore	USAF USAF	F-111F	73-0717
Maj Gary A. Mekash Lt Col Eugene M. Soeder	USAF USAF	F-111A	67-0105
Capt David W. Powell Capt Douglas A. Pearce	USAF USAF	F-111E	68-0042
2Lt Larry E. McFarland Capt Myles D. Hammon	USAF USAF	F-111A	66-0052
Capt Phillip B. Donovan Capt William J. Full	USAF USAF	FB-111A	68-0261
Capt Richard A. Hetzner Capt Raymond C. Spaulding	USAF USAF	F-111E	68-0003
Capt Roy W. Westerfield 2Lt Steven P. Anderson	USAF USAF	F-111D	68-0119
Capt Jack A. Hines Capt Richard J. Franks	USAF USAF	F-111E	68-0057
Capt Joseph G. Raker Capt Larry R. Honza	USAF USAF	F-111A	67-0097
Maj Ulysses S. "Sam" Taylor III 1Lt Paul E. Yeager	USAF USAF	F-111D	68-0139
Maj Thomas M. Mullen Capt Gary A. Davis	USAF USAF	FB-111A	68-0268
Maj Howard L. Tallman III Capt William R. Davy	USAF USAF	F-111D	68-0160
Maj Burnley L. Rudiger 1Lt Steven J. Pitt	USAF USAF	F-111F	70-2377
Capt Charles Michael Vidas 1Lt Steven A. Groark	USAF USAF	F-111F	74-0188
Capt Steven F. Locke Capt David Kirk Peth	USAF USAF	F-111A	66-0026

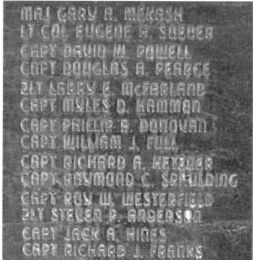

Crew Member Names	Aircraft Operator	Model Type	Tail #
Capt Alan J. "Tex" Pryor	USAF	F-111D	68-0164
1Lt Albert Heinrich "Rip" Torn	USAF		
FLTLT Stephen M. Erskine	RAAF	F-111C	A8-139
Capt Gregory S. Angell	USAF	Exchange with RAAF	
Maj Fernando L. Ribas-Dominicci	USAF	F-111F	70-2389
Capt Paul Franklin Lorence	USAF		
FLTLT Mark "Speed" Fallon	RAAF	F-111C	A8-128
FLGOFF William X. Pike	RAAF		
Capt Taylor F. "Chip" Stem III	USAF	F-111F	70-2375
Capt Philip D. "Phil" Baldwin	USAF		
Capt Robert A. Meyer Jr.	USAF	F-111A	67-0102
Capt Frederick A. Gerhart	USAF		
Capt Glenn E. Troster	USAF	F-111D	68-0098
Capt Michael A. Barritt	USAF		
1Lt J Robert "Bob" Boland	USAF	F-111F	70-2397
Capt James A. Gleason	USAF		
Capt Clifford W. Massengill	USAF	F-111E	68-0001
1Lt Thomas G. Dorsett	USAF		
Capt Frederick Arthur "Art" Reid	USAF	F-111F	74-0183
Capt Thomas R. "TC" Caldwell	USAF		
Capt Douglas M. Bradt	USAF	EF-111A	66-0023
Capt Paul R. Eichenlaub II	USAF		
Capt Jerry C. Lindh	USAF	F-111E	68-0052
Maj David Michael McGuire	USAF		
FLTLT Jeremy "'Jez" McNess	RAAF	F-111C	A8-127
FLTLT Mark 'CC' Cairns-Cowan	RAAF		
Capt Randolph P. Gaspard	USAF	F-111E	68-0045
Maj Frank B. Slusher	USAF		
FLTLT Anthony "Shorty" Short	RAAF	F-111G	A8-291
SQNLDR Stephen "Nige" Hobbs	RAAF		

A

DEFINITION OF ACRONYMS AND TERMS USED IN THIS BOOK

How to Decode the Mishap Page Titles:
66-0025 (USAF Serial Number) **F-111A** (F = Fighter, FB = Fighter Bomber, EF = Electronic "warfare" Fighter) **111** (Version or Series) and **A, B, C** and on: (Model Designator) **# 43** (the 43rd Production F-111A) **GD/FW Production Run # A1-43** (how GDFW identified individual airframes per contract and while the aircraft was on their production line) **USAF Delivery Date: February 13, 1968** (the date the USAF accepted the aircraft from the factory).
Note: the RAAF identified their aircraft with serial numbers, such as A8-125, for example.

AAA	Anti-Aircraft Artillery – pronounced "Triple A"
AB	Afterburner – Maximum Thrust; thrust augmentation by introduction of extra fuel beyond the turbine section
ABCCC	Airborne Command Center
ADI	Attitude Director Indicator, an artificial horizon instrument centered on the pilot's instrument panel
AC	Aircraft Commander (Left Seat Pilot in the F-111) – or an electrical acronym used to denote "Alternating Current"
Acft	Abbreviation for "Aircraft"
AFB	Air Force Base
AGL	Above Ground Level – an aircraft's altitude above the ground; versus above sea level
AHC	Advanced Handling Characteristics – training profile flown to explore unique aircraft response to maneuvers
AIM	Air Intercept Missile; e.g. AIM-9 Infra-red Heat Seeker, AIM-54 Phoenix radar guided
AMARC	Aerospace Maintenance and Regeneration Center (a.k.a. The Boneyard) at Davis-Monthan AFB, Arizona
AOA	Angle of Attack or Alpha Angle
AOS	Angle of Sideslip or Beta Angle
AR/AAR	Aerial Refueling / Air-to-Air Refueling respectively. AR-302 would designate a numbered Air Refueling track
ARCP	Air Refueling Contact Point
ARIP	Air Refueling Initial Point
ARTCC	Air Route Traffic and Control Center
ARS	Attack Radar Set – large radar antenna on the F-111 used for navigation, target identification, and bombing.
ASR	Approach Surveillance Radar – Ground based radar providing Non-Precision guidance to a landing runway

Attrited	An aircraft removed from the inventory due to sustained damage; not feasible to repair or return to service
AYC	Adverse Yaw Compensation – See Chapter 1 Flight Controls
BDA	Bomb Damage Assessment
BDU	Bomb, Dummy Unit – small practice bomb with similar ballistics as actual ordnance
BFM	Basic Fighter Maneuvers – used to engage or defend against a visual encounter with another aircraft
BINGO	Fuel state - term used to denote minimum fuel onboard necessary to return to the planned recovery airfield
Bold Face	Required critical action memory steps used by a USAF pilot during an emergency procedure
BRU	Bomb Release Unit - a Multiple Ejector Rack (MER), designed to carry up to six bombs
BSA	Basic Surface Attack – training sortie using practice bombs on a controlled and scored range
BS	Bombardment Squadron in Strategic Air Command
BW	Bombardment Wing in Strategic Air Command
CADC	Central Air Data Computer; receives pneumatic pressures from the static ports and the pitot-static tube, angle of attack from the AOA vane sensor, etc. and converts to airspeed, altitude, Mach, AOA, etc. for use by many instruments and avionics systems, including AMI, AVVI, INS, NCU, IFF, etc.)
CARA	Combined Altitude Radar Altimeter
CAS	Close Air Support – bombing mission in support of ground forces
CBU	Cluster Bomb Unit
CCTS	Combat Crew Training Squadron (obsolete) – provided initial or instructor training for a particular fighter type.
CEA	Circular Error Average - The bombing error or the mean points of impact from the center of the target.
CFIT	Controlled Flight into Terrain – pilot on the controls impacts the ground
Channel	F-111 automated systems were "Channels," ex, each TFR antenna was a channel or Flight Control "Pitch" channel
Cleared Hot	Radio clearance to employ ordnance

CONUS Continental United States

CPLT Cold Proof Load Test

Destroyed An aircraft where damage was extreme; destruction was complete

Det Detachment – a deployed squadron's operating base of operations e.g. Det 1 Takhli RTAFB vs at Nellis AFB

DME Distance Measuring Equipment – a radio beacon providing range or distance information

ECM Electronic Counter Measures

ECS Environmental Control System, also an abbreviation for Electronic Combat Squadron

EGT Exhaust Gas Temperature

EMI Electromagnetic Interference

EOR End-of-Runway; A safety inspection, departing- safety pins removed, Returning- safety pins installed.

FCF Functional Check Flight – a flight to ensure airworthiness after major maintenance

FL Flight Level – altitudes at or above 18,000 feet mean sea level, e.g. FL210 pronounced Flight Level Two-One-OH

FLSC flexible liner shaped charge – a severance component for the crew module.

FS Fighter Squadron

FTD Field Training Detachment – School House for USAF maintenance training

FW Fighter Wing

FWIC Fighter Weapons Instructor Course

Frag/fragged A squadron specific target break-out from the Air Tasking Order (ATO) is known as the "Frag" or "Fragged" target

Galling A condition when two rubbing metal surfaces experience excessive friction, causing localized welding together. Subsequent movement shears the materials and a tearing of the base material occurs, destroying the smooth surface. i.e. A transfer of metal to a mating part.

GCA Ground Controlled Approach – normal terminal approach control

GCI Ground Controlled Intercept – ground based radar controller directing an aircraft in flight, on approach, or in battle.

GDFW General Dynamics Fort Worth – Pronounced "Gee Dee Fort Worth." May also be printed as GD/FW

GM Ground Mapping – a radar display on the ARS Scope or E-Scope depicting radar detected terrain feature

HDGP High Drag General Purpose –Bombs with a high drag device such as clam shell, parachute, or ballute retarder

HF High Frequency – used for long range radio communication

HTSA Horizontal Tail Servo Actuator – individual hydraulic actuators used to pivot the all-moving horizontal stabilizers

HP High Pressure Compressor (HPC) or High Pressure Turbine (HPT)

ID Identification – by visual means (VID) for example

IFE In-Flight Emergency

IFF Identification Friend or Foe – aircraft with a transponder radio beacon transmit an IFF code for identification

IFR Instrument Flight Rules – Flight Rules at or above Flight Level (FL) 18000, or at any altitude when ceiling and visibility are below stated minimum values.

ILS Instrument Landing System – provides course and glideslope guidance via radio beams

Inop Inoperative - abbreviation

INS Inertial Navigation System – A gyro stabilized platform providing geographic position and navigation information

IP Instructor Pilot, or in bombing terms, the Initial Point, a last chance geographic point to update navigation/position

IR Route Instrument Route, a low-level route with width and height boundaries facilitating flight in IFR conditions.

Knots or Kts Nautical Miles / Hour: (KCAS) Kts Calibrated Airspeed, (KIAS) Kts Indicated Airspeed, (KTAS) Kts True Airspeed

LDGP Low Drag General Purpose – Slick Bombs

LP Low Pressure Compressor (LPC) or Low Pressure Turbine (LPT)

LARA Low Altitude Radar Altimeter

LOC Loss of Control - aircraft was stalled or entered a post-stall gyration, control was not regained, crew ejected

LOFT or TOSS; a bomb released in an upward trajectory; the parabolic arc terminating on the desired target

LOX/GOX Liquid Oxygen or Gaseous Oxygen respectively

LRU Line Replaceable Unit

Mach The speed of sound being Mach 1. Lesser speeds are annotated as 0.95 or .95 Mach for example.

MEA Minimum Enroute Altitude – minimum altitude to fly in an area or along a route to avoid terrain or obstacles

MER Multiple Ejector Rack – bomb suspension rack with six ordnance positions

MIL Military Power, full rated engine thrust without the use of Afterburner

MOA Military Operating Area

MSL Mean Sea Level – altitude reading above sea level

MX Abbreviation for Maintenance

NM Nautical Miles – used in aeronautical routes; a measure of 6,076 feet, pilot math rounded to 6,000 feet.

no-spot A bomb score indicating no bomb impact was observed even though the delivery aircraft was cleared to drop

NVN North Vietnam

OB Route Olive Branch or "Oil Burner" Low Level Routes e.g. OB-32. OB was subsequently replaced by IR and VR

OAP Offset Aim Point – a radar significant object used to update or verify navigation accuracy

OT&E Operational Test & Evaluation; develops procedures for operational training, tactics, and weapons employment

OVRD Override – to disengage an automated system manually; to "Paddle Off" the Terrain Following Radar (TFR)

PAR Precision Approach Radar, A ground based radar providing precision course and glidepath guidance to the runway

PDM Programmed Depot Maintenance

PIO Pilot Induced Oscillation

PW /P&W Pratt & Whitney Corporation

RAF Royal Air Force

RAAF Royal Australian Air Force

RBS Radar Bomb Scoring – A simulated bomb release initiated by a tone, radar position determines ballistic scoring

RDT&E Research Development Test and Evaluation- earliest variant of the F-111A used in flight testing

RLD Radar Lay-Down or Radar Level Deliveries. A low-altitude level bomb delivery using radar –acquisition

ROE Rules of Engagement

Route Pack (abbrev: RP) North Vietnam was divided into Route Packs 1 thru 6. RP 5 and 6 considered the highest threat

RTAFB Royal Thai Air Force Base

RTB Return to Base

RHAW | Radar Homing and Warning Receiver- same as RWR
RTU | Reserve Training Unit – replaced CCTS and TFTS – designated training unit for a specific fighter aircraft
RWR | Radar Warning Receiver – Indicates Air or Ground Radar tracking, threat warning, or missile/AAA guidance

SA | Situational Awareness or Surface Attack (practice bombing sortie)
SAC | Strategic Air Command
SAM | Surface to Air Missile
SAR | Search and Rescue
SAT | Surface Attack Tactics – bombing mission to an uncontrolled range using visual deliveries
SCP | Set Clearance Plane – the pilot preselected terrain clearance altitude to be maintained by the TFR when engaged
SEA | Southeast Asia
SEAD | Suppression of Enemy Air Defense – by electronic jamming or direct attack munitions.
SID | Standard Instrument Departure – a system of standardized departure routes from a terminal airport
SIS | Stall Inhibitor System
Slant Load | Ordnance loaded on both the outboard and lower position of a MER / TER pylon; the inboard position is empty
SMALC | Sacramento Air Logistics Center – Major Depot Maintenance for the F-111
SPO | System Program Office – A USAF organization which controls and directs the development phase of each aircraft program. After Program Management Responsibility Transfer (PMRT), the Depot, e.g. SMALC, is in charge to the end of the aircraft's service, at which time the SPO is disbanded.
SOF | Supervisor of Flying – pilot qualified officer who assists with emergencies, normally on duty in the control tower
STAR | Standard Terminal Arrival Routes – similar to a SID except used for standardized arrival routes
Stricken | An aircraft removed from the active inventory or from service due to damage, obsolesces, or destruction.
SUU | SU-spension Unit – BDU practice bomb dispenser – a SUU-20 for example carried up to six BDU training bombs

TACAN | Tactical Air Navigation – Radio Beacon with Bearing and Range
TER | Triple Ejector Rack – bomb suspension rack with three ordnance positions
TF | Terrain Following – the mode of flight selected, as in - Automatic (Auto) or Manual (Man) ex. Auto TF
TFR | Terrain Following Radar
TFX | Tactical Fighter Experimental – Runoff design competition leading to the F-111
TIT | Turbine Inlet Temperature
TFS | Tactical Fighter Squadron
TFTS | Tactical Fighter Training Squadron
TFW | Tactical Fighter Wing
TR | Transition Ride – a series of sorties to become familiar with basic flight characteristics in a fighter

Vark Hospital | Major aircraft repair facility at GDFW – may also have been known as "The Phoenix Line"
VFR | Visual Flight Rules – Flight Rules below 17,999 feet MSL, when ceiling and visibility are above stated minimums
VHF | Very High Frequency – radio communication
VOR | VHF Omni-directional Radio – provides a radio bearing only
VR Route | VFR Low Level Route – must be flown visually

UHF | Ultra High Frequency – radio communication
UPT | Undergraduate Pilot Training

WCTB | Wing Carry Through Box – structure within the F-111 fuselage supporting and joining the wing pivots
Write-Off | Denotes an aircraft that was substantially damaged and assessed uneconomical to repair
WSO | Weapons System Officer "Wizzo" (Right Seat position in F-111) PWSO –Pilot qualified WSO
WX | Weather

B

PRODUCTION TOTALS

	F-111A	F-111B	F-111C	F-111D	F-111E	F-111F	FB-111A	EF-111A	F-111G
Built	159[1]	7 (**1**)	24	96 (**1**)(**3**)	94	106	76 (**2**)(**3**)	42[2]	34[3]
Destroyed	42	2	8	17	18	26	14	3	1
Damaged	17	2	2	13	3	7	6	5	1
Repaired GDFW	2 (**4**)	0	0	6 (**4**)	2 (**4**)	0	2 (**4**)	0	0
Repaired									
Other	15	2	2	7	1	7	4	5	1
Museum	16	1	3	2	9	4	11	5	2
Scrapped	101	6	21	77	67	102	51	37	32

[1] Five (5) F-111As were eventually sold to RAAF as attrition replacements (see Appendix 3).
[2] Forty-two (42) F-111As were converted by Grumman Aerospace to EF-111As (see Appendix 3).
[3] F-111Gs: Thirty-four (34) were converted from FB-111A to the G Model – the SAC Astro-Tracker and SRAM / Nuclear Warfare systems were removed (see Appendix 3).

Sixteen (16) F-111Gs served with the USAF
Eighteen (18) F-111Gs were sold to RAAF
Fifteen (15) F-111Gs were delivered to RAAF. Three (3) remained in AMARC storage

Note (1): Twenty-two (22) cancelled F-111B airframes went into the F-111D production run.
Note (2): Cancelled F-111K assets diverted to the FB-111A production run.
Note (3): Thirty-six (36) FB-111A airframes went into the F-111D production line-up after the original FB-111 order was reduced from 112 to 76 aircraft.
Note (4): Fourteen (14) damaged F-111s were restored at the Vark Hospital. Thirty-six (36) F-111s were repaired "in the field."

Vark Hospital Restorations:

FB-111A	67-7194 twice, 68-0259
F-111A	67-0079, 67-0101
F-111E	68-0082, 67-0118, 68-0050
F-111D	68-0095, 68-0174, 68-0148, 69-0136, 68-0127, 68-0101

GDFW Production Line, *Courtesy of Author's Collection*

C

F-111 PRODUCTION NUMBERING SYSTEM / ENGINEERING TEST ARTICLES

Pre-Production A Models

A1 – 01 thru A1 – 18:	63-9766 thru 63-9783	Research, Development, Test & Evaluation (RDT&E)
A1 – 19 thru A1 – 28:	65-5701 thru 65-5710	(RDT&E)
A1 – 29 thru A1 – 30:	66-0011 and 66-0012	(RDT&E)

Production A Models

A1 – 31 thru A1 – 76:	66-0013 thru 67-0058	F-111A
A1 – 77 thru A1 – 159:	67-0032 thru 67-0114	F-111A

EF Models EFs were converted by Grumman Aerospace at Calverton NY

A1 – 31 thru A1 – 97:	Select airframes converted to EF-111A's, Production Numbers (EF-01 thru EF- 42)

D Models

A6 – 01 thru A6 – 96:	68-0085 thru 68-0180	F-111D

E Models

A1 – 160 thru A1 – 169:	67-0115 thru 67-0124	F-111E (E-1 thru E-10)
A1 – 170 thru A1 – 253:	68-0001 thru 68-0084	F-111E (E-11 thru E-94)

F Models

E2 – 01 thru E2 – 58:	70-2362 thru 70-2419	F-111F (F-01 thru F-58)
E2 – 59 thru E2 – 70:	71-0883 thru 71-0894	F-111F (F-59 thru F-70)
—	71-0895 thru 71-0906 not built	—
E2-71 thru E2-82:	72-1441 thru 72-1452	F-111F (F-71 thru F-82)
E2-83 thru E2-94:	73-0707 thru 73-0718	F-111F (F-83 thru F-94)
E2-95 thru E2-106:	74-0177 thru 74-00188	F-111F (F-95 thru F-106)

FB Models

B1-01 thru B1-05:	67-0159 thru 67-0163	FB-111A
B1-06 thru B1-10:	67-7192 thru 67-7196	FB-111A
B1-11 thru B1-64:	68-0239 thru 68-0292	FB-111A
B1-65 thru B1-76:	69-6503 thru 69-6514	FB-111A

USAF G Models:

Thirty-four (34) select FB-111A airframes with original production numbers B1-04 thru B1-76 were converted to F-111G.

(16) Remained in active USAF service until retired.

B Models:

B Models were built by Grumman Aerospace and assigned Navy Bureau Numbers (Bu. Nos)		
A2-01 thru A2-05:	151970 thru 151974	F-111B Navy Preproduction Version
A2-06 and A2-07:	152714 and 152715	F-111B Navy Production Version

C Models (RAAF):

D1-01 thru D1-24:	A8-125 thru A8-148	F-111C RAAF

A Models (RAAF):

A1-154, A1-157 thru A1-159:	A8-109, A8-112 thru A8-114	Ex-USAF F-111A attrition replacements
A1-03:	A8-106 tail number 63-9768	Ex- USAF RDT&E F-111A airframe; non-flying, ground trainer

(RAAF) G Models

F-111Gs sold and delivered to RAAF A8-259 / A8-264 / A-265 / A8-270 / A8-271 / A8-272 / A8-274 / A8-277 / A8-278 / A8-281 / A8-282 / A8-291 / A8-506 / A8-512 / A8-514

F-111Gs sold but not delivered and remained at AMARC 67-7193 / 67-7194 / 69-0260

Engineering Test Articles:

The F-111 Test Articles were actual airframes or components created for engineering studies at the Fort Worth factory. In most cases they were never intended to fly. Some, like articles B5 and B6, were donor airframes from the cancelled F-111K program and were never factored into the original plan. The F-111K components were recycled into the system to broaden the engineering database. The Test Articles *were the drivers* in making the F-111 the most tested combat aircraft in aviation history, for that era.

How the Engineering Test Numbers Relate:

A1-----F-111A	1963 F-111A-----RDT&E—flyable
A2— F-111A	1965 F-111A-----PRE-PRODUCTION—flyable
A3— F-111A	STATIC TESTA4-----F-111A/B FATIGUE TESTA6-----F-111D OPERATIONAL
A7— F-111B	STATIC / FATIGUE
A9— F-111	ALL WING AIRLOADS FLIGHT TEST
B4—FB-111A	FATIGUE TEST
B5—FB-111A	LANDING GEAR DROP TEST
B6—FB-111A	LANDING GEAR FATIGUE TEST
D1— F-111C	OPERATIONAL
E1— F-111K	PRODUCTION CANCELLED
E2— F-111F	PRODUCTION

Definition of Category (CAT) Flight Testing for USAF Aircraft

CAT I =	Contractor Development, Test & Evaluation conducted by the contractor. Opportunity for General Dynamics (Civilian Test Pilots) to validate contract specifications and performance.
CAT II =	USAF Development, Test & Evaluation conducted by the Air Force. Opportunity for (USAF Test Pilots) to validate contract specifications and performance.
CAT III =	USAF Follow-on Operational Test & Evaluation conducted by the Air Force. Conducted by USAF Test Pilots and Initial Cadre of experienced fighter pilots to develop training, tactics, manuals, and procedures for line squadrons. Category III testing is continuous throughout an aircraft's flying career, mostly involving new weapon system employment tests.

RDT&E F-111A 63-9778 was used in two joint USAF/NASA advanced fighter studies; TACT (Transonic Aircraft Technology) tested a completely new supercritical wing, and then the AFTI (Advanced Fighter Technology Integration) tested a "mission adaptive wing" that would flex and reshape the wing to maximize wing performance in all flight profiles. *Courtesy of USAF/NASA*

A-3 STATIC PROOF TEST COMPLETED   NOV 1970

FATIGUE TEST COMPLETED   MAY 1973

A-3 Undergoing Static Proof Testing, *Courtesy of GDFW*

Additional Test Article Pictures:

FB-111A FATIGUE TEST SET-UP DURING ASSEMBLY

FB-111A FATIGUE TEST SET-UP DURING ASSEMBLY

B-4 shown during Fatigue testing for the FB-111A, *Courtesy of GDFW*   *Courtesy of GDFW.*

F-111 Main Landing Gear Training Device

This trainer started out at Cannon AFB as an FTD School Trainer. I actually trained on this device for F-111 Electrical Systems 7 Level Cross-Training / Electrical Systems Master Technician Certification. *Courtesy of Author's Collection*

F-111 FUEL SYSTEM TEST STAND

Not a test article or production airframe, just all the fuel system components on a motion test rig. Notice the General Dynamics employee between the middle and outboard external fuel tanks!

F-111 HIGH-LIFT SYSTEM FUNCTIONAL AND RIGGING TEST

A-9---Wing and Air Loading Test Article A-9 was a "Recycled" F-111K Left Wing. *Courtesy of GDFW.*

2-44909   11-24-69
FW #2-2 – OVERALL VIEW LKG
INBD FROM L/H SIDE
10-7826
GD/FORT WORTH

F-111 CARRY-THRU STRUCTURE COMP 4 LIFE TIMES FATIGUE TEST
MAY 1970

Wing Carry Through Box (WCTB) Fatigue Test. *Courtesy of GDFW*

The first F-111 63-9766, with fresh paint applied, enters preflight weight and balance checks in December 1964. *Courtesy of GDFW.*

One of the most unique F-111 photos captures RDT&E F-111A 63-9769 with four (4) mockup AIM-54 Phoenix missiles. A series of performance flight tests validated stability and control, wing sweep limits, and jettison tests for the Phoenix missile load-out on the F-111's swivel pylons prior to F-111B trials. *Courtesy of GDFW.*

D

ALL CRASH MASTER DOCUMENT
(SEQUENTIAL ORDER OF OCCURRENCE)

Bold Type denotes those crew members who were fatally injuried;
their names also appear on the F-111 Memorial, Verterns Park, Clovis New Mexico.

	Event Date, Crew Statistics	Ejection #, Mishap Results	Crew Members Involved	Tail #	Pro-duc-tion #	Full Model Type	Call Sign	Aircraft Operator
1	**May-66** **Crash Land**	Crash Land-1 Repaired 1	Mr Charles McDaniels Mr Barton Warren	151972	A2-03	F-111B	972	Hughes Aircraft **Incident #1**
2	**19-Jan-67** **Fatal / Crash Land**	Crash Land-2 Destroyed 1	**Maj. Herbert F. Brightwell-Killed** Col. Donovan L. McCance-Survived	63-9774	A1-09	F-111A	774	6510 TW / 6512 TS
3	**21-Apr-67** **Fatal/ Ejection**	Ejection-1 Destroyed 2	**Mr. Ralph H. Donnell** **Mr. Charles E. Wangeman**	151973	A2-04	F-111B	Grumman 67	Grumman Test Flight
4	**19-Oct-67** **OK/ Ejection**	Ejection-2 Destroyed 3	Mr. David J. Thigpen Mr. Max E. Gordon (Engineer)	63-9780	A1-15	F-111A	Swing 7	Bailed to GDFW for CAT I Testing
5	**2-Jan-68** **OK/ Ejection**	Ejection-3 Destroyed 4	Maj. Joseph B. Jordan Col. Henry W. Brown	65-5701	A1-19	F-111A	5701	6510 TW / 6512 TS
6	**27-Mar-68** **No Ejection**	Combat Loss-1 Destroyed 5	**Maj. Henry Elmer MacCann** **Capt. Dennis Lee Graham**	66-0022	A1-40	F-111A	Omaha 77	474th TFW / 428th TFS
7	**30-Mar-68** **OK/ Ejection**	Ejection-4 **Combat Loss-2** Destroyed 6	Maj. Alexander A "Sandy" Marquardt Capt. Joseph Hodges	66-0017	A1-35	F-111A	Hotrod 76	474th TFW / Det 1 428th TFS
8	**22-Apr-68** **No Ejection**	**Combat Loss-3** Destroyed 7	**Comdr. David Leo Cooley USN** **Lt. Col Edwin David Palmgren**	66-0024	A1-42	F-111A	Tailbone 78	474th TFW / 428th TFS
9	**8-May-68** **OK/ Ejection**	Ejection-5 Destroyed 8	Maj. Charles E. Van Driel Maj. Kenneth A. Schuppe	66-0032	A1-50	F-111A	Hulu 16	4527 CCTS / 474th TFW
10	**18-May-68** **Crash Land**	Crash Land-3 Destroyed 9	Mr. Frederick J Voorhies Pilot Only--No WSO-	63-9769	A1-04	F-111A	Swing 6	GDFW Bailed for USAF Cat I Testing
11	**13-Aug-68**	**Inflight Damage** Repaired 2	Mr. Frederick J Voorhies Mr. Grover C Tate Jr	63-9783	A1-18	F-111A	9783	6510 TW / 6512 TS
12	**11-Sep-68** **Fatal/ Ejection**	Ejection-6 Destroyed 10	**Mr. Barton Warren** **Mr. Anthony Byland**	151971	A2-02	F-111B	Bartender 201	Hughes Aircraft
13	**23-Sep-68** **OK/ Ejection**	Ejection-7 Destroyed 11	Lt. John M Nash USN FLTLT. Neil M. Pollack	66-0040	A1-58	F-111A	PASHTO 01	4527thCCTS / 474th TFW
14	**12-Feb-69** **Fatal Crash**	No Ejection Destroyed 12	**Capt. Robert E. Jobe** **Capt. William D. Fuchlow**	66-0042	A1-60	F-111A	Fruity 01	4527 CCTS / 474th TFW
15	**4-Mar-69** **OK/ Ejection**	Ejection-8 Destroyed 13	Maj. William Baechle Maj. Edward P. Schmit	66-0043	A1-61	F-111A	PowWow 08	474th TFW
16	**29-Apr-69**	**Inflight Fire** Repaired 3	Maj John O Hanford Maj Grover C Poole	66-0013	A1-31	F-111A	Tartan 01	474th TFW / 4527th CCTS
17	**22-May-69** **OK/ Ejection**	Ejection-9 Destroyed 14	Capt. Kent M. May Maj John C. Morrow	67-0043	A1-88	F-111A	Soon 31	474th TFW / 429 TFS
18	**6-Oct-69**	Crash Land-4 Repaired 4	Mr. George Marrett Mr. William Bush	151972	A2-03	F-111B	972	Hughes Aircraft **Incident # 2**
19	**30-Oct-69** **Landed**	**Inflight Damage** Write Off-1	Lt Col Michael F McNamara Jr. 1Lt Howard J Kotlicky	66-0012	A1-30	F-111A	**Still Classified**	AFFTC / Edwards AFB, CA could be Nellis

	Event Date, Crew Statistics	Ejection #, Mishap Results	Crew Members Involved	Tail #	Produc- tion #	Full Model Type	Call Sign	Aircraft Operator
20	**6-Nov-69** Landed	**Inflight Fire** Repaired 5	Lt Col Donald G Mueller Capt Brian K O'Riordan	67-0057	A1-102	F-111A	Not on Report	474th TFW/ 430th TFS
21	**12-Nov-69** Landed	**Inflight Fire** Repaired 6	Capt Richard M Matteis Capt Harry J Richard	67-0097	A1-142	F-111A	Not on Report	474th TFW/ 429th TFS **Incident # 1**
22	**22-Dec-69** Fatal/ Ejection	Ejection-10 Destroyed 15	**Lt. Col Thomas J. Mack Maj. James L. Anthony**	67-0049	A1-94	F-111A	Advice 02	474th TFW /428th TFS Wing Pivot Failure
23	**7-Oct-70** Fatal/ Ejection	Ejection-11 Destroyed 16	**Lt. Col Robert S. Montgomery Jr Lt. Col Charles G. Robinson**	68-0253	B1-25	FB-111A	Not on Report	340th BG / Carswell AFB
24	**8-Jan-71** Fatal/ Ejection	Ejection-12 Destroyed 17	**Lt. Col Bruce D. Stocks Maj. Billy C. Gentry**	68-0283	B1-55	FB-111A	EEl 05	GDFW / Carswell AFB
25	**23-Apr-71** Fatal/ Ejection	Ejection-13 Destroyed 18	**Maj. James W. Hurt III Maj. Robert J. Furman**	67-0117	A1-162	F-111E	Junco 08	6510 TW / 6512 TS
26	**18-Aug-71**	Crash Land-5 Repaired 7	Lt. Col Bob Russell Maj. Arben R. Ely	69-6512	B1-74	FB-111A	NO DATA	509th BW(M)
27	**1-Sep-71** OK/ Ejection	Ejection-14 Destroyed 19	Capt. Donald M. Severance Capt. Edward Silverbush	66-0029	A1-47	F-111A	Canard 01	27th TFW / 522nd TFS
28	**29-Nov-71** Vark Hosp-1	Crash Land-6 Repaired 8	Maj Edwin M Moorman Maj James M Brighenti	67-7194	B1-08	FB-111A	Not on Report	509th BW / 393rd BS **Incident # 1**
29	**18-Jan-72** Fatal Crash	**No Ejection** Destroyed 20	**Lt. Col Floyd B. Sweet Lt. Col Kenneth T. Blank**	68-0018	A1-187	F-111E	Sewn 11	20th TFW / 55th TFS
30	**28-Jan-72**	**Landing Incident** Repaired 9	Unknown Unknown	70-2387	E2-26	F-111F	Unknown	347th TFW
31	**2-Feb-72**	**Run Station Fire** Write Off-2	Fire at Run Station # 5-GD/FW	70-2407	E2-46	F-111F	E2-46	GDFW
32	**20-Apr-72**	Crash Land-7 Repaired 10	Unknown Unknown	68-0241	B1-13	FB-111A	NO DATA	380th BW(M)
33	**24-Apr-72** OK / Ejection	Ejection-15 Destroyed 21	Capt. Richard W. Dabney Capt. Donald R. Joyner	67-0036	A1-81	F-111A	Trig 1	474th TFW / 442 TFTS
34	**15-Jun-72** OK / Ejection	Ejection-16 Destroyed 22	Capt. Henry R. Hutson Maj. John S Sinclair	70-2410	E2-49	F-111F	Racer 42	347th TFW
35	**18-Jun-72** Fatal / Ejection	Ejection-17 Destroyed 23	**Col Keith E. Brown Lt. Col James D. Black**	67-0082	A1-127	F-111A	Flick 79	474th TFW / 430th TFS
36	**11-Sep-72** OK / Ejection	Ejection-18 Destroyed 24	Maj. Charles P. Winters Sgt. Patrick S. Sharpe	65-5703	A1-21	F-111A	Snowman 11	6510 TW / 6512 TS
37	**28-Sep-72** No Ejection	**Combat Loss-4** Destroyed 25	**Maj. William Clare "Bill" Coltman 1Lt. Robert Arthur "Lefty" Brett Jr.**	67-0078	A1-123	F-111A	Ranger 23	474th TFW / 430th TFS
38	**29-Sep-72**	Crash Land-8 Repaired 11	Maj. Bennie L. Woytovich Capt. Andrew F. Stepniewski	69-6508	B1-70	FB-111A	Prior 47	380th BMW / 4007 CCTS
39	**16-Oct-72** No Ejection	**Combat Loss-5** Destroyed 26	**Capt. James Alan Hockridge 1Lt. Allen Upton Graham**	67-0066	A1-111	F-111A	Coach 33	474th TFW / 430th TFS
40	**7-Nov-72** No Ejection	**Combat Loss-6** Destroyed 27	**Maj. Robert Mack Brown Capt. Robert David Morrissey**	67-0063	A1-108	F-111A	Whaler 57	474th TFW / 430th TFS
41	**20-Nov-72** No Ejection	**Combat Loss-7** Destroyed 28	**Capt. Ronald Dean Stafford Capt. Charles Joseph Cafferrelli**	67-0092	A1-137	F-111A	Burger 54	474th TFW / 429th TFS
42	**18-Dec-72** No Ejection	**Combat Loss-8** Destroyed 29	**Lt. Col Ronald Jack Ward Maj. James Richard McElvain**	67-0099	A1-144	F-111A	Snug 40	474th TFW / 429th TFS
43	**22-Dec-72** OK / Ejection	Ejection-19 **Combat Loss-9** Destroyed 30	Capt. Robert D. Sponeybarger 1Lt. William Wallace "Bill" Wilson	67-0068	A1-113	F-111A	Jackel 33	474th TFW / 430th TFS
44	**11-Jan-73** OK / Ejection	Ejection-20 Destroyed 31	Maj. Robert J. Kroos Maj. Roger A. Beck	68-0024	A1-193	F-111E	Sewn 12	20th TFW / 55th TFS
45	**17-Feb-73** Landed	**Mid-Air** Repaired 12	Capt. Glen G. Perry Jr. Capt Kenneth M. "Alleycat" Alley	67-0098	A1-143	F-111A	Igloo 47	474th TFW / 429th TFS **Incident # 1**
46	**17-Feb-73** Landed	**Mid-Air** Repaired 13	Capt. Richard S. Skeels Capt. Robert Price McConnell Jr.	67-0071	A1-116	F-111A	Igloo 50	474th TFW / 430th TFS
47	**21-Feb-73**	**Takeoff Accident** Destroyed 32	Capt.Charles E. Sudberry Capt. Eric R. Puschmann	67-0072	A1-117	F-111A	Igloo 55	474th TFW / 428th TFS
48	**20-Mar-73** Fatal / Ejection	Ejection-21 Destroyed 33	**Maj. Richard Leon Brehm Capt. William Ty Halloran**	68-0105	A6-21	F-111D	Bert 73	27th TFW / 4427 TFRS

	Event Date, Crew Statistics	Ejection #, Mishap Results	Crew Members Involved	Tail #	Pro-duc-tion #	Full Model Type	Call Sign	Aircraft Operator
49	20-Mar-73 Fatal / Ejection	Ejection-22 Destroyed 34	**Maj. William Warren Gude** **Capt. David Carl Blackledge**	68-0158	A6-74	F-111D	Bert 74	27th TFW / 4427 TFRS
50	4-May-73 Landed	**Inflight Fire** Repaired 14	Capt Robert S Pahl Capt Thomas M Heyde	67-0053	A1-98	F-111A	Chaps 03	474th TFW / 442nd TTFS
51	8-May-73 Landed	**Inflight Fire** Repaired 15	Maj. Lester G. Frazier 1Lt. Gary R. Rundle	67-0083	A1-128	F-111A	Jumbo 41	474th TFW **Incident #1**
52	15-May-73 OK / Ejection	Ejection-23 Destroyed 35	Capt Andrew J. Peloquin Maj Ariel Alvarez	68-0008	A1-177	F-111E	Akee 54	20th TFW / 79th TFS
53	16-Jun-73 OK / Ejection	Ejection-24 Destroyed 36	Maj. Charles R. Stolz 1Lt. William R. Roberts Jr.	67-0111	A1-156	F-111A	Whaler 21	474th TFW / 428th TFS
54	16-Jun-73 Vark Hosp Field Team 1	**Mid-Air** Repaired 16	Lt. Col. Clarence J. Beaudoin Capt. Thomas David Evans	67-0094	A1-139	F-111A	Popper 11	474th TFW / 428th TFS
55	25-Jun-73	Crash Land-9 Repaired 17	Capt Robert D Ramsey Capt John C McFarren	68-0142	A6-58	F-111D	Age 15	27th TFW / 522nd TFS
56	11-Jul-73 OK / Ejection	Ejection-25 Destroyed 37	Maj. Robert N Hopkins Maj. Kirby F. Ludwick	67-0040	A1-85	F-111A	Chaps 01	474th TFW / 442nd TFTS
57	21-Dec-73 Fatal / Ejection	Ejection-26 Destroyed 38	**Capt. William K. Delaplane III** **1Lt. Robert J. Kierce**	68-0113	A6-29	F-111D	Age 39	27th TFW / 523rd TFS
58	22-Jan-74	Crash Land-10 Repaired 18	Capt Robert H Jones II Capt George G Giddens	68-0160	A6-76	F-111D	News 75	27th TFW / 4427th TFTS **Incident # 1**
59	14-Feb-74	Ground Accident Repaired 19	Unknown Unknown	68-0244	B1-16	FB-111A	NO DATA	380th BW(M)
60	1 May 74	**Crash Land** Repaired 20	Capt Dick Korich Capt Denny Blodgett	68-0287	B1-59	FB-111A	NO DATA	380th BW(M)
61	11-Sep-74 Fatal Crash	**No Ejection** Destroyed 39	**Capt. William Arthur Kennedy Jr** **2 LT. David C. McKennon**	70-2395	E2-34	F-111F	Chomp 81	366th TFW / 390th TFS
62	12-Nov-74 OK / Ejection	Ejection-27 Destroyed 40	Capt. Peter A. Granger Capt. Paul D. Sperry	67-0055	A1-100	F-111A	Sigma 71	474th TFW / 442nd TFTS
63	8-Jan-75	Crash Land-11 Repaired 21	LtCol Carl L Hamby WSO Unknown	67-0050	A1-95	F-111A	NO DATA	474th TFW / 428th TFS
64	3-Feb-75 OK / Ejection	Ejection-28 Destroyed 41	Capt Larry L. McMaster 1Lt James D. Kotten	69-6505	B1-67	FB-111A	Dowel 46	380th BMW / 528th BMS
65	3-Feb-75 OK / Ejection	Ejection-29 Destroyed 42	Capt. John E. Hockenberger Capt.Donald G. Vann	68-0280	B1-52	FB-111A	Dowel 45	380th BMW / 528th BMS
66	5-Mar-75 OK / Ejection	Ejection-30 Destroyed 43	Maj. Richard A. Wolfe Maj. Jay K Miller	68-0081	A1-250	F-111E	Not on Report	20th TFW / 55th TFS
67	6-Jun-75 OK / Ejection	Ejection-31 Destroyed 44	1LT. Martin L. Perina Maj Merle D Kenney	66-0034	A1-52	F-111A	Ned 70	474th TFW / 430th TFS
68	20-Jun-75 OK / Ejection	Ejection-32 Destroyed 45	Col. William F. Palmer Lt. Col. Robert L. Tidwell	66-0025	A1-43	F-111A	Chaps 01	474th TFW
69	14-Aug-75	**EOR FIRE** Repaired 22	Capt Wayne C Spelius Capt Donald R Westbrook	67-0089	A1-134	F-111A	Trick 02	442nd TFTS / 474th TFW 430th TFS / 474th TFW
70	7-Oct-75 Fatal Crash	**No Ejection** Destroyed 46	**Capt. Ralph David Bowles** **Maj. Merle D. Kenney**	66-0058	A1-76	F-111A	Tasty 15	474th TFW / 428th TFS
71	5-Nov-75 OK / Ejection	Ejection-33 Destroyed 47	Capt. James E. Stieber Capt. Robert L. Gregory	68-0060	A1-229	F-111E	Akee 46	20th TFW / 77th TFS
72	8-Nov-75 OK / Ejection	Ejection-34 Destroyed 48	Capt. Eddie L. Ortego 1LT Richard B Lewis	70-2393	E2-32	F-111F	Not on Report	366th TFW
73	23-Dec-75 OK / Ejection	Ejection-35 Destroyed 49	Capt. Robert J. Pavelco Lt Michael R Sprenger USN	68-0290	B1-62	FB-111A	Not on Report	380th BMW / 529 BMS
74	10-Feb-76	**EOR Fire** Repaired 23	Capt Jay D Milstead Capt James R Hussey	68-0099	A6-15	F-111D	Maggy 68	27th TFW / 523rd TFS
75	25-Feb-76 Vark Hosp-2	Crash Land-12 Repaired 24	Capt. James N. Gabriel Capt. Michael H. Labeau	67-7194	B1-08	FB-111A	Radon 19	509th BW / 715th BMS **Incident # 2**
76	26-Feb-76 Vark Hosp-3	Crash Land-13 Repaired 25	Capt. Victor D. Grahn Lt. Col. Clarenece R. "Ray" Reed	68-0095	A6-11	F-111D	Dryly 62	27th TFW / 481st TFTS
77	11-Mar-76 OK / Ejection	Ejection-36 Destroyed 50	Capt. Paul F. Reitschel 1LT. Gary L. Fullington	67-0080	A1-125	F-111A	Tasty 12	474th TFW / 430th TFS

	Event Date, Crew Statistics	Ejection #, Mishap Results	Crew Members Involved	Tail #	Production #	Full Model Type	Call Sign	Aircraft Operator
78	16-Mar-76 OK / Ejection	Ejection-37 Destroyed 51	Flt Lt.Richard E O'Ferrall RAAF Capt. Joseph Dale Freeman USAF	70-2388	E2-27	F-111F	Noman 87	366th TFW / 390th TFS
79	7-Apr-76 OK / Ejection	Ejection-38 Destroyed 52	Capt. Benjamin L. Alexander 1Lt Robert J Short	67-0060	A1-105	F-111A	Doxy 53	429th TFS / 474th TFW
80	21-May-76 Vark Hosp-4	Taxi Mishap Repaired 26	Capt Gregory L Smith 1Lt John C Hall	68-0174	A6-90	F-111D	Not on Report	27th TFW / 523rd FS
81	7-Jun-76 OK / Ejection	Ejection-39 Destroyed 53	Capt. Raymond T. Wilson Capt. Richard A. Bernardi	69-6511	B1-73	FB-111A	Peter 36	380th BMW / 529 BMS
82	10-Oct-76 OK / Ejection	Ejection-40 Destroyed 54	Capt. Richard J. McEwen Capt. Larry F. King	68-0167	A6-83	F-111D	Kino 05	27th TFW
83	27-Oct-76 OK / Ejection	Ejection-41 Destroyed 55	Capt. Douglas A. Joyce Capt. Richard M. Mullane	67-0116	A1-161	F-111E	Not on Report	3246th TW / 3214th TS
84	1-Dec-76	Ground Incident Repaired 27	Unknown Unknown	68-0111	A6-27	F-111D	Unknown	27th TFW
85	14-Feb-77 Fatal Crash	No Ejection Destroyed 56	**Capt. Edward A. Riley Jr Capt. Jeremiah F. Sheehan**	68-0266	B1-38	FB-111A	Orb 16	509th BW / 715th BS Pease AFB, NH
86	21-Apr-77 OK / Ejection	Ejection-42 Destroyed 57	Capt. Peter G. Ganotis Capt. Harold L. Peterson	73-0709	E2-85	F-111F	NOMAN 67	366th TFW / 391st TFS
87	28-Apr-77 OK / Ejection	Ejection-43 Destroyed 58	Capt. William H. Baker USAF FLTLT David Clarkson	A8-136	D1-12	F-111C	Falcon 33	82 WG / # 6 SQ
88	2-Sep-77 OK / Ejection	Ejection-44 Destroyed 59	Capt. Roy W. Westerfield Capt. Jonas l Blank Jr.	68-0146	A6-62	F-111D	Tempest 12	27th TFW / 524th TFTS
89	29-Sep-77 Fatal Crash	Ejection-45 Destroyed 60	**SQLDR. John Holt FLTLT A.P. "Phil" Noordink**	A8-133	D1-09	F-111C	Falcon 32	82 WG / #6 Sq.
90	3-Oct-77 Fatal Crash	No Ejection Destroyed 61	**Capt. Richard L. Cardenas 1Lt. Steven G. Nelson**	68-0093	A6-09	F-111D	Crazy 46	27th TFW / 524th TFS
91	5-Oct-77 Fatal Crash	No Ejection Destroyed 62	**Capt. Stephen H. Reid Capt. Carl T. Poole**	73-0718	E2-94	F-111F	F367	48th TFW / 494th TFS
92	28-Oct-77 OK / Ejection	Ejection-46 Destroyed 63	Capt. John D. Miller Capt. John J Blewitt Jr	68-0285	B1-57	FB-111A	Not on Report	380th BMW 4007th CCTS Plattsburgh AFB, NY
93	31-Oct-77 Fatal Crash	No Ejection Destroyed 64	**Capt. John J. Sweeney Capt. William W. Smart**	68-0070	A1-239	F-111E	Lay 198	20th TFW / 79th TFS
94	30-Nov-77 Fatal Crash	No Ejection Destroyed 65	**Capt. Arthur L Stowe Maj. Loreley O Wagner**	67-0083	A1-128	F-111A	Cub 21	366th TFW / 389th TFTS **Incident # 2**
95	15-Dec-77 OK / Ejection	Ejection-47 Destroyed 66	Capt.Jerry L. Kemp Capt.Thomas E. Bergam	70-2380	E2-19	F-111F	Trest 07	48th TFW / 492nd TFS
96	24-Mar-78	Ground Mishap Repaired 28	Maj James K Dozier Jr. Capt Brian J Teague	66-0030	A1-48	F-111A	Not on Report	SMALC Flight Test
97	29-Mar-78 Fatal / Ejection	Ejection-48 Destroyed 67	**Capt. Charles H. Kitchell 1Lt Jeffrey T. Moore**	73-0717	E2-93	F-111F	Hid 34	48th TFW / 492nd TFS
98	14-Aug-78	Ground Mishap Repaired 29	Unknown Unnown	67-0085	A1-130	F-111A	Unknown	Mountain Home AFB
99	25-Oct-78 OK / Ejection	Ejection-49 Destroyed 68	WGCDR David N Rogers SQNLDR Peter Growder	A8-141	D1-17	F-111C	Falcon Sabre 1	82 WG / # 6 SQ
100	18-Nov-78 OK / Ejection	Ejection-50 Destroyed 69	1Lt. Richard P.McKee Capt. Lee A. Bauer	68-0173	A6-89	F-111D	Patsy 05	27th TFW / 522nd TFS 481st TFTS
101	4-Jan-79 OK/ Ejection	Ejection-51 Destroyed 70	Capt. Gary E. Ryker Capt. William J. Locke	67-0059	A1-104	F-111A	Not on Report	366th TFW / 391st TFS
102	17-Jan-79 Vark Hosp-5	Crash Land-14 Repaired 30	Unknown Unknown	68-0148	A6-64	F-111D	NO DATA	27th TFW / 524th TFS
103	22-Jan-79	Landing Accident Repaired 31	Capt William M Blaesing 1Lt Roger F Kroph	68-0160	A6-76	F 111D	Crazy 46	27th TFW / 524th TFS **Incident #2**
104	16-Feb-79 OK/ Ejection	Ejection-52 Destroyed 71	Capt. Michael E."Stump" Damitz Capt. Randall C. Lambirth	68-0109	A6-25	F-111D	BEST 16	27th TFW / 522nd TFS
105	20-Apr-79 OK/ Ejection	Ejection-53 Destroyed 72	Capt. Joseph Peluso Capt. Timothy A Schlitt	70-2367	E2-06	F-111F	Hid 24	48th TFW / 492nd TFS
106	20-Apr-79 OK/ Ejection	Ejection-54 Destroyed 73	Capt. Stephen R Ruttman Capt. Roger L Webb	73-0714	E2-90	F-111F	Hid 23	48th TFW / 492nd TFS
107	1-May-79 In Flight Fire	Inflight Fire Repaired 32	Unknown Unknown	70-2378	E2-17	F-111F	NO DATA	48th TFW / 492nd TFS

	Event Date, Crew Statistics	Ejection #, Mishap Results	Crew Members Involved	Tail #	Production #	Full Model Type	Call Sign	Aircraft Operator
108	5-Jul-79 Fatal Crash	No Ejection Destroyed 74	Maj. Gary A. Mekash Lt. Col Eugene H. Soeder	67-0105	A1-150	F-111A	Iceman 1	366th TFW / 390th TFS
109	24-Jul-79 Fatal Crash	No Ejection Destroyed 75	Capt. David W. Powell Capt. Douglas A. Pearce	68-0042	A1-211	F-111E	Lay 26	20th TFW / 55th TFS
110	31-Jul-79 Fatal Crash	No Ejection Destroyed 76	2 Lt Larry E. McFarland Capt. Myles D. Hammon	66-0052	A1-70	F-111A	Sulk 82	366th TFW / 389th TFTS
111	24-Aug-79 OK/ Ejection	Ejection-55 Destroyed 77	FLGOFF Mark Kelly FLTLT Alan Joseph "Big Al" Curr	A8-137	D1-13	F-111C	Buckshot 3	82 WG / #1 SQ
112	18-Sep-79 Fatal Crash	No Ejection Destroyed 78	Capt. Phillip B. Donovan Capt. William J. Full	68-0261	B1-33	FB-111A	Not on Report	509th BMW / 393rd BMS
113	20-Sep-79 Vark Hosp-6	Crash Land-15 Repaired 33	Capt. Stephen J. Feaster 1Lt. Roy A Gilbert	68-0136	A6-52	F-111D	Not on Report	27th TFW / 481st TFS 522nd TFS
114	30-Oct-79 OK/ Ejection	Ejection-56 Destroyed 79	Capt. Eugene S. Ogilvie Capt. Albert P. Manzo	68-0012	A1-181	F-111E	Not on Report	20th TFW/ 79th TFS
115	12-Dec-79 Fatal Crash	No Ejection Destroyed 80	Capt. Randolph P. Gaspard Maj. Frank B. Slusher	68-0045	A1-214	F-111E	Lay 40	20th TFW / 79th TFS
116	12-Dec-79 Vark Hosp Field Team 2	Crash Land-16 Repaired 34	Maj Robert G. Little Capt. Steven J. Austin	73-0715	E2-91	F-111F	Trest 56	48th TFW / 492nd TFS
117	19-Dec-79 Fatal Crash	No Ejection Destroyed 81	Capt. Richard A. Hetzner Capt. Raymond C. Spaulding	68-0003	A1-172	F-111E	Rerun 16	20th TFW / 79th TFS
118	6-Feb-80 Fatal / Ejection	Ejection-57 Destroyed 82	Capt. Roy W. Westerfield 2Lt. Steven P. Anderson	68-0119	A6-35	F-111D	Leggs 45	27th TFW / 524th TFTS
119	26-Mar-80 Fatal / Ejection	Ejection-58 Destroyed 83	Capt. Joseph G. Raker Capt. Larry A. Honza	67-0097	A1-142	F-111A	Able 21	366th TFW / 390th TFS **2nd Incident**
120	29-Apr-80 Fatal Crash	No Ejection Destroyed 84	Capt. Jack A. Hines 2 Lt. Richard J. Franks	68-0057	A1-226	F-111E	Lay 32	20th TFW / 77th TFS
121	14-Jul-80 Fatal / Ejection	Ejection-59 Destroyed 85	Maj. Ulysses S. "Sam" Taylor III 1Lt. Paul E. Yeager	68-0139	A6-55	F-111D	Vark 22	27th TFW / 522nd TFS
122	30-Jul-80 OK/ Ejection	Ejection-60 Destroyed 86	Maj. Walter L. Mosher Capt. Jackie T. Shallington	68-0279	B1-51	FB-111A	Not on Report	509 BMW / 393rd BMS Pease AFB
123	28-Aug-80	Inflight Incident Repaired 35	Maj Rowland H Worrell III Capt John A Osborn	68-0106	A6-22	F-111D	Unknown	27th TFW / 481st TFS
124	6-Oct-80 Fatal Crash	No Ejection Destroyed 87	Maj. Thomas M. Mullen Capt. Gary A. Davis	68-0268	B1-40	FB-111A	Touch 55	380th BMW / 4007 CCTS Plattsburgh AFB, NH
125	21-Jan-81 Vark Hosp-7	Crash Land-17 Repaired 36	Maj Daniel P Kallenbach 1Lt Harry E Pauley	67-0079	A1-124	F-111A	Davit 21	366th TFW/ 390th TFS
126	30-Jan-81 OK/ Ejection	Ejection-61 Destroyed 88	Capt. Peter Carellas Maj. Ronald J Reppe	68-0263	B1-35	FB-111A	Salic 16	509th BMW / 715th BMS Pease AFB, NH
127	4-Feb-81 OK/ Ejection	Ejection-62 Destroyed 89	Capt. Barry E. Horne Capt. Lawrence P. Apel	72-1441	E2-71	F-111F	Pall 35	48th TFW / 494th TFS
128	25-Mar-81 Vark Hosp-8	Take-Off Mishap Repaired 37	1Lt Timothy E. Collins Capt Robert N. Miglin	68-0082	A1-251	F-111E	Not on Report	20th TFW/ 79th TFS
129	12-Jun-81 Vark Hosp-9	Ground Mishap Repaired 38	**No Crew Ground Accident**	67-0118	A1-163	F-111E	**Ground Incident**	3246th TW/ 3247th TS
130	7-Jul-81 Vark Hosp-10	**Inflight Fire** Repaired 39	Capt Ralph R Inman Capt George H Stilwell	68-0127	A6-43	F-111D	Hound 21	27th TFW / 523rd TFS
131	13-Aug-81 Vark Hosp-11	Ground Mishap Repaired 40	**No Crew Ground Accident**	68-0259	B1-31	FB-111A	**Ground Incident**	509th BMW / 715th BMS Pease AFB, NH
132	19-Jan-82 OK/ Ejection	Ejection-63 Destroyed 90	Lt. Col. Roland J. McDonald Jr. Capt. Alan D. Walker Jr.	67-0073	A1-118	F-111A	Nomex 71	366th TFW / 391st TFS
133	27-Jan-82 OK/ Ejection	Ejection-64 Destroyed 91	Capt. Jack V. Leslie Maj Theodore S Sieniki	68-0110	A6-26	F-111D	Not on Report	SMALC-PDM FCF Takeoff
134	12-May-82 OK/ Ejection	Ejection-65 Destroyed 92	Maj. Francis B. Morris Maj. George Earles III	66-0045	A1-63	F-111A	Sulk 85	366th TFW / 389th TFTS
135	23-Jun-82 OK/ Ejection	Ejection-66 Destroyed 93	Capt. Stanley J. Szybillo Capt. William S. Clendenen	72-1447	E2-77	F-111F	Cuppy 32	48th TFW / 492nd TFS

	Event Date, Crew Statistics	Ejection #, Mishap Results	Crew Members Involved	Tail #	Pro-duc-tion #	Full Model Type	Call Sign	Aircraft Operator
136	2-Aug-82 Vark Hosp-12	Inflight Fire Repaired 41	Maj. William D. Patton 1Lt. Chritopher A. Singalewitch	67-0101	A1-146	F-111A	Alton 2	366th TFW / 390th TFS
137	14-Sep-82 **Fatal Crash**	**No Ejection** Destroyed 94	**Maj. Howard L. Tallman III Capt. William R. Davy**	68-0160	A6-76	F-111D	Excit 76	27th TFW / 524th TFTS **Incident # 3**
138	16-Sep-82 OK/ Ejection	Ejection-67 Destroyed 95	2Lt. William C. Coutts Capt. Michael J. Artese	74-0179	E2-97	F-111F	Not on Report	48th TFW / 495th TFTS
139	8-Oct-82 OK/ Ejection	Ejection-68 Destroyed 96	Col. Ernest L. Coleman 1Lt. Scott L. Springer	67-0098	A1-143	F-111A	NOMEX 65	366th TFW / 391st TFS **Incident # 2**
140	1-Nov-82 OK/ Ejection	Ejection-69 Destroyed 97	1Lt. Steven J. Bowling Capt. John E. "Jack" Clay	73-0716	E2-92	F-111F	Fort 51	48th TFW / 492nd TFS
141	9-Nov-82	Ground Mishap Destroyed 98	Crew Chief Sra Randy Fancher Pro Super SMsgt Dean Federhart	67-0093	A1-138	F-111A	**Ground Incident**	366th TFW / 391st TFS
142	7-Dec-82 **Fatal Crash**	**No Ejection** Destroyed 99	**Maj. Burnley L. Rudiger Jr. 1Lt. Steven J. Pitt**	70-2377	E2-16	F-111F	Vixen 31	48th TFW / 494th TFS
143	13-Apr-83 OK/ Ejection	Ejection-70 Destroyed 100	2Lt. James M. Dahl Maj. J. Thomas Shealy	66-0054	A1-72	F-111A	Horse 91	366th TFW / 389th TFTS
144	26-Apr-83 **Fatal Crash**	**No Ejection** Destroyed 101	**Capt. Charles Michael Vidas 2Lt. Steven A. Groark**	74-0188	E2-106	F-111F	Hair 028	48th TFW / 492nd TFS
145	7-Jun-83 OK/ Ejection	Ejection-71 Destroyed 102	Maj Richard B. Young Capt Raymond A. Drogan	68-0242	B1-14	FB-111A	Maul 42	509th BMW / 393 BMS Pease AFB, NH
146	28-Oct-83 Vark Hosp-13	Ground Mishap Repaired 42	No Crew Ground Accident Lox Bottle Exploded	68-0101	A6-17	F-111D	Unknown	27th TFW / 522nd FS
147	21-Dec-83 OK/ Ejection	Ejection-72 Destroyed 103	1Lt. James P. "Dirt" Marcouiller 1Lt. Terry A. "Tater" Tatterfield	70-2366	E2-05	F-111F	Seeker 36	48th TFW / 493rd TFS
148	13-Mar-84 **Fatal/ Ejection**	Ejection-73 Destroyed 104	**Capt. David Kirk Peth Capt. Steven F. Locke**	66-0026	A1-44	F-111A	Zipgun 01	366th TFW / 389th TFTS FWIC Aircraft
149	9-Aug-84 OK/ Ejection	Ejection-74 Destroyed 105	Capt. Ralph J. Jodice II Maj. Paul D. Emrich	68-0019	A1-188	F-111E	Roar 21	20th TFW / 79th TFS
150	17-Oct-84 **Fatal Crash**	**No Ejection** Destroyed 106	**2Lt. Albert Heinrich. Torn Capt. Alan J. Pryor**	68-0164	A6-80	F-111D	Hound 34	27th TFW / 524th TFTS
151	10-Apr-85	Crash Land-18 Repaired 43	Maj. Fernando L. Ribas-Dominicci WSO Unknown	70-2413	E2-52	F-111F	NO DATA	48th TFW / 494th TFS
152	1985 Vark Hosp-14	Ground Mishap Repaired 44	Unknown Unknown	68-0050	A1-219	F-111E	NO DATA	30thTFW Upper Heyford
153	16-Dec-85	Fire Damage Repaired 45	Unknown Unknown	67-0035	A1-80	EF-111A		30thTFW Upper Heyford
154	28-Jan-86 **Fatal Crash**	**No Ejection** Destroyed 107	**FltLt. Stephen M. Erskine RAAF Capt. Gregory S. Angell USAF**	A8-139	D1-15	F-111C	Buckshot 1	82 WG / #1 Sq.
155	15-Apr-86 **Fatal/ Ejection**	**Combat Loss-10** Destroyed 108	**Maj. Fernando L. Ribas-Dominicci Capt. Paul Franklin Lorence**	70-2389	E2-28	F-111F	Karma 52	48th TFW / 495th TFTS
156	23-Feb-87 OK/ Ejection	Ejection-76 Destroyed 109	Capt. Scott E. Lewis Capt. Frank E. Casella	70-2418	E2-57	F-111F	Trest 01	48th TFW / 492nd TFS
157	3-Apr-87 **Fatal Crash**	**No Ejection** Destroyed 110	**FLTLT Mark "Speed' Fallon RAAF FLTOFF William X. Pike RAAF**	A8-128	D1-04	F-111C	Falcon Sabre 1	82 WG / # 6 Sq.
158	28-Jul-87 **Fatal/ Ejection**	Ejection-77 Destroyed 111	**Capt. Taylor F. "Chip" Stem III Capt. Philip D. "Phil" Baldwin**	70-2375	E2-14	F-111F	Duece 31	48th TFW / 493rd TFS
159	11-Sep-87 OK/ Ejection	Ejection-78 Destroyed 112	Maj. John W. "Juan" Sides Maj. Russell C. "Rusty" Stricker	68-0125	A6-41	F-111D	Captor 74	27th TFW / 524th TFS
160	12-Jan-88 **Fatal/ Ejection**	Ejection-79 Destroyed 113	**Capt. Robert A. Meyer Jr. Capt. Frederick A. Gerhart**	67-0102	A1-147	F-111A	Honest 2	366th TFW / 389th TFTS
161	15-Mar-88 **Crash Land**	Crash Land-19 Repaired 46	Lt Col Brusting Capt Keller	67-0085	A1-130	F-111A	NO DATA	366th TFW / 389th TFS
162	17-Mar-88 OK/ Ejection	Ejection-80 Destroyed 114	1Lt. Philip E. Walgren Maj. Juergen Nuemann (German AF)	68-0132	A6-48	F-111D	Not on Report	27th TFW / 522nd TFS
163	8-Jun-88 **Fatal Crash**	**No Ejection** Destroyed 115	**Capt. Glenn E. Troster Capt. Michael A. Barritt**	68-0098	A6-14	F-111D	Cubid 1	27th TFW / 523rd TFS

	Event Date, Crew Statistics	Ejection #, Mishap Results	Crew Members Involved	Tail #	Pro-duc-tion #	Full Model Type	Call Sign	Aircraft Operator
164	21-Oct-88 OK/ Ejection	Ejection-81 Destroyed 116	Capt. David A. Swanson Capt. Timothy P. Gaffney	68-0130	A6-46	F-111D	Snip 01	27th TFW / 524th TFTS
165	2-Feb-89 OK/ Ejection	Ejection-82 Destroyed 117	Capt. Randall S. Voorhees Capt. Leonard J. Esterly, Jr.	68-0243	B1-15	FB-111A	Heat 22	380th BW / 529th BMS
166	5-Apr-89 OK/ Ejection	Ejection-83 Destroyed 118	**1Lt J. Robert "Bob" Boland Capt. James A. Gleason**	70-2397	E2-36	F-111F	Greebie 54	48th TFW / 494th TFS
167	15-Sep-89	**Bird Strike** Write Off-3	Unknown Unknown	68-0140	A6-56	F-111D	NO DATA	27th TFW / Cannon AFB
168	5-Feb-90 Fatal Crash	**No Ejection** Destroyed 119	**Capt. Clifford W. Massengill 1Lt. Thomas G. Dorsett**	68-0001	A1-170	F-111E	Not on Report	20th TFW / 77th TFS
169	26-Mar-90	Bird Strike Write Off-4	Lt. Col. Hill Capt. Gregory Wiley	68-0168	A6-84	F-111D	Not on Report	27th TFW / 524th TFTS
170	2-May-90 OK/ Ejection	Ejection-84 Destroyed 120	Capt. David E. Ratcliff Jr 1LT Brian W. Kirkwood	70-2368	E2-07	F-111F	Rex 62	48th TFW / 492nd TFS
171	20-Jul-90 OK / Ejection	Ejection-85 Destroyed 121	Capt. Robert W. Travis Capt. Richard. M. Basak	68-0066	A1-235	F-111E	Not on Report	20th TFW / 55th TFS
172	23-Aug-90 OK/ Ejection	Ejection-86 Destroyed 122	Maj. Richard C. Davidage Maj. Valdimar "Valdo" L. Smith	68-0131	A6-47	F-111D	Captor 46	27th TFW / 522nd TFS
173	10-Oct-90 Fatal Crash	**No Ejection** Destroyed 123	**Capt. Frederick Arthur Reid Capt. Thomas R. "TC" Caldwell**	74-0183	E2-101	F-111F	Cougar 41	48th TFW (P) / 494th TFS 493rd Aircraft
174	17-Jan-91 Midair	Hit Tanker Boom Repaired 47	Capt Dwayne Mathers Maj Terry Phillips	70-2384	E2-23	F-111F	NO DATA	48th TFW (P) / 493rd TFS Taif AB
175	14-Feb-91 Fatal Crash	**Combat Loss-11** Destroyed 124	**Capt. Douglas M. Brandt Capt. Paul R. Eichenlaub II**	66-0023	A1-41	EF-111A	Wrench 54	48th TFW(P) / 42nd ECS 390th ECS Crew
176	31-May-91	Bird Strike Write Off-5	Unknown Unknown	68-0133	A6-49	F-111D	NO DATA	27th FW / 524th FS
177	29-Oct-91 In-Flight Fire	**Inflight Fire** Repaired 48	Capt Craig E Brown 1Lt Jeffrey M Zeller	72-1444	E2-74	F-111F	BOSOX 41	48th TFW / 494th TFS
178	2 Apr-92 OK/ Ejection	Ejection-87 Destroyed 125	Capt. Jeffery N. Coombe Capt. David E. Genevish	66-0056	A1-74	EF-111A	Not on Report	20th TFW / 42nd ECS
179	17-Sep-92 Fatal/ Ejection	Ejection-88 Destroyed 126	**Capt. Jerry C. Lindh Maj. David Michael McGuire**	68-0052	A1-221	F-111E	Lay 43	20th TFW / 55th TFS
180	13-Sep-93 Fatal Crash	**No Ejection** Destroyed 127	**FltLt Jeremy "Jez" McNess RAAF FltLt Mark "CC" Cairns-Cowan RAAF**	A8-127	D1-03	F-111C	Buckshot 18	82 WG / # 1 Sq.
181	6 Aug-93	Ground Mishap Write Off-6	Maintenance Run Weapons Bay Fire Run Man-Unknown	70-2370	E2-09	F-111F	Run # 370 Nellis MOC	27th FW / 524th FS **Nellis Trim Pad**
182	22-Sep-93 OK/ Ejection	Ejection-89 Destroyed 128	Capt. Robby A. "KY" Kyroauc Capt. Gregory "Pud" Wilson	70-2412	E2-51	F-111F	Leggs 12	27th FW / 522nd TFS
183	1-Aug-94	Bird Strike Write Off-7	Unknown Unknown	70-2408	E2-47	F-111F	Not on Report	27th FW / 522nd FS
184	1994/95	Bird Strike Write Off-8	Unknown Unknown	70-2364	E2-03	F-111F	Not on Report	27th FW / 522nd FS
185	16-Feb-95 OK/ Ejection	Ejection-90 Destroyed 129	Capt James E. "Fig" Newton 1Lt. Randolph L. Winge	68-0040	A1-209	F-111E	Hypo 01	27th FW / 428th TFTS
186	17-Jun-96 OK/ Ejection	Ejection-91 Destroyed 130	Capt. James D. Wingo Jr. Capt. Donald R. "Rick" Watson Jr.	66-0044	A1-62	EF-111A	Jamup 2	27th FW / 429th ECS
187	18-Apr-99 Fatal Crash	**No Ejection** Destroyed 131	**SQLDR Stephen "Nige" Hobbs FLLT Anthony "Shorty" Short**	A8-291	B1-63	F-111G	Pisces 01	82WG/ #6 Sq / RAAF
188	22 Feb 97	Ground Accident Repaired 49	Unknown Unknown	Unkwn		F-111G	Unknown	82WG/ #6 Sq / RAAF
189	18-Jul-06	Crash Land-20 Repaired 50	PLTOFF Peter Komar FLTLT Luke Warner	A8-143	D1-19	F-111C	Colt 2	82WG/ #6 Sq / RAAF

MAJOR F-111 MISHAPS
BY MODEL / TAIL NUMBER / PRIMARY CAUSE

Definition of Terms or Acronyms:

Landing Accident = Occurred during or with intent to Land

N/R Land = Ejection Not Required/ Aircraft Landed

N/R Gnd = Ejection Not Required - Ground Accident

No/Attp = Ejection Not Attempted - Reason Unknown

UnS/OoE = Unsuccessful Ejection / Out of Envelope

UnS/Malf = Unsuccessful Ejection / Malfunction of Ejection System

* Asterisk = Combat Loss

LOC = Loss of Control

Mid-Air = Mid-Air Collision

Ground Accident = With or Without Intent to Fly

Mechanical = Some form of Aircraft Systems Failure

Engine = Engine Failure/Fire

CFIT = Controlled Flight Into Terrain

Tail No.	Date	Ejection	Contributing Factors Leading to the Crash	ACFT Status	Primary Cause
General Dynamics F-111A					
63-9769	18-May-68	N/R land	Slow Flight Stall during Air show fly-by, crash landed	Destroyed	LOC
63-9774	19-Jan-67	N/R land	Improper Flap/Slat / Wing Sweep Configuration, Stall, crash landed	Destroyed	LOC
63-9780	19-Oct-67	Successful	Mechanical failure of speed brake, Loss of Hydraulics / **LOC**	Destroyed	Mechanical
63-9783	13-Aug-68	N/R land	Substantial aft fuselage structural damage during fuel tank jettison	Repaired	Mechanical
65-5701	2-Jan-68	Successful	Gun rounds cooked off in weapons bay causing loss of Hyd/ Fire /LOC	Destroyed	Mechanical
65-5703	11-Sep-72	Successful	Spin Test, uncommanded spin chute separation, LOC	Destroyed	LOC
66-0012	30 Oct-69	N/R land	Triple Plow II Inlet Splitter Plate separated, substantial fuselage damage	Write-Off	Mechanical
66-0013	22-Apr-69	N/R land	Engine Fire combustion chamber heat shield not installed	Repaired	Engine
66-0017	30-Mar-68	Successful	Horizontal Stab servo actuator spool valve failure LOC	Destroyed	Mechanical*
66-0022	28-Mar-68	No/Attp	Undetermined TFR related anomaly, CFIT	Destroyed	CFIT*
66-0024	21-Apr-68	No/Attp	Undetermined, TFR related, Self-Fragged with MK-117 High Drag	Destroyed	CFIT*
66-0025	20-Jun-75	Successful	Engine Failure, Fire, and LOC	Destroyed	Engine
66-0026	13-Mar-84	UnS/OoE	Accelerated Stall, LOC, Late Ejection Attempt	Destroyed	LOC
66-0029	1-Sep-71	Successful	Bird Strike, through windscreen, LOC	Destroyed	Bird strike
66-0032	8-May-68	Successful	HTSA servo valve input spool rod end separation failure, LOC	Destroyed	Mechanical
66-0034	6-Jun-75	Successful	Engine failure, ruptured fuel manifold, Uncontained Fire, LOC	Destroyed	Engine
66-0040	23-Sep-68	Successful	Undetected Fuel Imbalance, Aft CG, LOC	Destroyed	LOC
66-0042	12-Feb-69	No/Attp	Overrode TFR during low-level route abort, CFIT	Destroyed	CFIT
66-0043	4-Mar-69	Successful	Improper Flap/Slat Configuration, Stall, LOC	Destroyed	LOC
66-0045	12-May-82	Successful	Engine failure, Inflight Fire, LOC	Destroyed	Engine
66-0052	31-Jul-79	No/Attp	Passed through lead's jet wash dual engine compressor stalls, Flame out,	Destroyed	Engine
66-0054	13-Apr-83	Successful	Departure from controlled flight, SIS inoperative, LOC	Destroyed	LOC
66-0058	7-Oct-75	No/Attp	Engine Failure, TFR paddled off, CFIT	Destroyed	CFIT
67-0036	24-Apr-72	Successful	Departed controlled flight while conducting rudder rolls, LOC	Destroyed	LOC
67-0040	11-Jul-73	Successful	Bird strike, windshield disintegrated, disorientation	Destroyed	Bird strike
67-0043	22-May-69	Successful	Bird strike, windshield disintegrated, disorientation	Destroyed	Bird strike
67-0049	22-Dec-69	UnS/OoE	Wing Pivot Forging failed, LOC, Out of Envelope Ejection	Destroyed	Mechanical
67-0053	4 May 73	N/R Land	Engine Fire, Reverse Flow phenomena, Landed Safely	Repaired	Engine

Tail No.	Date	Ejection	Contributing Factors Leading to the Crash	ACFT Status	Primary Cause
67-0055	12-Nov-74	Successful	Mid-Air Collision with Civilian Acft, LOC	Destroyed	Mid-Air
67-0057	6-Nov-69	N/R land	Engine Bay heat damage due to nacelle ejector duct failure	Repaired	Mechanical
67-0059	4-Jan-79	Successful	Engine failure, inflight fire, Reverse Flow, LOC	Destroyed	Engine
67-0060	7-Apr-76	Successful	Engine failure, inflight fire, LOC	Destroyed	Engine
67-0063	7-Nov-72	No/Attp	Undetermined TFR related anomaly, CFIT	Destroyed	CFIT*
67-0066	16-Oct-72	No/Attp	Undetermined, TFR related, Self-Fragged with MK-84 Low Drag	Destroyed	CFIT*
67-0068	22-Dec-72	Successful	Loss of Hydraulics due to ground fire, SHOT DOWN	Destroyed	Shot Down*
67-0071	17-Feb-73	N/R land	Mid-Air Collision with another F-111, substantial damage	Repaired	Mid-Air
67-0072	21-Feb-73	N/R Gnd	Landing Gear Failure during Takeoff Roll, Ground Accident	Destroyed	Ground Accident
67-0073	19-Jan-82	Successful	Fuel leak from F-2 tank ,Engine Fire, Reverse Flow phenomena, LOC	Destroyed	Engine
67-0078	28-Sep-72	No/Attp	Undetermined TFR related anomaly, CFIT	Destroyed	CFIT*
67-0079	21-Jan-81	N/R land	Electrical Wire Arcing, Well Well Fire, Substantial Damage	Repaired	Mechanical
67-0080	11-Mar-76	Successful	During a rejoin , pilot departed the aircraft while maneuvering, Stall, LOC	Destroyed	LOC
67-0082	18-Jun-72	UnS/Malf	Inflight Fire, LOC, fuel cap siphoning, Main recovery parachute streamed	Destroyed	Mechanical
67-0083	30-Nov-77	No/Attp	Skip Hit ground during Low Alt Bomb Delivery, CFIT, TFR not in use	Destroyed	CFIT
67-0089	14-Aug-75	N/R Gnd	Engine explosion and Fire on takeoff run-up. Substantial Damage	Repaired	Ground Accident
67-0092	20-Nov-72	No/Attp	Undetermined TFR related anomaly with overwater transition, CFIT	Destroyed	CFIT*
67-0093	9-Nov-82	N/R Gnd	Gaseous Oxygen explosion and Fire on the ground	Destroyed	Ground Accident
67-0094	16-Jun-73	N/R land	Mid-Air Collision with another F-111, substantial damage	Repaired	Mid-Air
67-0097	26 Mar 80	UnS/OoE	Unrecognized sink rate with Right Engine stalled, Left engine in full AB	Destroyed	LOC
67-0098	8-Oct-82	Successful	Power loss to Flight Control Computers due to loose wire connection, LOC	Destroyed	Mechanical
67-0099	18-Dec-72	No/Attp	Undetermined TFR related anomaly with overwater transition, CFIT	Destroyed	CFIT*
67-0101	2-Aug-82	N/R land	Bird strike right engine, substantial damage, single engine landing	Repaired	Bird strike
67-0102	12-Jan-88	UnS/OoE	Right Canopy opened on T/O, Stall, LOC	Destroyed	LOC
67-0105	5-Jul-79	No/Attp	Descending turn to Low Altitude, TFR not engaged, CFIT	Destroyed	CFIT
67-0111	16-Jun-73	Successful	Mid-Air Collision with another F-111, LOC	Destroyed	Mid-Air

Grumman F-111B

Tail No.	Date	Ejection	Contributing Factors Leading to the Crash	ACFT Status	Primary Cause
151971	11-Sep-68	UnS/OoE	Rudder Hardover, LOC Ejection Seats /Ejection Attempted OoE	Destroyed	Mechanical
151972	6-Oct-69	N/R land	Overwing panel Jammed pitch control mechanism, Hard Landing,	Repaired	Mechanical
151973	21-Apr-67	UnS/Malf	Inlet Cowl Fairings closed on T/O, Dual Engine Compressor Stall	Destroyed	Engine

Royal Australian Air Force F-111C

Tail No.	Date	Ejection	Contributing Factors Leading to the Crash	ACFT Status	Primary Cause
A8-127	13 Sep 93	No/Attp	Aircraft impacted the ground after bomb delivery, TFR not engaged	Destroyed	CFIT
A8-128	3-Apr-87	No/Attp	CFIT during egress, overbanked descent, Auto TFR engaged	Destroyed	CFIT
A8-133	29-Sep-77	UnS/OoE	Birds trike, windshield disintegrated, disorientation, Auto TFR	Destroyed	Bird strike
A8-136	28-Apr-77	Successful	Failure of a engine Hot Bleed Air Duct, Inflight Fire, LOC	Destroyed	Mechanical
A8-137	24-Aug-79	Successful	T/O water ingestion, engine flameout, High Speed Abort, Ground	Destroyed	Ground Accident
A8-139	28-Jan-86	No/Attp	Collided with water surface after Harpoon attack, TFR not engaged	Destroyed	CFIT
A8-141	25-Oct-78	Successful	High Pressure Bleed Air Duct Failure, Inflight Fire, LOC	Destroyed	Mechanical
A8-291	18-Apr-99	No/Attp	CFIT with a small island during ingress for Harpoon Attack, TFR not engaged	Destroyed	CFIT

General Dynamics EF-111A

Tail No.	Date	Ejection	Contributing Factors Leading to the Crash	ACFT Status	Primary Cause
66-0023	14-Feb-91	No/Attp	CFIT during defensive threat reaction maneuver, TFR not engaged	Destroyed	CFIT*
66-0044	17-Jun-96	Successful	Right Engine fuel dutct failure, Inflight Fire, LOC	Destroyed	Mechanical
66-0056	2 Apr-92	Successful	Fuel System distribution duct failure, Inflight Fire, LOC	Destroyed	Mechanical

General Dynamics F-111D

Tail No.	Date	Ejection	Contributing Factors Leading to the Crash	ACFT Status	Primary Cause
68-0093	3-Oct-77	No/Attp	CFIT during night low altitude bomb run, TFR paddled off	Destroyed	CFIT
68-0095	26-Feb-76	N/R land	Wire chaffing to hydraulic lines, inflight wheel well fire	Repaired	Engine
68-0098	8-Jun-88	No/Attp	CFIT during low altitude bomb delivery, TFR not engaged	Destroyed	CFIT
68-0099	10-Feb-76	N/R land	Engine Failure and inflight fire. Successfully landed, major damage	Repaired	Engine
68-0101	28 Oct 83	N/R Gnd	LOX Converted bottle exploded, extensive damage to capsule floor	Repaired	Ground Accident
68-0105	20-Mar-73	UnS/Malf	Mid-Air Collision during night RBS attack, Unsuccessful Ejection	Destroyed	Mid-Air
68-0109	16-Feb-79	Successful	Accelerated departure, during recovery from bomb delivery, LOC	Destroyed	LOC
68-0110	27-Jan-82	Successful	Engine failure, Inflight Fire, Reverse Flow Phenomena, LOC	Destroyed	Engine
68-0113	21-Dec-73	UnS/Malf	CFIT during low altitude bomb delivery, TFR not engaged, LARA Inop	Destroyed	CFIT
68-0119	6-Feb-80	UnS/Malf	Mid-Air Collision with Civilian Acft, LOC	Destroyed	Mid-Air
68-0125	11-Sep-87	Successful	One engine shutdown, 2nd engine failed during approach to land	Destroyed	Engine
68-0127	7-Jul-81	N/R land	Wire chaffing to hydraulic lines, inflight wheel well fire	Repaired	Engine

Tail No.	Date	Ejection	Contributing Factors Leading to the Crash	ACFT Status	Primary Cause
68-0130	21-Oct-88	Successful	Engine failure, Inflight Fire, Reverse Flow Phenomena, LOC	Destroyed	Engine
68-0131	23-Aug-90	Successful	Electrical generator malfunction, flight computer interruption, LOC	Destroyed	Mechanical
68-0132	17-Mar-88	Successful	Fuel leak, Engine shut down, High Sink rate on landing, LOC	Destroyed	Mechanical
68-0136	20-Sep-79	N/R land	Engine Failure and inflight fire. Successfully landed, major damage	Repaired	Engine
68-0139	14-Jul-80	UnS/Malf	One engine shutdown, 2nd engine failed during approach to land	Destroyed	Engine
68-0142	25-Jun-73	N/R land	HTSA galling, Landing oscillations, Substantial damage	Repaired	Mechanical
68-0146	2 Sep 77	Successful	Departure from controlled flight during rudder rolls, T/O and Lnd gains, LOC	Destroyed	LOC
68-0148	17 Jan 79	N/R Gnd	9th stage fan blade disintegrated, pre-takeoff engine run-up, extensive damage	Repaired	Ground Accident
68-0158	20 Mar 73	UnS/Malf	Mid-Air Collision during Night RBS attack rejoin	Destroyed	Mid-Air
68-0160	14-Sep-82	No/Attp	CFIT, during Auto TFR descent to low alt, no recovery	Destroyed	CFIT
68-0164	17-Oct-84	No/Attp	Night TFR, CFIT after fly-up recovery maneuver, spatial disorientation	Destroyed	CFIT
68-0167	10-Oct-76	Successful	HTSA galling, LOC	Destroyed	Mechanical
68-0173	18-Nov-78	Successful	Engine failure, Inflight Fire, Reverse Flow Phenomena, LOC	Destroyed	Engine
68-0174	21 May 76	N/R land	Engine failure and fire during T/O runup, Major Damage	Repaired	Engine

General Dynamics F-111E

Tail No.	Date	Ejection	Contributing Factors Leading to the Crash	ACFT Status	Primary Cause
67-0116	27-Oct-76	Successful	Low fuel emergency, Landed Fast, Porpoised, LOC, Test Acft	Destroyed	Landing Accident
67-0117	23-Apr-71	UnS/Malf	LOC during test flight, LOC, Unsuccessful Ejection due to Malfunction	Destroyed	LOC
67-0118	12 Jun 82	N/R Gnd	Hi Press impact attenuation bag inflation bottle exploded, Extensive damage	Repaired	Ground Accident
68-0001	5-Feb-90	No/Attp	Night Radar Pattern, CFIT in base turn, TFR not engaged	Destroyed	CFIT
68-0003	19-Dec-79	No/Attp	CFIT with hill nearly inverted during low-level mission, TFR not engaged	Destroyed	CFIT
68-0008	15 May 73	Successful	Bird strike in Engine, Engine Fire, LOC	Destroyed	Bird strike
68-0012	30-Oct-79	Successful	Uncorrected airspeed decay, Stall, while in holding, post stall gyration	Destroyed	LOC
68-0018	18-Jan-72	No/Attp	Improper Flap/Slat, wing sweep config, Stall, in GCA pattern	Destroyed	LOC
68-0019	9-Aug-84	Successful	Bird strike, debris in Engines plus damage to SIS, LOC	Destroyed	Bird strike
68-0024	11-Jan-73	Successful	Engine failure, Inflight Fire on Takeoff, Reverse Flow Phenomena, LOC	Destroyed	Engine
68-0040	16-Feb-95	Successful	One engine in idle, 2nd engine failed during approach to land	Destroyed	Engine
68-0042	24-Jul-79	No/Attp	CFIT with water during base turn, bomb pattern, TFR not engaged	Destroyed	CFIT
68-0045	12-Dec-79	No/Attp	CFIT with water, downwind in bomb pattern, TFR not engaged	Destroyed	CFIT
68-0050	1985	N/R Gnd	LOX Bottle Exploded, extensive damage to Module, Wheel Well, Avionics bay	Repaired	Ground Accident
68-0052	17-Sep-92	UnS/Malf	No slat, no flap approach, excessive sink rate, slow, stalled, LOC	Destroyed	CFIT
68-0057	29-Apr-80	No/Attp	In the weather, spoiler stuck up, LOC, ground impact	Destroyed	LOC
68-0060	5-Nov-75	Successful	Bird strike, windshield disintegrated, disorientation	Destroyed	Bird strike
68-0066	20-Jul-90	Successful	Smoke in cockpit, pilot turned off CADC and Flight Control Dampers, LOC	Destroyed	LOC
68-0070	31-Oct-77	No/Attp	CFIT during night low-level, while rejoining with flight lead, TFR not engaged	Destroyed	CFIT
68-0081	5-Mar-75	Successful	Bird strike, windshield disintegrated, disorientation	Destroyed	Bird strike
68-0082	25 Mar 81	N/R Gnd	T/O abort due to stall warning indication due to AOA Probe damage	Repaired	Ground Accident

General Dynamics F-111F

Tail No.	Date	Ejection	Contributing Factors Leading to the Crash	ACFT Status	Primary Cause
70-2366	21-Dec-83	Successful	Departed controlled flight, possible flight control problem, LOC	Destroyed	LOC
70-2367	20-Apr-79	Successful	Mid-Air Collision while rejoining after range work, LOC	Destroyed	Mid-Air
70-2368	2-May-90	Successful	Engine failure, engine blades penetrated aft fuel tank, Fire, LOC	Destroyed	Engine
70-2375	28-Jul-87	UnS/OoE	During bomb delivery recovery maneuver, entered IMC, exited nose low, CFIT	Destroyed	CFIT
70-2377	7-Dec-82	No/Attp	CFIT during Night TFR Letdown, TFR Inop due to misalignment	Destroyed	CFIT
70-2380	15-Dec-87	Successful	HTSA mounting bold dislodged, LOC	Destroyed	Mechanical
70-2388	16 Mar 76	Successful	One throttle stuck, on landing, aircraft porpoised, crew ejected	Destroyed	Landing Accident
70-2389	18-Apr-86	Successful	SHOTDOWN during target ingress, rough seas, aircrew drowned	Destroyed	Shot Down*
70-2393	8-Nov-75	Successful	Failed Adverse Yaw Computer, LOC after configuring to land, Night	Destroyed	Mechanical
70-2395	11-Sep-74	No/Attp	CFIT during Night low altitude bomb delivery, TFR paddled off	Destroyed	CFIT
70-2397	5-Apr-89	UnS/OoE	CFIT, Accelerated Stall during threat reaction maneuver, LOC	Destroyed	LOC
70-2407	2-Feb-72	N/R Gnd	Internal failure of the right engine during pre-delivery engine run test	Write-Off	Ground Accident
70-2410	15-Jun-72	Successful	LOC during spacing maneuver with flight lead, exceeded critical AOA	Destroyed	LOC
70-2412	22-Sep-93	Successful	Engine failure, Inflight Fire, LOC	Destroyed	Engine
70-2418	23-Feb-87	Successful	HTSA galling, LOC	Destroyed	Mechanical
72-1441	4-Feb-81	Successful	Uncommanded pitch down on approach HTSA galling, LOC	Destroyed	Mechanical
72-1444	29-Oct-91	N/R land	Engine failure and fire during flight, landed safely, Major Damage	Repaired	Engine
72-1447	23-Jun-82	Successful	Foreign Object in HTSA servo control valve, LOC	Destroyed	Mechanical
73-0709	21-Apr-77	Successful	LOC during low altitude bombing maneuver	Destroyed	LOC
73-0714	20-Apr-79	Successful	Mid-Air Collision while rejoining after range work, LOC	Destroyed	Mid-Air
73-0715	12-Dec-79	N/R land	During go-around with gear damage, engaged cable in AB, hard landing	Repaired	Landing Accident

Tail No.	Date	Ejection	Contributing Factors Leading to the Crash	ACFT Status	Primary Cause
73-0716	1-Nov-82	Successful	Engine Fire, Reverse Flow Phenomena, LOC	Destroyed	Engine
73-0717	29 Mar 78	UnS/Malf	Aircraft departed controlled flight after lightning strike, LOC	Destroyed	LOC
73-0718	5-Oct-77	No/Attp	CFIT during low-level mission, TFR not engaged	Destroyed	CFIT
74-0719	16-Sep-82	Successful	Wheel Well Hot Light, Loss of Utility Hyd, LOC due to low hydraulic pressure	Destroyed	Mechanical
74-0183	10-Oct-90	No/Attp	CFIT during night PAVE TACK recovery maneuver, TFR not engaged	Destroyed	CFIT
74-0188	26-Apr-83	No/Attp	CFIT during low-level mission, TFR not engaged, overwater egress	Destroyed	CFIT

General Dynamics FB-111A

Tail No.	Date	Ejection	Contributing Factors Leading to the Crash	ACFT Status	Primary Cause
67-7194	29 Nov-81	N/R land	Aircraft struck approach lights during approach in poor WX,	Repaired	Landing Accident
68-0242	7-Jun-83	Successful	Engine Fire, Reverse Flow Phenomena, LOC	Destroyed	Engine
68-0243	2-Feb-89	Successful	External Fuel Tank on wing swivel pylon yawed, LOC	Destroyed	Mechanical
68-0253	7-Oct-70	UnS/OoE	Improper Flap/Slat, wing sweep config, Stall, in GCA pattern	Destroyed	LOC
68-0259	13 Aug 81	N/R Gnd	BDU-38 spotting charge went off in weapons bay, extensive fire damage	Repaired	Ground Accident
68-0261	18-Sep-79	No/Attp	LOC during low altitude maneuvering , Post Stall Gyration	Destroyed	LOC
68-0263	30-Jan-81	Successful	Uncommanded Roll input, during descent HTSA galling, LOC	Destroyed	Mechanical
68-0266	14-Feb-77	No/Attp	CFIT during low-level mission, TFR not engaged	Destroyed	CFIT
68-0268	6-Oct-80	No/Attp	CFIT during night IMC low-level mission, TFR engaged, overwater flight	Destroyed	CFIT
68-0279	30-Jul-80	Successful	LOC due to uncommanded roll input during Auto TFR Letdown ,	Destroyed	LOC
68-0280	3-Feb-75	Successful	Mid-Air Collision while rejoining at night after range work, LOC	Destroyed	Mid-Air
68-0283	8-Jan-71	UnS/OoE	During Auto TFR flight, aircraft pitched over at low alt, no recovery	Destroyed	CFIT
68-0285	28-Oct-77	Successful	Engine Fire, Reverse Flow Phenomena, LOC	Destroyed	Engine
68-0290	23-Dec-75	Successful	Engine failure, engine blades penetrated aft fuel tank, Fire, LOC	Destroyed	Engine
69-6505	3-Feb-75	Successful	Mid-Air Collision while rejoining at night after range work, LOC	Destroyed	Mid-Air
69-6508	29-Sep-72	N/R land	Aircraft landed at the wrong airport, heavy weight, departed runway end	Repaired	Landing Accident
69-6511	7-Jun-76	Successful	LOC after flight control malfunction, Roll Coupled Departure	Destroyed	Mechanical

F

FLIGHT RELATED CRASHES AND EJECTION STATISTICS

	Date	Tail	(Ejection #) Results	Comments
1.	21-Apr-67	151973	(1) Unsuccessful / Ejection	Module failed to eject (Malfunction)
2.	19-Oct-67	63-9780	(2)Successful / Ejection	First successful use of Escape Pod
3.	2-Jan-68	65-5701	(3)Successful / Ejection	
4.	27-Mar-68	66-0022	**Combat Loss** / No Attempt	
5.	30-Mar-68	66-0017	(4)**Combat Loss** /Successful	Rescued in Thailand
6.	22-Apr-68	66-0024	**Combat Loss** / No Attempt	
7.	8-May-68	66-0032	(5)Successful/ Ejection	Capsule experienced a Right Glove Boom failure
8.	11-Sep-68	151971	(6)Unsuccessful / Ejections	Ejection Seat equipped / Out of the envelope
9.	23-Sep-68	66-0040	(7)Successful / Ejection	
10.	12-Feb-69	66-0042	Fatal / No Attempt	
11.	4-Mar-69	66-0043	(8)Successful/ Ejection	
12.	22-May-69	67-0043	(9)Successful / Ejection	
13.	22-Dec-69	67-0049	(10)Unsuccessful / Ejection	Out of the envelope
14.	7-Oct-70	68-0253	(11)Unsuccessful/ Ejection	Out of the envelope
15.	8-Jan-71	68-0283	(12)Unsuccessful/ Ejection	Out of the envelope
16.	23-Apr-71	67-0117	(13)Unsuccessful / Ejection	Main Parachute failed to deploy (Malfunction)
17.	1-Sep-71	66-0029	(14)Successful / Ejection	
18.	18-Jan-72	68-0018	Fatal / No Attempt	
19.	24-Apr-72	67-0036	(15)Successful / Ejection	
20.	15-Jun-72	70-2410	(16)Successful / Ejection	
21.	18-Jun-72	67-0082	(17)Unsuccessful / Ejection	Main Chute became entangled (Malfunction)
22.	11-Sep-72	65-5703	(18)Successful / Ejection	
23.	28-Sep-72	67-0078	**Combat Loss** / No Attempt	
24.	16-Oct-72	67-0066	**Combat Loss** / No Attempt	
25.	7-Nov-72	67-0063	**Combat Loss** / No Attempt	
26.	20-Nov-72	67-0092	**Combat Loss** / No Attempt	
27.	18-Dec-72	67-0099	**Combat Loss** / No Attempt	
28.	22-Dec-72	67-0068	(19)**Combat Loss** /Successful	N. Vietnam POW's
29.	11-Jan-73	68-0024	(20)Successful / Ejection	
30.	20-Mar-73	68-0105	(21)Unsuccessful / Ejection	Mid-Air Main Chute burned (Malfunction)
31.	20-Mar-73	68-0158	(22)Unsuccessful/ Ejection	Mid-Air Main Chute damaged (Malfunction)
32.	15-May-73	68-0008	(23)Successful / Ejection	
33.	16-Jun-73	67-0111	(24)Successful / Ejection	
34.	11-Jul-73	67-0040	(25)Successful / Ejection	
35.	21-Dec-73	68-0113	(26)Unsuccessful / Ejection	Main /Stabilization Chute (Malfunction)
36.	11-Sep-74	70-2395	Fatal / No Attempt	
37.	12-Nov-74	67-0055	(27)Successful / Ejection	
38.	3-Feb-75	69-6505	(28)Successful / Ejection	Mid-Air Collision
39.	3-Feb-75	68-0280	(29)Successful / Ejection	Mid-Air Collision
40.	5-Mar-75	68-0081	(30)Successful / Ejection	

	Date	Tail	(Ejection #) Results	Comments
41.	6-Jun-75	66-0034	(31)Successful / Ejection	
42.	20-Jun-75	66-0025	(32)Successful / Ejection	
43.	7-Oct-75	66-0058	Fatal / No Attempt	Impacted a hill only 30' from the top
44.	5-Nov-75	68-0060	(33)Successful / Ejection	Over water landing / Pod Sank
45.	8-Nov-75	70-2393	(34)Successful / Ejection	
46.	23-Dec-75	68-0290	(35)Successful / Ejection	
47.	11-Mar-76	67-0080	(36)Successful / Ejection	
48.	16-Mar-76	70-2388	(37)Successful / Ejection	
49.	7-Apr-76	67-0060	(38)Successful / Ejection	
50.	7-Jun-76	69-6511	(39)Successful / Ejection	
51.	10-Oct-76	68-0167	(40)Successful / Ejection	First Supersonic Ejection
52.	27-Oct-76	67-0116	(41)Successful / Ejection	
53.	14-Feb-77	68-0266	Fatal / No Attempt	
54.	21-Apr-77	73-0709	(42) Successful / Ejection	Capsule Forward Bridle Malfunction
55.	28-Apr-77	A8-136	(43)Successful / Ejection	
56.	2-Sep-77	68-0146	(44)Successful / Ejection	
57.	29-Sep-77	A8-133	(45)Unsuccessful / Ejection	Out of the envelope
58.	3-Oct-77	68-0093	Fatal / No Attempt	
59.	5-Oct-77	73-0718	Fatal / No Attempt	
60.	28-Oct-77	68-0285	(46)Successful / Ejection	
61.	31-Oct-77	68-0070	Fatal / No Attempt	
62.	30-Nov-77	67-0083	Fatal / No Attempt	
63.	15-Dec-77	70-2380	(47)Successful / Ejection	
64.	29-Mar-78	73-0717	(48)Unsuccessful / Ejection	Rocket Nozzle burn-through (Malfunction)
65.	25-Oct-78	A8-141	(49)Successful / Ejection	Ocean landing
66.	18-Nov-78	68-0173	(50)Successful / Ejection	
67.	4-Jan-79	67-0059	(51)Successful / Ejection	
68.	16-Feb-79	68-0109	(52)Successful / Ejection	
69.	20-Apr-79	70-2367	(53)Successful / Ejection	Mid-Air Overwater
70.	20-Apr-79	73-0714	(54) Successful / Ejection	Mid-Air Overwater –pod capsized
71.	5-Jul-79	67-0105	Fatal / No Attempt	
72.	24-Jul-79	68-0042	Fatal / No Attempt	
73.	31-Jul-79	66-0052	Fatal / No Attempt	
74.	24-Aug-79	A8-137	(55) uccessful / Ejection	
75.	18-Sep-79	68-0261	Fatal / No Attempt	
76.	30-Oct-79	68-0012	(56)Successful / Ejection	
77.	12-Dec-79	68-0045	Fatal / No Attempt	
78.	19-Dec-79	68-0003	Fatal / No Attempt	
79.	6-Feb-80	68-0119	(57)Unsuccessful / Ejection	Main Parachute failed to deploy (Malfunction)
80.	26-Mar-80	67-0097	(58)Unsuccessful / Ejection	Out of the Envelope
81.	29-Apr-80	68-0057	Fatal / No Attempt	
82.	14-Jul-80	68-0139	(59)Unsuccessful / Ejection	Main parachute failed to deploy (Malfunction)
83.	30-Jul-80	68-0279	(60) Successful / Ejection	Escape Module landed in a lake
84.	6-Oct-80	68-0268	Fatal / No Attempt	CFIT Flew into Ocean
85.	30-Jan-81	68-0263	(61)Successful / Ejection	
86.	4-Feb-81	72-1441	(62)Successful / Ejection	
87.	19-Jan-82	67-0073	(63)Successful / Ejection	
88.	27-Jan-82	68-0110	(64)Successful / Ejection	
89.	12-May-82	66-0045	(65)Successful / Ejection	
90.	23-Jun-82	72-1447	(66)Successful / Ejection	
91.	14-Sep-82	68-0160	Fatal / No Attempt	
92.	16-Sep-82	74-0179	(67)Successful / Ejection	
93.	8-Oct-82	67-0098	(68)Successful / Ejection	Impact Attenuation Bags Failed
94.	1-Nov-82	73-0716	(69)Successful / Ejection	
95.	7-Dec-82	70-2377	Fatal / No Attempt	
96.	13-Apr-83	66-0054	(70)Successful / Ejection	
97.	26-Apr-83	74-0188	Fatal / No Attempt	CFIT Flew into Ocean
98.	7-Jun-83	68-0242	(71)Successful / Ejection	
99.	21-Dec-83	70-2366	(72)Successful / Ejection	
100.	13-Mar-84	66-0026	(73)Unsuccessful / Ejection	Out of the envelope

	Date	Tail	(Ejection #) Results	Comments
101.	9-Aug-84	68-0019	(74)Successful / Ejection	
102.	17-Oct-84	68-0164	Fatal / No Attempt	
103.	28-Jan-86	A8-139	Fatal / No Attempt	CFIT flew into the water
104.	15-Apr-86	70-2389	(75) **Combat Loss**/Successful Ejection	over water / aircrew drowned
105.	23-Feb-87	70-2418	(76) Successful / Ejection	Forward bridle cable failed
106.	3-Apr-87	A8-128	Fatal / No Attempt	
107.	28-Jul-87	70-2375	(77) Unsuccessful / Ejection	Out of the envelope
108.	11-Sep-87	68-0125	(78) Successful / Ejection	
109.	12-Jan-88	67-0102	(79) Unsuccessful / Ejection	Ejected inverted < 800' /Out of the envelope
110.	17-Mar-88	68-0132	(80) Successful / Ejection	
111.	8-Jun-88	68-0098	Fatal / No Attempt	
112.	21-Oct-88	68-0130	(81) Successful / Ejection	
113.	2-Feb-89	68-0243	(82) Successful / Ejection	
114.	5-Apr-89	70-2397	(83) Unsuccessful / Ejection	Out of the envelope
115.	5-Feb-90	68-0001	Fatal / No Attempt	over the water
116.	2-May-90	70-2368	(84) Successful / Ejection	
117.	20-Jul-90	68-0066	(85) Successful / Ejection	
118.	23-Aug-90	68-0131	(86) Successful / Ejection	
119.	10-Oct-90	74-0183	Fatal / No Attempt	
120.	14-Feb-91	66-0023	**Combat Loss** / No Attempt	
121.	2 Apr- 92	66-0056	(87) Successful / Ejection	
122.	17-Sep-92	68-0052	(88) Unsuccessful / Ejection	Impact damage to Rocket Motor(Malfunction)
123.	13-Sep-93	A8-127	Fatal / No Attempt	
124.	23-Sep-93	70-2412	(89) Successful / Ejection	
125.	16-Feb-95	68-0040	(90) Successful / Ejection	
126.	17-Jun-96	66-0044	(91) Successful / Ejection	
127.	18-Apr-99	A8-291	Fatal / No Attempt	

Totals

Attempted Ejections	**91**
Successful	71
System Malfuncion	10
Out of the Envelope	10
No Attempt	**36**
In Training	28
In Combat	8

Note 1: Includes 4 Aircraft destroyed by Ground Accidents and Crash Landings

Note 2: Line Number 8 may or may not have attempted ejection. In each case, both out of the envelope. Two ejection seats counted as one event / only one chute seen floating on ocean surface.

G

CRASH DATA ANALYSIS

Total Aircraft Destroyed	
Flight Related Event	127
Ground Accident	4
	131

Aircraft Written-Off	8
Aircraft Mishap Events-No Aircrew involved	8

F-111 Aircraft Damaged and Repaired	
Vark Hospital-GDFW	14
Vark Hospital-Field Team	2
USAF Maintenance Repair Team	34
	50

Total Crew Involved in all Mishap Events	363
Total Aircrew Fatalities	115

Total Ejection Events	
Successful Ejection	71
Unsuccessful Ejections	
Out of the Envelope	10
System Malfunction	10
	91

Aircraft Crashed - No Ejection	36
Crew Killed No Ejection	72

Total Crew that Ejected	
Crew Survived Ejection	140
Drowned after Successful Combat Ejection	2
Crew Killed Ejection	40
	182

Crew Injured as a result of Ejection	54

Escape Module Water Landings	6
Ejected Supersonic	1
Ejected Inverted	1

Crash Landing Events resulting in damage	20
Crew-Killed in a Landing Accident	1

Aircraft Lost in Combat	11
Aircraft Shot Down	2
Aircraft Lost due to Self-Fragmentation	2
Aircraft Lost Enroute to Target via Mechanical Failure	1
Aircraft Lost Due to CFIT related to TFR Anomalies	6
Crew Killed in Action (Combat Related)	18
Crew Survived Combat Ejection	6

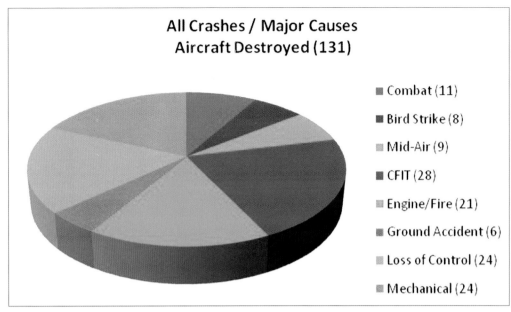

All Crashes / Major Causes
Aircraft Destroyed (131)

- Combat (11)
- Bird Strike (8)
- Mid-Air (9)
- CFIT (28)
- Engine/Fire (21)
- Ground Accident (6)
- Loss of Control (24)
- Mechanical (24)

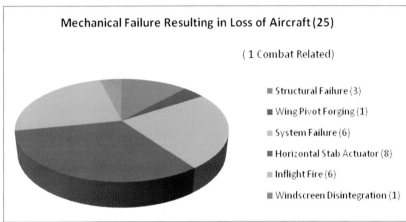

Mechanical Failure Resulting in Loss of Aircraft (25)

(1 Combat Related)

- Structural Failure (3)
- Wing Pivot Forging (1)
- System Failure (6)
- Horizontal Stab Actuator (8)
- Inflight Fire (6)
- Windscreen Disintegration (1)

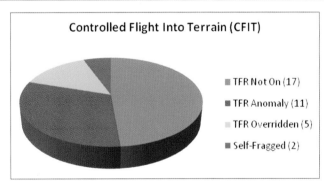

Controlled Flight Into Terrain (CFIT)

- TFR Not On (17)
- TFR Anomaly (11)
- TFR Overridden (5)
- Self-Fragged (2)

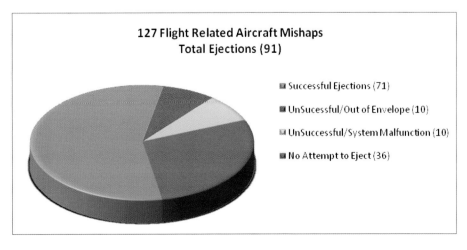

127 Flight Related Aircraft Mishaps
Total Ejections (91)

- Successful Ejections (71)
- UnSucessful/Out of Envelope (10)
- UnSucessful/System Malfunction (10)
- No Attempt to Eject (36)

H

F-111 WORLDWIDE CRASH LOCATION
(IN ORDER OF OCCURRENCE)

Model	Tail	GDFW Sequence #	Loss Date	Loss Location
F-111A	63-9774	A1-09	19 January 1967	Edwards AFB, CA 1 1/2 miles short of runway
F-111B	151973	A2-04	21 April 1967	Grumman Aerospace Calverton, NY Crashed on Take-off
F-111A	63-9780	A1-15	19 October 1967	14 NM West of Bowie, TX
F-111A	65-5701	A1-19	2 January 1968	Edwards AFB, CA.
F-111A	66-0022	A1-40	27 March 1968	Phu Phan Mountain Range, Northern Thailand
F-111A	66-0017	A1-35	30 March 1968	65 NM from Nakhon Phanom on the 185 degree radial
F-111A	66-0024	A1-42	22 April 1968	Quang Bien, N Vietnam N 17 19 20 / W 106 37 50
F-111A	66-0032	A1-50	8 May 1968	60 NM NNE of Nellis AFB
F-111A	63-9769	A1-04	18 May 1968	Holloman AFB, NM Runway
F-111B	151971	A2-02	11 September 1968	90 NM off Point Magi NAS Calif. Coast
F-111A	66-0040	A1-58	23 September 1968	Nellis AFB Runway 03L 1300 Feet short of Runway
F-111A	66-0042	A1-60	12 February 1969	South Pequop Mountain, near Elko Nevada
F-111A	66-0043	A1-61	4 March 1969	Nellis AFB Range N 37 26 55 W 114 51 20
F-111A	67-0043	A1-88	22 May 1969	50 NM NE of Tuba City, AZ
F-111A	67-0049	A1-94	22 December 1969	6 NM N of Indian Springs AFS Nellis AFB Range 5
FB-111A	68-0253	B1-25	7 October 1970	8.5 NM N of Carswell AFB, TX. N 32 54 41.24 / W 97 27 41.76
FB-111A	68-0283	B1-55	8 January 1971	4.5 NM East of Mandeville
F-111E	67-0117	A1-162	23 April 1971	67 NM NE of Edwards AFB, CA. Leach Lake Gunnery Range
F-111A	66-0029	A1-47	1 September 1971	near Van Horn Texas
F-111E	66-0018	A1-187	18 January 1972	14.5 NM NW of RAF Leuchars, Scotland GCA approach
F-111F	70-2407	E2-46	2 February 1972	Fire Run Station #5 General Dynamics Ft Worth, TX
F-111A	67-0036	A1-81	24 April 1972	Mohave County Arizona 58 NM East of Nellis AFB, NV
F-111F	70-2410	E2-49	15 June 1972	59 NM NE of NAS Fallon, Nevada
F-111A	67-0082	A1-127	18 June 1972	12 NM from Eglin AFB on the 095 Radial Eglin AFB, FLA.
F-111A	65-5703	A1-21	11 September 1972	8NM @ the 318 Degree Radial from Edwards AFB, CA.
F-111A	67-0078	A1-123	28 September 1972	Route Pack 5 North Vietnam N213551 / E1045921
F-111A	67-0066	A1-111	16 October 1972	Route Pack 6A North Vietnam
F-111A	67-0063	A1-108	7 November 1972	Route Pack 1 North Vietnam
F-111A	67-0092	A1-137	20 November 1972	N of Danang AB / S. China Sea
F-111A	67-0099	A1-144	18 December 1972	Route Pack 6A North Vietnam
F-111A	67-0068	A1-113	22 December 1972	Route Pack 6A Hanoi, North Vietnam
F-111E	68-0024	A1-193	11 January 1973	24 NM ENE of RAF Upper Heyford
F-111A	67-0072	A1-117	21 February 1973	Takhli RTAFB, Thailand Runway 18
F-111D	68-0105	A6-21	20 March 1973	1 NM N of Holbrook / Ejection, AZ 123 NM NE of Luke AFB, AZ
F-111D	68-0158	A6-74	20 March 1973	1 NM N of Holbrook / Ejection, AZ 123 NM NE of Luke AFB, AZ
F-111E	68-0008	A1-177	15 May 1973	23 NM NNE of RAF Macrihanish N 55 46 25.28 / W 5 21 18.80
F-111A	67-0111	A1-156	16 June 1973	41 NM NW of Phnom Penh Cambodia on 323 Degree Radial
F-111A	67-0040	A1-85	11 July 1973	5 NM N of Springdale Utah near Zion National Park Utah
F-111D	68-0113	A6-29	21 December 1973	10 NM West of Melrose, NM 26 NM W of CAFB NM
F-111F	70-2395	E2-34	11 September 1974	44 NM on 143 Radial from MHAFB on Saylor Creek Range
F-111A	67-0055	A1-100	12 November 1974	8 NM SSE of Kingston, Utah N 38 11 50 / W 112 11 20
FB-111A	68-0280	B1-52	3February 1975	S. Londonderry, VT Mid-Air Collision with 69-6505

Model	Tail	GDFW Sequence #	Loss Date	Loss Location
FB-111A	69-6505	B1-67	3 February 1975	S. Londonderry, VT Mid-Air Collision with 68-0280
F-111E	68-0081	A1-250	5 March 1975	4.5 NM SSW of Shap, near RAF Leeming Bar, UK
F-111A	66-0034	A1-52	6 June 1975	7 NM SSE of Peach Springs, AZ
F-111A	66-0025	A1-43	20 June 1975	Nellis AFB, Nevada Runway 21L
F-111A	66-0058	A1-76	7 October 1975	10 NM N of Indian Springs Auxiliary Airfield, NV
F-111E	68-0060	A1-229	5 November 1975	5 NM ESE of Boston, Lincolnshire, UK Wainfleet Range
F-111F	70-2393	E2-32	8 November 1975	Tonopah Test Range 120 NM NW of Nellis AFB NV
F-111F	70-2388	E2-27	16 March 1976	Runway 12 Mountain Home AFB Idaho
F-111A	67-0060	A1-105	7 April 1976	25 NM SE of Ely, NV N 38 53 / W 114 36
FB-111A	69-6511	B1-73	7 June 1976	1.5 NM NE of New Haven. VT N 44 08 5 / W 73 08
F-111D	68-0167	A6-83	10 October 1976	US Highway 82 15NM W of Hope, NM
F-111E	67-0116	A1-161	27 October 19768	Eglin AFB, FL Runway 01
FB-111A	68-0266	B1-38	14 February 1977	Beartown Mountain Russell County, Virginia
F-111F	73-0709	E2-85	21 April 1977	China Lake NAS COSO Target Area
F-111C	A8-136	D1-12	28 April 1977	Armidale NSW, Australia
F-111D	68-0146	A6-62	2 September 1977	10 NM South of Des Moines, NM
F-111C	A8-133	D1-09	29 September 1977	Evans Head Range NSW, Australia
F-111D	68-0093	A6-09	3 October 1977	12 NM W. of Floyd, NM
F-111F	73-0718	E2-94	5 October 1977	1.2 NM SE of Anweiler, Germany
FB-111A	68-0285	B1-57	28 October 1976	NM WSW of Ashland, Maine
F-111E	68-0070	A1-239	31 October 1977	NM NW of Llangadfan, Wales, UK
F-111A	67-0083	A1-128	30 November 1977	36 NM E of Goldfield, Nevada
F-111F	70-2380	E2-19	15 December 1977	Exning, UK 12.5 NM SW of RAF Lakenheath
F-111F	73-0717	E2-93	29 March 1978	7 NM from RAFL on the 027 Radial
F-111C	A8-141	D1-17	25 October 1978	Auckland NZ Harbor
F-111D	68-0173	A6-89	18 November 1978	12 NM NE of Kingman, Arizona
F-111A	67-0059	A1-104	4 January 1979	11 NM W of Murphy, Idaho
F-111D	68-0109	A6-25	16 February 1979	25 NM on the 253 Radial from Cannon AFB NM
F-111F	70-2376	E2-15	20 April 1979	2NM SSE of Dornock Scotland N 57 51.5 / W 004 00
F-111F	73-0714	E2-91	20 April 1979	2NM SSE of Dornock Scotland N 57 51.5 / W 004 00
F-111A	67-0105	A1-150	5 July 1979	15 NM ESE of Goldfield NV N 37 39 0 / W 116 56 0
F-111E	68-0042	A1-211	24 July 1979	1.5 NM N of Withernsea, UK N 53 45 3 / E 001 01 00
F-111A	66-0052	A1-70	31 July 1979	72 NM SW of MHAFB near Malheur, Oregon
F-111C	A8-137	D1-13	24 August 1979	RNZAF Ohakea, New Zealand off of Runway 27
FB-111A	68-0261	B1-33	18 September 1979	15 1/4 NM N of Pioche, Nevada
F-111E	68-0012	A1-181	30 October 1979	5 NM SW of Cambridge, UK N 59 02 25 / E 000 01 20
F-111E	68-0045	A1-214	12 December 1979	7.5 NM S of Skegness, Lincolnshire UK
F-111E	68-0003	A1-172	19 December 1979	10 NM NNE of Newton Stewart, Wigtownshire, Scotland
F-111D	68-0119	A6-35	6 February 1980	11 NM NE of Cannon AFB, NM
F-111A	67-0097	A1-142	26 March 1980	31 NM SE of Mountain Home AFB, ID
F-111E	68-0057	A1-226	29 April 1980	6 NM W of Winborne, Dorset, UK N 50 47 40 / W 002 08 40
F-111D	68-0139	A6-55	14 July 1980	9 NM NE of Cannon AFB New Mexico
FB-111A	68-0279	B1-51	30 July 1980	54 NM N of Bagotville Quebec, Canada
FB-111A	68-0268	B1-40	6 October 1980	7.4 NM from Coast Guard Jonesport on the 227 Radial
FB-111A	68-0263	B1-35	30 January 1981	2 NM E of Pease AFB, NH N 43 05 / W 70 46
F-111F	72-1441	E2-71	4 February 1981	East Wrentham near RAF Lakenheath UK
F-111A	67-0073	A1-118	19 January 1982	18 NM W of MHAFB on the 288 Radial
F-111D	68-0110	A6-26	27 January 1982	5 NM WSW of Woodlin, CA. N 38 38 38.6 W 121 55 21.7
F-111A	66-0045	A1-63	12 May 1982	27 NM from MHAFB, ID on the 124 degree radial
F-111F	72-1447	E2-77	23 June 1982	22 NM NW of Inverness, Scotland N 57 34 00 W 04 50 00
F-111D	68-0160	A6-76	14 September 1982	Wagon Mound, NM N 36 56 45 W 104 35 15
F-111F	74-0179	E2-97	16 September 1982	Crashed on approach to RAF Leuchars, Scotland
F-111A	67-0098	A1-143	8 October 1982	6.3 NM S of MHAFB, ID
F-111F	73-0716	E2-92	1 November 1982	near Tomek, Turkey
F-111A	67-0093	A1-138	9 November 1982	Gaseous Oxygen Fire; Burned on the MHAFB SAC Pad
F-111F	70-2377	E2-16	7 December 1982	89 NM on the 263 Radial from RAF Kinloss Scotland
F-111A	66-0054	A1-72	13 April 1983	73 NM from MHAFB on the 194 degree radial; Whiterock, NV
F-111F	74-0188	E2-106	26 April 1983	East end of Borkum Island, Germany
FB-111A	68-0242	B1-14	7 June 1983	36 NM SE of Mesquite, Nevada in Arizona
F-111F	70-2366	E2-05	21 December 1983	22 NM N of Flamborough UK N 54 28 00 W 00 05 00

Model	Tail	GDFW Sequence #	Loss Date	Loss Location
F-111A	66-0026	A1-44	13 March 1984	53 NM from MHAFB on the 270 degree radial
F-111E	68-0019	A1-188	9 August 1984	15 NM on the 295 radial from RAF Kinloss, Scotland
F-111D	68-0164	A6-80	17 October 1984	15 NM N of Carrizozo, NM on the Harkey Ranch
F-111C	A8-139	D1-15	28 January 1986	near Moruya New South Wales, Australia
F-111F	70-2389	E2-28	15 April 1986	Off Libya Coast near Sidi Bilal N 32 59 04.64 / E 012 59 09.8
F-111F	70-2418	E2-57	23 February 1987	Newmarket, Suffolk, UK N 52 15.35 E 00 26.20
F-111C	A8-128	D1-04	3 April 1987	Tenterfield New South Wales, Australia
F-111F	70-2375	E2-14	28 July 1987	3 NM E of Lauder, Scotland N 55 42.17 W 02 42.67
F-111D	68-0125	A6-41	11 September 1987	1.57 NM East of Runway 22 CAFB N 34 25 0 W 103 17 3
F-111A	67-0102	A1-147	12 January 1988	3 NM NW of MHAFB N 43 04 48 W 115 55 42
F-111D	68-0132	A6-48	17 March 1988	off the Cannon AFB, NM Runway EOR
F-111D	68-0098	A6-14	8 June 1988	1 Mi. W. of Melrose, NM N 34 20 00 W 103 48 50
F-111D	68-0130	A6-46	21 October 1988	6 NM SW of Cannon AFB, NM N 34 19 00 W 103 25 00
FB-111A	68-0243	B1-15	2 February 1989	Kirby, VT. 70NM E of Plattsburgh AFB, NH
F-111F	70-2397	E2-36	5 April 1989	Nellis AFB Range Complex near Tonopah, NV
F-111E	68-0001	A1-170	5 February 1990	13 NM at the 140 Radial from RAF Coningsby, UK
F-111F	70-2368	E2-07	2 May 1990	Binham, Norfolk UK near RAF Sculthorpe
F-111E	68-0066	A1-235	20 July 1990	62 NM W of Incirlik AB Turkey in Sorgun, Turkey
F-111D	68-0131	A6-47	23 August 1990	30 NM N of Truth or Consequences, NM
F-111F	74-0183	E2-101	10 October 1990	Askr Range N. of Taif AB Saudi Arabia
EF-111A	66-0023	A1-41	14 February 1991	N. of Taif AB Saudi Arabia near the Iraq border
EF-111A	66-0056	A1-74	2 April 1992	8 NM E of RAF Upper Heyford, Finmere, UK
F-111E	68-0052	A1-221	17 September 1992	1720' W of Runway 09 at RAF Upper Heyford
F-111F	70-2370	E2-09	6 August 1993	Nellis AFB, NV Trim Pad #1
F-111C	A8-127	D1-03	13 September 1993	near Black Mountain 6 Kilometers from Guyra NSW, Australia
F-111F	70-2412	E2-51	22 September 1993	18 NM W of CAFB, NM 6 mi S. of the Melrose Bomb Range
F-111E	68-0040	A1-209	16 February 1995	04 End of Runway Cannon AFB, NM
EF-111A	66-0044	A1-62	17 June 1996	14 NM NW of Tucumcari, NM on the T-4 Ranch
F-111G	A8-291	B1-63	18 April 1999	Island of Palau Aur 50NM off Malaysian Coast

Additional Aircraft Damaged but not Repaired

Model	Tail	GDFW Sequence #	Loss Date	Loss Location
Note: These aircraft were stricken from the USAF inventory due to substantial damage during a ground accident				
F-111F	E2-46	70-2407	2 February 1972	Run Station #5 Fire at GDFW
F-111F	E2-09	70-2370	6 August 1993	Nellis AFB Trim Pad Fire in Weapons Bay
Author's Note: These aircraft were stricken from the USAF inventory due to substantial damage from "Bird Strikes."				
F-111D	68-0140	A6-56	15 September 1989	Cannon AFB, NM
F-111D	68-0168	A6-84	26 March 1990	Cannon AFB, NM
F-111D	68-0133	A6-49	31 May 1991	Cannon AFB, NM
F-111F	70-2408	E2-47	1 August 1994	Cannon AFB, NM
F-111F	70-2364	E2-03	1994 or 1995	Cannon AFB, NM

NOTES AND REFERENCES
ALL CRASH DOCUMENTS

	Tail Number	Date	Main Info Source	2nd Source
1.	151972	May 1966	Tommy Thomason	George Marrett
2.	63-9774	19 January 1967	711 Mishap Report	GDFW
3.	151973	21 April 1967	Tommy Thomason	Nav Air Report
4.	66-0011	21 August 1967	GDFW Files	—
5.	63-9780	19 October 1967	711 Mishap Report	GDFW Attrited List
6.	65-5701	2 January 1968	711 Mishap Report	GDFW Attrited List
7.	66-0022	27 March 1968	474th Wing Histories	JTFFA
8.	66-0017	30 March 1968	474th Wing Histories	GDFW Incident
9.	66-0024	22 April 1968	474th Wing Histories	Doug Loeffler
10.	66-0032	8 May 1968	711 Mishap Report	GDFW Incident
11.	63-9769	18 May 1968	711 Mishap Report	GDFW Attrited List
12.	63-9783	13 August 1968	711 Mishap Report	GDFW Attrited List
13.	151971	11 September 1968	Tommy Thomason	Nav Air Report
14.	66-0040	23 September 1968	711 Mishap Report	GDFW Incident
15.	66-0042	12 February 1969	711 Mishap Report	GDFW Incident
16.	66-0043	4 March 1969	711 Mishap Report	GDFW Incident
17.	66-0013	29 April 1969	711 Mishap Report	GDFW Attrited List
18.	67-0043	22 May 1969	711 Mishap Report	GDFW Attrited List
19.	151972	6 October 1969	Tommy Thomason	George Marrett
20.	66-0012	30 October 1969	USAF Safety Center	Report Classified
21.	67-0057	6 November 1969	711 Mishap Report	GDFW Attrited List
22.	67-0097 #1	12 November 1969	711 Mishap Report	GDFW Attrited List
23.	67-0049	22 December 1969	711 Mishap Report	GDFW Attrited List
24.	68-0253	8 October 1970	711 Mishap Report	GDFW Incident
25.	67-0117	23 April 1971	711 Mishap Report	GDFW Attrited List
26.	69-6512	18 August 1971	GDFW Incident Listing	GDFW Attrited List
27.	66-0029	1 September 1971	711 Mishap Report	GDFW Incident
28.	67-7194 #1	29 November 1971	711 Mishap Report	GDFW Incident
29.	68-0283	8 January 1972	GDFW	GDFW Attrited List
30.	68-0018	18 January 1972	711 Mishap Report	GDFW Attrited List
31.	70-2387	28 January 1972	GDFW Crash Data	GDFW Attrited List
32.	70-2407	2 February 1972	GDFW Safety	Author's pictures
33.	68-0241	20 April 1972	Chris McWilliams	—
34.	67-0036	24 April 1972	711 Mishap Report	GDFW Attrited List
35.	70-2410	15 June 1972	711 Mishap Report	GDFW Incident
36.	67-0082	18 June 1972	711 Mishap Report	474th Wing Histories
37.	68-0142	25 June 1972	GDFW Crash Data	GDFW Attrited List
38.	65-5703	11 September 1972	711 Mishap Report	GDFW Attrited List
39.	67-0078	28 September 1972	474th Wing Histories	GDFW Attrited List
40.	69-6508	29 September 1972	711 Mishap Report	GDFW Attrited List
41.	67-0066	17 October 1972	474th Wing Histories	GDFW Attrited List
42.	67-0063	7 November 1972	474th Wing Histories	GDFW Attrited List
43.	67-0092	20 November 1972	474th Wing Histories	GDFW Attrited List
44.	67-0099	18 December 1972	474th Wing Histories	GDFW Attrited List
45.	67-0068	22 December 1972	474th Wing Histories	GDFW Attrited List
46.	68-0024	11 January 1973	711 Mishap Report	GDFW Incident
47.	67-0098 #1	17 February 1973	711 Mishap Report	GDFW Incident
48.	67-0071	17 February 1973	711 Mishap Report	GDFW Incident
49.	67-0072	21 February 1973	711 Mishap Report	GDFW Attrited List
50.	68-0105	20 March 1973	711 Mishap Report	GDFW Attrited List
51.	68-0158	20 March 1973	711 Mishap Report	GDFW Attrited List

	Tail Number	Date	Main Info Source	2nd Source
52.	67-0053	4 May 1973	711 Mishap Report	GDFW Attrited List
53.	67-0083	8 May 1973	474th Wing Histories	GDFW Attrited List
54.	68-0008	15 May 1973	711 Mishap Report	GDFW Attrited List
55.	67-0111	16 June 1973	711 Mishap Report	474th Wing Histories
56.	67-0094	16 June 1973	711 Mishap Report	474th Wing Histories
57.	68-0142	25 June 1973	711 Mishap Report	GDFW Incident
58.	67-0040	11 July 1973	711 Mishap Report	GDFW Attrited List
59.	68-0113	21 December 1973	711 Mishap Report	GDFW Attrited List
60.	68-0160 #1	22 January 1974	711 Mishap Report	GDFW Attrited List
61.	68-0287	May 1974	Chris McWilliams	
62.	70-2395	11 September 1974	711 Mishap Report	GDFW Attrited List
63.	67-0055	12 November 1974	711 Mishap Report	NTSB Report
64.	67-0050	8 January 1975	Don Logan	Don Logan pictures
65.	69-6505	3 February 1975	711 Mishap Report	GDFW Attrited List
66.	68-0280	3 February 1975	711 Mishap Report	GDFW Attrited List
67.	68-0081	5 March 1975	711 Mishap Report	GDFW Attrited List
68.	66-0034	6 June 1975	711 Mishap Report	GDFW Incident
69.	66-0025	20 June 1975	711 Mishap Report	GDFW Attrited List
70.	67-0089	14 August 1975	711 Mishap Report	GDFW Attrited List
71.	66-0058	7 October 1975	711 Mishap Report	GDFW Attrited List
72.	68-0060	5 November 1975	711 Mishap Report	GDFW Attrited List
73.	70-2393	8 November 1975	711 Mishap Report	GDFW Incident
74.	68-0290	23 December 1975	711 Mishap Report	GDFW Incident
75.	68-0099	10 February 1976	711 Mishap Report	GDFW Attrited List
76.	67-7194 #2	25 February 1976	711 Mishap Report	GDFW Attrited List
77.	68-0095	26 February 1976	711 Mishap Report	WSO Written Story
78.	67-0080	11 March 1976	711 Mishap Report	GDFW Attrited List
79.	70-2388	16 March 1976	711 Mishap Report	GDFW Incident
80.	67-0060	7 April 1976	711 Mishap Report	GDFW Attrited List
81.	68-0174	21 May 1976	711 Mishap Report	GDFW Attrited List
82.	69-6511	7 June 1976	711 Mishap Report	GDFW Attrited List
83.	68-0167	10 October 1976	711 Mishap Report	GDFW Attrited List
84.	67-0116	27 October 1976	711 Mishap Report	GDFW Attrited List
85.	68-0111	1 December 1976	GDFW Safety Listing	
86.	68-0266	14 February 1977	711 Mishap Report	GDFW Attrited List
87.	73-0709	21 April 1977	711 Mishap Report	GDFW Attrited List
88.	A8-136	28 April 1977	Gen Kym Osley RAAF	GDFW Attrited List
89.	68-0146	2 September 1977	711 Mishap Report	GDFW Attrited List
90.	A8-133	29 September 1977	Gen Kym Osley RAAF	GDFW Attrited List
91.	68-0093	3 October 1977	711 Mishap Report	GDFW Attrited List
92.	73-0718	5 October 1977	711 Mishap Report	GDFW Attrited List
93.	68-0285	28 October 1977	711 Mishap Report	GDFW Attrited List
94.	68-0070	31 October 1977	711 Mishap Report	GDFW Attrited List
95.	67-0083	30 November 1977	711 Mishap Report	GDFW Attrited List
96.	70-2380	15 December 1977	711 Mishap Report	GDFW Attrited List
97.	66-0030	24 March 1978	711 Mishap Report	GDFW Attrited List
98.	73-0717	29 March 1978	711 Mishap Report	Wingman Statement
99.	67-0085	14 August 1978	GDFW Safety Listing	
100.	A8-141	25 October 1978	Gen Kym Osley RAAF	GDFW Attrited List
101.	68-0173	18 November 1978	711 Mishap Report	GDFW Attrited List
102.	67-0059	4 January 1979	711 Mishap Report	GDFW Attrited List
103.	68-0148	17 January 1979	27th TFW Histories	
104.	68-0160 #2	22 January 1979	711 Mishap Report	GDFW Attrited List
105.	68-0109	16 February 1979	711 Mishap Report	GDFW Attrited List
106.	70-2367	20 April 1979	711 Mishap Report	GDFW Attrited List
107.	73-0714	20 April 1979	711 Mishap Report	GDFW Attrited List
108.	70-2378	1 May 1979	48th TFW Histories	
109.	67-0105	5 July 1979	711 Mishap Report	GDFW Attrited List
110.	68-0042	24 July 1979	711 Mishap Report	GDFW Attrited List
111.	66-0052	31 July 1979	711 Mishap Report	GDFW Attrited List

	Tail Number	Date	Main Info Source	2nd Source
112.	A8-137	24 August 1979	Gen Kym Osley RAAF	WSO's pictures
113.	68-0261	18 September 1979	711 Mishap Report	GDFW Attrited List
114.	68-0136	20 September 1979	711 Mishap Report	GDFW Attrited List
115.	68-0012	30 October 1979	711 Mishap Report	GDFW Attrited List
116.	68-0045	12 December 1979	711 Mishap Report	GDFW Attrited List
117.	73-0715	12 December 1979	711 Mishap Report	GDFW Attrited List
118.	68-0003	19 December 1979	711 Mishap Report	GDFW Attrited List
119.	68-0119	6 February 1980	711 Mishap Report	GDFW Attrited List
120.	67-0097 #2	26 March 1980	711 Mishap Report	GDFW Attrited List
121.	68-0057	29 April 1980	711 Mishap Report	GDFW Attrited List
122.	68-0139	14 July 1980	711 Mishap Report	GDFW Attrited List
123.	68-0279	30 July 1980	711 Mishap Report	GDFW Attrited List
124.	68-0106	28 August 1980	711 Mishap Report	GDFW Attrited List
125.	68-0268	6 October 1980	711 Mishap Report	GDFW Attrited List
126.	67-0079	21 January 1981	711 Mishap Report	GDFW hospital book
127.	68-0263	30 January 1981	711 Mishap Report	GDFW Attrited List
128.	72-1441	4 February 1981	711 Mishap Report	GDFW Attrited List
129.	68-0082	25 March 1981	711 Mishap Report	GDFW hospital book
130.	68-0127	7 July 1981	711 Mishap Report	GDFW hospital book
131.	68-0259	13 August 1981	GDFW Safety List	GDFW hospital book
132.	67-0118	12 June 1982	GDFW Safety List	GDFW hospital book
133.	67-0073	19 January 1982	711 Mishap Report	Author was Eyewitness
134.	68-0110	27 January 1982	711 Mishap Report	GDFW Attrited List
135.	66-0045	12 May 1982	711 Mishap Report	GDFW Attrited List
136.	72-1447	23 June 1982	711 Mishap Report	GDFW Attrited List
137.	67-0101	2 August 1982	711 Mishap Report	WSO Statement
138.	68-0160 #3	14 September 1982	711 Mishap Report	GDFW Attrited List
139.	74-0179	16 September 1982	711 Mishap Report	GDFW Attrited List
140.	67-0098	8 October 1982	711 Mishap Report	GDFW Attrited List
141.	73-0716	1 November 1982	711 Mishap Report	GDFW Attrited List
142.	67-0093	9 November 1982	MHAFB 366 TFW News	Author was Witness
143.	70-2377	7 December 1982	711 Mishap Report	GDFW Attrited List
144.	66-0054	13 April 1983	711 Mishap Report	GDFW Attrited List
145.	74-0188	26 April 1983	711 Mishap Report	GDFW Attrited List
146.	68-0242	7 June 1983	711 Mishap Report	GDFW Attrited List
147.	68-0101	28 October 1983	27th TFW Histories	GDFW History
148.	70-2366	21 December 1983	711 Mishap Report	GDFW Attrited List
149.	66-0026	13 March 1984	711 Mishap Report	GDFW Attrited List
150.	68-0019	9 August 1984	711 Mishap Report	GDFW Attrited List
151.	68-0164	17 October 1984	711 Mishap Report	GDFW Attrited List
152.	70-2413	10 April 1985	48th TFW History	—
153.	67-0035	16 December 1985	67-0035 Jacket File	—
154.	A8-139	28 January 1986	Gen Kym Osley RAAF	GDFW Attrited
155.	70-2389	15 April 1986	GDFW Attrited Listing	Eyewitness Account
156.	70-2418	23 February 1987	711 Mishap Report	GDFW Attrited List
157.	A8-128	2 April 1987	Gen Kym Osley RAAF	GDFW Attrited
158.	70-2375	28 July 1987	711 Mishap Report	GDFW Attrited List
159.	68-0125	11 September 1987	711 Mishap Report	GDFW Attrited List
160.	67-0102	12 January 1988	711 Mishap Report	GDFW Attrited List
161.	67-0085	15 March 1988	366th TFW Histories	Al Green witness
162.	68-0132	17 March 1988	711 Mishap Report	GDFW Attrited List
163.	68-0098	8 June 1988	711 Mishap Report	GDFW Attrited List
164.	68-0130	21 October 1988	711 Mishap Report	GDFW Attrited List
165.	68-0243	2 February 1989	711 Mishap Report	GDFW Attrited List
166.	70-2397	5 April 1989	48th TFW Histories	Range & PT video
167.	68-0140	15 September 1989	27th TFW Histories	—
168.	68-0001	5 February 1990	711 Mishap Report	GDFW Attrited List
169.	68-0168	26 March 1990	711 Mishap Report	GDFW Attrited List
170.	70-2368	2 May 1990	711 Mishap Report	GDFW Attrited List
171.	68-0066	20 July 1990	711 Mishap Report	GDFW Attrited List

	Tail Number	Date	Main Info Source	2nd Source
172.	68-0131	23 August 1990	711 Mishap Report	GDFW Attrited List
173.	74-0183	10 October 1990	711 Mishap Report	GDFW Attrited List
174.	70-2384	17 January 1991	48th TFW Video	Craig Brown confirmed
175.	66-0023	14 February 1991	390th / 429th ECS Histories	Walt Manwill
176.	68-0133	31 May 1991	27th TFW Histories	—
177.	72-1444	29 October 1991	711 Mishap Report	Pilot Statement
178.	66-0056	2 April 1992	711 Mishap Report	GDFW Attrited List
179.	68-0052	17 September 1992	711 Mishap Report	GDFW Attrited List
180.	70-2370	7 August 1993	Tear Down Pictures	—
181.	A8-127	13 September 1993	Gen Kym Osley RAAF	GDFW Attrited List
182.	70-2412	22 September 1993	711 Mishap Report	GDFW Attrited List
183.	70-2408	1 August 1994	27th TFW Histories	—
184.	68-0040	16 February 1995	711 Mishap Report	GDFW Attrited List
185.	66-0044	17 June 1996	711 Mishap Report	GDFW Attrited List
186.	F-111G	22 February 1997	GDFW Safety Listing	—
187.	A8-291	18 April 1999	Gen Kym Osley	WCDR Mike Smith
188.	A8-143	18 July 2006	RAAF Pictures	Australian News

Totals	Sources
134	AF 711 Reports
2	Nav Air Reports
52	GDFW Unclassified Listings / Fighter Wing Histories/Contributing Individuals

	Tail Number	Date	Main Info Source	2nd Source
1.	63-9771	14 November 1966	GDFW History	
2.	63-9772	6 July 1966	GDFW History	
3.	68-0011	21 August 1967	GDFW Files	
4.	66-0012	30 October 1969	USAF Safety Center	Report Classified
5.	66-0013	22 April 1969	711 Mishap Report	GDFW Attrited List
6.	66-0018	23 January 1981	Author's Pictures	
7.	66-0030	24 March 1981	GDFW History	
8.	67-0033	5 May 1981	Aircraft Jacket File	
9.	67-0050	8 January 1975	Don Logan	Don Logan Pictures
10.	67-0057	6 November 1969	711 Mishap Report	GDFW Attrited List
11.	67-0059	23 November 1972	474th TFW CGV History	
12.	67-0059 #2	16 April 1973	474th TFW CGV History	
13.	67-0065	29 December 1972	474th TFW CGV History	
14.	67-0065 # 2	18-19 May 1980	Eyewitness	
15.	67-0069	27 December 1972	474th TFW CGV History	
16.	67-0080	21 October 1972	474th TFW CGV History	
17.	67-0083	20 December 1972	474th TFW CGV History	
18.	67-0085	15 March 1988	Authors Video	Al Green Witness
22.	67-0100	21 October 1972	474th TFW CGV History	
23.	67-0100 #2	February 1991	366th Wing History	
24.	67-0103	23 October 1972	474th TFW CGV History	
25.	67-0106	12 May 1973	474th TFW CGV History	
26.	67-0112	11 October 1972	474th TFW CGV History	
27.	67-0113	11 October 1972	474th TFW CGV History	
28.	67-0114	5 November 1972	474th TFW CGV History	
29.	151972	May 1966	Tommy Thomason	
30.	A8-114	3 March 1983	82 Wing/RAAF History	
31.	A8-131	12 March 1986	82 Wing/RAAF History	
32.	A8-131 #2	18 January 1988	82 Wing/RAAF History	
33.	A8-114	26 May 1988	82 Wing/RAAF History	
34.	A8-112	26 June 2002	82 Wing/RAAF History	
35.	A8-143	18 July 2006	82 Wing/RAAF History	
36.	Unknown F-111G	22 February 1997	GDFW Safety Listing	
37.	68-0090	11 June 1977	27th TFW History	
38.	68-0097	21 March 1978	27th TFW History	
39.	68-0098	10 May 1975	27th TFW History	
40.	68-0099	10 February 1976	27th TFW History	
41.	68-0101	28 October 1983	27th TFW History	GDFW History
42.	68-0104	2 June 1977	27th TFW History	
43.	68-0106	28 August 1980	27th TFW History	
44.	68-0108	8 January 1976	27th TFW History	
45.	68-0108 #2	April 1977	27th TFW History	
46.	68-0108 #3	June 1977	27th TFW History	
47.	68-0108 #4	March 1978	27th TFW History	
48.	68-0110	27 November 1978	27th TFW History	
49.	68-0111	1 December 1976	27th TFW History	
50.	68-0115	1980's	27th TFW History	Authors Pictures
51.	68-0115 #2	8 December 1978	27th TFW History	
52.	68-0115 #3	21 January 1988	27th TFW History	
53.	8-0121	1980's	27th TFW History	Authors Pictures
54.	68-0127	17 January 1979	27th TFW History	
55.	68-0129	5 February 1979	27th TFW History	
56.	68-0129 #2	Late 1985 early 86	Authors Pictures	Greg Weigl Verified

	Tail Number	Date	Main Info Source	2nd Source
57.	68-0129 #3	1980 's	Authors Picture	
58.	68-0133	31 May 1991	27th TFW History	
59.	68-0135	10 May 1977	27th TFW History	
60.	68-0135 # 2	March 1978	27th TFW History	
61.	68-0136	15 January 1976	27th TFW History	
62.	68-0138	20 September 1979	27th TFW History	
63.	68-0140	15 September 1989	27th TFW History	
64.	68-0142	25 June 1972	27th TFW History	
65.	68-0148	17 January 1979	27th TFW History	Author's pictures
66.	68-0150	3 December 1975	27th TFW History	
67.	68-0150 #2	7 November 1975	27th TFW History	
68-	0150 #3	16 January 1978	Tom Roger's Picture	27th TFW History
69.	68-0152	9 January 1976	27th TFW History	
70.	68-0159	20 February 1976	27th TFW History	
71.	68-0168	26 March 1990	711 Mishap Report	GDFW Attrited List
72.	68-0168 #2	25 February 1976	27th TFW History	
73.	68-0178	30 December 1975	27th TFW History	
74.	68-0180	6 January 1976	27th TFW History	
75.	68-0180 #2	19 January 1978	27th TFW History	
76.	67-0118	12 June 1982	GDFW History	
77.	68-0038	20 July 1970	GDFW History	
78.	68-0039	Unknown Date	Bill Allen	
79.	68-0043	1986-1989	BAe Bristol Pictures	
80.	68-0050	1985	Joe Betts GDFW	
81.	70-2413	10 April 1985	48th TFW History	
82.	70-2384	17 January 1991	Taif Video	
83.	70-2387	29 January 1974	GDFW Safety Files	
84.	70-2370	22 August 1993	Tear Down Pictures	
85.	70-2364	Unknown	Pedestal Pictures	
86.	70-2408	15 June 1994	27th TFW History	
87.	70-2387	28 January 1972	366th Wing History	
88.	70-2378	1 May 1979	48th TFW Histories	
89.	70-2401	17 January 1991	USAF	
90.	71-0888	1987-1990	Author was Witness	
91.	71-0891	16 June 1995	Author was Witness	
92.	72-1444	17 January 1991	USAF	
93.	Unknown F-111F	10 August 1982	GDFW Safety Files	
94.	69-6512	18 August 1971	GDFW	Author's Pictures
95.	68-0241	20 April 1972	GDFW	
96.	68-0287	17 May 1974	Chris McWilliams	
97.	68-0259	13 August 1981	GDFW	
98.	68-0244	14 February 1974	GDFW Safety Files	
99.	68-0245	15 July 1974	GDFW Safety Files	
100.	66-0021	6 March 1997	429th ECS History	
101.	66-0027	16 August 1995	429th ECS History	
102.	67-0032	prior to 1992	Scott MacManus	
103.	67-0034	12 November 1991	GDFW Safety Files	
104.	67-0035	16 December 1985	Jacket File	
105.	67-0037	15 or 16 February 1991	USAF	
106.	68-0038	December 1991	GDFW Safety Files	

INDEX BY TAIL / SERIAL NUMBER RECOGNITION

67-0102	F-111A	72
67-0105	F-111A	73
67-0111	F-111A	73

F-111B

SERIAL NUMBER	TYPE / MODEL	PAGE
151971	F-111B	41-42
151972	F-111B	43, 186
151973	F-111B	43-44

F-111C / F-111G

SERIAL NUMBER	TYPE / MODEL	PAGE
A8-127	F-111C	75
A8-128	F-111C	75-76
A8-133	F-111C	76
A8-136	F-111C	77
A8-137	F-111C	77-78
A8-139	F-111C	78
A8-141	F-111C	79
A8-143	F-111C	186
A8-291	F-111G	79

F-111D

SERIAL NUMBER	TYPE / MODEL	PAGE
68-0093	F-111D	109
68-0095	F-111D	109-110
68-0098	F-111D	110-111
68-0099	F-111D	111
68-0101	F-111D	187
68-0105	F-111D	112-113
68-0106	F-111D	187
68-0109	F-111D	113-114
68-0110	F-111D	114
68-0111	F-111D	187
68-0113	F-111D	115
68-0119	F-111D	116
68-0125	F-111D	117
68-0127	F-111D	118
68-0130	F-111D	118-119
68-0131	F-111D	119
68-0132	F-111D	120
68-0133	F-111D	188
68-0136	F-111D	120
68-0139	F-111D	121
68-0140	F-111D	189
68-0142	F-111D	122-123, 189

68-0146	F-111D	123-124
68-0148	F-111D	189
68-0158	F-111D	112-113
68-0160	F-111D	124-125
68-0164	F-111D	125
68-0167	F-111D	126
68-0168	F-111D	190
68-0173	F-111D	126
68-0174	F-111D	127

F-111E

SERIAL NUMBER	TYPE / MODEL	PAGE
67-0116	F-111E	129
67-0117	F-111E	129
67-0118	F-111E	190
68-0001	F-111E	130
68-0003	F-111E	130
68-0008	F-111E	131
68-0012	F-111E	132
68-0018	F-111E	132-133
68-0019	F-111E	133
68-0024	F-111E	134
68-0040	F-111E	134-135
68-0042	F-111E	136
68-0045	F-111E	136
68-0050	F-111E	191
68-0052	F-111E	137
68-0057	F-111E	137-138
68-0060	F-111E	138-140
68-0066	F-111E	140
68-0070	F-111E	141-142
68-0081	F-111E	143
68-0082	F-111E	143-144

F-111F

SERIAL NUMBER	TYPE / MODEL	PAGE
70-2364	F-111F	191
70-2366	F-111F	146
70-2367	F-111F	146-147
70-2368	F-111F	148
70-2370	F-111F	191-192
70-2375	F-111F	148
70-2377	F-111F	149-150
70-2378	F-111F	192
70-2380	F-111F	151-152
70-2384	F-111F	192
70-2387	F-111F	192

70-2388	F-111F	153		**FB-111A**		
70-2389	F-111F	100-106		SERIAL NUMBER	TYPE / MODEL	PAGE
70-2393	F-111F	154		67-7194	FB-111A	168-169
70-2395	F-111F	154		68-0241	FB-111A	193
70-2397	F-111F	155		68-0242	FB-111A	169
70-2407	F-111F	156		68-0243	FB-111A	170
70-2408	F-111F	192		68-0244	FB-111A	218
70-2410	F-111F	156-157		68-0253	FB-111A	170-171
70-2412	F-111F	158		68-0259	FB-111A	193
70-2413	F-111F	192		68-0261	FB-111A	171
70-2418	F-111F	159		68-0263	FB-111A	172
72-1441	F-111F	160		68-0266	FB-111A	173
72-1444	F-111F	160-161		68-0268	FB-111A	172
72-1447	F-111F	161		68-0279	FB-111A	173
73-0709	F-111F	162		68-0280	FB-111A	174
73-0714	F-111F	146-147		68-0283	FB-111A	176-177
73-0715	F-111F	162-163		68-0285	FB-111A	178
73-0716	F-111F	163		68-0287	FB-111A	193
73-0717	F-111F	164		68-0290	FB-111A	178-179
73-0718	F-111F	165		69-6505	FB-111A	174
74-0179	F-111F	165		69-6508	FB-111A	179-181
74-0183	F-111F	166		69-6511	FB-111A	182
74-0188	F-111F	166		69-6512	FB-111A	193

INDEX BY NAME RECOGNITION

NAME	A/C TYPE	SERIAL #	PAGE	NAME	A/C TYPE	SERIAL #	PAGE
Riley, Edward A	FB-111A	68-0266	173	Sweet, Floyd B	F-111E	68-0018	132-133
Roberts, William R Jr	F-111A	67-0111	73	Sweeney, John J	F-111E	68-0070	141
Robinson, Charles G	FB-111A	68-0253	170-171	Szybillo, Stanley J	F-111F	72-1447	161
Rogers, David N	F-111C	A8-141	79	Tallman, Howard L	F-111D	68-0160	124-125
Rudiger, Burnley L Jr	F-111F	70-2377	149-150	Tate, Grover C	F-111A	63-9783	39-40
Rundle, Gary R	F-111A	67-0083	185	Taterfield, Terry A	F-111F	70-2366	146
Russell, Bob	FB-111A	69-6512	193	Taylor, Ulysses S III	F-111D	68-0139	121
Ruttman, Stephen R	F-111F	73-0714	146-147	Teague, Brian J	F-111A	66-0030	184
Ryker, Gary E	F-111A	67-0059	64	Thigpen, David J	F-111A	63-9780	37-39
Schlitt, Timothy A	F-111F	70-2367	146-147	Tidwell, Robert L	F-111A	66-0025	46
Schmit, Edward P	F-111A	66-0043	52	Torn, Albert Heinrich	F-111D	68-0164	125
Schuppe, Kenneth A	F-111A	66-0032	48	Travis, Robert W	F-111E	68-0066	140
Severance, Donald M	F-111A	66-0029	47	Troster, Glenn E	F-111D	68-0098	110-111
Shallington, Jackie T	FB-111A	68-0279	173	Van Driel, Charles E	F-111A	66-0032	48
Sharpe, Patrick S	F-111A	65-5703	40-41	Vann, Donald G	FB-111A	68-0280	174-175
Shealy, J Thomas	F-111A	66-0054	53-54	Vidas, Charles Michael	F-111F	74-0188	166
Short, Anthony	F-111C	A8-291	79	Voorhees, Randall S	FB-111A	68-0243	170
Short, Robert J	F-111A	67-0060	64	Voorhies, Frederick J	F-111A	63-9769	36
Sides, John W	F-111D	68-0125	117	Voorhies, Frederick J	F-111A	63-9783	39-40
Sieniki, Theodore S	F-111D	68-0110	114	Wagner, Loreley O	F-111A	67-0083	68
Silverbush, Edward	F-111A	66-0029	47	Walgren, Phillip E	F-111D	68-0132	120
Sinclair, John S	F-111F	70-2410	156-157	Walker, Alan D Jr	F-111A	67-0073	66
Singalewitch, Christopher A	F-111A	67-0101	72	Wangeman, Charles E	F-111B	151973	43-44
Skeels, Richard S	F-111A	67-0071	65	Ward, Ronald Jack	F-111A	67-0099	96-97
Slusher, Frank B	F-111E	68-0045	136	Warner, Luke	F-111C	A8-143	186
Smart, William W	F-111E	68-0070	141	Warren, Barton	F-111B	151971	41-42
Smith, Gregory L	F-111D	68-0174	127	Warren, Barton	F-111B	151972	186
Smith, Valdimar L	F-111D	68-0131	119	Watson, Donald R Jr	EF-111A	66-0044	56
Soeder, Eugene H	F-111A	67-0105	73	Webb, Roger L	F-111F	73-0714	146-147
Spaulding, Raymond C	F-111E	68-0003	130	Westbrook, Donald R	F-111A	67-0089	68
Spellus, Wayne C	F-111A	67-0089	68	Westerfield, Roy W	F-111D	68-0119	116
Sperry, Paul D	F-111A	67-0055	62	Westerfield, Roy W	F-111D	68-0146	123-124
Sponeybarger, Robert D	F-111A	67-0068	97-99	Wiley, Gregory	F-111D	68-0168	190
Sprenger, Michael R	FB-111A	68-0290	178-179	Wilson, Gregory	F-111F	70-2412	158
Springer, Scott L	F-111A	67-0098	71	Wilson, Raymond T	FB-111A	69-6511	182
Stafford, Ronald Dean	F-111A	67-0092	95-96	Wilson, William W	F-111A	67-0068	97-99
Steiber, James E	F-111E	68-0060	138-139	Winge, Randolph L	F-111E	68-0040	134-135
Stem, Taylor F III	F-111F	70-2375	148	Wingo, James D	EF-111A	66-0044	56
Stepniewski, Andrew F	FB-111A	69-6508	179-180	Winters, Charles P	F-111A	65-5703	40-41
Stillwell, George H	F-111D	68-0127	118	Wolfe, Richard A	F-111E	68-0081	143
Stocks, Bruce D	FB-111A	68-0283	176-177	Worrell, Rowland H III	F-111D	68-0106	187
Stolz, Charles R	F-111A	67-0111	73	Woytovich, Bennie L	FB-111A	69-6508	179-180
Stowe, Arthur L	F-111A	67-0083	68	Yeager, Paul E	F-111D	68-0139	121
Stricker, Russell C	F-111D	68-0125	117	Young, Richard B	FB-111A	68-0242	169
Sudberry, Charles E	F-111A	67-0072	65	Zeller, Jeffery M	F-111F	72-1444	160-161
Swanson, David A	F-111D	68-0130	118-119				

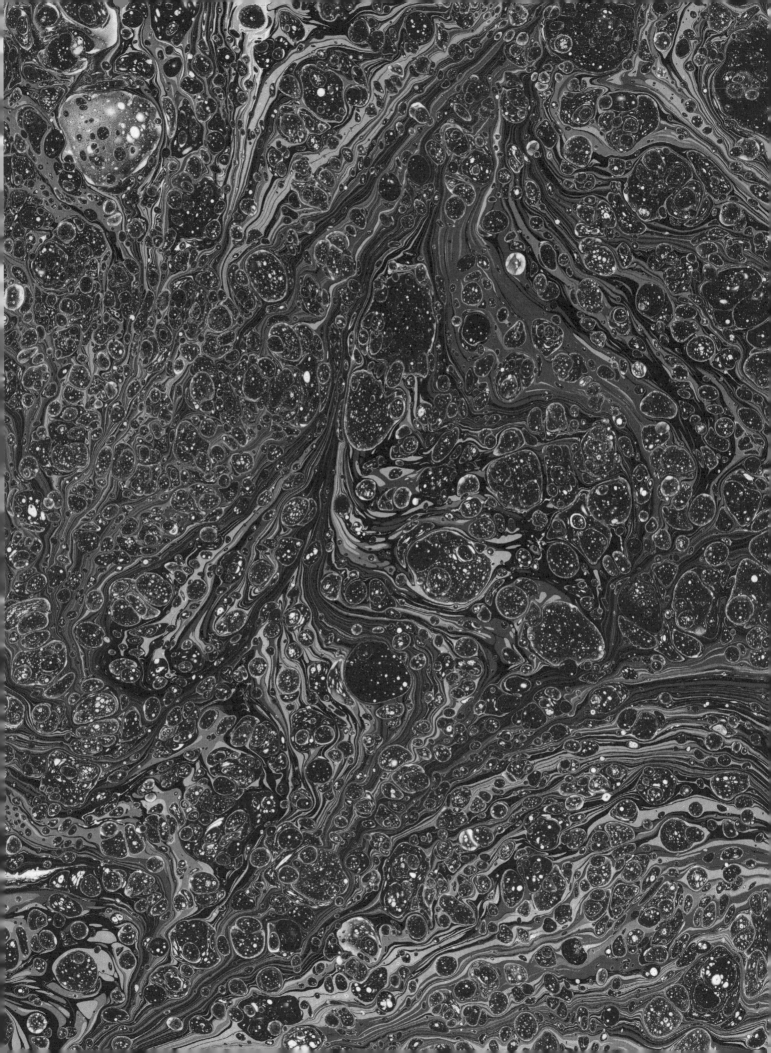